D0070614

AMERICAN FOREIGN POLICY IN CANADIAN RELATIONS

THE MACMILLAN COMPANY
NEW YORK · BOSTON · CHICAGO · DALLAS
ATLANTA · SAN FRANCISCO

MACMILLAN & CO., LIMITED
LONDON · BOMBAY · CALCUTTA
MELBOURNE

THE MACMILLAN COMPANY
OF CANADA, LIMITED
TORONTO

AMERICAN FOREIGN POLICY IN CANADIAN RELATIONS

By

JAMES MORTON CALLAHAN

NEW YORK
THE MACMILLAN COMPANY
1937

Set up and printed. Published January, 1937.

PRINTED IN THE UNITED STATES OF AMERICA
NORWOOD PRESS LINOTYPE, INC.
NORWOOD, MASS., U.S.A.

PREFACE

THE recent establishment of direct diplomatic representation between Washington and Ottawa, a realization of Canadian wishes and earlier American suggestions, provides a fortunate and fitting occasion for the appearance of the first general historical volume on American policy in Canadian relations during the long period in which all negotiations in regard to American-Canadian questions were complicated and embarrassed by the necessity of constant reference to the British imperial government at London.

This volume is justified by the importance of the subject. America's relations with Great Britain, chiefly concerned with American problems pertaining to the American Canadian border frontier and the British North American provinces, have exceeded in importance its relations with other nations. Its Canadian relations with the accompanying series of adaptations and adjustments, as revealed in the archives, furnish a key to the interpretation of the significance of the long peace which persisted in the face of many provocative circumstances arising from numerous controversies and contentions along the unfortified frontier at a period of the American aggressive westward movement. A study of its policies in connection with these relations leads to the conclusion that a retrospective view of the origin and determining factors, and of the discussion and the adjustment or settlement, of difficult and irritating international problems which at times threatened to result in serious consequences, might prove useful in establishing a better understanding under new conditions of economic interdependence, and in the improvement of future neighborhood contacts and trans-frontier relationships.

The author of this volume first became interested in American Canadian policy long ago in connection with some historical researches on the disarmament agreement of 1817 which stimulated him to publish a small volume on the "Neutrality of the American Lakes" and to begin the collection of original historical materials on American problems along the Canadian border. Later, in 1929, with renewed interest stimulated by the success of the permanent international joint commission established by the Root-Bryce treaty of 1909 for the judicial settlement of border disputes and by the success of direct American Canadian diplomatic communication, he began a new series of researches which finally resulted in the completion of this volume.

Although the chief purpose of the volume is to present logically and judicially the dominant or significant facts and factors of American policy, the author has given considerable attention to the collection and interpretation of data relating to the basis and influence of Canadian policy and to the more general subject of diplomatic relations.

In addition to careful and arduous researches in the original official manuscript archives of the American Department of State upon which the narrative is chiefly based, and which have been supplemented by the use of the letters and papers of public men at the Manuscript Division of the Library of Congress, he has examined incidentally many manuscript records in the Canadian Archives at Ottawa and in the Public Record Office at London, in order to ascertain to what extent American policies have been influenced by British and Canadian policies or views. At Ottawa he especially studied the correspondence of the British ministers at Washington with the Canadian governors-general and the Canadian correspondence with the Colonial Office at London, and accompanying enclosures of correspondence of the British minister with the Secretary of State and the Foreign Office and of the latter with the Colonial Office. He also used extensively the valuable collections of the manuscript papers of Sir John Macdonald and Sir Wilfrid Laurier. He has been diligent in the pursuit of evidence needed to avoid the ordinary dangers of error in statements of narrative or of conclusions.

Besides mansucript sources he has also used the various government publications, the newspaper files and other periodic literature, as indicated by the bibliographical references inserted at the close of each chapter.

The author gratefully acknowledges his obligations to the Social Science Research Council for liberal coöperative financial aid in facilitating the collection of part of the manuscript materials used as a basis for completion of the narrative. He also acknowledges a debt of gratitude to the Carnegie Endowment for International Peace for financial aid in connection with the publication.

JAMES MORTON CALLAHAN

CONTENTS

I. PROBLEMS AND POLICIES OF THE REVOLUTION 1
II. LAKE POSTS AND THE JAY TREATY 22
III. ANTECEDENTS AND OPERATIONS OF THE WAR OF 1812 46
IV. NEGOTIATIONS OF THE PEACE TREATY OF GHENT 70
V. EARLY POST-WAR ADJUSTMENT 87
VI. PEACETIME ECONOMIC QUESTIONS: FISHERIES, COMMERCE AND NAVIGATION 105
VII. PEACETIME BOUNDARY QUESTIONS 127
VIII. LAKE FRONTIER PROBLEMS OF THE CANADIAN REVOLUTION 161
IX. THE WEBSTER-ASHBURTON TREATY 185
X. THE NORTHWEST BOUNDARY: THE OREGON QUESTION 215
XI. THE RECIPROCITY TREATY OF 1854 241
XII. BORDER PROBLEMS OF THE CIVIL WAR PERIOD 270
XIII. ANNEXATION AGITATION AND CANADIAN DESTINY, 1861-71 299
XIV. NEGOTIATIONS OF THE TREATY OF 1871 326
XV. NEW PROBLEMS OF RECIPROCITY AND FISHERIES, 1872-89 354
XVI. INDIANS, RAILWAYS, WATERWAYS AND EXTRADITION, 1872-89 387
XVII. POLICY OF THE HARRISON ADMINISTRATION, 1889-93 411
XVIII. THE BERING SEA FUR SEALS CONTROVERSY AND AFTER 438
XIX. THE ALASKA BOUNDARY CONTROVERSY 465

XX. THE WAY OF TRANSITION TO EASIER ADJUSTMENTS 493
XXI. THE LATEST ERA OF EASIER ADJUSTMENT 534
INDEX 563

MAPS

The Maine Boundary Dispute 187
The Alaska Boundary Dispute 467

AMERICAN FOREIGN POLICY IN CANADIAN RELATIONS

CHAPTER I

PROBLEMS AND POLICIES OF THE REVOLUTION

THE United States, in 1776, in its determination to secure independence, was largely animated by a desire to avoid complications resulting from European wars and colonial systems. It desired separation from the European system and the opportunity to promote a system of self government and free trade without European foreign interference either direct or through European colonial establishments on the American continent. In its earliest international policy in connection with the Revolution, it was largely guided by influences originating in the long Anglo-French struggle for colonial trade control along the Lakes and in the interior south of the Lakes. It was influenced by knowledge of the inconveniences and difficulties and dangers which had arisen during the long period of international rivalry before the British victory of 1763, and by the later British policy (of the Quebec Act) to add to Canadian jurisdiction the valuable hinterland south of the Lakes to the Ohio, and also by considerations of future security and defense which might be facilitated by withdrawal of trans-Atlantic British rule from contiguous territory in North America.

Therefore, the Continental Congress, in guiding the policies and destinies of the prospective American republic, sought to establish a continental union by the peaceful incorporation of the inhabitants of Canada who, apparently, could offer no assurance of aid.

The first Continental Congress, which met at Philadelphia in September, 1774, expressed the general desire to include Canada in the organization for opposition to the British government. On October 26, it ordered the printing of an address inviting Canadians to coöperate in a united opposition. Later (in February, 1775), encouraged by expressions of sympathy from Canadian merchants, it authorized the Boston Committee of Correspondence to send a more formal invitation to the merchants of Montreal to join the struggle by sending delegates to the next session of the Congress—an invitation which was declined, possibly because of the fear that acceptance might result in injury to business interests.[1] On May 29, John Jay wrote a similar letter, which was sent to the "oppressed" country as a step toward its acquisition, and to prevent its adoption of a policy of neutrality.[2]

After the opening of the Lake Champlain route through the capture of Crown Point and Ticonderoga by the militia of Vermont and New Hampshire in May, 1775, and in response to a suggestion of Ethan Allen that this key should be held and that through it the conquest of Canada might be effected by an American force of two or three thousand men, Congress disavowed any hostile intentions in that direction and for a short time refused to change its policy. It proceeded to distribute in Canada copies of a friendly letter, and sent Ethan Allen as a propagandist to "preach politics."

Later, however, it was led to change its policy. In this change it was influenced by the report that the Canadian people had opposed the efforts of Sir Guy Carleton to induce them to join the British cause and were disposed to be neutral. Finding that Canadians did not seem inclined to enlist, it finally decided to adopt the view of Arnold that an invasion of Canada was a necessary defensive measure. In August, with a desire to promote the peace of all the colonies, it authorized a friendly invasion by a force of 1500 men to capture Montreal and Quebec with a view to securing Canadian adhesion to the war for independence. In the interest of border security, and trusting to friendly persuasion, it sent Schuyler and Montgomery to occupy the incorporation of Canada as a fourteenth state. Apparently with little doubt concerning the ultimate destiny of the region between the Appalachians and the Mississippi, it concentrated its earlier policy on the more doubtful problem of securing the accession of Canada.

General Schuyler, who replaced Arnold in the command at Ticonderoga, adopted plans for a simultaneous attack on Montreal and Quebec. He promptly sent to Canada a personal representative, who reported in July, 1775, that the Canadians were friendly and that many would join the invading force. Following the French route via Lake Champlain and the Richelieu River, he besieged St. Johns which was surrendered on November 1 to his successor, Montgomery. The latter on November 13 reached Montreal, where he captured military stores which General Carleton in departing for Quebec had left behind. He also considerably increased his force by many Canadian accessions.[3]

Americans were elated by the news. On November 21, 1775, after the arrival of information of the capture of St. Johns, and in the expectation that Montreal and the Upper St. Lawrence would be taken, Jefferson wrote to Eppes: "We consider this as having determined the fate of Canada. A committee of Congress is going to improve circumstances so as to bring the Canadians into our Union." On November 29, having heard the news that General Montgomery had been received in Montreal, he also expected to hear that Quebec had opened its arms to Arnold. He wrote John Randolph: "In a short time, we have reason to hope the delegates of Canada will join us in Congress and complete the American Union."[4]

Meantime, Arnold, after many hardships on a difficult march from Cambridge, Massachusetts, had crossed the St. Lawrence at Quebec on November 11, eight days before the arrival of General Carleton from Montreal. Failing in his demand of November 14 for the surrender of the city, and with no naval force by which to establish a blockade, he retired up the river after the arrival of Carleton. He decided to await the arrival of Montgomery, whose success at Montreal had been followed by the threatened retirement of many of his troops (whose terms of enlistment had expired) and, later, by friction between his forces and the inhabitants.

On December 2, Montgomery with three hundred men joined Arnold. On December 5, he encamped before Quebec with a combined force of about one thousand Americans and five hundred Canadian volunteers. In a written demand for surrender, he confidently stated that the citizens and most of the sailors assisting in the defense of the city were friendly to the Americans. He overestimated the strength of the pro-American sentiment, which had been greatly reduced by the firm policy of Governor Carleton; and as the siege continued he soon had reason to apprehend possible defection among his own poorly housed and poorly fed troops, some of whom notified him that their term of enlistment would expire at the close of December. Finally, on the night of December 31, in the midst of a heavy snowstorm he directed a sudden surprise attack during which he was killed by the fire of the enemy before he reached the appointed place of junction with the larger force led by Arnold.[5]

Arnold, although over four hundred of his men surrendered after a hard fight, decided to continue the siege with his remaining force, which was later increased (in March) by a small additional force which General Washington sent in January, via Albany and Lake Champlain, in response to General Schuyler's urgent request. Although he remained at his post through the winter and received reinforcements in the following May, he encountered constantly increasing difficulties —including animosities between the American Protestant soldiers and the Catholic Church.[6]

Meantime, on January 15, 1776, seeking to placate the growing resentment in Canada, Congress appointed a commission of three men (Franklin, Chase and Charles Carroll) to use all suitable means to induce the Canadians to join in the contest for independence. It authorized a promise of the same privileges and terms of union which had united the other colonies. The commission enlisted the services of the Reverend John Carroll (a Catholic clergymen of Maryland) who unsuccessfully attempted an adjustment by a trip to Montreal. It found no basis for hope of Canadian coöperation. It reported that the clergy were in unanimous opposition to the American cause.[7]

In April, although advocating a policy of making Canada secure by "taking strong hold of the affections and the confidence of the inhabitants," Washington (at Schuyler's suggestion) sent all the troops he could spare; and Congress now became determined to secure Canada. About May 1 General Thomas, sailing under the Union flag, arrived before Quebec with three war-ships, which had sailed from Plymouth, via the St. Lawrence, bringing reinforcements to the Americans. After a brief battle, the Americans retreated, leaving prisoners and sick who were well treated by Carleton.

What might have been effected in Canada the year before, possibly without great difficulty, had now become arduous work. Washington wrote Schuyler (May 17) that he feared "the prospects we had of possessing that country, of so much importance in the present controversy," were almost over, or at least would require more bloodshed than would have been necessary if exertions had been applied earlier. President Hancock, in June, wrote Washington in the same tone, stating that the failure was a misfortune, as the continent had been put to a great expense in endeavoring to get possession. Washington, in his reply of June 30, said: "Canada . . . would have been an important acquisition, and well worth the expenses incurred in the pursuit of it, but as we could not reduce it to our possession, the retreat of our army with so little loss . . . must be esteemed as a most fortunate event." [8]

Failure of the American expedition to Canada was due in part to lack of American plans to utilize the potential strength of the friendly Canadians, and in part to the inexperienced and unstable character of the American troops, and to insufficient financial support from Congress.

Finally, finding his position had become precarious by decreasing supplies and an increasing mutinous spirit among his troops and by a coincident growth of Canadian resentment, Arnold withdrew his forces to Crown Point on Lake Champlain, followed slowly by the advance of Governor Carleton to the northern end of the lake. After constructing a fleet of ten vessels on Lake Champlain, he sailed northward on August 24 and met the newly constructed British fleet (of twenty-nine vessels) on October 11. In the curious naval battle which ensued he was defeated and forced to escape via Crown Point and Ticonderoga. By his defense, however, he arrested the advance of Carleton, who returned to Canada with his troops in preference to the conduct of a winter campaign against the Americans.[9]

Possibly the only importance of the American Canadian expedition was its strategic influence in dividing General Howe's opposing army into two parts.

Later, Congress persisted in looking forward to the broader expansion of the Confederacy. In the Articles of Confederation which it completed on November 15, 1777, it inserted the provision that "Canada, acceding to the Confederation and joining in the measures of the United States, shall be admitted into, and entitled to all the advantages of the Union."

In January, 1778, the American commissioners at Paris (Franklin, Lee and Deane), in reply to an inquiry from Gerard concerning the terms upon which they would agree to reject British proposals to return to their former place within the empire, requested an immediate engagement "to guarantee the present possessions of the Congress in America, with such others as they may acquire on the Continent during the war" and a promise from the French that they would furnish aid in the war until all English possessions on the continent were conquered. In the treaty of defensive alliance of February 6, the United States obtained a guarantee of all its possessions "from any of the dominions now or heretofore possessed by Great Britain in North America."[10]

American plans for further attempts at invasion of Canada were terminated by the formal entrance of France into the war as an ally of the United States. M. Gerard, the French minister in Philadelphia, discouraged designs on Canada; and it appears that the French government was actually opposed to any expedition that would give that region to the United States. To this French policy, however, some prominent Frenchmen were opposed. Cerisier, the secretary of the French legation at the Hague in 1778, suggested that England, in order to prevent future dispute, should abandon to the United States all its neighboring possessions, and proposed that Canada should become a fourteenth state of the Union.

Lafayette and a committee of Congress drew up a plan for a combined Franco-American attack. This unexecuted plan was opposed by Washington who, desiring to avoid an increase of American national obligation to foreign powers, and being unwilling to ask for any assistance not indispensable, objected (November, 1778) to the introduction of a large body of French troops into Canada. The basis of this opposition was the fear that France, if it aided in conquering the country, would insist upon retention of the region, and that it would thereby obtain too much advantage on the American continent. On November 20, however, preparatory to plans for future American expeditions in case they should be found expedient, Washington began to inquire as to the best route and "how far short of entire conquest and annexation of Canada to the Union would give permanent peace and security to the frontiers." [11]

Leading men continued to urge expeditions for the acquisition of Canada. In August 1778, Timothy Pickering at Philadelphia wrote that "The United States will not make peace until Canada, Nova Scotia, and the two Floridas are also recovered to freedom and independence, and a free fishery secured to New England." As late as December, 1779, General Gates and others still had a desire to send an expedition to make overtures to the Canadians that their country become a state of the Union. From M. Luzerne, representing the French government and objecting to this policy, he received the reply that if the United States (while the enemy held so much of its territory) had means of offensive operations it had better apply them to the conquest of the Floridas.

Although the policy of the French government was not to aid American expansion either north or south, Lafayette, with the approval of Washington, in May, 1780, issued to the Canadians an ineffective proclamation asking them to join the French arms and help to make their country a part of the United States; but his dream was never realized.[12]

After abandonment of plans for military invasion, Congress sought to obtain Canada by diplomacy. Although it wisely refrained from demanding cession as a *sine qua non,* it instructed the American peace commissioners to try to persuade the British to agree to a cession for reparations, as compensation for indemnities, and to prevent future wars.

The Americans were more successful in their attempt to conquer the trans-Appalachian territory between the Ohio and the Lakes. In 1778, with instructions from Governor Patrick Henry of Virginia, George Rogers Clark hastened to the British post at Kaskaskia and seized it on July 4. Then, in 1779, with only 130 men, he advanced to Vincennes on the Wabash, where by stratagem, he induced the town to surrender and captured the fort. American occupation of the Northwest was further made possible by the failure of the attempt of General Haldimand to reduce the Spanish posts on the Mississippi. American claim to the region was also strengthened by the action of Governor Jefferson of Virginia in directing Colonel Clark to establish a fort on the Mississippi near 36° 30′ and to construct others in the direction of the Lakes, both for occupation and for protection.[13]

In all the instructions for negotiating treaties, the Continental Congress claimed the Mississippi as the western boundary north of the parallel of 31°. Although this claim was opposed by France and Spain, it was finally successful by the concession of the British government which, lessening its own power to exert control in that region, ceded to the United States the large tract of country to which Hamilton said "we had even no plausible claim."[14]

The question of future American-Canadian boundaries was discussed in Congress several times before the close of the Revolution. In 1779 a committee report, to which Congress agreed on March 19, proposed a line "running from Nova Scotia southwesterly, west and northwesterly to Lake Nipissing, thence westerly to the source of the Mississippi (which was then supposed to be the Lake of the Woods), and thence following the Mississippi to the northern boundary of Florida." It also proposed to negotiate for the acquisition of Nova Scotia and Florida, and for the right of settling alien territories. Later, through Gouverneur Morris, it presented its views to Congress which accepted them. It stated that America, while regarding the cession of Canada and Nova Scotia as of the utmost importance to the peace and commerce of the United States, and while claiming that an equal common right to the fisheries should be guaranteed, did not present these subjects in the form of an ultimatum.

On August 14, 1779, Congress adopted instructions defining the boundaries of the United States as the St. John River (to its northern source), the highlands from the northwest angle of Nova Scotia to the northwesternmost head of the Connecticut, the Connecticut to 45°, the latter to the St. Lawrence, thence a straight line to the south end of Lake Nipissing, thence direct to the source of the Mississippi, the middle of the latter to 31°, thence east on 31° to the Appalachicola, down the latter to the mouth of Flint, thence direct to the head of the St. Marys, and down the latter to the Atlantic. In these instructions authority was given, if necessary, to agree upon some other line west of Lake Nipissing (but not south of 45°) and upon the adjustment of the eastern boundary by commissioners "according to such line as shall be by them settled and agreed on as the boundary between . . . Maine and the colony of Nova Scotia."[15]

In the later, and more elastic instructions of June 15, 1780, to the commissioners, Congress requested them "to secure the interest of the United States . . . as circumstances may direct . . . provided Great Britain be not left in possession of any part of the Thirteen United States." On October 18, 1780, it approved a committee resolution informing Adams that a short truce would be highly dangerous to the United States, but authorizing him, with the concurrence of France, to agree to a long or indefinite truce on condition that Great Britain agree to remove the British land and naval armaments from the United States.[16]

In later instructions (of 1781), issued at the time of Cornwallis's invasion of Virginia, and apparently influenced by possible French views concerning boundaries, and by a sincere desire for peace, Congress submitted to the commissioners, through Gouverneur Morris, its views that circumstances might necessitate some alterations of the earlier instructions which had been submitted to Adams on August 14, 1779, and October 18, 1780; and it suggested certain proposals which "ought to be obtained if possible." In the new instructions Morris insisted that there could be no doubt of the American right to the territory within the lines marking the eastern boundary of Maine, the high grounds (dividing Atlantic waters from St. Lawrence waters) to the head of the Connecticut, the latter river to 45° N., the parallel of 45° to the St. Lawrence, the latter and Lake Ontario to the mouth of the Oswego or Onondaga, thence upstream southwardly to 43° N., the parallel of 43° to the western limit of Pennsylvania, the western boundary of Pennsylvania, the southern boundary of Pennsylvania eastward to Maryland, the western boundary of Maryland, thence the Lord Fairfax line to the Allegheny watershed, the latter to the southern boundary of Georgia, and thence to the Atlantic. He conceded that the eastern boundary of Maine was open to negotiation provided it should not be moved farther westward than the Kennebec. He urged that efforts should be made to continue the northern boundary on Lake Ontario and on Lake Erie and west of the western boundary of Pennsylvania, in order to include the Fort of Niagara and the territory ceded by the Indians at Fort Stanwix on November 5, 1768. Concerning the latter he especially urged strong contention for the line of the Ohio to the mouth of the Great Kanawha, thence the latter river to its head "in the Allegheny Mountains."

He further instructed the commissioners to obtain an admission that the cis-Mississippi territory not included within the boundaries of the United States (including Nova Scotia, the Floridas and the trans-Allegheny territory) would be subject to the free and independent Indian tribes, and (without receding except in the last necessity) to insist upon the demolition of all frontier fortresses. In authorizing ultimate consent to the restricted boundaries, if expressly required by the King of France, he directed the commissioners to act entirely in concert with the French ministers and "not to swerve from the principles of our alliance in any possible case." [17]

In August, 1782, following a report of the Massachusetts

legislature, a special committee of Congress reported that the Sagadahoc region "cannot be proved to extend to the St. John" as clearly as to the St. Croix.[18]

Meantime Congress had considered the question of the Loyalists. In October, 1780, it approved a committee resolution prohibiting any stipulation for re-admittance to the United States of persons who had abandoned any of the states, or had been banished, since the beginning of the war, and authorized consideration of the equivalent for their property only on condition of a British reciprocal stipulation to make full compensation for all wanton destruction of property of American citizens by British subjects. It also expressed the wish not to be bound by any public engagement to admit British subjects to any of the rights or privileges of citizens of the United States, since it was determined not to admit them to a full equality in this respect unless Adams should decide that such a concession was necessary to prevent a continuance of the war.[19]

Toward friendly Canadians, however, it favored a more liberal policy. On November 10 it approved the order of General Washington for extending protection and assistance to distressed Canadians who, because of attachment to the American cause, had left their own country and were residing in New York State.[20]

In the spring of 1782 the preliminary peace negotiations were begun at Paris. In April, Franklin, who in 1760 had favored a British demand for the possession of Canada as indemnification and to prevent France from being a check on the British colony, suggested to Oswald that some Americans, although they might have no desire to incorporate Canada which as a foreign neighbor might prove beneficial in stimulating closer union among the thirteen commonwealths, would be favorably affected by a British conciliatory offer to cede it. He especially suggested a cession as compensation for losses during the war, for indemnification of Loyalists, and to prevent future wars.

In one of the earliest conferences (in May, 1782), he insisted that in the division of the empire, which must result from a treaty of peace, the United States should share in the imperial assets, among which he included the Newfoundland fisheries and at least a part of Canada.

He suggested that in order to promote an enduring peace a cession of Canada was desirable, and that for this British sacrifice America might agree to grant to the American Loyalists wild Canadian lands as compensation for their losses resulting from the Revolution. He especially proposed that the extent of Canada should be reduced, at least to the boundaries which existed before its extension to the Indian country south of the Lakes by the Quebec Act of 1774—an extension which the Americans regarded as illegal so far as it had diminished the extent of earlier English colonial boundaries.

Oswald was inclined to favor the proposed cession of Canada and Nova Scotia on the ground that the cession would remove the occasions for future wars which might result from differences between frontier settlers. Later, however, he received information from Lord Shelburne that the British government could not cede Canada as reparation and hoped some more friendly way could be found to prevent future wars. In May, still regarding British possession of Canada as detrimental to British interests, he expressed to Franklin the opinion that the Canada question would be settled to American satisfaction before the close of the negotiations; but he was unable to induce the British ministry to cede more than the region south of the St. Lawrence drainage and of the Lakes, including the territory north of the Ohio which had been added to Quebec in 1774. The British government soon thereafter sent to Paris a new commissioner, Mr. Strachey, under renewed instructions against any surrender of Canada.[21]

Later, finding that France would not support the American demand for cession of Canada which Congress had not made a *sine qua non*, the American commissioners directed their efforts to more promising discussions. In the subsequent diplomatic negotiations with the British, after elimination of their proposal for a cession of Canada, they secured better terms than they expected. Secret direct negotiations with Great Britain were begun in September on the suggestion of John Jay. The latter, having no confidence in the rectitude of the French monarchy with which he regarded Franklin as too conciliatory, rightly suspected a French commitment with Spain to confine the new-born American republic within narrow geographical limits, and even French views in favor of a continuation of British possession of the northern part of the trans-Allegheny territory which some affected to regard as Indian property not included in the limits of the old English colonies.[22]

The Americans explained that the recognition of independence which they asked involved the acceptance of boundaries which the states legally possessed as colonies, together with all the jurisdictions and territorial rights which had belonged to the British crown therein after the treaty of 1763. Their first treaty draft was drawn by Jay. As a boundary on the north-east they proposed the southern boundary of Quebec as fixed by the proclamation of 1763: the parallel of 45° from the St. Lawrence to the Connecticut, the latter to its head, thence the crest of the highlands (which formed a watershed separating the St. Lawrence tributaries from the streams which emptied into the sea) to the northwestern angle of Nova Scotia, thence a line due south to the St. John and the latter to its mouth.

Following Oswald's statement of October 23 that the lower St. John was beyond the existing limits of Massachusetts (which then included Maine) and that Nova Scotia extended to the Kennebec, they agreed to accept as the eastern boundary the south line from the northwest angle of Nova Scotia across the St. John to the head of the St. Croix and the latter stream to its mouth. This decision was reached after October 26, following the arrival of Adams who was not prepared to maintain the claim of Massachusetts beyond the St. Croix.

From their first proposal of the Kennebec, the British commissioners soon retired to the Penobscot, from which (after a brief, obstinate defense) they finally retreated reluctantly to the St. Croix. The second treaty draft containing this agreement was carried to London on November 5 by Mr. Strachey, the British assistant in the negotiations.[23]

Westward from the intersection of the parallel of 45° on the St. Lawrence the American commissioners first proposed (on October 8) to accept a direct line to the southern point of

Lake Nipissing and thence a direct line to the source of the Mississippi. This proposal of an illogical line of extension, which was a part of the American second treaty draft, the British cabinet fortunately rejected. Later, after further examination of maps, and after receiving Oswald's reply that Quebec included the territory north of the Ohio, the Americans suggested a choice between two alternative propositions: (1) the parallel of 45° from the St. Lawrence to the Mississippi, or (2) a line by river and lake to the northwest corner of the Lake of the Woods, and thence a direct line due west to the Mississippi. The latter proposal, by which America obtained a line through the middle of the Great Lakes and valuable mineral deposits on Lake Superior, the British accepted in preference to the other proposals.[24] In a third draft of the provisional treaty the proposed boundary was substantially the same as that later adopted in the definitive treaty of September 3, 1783.

Successful in obtaining a boundary through the middle of the Lakes, and an agreement of the British to withdraw from the posts within American jurisdiction, the Americans did not make an issue of the British fur trade across the boundary in the Maumee region where it later encountered the increasing competition of traders from Pennsylvania and New York.

On November 29, after several conferences and considerable discouraging controversial discussion on several knotty problems (pre-Revolution debts, Loyalist claims to compensation, and American claims to fishery rights), the commissioners reached compromise agreements which were included in the fourth and final draft of the preliminary or provisional treaty. This provisional draft treaty, which was signed on November 30, 1782, was practically the same as the later definitive treaty of September 3, 1783, except that in the latter the article on fisheries was made more specific.[25]

Article II of the provisional treaty designated the northern boundaries of the United States as follows: on the east, the St. Croix and a line to the northwest angle of Nova Scotia; on the north, the highlands south of the St. Lawrence, the upper Connecticut to 45°, the latter to the St. Lawrence, thence through the middle of the river and the lakes and water communications to the northwest corner of the Lake of the Woods, and thence "a due west course" to the Mississippi.

In the treaty terms concerning the northern boundary were involved geographical questions whose elucidation required the efforts of sixty years. The provision concerning the highlands south of the St. Lawrence encountered some prompt objections from the British opposition which claimed that the approach of the boundary line so near to Montreal (twenty-four miles) was inconsistent with the security of Canada. Montreal merchants, especially, continued to urge a new boundary line south of the Lakes.

To Canadians and others who censured the surrender of Illinois and the country on the Ohio, including the Muskingum connection south of the Lakes, Richard Champion announced his refusal "to walk in mournful procession over the calamitous scenes of the late unhappy war." He declared that this ceded territory had no intrinsic value to Great Britain, and that the latter would have been benefited if Canada and Nova Scotia had been ceded in exchange for the Newfoundland and Labrador fisheries. He also opposed the dispute concerning the Lake of the Woods boundary in a region in which he predicted that neither the United States nor England would ever occupy except on paper (!).

Canadians were later inclined to blame British cabinet officers for neglecting the interests of Canada in agreeing to "amputation of territory" in 1783, but they attributed British policy chiefly to ignorance of geography and to depreciation of the ability of American diplomats.[26]

Some American leaders continued to expect the later annexation of Canada. In October, 1785, John Adams still contemplated the possible acquisition of Canada in the interests of peace, even if war was necessary to secure it. Hamilton, however, suggested that Canada, if well governed, might become well populated by people attached to their own government. In 1787 he was apprehensive of a growing connection of Vermont with Canada, which he sought to discourage by a proposal to the legislature of New York to release the New York claim to the territory of Vermont, provided the latter would immediately become a member of the American Union.[27]

After the article on boundaries, one of the chief articles of the treaty was that relating to fisheries on the coasts of British American dominions (Article III). This article reserved to the United States important American fishing rights in British North America, which Congress in its instructions had declared necessary to American welfare, and some of which had been strenuously resisted by the British. It provides that the American people "shall continue to enjoy unmolested the right to take fish of every kind on the Grand Bank, and on all the other banks of Newfoundland; also in the Gulph of St. Lawrence, and at other places in the sea where the inhabitants of both countries used at any time heretofore to fish." It also stated that they "shall have liberty to take fish of every kind on such part of the coast of Newfoundland as British fishermen shall use . . . and also on the coasts, bays and creeks of all other of His Britannic Majesty's dominions in America; and . . . shall have liberty to dry and cure fish in any of the unsettled bays, harbours, and creeks of Nova Scotia, Magdalen Islands and Labrador, so long as the same shall remain unsettled." On this liberty, however, was placed a restriction that, after these places became settled, the agreement of the inhabitants, proprietors or possessors of the ground must be obtained.

Associated with this article in the negotiations was Article VIII which declared that the navigation of the Mississippi from its source to its mouth "shall forever remain free and open" to British subjects and American citizens.

Of especial interest were articles in regard to debts and the Loyalists, upon which the British had insisted. Article IV provided that creditors of either country should meet with no lawful impediment to the full recovery of all *bona fide* debts previously contracted. Article V was inserted to satisfy the British request for a compensation adjustment of losses by Loyalists in the Revolution. In it the Americans, claiming that Congress had no power to provide compensation or to compel the states to do so, agreed that Congress would earnestly recommend to the states provisions for restitution of property and rights confiscated under a radical defensive policy which, after the failure of American plans to incorporate Canada, had resulted in an expedient resort to harsh measures of compulsion (both legal and illegal). These measures the Revolutionary leaders in Congress and in the new states (and the Whig mobs) had attempted to justify as necessary to preserve the new freedom and to secure the success of the movement for independence.[28]

From the standpoint of the result, this American domestic policy in the treatment of the Tories was shortsighted. Unfortunately, it resulted in the forced emigration of many conservative Loyalist citizens whose settlement in Canada near the American border was a large determining factor in later American-Canadian contacts—especially in the hostile contacts before 1815. It strengthened the neighboring antipathy against Americans and instilled in the latter a deep antipathy which only time could remove.

After the treaty of 1783, the American Congress under the Articles of Confederation was unable to enforce its recommendations that the states should provide for cessation of all persecution of the Loyalists, for restoration of the property of those who had not borne arms, and for permission of all to return for a year to settle their business affairs (including prosecution of their rights in confiscated lands). As a result, the banishments and emigrations which had begun during the Revolution were continued in large numbers in 1783–84—especially contributing to the increase in the population of the western part of Nova Scotia (from which New Brunswick was separated in 1784) and to the establishment of permanent settlers in the region later known as Upper Canada.

The total Loyalist emigration was later estimated at 100,000 persons. A large number of these submitted claims to the British government for indemnities for losses and hardships which they had suffered in the Revolution and the memory of which created in their minds a deep hostility toward the authors of their misfortunes. These claims, for which the American government declined to assume responsibility and for which the state legislatures refused to provide restitution, were finally adjusted by the British government by an appropriation of £3,000,000 in 1790.[29]

In New Brunswick the loyal refugees, immediately after the treaty of peace, built the town of St. Andrews on the eastern bank of the Schoodic, which was regarded by the British government as the St. Croix designated as the international boundary in the treaty. At Nantucket, the Loyalist inhabitants, in opposition to American interests, desired "to separate themselves from the United States, and become either a neutral Island, or annexed to Great Britain," or "to emigrate to some part of the British Dominions, thereby exonerating themselves from the Foreign Duties on whale oil." Leaders of Nova Scotia, fearing injury from the smuggling which would result from the Nantucket project, sought to induce the British government to pursue a policy which might cause the whole American whale fishery to center in Nova Scotia.[30]

In Canada the Loyalists especially contributed to economic, social and political growth. As pioneers across the American northern border they laid the foundations of the new province of Ontario which became a barrier to later American plans for annexation, and otherwise became a leading factor in establishing the foundation of Canadian destiny.

In the treaty negotiations the Americans were unable to induce the English to agree to an arrangement for commercial privileges. After the completion of the treaty of 1783, they still expected satisfactory trade relations. In this they were encouraged by the early policy of Pitt, who, hoping to eradicate all sources of irritation which had caused the recent war, proposed (in 1783) as a temporary regulation to admit American vessels and merchandise to all British ports (including colonial ports) on terms of equality with the trade of British subjects, but who was finally forced by important hostile interests to abandon his measure of liberal concession to America.[31]

American interests after 1783 were threatened by the new British policy of encouraging Canadian development at the expense of the earlier trade in colonial vessels between New England and the British West Indies. The American government doubted the wisdom of the British attempt to supply the West

Indies from the British North American colonies, since its success would involve restrictions on the more convenient trade with the United States which seemed essential to the prosperity of the sugar islands.[32] In vain, it sought to secure a modification of the illiberal antiquated British principle of colonial monopoly which had caused the American struggle for independence, and which was especially urged by Lord Sheffield, although in opposition to the opinion of British planters in the West Indies[33] and the views of Richard Champion.[34] A remaining American hope of more liberal trade relations after the inauguration of the new American government under the new constitution was dispelled by the British orders in council of January, 1791.[35]

Meantime, after 1783, anticipating early British withdrawal from the occupation of the border posts of the Lakes, Americans had hopes for an expansion of the trade of the East with the Lakes and the Ohio, via Oswego and the Mohawk and the Potomac—hopes which were expressed in proposals to establish inland communication with the Northwest.[36]

REFERENCES

1. LODGE (ed.), *The Works of Hamilton,* I, 173–88; *Franklin's Works,* V, 65; *John Adams' Works,* X, 251; *C.A.,* Q., Vol. 2, 129.
2. JARED SPARKS, *Life of G. Morris,* I, 64; *Journal of Congress,* I, 100, 104, 109; *Secret Journal of Congress,* I, 42, 283 and 290; *4 Am. Archives,* II, 976; C. H. JONES, *Campaign for Conquest of Canada.*
3. *4 Am. Archives,* II, 1685; *Ib.,* III, 841.
4. FORD (ed.), *Writings of Jefferson,* I.
5. JUSTIN SMITH, *Arnold's March from Cambridge to Quebec; 4 Am. Archives,* III, 796 and 1688; *Ib.,* IV, 190 and 309 and 1513; *C.A.,* Q., Vol. 12, 16.
6. *4 Am. Archives,* IV, 1513.
7. *Ib.,* V, 1166–67, 1237, 1643–45; *Writings of Washington,* III, 390.
8. *Ib.,* II, 444.
9. *4 Am. Archives,* VI, 129, 456; *5 Am. Archives,* I, 925–30 and 937–48; *Ib.,* II, 1058; *Scribner's Monthly,* Feb., 1898; *Lieut. Haddon's Journal and Orderly Books,* 1776–78, p. 221.

10. *The Deane Papers,* II, 313.
11. *Writings of Washington,* VI, 107–13, 298, 432–37; WHARTON, *Diplomatic Correspondence of the Am. Revolution,* III, 321.
12. PICKERING and UPHAM, *Life of Timothy Pickering,* p. 234; *Writings of Washington,* VII, 44–45.
13. WINSOR, *Narrative and Critical History,* VI, 742; GEORGE TUCKER, *Life of Jefferson,* I, 141.
14. *Journals of Congress,* XVIII, 900; *Madison's Letters and Other Writings,* Vol. 4, 444; *Hamilton's Works,* IV, 294.
15. *Journals of Congress,* Vol. 14, 959–60; *Papers of the Continental Congress,* Vol. 1 (folio 147), No. 25; *Secret Journals, Foreign,* II, 225–26; *Am. State Papers, Foreign Relations,* VI, 806; WHARTON, *Dip. Cor. of the Am. Revolution,* III, 301; J. B. MOORE, *International Arbitrations,* I, 95–96; J. M. CALLAHAN, *Neutrality of the American Lakes,* Chap. 2.
16. MOORE, *Int. Arbs.,* I, 97; *Journals of Congress,* XVIII, 948–50; *Instructions to Peace Commissioners,* Oct. 18, 1780 (in Mss. Division of Library of Congress).
17. *Misc. Letters, Jan.–Feb., 1842* (Jared Sparks to Webster, Feb. 15, 1842).
18. WHARTON, *Dip. Cor. of the Am. Revol.,* IV, 504–05; *Secret Journals of Congress, Foreign Affairs,* III, 161–71.
19. *Resolutions of Congress,* Oct. 18, 1780.
20. *Journals of Congress,* XVIII, 1042.
21. *Franklin's Works,* VIII, 12–15; *Ib.,* IX, 69, 354; *John Adams' Works,* I, 360; WHARTON, *Dip. Cor. of the Am. Revol.,* V, 540–41; SPARKS: *Dip. Cor. of the Am. Revol.,* VI; FITZMAURICE, *Life of Lord Shelburne,* I, 175–82 and 188– ; *Imperial and Asiatic Quart. Rev.,* Jan., 1898, 93–119; WINSOR, *Narrative and Critical History,* III, 101, 109, 175–81.
22. *Cont. Cong. Papers, Rps. Committees,* I, 35; SPARKS, *Dip. Cor. of the Am. Revol.,* III, 286; WHARTON, *Dip. Cor. of the Am. Revol.,* III, 295; *Am. Hist. Rev.,* X, 249–55 (F. J. TURNER).
23. WHARTON, *Dip. Cor. of the Am. Revol.,* V, 452; J. B. MOORE, *International Arbitrations,* I, 99.
24. *Ib.,* I, 99; SPARKS, *Dip. Cor. of the Am. Rev.,* V, Nov. 6, 1782; WHARTON, *Dip. Cor. of the Am. Revol.,* V, 461, 851.
25. *Ib.,* V, 452; *Franklin's Writings,* VIII, 527, 621– ; *John Adams' Works,* III, 333 and 336.
26. RICHARD CHAMPION, *Considerations of the Present Situation of Great Britain and the United States,* 256; *Asiatic Quart. Rev.,* V (1898), 93–119; *Ib.,* VI, 196–97.
27. *John Adams' Works,* IV, 293; *Jefferson's Papers,* M, 1°, Vol. 57, Nos. 8 and 9; *Hamilton's Works,* I, 407; *Ib.,* II, 374.
28. FITZMAURICE, *Life of Lord Shelburne,* I, 175–82 and 188– ; *4 Am. Archives, passim.*

29. H. L. Keenleyside, *Canada and the United States*, pp. 36–55; *Malloy Treaties*, I, 588–89; *Transactions of the Royal Society of Canada*, VII–X (W. H. Siebert); *N. Y. Packet*, March 3 and 8, 1794.
30. *121 Foreign Letters* (Cont. Cong. Archives), 121–55; *C.A.*, *A 107 N.S.*, *C.O. Records*, 1795, 109–14.
31. *Trade of Great Britain with the United States, 1791* (Washington, 1888).
32. G. S. Graham, *British Policy and Canada*, 1774–91; *Am. State Papers*, 15–1, Vol. 4, No. 87, Feb. 19, 1818; *Exec. Docs.*, 27–2, No. 68, Feb. 8, 1842, 190; *C.A.*, G., 127, pp. 322–64 (especially pp. 330), *Rp. of the Lords of the Com. of the P.C. for Trade*, Nov. 14, 1846, enclosure in Grey to Elgin, No. 38, Mar. 19, 1847.
33. *37 Hazard Pamphlets*, No. 15 (Library of Congress); *Intercourse between the [British] Sugar Colonies and the United States.*
34. Richard Champion, *Considerations on the Present Situation of Great Britain and the United States;* George Chalmers, *Opinions on Subjects of Public Law and Commercial Policy Arising from Am. Independence;* Tench Coxe, *Examination of Lord Sheffield's Observations on the Commerce of the United States* (Misc. Pamphlets, Library of Cong.); *Jefferson Papers* (M), 2°, Vol. 57, No. 26, Monroe to Jefferson, Nov. 1784.
35. *Am. State Papers, Foreign Affairs*, I; *Rp. of the Privy Council*, Jan. 28, 1791; *Jefferson's Works*, VIII, 642.
36. *Miss. Valley Hist. Rev.*, Dec. 1920, pp. 228–41; *Ib.*, March 1922, pp. 327–66; McMaster, *United States*, I, 58 and 61; *Washington's Diary of 1784.*

CHAPTER II

LAKE POSTS AND THE JAY TREATY

ONE of the earliest problems of the young American republic was that of the control of frontier hinterland over whose native inhabitants British control was threatened through the influence of the Canadian fur trade. In the first two decades after 1783, the American government, which had failed to achieve its defensive policy of including Canada in a continental union, found reasons for apprehension in Britain's Canadian policies, which threatened to restrict the expansion and jurisdiction of the United States in its own hinterland territory, and also the future of American commercial activity on the boundary Lakes and the St. Lawrence.

For twelve years after the ratification of the treaty of 1783, which was proclaimed by Congress on January 14, 1784, the question of the border posts (which the British had agreed to evacuate with "convenient speed") remained one of the chief issues in Anglo-American relations. In the discussions of the subject, the Americans reached the conclusion that apparently the dominant reason for British policy in holding the posts was to protect the profitable Canadian fur trade with the Indians of the American Northwest—a trade with the interior which after 1763 had greatly increased under the business management of Sir Alexander Mackenzie and other Scotch merchants of Montreal who exported their furs to England. In this conclusion they were probably correct.

The British government was influenced in its action by the Canadian merchants, who were astonished at the boundary provisions of the treaty which manifestly would soon result in the extension of American settlements into the Indian country south of the Lakes, and who were apprehensive that the admission of Americans to the navigation of the Lakes might result in a diversion of the furs of the Northwest to New York via Albany. It was also influenced by the fear that the Indians who had been their allies would resent the transfer of territory which, in 1768, had been recognized as Indian territory by the treaty of Fort Stanwix.

The Canadian fur traders especially influenced the authority of the British commander at Detroit in efforts to control the trade of the Maumee and the upper Wabash and Mackinac, under the supervision of the post commanders. They also encouraged the British policy to hold the confidence and loyalty of the Indians of the Northwest during their conflict with the American settlers and the American government. These efforts to influence British Indian policy they continued until the American expeditions against the Indians were finally terminated by Wayne's victory and the treaty of Greenville in 1795.[1]

The resulting controversy was essentially a conflict between the steel trap and the plow. The American government felt the obligation to encourage the extension of settlement westward into the wilderness, in order to provide homes for migrating sons of New England whose dispersion was stimulated by a depression caused in part by the loss of the British West India trade.

The American Congress, following a resolution of May 1, 1783, announced a policy of conciliation in relations with the Indians. In pursuance of plans to confer with the hostile tribes, it sent to Detroit commissioners who found that the British officers were not disposed to coöperate. It soon found that its peace policy was opposed by the western tribes, who were led by Chief Joseph Brant of the Mohawks, and who were encouraged by British commanders of the American border posts and by agents of the well-organized Canadian Department of Indian Affairs who executed British orders in communicating with the Indians in American territory.

In July, 1783, General Baron von Steuben, who was sent to Canada with orders from General Washington to arrange the details of British evacuation of the American posts, reported that General Haldimand (the British governor-general) declined to treat—apparently with the purpose to delay evacuation long enough to enable traders to withdraw without serious loss, and to protect the Indians long enough to reconcile them to the new situation. In July, 1784, Lieutenant-Colonel Hull, who arrived in Canada with American orders to arrange the details of evacuation, learned from General Haldimand that no orders had been received and that the delay was probably due to American treatment of Loyalists who had returned to the United States after the Revolution. This information was in accord with the views of Lord Sydney, Secretary of the British Office for Home Affairs, who early in the previous April had suggested to Haldimand that, as the United States had not yet complied with the provisions of the treaty, evacuation might be delayed until the fur traders could withdraw their property. Later, the British government offered as an excuse for retention of the posts the failure of Congress to execute the treaty provisions concerning the collection of British debts in United States territory.[2]

The British attitude toward Indian opposition to the American advance was uncertain. In November, 1785, Sir John Johnson, head of the Canadian Indian Department, in a speech at Quebec to Indian representatives, expressed approval of this opposition to American encroachment. In April, 1786, however, Lord Sydney, at London, after refusing Brant's personal request for aid, sent secret instructions to Quebec prohibiting any "open encouragement" to Indian hostilities. Apparently the policy of the British government in holding the posts did not include plans to incite the Indians against the American government.

In October, 1786, in reply to the British refusal to evacuate the posts, John Jay submitted to Congress in secret session a report in which he stated that British retention of the posts was justified by state legal impediments which prevented British recovery of debts. At the same time he recognized the unsalutary influence of the retention. In a letter to John Adams he suggested that possibly British influence had encouraged insurgent citizens of Vermont to conduct a secret correspondence with Canada.

In April, 1787, fearing that American success in attacks on the Indians might result in an attack on the British posts, Sydney intimated to Lord Dorchester that the supply of ammunition to the Indians, for defense, was not regarded as active assistance. In the following September, he wrote Dorchester that the posts must be held, and suggested that the aid of the Indians might be needed in case of an American attempt to capture them. Later, John Adams, at London, continued unsuccessful demands for British evacuation, until he finally severed diplomatic relations, and withdrew from the British capital. Coincidentally the British became more determined to retain the posts and to thwart American influence on the Lakes. In 1789 the British commander at Niagara refused to allow Americans to view Niagara Falls.[3]

Meantime, between 1784 and 1789, Congress had concluded with different Indian tribes several treaties of cession by which it claimed the extinguishment of Indian title to all the region later included within the later limits of Ohio except the northwestern part which was drained into Lake Erie. In 1786, it established Fort Harmar on the Ohio, at the mouth of the Muskingum. In 1787 it enacted the famous Ordinance for government of the Northwest, resulting in the beginning of the settlement of Marietta in May, 1788. By this action it aroused the opposition of some western Indian tribes which regarded the new settlement as an encroachment upon land claimed by them.

In January, 1789, at Fort Harmar some local tribes unwillingly joined in a council which re-affirmed the earlier grants by Indians who did not occupy the territory; but they probably did not understand the nature of their act of cession. Later, the act of the chiefs who signed was repudiated by tribal members who had not signed, and who threatened danger to the new white settlements in the region.

After the organization of hostile Indians who expected Canadian assistance in resisting the American advance into former Indian territory, President Washington adopted an American policy of military defensive under General St. Clair, which by 1791 resulted in the organization of a military expedition with plans to erect a chain of border police forts from Fort Washington on the Ohio (near the site of Cincinnati) northward to the Maumee.[4]

In 1790, when the Anglo-Spanish controversy concerning the Nootka Sound affair threatened to precipitate a war, Washington recognized that the foreign situation and the strategic position of the United States between Canada and Louisiana necessitated the formulation of an American foreign policy relative to both the Northwest posts and the Southwest problem of Louisiana. Early in 1790, he sent Gouverneur Morris from Paris to London on an informal personal mission to clear the way for adjustment of the chief issues with Great Britain, including commerce and the posts. From Morris, he soon received the information that British government, under Pitt, although it instructed Lord Dorchester to restrain the Indians from depredations against American settlers on the Ohio, offered no encouragement in regard to British evacuation of the posts, which it claimed to hold only to secure fulfillment of treaty obligations. In the following October, he had reason to believe that all British consideration of plans for voluntary withdrawal from the posts was ended by the news that Spain agreed to the British demands in the Nootka affair.[5]

In July, following the informal conferences of Morris at London, Hamilton held some interesting intimate conferences at New York, with George Beckwith, an unofficial (or semi-official) British agent, whom Lord Dorchester had sent to ascertain the American attitude toward the apprehended British war with Spain, the nature of American negotiations with the Indians of the Northwest, and a possible basis for an American alliance with Great Britain. After consultation with Washington, he cautiously notified Beckwith that a more definite detailed statement representing the views of the British cabinet in regard to the irregular proposal of alliance would furnish a better basis for conversation.[6] Apprehending a possible British request for permission to send a military force across American territory from Canada to Louisiana, and with a view to possible British co-operation in American plans to secure a post or territory at the mouth of the Mississippi, Washington asked members of his cabinet to submit their written opinions.[7] Anxious to adjust all differences with Great Britain, he authorized frank assurances concerning American plans to chastise the western Indians—plans which did not contemplate a military advance against the unevacuated posts. Hamilton, in suggesting to Beckwith the wisdom of avoiding a source of future border collision and of encouraging more satisfactory trade relations, stated that American friendship might become important in relation to the security of British North American possessions.[8]

In December, Jefferson expressed his opinion that the British government had no intention either to evacuate the posts or to negotiate a commercial treaty unless it could obtain American agreement to a treaty of alliance. In the following February, he recommended reprisals against British commerce. In April, 1791, after Knox had instructed General St. Clair to establish a post at the northern Miami village as a means of warning to prevent future Indian hostilities, he notified the British of the President's suggestion that the American government objected to any activities of British traders (at the posts) which might result in supplying the American Indians with war materials. Later, in July, in directing St. Clair to attack the hostile Indians on the Maumee, Knox authorized a courteous (but unnecessary) explanation, to the British commander at Detroit, that the expedition had no plans of hostility against the British forces at the border posts.[9]

Meantime, in February, 1791, Hamilton had intimated to Beckwith that the Canadian government and the fur traders should use their influence to induce the Indians to make peace. Promptly thereafter, Lord Dorchester authorized Canadian officials to obtain from the Indians a statement of their peace terms. In the following August, following an Indian council at Maumee Rapids and nearly three months before St. Clair's disastrous defeat, he received at Quebec a delegation of Indian chiefs who requested him to aid them to secure a boundary along the Ohio below the Muskingum and from the head of the latter eastward to Venango and the Pennsylvania purchase of 1784. A few weeks later, on a visit to London, he submitted his views of British policy and thereby influenced the supplemental instructions of George Hammond who had recently been appointed the first British minister to the United States.[10]

In October, Hammond arrived at Philadelphia with his earlier instructions (of September 1) based upon the views of Hawkesbury who advocated British retention of the posts as a means to control the navigation of the Lakes and Canadian monopoly of the fur trade, and as a security for the fidelity of the Indians. He was directed by Grenville to insist upon American execution of treaty obligations, to offer his (or Canadian) interposition for termination of hostilities between the American government and the Indians by measures not inconsistent with the security of the Indians, and to receive *ad referendum* any American proposals concerning a trade treaty on a reciprocal basis.[11] He postponed the presentation of his credentials until late in October, a few days before St. Clair's defeat which encouraged Canadians to suggest plans for British mediation to secure an Indian barrier south of the Lakes and north of the Ohio.[12] In later (supplemental) instructions (of March, 1792), he was authorized to make discretionary efforts to secure to the Indians lands defined by them, to establish this area as a permanent independent barrier territory and to extend a barrier strip eastward along the shore of Lake Ontario and the St. Lawrence, south of the entire boundary as defined in 1783. Soon thereafter, he received Dorchester's project for rectification of the boundary in the region of Lake Champlain.[13]

In the discussions with Hammond, in March, 1792, Jefferson enlivened the diplomatic contest by a review of the various American complaints and especially by a long and severe reply in which he declared that the original treaty infraction was the British retention of the posts. By his intemperate irritating tone, he drove Hammond to seek consolation of Hamilton who unofficially stated that after British evacuation of the posts, some arrangement might be made to secure the interests of the Canadian fur traders. Early in June, after another interview which seemed to indicate no chance for an agreement,[14] he decided that the British government did not intend to retire from the posts, and he suspected that through plans for adjustment of the doubtful Northwest boundary, it sought to secure a cession of American territory which would furnish Canada a practical outlet to the navigable waters of the Mississippi.

Jefferson agreed with Hamilton and Knox that the American government could accept no mediation in its relations with the Indians and no British proposition for cession of territory or interference in American disputes with the Indians, but that it would adjust any British inconveniences which might result from evacuation of the posts and that possibly it might even agree to a mutual restriction of armaments on the Lakes, or other measures necessary for the security and protection of the Canadian fur traders there. He and the President, however, opposed Hamilton's proposal to offer the British access to the navigable waters of the Mississippi (by streams tributary to Lake Superior) as an exchange concession for an alliance in efforts to secure free navigation of the Mississippi to the Gulf. Hamilton had suggested to Hammond an arrangement for mutual free trans-border intercourse with the Indians.[15]

In reporting the American views to Grenville, in June and July, Hammond stated that a formal proposal of mediation and the project of a neutral Indian barrier were impracticable.

Meantime, Colonel John Graves Simcoe, who in the spring of 1791 had favored Levi Allen's plans for union of Vermont with Canada,[16] had been appointed the first governor of the newly organized province of Upper Canada, and had proposed another impracticable program for adjustment of border problems.[17] Desiring to continue British control of the Lakes and to guard the security of Canada, he had unsuccessfully requested an increased military force for defense of Canada from American invasion and had also urged the necessity of retaining the barrier forts.[18] Influenced by representations and suggestions from Montreal and Quebec commercial interests which urged a new revised boundary south of all the Lakes,[19] he proposed (in June, 1792), in addition to the establishment of an Indian barrier, an American cession of Detroit as compensation for American retention of the Genesee region in New York. Establishing his temporary headquarters at Niagara, he managed (through Alexander McKee) to obtain from the Indians, at their Maumee council of October, 1792, a "voluntary" request for his mediation at a proposed peace conference with American commissioners at Sandusky early in 1793, at which the Indians proposed to insist upon the Ohio as a boundary.[20]

Jefferson, to whom Hammond officially mentioned the new mediation proposal, replied that such a mediation between a sovereign power and dependent tribes within its jurisdiction would create a source of embarrassment which should never be permitted, but he agreed that Simcoe might appear at the council conference as a spectator and that British agents might attend to explain the American offers to the natives. At the same time, he urged renewal of negotiations on the unexecuted treaty articles of 1783 which had been suspended since his note of May 29, 1792.[21] On December 30, while waiting for Hammond to obtain instructions on the subject, he suggested to Pinckney at London that he should urge upon the British government the necessity of instructions wide enough to enable Hammond to proceed without waiting for new instructions for every new move in the negotiations. Two days later, he also requested accurate data relating to any embarkation of British troops to Canada. Over three months later, he reported that Hammond was still waiting for expected instructions.[22]

Meantime, early in 1793, while General Anthony Wayne was descending the Ohio with plans to march troops northward on the St. Clair route to the Maumee, President Washington decided to make a last effort to negotiate a peace with the Indians. While Wayne halted, he appointed three peace commissioners who were instructed to ask the Indians to confirm the Fort Harmar treaty of 1789, which confined them to the Lake Erie region between the Cuyahoga and the Maumee. From May 17 to July 11, while awaiting the assembling of the tribes at Sandusky, these commissioners accepted the hospitality of Governor Simcoe at Niagara. From there, they were conveyed on Lake Erie in British vessels with an escort of British officers whom they invited to be present at the peace council. At the council, they conferred with twenty chiefs who arrived directly from the divided Maumee camp where preliminary discussions had been influenced by McKee, an officer of the Canadian Indian Department. They soon found that their plans were defeated by McKee's unreasonable demand for the old line of 1768 as a basis for negotiations.[23] They had been outwitted by the aggressive Simcoe who had hostile frontier plans to prevent the advance of Wayne to the Maumee and to secure the establishment of a new boundary line—plans which he probably regarded as aids to a larger plan for British control of the mouth of the Mississippi as a check upon American strength in the trans-Allegheny region.[24] Coincident with trading activities which were establishing a basis for later extension of American territorial limits on the distant Pacific coast,[25] they had reason for apprehension of British strategic plans to restrict American recognized limits between the Lakes and the Mississippi (!).

In the summer of 1793, American relations with Great Britain concerning the frontier situation were complicated by the activities of Genêt, the French minister, who planned expeditions from American territory against both the Canadian border and the Louisiana border, and by October they were affected by increase of American settlements in the Genesee country and other points south of Lakes Ontario and Erie, which caused Dorchester to suggest to Simcoe the importance of encouraging the development of settlements at Toronto and other points along the north side of the Lakes.[26] Apparently both Dorchester and Simcoe, contemplating the increasing sources of border friction, regarded war as inevitable. At the same time, Jefferson informed the cabinet that Hammond was still waiting for instructions, and Pinckney reported from London that the British government was not yet convinced of its duty to evacuate the border posts.[27]

Early in 1794 (in February), influenced by General Wayne's renewed activity in his campaign to control the Indians and by the resulting wild rumors of an expected American aggressive advance to Detroit, and also by Simcoe and several incidents of border friction along the frontier of New York and Lake Champlain, Dorchester delivered to a visiting delegation of Indians an indiscreet and inflammatory address and ordered Simcoe to erect British defensive fortifications at the rapids of the Maumee on American territory. He also suggested that the arming of British vessels on the Lakes might be necessary to preserve British control there.[28]

Simcoe promptly responded by marching a small British force to the Maumee to build a fort, against which Secretary Randolph complained (on May 20) through Hammond.[29] In June, expecting coöperation of the Cherokees, he said that Canada by a successful war could separate Kentucky and other trans-Allegheny territory from the American Union. He expected Vermont to remain neutral. Later, by authority of Dorchester, he sent a military force to prevent Americans from settling at Sodus Point on Lake Ontario, fearing that they planned to establish there a naval force which might endanger Canadian commerce and safety.[30]

Late in July, apparently with some reason for suspicion concerning Canadian movements, President Washington sought better facilities for obtaining definite information of British hostile preparations. For this purpose, Randolph confidentially requested the governor of Vermont to procure means for regular reports of accurate and secret information by posting at Montreal a discreet and penetrating secret agent of the United States with authority to forward his observations by special messengers. Possibly he may have had some intimation of Simcoe's expressed expectation that in case of war Vermont might unite with Canada.[31]

In July, following the British erection of a new fort on the Maumee, Wayne marched northward from Fort Recovery and built Fort Defiance. In August, he advanced down the Maumee. On August 20, at Fallen Timbers (a few miles above the new British fort), he fought a decisive battle in which he defeated the Indians who had received large war supplies from Detroit. Although he demanded the surrender of the new British fort on the Maumee, he refrained from attack. He considered that the object of his campaign was completed.. He soon withdrew southward and thence westward to the Wabash where he built Fort Wayne, leaving the excited Canadian authorities to continue active preparations for war until they received news of the

Jay-Grenville agreement for a frontier *status quo* during a period of treaty negotiations at London to settle the question of the posts in an orderly way.[32]

On September 1, in referring to Wayne's movements, Randolph made certain statements displeasing to Simcoe, who promptly, but unsuccessfuly, attempted to draw him into a discussion. While declining discussion with Simcoe, he pressed Hammond to say whether he or his government approved Simcoe's views in explanation of British purpose in "re-occupying the post on the Miamis" and in suggesting the right of one nation to intermeddle with the Indians within the territory of another nation. While intimating that British officers and soldiers had aided the attack of the Indians at Fort Recovery, he sought to avoid a recurrence to the circumstances which prevented a treaty with the northern tribes of Indians in the last year. Hoping that the conduct of Governor Simcoe would soon be "consigned to oblivion by the reparation of our injuries and the restitution of our rights," he stated that he would "not willingly open a new source of altercation." He received from Hammond a prompt and courteous reply stating that, as he had resolved not to regard himself responsible for the conduct of British officers in Canada, it was "totally unnecessary" for him to express his personal opinion of the doctrines, assertions and statements contained in Simcoe's letter.[33]

Meantime, Chief Justice John Jay, a diplomat of established reputation, was engaged in efforts with the British government to negotiate a treaty to provide for peaceful adjustment of the difficult problems which had produced a crisis in the spring of 1794 and had threatened to result in war. Appointed by Washington on the recommendation of Hamilton, he had sailed for England on May 12 with instructions to induce Great Britain to restrain British agents on the Canadian border and to find a way to terminate the discussions, concerning the inexecution and infraction of the treaty of peace, whose transfer from one side of the ocean to the other had been regarded with considerable amusement.[34]

Jay's instructions of May 6, although signed by Randolph, were largely based on Hamilton's memorandum of Federalist views which included five chief proposals: (1) demands for indemnification for depredations or spoliations of commerce and for negroes carried away, (2) demand for a treaty of commerce and especially for trade with the British West Indies in vessels of limited tonnage, (3) mutual consent for disarmament on the Lakes and within a limited distance of their shores and for reciprocal free trade with Indian tribes on each side of the boundary, (4) agreements for surrender of the posts and settlement of all other points of difference concerning the treaty of 1783, and (5) insistence on a provision requiring each party to refrain from furnishing anything but the usual supplies to hostile Indians, and on the principle that no nation should interfere with Indians outside its territorial jurisdiction.[35]

On May 27, aroused by the report that Simcoe had marched to the rapids of the "Miami of the Lake," Randolph forwarded to Jay additional instructions emphasizing the manifest necessity of an immediate adjustment of disputes, and again reminding him of the irrevocable sense of the President against any surrender of any part of American territory upon any consideration. On July 30, following the "unfortunate tumult" near Pittsburgh against the whiskey excise tax, he wrote Jay that the reports of British determination to abet the Indians against General Wayne were daily growing more serious.[36]

At London, Jay found his mission was favored by the diplomatic situation, and by the influence of the pressure of the American embargo on Jamaica and other British West India Islands. He received very courteous attention from the British government whose desire to relieve the situation was illustrated by its reprimand of Lord Dorchester for his indiscreet hostile speech of February 10. In conference on disputes concerning the treaty of 1783 he agreed with Grenville that further pursuit of the question of the original infraction (which had been argued by Jefferson and Hammond) would be useless. Personally, he did not blame the British government for refusing to withdraw from the American posts after the American treaty violations concerning British recovery of debts.

By September 13 he reached an agreement on the chief issues

except commerce and rights of neutrals. He proposed to arrange for British evacuation of the posts on June 1, 1795; but at the request of Grenville he agreed to extend the time another year, an extension which Randolph considered as dangerous and unnecessarily long. Other agreements were: (1) mutual trans-boundary trade with the Indians, which Randolph feared would produce in the Northwest "great embarrassment and all the heart burnings of rivalry"; (2) appointment of a mixed commission to determine the identity of the St. Croix River which marked the beginning of the northeast boundary; (3) appointment of a mixed commission to decide British claims for compensation for unrecovered debts, which the American government agreed to pay in specie; (4) British admission of American ships of a limited tonnage (seventy tons) to the British West Indies to carry American products and to return to the United States with West India products, provided the United States would agree to prohibit the reexport of West India products thus imported.[37]

Another question concerning Canada originated in the British demand for rectification of the northwest end of the boundary of 1783 (west of Lake Superior), in order to give Canada free access to the navigation of the Mississippi without passing through foreign territory. This demand Jay fortunately declined to consider. To Grenville's suggestion to agree upon a line from West Bay (on Lake Superior) due west to the Red Lake River branch of the Mississippi, or upon a line due north from the mouth of the St. Croix branch to the water passage west of Lake Superior, he declared (September 4) that the only proper way to adjust the controversy was by an arrangement for a joint survey to determine whether the Mississippi would be intersected by a line drawn due west from the Lake of the Woods. He then suggested that if the line did not intersect the Mississippi, the question should be settled by a joint commission—or, in the words of the treaty of 1783, that the two parties proceed "by amicable negotiation to regulate the boundary in that quarter . . . according to justice and mutual convenience, and in conformity to the intent of said treaty."[38]

Jay could not induce Grenville to consent that neither government should interfere with Indians in the territory of the other, nor that each should try to restrain its Indians from hostility against the other. Neither could he obtain consent to Hamilton's proposal to prohibit naval armaments on the Lakes, nor to plan for later limitation of military force on the international frontier.

As the chief equivalent for British evacuation of the posts, Jay, while guarding against British plans to secure a back-door free trade entrance of British goods into the United States, agreed to a reciprocal provision relating to the frontier trans-boundary trade with the Indians, including freedom from duty on peltries and on regular Indian goods carried by Indians, and also including freedom of passage (without payment of duties) over portages or carrying places on either side by the usual or direct road for reshipment, and without purpose of sale during passage.

This reciprocal provision restricted American traders in Canada to territory outside of the jurisdiction of the Hudson Bay Company. It provided for mutual right to navigate all the Lakes and communicating waters and to conduct trade and commerce, but did not authorize the admission of American vessels into the seaports, harbors, bays or creeks of Canadian territories, "nor into such parts of the rivers . . . as are between the mouth thereof, and the highest port of entry from the sea, except in small vessels trading *bona fide* between Montreal and Quebec, under such regulations as shall be established to prevent the possibility of frauds in this respect." Under this provision, by British regulation, St. John on the Richelieu was designated the sole Canadian inland port of entry for American goods.

Especially significant was the stipulation exempting from duty all goods in transit by usual and direct route across portages for purpose of immediate reëmbarkment for some other place—a stipulation which may be regarded as the antecedent of the later arrangement for shipment in bond.

The Mississippi remained entirely open to both parties. Article IV provided for a joint survey of the upper Mississippi above the falls of St. Anthony to its source, in order to ascertain whether it was intersected by a line drawn west from the Lake of the Woods as designated in the treaty of 1783, and (if necessary) for amicable negotiation to regulate the boundary in that quarter.

Another article (V) provided for the determination of the identity of the St. Croix by a commission (which reported its decision in 1798). Another (Article XII) conceded to Americans a *restricted* West India trade which the Senate refused to accept. The other articles had no direct bearing upon Canadian border relations.[39]

On November 19, five days after the signing of the treaty, Jay sent to Randolph a dispatch in which he defended the treaty provisions partly on grounds of reason and partly on grounds of expediency.

Before the arrival of this dispatch at Philadelphia, Randolph in his instructions of December 15 reiterated the information that the extension of the time for British surrender of the posts was repugnant to the President, who remained fixed in his opinion that the arrangment would be injurious to the United States—because he was convinced that tranquillity with the Indians could not be obtained as long as the British retained Detroit and other frontier posts within American limits. "In short," said Randolph, "the interval will be employed in rendering the transference of the British fort from one side of the river to the other as little operative as possible on the minds of the Indians, by gradually managing and persuading them to believe that the new position is more convenient to them and that the removal was the effect of choice and by an infinity of other pretenses."[40]

After an extended visit in London, Jay finally arrived in New York on May 28, 1795. A month later, after the Senate had agreed to advise in favor of ratification of the amended treaty, he was severely criticized for agreeing to the delay in the date of the British evacuation of the posts, and for postponing American participation in the fur trade during that period. He was also criticized for other parts of the treaty. Madison especially expressed disappointment that its unreciprocal terms concerning frontier trade and navigation gave the British an advantage on the Lakes. In the failure of the United States to obtain egress and ingress between the Lakes and the Atlantic he recognized a basis for future British shipping monopoly on the Lakes, and he thought that the treaty should have prevented the importation of arms and warlike stores via the Lakes.

In defense of the terms of the treaty, Hamilton stated reasons for delay in the transfer of the posts from British to American possession. He declared that the United States in its trade with the neighboring Canadian territory would have a balance of advantage, especially through its easier and safer sea communication which would provide a cheaper route than the route via the St. Lawrence for transportation of East India products to Canada.[41]

After considerable expression of opposition, which was increased by reported evidence of British influence in the West to secure the aid of American frontiersmen against Spanish Louisiana, the Senate in secret session (on June 24, 1795) finally advised ratification, subject to an amendment suspending the unsatisfactory article relating to American trade with the West Indies.

The treaty was proclaimed by President Washington on February 29, 1796, four months after exchange of ratifications. The appropriation necessary for its execution was delayed for several weeks by the House which, after a strong and convincing speech of Fisher Ames, finally assented (on April 28) by only a small majority of three (by a vote of fifty-one to forty-eight). In the final debate in the House, the van of the opposition was led by Madison.

Meantime, in August, 1795, American policy concerning the northwest border attained an additional safeguard for peace by the treaty of Greenville. By this treaty the Indians, through the diplomacy of General Wayne and evidently against the efforts of the Canadian Department of Indian Affairs, agreed to cede the larger part of their Ohio territory, retaining title only to the northwestern region on Lake Erie (between the Cuyahoga River and the Maumee) which was extinguished by a later treaty.[42] The American government, however, had not extinguished Canadian hopes for mediation and for a neutral Indian barrier, which especially appeared again in the negotiations of 1814 at Ghent.

The Jay treaty, coincident with Wayne's victory against the Indians, practically terminated the Montreal struggle for monopoly of the trade, although Detroit continued as the chief outlet for the fur trade even after the American acquisition of Louisiana.

In the summer of 1796 Wayne's army advanced to Detroit to receive that post from the retiring British, who later developed for control of the fur trade a Canadian center at Malden (later Amherstsburg)—which was visited by large numbers of American Indians from the Wabash villages during the yearly trading season, and which fifteen years later was regarded by Indiana white settlers as a source of evil influence in creating an anti-American attitude among the Indians.

On July 12, 1797, within a year after the transfer of Detroit to the United States, General James Wilkinson, the commander of the American troops, declared martial law within the limits of the fortifications. He explained that his purpose was "to guard national interests against machinations of enemies, to baffle the Arts of Seduction which [had] led to numberless desertions . . . and to restrain . . . the infamous habits of drunkenness encouraged among the troops by the disorderly conduct of venders of Ardent Spirits." Four days later, stimulated by this purpose, he issued an address to the British justices of the western region of Upper Canada, suggesting concerted action or "coincidence of plan and arrangement to preserve tranquillity" in the settlements bordering on the Strait which, he said, were menaced by common dangers liable to result from the apprehended insurrection. At the same time, he ordered a larger armed force for defense and to prevent desertions. He especially complained that American deserters who crossed the Strait into Upper Canada were received as British subjects.

In the following November, Peter Russell, writing from York, Upper Canada, submitted to Robert Liston (the British minister at Philadelphia) complaints of British merchants that Wilkinson had driven their agents from the trading houses in the Indian country, in violation of the spirit and principle of the recent treaty.[43]

In March, 1799, Congress definitely provided for British participation in the trade along the boundary, subject to the earlier license requirement under the law of May, 1796. This participation became a source of controversies and, in response to the wish of American traders, it was finally forbidden after the close of the War of 1812 (by act of March 29, 1816).

The recovery of the northwestern posts and the extension of American control over the Indians of that region may be regarded as important steps toward the future solution of the Mississippi question, which had become more uncertain in connection with the British struggle against revolutionary France. In February, 1797, Secretary Pickering considered with some apprehension various earlier reports that the French government contemplated the repossession of Louisiana, and especially Adet's recent explicit avowal to Randolph that France would insist on the cession of Louisiana as a preliminary to negotiations with Spain. He instructed Rufus King at London to discover any available evidence that the French design still existed, and to use any opportunities or situations to counteract the project. Later he mentioned to Liston the suspicions expressed by the Spanish minister respecting a British expedition supposed to be preparing on the Lakes with a view to an attack on the Spanish posts in Louisiana. In the following June, he received from Liston authoritative assurance that the British government in Canada planned no such expedition and would reject any such plan which involved the impropriety of violating neutral territory of the United States. In response to a further delicate request for further information, he received from Liston a statement that in the preceding winter he had received from residents of the United States (whom he declined to name) a proposal of such a plan, which he and his government had declined to countenance on the ground that it contemplated the aid of Indians and "tended to a violation of the neutrality of the United States." [44]

In March, 1798, when the aspect of American affairs with

France was threatening, Secretary Pickering requested the views of Hamilton in regard to a treaty of alliance with Great Britain. He received from Hamilton a reply of March 27 advising against a treaty which might entangle the American government, but suggesting that the British government might be persuaded to lodge with its minister at Washington "powers commensurate with such arrangements as exigencies may require, and the progress of opinion permit," and that it might wisely send to America a dozen frigates to act under directions of the American government.

Later, on April 2, after consultation with Hamilton, and in connection with his instructions to Rufus King, Pickering contemplated the possibility of formal concerted action with Great Britain (through Liston) in plans of common defense, in case French aggressions and dangerous ambitions should result in open hostilities with the United States. He especially suggested that the United States, besides planning a possible necessary seizure of Louisiana (with West Florida) to prevent its transfer to France, might arrange its frontier troops with a view to effectual resistance to any attempt of French invasion of Canada from Louisiana, and, if necessary, "to overawe Canadians on the western borders." He added that it might also send troops to protect Lower Canada against insurrection of Canadians or against French attempts at conquest, and that it could also furnish similar aid to Nova Scotia and New Brunswick.[45]

Such plans, if they had been put into operation, probably would have met with violent opposition from a strong American party. Liston, in a dispatch of September 9, 1799, to Governor-General R. S. Milnes of Canada, stated that, notwithstanding the favorable inclinations of the federal administration which recognized that the security of the United States depended upon the safety of Canada, a numerous and active American party with violent animosities against Great Britain "would eagerly embrace an opportunity of aiding . . . to promote a democratick revolution in the King's American Dominions." Therefore, he suggested that serious attention should be given to the political and moral character of emigrants from the United States who sought to settle in Canada and of travelers who were suspected of being French emissaries or adherents of the American "Jacobinical party."[46]

Meantime, in 1798, commissioners (chosen in accord with Article V of the Jay treaty) decided the controversy concerning the identity of the St. Croix River by agreeing upon the stream known as the Schoodic and by agreeing that its source was the northernmost source of the Chiputneticook. For this decision, Liston assumed responsibility for Great Britain at a conference at Providence, Rhode Island on October 23, 1798. Three years later, the American government instructed King at London to negotiate for the settlement of the questions of jurisdiction and navigation in Passamaquoddy Bay, which however, remained undetermined until 1817.

The boundary north of the source of the St. Croix, although defined in the treaty of 1783, was still uncertain because the negotiators of the treaty had never filed with the treaty any map or other official record of their intentions. Its determination was regarded as difficult. In 1802, Secretary Madison in his instructions to Rufus King admitted that the "highlands" mentioned in the treaty of 1783 apparently had "no definite existence." In October, 1803, President Jefferson, in his message to Congress, admitted that the boundaries designated in 1783 were "too imperfectly described to be susceptible of execution."[47]

With the stimulation of American settlement and interest on the Lakes the question of more specific designation of the boundary through the Lakes (for which the treaty failed to provide) soon assumed larger practical importance. On December 5, 1801, Secretary W. Dearborn of the War Department suggested to President Jefferson the propriety of proposing to Congress some provision for a clear designation of the boundary from the outlet of Lake Ontario to Lake Superior, in order to facilitate the settlement of disputes concerning the ownership of valuable islands in the Lakes and connecting rivers. In the following February a copy of this letter was promptly submitted to the British government.[48]

REFERENCES

1. *Transactions of the Royal Canadian Institute*, III and V (E. A. Cruikshank); *The John Askin Papers* (Burton Collection, Detroit Public Library); *Report of the Am. Hist. Ass'n.*, 1894, pp. 426–30 (A. C. McLaughlin).
2. *Canadian Archives*, Q, 26–2, p. 378; *Ib.*, Q, Vol. 21, pp. 229 and 388, Haldimand to Lord North, June 2 and Aug. 20, 1783; *Ib.*, Q, Vol. 21, p. 405; *Ib.*, Vol. 22, p. 329; *Ib.*, B, Vol. 50, p. 142.
3. *Ib.*, Q, 26–1, p. 73; *Ib.*, Q, 27–1, p. 44; *Ib.*, Q, Vol. 28, p. 28; *Secret Journals of Congress*, Vol. 4, p. 185; *Continental Congress Archives, 121 Foreign Letters*, pp. 215–18; J. Adams' *Works*, VIII, 394.
4. F. L. Paxson, *The Am. Frontier*, pp. 61, 72, 76.
5. *Am. State Papers, Foreign Relations*, I, 123–25; *Rp. Am. Hist. Ass'n*, 1904, pp. 363–87 (W. R. Manning); *Am. Hist. Rev.*, July, 1902, pp. 706–35 (F. J. Turner); Hamilton's *Works*, IV, 33–34, 48; Jefferson's *Writings* (Ford, ed.), V, 224, 238; *C.A.*, Q, 45–2, p. 510; *Ib.*, 46–2, p. 529.
6. *Rp. C.A.*, 1890, pp. 133–34; *Am. Hist. Rev.*, July, 1902, pp. 706–35; Hamilton's *Works*, IV, 33–34; Jefferson's *Writings*, V, 224.
7. *Ib.*, V, 238; Hamilton's *Works*, IV, 48; J. Adams' *Works*, VIII, 497; *Rp. C.A.*, 1890, p. 162.
8. *Ib.*, pp. 162–63; *C.A.*, Q, Vol. 49, p. 105; Hamilton's *Works*, IV, 64–65.
9. Jefferson's *Writings*, V, 262, 321, 324; *C.A.*, 1A, *British Legation, Notes from*; Washington's *Writings*, XII, 31; S. F. Bemis, *Jay's Treaty*, pp. 112–13.
10. *Ib.*, pp. 113, 116.
11. *Ib.*, pp. 89–94.
12. Wm. Kingsford, *History of Canada*, Vol. 7, p. 343.
13. Bemis, *Jay's Treaty*, pp. 117–20; *C.A.*, Q, 58–1, 63; *Am. State Papers, Foreign Relations*, I, 392.
14. *Ib.*, pp. 189, 193–237; Jefferson's *Writings*, VI.
15. *Ib.*, I, p. 207; *Record Office, Foreign Office Papers*, July 3, 1792; *Am. Hist. Rev.*, XXVII, 465; Bemis, *Jay's Treaty*, pp. 119–23.
16. *Rp. C.A., State Papers, 1891, U.C.*, p. 27; *Am. Hist. Rev.*, XXI, 547; *C.A.*, Q, Vol. 228, p. 226.
17. *Ib.*, Q, 54, *C.O. Records, Minutes of the Council of Quebec, 1791*, pp. 698–705 (and Part 2, pp. 721–23).
18. *Ib.*, Q, Vol. 278, pp. 257 and 327.
19. *C.A., Br. Legation Notes* (with George Hamilton, 1794–95).
20. *C.A.*, Q, Vol. 278, p. 191; *Ib.*, Q, 279–1, Vol. 13, p. 169 (Aug. 30, 1792), and p. 31.

21. Washington's *Writings,* XII, 292; *Am. State Papers, Foreign Relations,* I, 238.
22. *1 U.S. Ministers, Instructions,* pp. 224–27, and 272–73.
23. *Am. State Papers, Internal Affairs,* I, 337–61.
24. *C.A.,* Q, 279–1, p. 264; Bemis, *Jay's Treaty,* pp. 169–70.
25. *H. Rps.,* 25–3, No. 101; Greenhow, *Hist. of Oregon and California; Territorial Papers* (Dept. of State), I (Oregon), Parts 1 and 2, pp. 1, 16, and 33–36; *Jefferson's Works,* Vol. 1, p. 68; Jared Sparks, *Life of John Ledyard;* Greenhow, *Memoir of the Northwest Coast,* p. 149.
26. *C.A.,* Q, 67, *Canada, C.O. Records,* p. 99 (Oct. 7, 1793); *Ib.,* Q, 280, pp. 307–57.
27. Hamilton's *Works,* IV, 480; *Am. State Papers,* I, pp. 238, 327; *3 Great Britain, Despatches, Private,* Nov. 27, 1793.
28. *C.A.,* Q, 67, *Canada, C.O. Records,* pp. 97–99.
29. *7 Domestic Letters,* pp. 417–20; Edward Smith, *England and Am. after Independence,* p. 47.
30. *Corres. of John Jay,* IV, 55; *C.A.,* Q, Vol. 69–1, pp. 38 and 41; *Ib.,* Q, 280, *Canada, C.O. Records,* p. 202; *Ib.,* 280–2, pp. 280 and 289.
31. *7 Domestic Letters,* pp. 421–23 (July 28, 1794); *C.A.,* Q, 280, pp. 269–70.
32. *Am. State Papers, Indian Affairs,* I, 490.
33. *7 Domestic Letters,* pp. 417–20 (Nov. 30, 1794); 1A, *British Legation, Notes from,* Dec. 1, 1794.
34. *Am. State Papers, Foreign Relations,* I; *1 England, Despatches, Instructions to John Jay,* May 6, 1794.
35. *Am. State Papers, Foreign Relations,* I, 433.
36. *2 U.S. Ministers, Instructions,* pp. 80–85 (May 27), and 118–19 (July 30).
37. *Am. State Papers, Foreign Relations,* I, 486; *Ib.,* pp. 89–100; *2 U.S. Ministers, Instructions,* pp. 229–31 (Nov. 12, 1794).
38. *Am. State Papers, Foreign Relations,* I, 490.
39. Malloy, *Treaties,* I, 592–94, 609–10; Shortt and Doughty, IV, 546–47.
40. *Am. State Papers, For. Rels.,* I, 503; *2 U.S. Ministers, Instructions,* Dec. 15, 1794.
41. *Madison Papers,* V; Hamilton's *Works,* VII, 226–29, 258–59.
42. *Am. State Papers, Interior Affairs,* I, 547.
43. *2 British Legation, Notes from.*
44. *U.S. Statutes,* Mar. 2, 1799; *4 U.S. Ministers, Instructions,* p. 7, Feb. 15, 1797; *2 British Legation, Notes from,* June 19 and July 2, 1797; *10 Domestic Letters,* pp. 72–73, July 1 and July 2, 1797.
45. Hamilton's *Works,* VI, 278; *Ib.,* Vol. 7, p. 722; *U.S. Ministers, Instructions,* pp. 256–64, Apr. 2, 1798.

46. *C.A.*, G, 240, pp. 1–5 (Despatches of British Ministers at Washington to the Governors of Canada).
47. *U.S. Mins.*, pp. 150–51, Pinckney to King, Oct. 19, 1797; J. B. Moore, *International Arbitrations*, I, 1–43 and 45–64; *21 Great Britain, Notes from*, June 13, 1842.
48. *C.A.*, G, 240, pp. 26–27; *Canada Public "S" Series, Diplomatic and Secret Service Reports*, 1797–1822.

CHAPTER III

ANTECEDENTS AND OPERATIONS OF THE WAR OF 1812

IN the decade before the War of 1812, following the acquisition of Louisiana to remove foreign restrictions on American commerce at the mouth of the Mississippi, and influenced by British-Canadian policies in the control of trade with the American Indians of the Lakes frontier and British sea policies in the gigantic struggle to defeat Napoleonic policies in Europe, the American government again reached a decision to attempt to secure the annexation of Canada. In this it had a double purpose: to avoid border inconveniences and friction and to separate American problems from the control or influence of trans-Atlantic policies. The drift toward the war of 1812 "began in Napoleon's bath-tub where . . . he made his inexorable decision to sell Louisiana." At the close of the war a British writer, proposing plans to check American growth, stated that the American acquisition of Louisiana had been a step toward American acquisition of Canada and never should have been permitted by England who (he said) needed it in order to open to British merchandise the entire internal frontier of the United States.[1]

Jefferson began his administration with plans of coöperation with the British government to circumvent Napoleon's territorial designs on trans-Mississippi territory. He recognized that these plans involved consideration of friendly relations with Canada. He was prompt in ordering an investigation of representations from Montreal concerning certain democratic projects and machinations agitated by seditious pro-French inhabitants of Vermont against the peace of Canada.

In February, 1802, Thornton suggested that Jefferson, influenced by renewed reports of the French acquisition of Louisiana from Spain, might even find necessary a policy of coöperation with the British government in opposition to the French system, which he said was seeking to obtain a preponderating influence on American councils. Feeling that the United States and Canada were involved in the same danger of sedition and of consequent war which they would be obliged to repel by a common effort, he suggested to his government the propriety of adjusting the northern and western boundaries of the United States and Canada "before the French can avail themselves of their new neighborhood to interfere in the adjustment." In this connection he was inclined to offer no objection to the favorite plan of the United States to detach the Indian nations, within the American limits and on the borders, from the influence of other countries and to lead them gradually into an agricultural and civilized mode of life.[2]

In the following April, when considering the recent French acquisition of Louisiana from Spain, Jefferson suggested a possible Anglo-American alliance against France. Soon thereafter, acting through Rufus King, at London, he attempted to settle the remaining questions of the northern boundary, including the adjustment of the line between the Lake of the Woods and the source of the Mississippi and the actual location of the line from the northwest angle of Nova Scotia to the source of the Connecticut.

King found the British government receptive to plans for coöperation. Believing that French acquisition of Louisiana and the Floridas was not conducive to the preservation and perpetuation of the American Union, he sought British information and views concerning the uncontradicted reports of French plans. In a confidential letter of April, 1802 to Hawkesbury, he requested in confidence a frank statement of British official views. From the reply of May 7, he learned that the British government was opposed to the reported cession of Louisiana to France. From it, he also received the suggestion that the cession "should render it more necessary than ever that there should subsist between the two Governments that spirit of confidence which is become so essential to the security of their respective territories." [3]

Near the close of 1802, viewing with increased apprehension the possible dangers at New Orleans, the Jefferson administration felt the need of some more direct arrangement for adjustment of difficulties arising in relations with authorities of neighboring territories under European control. This feeling Madison mentioned in his instructions of November 27, 1802, to Charles Pinckney at Madrid. After referring to the inconvenience of applying to sovereigns in distant Europe for repair of injuries to the United States from colonial officers in America, he suggested that in order to prevent the long delays and dangers resulting from trans-Atlantic negotiations concerning emergencies in the American neighborhood, all governments of Europe which had colonies in the new continent should invest their representatives at Washington with authority to control or correct the mischievous acts of their colonial officers.[4]

At Paris, Livingston was considering the Louisiana question from the standpoint of American policy in Canadian relations. He was suspicious that Great Britain, in seeking to connect Canada with the navigable part of the upper Mississippi, was looking forward to future possession of the mouth of the river. He suggested (on December 24) that France by sound policy should either relinquish its designs on Louisiana or cover its frontier by a cession to the United States. He urged that the American boundary with Canada should be moved up the Mississippi as far as possible in order to prevent communication of Canada with the river by tributary streams between the Lakes and the river. Two weeks later, in a memoir which he submitted for the consideration of Napoleon, he emphasized the importance of an arrangement to interpose the United States between Canada and the French establishment on the lower Mississippi, with a view to the prevention of British plans of communication of Canada with the Gulf of Mexico via the Mississippi.[5]

Finally, on January 29, 1803, following the selection of Monroe as envoy on the extraordinary mission required by the importance of the crisis at New Orleans, Madison submitted the

President's views to King at London to enable the latter to explain to Hawkesbury the American policy on the subject mentioned in King's letter of May 7, 1802. He gave assurance that the mission contemplated nothing not consistent with prior engagements concerning the navigation of the Mississippi.

A few weeks later, in response to a verbal observation of M. Addington that in case of renewal of war against France, the British government would probably take prompt steps to occupy New Orleans, King frankly declared that the American government "looked forward without impatience to events which in the ordinary course of things must annex this country to the United States" and would view with much concern its possession by England. Thereupon he was assured that England would not accept the country as a permanent possession but desired only to prevent its possession by France, an end which he suggested could best be effected by transfer to American ownership. He was further assured that the British government, if it found British occupation of the territory necessary, would do nothing injurious to American interests.[6]

Satisfied with the friendly attitude of the British government, Jefferson was ready to consider more definitely the question of American policy in case the American negotiations with France should fail to secure a friendly arrangement. On April 18, Madison directed Livingston and Monroe, in case of threatened hostilities with France, prudently to sound the British government (preferably through the British minister at Paris) to ascertain its disposition and to invite its concurrence in the war. In proposing such joint action he said: "Notwithstanding the just repugnance of this country to a coalition of any sort with the belligerent policies of Europe, the advantages to be derived from the coöperation of Great Britain in a war . . . against France and her allies, are too obvious and too important to be renounced." Concerning the possible terms upon which Great Britain might agree to coöperate, he declared that any proposition for a mutual guarantee of existing possessions or of conquests must be rejected explicitly, and that any British pressure of a pretension to the acquisition of territory between the Mississippi and the Missouri would be regarded as objectionable and must be resisted as repugnant to American sentiment and sound American policy; but to alleviate any British disappointment, he was willing to agree that France would not be allowed to retain or acquire any part of territory from which Great Britain would be precluded. He authorized a promise of free trade with all ports which the United States might acquire within the Mississippi.[7]

On May 28, after reception of the information of Addington's friendly assurances, Madison instructed Livingston and Monroe that the prospect of a bargain with the British government would justify an expectation of better French terms than their original instructions indicated, and of as little concession as possible on points disagreeable to Great Britain. He especially advised the avoidance of any guarantee of any territory beyond the Mississippi, desiring to avoid any cause of embarrassment in connection with British meditated plans for emancipation of all Latin America.[8]

Meantime the question of frontier boundaries, at the northwest and also in Passamaquoddy Bay, had been a subject of negotiation with the British government. In June, 1802, following earlier instructions concerning the proposed settlement of the questions of jurisdiction and navigation in Passamaquoddy Bay, Secretary Madison instructed King that the error in the northwest boundary from the Lake of the Woods to the source of the Mississippi might be rectified by agreement on a line from the source of the river nearest the lake to a tangent drawn from the northwestern point of the lake. After referring to the difficulty in attempting to fix the northwest angle of Nova Scotia on the northeast boundary, because of the recent discovery that the "highlands" of the treaty of 1783 seemed to have no definite existence, he suggested the appointment of a joint commission "to determine on a point most proper to be substituted for the description in Article II of the treaty of 1783."

In accord with these instructions, King negotiated with Hawkesbury (by April 11, 1803) a draft convention which was signed on May 12, 1803, before he learned of the American acquisition of Louisiana by treaty of April 30.

Later, on October 17, 1803, President Jefferson informed

Congress that "a further knowledge of the ground in the northeastern and northwestern angles of the United States has evinced that the boundaries established by the treaty of Paris, . . . in those points, were too imperfectly described to be susceptible of execution."[9]

On the recommendation of John Quincy Adams, the northwest boundary article of King's draft treaty, providing for a direct line from the source of the Mississippi to the tangent of the Lake of the Woods, was disapproved and expunged by the Senate on the ground that it might be in conflict with the northern boundary of the newly acquired Louisiana, which was believed to have been fixed at 49° west of the Lake of the Woods by commissioners under the treaty of Utrecht. Monroe, who was sent to London from Paris to explain the action of the Senate and to secure British ratification of the modified treaty, could not persuade the British government to accept the change.[10]

After the acquisition of Louisiana, new possible sources of future controversy were apprehended. Thornton, although he recognized that the undefined boundary between the Louisiana territory and Upper Canada might not become a subject of Anglo-American dispute for many years, promptly expressed to Governor Milnes (on July 22) his fear that American customs regulations concerning passage of goods of fur traders across the portages might be extended at once to Louisiana. He suggested that such extension would result in serious loss to the Canadian fur trade with the Indians and possibly in the consequent disuse of the American portages.[11] At St. Louis, which had been the Montreal of the Mississippi for four decades and had some advantage over the older Montreal route, Canadian traders began to arrive by 1805 with expectations of conducting commerce with the Indian nations under the provisions of the Louisiana treaty. They were soon disappointed. In May, 1805, Madison announced the President's policy to oppose any proposition to open any part of Louisiana to British trade with the Indians. On August 26, 1805, General Wilkinson issued a proclamation prohibiting citizens of a foreign country from entering the Missouri for the purpose of Indian trade and also prohibiting the conveyance of foreign goods up the river except by citizens or residents of the United States.[12]

For several years questions of trade were most prominent in negotiations concerning the British American provinces. In 1804, Monroe suggested to Lord Harrowby that, in view of the growth of American interests, the question of renewing the temporary provisions of the Jay treaty should be determined by negotiations for a new treaty. In March, 1805, Madison, through Monroe, complained of the injustice of the British policy which attempted to force the growth and prosperity of Nova Scotia and other expensive northern provinces by an interdiction of American trade with the British West Indies, which without American supplies would be impoverished. In submitting this complaint at London, Monroe urged the unreasonableness of the British policy which impoverished the productive island colonies (naturally dependent upon American trade) by an attempt to force the growth and prosperity of the expensive British North American colonies "which from local causes must eventually detach themselves from the parent state, and the sooner in proportion as their growth may be stimulated." In October, 1805, after returning to London from a trip to Spain, he reported that the British government evidently sought to delay negotiations concerning boundaries and commerce, possibly because of the question of impressment of American seamen which seemed to indicate a general purpose to check the growing importance of the United States. Early in 1806, however, he reported prospects more favorable.[13]

Meantime, American trade with the northern British colonies since 1802 had improved. According to a report of Secretary Gallatin of the treasury for 1802–04, the annual exports had exceeded the imports. The value of exported articles of domestic production had increased from $512,581 in 1802 to $983,306 in 1804. The value of imports had increased from $437,948.47 in 1802 to $791,719.69 in 1804. The duties collected on these imports increased from $62,153.98 in 1802 to $111,577.51 in 1804 and to $244,125 in 1807.[14]

In 1808, American fishermen, whose business had increased since 1789 (and especially since 1783), complained of British colonial interference with their industry, by search and by tolls and anchorage dues levied to favor British-Canadian interests.

In connection with the proposed negotiations to secure a treaty to replace the temporary commercial provisions of the Jay treaty, the American government sought reciprocity in trade. On May 17, 1806, Madison instructed Monroe and Pinckney that the American government desired intercourse with the West Indies and the North American colonies as free as that with Europe. Urging the reasonableness of the American policy to secure free intercourse on terms of perfect reciprocity, he declared that in the commerce of Nova Scotia and New Brunswick, notwithstanding the British policy of exclusion, the Americans had a greater share of the trade by a system of connivance between Halifax and Boston and between the Bay of Fundy and Maine. On May 20, while stating that the President refused to accept any arrangement which did not include provision against impressments, he particularly indicated that among the objectionable proposals which required essential alteration was one limiting American trade with British West Indies to a direct trade which would stop American reëxport of the products of British American colonies.

In further instructions of May 30, he opposed the renewal of Article III of the treaty of 1794 concerning the Indian trade, which in its operation he considered as seriously detrimental to the United States. As objections to the renewal of the trade, he mentioned the bad influence on the Indians, the collisions with rival American traders, the consequent hostile attitude of the British trader against the American nation, the conflict of the trade with the American policy to substitute the arts of civilized life for savage manners, and the unreciprocal character of the trade in practice. He urged an amendment which would mutually authorize the two governments "to confine Indian trade within their respective limits to their own traders," thereby removing a source of jealousy and ill will, and contributing to the advancement of friendship and harmony which was far more valuable than the trans-boundary Indian trade.[15]

In connection with the negotiations the British submitted a communication of Canadian merchants asking from the American government redress for injuries to regular Canadian trade. This request for indemnity was based upon exclusion from Louisiana territory, duties charged on imports from Canada in excess of duties charged American citizens on the same kind of goods in American vessels at Atlantic ports, attempts to collect duties at the American portages, and acts of American revenue officers in harassing and impeding the trade of British merchants on the Lakes by stopping vessels on frivolous pretenses "without considering the difficulty of observing on lakes and rivers of Canada those regulations with regard to the approach of shores and ports which are applicable to the ports of the ocean."[16]

After several delays, the last of which was caused by the arrival (at London) of Napoleon's famous Berlin decree of November 21 and the consequent British demand for American assurance of resistance to this unjust pretension, a draft treaty was finally completed and signed on December 31, 1806, in the face of a situation which threatened to involve the United States in the European war.

Early in January, 1807, Monroe and Pinckney, in explaining the negotiations which resulted in Article II of the draft treaty, reported that the British commissioners had earnestly insisted that Canadian traders and the Hudson's Bay Company should be admitted to participation in the trade with the Indian tribes of the Louisiana territory. Later (on April 25), they explained that the proposed arrangement, although it opened to the United States the trade of the territories of the Hudson's Bay Company, was a concession to Great Britain (and to Canada). By Article VII, it extended the privileges of intercourse and trade, by land or inland navigation, to all the territories belonging to either party on the continent of America, by payment of the regular duties and without extra fees for licenses to trade with the Indians. By Article VI, it allowed to British subjects free access across American territory to the Mississippi River to enable them to enjoy the navigation of that river.[17]

This draft treaty, which also contained provisions concerning the settlement of boundary questions, the President did not approve and did not submit to the Senate. In new instructions (of March, 1807) to the joint commission Madison indicated that the President was opposed to the opening of any part of Louisiana to British trade with the Indians. By later instructions of July 30 he definitely forbade any agreement to renew the previous privilege of British trade and intercourse with the Indians within American jurisdiction. He declared that the American government would permit the access of British traders to the Mississippi through American territory only after the payment of all duties on the goods imported as required of American citizens engaged in the same trade. Unable to see any good reason for the Canadian request for free access to the Mississippi for their goods (which were for consumption within American territory), he stated that the previous motives for excluding foreign traders from American territory west of the Mississippi had been strengthened by recent experience, and especially because the English proposition of mutual trans-boundary trade failed essentially in the point of real and fair reciprocity.[18]

The administration also declined to approve the language of the British treaty project for agreement on boundary limits west of the Lake of the Woods—language in which was forecast the later Anglo-American contest for Oregon. Monroe and Pinckney had proposed that the parallel of 49° should be the boundary west of the intersection of a line drawn due north or south from the northwestern point of the Lake of the Woods. To this line, which was not construed to extend to territory west of the Rockies, the British commissioners agreed. In the negotiations, however, they had sought to apply to the territories of the United States, and not to those of Great Britain, the indefinite limit of extension "as far as the territories extend," thereby leaving a nest-egg for future British pretensions south of 49°. Monroe had added a clause proposing that the line of 49° "should extend west as far as the respective territories of the parties extend in that quarter." To this the American government, for politic reasons, hesitated to agree. Unwilling to risk possible offense to Spain by discussing the extension of the line from the Rockies to the Pacific "which it considered of little immediate importance," it preferred to leave the question in abeyance. Madison instructed the commissioners to omit any impolitic proviso which might be regarded by Spain as an offensive intimation and which might at that time strengthen Spanish jealousies of the United States.[19]

At that time the definite marking of the eastern water boundary was regarded as more important. In May, 1807, following communications from the Governor of New York and the Governor of Vermont concerning the St. Lawrence boundary, Madison suggested to Monroe the advisability of an arrangement to provide for a joint examination of the islands and channels of the St. Lawrence with a view to a report on impartial information required as a basis for demarcation of the boundary in the river.

Meantime, events were preparing the way for the later American claim to Oregon. In 1803 President Jefferson had sent Meriwether Lewis and William Clarke on an expedition to explore the Missouri and to trace some convenient stream to the Pacific with a view to opening a trade route to the northwest coast. By this expedition he stimulated interest in the fur trade of the Missouri and the Northwest, the larger possibilities of which were first seen by John Jacob Astor (of New York). By private enterprise Astor quickly seized the opportunity to gain American advantage in competing with Canadian traders on the upper Mississippi and the Missouri. Succeeding to the earlier plans of the Missouri Fur Company, and enlarging them, he formed the Pacific Fur Company with plans to establish a factory at the mouth of the Columbia. These plans Jefferson favored. In a letter of April, 1808, to Astor, he stated that the Executive, in order to oust the foreigners who had a bad influence on the Indians, would use every reasonable facility and patronage to encourage the trade of American citizens in the direction of the Columbia. Two years later, after his retirement from the presidency, he considered that an early American settlement on the western coast would be a "great public acquisition," and he looked forward to the time "when its descendants should spread themselves throughout the whole length of the coast," covering it with free Americans, independent and self-governing.

Thus encouraged by promise of government protection, Astor sent (in September, 1810) by sea from New York the vessel *Tonquin* which, in March, 1811, landed its goods and

120 passengers on the Columbia, at a site on which the settlement of Astoria was established. This settlement was made about four months before the arrival of a party of Englishmen which was sent by the Northwest Company with plans to occupy the region, but which promptly retired.[20] In the spring of 1812 the Astoria settlement was reinforced by the arrival of an overland party which left St. Louis in January, 1811, traveled via the Missouri and the Black Hills thence across the Rockies and down the Salmon River, and suffered many hardships on the route. In May, 1812, after learning that Astor had encountered difficulties, Jefferson encouragingly wrote that he did not expect Congress and the government to stand in the way of "so interesting an object as that of planting the germ of an American population on the shores of the Pacific."

New difficulties soon arose. On October 16, 1812, discouraged by reverses and by an alarming report of British plans to take possession, the local partners of Astor consented to sell the property of the company to the Northwest Fur Company. Six weeks later, the captain of a British war vessel raised over the factory the British flag, which remained as a sign of British jurisdiction until after the close of the War in 1812.[21]

The War of 1812 was preceded by premonitory clouds and strains. Along the Lakes and St. Lawrence frontier the signs of approaching war appeared by 1808. Following a period of threatened commercial war which resulted from the search of the *Chesapeake* on the high seas near Norfolk (in June, 1807), American-Canadian relations became severely strained. In the summer of 1807 the pamphleteers had threatened to take Canada and Nova Scotia and to make peace at Halifax. Late in December Congress enacted into law Jefferson's proposed policy of an embargo on exports, including a prohibition on transport of American produce to Canada.

John Henry, a Canadian agent who attributed the origin of the embargo act to the "inveterate hostility of the American executive towards Great Britain" and who reported to Quebec that the act was opposed and violated in Vermont, suggested that the American policy might result in a collision between the "sovereign people" and American government officials and in a consequent division which might prove beneficial to Canada. On April 14, after returning from the United States to Montreal, he reported that the northern part of Vermont was "favorable to coalition with England," and that in case of war it would seek protection from "the Governor of Lower Canada." On April 25 he reported that the accession of northern Vermont and the command of the navigation of Lake Champlain would provide "an effectual barrier to any inroad which might be attempted by the usual and most practical route into Canada." On May 5, in forwarding the later correspondence of Henry to Lord Castlereagh, Governor Craig reported that the disposition of the people of Vermont and their defiance of American customs vessels had been verified. On May 13 he informed Erskine that he had taken prompt measures to bind the Indians more closely to British interests in order "to render abortive the intrigues of our artful and persevering enemy." [22]

By the middle of 1808 the British government, which in 1806 had refused to agree upon any arrangement for trade between the United States and the colonies in American vessels, temporarily changed its trade policy. Although it began to enforce its colonial system against the interests of American trade, it decided to encourage American exports to the British sugar colonies via Canada. On June 30, 1808, during the operation of the American embargo, it obtained an act of Parliament which authorized the governors of the North American provinces to open their ports for importation of articles from the United States for reëxport to the West Indies. As a result considerable illicit American export trade was conducted along the Canadian boundary by successful evasions of the American embargo act. The commerce of Lakes Champlain, Ontario and Erie was largely increased, both by exports and by imports. At Atlantic ports coasting vessels which cleared for distant American ports were often driven by "stress of weather" into a Nova Scotian harbor.

As a result of the American embargo act and British policy, however, the total American trade with the British American colonies suffered a heavy decline compared to that of 1807. American export of American products fell from $1,338,199 to

$308,635 and American imports fell from $244,125 to $112,177.[23]

In considering the border situation of 1808, General Hull suggested to the administration the expediency of placing armed vessels on Lake Erie in order to protect the communication with the Northwest Territory.

Canadians complained that American revenue officers had from time to time "attempted to exact duties upon goods crossing the portages." The Canadian traders resisted such duties on the ground that the Jay treaty gave them freedom of commerce and intercourse. They also claimed that the situation of American ports of entry on the boundary lakes and rivers, and the nature of the navigation, made difficult the rigid observance of regulations which were applicable to Atlantic ports. Referring to Canadian vessels which had been seized because of their too great proximity to particular ports or shores, they disclaimed any intention of infringing the revenue laws of the United States. To the British government they submitted their complaints which Canning promptly presented to the American minister at London. At the same time, they were using every effort to retain the control of the lake trade in which their influencc was lessened by the events of the next four years.[24]

On October 20, 1808, Canadian merchants of Montreal, representing the Michilimackinac Company, complained of an American outrage at Niagara by American military authorities against vessels which had been sent from Lachine to St. Josephs in May to trade with the Indians there. They stated that two boats had been seized, that six others had been intercepted in the open lake (Ontario), and that nine others had been pursued eastward until they were compelled to return to Kingston. Claiming that the vessels, coasting from one British port to another, could not be governed by the American embargo or other American legislative act, they asked for reparations for damages (£26,000) for property detained at Niagara. Regarding the American acts as a part of American plans to drive British Indian traders from American territory by every species of vexation (including fiscal extortions), they urged counter-action by the British government. At the same time they submitted a warning that the Indian trade within American limits, unless properly protected against interruptions of free navigation on the Lakes and unless strengthened by recognition of rights west of the Mississippi, would be abandoned and that the abandonment would terminate British influence with Indians residing within the limits of Canada.

On November 3 the traders of the Northwest Company submitted through Governor Craig an interesting memorial against a British bill in Parliament to prohibit the use of spirituous liquors among the savages of British America. They stated that the bill, if it became a law, "would transfer the Fur Trade of the Canadas to the neighboring states; and with it the ascendency possessed by Great Britain over the Indian nations." Following the memorial was an annexed inquiry into the merits of the bill, indicating political objections "more cogent than even those which flow from the personal rights and interests of your memorialists." [25]

Frontier difficulties arising from the embargo were soon terminated. In the summer of 1809 the American government issued a circular to collectors on the Lakes indicating that exportation to British territories by land was not forbidden.[26]

Meantime, in 1808, Americans had reason to be apprehensive of future British trade policy, and especially future British policy in South America, affecting American interests both north and south of the Caribbean.[27]

In the decade before 1812 the advance of American settlements in the region contiguous to the southern shores of the Great Lakes was retarded by the diverting geographic influence of the Ohio River in the westward movement. American expansion south of Lake Erie, and westward along the Wabash and to Lake Michigan, was also delayed by the danger of Indian obstruction. West of Detroit the only American post on the international border was at Michilimackinac. Southward from this the nearest American posts were at Fort Wayne and at Fort Dearborn (on the site of Chicago).[28]

After 1808, Governor Harrison of Indiana Territory watched with increasing suspicion and alarm the increasing discontent and antipathy which Tecumseh encouraged at the Shawnee village of Tippecanoe on the Wabash, which had continuous intercourse with the Canadian town of Malden. Finally, in 1811, he advanced up the Wabash and (on November 7) defeated the Shawnees and their allies and prepared the way for the later American plans in the War of 1812.

The American government was convinced that the Indian hostilities were largely a result of the influence of British trading agents and of general British policy in the West, an influence which it regarded as distinctly antagonistic to the American policy of Indian control. This conviction Secretary Monroe diplomatically expressed to the British minister (Foster) who promptly (in January and again in June, 1812) disavowed any agency of the British government in encouraging any Indian depredations in American territory.[29]

Possibly the American attitude toward Canada at the beginning of the War of 1812 may be explained in part by the view later asserted by David Anderson (in a British book on Canada): that the American government was jealous of Canadian advantage from the border trade and from the commercial value of the St. Lawrence as a natural outlet. This advantage was expected to increase with the advance of American settlement along the lengthy frontier across which smuggling could be continued without difficulty, with a consequent prospect of Canadian export of the American products of the North and Northwest.[30]

In the West the chief motive of the war was the conquest of Canada (especially of western Canada) which was regarded as the easiest way to relieve the frontier from Indian troubles. This motive was influenced in part by the attitude of Canadian fur-trading interests, which under the Jay treaty had free access to trade with Indian tribes within American territory. To stop this Canadian trade, to terminate its stifling competition, was regarded as necessary to future peace and security. With that end in view, and influenced also by plans in the strategy of defense and by a policy to obtain greater future security through withdrawal of British rule from the American continent, the American government first directed an invasion of Canada and later attempted negotiations for British cession of Canadian territory.

The Madison administration, influenced by the fiery speeches of fascinating leaders and the slowness of the British government in deciding to repeal the Orders in Council, was forced into what has since been called an "unnecessary and unwise war." On June 1, 1812, under the influence of Secretary Monroe, the President recommended to Congress a declaration of war. On June 18 Congress adopted an act declaring war, which the President promptly approved.

On June 29, 1812, Jefferson wrote Madison that in order to continue the popularity of the war the Indian barbarities should be stopped by a conquest of Canada. In this statement of policy he was probably influenced by the views of Du Pont de Nemours, who (in 1807–08) had offered to him confidential suggestions that possession of Canada was indispensable to American political security.[31]

The principal theatre of military operations in the war was on the Lakes frontier. The first strategic point was Detroit. It was in an exposed situation and its possession depended primarily upon the control of Lake Erie. This control Governor Hull promptly recommended as the most expedient measure of the war. At Washington, before the declaration of war, when plans for invasion of Canada as a future war measure were under discussion, he doubted whether either invasion or a fleet was necessary to obtain command of the Lakes. He believed that the mere American protection of Detroit, which he expected to result in keeping the Indians from Malden, would be sufficient. Later the American government adopted a plan to send him from Urbana to occupy Upper Canada by an advance from Detroit in order to control Lake Erie without a naval force. To aid this movement it planned to send an army across New York to seize the Niagara peninsula.

On June 25, the Senate approved a House resolution authorizing the President, in case of the necessity of an invasion and occupation of British American continental provinces to vindicate American rights or to secure American safety, to issue a proclamation to the inhabitants of those provinces assuring them of full security and protection under the American Constitution.[32]

Meantime, on June 11, Hull had advanced from Urbana. On June 29, after a difficult march, he reached the Maumee. On July 12, he crossed from Detroit into Canada. At Sandwich he issued to the inhabitants a proclamation promising American protection and hinting at the advantage of participation in the American type of government. Although he was joined by many Canadians, he soon learned that Americans in their optimistic expectations concerning the easy conquest of Canada had not estimated the spirit and influence of the Loyalist exiles of 1783. He soon discovered that his position was threatened by General Isaac Brock who, after improving the Canadian situation by a counter proclamation to counteract the influence of that of Hull, summoned the legislature on July 27 to rally public opinion, and promptly ordered additional forces westward by water from the Niagara frontier to Amherstsburg which he reached on August 13.[33] Confronted by the awakened spirit of resistance of the American Tory exiles who were able to turn the tide of battle against the invading forces, he abandoned his advance.

Deciding that he was unable to capture Malden, where the British were concentrated and where they were joined by their Indian allies under Tecumseh, he recrossed the river to Detroit. On August 16 he surrendered to Brock's British force, resulting in British control on the American frontier of the Northwest, including control of the Lakes. Western hopes, thus dampened, were further disappointed and depressed at the River Raisin in the following January by the defeat of an American force under Winchester.

Meantime, the Americans had lost control of forts at each end of Lake Michigan. The American commander at Michilimackinac had surrendered to a British force on July 17, before he had any notice of the declaration of war. This surrender had facilitated the defeat of Hull at Detroit and, by influencing the Indians in favor of the British, proved to be a decisive event of the war. The American occupants of Fort Dearborn (Chicago) abandoned it on August 15, a day preceding Hull's surrender.

General Dearborn, who had been appointed to command operations at Niagara and eastward of Lake Ontario in the direction of Kingston and Montreal, had delayed hostilities partly because he had expected Hull to reach Niagara by a victorious march, and partly because of difficulties in recruiting an army in New York and New England. Finally, on October 8, Lieutenant J. D. Elliott of the American navy, near his station at Black Rock, began operations on Lake Erie by the capture of two British vessels which had just arrived from Amherstsburg. By this success he hastened an American attack (of October 13) on Queenston. The latter, however, resulted in failure—to which contributing factors were the differences of plans of the two generals and the refusal of New York militia to cross the river.[34]

Meantime, after Hull's surrender, the American government, acting in accord with the views of Secretary Armstrong of the navy and General Harrison of the American army of the Northwest, decided to create a superior inland naval force which would secure control of the Lakes and thereby aid in the separation of Upper Canada from Lower Canada. On March 3, 1813, it authorized the construction of war vessels needed. On May 25, the President announced "On the lakes our superiority is near at hand where it has not already been established."

Commander Oliver H. Perry, who succeeded Elliott on Lake Erie, removed the naval base from Black Rock to Presqu' Isle (Erie) which had a better harbor and other advantages. On August 5, after overcoming many difficulties, he moved his new hastily-prepared fleet from Erie where the British had sought to blockade him. He anchored at Put-in-Bay where he soon obtained control of the lake. There, on September 10, he defeated the British fleet which attacked him only from the necessity of securing food for Amherstsburg.

Following this victory, General Harrison, whose army had long been idle on the lower Maumee (at Fort Meigs) and on the neighboring Portage and Sandusky rivers, immediately seized the opportunity for a second invasion of Canada. Arriving at Fort Malden on September 27, three days after the British under Proctor and Tecumseh had retired eastward from Detroit and Amherstsburg, he promptly pursued the retreating forces through the woods. He defeated them on October 5 at the battle of the Thames, which completed the military events on the Michigan frontier and resulted in safety to the Ohio and Indiana frontiers.[35]

East of Lake Erie Commodore Isaac Chauncey had established his naval base at Sackett's Harbor on Lake Ontario. He had accomplished little in his random encounters with the opposing British fleet which had played with him games of alternating flight and pursuit. In April he and General Dearborn, with their attention diverted from logical plans for an attack on the British strategic center at Kingston, sailed westward with an expedition which attacked York (Toronto) and burned its capitol building as an act of vengeance for losses resulting from an explosion of a British powder magazine. On May 27, after abandoning York, they captured the British Fort George at the mouth of the Niagara. This action was followed by a period of inaction and depression which resulted finally in the British occupation of Fort Niagara on the American side of the river (in December, 1813).

Chauncey was recalled from his dreams of westward conquest by a British naval attack on his naval base at Sackett's Harbor, on May 29. From this base the notorious and pompous General James Wilkinson, who arrived in August, started down the St. Lawrence early in November with expectation that another force under General Wade Hampton would join him at Isle Perault for a concentrated attack on Montreal. This plan was abandoned, following an attack on Hampton (on October 26) which prevented him from reaching Isle Perault, and after a later attack on part of Wilkinson's force at Chrystler's Farm (on November 11).

In 1814 General Jacob Brown led an American force across the Niagara to Fort Erie and thence to Lake Ontario; but, disappointed by the failure of Chauncey to arrive with a fleet to coöperate with him, he retired westward, fought an indecisive battle at Lundy's Lane (on July 25), and soon returned to Fort Erie from which he later (in September) crossed to the American side of the river.

Meantime interest on Lake Ontario had shifted to Sackett's Harbor where, following a competition in construction of fleets for control of the lake, Chauncey's fleet was rendered useless by the British blockade of the harbor.[36]

The only decisive American victory on the Canadian frontier in 1814 was at Plattsburg, a village of 1500 people at the mouth of the Saranac River, on the west side of Lake Champlain. Here, at the period of the embargo, had begun a brisk illicit trade from New York and Vermont via Lake Champlain to Canada. Later, in the period of the war it had greatly increased by the stimulation of large profits from trade with the enemy. In September, 1814, with a view to protection of its source from any possible action of the American government or of Congress, the British attempted military occupation of the region by a force under Sir George Prevost; but an American force under Commodore Macdonough, by a complete naval victory over the superior British fleet, effected American control on the lake and the prompt retreat of Prevost's land force northward from the position which it had occupied at the mouth of the Saranac.[37]

In addition to the special problems of illicit trade through Vermont, the American government during the war encountered much difficulty in its efforts to prevent illegitimate but lucrative trade with the enemy between Massachusetts and Nova Scotia. To prevent the latter trade became more difficult in the summer of 1814, after the British occupation of the eastern part of Maine, between the St. Croix and the Penobscot. This occupation, under the immediate direction of Governor Sir John Sherbrooke of New Brunswick, followed Cochrane's April proclamation of a blockade of the entire American coast from Eastport, Maine, to New Orleans, Louisiana. It was accomplished by an invasion of British forces which conquered the territory and annexed it to New Brunswick—beginning with Eastport, then advancing to Moose and Nantucket Islands of the Passamaquoddy group and finally (by September) to Castine in Penobscot Bay.[38]

The American failure to acquire Canada in the War of 1812, largely due to the Canadian settlements resulting from the Tory emigration from the United States after the Revolution, was also largely influenced by the opposition of New England. Quincy and Wheaton of Massachusetts, neither willing to admit British subjects of Canada as citizens of the United States nor desirous of attempting the difficult task of holding them as conquered people, opposed any attempt to conquest. Quincy feared that the capture of Quebec might result in an American "dynasty by the sword," and he declared that the United States had enough territory.[39]

Unsuccessful in defensive plans for acquisition of Canada by military operations, the American government unsuccessfully sought to secure the same object by diplomacy.

REFERENCES

1. A British Traveller, *The Colonial Policy of Great Britain with Relation to Her North American Provinces* (1816).
2. *Canadian Archives,* G, 240, pp. 22–26 and 28–30, Edward Thornton to Sir Robert S. Milnes, Feb. 25, 1802; *Ib.,* Thornton to Milnes, Nov. 21, 1801; also see *C.A.,* S, 61, Merry to Milnes, Sept. 27, 1804.
3. *10 Great Britain, Despatches,* No. 66, May 7, 1802; C. R. King, *Rufus King,* Vol. 3, p. 469.
4. *6 U.S. Ministers, Instructions,* pp. 62–64, Nov. 17, 1802; *Ib.,* pp. 78–79, Feb. 17, 1803; *Ib.,* pp. 131–33, May 28, 1803.
5. *H. Docs.,* 57–2, Vol. 92, No. 431, pp. 82–84, Dec. 24, 1802; *Ib.,* pp. 109–10, 220 and 223; *Annals of Congress,* 7–2, pp. 1069–71, and 1078–83.
6. *6 U.S. Ministers, Instructions,* pp. 75–77, Jan. 29, 1803; *10 Great Britain, Despatches,* No. 89, Apr. 2, 1803.
7. *6 U.S. Ministers, Instructions,* pp. 113–18, Apr. 18, 1803.
8. *Ib.,* 131–33, May 28, 1803.
9. J. B. Moore, *International Arbitrations,* I, 45–64; *Am. State Papers, Foreign Relations,* II, 584–91; *21 Great Britain, Notes* [*from*], June 13, 1842; *10 Great Britain* [*Despatches*], No. 98, May 13, 1803; *8 U.S. Ministers, Instructions,* pp. 223–32, July 28, 1818.
10. *Exec. Journal of Senate,* I, 452–53; *Am. State Papers, Foreign Relations,* II, 584, 591; *Ib.,* III, pp. 89, 93, 95, 97, Feb. 14, 1804; *12 Great Britain* [*Despatches*], No. 1, Sept. 5, 1804 (Enclosure); *Diplomatic Correspondence* (Washington, 1808), Part 2, p. 72.
11. *C.A., Canada Public "S" Series, Diplomatic and Secret Service Reports,* 1797–1822, July 22, 1803.

12. *C.A.*, G, 240, pp. 48–55, Merry to Madison, Jan. 7, 1806; *C.A.*, G, 410, Thomas Dunn to Merry, Nov. 15, 1805.
13. *Dip. Cor.* (Washington, 1808), Part 2, p. 67, Monroe to Madison, Aug. 7, 1804; *Ib.*, Madison to Monroe, Mar. 6, 1805 and May 22, 1807; *6 U.S. Ministers, Instructions*, pp. 271–77, Mar. 6, 1805; *12 Great Britain, Despatches*, No. 35, Oct. 18, 1805; *Ib.*, No. 41, Feb. 12, 1806.
14. *U.S. Official Reports*, 1805–06, No. 4; *Exec. Docs.*, 9–1, Feb. 28, 1806; *State Papers*, 14–2, *Exec. Reports*, Dec. 23, 1816; McMaster, *U.S.*, IV, p. 460.
15. *H. Docs.*, 27–2, No. 68, Feb. 8, 1842; *Dip. Cor.* (Washington, 1808), Part 3, pp. 19, 39, 42; *6 U.S. Ministers, Instructions*, pp. 340–55, May 17, 1806; *Ib.*, pp. 359–60, May 30, 1806.
16. *Dip. Cor.* (1808), Part 3, pp. 172–76.
17. *Ib.*, p. 121, Madison to Monroe and Pinckney, Jan. 3, 1807; *Ib.*, p. 190, Apr. 25, 1807.
18. *6 U.S. Ministers, Instructions*, pp. 413–17, May 22, 1807; *Ib.*, pp. 421–23, July 30, 1807; *Dip. Cor.* (1808), Part 3, p. 65, July 30, 1807; J. B. Moore, *Int. Arb's.*, I, 45–64.
19. *Am. State Papers, Foreign Relations*, III, 162, 165, 185; *8 U.S. Ministers, Instructions*, pp. 223–32, July 28, 1818; *6 U.S. Ministers, Instructions*, pp. 421–23, July 30, 1807.
20. *Ib.*, pp. 413–17, May 22, 1807; Washington Irving, *Astoria.*
21. Jefferson's *Works*, Vol. 6, May 24, 1812; *1 Despatches to Sumter* (Rio Janeiro), Nov. 12, 1812.
22. *C.A.*, Q, *107 Colonial Office Records*, pp. 111–14, 150–53 and 154–56, Gov. Craig to Lord Castlereagh, Apr. 10 (Enclosure), Apr. 14, and Apr. 25, 1808; *Ib.*, pp. 148–49 and 260–66, May 5 and 13, 1808.
23. Israel De Wolfe Andrews, *Reciprocity and Fishery Treaty* (Washington, 1862); Timothy Pitkin, *Statistical View of the Commerce of the U.S.* (1817), pp. 217–18; *H. Docs.*, 27–2, No. 68, Feb. 8, 1842; David Anderson, *Canada* (a view of the importance of the British colonies); *State Exec. Papers*, 15–1, Vol. 4, No. 87, Feb. 9, 1818; *Ib.*, 16–1, Vol. 7, No. 102, Feb. 19, 1820.
24. *Am. State Papers, Foreign Relations*, III, p. 226.
25. *C.A.*, Q, *108 Canada, C.O. Records*, pp. 2–15, Craig to Castlereagh, No. 37, Oct. 29, 1808; *Ib.*, pp. 50–68, No. 43, Nov. 15, 1808 (Enclosure).
26. *C.A.*, *Canada Public "S" Series, Diplomatic and Secret Service* (Reports, 1797–1822), Aug. 11, 1809.
27. *15 England, Despatches, Private*, Sept. 7, 1808.
28. McMaster, *U.S.*, III, 460–64.
29. *Am. State Papers, Indian Affairs*, I, 776; *Ib.*, *Foreign Relations*, III, 715–23; *2 Foreign Legations, Notes to*, p. 19; *C.A.*, *Canada*

Public "S" Series, Diplomatic and Secret Service (Reports, 1797–1822).

30. DAVID ANDERSON, *Canada;* H. ADAMS, *U.S.*, VI, 136–37.
31. *Monroe Papers,* Vol. 13, No. 1696, Jefferson to Monroe, June 19, 1813; *7 U.S. Ministers, Instructions,* pp. 238–70 and 296–300, Apr. 15, and June 23, 1813; PRATT, *The Expansionists of 1812; Annals of Congress, 11th Congress, 1st Session,* p. 580; G. MORRIS, *Diary and Letters,* Apr. 5, 1813; JEFFERSON'S *Works,* V, 444; HENRY M. BRACKENRIDGE on South American Affairs, in *Pamphleteer,* Vol. 13 (1818), p. 67.
32. RICHARDSON (ed.), *Messages and Papers,* I, 499–504; CHANNING, *U.S.*, IV, 453, 462–64; *Journal of Executive Proceeding of the Senate,* Vol. 2, p. 290.
33. CHANNING, *U.S.*, IV. 465, 469; *C.A.*, C, 676, Duplicate Q, 118, p. 71.
34. *Ib.*, pp. 332–36; CRUIKSHANK, *Documents Relating to the Invasion of Canada in 1812.*
35. *Am. State Papers, Foreign Relations,* I, pp. 80, 83; *Ib., Naval Affairs,* I, 294–95.
36. *Ib., Military Affairs,* I, 458–63; *C.A.*, Q, 123, p. 11; *C.A.*, C, 681, p. 62; *C.A.*, Q, 128–1, p. 119; MAHAN, *Sea Power in its Relation to the War of 1812,* Vol. 2, p. 104.
37. MCMASTER, *U.S.*, IV, 65; H. ADAMS, *U.S.*, VIII, 94; MAHAN, II, 360–82; *C.A.*, M, 389, pp. 176–83; *C.A.*, Q, 128–1, p. 220; *Am. State Papers, Naval Affairs,* III, 309– .
38. *Annals of Congress,* 1813–14, p. 2021; *Ib.*, 1815–16, p. 1651; *Ib., 13th Congress,* II, p. 2781; *C.A., Report,* 1896, p. 37.
39. *Annals of Congress,* 12–2, Jan. 1813.

CHAPTER IV

NEGOTIATIONS OF THE PEACE TREATY OF GHENT

In the peace negotiations of 1813–14 the Madison administration persistently continued its proposals to acquire contiguous Canadian territory until it was practically forced to abandon them in the struggle to defeat British counter plans against American rights upon the Lakes and the adjacent southern shores.

The basis of American policy was security. In 1812 Jefferson declared that a cession of Canada was a *sine qua non* of peace. In January, 1813, Robertson of Louisiana, urging the necessity of making the frontiers secure, said: "The power of Great Britain must be extinguished in America." Macon of North Carolina, suggesting the possibility of canal connection between the St. Lawrence and the Mississippi systems, declared that Canada was "absolutely necessary . . . to the peace and happiness of the nation." In June, 1813, Jefferson suggested to Secretary Monroe that acquisition of the territory by military operations would at least enable the American government in the proposed negotiations at St. Petersburg to insist successfully on retention of "all westward of the meridian of Lake Huron, or Lake Ontario, or on Montreal . . . as an indemnification for the past and security for the future."[1]

On April 15, 1813, under the proffered Russian mediation, Secretary Monroe issued his first instructions to the American peace commissioners (Albert Gallatin, J. Q. Adams and James A. Bayard). Influenced by the causes and progress of the war along the Canadian border, and confident that the consequence of the war (if continued) would be the annexation of the British North American provinces, he took a firm stand on the control of the Indian trade and the navigation of the Lakes. He said:

"The Article in the Treaty of 1794, which allows British Traders from Canada and the North West Company to carry on trade with the Indian tribes within the limits of the United States, must not be renewed. The pernicious effects of this privilege have been most sensibly felt in the present War by the influence which it gave to the traders over the Indians whose whole force has been wielded by means thereof against the Inhabitants of our western States and Territories. You will avoid also any stipulation which might restrain the United States from increasing their naval force to any extent they might think proper on the Lakes in common; or [from?] excluding the British Traders from the Navigation of the Lakes and Rivers exclusively within our own jurisdiction." [2]

In later instructions of June 23, encouraged by the improvements of the American military force and its achievements along the lake frontier, and with hopeful expectation of obtaining military possession of Upper Canada, he wrote to the commissioners detailed instructions in which he stressed the "advantages to both countries . . . promised by a transfer . . . of Canada to the United States," and especially by a transfer of upper Canada. After mentioning the advantages to Great Britain he proposed, in case of a cession, to stipulate for temporary trade advantages to Great Britain similar to those secured to France by the Louisiana treaty. At the same time, considering the question of an agreement for restitution of territory, he suggested the propriety and importance of a provision for a fair and equitable settlement of the international boundary on the upper St. Lawrence and the Lakes to the northwestern corner of the Lake of the Woods, in accord with the principles of the treaty of 1783. For this purpose he suggested the advisability of the appointment of commissioners on each side, with full powers.[3]

On January 1, 1814, following new advantages from success in Upper Canada and from the capture of British public documents which indicated British influence in exciting against the United States the hostility of Indians within the limits of the United States, he instructed the American commissioners to request a cession of Canada, or Upper Canada, or at least of that portion lying between the western end of Lake Ontario and the eastern end of Lake Huron. He suggested that the British government must be sensible of the impossibility of preserving a durable peace with the United States while it retained possession of the Canadian provinces.[4]

On January 28, after further reflection which strengthened official conviction on the reasons submitted in favor of a cession of Canada, he sent additional instructions. In these he emphasized his earlier views concerning the pernicious effects of British ascendancy over the Indians within American limits and expressed the opinion that experience had shown that British participation in the dominion and navigation of the Lakes would result in the danger of an early renewal of the war. Stating that new sources of controversy would probably result from extension of American settlements in the vacant territory westward from Detroit to Lake Michigan and beyond, and from the continued incontrollable cupidity of the British traders, he suggested that future evils (including possible colonial demand for independence) should be anticipated and avoided by a timely transfer arrangement between the two governments.[5]

In later instructions (of March 22, 1814), he mentioned the problem of future American security between the Lakes and the Pacific. Referring to the American post at Astoria on the Columbia, he declared: "On no pretext can the British Government set up a claim to territory south of the northern boundary of the United States [evidently implying that the line of 49° extended to the Pacific coast]. It is not believed that they have any claim whatever to territory on the Pacific ocean." Then he added: "You will be careful . . . not to countenance . . . a pretension in the British Government to territory south of that line."

On June 23, 1814, writing to the American commissioners at Gothenburg, he repeated the arguments which he had submitted a year earlier. Two days later, after learning that the British would probably demand a surrender of the right to the fisheries, an abandonment of all trade beyond the Cape of Good Hope, and a cession of Louisiana to Spain, he stated that negotiations must cease if the British insisted upon discussion of these American rights.[6]

Meantime, British-Canadian expressions of expectations were preparing a basis for extreme British demands in the peace negotiations. In February, 1814, the New Brunswick assembly, expressing recent views of the maritime provinces concerning the importance of securing a shorter and more desirable communication between Halifax and Quebec, proposed the alteration of the boundary in order to avoid possible future interruption of communication via the St. John. From elsewhere came suggestions to avoid other errors of previous treaties. One writer especially urged avoidance of the ambiguity of the treaty of 1794 in regard to inland navigation, under which Canadian fur traders were placed at the mercy of American revenue collectors in the payment of duties on goods passing inland from Canada to the Indians in American jurisdiction. Early in March, 1814, Nathaniel Atcheson, an employé of the British Society of Ship Owners of London, published a pamphlet on "Compressed View of the Points to be Discussed in Treating with the United States." Complaining that the boundary of 1783 had not been fixed according to the natural geographical conditions, and that the Northwest Territory never should have been ceded, he proposed that the new boundary should effectually curb the avowed American ambitions and give permanent security to Canada. This security he said could be obtained especially by "exclusion of the Americans from the navigation of the St. Lawrence and its tributary seas and waters" which he regarded as the "natural patrimony of the Canadas," and by establishment of the "prominent boundary at the heights of land separating the respective territories." The latter he desired as a means to give Canada the southern shores of all the Lakes (including Lake Champlain) and contact with a navigable portion of the Mississippi. If the latter could not be obtained, he proposed a boundary from Lake Erie up the Sandusky River, and thence across the portage and along the nearest stream flowing into the Ohio, with a stipulated limitation on the size of American vessels on the Lakes and a prohibition of American fortifications on the borders of boundary waters or the American streams tributary thereto. He also proposed that the new American claim to the Northwest coast as far as the Columbia "should be extinguished forever." He suggested as the best boundary of the proposed Indian territory a line up the Sandusky and down the nearest river flowing into the Ohio, the Ohio to the Mississippi, the latter to the mouth of the Missouri, and the Missouri to its principal source.[7]

About the same time, David Anderson, a British citizen who had resided in the colonies and had obtained much information from Atcheson, published a volume in which he claimed that under British policy after 1784 the United States had supplied the British colonies with masts and other timber products which could have been supplied by British North America, and that in the War of 1812 it sought Upper Canada and the St. Lawrence in order to obtain valuable timber above Quebec and to prevent the smuggling of British manufactures via Canada. He urged that the British government should retain the fisheries, prohibit all American intercourse with the British West Indies, and enforce the duty on foreign timber. This policy he advocated with a view to encouragement of Canadian shipment of American flour via the St. Lawrence and to encourage ample Canadian resources to supply the West Indies.[8]

On March 7, 1814, at Halifax, the assembly of Nova Scotia issued a significant address to the British Prince Regent stating that the sacrifice of British-Canadian interests in 1783 had resulted in "artful American insinuations to weaken the British colonists from allegiance and attachment" to Great Britain with the idea of easy America conquest. It urged that England should increase the strength of the Canadian provinces by encouragement of European immigration (as American strength had been increased).[9]

Later, hoping to recover British interests which had been sacrificed in 1783, Canada proposed to the British government terms to which the American government should be required to agree in the negotiations for a new treaty of peace: that it should be denied any fishery rights within the jurisdiction of British America; that it should be required to cede eastern Maine and to surrender a part of New York north of a line drawn from Plattsburg to Sackett's Harbor (to secure to Canada the control of the St. Lawrence); that (to provide for security of Canada) it should also be required to withdraw all American troops from the posts of the Northwest, to surrender the eastern bank of the Niagara and to agree to the establishment of an Indian territory north of a line drawn from Sandusky to Kaskaskia on the Mississippi; and that it must also be required to cede to Spain the territory of Louisiana which it had purchased from France.[10]

In accord with part of the Canadian proposals the British commissioners at Ghent, on August 8 at their first conference with the American commissioners, demanded a cession of soil and sovereignty of the Indian territory (as a *sine qua non*), revision of the Canadian boundary, and withdrawal of American fishery privileges in British American territorial waters. In seeking to justify the demand for cession of territory, they stated that the United States, with a spirit of conquest and aggrandizement which had been illustrated in the progressive occupation of Indian lands and acquisition of Louisiana, had begun the war chiefly with a view to annexation of Canada and that its alleged purpose to defend maritime rights was largely a pretense. They urged that Great Britain, being the weaker power on the North American continent, should have military occupation of the Lakes in order to prevent American conquest of the British dominions.[11]

The American commissioners, with no authority to cede territory, were surprised by the British proposal to revise the boundary "with a view to prevent future uncertainty and dispute." From a later explanation they learned that this proposal contemplated "such a variation of the line of frontier as may secure a direct communication between Quebec and Halifax," the interruption of which "was not in contemplation of the British Plenipotentiaries who concluded the treaty of 1783." They were also asked to agree to an Indian boundary south of the Lakes. They replied that the proposed Indian boundary was without example in the practice of European nations, and they proceeded to explain the American liberal and humane Indian policy under which uninterrupted peace with the Indians had existed for sixteen years after 1795. They had no power to agree to a cession of any part of American sovereignty and soil to the Indians. They, therefore, gladly agreed to the British proposal to suspend the conferences while awaiting the result of a consultation with the British government at London.[12]

In the earlier draft of general instructions to the British peace commissioners, probably written in July, 1814, Lord Castlereagh had shown a desire to prevent a contest for naval supremacy on the Lakes. He had added an unused suggestion that "the two contracting parties should reciprocally bind themselves not to construct any ships of war on the Lakes and should entirely dismantle those already in commission or in preparation for service." [13] By August he decided that in the interest of peace and economy the Lakes should belong exclusively to one power, stating that the previous mid-lake boundary tended to create "perpetual contest." In his instructions of August 14 he said that the British government, with strictly defensive views of the weaker power on the North American Continent, considered the course of the Lakes above the St. Lawrence as the natural military frontier of British possessions in North America and that therefore it was entitled to claim the use of those Lakes as a military barrier—a claim which apparently was suggested by the earlier doctrine of the "natural limit of Canada" south of the Lakes.[14] Although he stated that Great Britain should also have military command of the American shores of the Lakes, he was "disposed to leave the sovereignty of the soil undisturbed and, incident to it the free commercial navigation of the Lakes," provided the American government would stipulate "not to preserve or construct any fortifications upon or within a limited distance of the shores, or maintain or construct any armed vessel upon the Lakes in question or upon the rivers which empty themselves into the same."

On August 19, after the arrival of further instructions from London, the British commissioners stated the British purpose to create a permanent Indian barrier between Canada and the American settlements of the West, and proposed that its boundary should be the line of the Greenville treaty of 1795 (beyond which many thousand American citizens had already settled). They explained that the revision of boundary should include (1) a cession of all eastern Maine to the Quebec line, in order to facilitate a direct line of communication from Halifax and Quebec, and (2) a change in the boundary west of Lake Superior by a line from the latter to the Mississippi which they still claimed the right to navigate. They also demanded that, in order to avoid the dangers to peace resulting from joint possession of the Lakes and the consequent rivalry in armament, the United States (as the stronger power) should agree to disarm on the Lakes and its tributary streams, beginning with the dismantling of Fort Niagara and Sackett's Harbor. Such demands seemed to forebode the early termination of negotiations.[15]

The American commissioners, in a clear and dignified reply of August 24, refused to consider the unreasonable British demands. They said these demands were unrelated to the causes of the war, inconsistent with the principles of public law, an insult to American independence and sovereignty, and calculated to inflict vital injury on the American nation (by dismemberment, abandonment of its citizens, restriction on increase of population and dangers from exposed frontiers). As to the British proposal concerning the Lakes, they stated that they were "at a loss to discover by what rule of perfect reciprocity the United States can be required to renounce their equal right of maintaining a naval force upon those lakes, and of fortifying their own shores, while Great Britain reserves exclusively the corresponding rights to herself." They declared that they had "no authority to cede any part of the United States." A week later they sent George M. Dallas to Washington with dispatches announcing the failure of the mission and submitting a statement of the humiliating British demands which, arriving just after the news of American victories by Macdonough and others on the Canadian frontier, were promptly (on October 10) delivered to the House and published with good effect.[16]

Although they failed to persuade the British to abandon Canada to the United States, they firmly adhered to their determination to make no cession of territory. By this determination they caused the British to abandon the proposition to vary the line and to decide to submit more moderate proposals. On September 1 Adams, in a conversation with Goulburn, declared that the American people could not be prevented from settling and cultivating lands which the Indians did not improve—that no stroke of the pen could insure the wilderness of the Northwest to the Indian and the British trader.[17]

On September 4 the American commissioners, who had been preparing to leave Ghent, received from the British commissioners the information that the British government (in new instructions) had explained that the proposal of the Indian barrier and British exclusive military possession of the Lakes had been submitted to invite discussion with a view to plans to protect Canada from future American attempts at conquest and annexation and had not been intended as a *sine qua non*.

Regarding the demands as inadmissible, however, the Americans refused to discuss them and declined to refer them to Washington. On September 6 Gallatin proposed to offer at least to refer to Washington a stipulation for disarmament on both sides of the Lakes. Although Adams through Bayard manifested symptoms of concession on the points proposed by the British, all stood together in the reply of September 9. They denied that American policy was conquest. They declared that for the security of Canada from sudden invasion Great Britain had a sufficient pledge in the extensive American commerce upon the ocean—a commerce more valuable than Canada. They maintained a peaceful attitude which contributed to produce a better spirit in the British reply of September 19.

In reply the British commissioners explained that they had "never stated that the exclusive military possession of the Lakes . . . was a *sine qua non* in the negotiation"; and they added that after adjustment of the Indian question they could make a final boundary proposition founded on principles of moderation and justice.[18] Inconsistent with this reply, however, the *London Courier* asserted that peace should be subject to a condition that America would have no territory on the waters of the St. Lawrence and no settlements on the Lakes.

On September 26 the Americans pledged themselves to meet with perfect reciprocity a proposition for mutual reduction of armaments which they hoped the British intended to offer. Later, Clay favored the rejection of any proposition to disarm upon the Lakes if a proposed British article (an ultimatum on Indian pacification) was admitted. He considered that the two articles together would deliver the whole western country to the mercy of the Indians. Later, in view of a possible British proposal for mutual restriction "either partial or total," Gallatin asked Monroe whether the American commissioners should still adhere to the *sine qua non* of earlier instructions claiming the right to preserve American naval forces on the Lakes without restriction. He probably would have agreed with Gouverneur Morris, the former chairman of the Erie Canal Commission, who recently had suggested both naval and military disarmament on the Lakes as a matter of economy—"to avoid idle and useless expense."

Meantime, the American government was surprised by the news of the earlier British proposals which reached Washington on October 9, after the failure of the British attempt to invade New York from Canada. Madison, in a note of October 10, intimated to Jefferson that the American commissioners would arrive in a few days, unless the British policy had been modified by some sudden change in the British cabinet or as a result of news from America and Europe. Jefferson, convinced that "we should put our house in order for interminable war," suggested that, in order to counterbalance the intention of England to conquer the Lakes and the Northwest, the Americans "ought to propose . . . the establishment of the meridian of the Sorel northwardly" as the western boundary of all British possessions. Later, in a letter to Melish, he said: "As to repressing our growth they might as well attempt to repress the waves of the ocean." [19]

By the end of October, the American commissioners reported that the British had abandoned the demands as to the Indian boundary and as to British exclusive control of the Lakes. They also reported their rejection of the recent British *ultimatum* that the Indians must be admitted as parties to the treaty of peace. In place of the latter they proposed an offer of a general amnesty for Indians who had served as a part of the British military forces in the war—an offer which the British commissioners accepted in accord with new instructions from London.

Later, after arrival of news of American victories on the Canadian frontier, the Americans rejected the British proposal to treat on the basis of *status uti possidetis*. They proposed the basis of *status quo ante bellum*. This the British government accepted, after consultation with Wellington who said it had no right to demand territory, and after reaching a sensible decision that it could not hope to secure by treaty what it had failed to secure by force of arms.[20] In reaching this basis, which resulted in the British restoration of eastern Maine and the Pacific post at Astoria, the Americans had overcome the hesitation of Clay who was so largely responsible for the declaration of war and who had expected to dictate a peace at Quebec or Halifax.

With the British diplomatic change in the basis of the negotiations, Canadians were disappointed. The *Halifax Journal*, at the close of October, still asserted that British demands concerning fisheries, revision of boundary, Indian allies, and Indian barrier territory were necessary to the general interests and permanent security of the British American colonies.

A month before the completion of the treaty at Ghent, Canadian officials still hoped for some British advantage from American defection in New England. From Halifax, on November 20, J. C. Sherbrooke wrote to Earl Bathurst that a member of the Massachusetts House of Representatives, from the Maine region (Castine) which had been occupied by British troops, had brought to him from Boston a communication from the Massachusetts government inquiring whether Great Britain would furnish military aid to the Federalists to aid them in case they should attempt to separate New England from the Union with a view to the formation of an independent government. He suggested the wisdom of a British policy to send more troops promptly "to be in readiness" either to defend the new British frontier at the Penobscot or to assist possible New England plans for separation, and also to send secretly a skillful diplomatic "negotiator" who would be ready and able to treat with the subtle New Englanders and "to take advantage of circumstances as they occur"; but, while anxiously awaiting instructions, he planned "not to interfere in the Politics of the New England States in any way . . . unless circumstances should produce an open rupture between them and the Government of the United States sooner than is expected." [21]

In preparing a treaty draft which was submitted to the British, on November 10, the American commissioners could not reach an agreement upon the questions of the continuation of American rights in the northeastern fisheries and the British right to navigate the Mississippi as recognized in the treaty of 1783. Clay, representing the spirit of the West, strenuously opposed Gallatin's article which provided for confirmation of the British right to navigate the Mississippi as a corollary of the confirmation of the American rights in the northeast fisheries. He finally induced his colleagues to accept a compromise by which neither subject was mentioned in the treaty; but in an accompanying note appeared the statement that any renewed stipulation concerning the American rights in the fisheries was regarded as unnecessary.

When the British commissioners added to the draft a provision for free navigation of the Mississippi by British subjects, Clay firmly continued his objection. On December 1, through the influence of Gallatin, the Americans proposed to agree to British navigation of the Mississippi in exchange for American use of the fisheries; but, following a suggestion of the British that both subjects be postponed for future negotiation, the Americans obtained consent of the British to an agreement on the treaty without further mention of those issues at that time.[22]

The Americans, evidently regarding peace as more important than codfish, decided to postpone further diplomatic contention on the question of the fisheries which was so important to the recovery of New England business interests.

In the negotiations the British denial of American rights to fish in colonial waters was probably based on the grounds of colonial opposition. In 1813 this opposition had urged that the concession of 1783 had injured British interests, by furnishing greater American opportunities for illicit trade and for creation of discontent and insubordination among Canadians (many of whom were tempted to emigrate to the United States).[23]

On the question of the boundary west of the Lake of the Woods, although both parties were willing to agree to the line proposed in 1806, the American commissioners could not accept the new British condition that to the boundary agreement should be added a provision securing to British subjects access across American territory from Canada to the Mississippi and free navigation of the Mississippi to the Gulf. In the later conferences the Americans proposed that west of the meridian of the Lake of the Woods the boundary between American and British territories should be the parallel of 49° "as far as the said respective territories extend in that quarter." Finding that the British insisted that the line of 49° should be designated to extend only as far as the limit of American territories, they finally proposed to omit any mention of the northwestern boundary—a proposal to which the British agreed.[24]

In the negotiations the Americans were favored by time and events (and the advice of the Duke of Wellington) which influenced the British government and the British commissioners to view with more toleration the American pretensions and gradually to withdraw or drop the British demands until all the American commissioners could agree to sign a treaty which conceded none of the American demands, nor mentioned them.

The treaty of Ghent was silent on these issues and also on the issues which caused the war. It simply provided for peace, surrender of captured territory, and the appointment of three commissions to determine for definite location of the boundaries as already defined in the treaty of 1783.[25]

On December 25, in a dispatch supplementing the regular official report on the terms of the treaty, Gallatin explained to Secretary Monroe that the Indian article, proposed as an alternative to the termination of negotiations, was accepted only provisionally, subject to the approbation or rejection of the American government. He also explained that the exception of Moose Island from the general restoration of territory was accepted to avoid the hazard of risking the peace on the question of the temporary possession of a small island, the title to which was fully reserved for future adjustment.

Gallatin closed his letter with an interesting reference to the British foundation for a future dispute of the American claim to northern Maine. He said:

"I believe that G. Britain is very desirous of obtaining the northern part of Maine, say from about 47° north latitude to the northern extremity of that district as claimed by us. They hope that the river which empties into Bay des Chaleurs in the Gulf of St Lawrence has its source so far west as to intervene between the head waters of the River St John's & those of the streams emptying into the river St Lawrence; so that the line north from the source of the River St Croix will first strike the height of land which divide the waters emptying into the Atlantic Ocean (River St John's) from those emptying into the *Gulf* of St Lawrence (River des Chaleurs), and afterwards the height of land which divide the waters emptying into the *Gulf* of St Lawrence (River des Chaleurs) from those emptying into the River St Lawrence; but that the said line never can, in the words of the treaty strike any spot of land actually dividing the waters emptying into the Atlantic Ocean from those which fall into the *River* St Lawrence. Such will be the foundation of their disputing our claim to the northern part of that territory; but feeling that it is not very solid, I am apt to think that they will be disposed to offer the whole of Passamaquoddy bay and the disputed fisheries as an equivalent for the portion of northern territory which they want in order to connect New Brunswick and Quebec. This may account for their tenacity with respect to the temporary possession of Moose island & for their refusing to accept the recognition of their right to the navigation of the Mississippi provided they recognised ours to the fisheries."

To this he added:

"That northern territory is of no importance to us & belongs to the United States & not to Massachusetts which has not the shadow of a claim to any land north of 45° to the eastward of the Penobscot river, as you may easily convince yourself of, by recurring to her charters." [26]

Canada, which was not directly represented at Ghent, regarded highly the ability of the American commissioners in obtaining peace without concessions. In later expressions of disappointment with the results it especially stated that the British representatives should have been able at least to enforce the British demand for a cession of the northern half of Maine in order to link the maritime provinces with the St. Lawrence.

Some British expressions of disappointment also appeared. A British traveler, in a volume on British colonial policy, complained that British "oversights" in failing to insist upon the retention of upper Maine and the establishment of a straight line boundary south of the Lakes to the Mississippi had resulted in an American advantage on the frontier. He declared that peace should have been postponed until Canada secured its desire for a change of boundary, and that the British negotiators should have retained at least Oswego, Sackett's Harbor, Detroit and Buffalo, and also control of the Lakes by prohibition of an American fleet there or by limitation as to force. He urged that the United States, if it should again declare war, should be coerced to abandon Lake Michigan and Michigan Territory and to retire from the waters of the Lakes and the connecting rivers. Warning the British government of the dangerous tendency of American competition and of a possible loss of Canada which would be followed by the loss of the West Indies, he advocated a vigorous colonial policy, including restrictions concerning the fisheries, encouragement of emigration to the colonies, prevention of emigration to the United States, and a close watch on the United States by an observing minister and secret emissaries.[27]

Americans apparently were satisfied with the opportunity to turn their minds from the temptations of external expansion to the duties of internal growth. Turning their backs on Europe, they faced toward peace-time problems of the northern border and the rising West. Jefferson, although he boasted that Quebec and Halifax would have been taken if the war had continued, philosophically concluded that peace and reconciliation were better than conquest by war.[28] By experience of war, especially by observation of development of national patriotism in the British provinces, the American government had learned that it had been too sanguine in its belief in American destiny to annex Canada, and that attempts at annexation by force were less practical than disarmament along the border combined with efforts for peaceful adjustment of questions of controversy.

In considering future foreign policy, however, some leading Americans still regarded Canada as a problem. Madison still regarded its possession by England as a remaining danger to a permanent Anglo-American harmony. In November, 1818, after he had retired to private life, he wrote President Monroe that Canada in British hands must be ever a source of collision which both governments should be equally anxious to remove. Five years later, in November, 1823, following allusions in the British press and Parliament concerning the consideration of recommendations for alienation of Canada, he suggested to Richard Rush (the American minister at London) the expediency of an appeal to the British government for a cession of Canada as a policy conducive to permanent peace, especially by closing a wide door to smuggling and border collision. In February, 1827, A. H. Everett stated that the American government, without claiming to feel any wish for territorial extension, should be prepared to assent to a spontaneous proposal of annexation from British American colonies which he expected eventually to follow the fortunes of other European possessions in America and naturally to seek connection with the United States.[29]

REFERENCES

1. *Works of Jefferson* (FORD, ed.), VI, 70; *Monroe Papers,* Vol. 13.
2. *7 U.S. Ministers, Instrs.,* pp. 238–70, April 15, 1813.
3. *Ib.,* pp. 296–300, June 23, 1813.
4. *Ib.,* pp. 308–09, Jan. 4, 1814.
5. *Ib.,* pp. 311–21, Jan. 28, 1814; *Am. State Papers, Foreign Relations,* III, 700–01, 731; *Papers of James A. Bayard, 1796–1815* (*Ann. Rp. Am. Hist. Assoc.,* 1913, II, 263–65).
6. *U.S. Ministers, Instrs.,* pp. 360–62, June 23; *Ib.,* pp. 368–71, June 25, 1814.
7. BURRAGE, *Maine in the Northeast Boundary Controversy,* p. 98; *Pamphleteer,* Vol. 6, pp. 35, 43; *Ib.,* Vol. 5, No. 9, pp. 108–17 (and also No. 10).
8. DAVID ANDERSON, *Canada* (a view of the importance of the British American colonies).
9. *Canadian Archives,* A 152, *Nova Scotia, C.O. Records,* 217, Vol. 19.
10. MCMASTER, *U.S.,* IV, p. 261.
11. *Am. State Papers, Foreign Relations,* III, pp. 705 and 709; *Commissioners to Monroe,* Aug. 12, 1814; *Commissioners,* 1813–16, *Report of Conferences at Ghent,* No. 2, Aug. 12, 1814; *America,* Vol. 129 (Public Record Office, London); *Letters and Despatches of Castlereagh,* Vol. 2, 3rd Series.
12. J. B. MOORE, *International Arbitrations,* I, 69; *Am. Commissioners, 1813–16, Report of Conferences of Aug. 8–9 at Ghent,* No. 2, Aug. 12, 1814.
13. *America,* Vol. 128 (in Public Record Office at London).

14. *Parliamentary Debates* (Marquis Wellesley in the House of Lords, Apr. 13, 1815).
15. *Monroe Papers,* Vol. 14, Aug. 19, 1814; J. Q. ADAMS' *Memoirs,* Vol. 3, pp. 17–21.
16. *Am. State Papers, Foreign Relations,* III, 709 and 712; *Rp. Am. Hist. Ass'n,* 1913, II, 263–67 (Bayard Mss.).
17. MOORE, *International Arbitrations,* I, 70; J. Q. ADAMS' *Memoirs,* Vol. 3, pp. 24–25.
18. *Am. State Papers, Foreign Relations,* Vol. 1, pp. 713 and 718; H. ADAMS, *Writings of Albert Gallatin,* Vol. I, p. 640; J. Q. ADAMS, *Memoirs,* Vol. 3, Sept. 6 and 19, 1814; *America,* Vol. 129 (at Public Record Office, London).
19. *Madison Papers,* Vol. 7; *Jefferson Papers,* 2nd Series, Vol. 58, No. 59; *Monroe Papers,* Vol. 13, No. 1696; *Jefferson Papers,* 1st Series, Vol. 1 (to Monroe, Oct. 13; to Madison, Oct. 15; to Melish, Dec. 10).
20. *Ib.,* 2nd Series, Vol. 58 (Monroe to Jefferson, Nov. 30, 1814); *Castlereagh Correspondence,* Vol. 10, p. 168.
21. *Canadian Archives,* A 151, *Nova Scotia,* C.O. *Records,* 1814, pp. 399, and 405–08.
22. McMASTER, *U.S.,* IV, 270–73.
23. *Ib.,* IV, 460; NILES' *Register,* July 11, 1814.
24. *8 U.S. Ministers, Instrs.,* pp. 223–32, Adams to Gallatin and Rush, July 28, 1818; J. Q. ADAMS' *Memoirs,* III, 72, 84; *Am. State Papers, Foreign Relations,* III, 738 (and 709).
25. CHANNING, *U.S.,* IV, 355–57; McMASTER, *U.S.,* IV, 273–74; *Can. Hist. Rev.,* March, 1921.
26. *Am. Commissioners, 1813–16,* Gallatin to Monroe, Dec. 25, 1814.
27. A BRITISH TRAVELLER, *The Colonial Policy of Great Britain* (with relation to North Am. provinces).
28. *Jefferson Papers,* 1st Series, Vol. 14 (to Francis C. Grey), March, 1815.
29. MADISON'S *Writings,* III, 42, 113, 347–48; BELL'S *Weekly Messenger,* July 7, 1823; A. H. EVERETT, *America,* p. 208.

CHAPTER V

EARLY POST-WAR ADJUSTMENT

PROMPTLY after the proclamation of Anglo-American peace, the American government, wishing to establish better neighborhood relations and a lasting peace along the international boundary of the northern and northwestern frontier, sought to adapt measures to lessen the chances of possible sources of future misunderstandings and to guard against the danger of immediate future collision or friction. It especially sought an effective arrangement for reduction of naval armaments on the border Lakes and a consequent limitation of expensive competitive naval construction, with a view to mutual interests in connection with expected increase of frontier settlements and growth of commerce which stimulated plans for improvements in communication with the northern frontier and the American Northwest.

The President recognized that vigilant attention was required to preserve the peace which had been declared by the treaty of Ghent. He promptly issued orders to restore the part of Upper Canada which was occupied by American troops and to conclude treaties of peace with the Indian tribes. He also approved an act of Congress providing for reduction of the army from 62,000 to 10,000. At the same time he expected prompt restoration of posts held by the British at Michilimackinac, Niagara and Castine. He also claimed and expected restitution of Astoria on the Columbia. In May Monroe in his instructions to Adams expressed fear that the British delay in the surrender of Michilimackinac might inspire in the minds of the Indians doubts injurious to the United States. In July he stated that the delay had produced the effects anticipated, causing the Indians to treat coolly the requests to meet the American commissioners for conference. At the same time he complained of a recent British warning to American fishermen on the British colonial coasts whose right to fish he said was amply secured by the treaty of 1783 supplemented by the declaration of the American commissioners in the negotiations at Ghent.[1]

The British authority faced the new situation with some doubt and suspicion. To Lieutenant-General Sir Gordon Drummond, who had suggested desirable works for the defense of Upper Canada, Bathurst replied on October 16, 1815, that any proposed fortification should be postponed until the British government could decide upon some general plan. A month later, he suggested to Major-General Wilson of Lower Canada the question whether from a military point of view the frontier between Montreal and Lake Champlain should be left as far as possible in a state of nature by suspension of further grants there and by recovery of lands already granted. In September, 1816, Sherbrooke, accepting the suggestion, stated that as far as possible he would also prevent the extension of roads in that quarter.[2]

Following the British surrender of Michilimackinac, the American authorities enforced trade measures which caused considerable complaint of the British traders. They acted under a law of April 29, 1816 (supplementary to an act of March 13, 1802), by which all trade intercourse with Indian tribes within the United States was interdicted under heavy penalties, and by which all other intercourse was placed under restraints which resulted in exclusion of British subjects from the territories.

In June, Lieutenant-Colonel McDouall, writing to Governor Sherbrooke from Drummond's Island, said: "The most violent measures continue to be carried on at Mackina. All the furs which have yet arrived belonging to the British Traders have been seized, principally, as they alledge in their indication, because the duties were not paid to the American Government on the different equipments going into the Indian Country and which indeed could not be as Mackina was then in our possession." Referring to the possible effect of the American policy on the Indians, he proposed to occupy the heights for a proposed fort. In August, complaining of American plans to erect forts on Indian lands (especially on Green Bay) to facilitate the exclusion of the British from the Indian trade and to aid the American monopoly of the trade, he recommended government interposition in the unnatural contest between the two great rival fur companies, the Hudson's Bay and the Northwest companies, with a view to the creation of a united formidable barrier against American encroachment.[3]

The American policy against British participation in the trans-border fur trade with American Indians favored American fur interests which soon thereafter organized under the leadership of John Jacob Astor of the American Fur Company, with headquarters at St. Louis, or established competitive firms such as that of Alexander Ewing (and his sons) with chief headquarters at Fort Wayne, Indiana.

Farther east, across the Detroit River, a new Indian problem arose in the fall of 1819. Governor Cass of Michigan Territory complained to the Secretary of War that the British authorities in Upper Canada by invitations had attracted large numbers of Indians from American territory to Malden where in connection with distribution of presents they were instigated to hostility against the United States. By order of President Monroe, who believed that the action of the British local officers did not represent the intentions of the British government, Secretary Adams, with a view to the promotion of good understanding and harmony, suggested that the government at London should order all British authorities in Canada "to supersede for the future the practice of inviting any of the Indians, residing within our boundaries to Malden or any other place within British jurisdiction, and that of distributing to them any presents whatever." As to the reasonableness of this suggestion he said "there can be no possible motive, friendly to the United States, for inviting Indians under their protection from great distances to bestow presents upon them for which no equivalent is asked or expected."[4]

Meantime, following the treaty of peace, two questions concerning restitution of territory, one on the eastern maritime frontier and the other on the Pacific coast, were considered and adjusted.

The British government refused to restore Moose Island and two other islands (in Passamaquoddy Bay) which (with Eastport) it had occupied during the war, but to which it also set up a disputed claim under the treaty of 1783. The question of title was finally settled in favor of the United States on November 24, 1817, in conformity with the true intent of Article II of the treaty of 1783, by decision of a commission (Thomas Barclay and John Holmes) under the provision of Article IV of the treaty of Ghent—a decision based upon the provision of Rufus King's unratified draft treaty of May 12, 1803, and the similar arrangement attempted by Monroe and Pinckney in 1806–07. Under the decision, however, no steps to mark the water boundary were taken until 1892.[5]

After the conclusion of peace, the Madison administration, influenced by Astor's urgent representations in favor of American re-occupation of Astoria at the mouth of the Columbia where he had been planning to renew the earlier settlement, decided to send a vessel to coöperate in the restoration of the American flag. In July, 1815, Secretary Monroe notified the British chargé at Washington that the President planned to re-occupy Astoria at once under the treaty provision for restitution of territory seized in the war. From the British legation he received an expression of doubt as to the sufficiency of the American claim—a doubt which apparently was based upon a report of the Captain-General of Canada that the Americans had retired from Astoria under an agreement with the Northwest Company. Finally, in September, 1818, exercising his executive authority, he ordered the American sloop *Ontario,* commanded by Captain J. Biddle, who was jointly commissioned with J. B. Prevost (American agent) to proceed to the Columbia to assert in a friendly and peaceful manner the American claim to the adjacent country. In October the vessel sailed from New York for the voyage around Cape Horn. In November Secretary Adams informed Bagot of the American purpose in sending the expedition. From Bagot he received a remonstrance, which Lord Bathurst of the British government later disapproved. Lord Castlereagh, expressing regret and a desire to avoid collision, admitted the American right to be re-instated at Astoria until the claim could be settled by arbitration and negotiation. On May 20, 1818, Adams wrote to Rush at London that he had not anticipated that England was disposed to start questions of title with the United States on the shores of the South Sea. He suggested that if from the nature of things and in the course of events the American claim should become an object of serious importance to the United States, England could hardly find resistance useful; and he significantly added that if the United States should leave England in possession of its holds upon Europe, Asia and Africa, and its actual possessions in this hemisphere, "we may fairly expect that she will not think it consistent, either with a wise or a friendly policy, to watch with eyes of jealousy and alarm every possibility of extension to our natural dominion, in North America, which she can have no solid interest to prevent until all possibility of her preventing it shall have vanished."[6] Captain Biddle took temporary possession of the territory on August 9, 1818. Later, on October 6, Prevost, who had disembarked from the *Ontario* in Chile and had sailed for the Columbia from Valparaiso (in August, 1818) on the British sloop *Blosssom*,[7] officially received the surrender of the Columbia post which the British had named Fort George, but which was re-christened Astoria. Although the post was left in the hands of the British traders, the American flag replaced the British flag as a token of the change of sovereignty. By this action, in accord with orders of the British government, the American government obtained an advantage in the later claims to rights of sovereignty in the Oregon controversy.

Probably the most significant and important of the early post-war adjustments was the Agreement of 1817 for mutual reduction of Lakes armaments—resulting in the prompt dismantling of naval vessels which remained as a reminder of the former warring fleets and which their owners at that time were unable to remove from the Lakes to the sea.

While arranging mutual compliance with the *status quo ante bellum* provision of the treaty of Ghent, and while considering the several sources of dissension—such as Indian restlessness and hostility, the conduct of British local authorities in Canada, and the desertion of British soldiers to the American side of the boundary—the American authorities at Washington saw a greater probable source of future trouble and a danger of collision in the evident intention of the British government to increase the British naval force upon the Lakes where it had built several new vessels just before the peace. They were apprehensive of an item, which appeared in the London newspapers of August, 1815, announcing that the British cabinet had determined not only to maintain, but also to augment the armed naval force on the Lakes. Considering the fact that upon Lake Erie (where the Americans had been dismantling their vessels) an American merchant vessel had been fired upon by a British armed vessel, they had reason to fear the results of further augmentation which would necessitate a policy of rival fleets in time of peace. On July 22, when taking measures to prevent a United States officer from influencing soldiers to desert from the British service, Secretary Monroe, in a letter to the representative of the British legation at Washington, intimated the necessity of a reciprocal stipulation in regard to naval forces. Later, on December 6, after reporting an inquiry into the case of Lieutenant Vidal who had been fined for riot while pursuing offenders into American territory, he frankly wrote: "This Government is sincerely desirous, as I had the honor to intimate to you in a late interview, to make such arrangements relating to the force to be kept on the Lakes, and to the intercourse between the United States and the British provinces in that quarter, as will effectually prevent these evils." [8] Meantime, on November 16, expressing to Adams at London the American policy to disarm on the Lakes, he said:

"It is evident, if each party augments its force there, with a view to obtain the ascendancy over the other, that vast expense will be incurred and the danger of collision augmented in like degree. The President is sincerely desirous to prevent an evil which it is presumed is equally to be deprecated by both governments. He therefore authorizes you to propose to the British Government such an arrangement respecting the naval force to be kept on the Lakes by both governments as will demonstrate their policy and secure their peace. He is willing to confine it, on each side, to a certain moderate number of armed vessels, and the smaller the number the more agreeable to him; or to abstain altogether from an armed force beyond that used for revenue."[9]

In accord with these instructions, Adams promptly (on January 25, 1816) proposed to Lord Castlereagh to disarm on the Lakes, stating that Canada had been a source of disagreement in the past, and might be a source of "great and frequent animosities hereafter, unless guarded against by the vigilance, firmness, and decidedly pacific dispositions of the two governments." This pacific proposal Castlereagh received with caution, although he apparently approved the principle of the policy. Probably he was influenced by suspicions of the British ministry as to some possible hidden strategy beneath the apparently amicable spirit and unsuspecting confidence shown by the offer. As at Ghent, he still thought that the "lakes should belong to our party, thereby rendering armaments unnecessary." He feared that an engagement for mutual disarmament would give the United States too much advantage in case of war. To this Adams replied that in such case the engagement would be in favor of Great Britain. He reported little hope for even an arrangement to limit the force to be kept in actual service. On March 21, still desiring that peace should be cemented by "that mutual reliance on good faith, far better adapted to the maintenance of national harmony than the jealous and exasperating defiance of complete armor" in an expensive armed peace which would "operate as a continual stimulus of suspicion and of ill will" between the people of the frontier, he renewed the proposal to "mutually and equally disarm upon the American lakes"; and, with the hope that it might be entertained in the same sincerely amicable spirit in which it was made, he emphasized the fact that there were abundant securities against the possibility of any sudden attack upon the colonies which the "guarded and cautious policy" of Great Britain might fear.[10]

In the debates in Parliament, reflecting jingo adherence to the principle of preserving peace by being prepared for war, Adams found little evidence that the proposal would be considered. In a letter to Monroe on March 30 he said: "In all the late debates in Parliament upon what they call their Military and Naval Peaces Establishment the prospect of a new war with the United States has been distinctly held up by the ministers and admitted by the opposition as a solid reason for enormous and unparalleled expenditure and preparation in Canada and Nova Scotia."

The crisis in Parliament appears to have been passed soon after April 5. A few days later Adams was much surprised when Lord Castlereagh requested an interview to inform him that the British government was ready to meet the proposal of the United States "so far as to avoid everything like a contention between the two parties which should have the strongest force" on the Lakes, and that they had no desire to have any ships in commission or active service except what might be needed "to convey troops occasionally." As Adams did not feel that he was authorized to conclude the arrangement without further instructions, he agreed with Castlereagh that the negotiations should be transferred to Washington, and that the British government should send power and instructions to Mr. Bagot, the British minister to the United States; but he desired to begin at once all the effects of a positive arrangement. In his letter of April 15, to Monroe, he expressed his impression that it was "agreed that no new or additional force should be commenced upon the lakes on either side for the present," although no notes to that effect were exchanged. After the interview Castlereagh was prompt in notifying Bagot of his power to act in arranging both the naval forces and the fisheries.[11]

Monroe would have been willing to let the force remain unchanged in order to stop the dangerous tendency of further increase. This was indicated in a conversation with Mr. Bagot on May 2 and in instructions to Adams on May 3 and May 21, before he had heard of the decision of the British government to meet the proposal to disarm, and was based on the consideration "that Great Britain has the ascendancy on Lake Ontario, which appears more immediately on Canada, and that the United States have it on Erie and Huron, which is important only in relation to the savages within our limits." [12]

Later events on the Lakes, however, soon made it apparent

that more efficient measures should be adopted. On June 8 General Cass sent the news that British naval officers at Malden had been boarding passing American vessels in search of deserters. None had actually been taken, and the conduct was "presumed not to have the sanction of the British Government," but it was none the less a violation of the rights of the United States, and Monroe asked Adams to invite the early attention of the British government to the incident. Graham (acting under Secretary Monroe), in a letter to President Madison, on June 25, threw the mantle of charity over the affair by saying that "possibly the measure was adopted more with a view of preventing their men from going on board United States vessels than with any serious intention of violating rights of the United States."[13]

When America learned the news of the apparently sudden change in the attitude of the British government, it naturally was influenced to enter into some speculation as to the probable cause. On June 26 Dallas wrote President Madison that "Lord Castlereagh's overtures to arrange the question of armament on the lakes are probably suggested by the apprehension of a new commotion in Europe."[14]

In the early part of July Monroe received from Mr. Bagot information of the new powers which had been given him, but he did not enter into a full discussion. On July 7, in a note to President Madison, he stated that Bagot had said that he would enter upon the subject of naval forces after the question of fisheries had been arranged. In his own mind the adjustment of the Lakes armaments was first, and he requested the President's opinion. Madison responded promptly, on July 11, that he did not see why Bagot should desire to suspend an arrangement of naval forces until the subject of fisheries had been disposed of. He saw no connection between the two, and he said that "an immediate attention to the former is the more necessary, as it is said an enlargement of the British forces, particularly on Erie, is actually going on." He suggested that it would be far better to suspend this enlargement until negotiations concerning it were concluded. To him it now seemed expedient to stipulate:

"(1) that no increase of existing armaments should take place
"(2) that existing armaments be laid up
"(3) that revenue cutters, if allowed at all, be reduced to the minimums of size and force."

Suggesting that the regulation of revenue cutters might be influenced by the question of jurisdiction, he asked, "What is the practice with respect to jurisdiction on the lakes? Is it common to both parties over the whole, or exclusive to each on its own side of the dividing line?" In a later note of July 21, in reply to a note from Monroe, he said:

"I hope Mr. Bagot, if willing to arrange in any mode a reciprocity on the lakes, will immediately issue instructions to discontinue augmentations, or preparations of force on the British side. The state of the size on our side will correspond without instructions, but a communication to the proper officers of what may be the British intentions will be proper. There can be no inconvenience to Mr. Bagot in taking such a course. The measure suggested may be provisional till a more formal arrangement be made; or converted into a permanent arrangement as may be found best." [15]

Returning from a visit to Loudoun county, Monroe had several conversations with Mr. Bagot upon the subject of the naval armaments upon the Lakes. He "thought at one time that they would agree"; but after submitting his ideas informally in writing, he found that Bagot, intimating some difficulty as to his powers, would not subscribe his name to them. Seeing "little probability of being able to do anything immediately with Mr. Bagot" in relation to the fisheries, and to the reduction of naval forces, he decided to return into the country.[16] After his departure from Washington, he received from Bagot a letter of July 26, which formally opened the negotiations at Washington by stating that in relation to the naval armaments on the Lakes the Prince Regent, "in the spirit of the most entire confidence," was ready to adopt "any reasonable system" which would contribute to economy, to peacefulness, and to the removal of jealousy. In reply he sent a letter of August 2, to which he first obtained the President's approval and in which he submitted the "precise project" which was desired. The details of the proposals were given as follows:

"I have the honor now to state that the President is willing, in the spirit of the peace which so happily exists between the two nations and until the proposed arrangement shall be cancelled in the manner hereinafter suggested, to confine the naval force to be maintained on the lakes on each side to the following vessels, that is: On Lake Ontario to one vessel not exceeding 100 tons burthen and one 18 pound cannon, and on the upper lakes to two vessels of like burthen and force, and on the waters of Lake Champlain to one vessel not exceeding the like burthen and force; and that all other armed vessels on those lakes shall be forthwith dismantled, and likewise that neither party shall build or arm any other vessel on the shores of those lakes

"That the naval force thus retained by each party on the lakes shall be restricted in its duty to the protection of its revenue laws, the transportation of troops and goods, and to such other services as will in no respect interfere with the armed vessels of the other party

"That should either of the parties be of opinion hereafter that this arrangement did not accomplish the object intended by it, and be desirous of annulling it, and give notice thereof, it shall be void and of effect after the expiration of —— months from the date of such notice." [17]

He suggested that immediate effect might be given to this project by convention or by interchange of notes, or that if Bagot had to wait for the sanction of his government, he was willing to concur in a provisional reciprocal arrangement or in a temporary suspension of further augmentation or equipment of vessels for the lakes named.

Mr. Bagot, although he offered no objection to any of the details of the proposition, announced his lack of authority to conclude definitely an agreement as to details without first submitting it to his government for its consideration of "points connected with the internal administration" of the provinces, and as to the naval assistance necessary for the ordinary business of a peace establishment. In the meantime, he was willing to give effect to any arrangement, to which they might agree, for the mutual suspension of construction, equipment, and exertion on the Lakes.[18]

On August 12, promptly after his return from the country, Monroe, seeking to make the arrangement equal, proposed to adopt the detailed project of August 2, as a "provisional arrangement." He found, however, that Bagot did not feel "authorized to make, even provisionally, any precise agreement as to the exact manner" of limiting the forces on the Lakes and that his power appeared to be limited "to a right to agree to suspend the further augmentation of the naval force on those waters, without fixing its maximum by any rational standard to the number of vessels which might be necessary."

Evidently Bagot was not satisfied at that time to make a reduction as large as that proposed by the American note. In a dispatch to Lord Castlereagh he also expressed doubt concerning "certain restrictions as to the employment of the Vessels to be retained, which appeared to have some object in view beyond the principal . . . one professed by the American Government."

Monroe then proposed that the American government, upon receipt of a statement of the British force on the Lakes and an assurance that it would not be further augmented, would confine the American force to the same limits. To this Bagot promptly agreed in a note closing with the assurance that all further augmentation of the British force would be immediately suspended. This, however, was subject to a condition that any of the British armed vessels far advanced under construction, if their dismantlement involved great injury to the materials, might be completed so far as necessary for their preservation.[19]

Monroe thought that the conclusion of the negotiations would probably revert to Adams at London, and so instructed him on August 13. At this information, indicating further delay, Adams was surprised, and he was inclined to question the sincerity of the existing cabinet whose policy appeared to him as one of the subterfuges, of refusals to negotiate, "or of expedients having all the features of refusal except its candor." He was led to suspect that the British government was simply amusing the United States while preparing British defenses. On September 27 he wrote Monroe that "while Mr. Bagot was negotiating, and receiving your specific proposition to be transmitted here, 52,000 tons of ordnance stores have been dispatched to Canada with the avowed purpose of arming their new constructed forts, and new built ships upon the lakes."[20]

Monroe, although he agreed with Adams concerning the apparent British policy to amuse, had been influenced by Bagot to increase his confidence in the sincerity of the British government. On August 15, apparently for the first time, he informed Cass of the President's discussions with Bagot, resulting in a "provisional arrangement for the present to suspend the further augmentation of the naval force of Great Britain in those waters, and to confine our force within the same limit." He also stated that Bagot expected an enlargement of his power. He sent to Cass in confidence a copy of the correspondence which had passed, and under a similar injunction of "confidence" authorized him to communicate the correspondence to Major General McComb. He also advised direct consultation with the Governor of Canada.[21]

Meantime, Monroe, with confidence in prompt British remedial action, had submitted to Bagot on August 14, for the consideration of the British government, certain complaints from General Cass and General McComb concerning the improper conduct of British officers of British armed vessels in permitting men from these vessels improperly to board and search American vessels passing under Fort Malden and at other points in Lake Erie. The resulting British action was satisfactory. Bagot, aware of the dangerous tendency of these acts, proceeded at once to request the Governor-General of Canada and the chief of the naval forces on the Lakes to direct inquiry into the matter. Castlereagh, to whom Adams submitted the complaints on August 29, promptly issued positive instructions to the civil and military and naval authorities in North America to discourage by every means such proceedings in the future, and to pursue a conduct showing an amicable disposition. The result was that the commander-in-chief (on the Lakes), who had "misconceived the nature of his instructions," immediately revoked his previous orders and adopted restraining means to prevent any similar occurrence. Late in November the American government coöperated by corresponding orders for proper restraint.[22]

Meantime, on November 4, Bagot submitted "an account of the actual state of His Majesty's naval force upon the lakes," and stated that further augmentation was suspended until the

British government reported upon the proposal of August 2. Monroe at once (November 7) submitted the statement of the American naval force in the same region and reported orders "to prevent any augmentation of it beyond the limit of the British naval force on those waters." This statement Bagot promptly forwarded to Sir Robert Hall of Canada with an explanation that the agreement was "merely provisional" and intended to have effect only until the British government could decide upon a more particular proposition.[23]

The reciprocal and definite reduction of the Lakes naval force did not occur until the next year, after Monroe had become President. On January 31, 1817, Castlereagh informed Bagot that the Prince Regent had agreed to the proposition (of August 2, 1816). Upon receipt of this information Bagot promptly notified Mr. Rush (who was acting as Secretary of State under President Monroe until Mr. Adams could arrive from London). On April 28–29, 1817, by exchange of notes they entered into a formal agreement which was practically the same as the proposed project of August 2. It became effective at once, and could be annulled by either party after a notice of six months. It limited the Lakes naval force of each party to four vessels of not more than one hundred tons burden and with arms limited to one eighteen-pound cannon —one vessel on Lake Ontario, two on the upper Lakes, and one on Lake Champlain. The British government had already issued orders to the officers on the Lakes, directing that the limited naval force should be restricted to such services as would "in no respect interfere with the proper duties of the armed vessels of the other party." By the request of Mr. Rush (April 30), orders to the same effect were issued on May 2 by Mr. Crowninshield, Secretary of the Navy, to the American commanding naval officers at Erie, Pennsylvania, Sackett's Harbor, New York, and Whitehall, New York. By these orders the schooner *Lady of the Lake* was assigned to Lake Ontario, the schooners *Porcupine* and *Ghent* to the upper Lakes, and the galley *Allen* to Lake Champlain.[24]

The agreement was regarded as effective at once, without consent of the Senate. Nearly a year later, however, on April 6,

1818, President Monroe formally notified the Senate of the arrangement and submitted to its consideration whether this was "such an arrangement as the Executive is competent to enter into by the powers vested in it by the Constitution, or is such a one as requires the advice and consent of the Senate, and, in the latter case, for their advice and consent, should it be approved." On April 16 the Senate gave its approval and consent, with no dissenting vote, and recommended that the arrangement be carried into effect by the President. On April 28 the President proclaimed the agreement, which appeared in the *National Intelligencer* of April 30.

The work of dismantling was begun promptly. Soon the forces on each side declined to "almost complete disappearance." By 1820 American feelings of danger had decreased so far that the House of Representatives refused to consider a resolution which proposed a western depot for arms "convenient to those points which are most vulnerable to the enemy." In 1822 Mr. Cooke, in the House, understanding that most of the vessels on the Lakes were sunk and "none fit for service, proposed an inquiry to ascertain whether the salaries of the naval officers and men had correspondingly declined." In January, 1824, the Secretary of the Navy reported that naval stations at Whitehall and Erie were no longer useful or necessary. In 1825 public vessels had practically disappeared.[25] Old forts also were disappearing. In 1826, at Detroit, Fort Shelby was demolished and its garrison was removed. Even revenue cutters had disappeared west of Lake Huron. In 1828, W. Astor urged the reestablishment of a revenue cutter on Lake Superior to prevent smuggling there.[26]

The example of the American government in promptly abandoning every vestige of its establishments at Sackett's Harbor, and in its later announced policy to keep no vessels on the Lakes, induced British authorities to decide to abandon completely their earlier "main effort to maintain British naval supremacy on the Lakes of Canada" which Canadians had regarded as one of the principal defenses against attack from the United States. In 1831 the British government decided to discontinue the repair of ships at Kingston and to abandon the dock yard, although from "prudent suggestions of caution" (for moral effect in Canada) it retained the commander "without a single sound ship except the schooner" which bore his pendant. According to a report of J. B. Martin, it had no ships on the Lakes except those which had decayed. In December, 1833, it announced that the discontinuance of repairs had produced no injurious effects but "would tend to remove one cause of jealousy" without diminishing future (military) means of defense which had been greatly improved by the recent completion of the Rideau Canal, securing the inland communication between Quebec and Kingston.[27]

Meantime, after the immediate post-war adjustments which contemplated a long period of peace, America was preparing for an active period of peaceful internal development, including expansion of American settlements on the Lakes frontier and increase of American commerce on the Lakes. In this purpose it received fresh stimulation from the admission of two new northern states—Indiana in 1816, and Illinois in 1818. It was also encouraged by the brisk western migration and the large immigration from Europe, especially the immigration from Ireland.

In the summer of 1817 in connection with a northern tour to examine American harbors and posts and fortifications, President Monroe visited several points along the frontier: Plattsburgh, Ogdensburg, Sackett's Harbor, Fort Niagara, Buffalo, and Detroit.[28] He returned with broadened views concerning the increased influence of the Northwest and the West which was foreseen in the continuous migrations across central New York to Buffalo, in the beginning of construction on the Erie Canal, the incorporation of the thriving village of Cleveland upon Lake Erie, the opening of steamboat navigation on Lake Ontario and Lake Erie, and extinguishment of Indian titles in Ohio and parts of Indiana and Michigan.[29]

REFERENCES

1. *7 U.S. Mins., Instrs.*, pp. 400–04, May 11, 1815; *Ib.*, 407–11, July 21; 2 *For. Legations, Notes to*, pp. 88–89, May 6.
2. *C.A.*, G 7, *Lower Can.*, 1815 (Oct. 16), pp. 84–85; *Ib.*, pp. 109–

10 (Nov. 16); *C.A.*, Q 137, *Canada, C.O. Records*, p. 169, No. 34, Sept. 23, 1816, Sherbrooke to Bathurst.

3. *C.A.*, G 222, *British Ministers at Washington to Governor-Generals of Canada*, Bagot to Drummond, June 1, 1816; *Ib.*, Bagot to Sherbrooke, Aug. 14, 1816; *C.A.*, Q 137, *Canada, C.O. Records, Gov. Sherbrooke, 1816*, pp. 15–20 (Enclosure in Sherbrooke to Bathurst, No. 3, July 15, 1816); *Ib.*, pp. 70–76 (Enclosure in Sherbrooke to Bathurst, No. 12, Aug. 9).
4. *8 U.S. Mins., Instrs.*, Adams to Rush, No. 20, Nov. 19, 1819.
5. Moore, *Int. Arb's.*, I, 45–64; Richardson, *Messages . . .* , II, 12.
6. Edward Smith, *England and America after Independence*, p. 274; *8 U.S. Mins., Instrs.*, pp. 188–96, No. 4; *Exec. Papers*, 17–1, Vol. 6, No. 112, Apr. 15, 1822.
7. *Rio Janeiro, Despatches* (Sumter), Oct. 3, 1818.
8. Campbell, *Political History of Michigan; 2 G.B., Notes to* (p. 110), July 22, 1815; *Ib.*, Dec. 6.
9. *8 U.S. Mins., Instrs.*, Nov. 16, 1815.
10. Adams, *Memoirs*, III; *20 G.B., Desps.*, Jan. 31 and Mar. 22, 1816.
11. *Ib.*, Apr. 5; *America*, Vol. 140, Apr. 23, 1816.
12. *8 U.S. Mins., Instrs.*, pp. 46 (May 3), and 61–66 (May 21); *America*, Vol. 141, Bagot to Castlereagh, May 3, 1816.
13. *Madison Papers*, Vol. 58.
14. *Ib.*, No. 74.
15. *8 U.S. Mins., Instrs.*, p. 65, July 8, 1816; *Monroe Papers*, Vol. 5, No. 643, July 7; *Ib.*, Vol. 15, Nos. 1969 (July 11), and 1973; *Madison Papers*, Vol. 58, No. 91, July 21.
16. *Ib.*, No. 107, July 29 (Graham to Madison).
17. *Annals of Congress*, 15–1, Vol. 2, p. 1943, *Appendix; Am. State Papers, For. Rels.*, Vol. 4, p. 202.
18. *Madison Papers*, Vol. 59, Aug. 9 (Graham to Madison).
19. *America*, Vol. 142, No. 24.
20. *U.S. Mins., Instrs.* (p. 94) Aug. 13 and Nov. 14, 1816; *21 G.B., Despatches* (*Dip. Cor.*), No. 56, Sept. 27.
21. *16 Domestic Letters*, p. 322, Aug. 15, 1816.
22. *8 U.S. Mins., Instrs.*, p. 99; *Ib.*, pp. 129–30, Nov. 14, 1816; *21 G.B.* (*Dip. Cor.*), Sept. 18, 1816; *9 G.B., Notes from*, Nov. 18; *2 G.B., Notes to.*
23. *America*, Vol. 142, Nov. 9, 1816; *C.A.*, Bagot, *Washington-Canadian Corres.*, 1816–19, pp. 44–45, Nov. 20; *Ib.*, p. 63, No. 13, Feb. 3, 1817 (Enclosure).
24. Richardson, *Messages . . .* , II, 12.
25. Niles' *Weekly Register*, July 12, 1817, p. 320; *Ib.*, Vol. 25, Feb. 14, 1824, pp. 575–76; *Annals of Cong.*, Jan. 4, 1820; Benton's *Abridgement*, Vol. 7.

26. J. Q. Adams, *Memoirs,* VII, 446, Feb. 23, 1828.
27. *C.A.,* Q 210, Canada, *C.O. Records,* 1833, pp. 17–23 and 24–64.
28. Niles' *Weekly Register,* XII, 46, 71–73, 143, 280–82, 315–17, 327–30, 360–61, 371–72, 374, 398, 415.
29. Richardson, II, 16–17.

CHAPTER VI

PEACETIME ECONOMIC QUESTIONS: FISHERIES, COMMERCE AND NAVIGATION

FOLLOWING the immediate adjustments contemplated in the peace treaty and the supplemental agreement for mutual disarmament on the Lakes, the American government sought to remove all remaining sources of border friction or possible sources of future friction, both along the nearer and older northeastern and the northern Lakes frontiers and at the distant Pacific outposts of the undefined and unsettled Oregon country which had a strategic importance in connection with American interests in the China trade.

The chief problems which were subjects of negotiation between 1817 and the early thirties were the northeastern fisheries and commerce and navigation (which are treated in this chapter), and boundaries (which are treated in the next chapter). By a convention of 1818 the question of fisheries was settled, the boundary from the meridian of the northwest corner of the Lake of the Woods westward to the Rocky Mountains was established on the parallel of 49°, the question of the establishment of the boundary west of the Rockies was postponed by an agreement for joint occupation for ten years, and a commercial treaty of 1815 was extended for ten years. By conventions of August, 1827, the commercial convention and the joint occupation of the trans-Rocky (Oregon) territory were renewed indefinitely with provision for annulment by a notice of one year, and the unsettled dispute concerning the northeastern boundary was submitted to arbitration with an unrealized hope that a friendly power could reach a satisfactory settlement.

In July, 1815, the American government learned that the

British colonial authorities, considering that all American fishing rights had been abrogated by the war, had decided to drive from the coast of Nova Scotia any Americans who attempted to fish within three miles of the coast. On July 18, after learning of the detention of American fishing vessels by a British naval authority who warned them not to approach within sixty miles of the coast, Secretary Monroe demanded an explanation. He was assured by the British chargé, Sir Anthony Baker, that the act was unauthorized. Declaring that fishery rights acknowledged by the treaty of 1783 were not abrogated by the recent war, he promptly instructed Adams at London to present a complaint to the British government, resulting in a disavowal of the act of the naval officer. To Lord Bathurst's statement of the British intention to exclude Americans from fishing in territorial waters after 1815, Adams declared on September 25 that American rights and liberties existed before their recognition by the treaty of 1783 and were not regarded as grants from the British sovereign by treaty. In October, 1815, although the British government denied that it had ever recognized American fishing concessions within British jurisdiction as a right, Lord Bathurst stated that his government was quite willing to negotiate for a modified renewal of a concession for liberty to fish.

Early in the following year Monroe sent Adams new instructions for adjustment of the fisheries in connection with an arrangement of other difficulties. At the same time he received from Bagot at Washington an offer to concede to Americans the liberty to dry and cure fish on the unsettled parts of Labrador east of Mount Joli on condition of the abandonment of claims to the right to fish elsewhere in British American territory. This offer he rejected as inadequate. A year later some American fishing vessels were captured by British forces outside the three-mile limits. In June, 1817, eighteen vessels were captured near the British coasts and sent for trial at Halifax where they were released on the ground that they were not engaged in fishing when arrested and that the British government had published no specific prohibition of the privileges so long enjoyed.[1]

In 1818 Secretary Adams, acting under President Monroe, instructed Rush (at London) to negotiate with Great Britain a new commercial treaty and to ask for a settlement of various questions, including American fishery rights, the boundary west of the Lake of the Woods and the American title to the settlement at the mouth of the Columbia. As a basis of the proposed new fisheries treaty he offered a concession to desist from the liberty of fishing and curing and drying fish in British jurisdiction generally, upon condition that the privilege within certain limits might be secured as a permanent right not liable to be impaired by future war. He authorized a proposal to confine the request for permanent liberty to fish within British jurisdiction to the west coast of Newfoundland and the western part of the south coast (to the Rameau Islands) and along the coast of Labrador east of Mount Joli.

On August 27 Rush and Gallatin began conferences with Frederick J. Robinson and Henry Goulburn, resulting in the signing of the convention of 1818 on October 20. On the question of fishery rights they obtained more than was expected by their instructions. In addition to limited jurisdictional area of permanent right proposed by Adams they obtained permanent permission to fish on the shores of the Magdalen Islands and to enter jurisdictional waters elsewhere for shelter, for repairs and for wood and water. By the convention, in accord with the agreement for the right of the fisheries forever, the American government renounced the liberty of taking, drying or curing fish within three miles of any bays of the British dominions in North America not included in the prescribed treaty limits. Under this convention, American fishing rights were satisfactorily observed without any controversy for nearly two decades, possibly excepting a brief period in 1823–25 when the American government complained of the British seizure or detention of certain fishing vessels.[2]

After 1815 American trade with Canada, which during the war had illegally existed by connivance and which was still desired by Canada, was prohibited by the British enforcement of the navigation acts—resulting in the exclusion of American vessels from the British provincial ports. The American government, after unavailing efforts to secure modification of the British policy, finally sought to retaliate by adoption of a similar policy in regard to British vessels whose owners sought to continue trade between the British provinces and the United States. By act of Congress of September 30, 1818, this policy was made effective. It resulted in a commercial struggle which lasted until 1830, when the British government, against the objections of the British maritime provinces, permitted American vessels to trade directly with the British West Indies on terms granted to the vessels of other foreign nations. With the question of trade after 1822 was associated the question of free navigation of the St. Lawrence.

On May 18, 1815, Clay and Gallatin, after an interview with Castlereagh, reported to Secretary Monroe that the British government, although not prepared to make any change in its colonial policy concerning the West Indies trade, was ready to receive propositions concerning trade with its North American possessions with a view to placing it on a footing mutually satisfactory. In opening negotiations they expressly stated that they were positively instructed not to consent to a renewal of trade between British subjects and the Indians within American territory. They explained that the American policy on this point was based entirely on political considerations—the result of a bitter experience of thirty years.

Early in June, 1815, Adams, Clay and Gallatin submitted to the British plenipotentiaries (Robinson, Goulburn and Adams) a project of a commercial convention, in which (without offering any article on intercourse with the West Indies) they were largely guided by three precedents: (1) by Article III of the Jay treaty of 1794 (omitting provisions relating to the Indian trade); (2) by the unratified treaty of 1806; and (3) by Secretary Madison's instructions of May 20, 1807. In the conferences which followed they found disagreement on intercourse with Canada. The British persistently refused to admit the right of American citizens to carry their produce down the St. Lawrence to Montreal, or down the Chambly (or Lord) to the St. Lawrence, and insisted upon other restrictions which made the trade useless or unequal in its practical operation.

Under the commercial convention of July 3, 1815, each party was free to regulate the trade between the United States and Canada (and the West Indies) by legislation.[3]

In the spring of 1816 Monroe urged in the interest of peaceful intercourse the necessity of a treaty arrangement to place the British colonial commerce on a footing of reciprocity. He threatened defensive economic measures by Congress as an alternative. He especially complained of a recent intercourse act of Upper Canada in establishing on imports from the United States a tariff of duties which he regarded as unfair and irritating—especially unfair because American supplies were needed by Canada.[4]

Canadian policy varied. Governor Sherbrooke, soon after his arrival in Canada, finding a great scarcity of flour and indications of a bad harvest, authorized importation from the United States (acting under the power vested in him by act of 30 George 3). In September, 1816, however, following information of measures adopted by Sir Gordon Drummond for regulation of the inland trade with the United States and in conformity with directions from Bathurst, he cancelled his predecessor's private instructions to provincial collectors for the admission of certain articles of provisions whose importation from the United States was not allowed by law. Later, New England commerce was injured by legislative acts of New Brunswick and Nova Scotia which placed an export tax on plaster of Paris shipped in American coasting vessels to ports east of Boston. After 1816, American commerce was also injured by British return to the policy to encourage Canada by excluding American ships from the West Indies and by limiting shipments of certain American products (such as flour, corn, potatoes, peas, pork, lumber, and live stock) to the West Indies. Loss of American trade resulted in the decline of American shipbuilding and related industries, the increase of unemployment, and the migration of American shipbuilders to New Brunswick. Between 1816 and 1822, however, as a result of the British struggle to maintain the colonial monopoly, American articles were smuggled into Canada through New Brunswick, Nova Scotia, Prince Edward Island, Cape Breton and along the international boundary.[5]

On March 3, 1817, following the revival of British policy to prevent American vessels from trade in the British West Indies, and after the action of Nova Scotia and New Brunswick in placing a duty on plaster of Paris, Congress by a retaliatory act forbade importation of plaster of Paris except from foreign ports from which American ships were allowed to transport it on terms of equality. By this act it was successful in securing a repeal of the provincial restrictions. In the following December, however, it received the information that the British government, after amicable negotiations, had declined the American proposal to extend to the British colonies the principle of the convention of London concerning commerce between American ports and British ports in Europe. Therefore it was asked to consider the question whether it would decide to make other regulations for protection and improvement of American navigation. Later, by act of April 18, 1818, it rejected a British offer (of 1817) for free commercial intercourse between American citizens and British North American provinces and for free British access to the Indians within American territory, and it authorized (after September 30) the closing of American ports to British vessels arriving from ports ordinarily closed against American vessels.[6]

Following the latter act, the American government renewed diplomatic negotiations on trade relations. In May, 1818, it had reason to believe that Lord Castlereagh was personally well-disposed to a more liberal expansion of colonial intercourse, and that the British cabinet was becoming more liberal in its policy, and hoping that the recent American navigation act might contribute to a change of attitude. Secretary Adams instructed Gallatin to take advantage of the favorable time to negotiate for adjustment of commercial relations with the British colonies; but, in case of continued British obstinacy in excluding American vessels from the colonial ports, he authorized a renewal of the convention of July, 1815. A few days later, after learning from Rush that Castlereagh's policy was less favorable than he had anticipated, he wrote Rush that the President, before the date set for operation of the recently enacted navigation law of Congress, again offered to Great Britain "the hand of liberal reciprocity," but directed him not to press the offer. "If not accepted," said he, "we must be content to abide by the issue of our own prohibitions."[7]

Among the articles which the British government proposed as additions to the commercial convention of 1815, and which the President rejected, was one which would have interfered with the settled American policy in relation to the Indians within American limits. The rejection of this was especially approved by a committee of the House in a printed report which affected the sensibility of the British cabinet and resulted in some correspondence from Lord Castlereagh (in June). Later (December 1), Secretary Adams, in a reply to Rush, stated that the British government had previously acquiesced in the determined American political policy (based on bitter experience of many years) to decline any proposal for renewal of Indian trade with British subjects.[8]

In July, still admitting American preference for promotion of good humor by removal of obstacles to commercial intercourse, Adams suggested that Great Britain in its pressing recommendation to Spain (to abandon its policy of commercial monopoly in South America) might profitably set the example with its own colonies. Declaring unreasonable the British argument against changing a system which had been long established, he philosophically concluded that, if the system must be tested by the experiment of the opposition of counter exclusions, the United States was ready to abide by the result. "Should your efforts prove ineffectual," said he, "we can only wait the result of the counteracting measures to which we have resorted, or which may be found necessary hereafter."

The British government, although it agreed to the general principle of reciprocity, urged its policy of reserving the right of surcharging with discriminatory duties the articles in American vessels; and it tenaciously insisted that the same articles should be received in the northern provinces (for shipment from those provinces to the West Indies in British vessels). To this the American negotiators were not authorized to agree.[9]

As a result of the British West India policy, Congress, by a supplementary act of May 15, 1820, closed American ports against British vessels arriving from Lower Canada, New Brunswick, Nova Scotia, Newfoundland, St. Johns, Cape Breton, or from the West Indies. This act, however, was later suspended in its application to commerce with St. John and St. Andrews (New Brunswick), Halifax, Quebec, and St. Johns, Newfoundland. Although it provoked a British retaliatory act of June 24, 1822, it induced the British government to admit American vessels with certain goods into specific ports of British North America, and into the West Indies by payment of a tax on American articles ten per cent higher than that charged on like articles from the British North American colonies.[10]

Following a period of a condition of non-intercourse, of which the British colonies complained, the British government partially opened the British colonial ports to direct trade in flour, rice, live stock and lumber. In consideration of this the United States opened its ports to a direct intercourse with the British colonies for all their products. In August, 1822, the President by proclamation, using the utmost extent of his authority under a recent act of Congress, opened American ports (under strictly reciprocal regulations) to British vessels employed in trade and intercourse between the United States and the islands and colonies in the West Indies and North America whose ports had been opened to American vessels by an act of Parliament of the preceding June.[11]

Meantime, on August 5, 1822, the British Parliament had passed the Huskisson Canada Trade Act ("to regulate the trade of Lower and Upper Canada"). This act, by applying along the land boundary the same duties as those levied on imports into the colonies by sea, was designed to restrict previous American freedom (since 1791) of intercourse for exports across the boundary and down the St. Lawrence. Against it Americans complained to the President and to Congress within the following year and later.

Apparently, the British policy encountered considerable opposition in England. In 1822 Robert Gourley published in London a book in which he stated that Canada could not compete with the United States in the West Indies markets. In criticizing the disposition of legislators of Upper Canada to impose provincial duties on American produce he declared that American timber and grain (in the face of British duties) were introduced into Lower Canada and shipped to England free. He urged that American land produce should be received at Quebec and other British American ports, in exchange for British manufactures, without question as to its origin.

In the early summer of 1823 a question arose at Montreal whether articles not enumerated in the Canada Trade Act (3 George 3, Chapter 119), although previously allowed to be imported under provincial acts, were admissible into the Province of Quebec from the United States, and whether admissible in American bottoms. It was temporarily settled by a Canadian executive order to admit them until the close of the navigation season.[12]

The injurious effect of the British act (of August, 1822) upon American trade was later summarized by Henry Clay in a statement that, by the duties which it imposed, it almost entirely destroyed the beneficial and innocent trade of the Americans of the Lakes frontier with the markets of Montreal and Quebec, where it was sold for subsequent exportation by sea to distant markets, principally to the West India colonies, in British ships. The irritation produced by this loss of trade was reflected in later memorials (of 1825) to the New York legislature requesting it to recommend to Congress a policy of retaliation by restrictions on Canadian navigation in its transit through the only navigable channel of the St. Lawrence at Barnhart's Island, which was exclusively within American jurisdiction.[13]

Congress promptly expressed the American opposition to the New British act. The House, stating that it was inconsistent with the liberal spirit recently avowed by both governments, submitted evidence to show that it was highly injurious to the immediate interests of the people of six large states and one territory. It requested the President to negotiate for such modifications as might remove all just cause of complaint. To regulate American commerce with certain British colonial ports Congress on March 1, 1823, enacted a law which encountered British protests.

Secretary Adams, through Rush, proposed a special convention to regulate intercourse with the British American colonies. Later, in reply to the British demand for indirect trade and for removal of the discriminating duty from British vessels, President Monroe explained that under the act of Congress of 1823 he had no power to repeal the existing law except upon assurance (with proofs) that no higher charges existed in colonial ports on American vessels and merchandise. The British government, unwilling to give the required assurance, soon laid on American vessels a duty equal to the American discriminating duty.[14]

Meantime the question of negotiations was under consideration at London. On October 9 (1823) Rush wrote that Canning had expressed a desire to consider all the questions except that relating to maritime rights, and had promised to appoint Huskisson and Stratford Canning to conduct the negotiations except on the question of the slave trade which he wished to retain as a separate question, but he stated that the negotiations would probably be delayed until the latter part of November.

The President, in his message of December 2, announced to Congress that, as experience had shown that no satisfactory commercial arrangement between the United States and the neighboring British colonies could be reached through legislative acts without agreement or concert, the American government had proposed to the British government to regulate this commerce by treaty and likewise to arrange the just claims of American citizens (of the region bordering on the Lakes and the rivers which empty into the St. Lawrence) to navigate the St. Lawrence to the ocean. At London in 1824, however, in a conference on colonial relations, the American representative was unable to induce the British government to yield the duty on American productions or to negotiate upon the question of the navigation of the St. Lawrence with which it was connected.[15]

In March, 1825, Rush was attracted by a speech in the Commons which announced contemplated alterations in the commercial system with a view to strengthening the British colonies (continental and island), on the avowed ground of lessening British colonial dependence upon the United States and of creating rivals to the United States. In a dispatch to Adams he declared that these projected changes were chiefly conceived in a spirit of jealousy which had begun to assume new forms since the emancipation of Latin America. He especially mentioned (1) plans to encourage the introduction of Canadian wheat into the ports of England, (2) the recent establishment of a London "Canada Company" under the immediate auspices of the British government with a view to the encouragement of emigration to Canada by provisions for sale of crown lands and by facilities for transportation, and (3) the contemplation of a commission to report on the state of the posts and fortifications along the American frontier line.

By British acts of June–July, 1825, based upon Huskisson's proposal to open British colonial commerce to the free intercourse of all friendly states (either in their own or in British ships), the American government had an opportunity to participate in this trade with privileges of free warehousing ports at Kingston (Jamaica), Halifax, Quebec and St. Johns, on condition that it place British commerce on a footing with the most favored nation. By British act of July 5, 1825, however, American products admitted to the British colonies were required to pay a duty not required on British products. By later act (of 7 George 4) American products seeking a market in the West Indies were forced to go through the indirect channels of the British northern ports. They were invited to the West Indies via Canada. At the same time the British government, seeking to prevent American illicit introduction of tea into Canada from the United States, made an arrangement with the East India Company to ship teas direct to Canada—an arrangement which later caused the American Senate (in February, 1826) to consider the question of reduction of the tariff on tea in order to prevent the smuggling of tea into the United States from Canada.[16]

The American government desired to obtain the West Indies trade upon equal terms with Great Britain and to the exclusion of Canada, Nova Scotia and New Brunswick. It contended that the United States, having no colonial possessions, was not benefited as much as other nations by the British act of 1825. Therefore, it postponed the required action until after the expiration of the period within which it could accept the privileges offered, and thereafter found itself confronted with a British interdict which Canning said the British government was not bound to remove to suit American convenience.[17]

Not satisfied with the results of the negotiations of the aged Rufus King who had been sent to London in May, 1825 with full power to treat the colonial question, together with four other questions, the Adams administration decided to renew its efforts. In May, 1826, embarrassed by King's illness, it sent Gallatin as minister plenipotentiary to assist the negotiations. In his instructions of June 19, 1826, Clay declared that the American government did not regard the British act of July, 1825 as satisfactory. In explaining American objections to the act he said that, although it allowed inland importation from the United States into Canada (in American vessels or boats or carriages) of any goods which might be lawfully imported by sea, it required that such goods must be taken to a port or place of entry, that they must pay the same duties required if imported by sea and that for exportation without duty they could be warehoused only at Quebec (under certain restrictions subject to the will of the local officers). He instructed Gallatin to negotiate for the privilege to sell (without duty) at Montreal and Quebec articles intended for reshipment to foreign countries (and also for right of deposit before sale and reshipment). For this he authorized an offer of free use of American channels on the upper St. Lawrence and reciprocal privilege of introducing the same kind of articles for reshipment by canals to New York. In an alternate (minimum) proposition he omitted the proposal for the privilege to sell goods in Canadian jurisdiction. He suggested that the situation might be considerably improved by British legislation to place on a more stable footing the privilege of warehousing American produce at Quebec for exportation and the privilege of exportation in American vessels.[18]

Suspecting that the British government might urge that the American admission of the British right to lay discriminating duties in the ports of the West India colonies in order to protect Canadian productions was equivalent to admission of a British right to impose similar duties on American produce descending the St. Lawrence, Clay explained that the cases were not analogous—that the produce in the latter case was in transit to places beyond Canada, and that by necessity it passed through the St. Lawrence to reach a market at which it would be required to pay a duty.[19] In connection with the discussion of the American claim to the right of free navigation of the St. Lawrence, he suggested that the necessity of immediate settlement of that question might largely be superseded by the enjoyment of a ready and certain market if the British government was not indisposed to consent voluntarily to repeal all prohibitory and other duties imposed on American produce, and thus to admit it into the ports of Montreal and Quebec on the same terms as the same kind of produce received from Upper Canada. He stated that, following such assurance of British liberality and good neighborhood, the President would "recommend to Congress to reciprocate . . . by acts of equal liberality and good neighborhood . . . in respect to the admission and sale of Canadian produce in the United States."[20]

In the tangled Anglo-American relations which followed, the British government, remaining firm, contemplated the possibilities of increasing competition and friction. British authorities in Canada were building canals to compete with the United States in securing the trade of the Lakes. Some went so far as to advise that in order to deprive the Americans of a means of attack upon Canada, and in order to make Great Britain mistress of the Lakes trade, the canals should be made large enough for steamers suited to the Lakes and "capable of being turned into military purposes without any expense."[21]

In August, 1826, two days after his arrival at London, Gallatin learned that negotiations on the colonial question were closed by peremptory decision of the British government, coincident with its action in issuing an interdict on colonial trade. When he offered to waive the question of right, he found the British government indisposed to reopen the question in any way and that it refused to consider with the colonial question the American claim to the right to navigate the St. Lawrence. On August 19, in reporting a conference with Canning, he stated that the recent retaliatory order in council (of July 27), under which American vessels would be prohibited from entering British West India ports after December 1, did not provide for suspension of intercourse with the British North American colonies after that date. He could not clearly see why the British government had allowed the latter intercourse to continue.

On September 13 he reported to Clay that Huskisson, while declining to negotiate concerning the West Indies as a question of right, had stated that the British government was willing to treat on the subject of intercourse by land or inland navigation between the United States and the adjacent northern colonies on the ground of mutual convenience. A few days later, September 22, after stating that Canada did not have enough surplus wheat to supply the West Indies, he said that the British government by a reduction or repeal of Canadian duties on American produce imported by inland navigation could control American export produce from the region bordering on the Lakes. On October 27 he wrote that the British could arrange the tariff so that this produce could be delivered in the West Indies cheaper by the circuitous route.[22]

Later he reported that in one of the September conferences Canning had complained that the American retaliatory act of March 1, 1823, resulting from the British act of June 24, 1822, had been continued fourteen months after the British act of July 25, 1825, which had abrogated the limitations of the act of 1822. He confessed that in these conferences he had found some difficulty in his efforts to discover what limitations on colonial trade had been repealed. To Clay, he wrote: "It seems to me that the intricacy of these several acts of Parliament and the difficulty of understanding their precise meaning might have been considered by the British government as a sufficient reason why the United States might not have been disposed to accept the conditions on which, by those acts, the intercourse was opened."[23]

On November 11, 1826, Clay sent new instructions to Gallatin. Briefly reviewing recent negotiations for British colonial trade, he ably answered the British argument that the United States, having no colonies (but local territorial organizations instead), should receive less liberal treatment by the British application of different principles to its intercourse with the British colonies. He also answered the British argument that, upon the ground of the control of coasting trade, a nation holding colonies was entitled to the exclusive enjoyment of the circuitous navigation between the parent country and a foreign country, through its colonies. He also stated that the American government, animated by a desire to maintain with Great Britain the forms of courtesy and the practice of friendship and liberal reciprocity in mutual intercourse, regretted to learn of the British resolution to close the door against the friendly avenues of diplomatic explanations, by rejecting the ordinary mode of treating through the established agency of accredited ministers and substituting that of mutual legislation, a less advantageous mode of negotiation.[24] These views, and an explanation of the American delay resulting from the illness of Mr. King, Gallatin submitted to Canning on December 28—evidently with a purpose to pour oil on troubled waters.

After December 1, 1826, no trade intercourse existed between the United States and the British American colonies, in either British or American vessels, excepting that resulting from the limited permission to American vessels to conduct direct trade with the northern provinces.[25]

In Congress a retaliatory interdict of intercourse was hopefully advocated, with the expectation that it would effect an important revolution in the commerce of the Lakes region. Senator Johnson predicted that it and the opening of the branch canal from Oswego to the Erie canal would divert trade to the Hudson and render the St. Lawrence no longer important to the United States.[26]

In his later correspondence, Gallatin reported further upon

the obvious British intention to encourage inland trade in American vessels from American ports on the Lakes to Montreal by legislation for warehousing ports at Kingston and Montreal but to consider any relaxation of the colonial system as an indulgence. Finding the London government immovable in its determination not to open the colonial intercourse of the West Indies and not to negotiate on the navigation of the St. Lawrence to the sea without an American disclaimer of a right to claim it, he suggested (in September, 1827) that the best immediate policy was mutual legislative regulation of American intercourse with the northern British colonies by inland navigation. Soon thereafter he embarked for the United States.[27]

Two years later, under the Jackson administration, Secretary Van Buren instructed McLane at London to renew trade negotiations. In this action he was influenced especially by the desire to improve Anglo-American relations and to avoid the necessity of American retaliatory legislation for prohibition of trade with Canada.[28] In opening the discussion with Lord Aberdeen, in March, 1830, McLane urged a correction of past errors of policy and significantly uttered a warning that the United States by shifting its indirect trade to other foreign islands of the West Indies had the power effectually to destroy the monopoly of direct trade with the British West Indies which the British northern provinces enjoyed under previous British policy.[29]

After some British delay, possibly due to the influence of the British northern provinces, Van Buren (in June) notified McLane of the President's intention to ask Congress to extend to the British northern colonies the interdict which was in operation for the British West Indies. In the following August, this hint resulted in a British agreement to extend to American vessels all the advantages of the British act of July 5, 1825.

Adjustments in execution of the new British agreement were prompt. In October (by authority of an American act of May, 1830), the President declared the repeal of the American acts of April 18, 1818, of May 15, 1820, and of March 1, 1823; and announced that American ports were open to British vessels from British colonial possessions in the West Indies and in North America.[30] He had reason to expect an improvement in American commerce and navigation which had recently declined while that of the British northern provinces had advanced.[31] In 1831, he was pleased by an unexpected and advantageous act of Parliament which repealed the duties in Canada on wheat, flour, live stock, wood and lumber imported for use there; but he found remaining cause for complaint against British discriminating duties in favor of importations from the northern provinces into the West Indies.[32]

In the decade after 1831, several new sources of complaint arose in regard to trade, usually on questions relating to British observance of the arrangement of 1830. In 1833, American authorities sought relief from certain Canadian charges levied upon American vessels at Kingston and St. Johns, apparently similar to American charges upon Canadian vessels entering American frontier ports from those places.[33] In 1838, the Maine legislature complained that certain ports of Nova Scotia and New Brunswick were not open to American vessels, but a committee of Congress found little basis for the complaint.[34] Late in 1840 citizens of Massachusetts and Maine complained of the inequalities and injurious effects of the existing arrangements under the American act of 1830 and the subsequent agreement of that year. The memorial signed by Maine citizens declared that the arrangement of 1830 had not benefited American trade and especially complained that the import of plaster was almost wholly in British vessels. This complaint was sustained by a report of the House which specifically stated that the reduced British duty between Canada and the West Indies had resulted in the exclusion of American vessels from the transportation of American products by the stimulation of the American flour trade to the British northern provinces whence British ships carried it to the West Indies.[35]

Early in 1836, Americans proposed a regulated free transit of British and Canadian goods across American territory between Canada and the sea, which they regarded as a more convenient route than the St. Lawrence. Their proposal, although rejected by the British government on legal grounds, was favored by

Upper Canada whose citizens were smuggling tea through American territory in order to avoid the import tax at the port of Quebec and became active in agitating for reciprocity in bonding privileges for shipments to foreign markets and reciprocity of trade in natural products, such as lumber, grain and fish.[36]

Closely associated with trade negotiations throughout the decade after 1822 was the discussion of the American claim to the right of free navigation of the St. Lawrence to the sea, which had been postponed in the negotiations of 1815 by the determined American opposition against British efforts to continue the trans-border trade with the American Indians, and which was revived by the needs of New York communities on the St. Lawrence frontier.

In 1823 Secretary Adams suggested to Rush that this claim was based upon a natural right antecedent to any right of sovereignty which might claim exclusive jurisdiction.[37] He found that the British government objected to the assertion of such a claim in connection with negotiations on the subject of colonial trade.[38]

Three years later, in June 1826, under the Adams administration, Secretary Clay renewed negotiations by instructions to Gallatin to ask the British to distinguish between innocent trackless water passage and ordinary land passage. In reply to the British inquiry whether he was ready by reciprocity to apply his St. Lawrence doctrine to the Mississippi, he said his government would consistently apply the same doctrine on the Mississippi if the circumstances and conditions of its upper connections should prove to be analogous to those of the St. Lawrence.[39] He justified his doctrine by the geographical conditions: by the size of the Great Lakes upon which bordered eight populous American states and one territory whose common navigation was guaranteed by the faith of treaties and whose only natural outlet to the sea was through the St. Lawrence. Significantly, he added that the United States, if it were willing to follow an unfriendly example, certainly had the power within its own jurisdiction on the upper St. Lawrence, in the single practicable navigation channel at Barnhart's Island, to place upon Canadian navigation restrictions similar to those by which the British had inconvenienced American citizens. He urged that Americans whose trade with Montreal and Quebec was prevented by high British duties should be allowed to carry their products down the St. Lawrence to the sea to seek a market elsewhere until American interest in that route and the Canadian capitals might be diverted to the Hudson and New York by the Erie Canal and its Oswego branch and by the projected canal between Lake Champlain and the St. Lawrence. For British recognition of American right of free navigation of the St. Lawrence and for certain free trade and deposit concessions at Montreal and Quebec, he authorized an offer of free navigation of American channels in the upper St. Lawrence and free admission of certain Canadian articles shipped via New York canals for the market at New York City. At the same time he declined to consider a vague British offer to combine the settlement of the St. Lawrence navigation question with negotiations for settlement of the northeastern boundary question, and he explicitly stated that the American government could not consent to waive or renounce the claim to navigation for any British offer of an equivalent elsewhere.[40] In the following August he instructed Gallatin that the President could neither renounce the right nor authorize the surrender of any territory south of 49° on the Pacific coast as a payment for British recognition of the right. Neither could he agree to Gallatin's suggestion that the United States might concede the navigation of Lake Michigan (or of Lake Champlain) if the British should request it.[41]

At London Gallatin directed all his observations to the question of terms upon which he might obtain a practicable temporary arrangement based upon mutual convenience and without any impairment of the American right, but he was unable to reach a basis of agreement.

In July, 1829, under Jackson's administration, Secretary Van Buren authorized McLane to renew Clay's proposal of June, 1826; but, seeing no hope of immediate success and apprehending that pressure might embarrass other important affairs, he authorized postponement on grounds of expediency and with a cautious suggestion to avoid any act which might be construed as an abandonment of the American claim—a suggestion which was repeated by Secretary Livingston in August, 1831.[42]

Apparently the two governments were as determined and obstinate in their opposing views on this subject as they were in their opposing views on the question of boundaries.

REFERENCES

1. *Am. State Papers, For. Rels.*, IV, 348, 352–54; *8 U.S. Mins., Instrs.*, May 24, 1816.
2. SIDNEY WEBSTER, *Can. Reciprocity Treaty of 1854; Sen. Exec. Docs.*, 32–1, Vol. 10, No. 100, Aug. 2, 1852.
3. SHORTT and DOUGHTY, IV, 585–86; *H. Docs.*, 14–1, *Monroe's report*, Apr. 18, 1816; *Am. Commissioners* [*Desps.*], 1813–16; *8 U.S. Mins., Instrs.*, pp. 279–85, No. 11, Adams to Rush, Dec. 1, 1818.
4. *Ib.*, pp. 61–66, Monroe to Adams, May 21, 1816.
5. *C.A.*, Q 137, *Canada, C.O. Records*, p. 169, No. 34, Sept. 23, 1816; ISRAEL D. ANDREWS, *Reciprocity and Fisheries Treaty* (1862).
6. RICHARDSON, *Messages . . .*, II, 12; *H. Docs.*, 27–2, No. 68, Feb. 8, 1842 (a review).
7. *8 U.S. Mins., Instrs.*, pp. 197–202, No. 6, Adams to Gallatin, May 22 and May 30, 1818.
8. *G.B., Desps.*, No. 22, Rush to Adams, June 19, 1818 (enclosure); *8 U.S. Mins., Instrs.*, pp. 279–85, No. 11, Dec. 1, 1818.
9. *Ib.*, pp. 223–32, Adams to Gallatin and Rush, July 28, 1818; *H. Docs.*, 27–2, No. 68, Feb. 8, 1842.
10. *Am. State Papers*, 19–2, III; *H. Exec. Docs.*, 19–2, No. 45, Dec. 19, 1826 (pp. 98, 100 and 103); *Ib.*, No. 68, Feb. 8, 1842.
11. *U.S. Dipl. Questions, State Dept. Pamphlets*, II, No. 14859; *9 U.S. Mins., Instrs.*, No. 59, Aug. 27, 1822.
12. *Can. Hist. Rev.*, VII, 9 (March, 1926); ROBT. GOURLEY, *General Introduction to a Statistical Account of Upper Canada* (1822); *C.A.*, Q 168, *Canada, C.O. Records*, pp. 37–39, Dalhousie to Bathurst, Feb. 27, 1824.
13. *11 U.S. Mins., Instrs.*, No. 1, June 19, 1826.
14. *H. Rps.*, 17–2, No. 96; *9 U.S. Mins., Instrs.*, pp. 324–57 and 358–75, Nos. 64 and 65, June 23 and 24, 1823; *U.S. Dipl. Questions, State Dept. Pamphlets*, II, No. 14859.
15. *29 England, Despatches*, No. 335, Oct. 9, 1823; RICHARDSON,

Messages . . . , II, 208; *U.S. Dipl. Questions, State Dept. Pamphlets,* II, No. 14859 (speech of Senator Johnston, Feb. 23, 1827).

16. *32 G.B., Desps.,* No. 436, Rush to Adams, Mar. 26, 1825; *Sen. Docs.,* 19–1, No. 5, Dec. 26, 1825; *Ib.,* 22–1, Vol. 3, No. 118, Apr. 4, 1832; *Ib.,* 19–1, Vol. 2, No. 31, Feb. 6, 1826.
17. *H. Exec. Docs.,* 27–2, No. 68, Feb. 8, 1842 (p. 16).
18. *U.S. Dipl. Questions, State Dept. Pamphlets,* II, No. 14859; *11 U.S. Mins., Instrs.,* No. 1, June 19, 1826.
19. *Ib.*
20. *Ib.*
21. *Rp. of Can. Archives,* 1890, Lieut.-Col. By to Gen. Mann, July 13, 1826.
22. *Sen.* [*Exec.*] *Docs.,* 22–1, Vol. 3, No. 132, Apr. 20, 1832 (pp. 8, 10 and 16).
23. *Am. State Papers,* 19–2, Vol. 2; *H. Exec. Docs.,* 19–2, No. 12, Dec. 8, 1826 (No. 16, Gallatin to Clay, Oct. 27, 1826); *Am. State Papers,* 20–1, Vol. 6; *H. Exec. Docs.,* 20–1, No. 259, Apr. 28, 1828; *33 England, Desps.,* pp. 437–38, No. 45, Dec. 28, 1828.
24. *11 U.S. Mins., Instrs.,* pp. 188–211, No. 14, Clay to Gallatin, Nov. 11, 1826.
25. *H. Exec. Docs.,* 21–2, No. 22, Jan. 3, 1831.
26. *U.S. Dipl. Questions, State Dept. Pamphlets,* II, No. 14859.
27. *11 U.S. Mins., Instrs.,* pp. 288–305, No. 26, Apr. 11, 1827; *England, Desps.,* No. 115, Sept. 14, 1827; *Am. State Papers,* 20–1, Vol. 6; *H. Exec. Docs.,* 20–1, No. 259, Apr. 28, 1828; *Sen. Exec. Docs.,* 22–1, Vol. 3, No. 132, June 13, 1827 (pp. 23 and 29–30).
28. *H. Exec. Docs.,* 21–2, No. 22, Jan. 3, 1831.
29. *Ib.* (McLane to Aberdeen, Mar. 16 and Apr. 6, 1830).
30. *Ib.; Sen. Exec. Docs.,* 22–1, Vol. 1, No. 28, Jan. 13, 1832; *Ib.,* Vol. 2, No. 85, Mar. 1, 1832.
31. Sir H. Douglas, *Considerations on the Value and Importance of the Br. N. Am. Provinces* (1831); *Sen. Docs.,* 21–2, Vol. 1, No. 20, Jan. 3, 1831; *Ib.,* 22–1, Vol. 1, No. 59, Jan. 13, 1831; *H. Exec. Docs.,* 21–2, Vol. 1, Jan. 31, 1831.
32. *14 G.B., Instrs.,* No. 2, Aug. 1, 1831.
33. *Sen. Docs.,* 22–1, Vol. 1, No. 52, Feb. 8, 1832; *Ib.,* Vol. 3, No. 132; *H. Docs.,* 22–1, Vol. 3, No. 118, Apr. 4, 1832; *C.A.,* G 233, pp. 73–87, Vaughan to Lord Aylmer, June 29, 1833; *Ib.,* Jan. 22 and June 13, 1834.
34. Andrews, *Reciprocity and Fisheries Treaty* (1862); *Sen. Docs.,* 25–2, Vol. 5, No. 423, May 7, 1838; *H. Reps* 25–3, Vol. 2, No. 301, Feb. 25, 1839.
35. *Sen. Docs.,* 26–2, Vol. 2, No. 31, Dec. 28, 1840; *H. Docs.,* 27–2,

No. 68, Feb. 8, 1842; *H. Rps.*, 27–2, Vol. 3, No. 650, Apr. 14, 1842.

36. *C.A.*, Q 230, *C.O. Records* (1836), pp. 55–56; SHORTT and DOUGHTY, *Canada and Its Provinces*, IV, 592–93.
37. *9 U.S. Mins., Instrs.*, No. 64, June 23, 1823; RICHARDSON, *Messages* . . . , II, 208.
38. *11 U.S. Mins., Instrs.*, pp. 99–129, No. 1, June 19, 1826.
39. *Ib.*; RICHARDSON, *Messages* . . . , VII, 104.
40. *11 U.S. Mins., Instrs.*, No. 1, June 19, 1826.
41. *Ib.*, No. 6, Aug. 8, 1826.
42. *33 England, Desps.*, No. 17, Oct. 30, 1826; RICHARDSON, *Messages* . . . , II, 394; *14 G.B., Instrs.*, pp. 12–45, No. 2 (to McLane), July 20, 1829; *Ib.*, No. 2 (to Van Buren), Aug. 1, 1831.

CHAPTER VII

PEACETIME BOUNDARY QUESTIONS

PARALLEL with the American negotiations to secure better commercial relations in the two decades after 1815 was a series of efforts to establish definite boundaries along the entire northern frontier, except at the St. Croix River (which had been determined in 1798). These efforts were made both by diplomatic negotiations and by conferences of the joint commissions under provisions of the treaty of Ghent. Diplomacy was used first in the efforts to establish the boundary west of the Lake of the Woods, and later in efforts to complete the work (east of that point) originally assigned to commissions.

Diplomatic efforts concerning the line between the Lake of the Woods and the Pacific were begun in 1818, in connection with the restoration of Astoria. In connection with a British expression of regret that the American government had given no notice concerning the departure of the *Ontario* to reoccupy the post of Astoria, Rush received from Castlereagh a proposal to refer to commissioners the question of title to territory on the northwest coast, with a provision for arbitration in case the commissioners could not agree. Without instructions, he declined to discuss the question.

On May 20, in reply to the report of Rush on his conference with Castlereagh, Secretary Adams expressed surprise at the British disposition to start questions of title with the United States on the borders of the South Sea. He boldly instructed Rush in an unoffensive manner to suggest that Great Britain would probably not find it useful or advisable to resist any future American claim to possession of territory on the northwest coast. At the same time, with his instructions to Gallatin concerning colonial intercourse and the fisheries, he enclosed instructions concerning the adjustment of the boundary west of the Lake of the Woods and the American title to the settlement on the Columbia. These instructions in more detail he also sent to Rush who was asked to aid in the negotiation. For settlement of the western boundary and Columbia questions he doubted the expediency of reference to a mixed commission. Referring to the dissatisfaction which had already been excited by two commissions employed to settle the northeastern boundaries, he suggested that "another commission to draw a line through the depth of the deserts and to an indefinite extent would be still more liable to censure" and would prove a source of apprehension concerning possible plans "to bring the British territory again in contact with the Mississippi."[1]

Later, on July 28, considering that at Ghent the British government had abandoned its pretensions to seek a boundary line from Lake Superior to the Mississippi and to renew its right to the navigation of the Mississippi, Adams again expressed surprise at the new British pretension to dispute the American title to the Astoria settlement on the Columbia. This pretension he said indicated either a design to encroach south of the parallel of 49° where it had no claim, or a jealous desire to check the progress of American settlements. Since the British government admitted explicitly its obligation (under the treaty of Ghent) to restore the post at Astoria, he had no knowledge of any basis for a British claim in territory on the shore of the South Sea claimed by Spain to the parallel of 56°. Nor could he see how or why the British proposed to refer settlement of the boundary and the question of the Columbia (entirely different in their nature) to a single mixed commission of two persons with provision for ultimate determination by the sovereign of Russia in case of a difference (almost unavoidable) between the two commissioners. Suggesting that Russia could not properly be selected as an arbiter in the case, he recommended direct negotiation between the two parties in an attempt to reach an agreement upon all objects which had not yet been thoroughly discussed between them. Regarding the British offer as an attempt at compromise, he stated that mutual concessions could be made with more convenience by direct and immediate agreement between the two governments than by solemn references to a foreign sovereign. "As to the line from the Lake of the Woods," said he, "you are authorized to agree to that which was agreed upon by the Plenipotentiaries on both sides in 1807, but not to any line which would bring the British in contact with the Mississippi, nor to anything which would authorize the British to trade with the Indians within the boundaries of the United States." He opposed any provision which would furnish to Great Britain "a nest-egg for future pretensions . . . south of latitude forty-nine." [2]

Meantime, by July 25, in an amicable conference with Castlereagh, Rush proposed to reopen negotiation of the northwest boundary and to join with it the question of title to the Columbia and other unsettled questions at the Northeast. This proposal Castlereagh promptly accepted.

On August 16, following the arrival of Gallatin at London, negotiations were promptly begun with British commissioners, Robinson and Goulburn. In the conferences Rush and Gallatin proposed as a boundary the line of 49°, from the meridian of the most northwest point of the Lake of the Woods to the Pacific, and also offered a provision that the inhabitants of each country should have free navigation of the rivers and free use of the ports and harbors in the territory of the other. In reply to the British declaration refusing to agree to any boundary which did not at least provide for common use of the mouth of the Columbia, they stated that rather than concede this they would prefer to leave open the entire question of trans-Rocky ownership and sovereignty. In reply to the British proposal of a joint occupation (without a time limit) of the transmontane region between the parallels of 45° and 49°, as a plan to prevent disputes and differences between the two parties, they declared that rather than acquiesce in such an arrangement they would sign no agreement as to territory either east or west of the Rockies. Unable to obtain British agreement to their proposition, however, they finally offered to agree to a compromise. They proposed to establish the line of 49° as the boundary from the meridian of the Lake of the Woods to the summit of the Rockies, and (in order to prevent disputes and differences) to accept the principle of joint occupation of the disputed territory west of the mountains as a practicable *modus vivendi* for ten years and without territorial limitations. To this the British commissioners reluctantly agreed.[3]

The resulting convention of October 20, which provided for joint occupation on the Northwest coast also confirmed the restoration of Astoria and was promptly accepted by President Monroe. It was approved by the Senate on December 29 with little debate, and was ratified on January 30, 1819—nearly a month before the signing of the Florida treaty by which Spain relinquished to the United States forever all Spanish territorial claims north of the parallel of 42° between the Rockies and the Pacific, and thereby established more firmly the basis of American claim to territorial title in that region.

The joint-occupation article of the convention encountered some American opposition. It was strongly opposed by Benton and others who suggested that the valley of the Columbia might soon become the granary of China and Japan to whose governments the American government might soon be able to send ministers.

Later, in December, 1820, the House appointed a committee to report on the condition of the Columbia settlement and the propriety of steps by the American government to take possession of the territory.

In 1821 John Floyd of Virginia started a movement for legal promotion of the occupation of the Columbia Valley. In a report of January 25, in which he denied that any territory on the continent had been open to settlement and discovery since the close of the War of 1812, he declared that American interests should be guarded. Stating that the United States could claim from 42° to 60° by retirement of Spain in its favor, and from 41° to 53° by establishment and exploration and otherwise, he maintained that the American government should no longer neglect to occupy a position so important to the Pacific fisheries, to the commerce between China and the natives of the Northwest, and to increasing American trade throughout the ocean. Calling attention to the menacing activities of Russia on coasts of the Pacific, he recommended an early establishment of American settlements on the Columbia. He proposed that settlers should take women and children with them. He also suggested that the Chinese might be encouraged to acquire homes in America.

In December, 1824, by support of President Monroe, Floyd's occupation bill was approved by the House by a vote of 113 to 57, but it did not pass the Senate. It was opposed by the American fur companies and by members of Congress who feared that Oregon after its settlement by Americans might ultimately separate from the Union.[4]

Meantime, Adams found occasion to resist Russian pretensions on the northwest coast as expressed in the Czar's ukase of September, 1821, by which Russian subjects were granted exclusive rights north of 51°. Demanding an explanation, he denied all Russian claims south of 55°. In the resulting discussion with the Russian minister (Poletica) at Washington, he stated (March 30, 1822) that the Russian claim to 51° was in excess of that of 1799 as indicated by the designation of the southern limit of the Russian grant to the Russian-American Company.

Soon thereafter, he mentioned the subject in his instructions to Rush. Later, he received from Rush a suggestion of Canning's that the subject of the adjustment of Russian pretensions might be allowed to rest provided Russia abstained from all steps tending to give activity to the claim. On July 29, 1823, in reply to this suggestion, he informed Rush that the Russian authorities had already driven from the northwest coast an American trading vessel, causing much injury for which he had asked the Russian government to furnish indemnity and reparation. He also offered a suggestion that the best adjustment of the question of the Russian claim would be an express convention denying the exclusive right of either party to trade or navigate on that coast, and upon the ocean.[5]

Meantime, Adams began negotiations with a view to delimitation of both Russian and British territorial claims, in accord with statements of policy which later reappeared in the assertion of Monroe in December, 1823. On July 22, 1823, in his instructions to Middleton at St. Petersburg, after proposing a tripartite joint convention between the three powers concerned, he asserted the unquestionable American right to territory between 42° and 49° which he said was especially important to the United States on grounds of continuity of possessions and future facility of communication. He also suggested that the time was suitable for a frank and explicit statement to Russia that the peace of the world would not be promoted by Russian settlements south of 60° upon any part of the American continents. These continents, "with the exception of the British establishments north of the United States" [east of the Rockies], he said "must henceforth be left to the management of American hands."

On the same date he presented to Rush a full statement of the bases of American territorial claims on the northwest coast: (1) the discovery of the Columbia by Captain Gray, (2) the settlement of Astoria and its recent restoration by the British under the terms of the treaty of Ghent, (3) the convention of 1818, and (4) the acquisition of Spanish rights north of 42° by the Spanish treaty of 1819. In connection with this statement, "with a view to draw a definite line of demarcation for the future," he authorized Rush to stipulate that "no settlement shall be made on the northwest coast or any of its islands thereto adjoining, by Russian subjects, south of 55°; by citizens of the United States north of latitude 51°, or by British subjects either south of 51° or north of 55°." Although he mentioned 51°, the possible northern limit of tributaries of the Columbia, as the bound within which he was willing to limit future American settlements, he authorized the acceptance of a continuation of the boundary on the parallel of 49° from the Rockies to the sea, "should it be earnestly insisted upon by Great Britain." [6]

In the following December, President Monroe announced the opening of amicable negotiations with Russia to arrange the rights and interests of the two nations on the northwest coast and, incident to the occasion, asserted as a principle, in which American rights and interests were involved, "that the American continents, by the free and independent condition which they have assumed and maintain, are henceforth not to be considered as subject to future colonization by any European powers." [7]

In the plans for British coöperation in negotiations with Russia, Adams failed, chiefly by his proposal to limit Great Britain on the north to 55° and by his assertion of the "non-colonization" principle which aroused British suspicions.

Finding that Canning refused to discuss the relative territorial pretensions of Russia and the United States, Rush offered to the British commissioners (Huskisson and Stratford Canning) a proposal to extend the joint-occupation of 1818 for ten years with a provision prohibiting British settlements between 51° and 55° and American settlements north of 51° during that period—a proposal which was promptly declined. In response to the British counter-proposition to extend the line of 49° west of the Rockies to the northeastern branch of the Columbia and thence to follow the middle of the river to the ocean, he offered the line of 49° to the ocean. This offer the British rejected.[8]

Meantime, Middleton had proceeded with negotiations with Russia. On April 17, 1824, he concluded a convention, agreeing that American citizens would form no settlements or establishment north of 54°40′ and that Russian subjects would form none south of that line, and that both Americans and Russians would have free access upon the coast for fishing and for trade with the natives.

In the following January, the British government signed with Russia a similar treaty agreeing to the same line of boundary at the coast, and a line eastward to the Portland channel, and thence a line designating the eastern limits of Russian America: northward along the Portland channel to the parallel of 56°, and thence along the summits of the mountains parallel to the coast to their intersection with the meridian of 141° W. and the latter to the Frozen Ocean.

Following these conventions the American government renewed negotiations with the British government to adjust conflicting boundary claims west of the Rockies. As a counter-proposal to the British offer of the parallel of 49° to the northeastern branch of the Columbia and thence the river to the ocean, the Adams administration offered the line of 49° to the ocean to which was added free navigation of the Columbia to the sea if found to be navigable to its intersection with 49°.

Late in March, 1825, after referring to the recent mission of Stratford Canning to St. Petersburg in relation to the Russo-American dispute concerning the navigation of the Pacific, and after reference to the recent debates in Congress on a bill respecting interests on the Columbia, Rush expressed the opinion that the later British tone on claims to the Columbia and the Pacific coast would be unyielding and that a future American attempt (by legislation or otherwise) to exercise exclusive jurisdiction over both sides of the Columbia south of 49° would result in a serious rupture in Anglo-American relations.[9]

In June of the next year, following a suggestion of Canning that negotiations for the settlement of the northwestern boundary should be renewed, President Adams and Secretary Clay decided to send Gallatin to London to reopen the question and to continue the negotiations. In his instructions of June 19 to Gallatin, in reply to the British pretensions to the mouth of the Columbia which had arisen since the negotiations of Ghent, Clay authorized an offer to establish a permanent boundary at the Northwest by extension of the line of 49° to the Pacific. He stated that Great Britain, by agreeing to this American liberal proposal, would acquire a clear title to five degrees of latitude which was but little less than that retained by the United States from the right (from 42° to 60°) acquired by the American government from Spain by the treaty of 1819, and later limited to the territory between 42° and 54°40′ by the American agreement with Russia in 1824. He furnished evidence to prove that the British claim to the mouth of the Columbia did not exist in 1814, and that the basis for such a claim was not specified in 1818 when Spain still claimed northward to 60°. In submitting as an ultimatum the proposed liberal compromise line at 49°, an extension of the line established from the Lake of the Woods to the Stony Mountains, he also authorized an agreement to recognize the British right of navigation on the Columbia (in common with American citizens) only in case any of its branches were navigable by boats to the point of intersection with the proposed boundary line of 49°; but, seeking to prevent future collision, he proposed regulations prohibiting citizens of either country from trading with the natives of the other or from hunting on the territory of the other.

In later instructions of August, 1826, he declared that the President could not consent to a boundary south of 49° on the northwest coast. He again sought to satisfy the British government by the conciliatory offer of a right (in common with the United States) to the navigation of the Columbia, and he also suggested an extension of time (to fifteen years) for removal of British subjects from south of 49°.[10]

Gallatin, before he sailed from New York, suggested to Clay the opinion that the American government, if it could secure the Columbia and its tributaries south of 49°, might abandon without inconvenience the American right to the strip of land watered by the Caledonia River and smaller streams which emptied into the Gulf of Georgia or the straits of Fuca. In this opinion he was strengthened by certain information which he submitted in a letter to Clay. From one of John Jacob Astor's agents who had resided for a time on the Columbia, he learned that the country north of the Columbia to the parallel of 49° was "extremely worthless, along the seashore rocky and poor . . . , farther inland sandy and destitute of timber, a very small portion of the whole fit for cultivation, and in the meanwhile affording hardly any furs." Influenced by this report and by the expectation that the British government would wish to retain possession of the mouth of the Caledonia, he was inclined to yield to a modification on that point in preference to a proposed renewal of the agreement for joint occupation for ten years, which he suggested might result in British consolidation of actual possession of the region in dispute; but later, finding that the President regarded his suggestion as inadmissible, he faithfully accepted his duty to follow instructions in seeking to execute the President's wishes.

On November 25 Gallatin notified Clay that, conjecturing that the British government might object to the terms of the proposal in regard to the Columbia, he had altered the instructions "so that the falls in the river should not be enclosed in the restriction"—so that, if the intersecting branch was navigable to the Columbia, the navigation of both the branch and the

Columbia would be "perpetually free" to British subjects. In the same dispatch he announced the British rejection of his proposal.

On February 24, 1827, Clay instructed Gallatin to declare officially that the American government would not hold itself bound thereafter by the rejected proposal but would consider itself at liberty to contend for the full extent of its claims.[11]

In the long negotiations of 1826–27 Gallatin, renewing the previous arguments of Rush, claimed to 54°40′. He encountered the previous British arguments based on the Nootka Sound convention, which he contended was abrogated by war in 1796.

Finally, convinced that the British were suspicious of the non-colonization doctrine of Monroe and that they would not agree to the line of 49°, he was driven to favor a temporary renewal of the stipulation of 1818 for joint occupation with the hope that it would preserve peace until the ultimate and conclusive determination of the question by the natural course of events resulting from future American settlements. On August 6, 1827, he signed with the British commissioners (Grant and Addington) a convention, indefinitely extending the joint occupation, subject to a provision for abrogation by notice of twelve months. Apparently this arrangement, which was subject to renewed negotiations at any time, was regarded as satisfactory. In the second session of the twentieth Congress (1828–29) a bill for occupation of Oregon was defeated in the House by a vote of ninety-nine to seventy-five.[12]

In August, 1831, Secretary Livingston, in his instructions to the American minister at London, suggested that American rights would suffer nothing by delay: that America was steadily gaining ability to assert its rights if later negotiation should fail.[13]

Before the beginning of negotiations on the boundary west of the Lake of the Woods, the two governments completed arrangements for the establishment of the northeastern and northern Lakes boundaries, extending from Passamaquoddy Bay to the Lake of the Woods (and for convenience divided into four sections). In accord with a provision of the treaty of Ghent, they selected joint boards or commissions of two members (one appointed by each government) whose disagreements were referable to the decision of a friendly sovereign or state. Two of the boundary sections, one from the upper St. Lawrence at 45° to the water communication between Lake Huron and Lake Superior, and the other from this water communication to the Lake of the Woods, they assigned to a single commission. The American members of the three commissions were promptly appointed by President Madison. In May, 1816, they were awaiting the arrival of the British members.[14]

John Holmes and Thomas Barclay, who were chosen to decide upon the division of the islands in Passamaquoddy Bay, a part of the Bay of Fundy, submitted an equitable decision at New York on November 24, 1817.

Peter B. Porter and Anthony Barclay, the members of the commission appointed to determine the water boundary from the junction of the parallel of 45° with the St. Lawrence and through Lakes Ontario, Erie and Huron to the water communication with Lake Superior, agreed upon a decision at Utica, New York, on June 22, 1822. Among the islands whose location they decided was on the American side of the line was Drummond's Island, which had been occupied by British authorities since the restoration of Michilimackinac after the treaty of Ghent and which remained under British authority until 1828 when a representation from Secretary Clay resulted in the prompt British order for withdrawal from it. To the United States, they also assigned the two Sault islands and Barnhart's Island as an equivalent or compensation for a large well-timbered and valuable island, Grand Isle (or Long Island). The latter, because of its location at the head of the St. Lawrence in front of the Kingston fortress and shipyard, they assigned to the British at the request of Barclay.[15]

In January, 1822, Secretary Adams considered the possibility of a disagreement of the commissioners on a point of considerable magnitude. General Porter, the American member of the commission, seeking to compromise a difference, had offered a middle line at the mouth of the Detroit River. To this line Barclay proposed to assent only on the inadmissible condition that Porter would assure him that the American government would agree not to fortify the three insignificant islands (Sugar, Fox and Strong) which the Americans would obtain by the compromise. To Stratford Canning, the British representative at Washington from whom Barclay had sought advice, Adams stated that the condition proposed was beyond the authority of the commissioners and was one to which the American government could agree only in the form of a treaty or a convention or an arrangement, like that recently concluded for disarming upon the Lakes, "to which the advice and consent of the Senate would be necessary to give it effect." However, he agreed that the American government had "no objection to the principle of disarming the Islands as well as the waters, provided the stipulation is made reciprocal and applicable to all the Islands at the mouth of the Detroit River." To this general arrangement Canning did not consider himself authorized to agree, nor could he otherwise satisfy the scruples of Barclay. In the interest of amicable negotiations, however, the British government directed Barclay to surrender the three islands (in front of Amherstsburg).[16]

After successfully closing their labors in the determination of the boundary on the St. Lawrence from the parallel of 45° and through the Lakes and communicating waters to the communication between Lakes Huron and Superior, the commissioners proceeded to the work of determining the boundary from that point through Lake Superior and to the Lake of the Woods. Their first meeting on the new work was held at Utica on June 22, 1822. Following the completion of the surveys and the conclusion of the arguments of the agents, they were unable to agree on two points—the line in the St. Marys River and the line from a point near Isle Royale in Lake Superior to the Chandière Falls in Lac la Pluie, between Lake Superior and the Lake of the Woods. Barclay sought to obtain British control of the navigation of St. Marys River by a cession of St. George's Island, but offered to stipulate for free navigation of the eastern Neebish channel if Porter would make a similar stipulation concerning the channels at Barnhart's Island, at the two Long Sault islands in the St. Lawrence and at the mouth of the St. Clair River. To the latter Porter declined to agree.

From the north side of Isle Royale Barclay claimed that the line should be located southwestwardly to Fond du Lac and up the St. Louis River and by its portage to the Chandière Falls. Porter contended for the more natural route farther north, first claiming the Kamanistiquia and later offering to compromise on the Pigeon River (Long Lake) route. He declined Barclay's proposal to compromise on a line farther south. At a meeting in New York on October 23, 1826, the commissioners recorded a description of their two disagreements; and, on December 24, 1827, they exchanged their separate reports and adjourned *sine die,* leaving unsettled the differences which were finally adjusted in 1842 by the Webster-Ashburton treaty—in accord with Porter's earlier views.[17]

Meantime, C. P. Van Ness and Thomas Barclay, who had been appointed as commissioners to determine and mark the boundary from the source of the St. Croix to the St. Lawrence at the parallel of 45°, had encountered greater difficulty. They had held their first conference at St. Andrews, New Brunswick, on September 23, 1816, and had adjourned on the following day to await the arrival of surveyors whose field explorations were planned to begin in the following summer. From the first, Barclay was apprehensive of difficulties in finding highlands to satisfy the treaty of 1783, and in locating the stream which constituted the northwesternmost head of the Connecticut. At a meeting of June, 1817, at Boston, the Commission issued instructions to the surveyors. On November 25, 1820, after the completion of the frontier surveys, which were especially costly through the wilderness from the St. Croix to the St. Lawrence and thence to the head of the Connecticut, it decided that no further surveys were necessary. In the meetings of 1821 it heard the arguments of the agents of each government—arguments which, in controversies relating to procedure and the location of responsibility for delays, were characterized by considerable acrimony.[18]

The American agent claimed that the northwest angle of Nova Scotia was at the head of the Metis River (a tributary of the St. Lawrence) 143 miles north of the source of the St. Croix. The British agent, who contested this, claimed that Mars Hill, only forty miles north of the source of the St. Croix (and about thirty-seven miles south of the St. John) was the desired point —although it was at least a hundred miles distant from any of the rivers which emptied into the St. Lawrence. This pretension he supported "by remarkable dexterity of reasoning," which, however, although accepted by Barclay, was not convincing to those who knew that the St. Lawrence watershed was north of the St. John. The agents also disagreed on what stream (Hall's or Indian) to find the northwesternmost head of the Connecticut River. Later, Van Ness, against the claim of the American agent that Hall's Stream was the head of the Connecticut, decided in favor of Indian Stream—although it was less advantageous to the United States. Another subject of controversy was the line of the parallel of 45°, which in the region of Lake Champlain (by an old survey) had been located about three-fourths of a mile north of its correct location—an error resulting in the American construction of an expensive border fort on British territory.[19]

The American fort at Rouse's Point had already been the source of some complaint. On September 4, 1818, the British minister (Bagot) submitted to Secretary Adams a complaint concerning a violation of Canadian territory by the irregular action of members of the American border garrison in the forcible return of American deserters from Odell Town in Lower Canada. Mr. Brent, acting for Adams, had promptly reported strict orders to prevent the repetition of such violation of British rights. Later, provincial commissioners reported that Rouse's Point was regarded as highly important to the British government, and that it should not be ceded to the American government which seemed determined to fortify it with a view to the exclusion of the British flag from Lake Champlain.[20]

After a declaration of disagreement, on October 4, 1821, the commissioners adjourned. After preparation of separate reports indicating their inability to agree upon a decision, they held their last meeting on April 13, 1822, at New York, without reaching an agreement, thus leaving to diplomacy an intricate and complicated problem whose solution required a long period of tedious negotiations.

Meantime, in January, 1822, while the commissioners were preparing their separate reports, Secretary Adams contemplated the provision for a reference of the questions between them to the determination of a sovereign friendly to both parties. He instructed Rush to ascertain whether the British government would be disposed (before resorting to the umpirage of a third power) "to make an effort for adjusting the difference by a direct communication between the two governments."[21]

Later, in June, 1823, considering the fact that the commissioners could not agree upon the map and declaration required by the treaty to fix the boundary, Adams regarded as serious the question of whether there was anything to refer to the decision of a friendly sovereign conformable to the stipulation of the treaty and the question of how and to whom the disagreement should be referred. In view of the situation, he instructed Rush to express the President's wish that further consideration of the problem should be by direct diplomatic negotiation and without reference to any foreign sovereign. For that purpose he authorized a proposal of a convention article, preferably designating negotiations through the British minister at Washington convenient to the documents and to the interests concerned. In case the British government should insist on arbitration, he authorized the nomination of the Emperor of Russia as umpire and an ultimate agreement to accept the King of Prussia if preferred by Great Britain; but he indicated reasons for refusing to accept the King of the Netherlands who, according to the intimation of Canning, was agreeable to the British government.

President Monroe in his annual message of December announced that, as the selection of a friendly power as umpire to settle the disagreement of the commissioners would involve great delay and much inconvenience to the umpire, the American government had proposed to establish the boundary by amicable negotiation, to which Great Britain had acceded.[22]

Meantime, the importance of an early determination of the exact boundary at the Northeast was emphasized by new economic and political development in that region. In 1820 Maine had been admitted to statehood. Its admission had been preceded by an advance of American settlers toward the New Brunswick border. By 1818 several American families from the Kennebec had settled at Madawaska which they claimed was in the United States, and there they had soon begun to cut wood for lumber. In December, 1818, acting upon a complaint of Sir Charles Bagot that irregular settlements had been attempted by American citizens on lands in controversy, Secretary Adams had requested the names of the "squatters" with a view to taking steps through the Governor of Massachusetts to remove them by peaceable means.

Later, the Maine government had complained of the intrusion of British squatters from New Brunswick. In February, 1822, Governor King of Maine had sent an agent to the Aroostook region to notify the British to cease trespassing on valuable timber lands there.

Later, in 1825, the situation became more serious. Governor Parres of Maine sent an agent to seize all timber found in possession of the trespassers on the Aroostook west of the due north line from the source of the St. Croix. Soon thereafter he submitted the problem to the legislature, which proceeded to authorize deeds, for the settlers of 1818 and thereafter, to lands on the St. John and Madawaska rivers. This resulted in a complaint of the lieutenant-governor of New Brunswick to the British minister at Washington.

Following an inquiry from the British legation, Clay requested the Governor of Maine to submit the facts. On March 27 he submitted to the British minister at Washington a report (of January 18) of a committee of the Maine senate concerning encroachments upon American territory by British citizens, who pretended to have licenses and permits from the New Brunswick government giving them authority to cut timber on lands within the limits of Maine and to transport the logs down the St. John for export. He also submitted a report concerning prospective colonial plans for granting lands within the territorial jurisdiction of Maine. By instructions of the President, he demanded immediate measures to stop such improper proceedings and stated his expectation of full indemnity and reparation to Maine and Massachusetts for the value of the timber which had been cut and removed.[23]

Early in 1826, following representations of Vaughan (the

British minister), Clay investigated a complaint of Sir Howard Douglas, Lieutenant-Governor of New Brunswick, concerning certain measures adopted by Massachusetts and Maine for the Maine frontier. On January 18 he reported that the measures were entirely precautionary, and had been adopted only to counteract possible effects of previous British colonial acts in asserting authority over the disputed territory. As the cause had been withdrawn, he urged upon the governors of Massachusetts and Maine a spirit of forbearance and moderation which he hoped would also be practiced by the Canadian authorities.

A year later, following British representations that the agents and surveyors of Maine and Massachusetts were marking townships and opening roads in the disputed territory bordering on New Brunswick, and promptly in response to a request from Vaughan for interposition of the American government to induce the state authorities to abstain from measures resembling a premature exercise of authority, he again requested the governors of Maine and Massachusetts to continue to practice the forbearance and moderation which to the President appeared expedient for both governments to observe.[24]

Meantime, early in August, 1826, Clay instructed Gallatin concerning the President's wish to negotiate an amicable settlement of all points of Anglo-American difference, on just principles which would command the concurrence of the Senate. He stated, however, that unadjustment was better than terms disadvantageous to the United States. Recognizing that the boundary dispute could be settled only by direct negotiation, either by compromise or according to the provisions of the treaty of 1783, he renewed the earlier instructions (of Adams to Rush) to urge the British government to substitute for the existing treaty-method of settling the question, a direct negotiation at Washington (convenient to the necessary facts and information). He stated that the President, although not prepared to authorize any specific proposal of compromise without consultation with the two states involved, was ready to receive proposals which the British government might desire to offer for consideration. He emphasized the importance of the first necessary step, to establish indispensable facts in order to determine whether attempt at adjustment should be by reference to a third power or by direct negotiation; and, therefore, he authorized the proposal of a survey of the disputed territory (a subject upon which the treaty of Ghent was silent). In referring to the question of reference to a third party as an umpire, he suggested that the name of the King of Prussia (who was in poor health) should be erased from the list of the nominees for referee.[25]

Gallatin, without any authority to consider compromise, found negotiations difficult. Acquiescing and concurring in the President's opinion and recognizing that a compromise based on assent of Maine and Massachusetts could not be concluded at that time, he decided that his first object was to open the difficult negotiations on the basis of the true construction of the treaty of 1783 with a view to making it more intelligible to the umpire, and that his second object was to transfer the negotiation to Washington with a view to an agreement on a joint statement or an attempt at a compromise. With William Huskisson and H. U. Addington he held informal conferences which were tedious and protracted. He characterized Addington as "extremely unmanageable." He was unable to obtain a reference of the question to Washington for direct negotiation and later could obtain no agreement on the choice of an arbitrator.[26]

Finally, at the nineteenth conference, he obtained from the British negotiators (Grant and Addington) an agreement to an arbitration convention which was signed on September 29, 1827. This convention provided for submission of the boundary question to arbitration by some friendly sovereign, who was to be chosen by concerted action and to whom each government was required to submit new and separate statements of the case. The arbiter was authorized to order additional surveys to supplement topographical evidence submitted, and was expected to make a decision (if practicable), within two years after his consent to act.[27]

The convention was ratified on February 12, 1828, in accord with the advice of the Senate (given on January 14). After exchange of ratifications at London on April 2, it was proclaimed by the President on May 15. It resulted in the transfer of the differences of the commissioners to diplomatic discussion, which was influenced by more concrete frontier expression.

On the Maine frontier, a few weeks before the convention was signed, occurred several irritating incidents resulting from local border rivalries, political and personal. Among these was the arrest of John Baker, an American resident on the Madawaska (within the American line), by authorities of New Brunswick. Apparently, this arrest was a direct result of Baker's refusal to obey a New Brunswick order to remove an American flag which he had raised on July 4, 1827, but possibly it was also influenced by his refusal to permit the British mail to pass over his land.[28]

Following some September correspondence with Vaughan concerning these irritating incidents, Clay obtained from Governor Lincoln information which he submitted to Vaughan on November 17. This information included the affidavit of witnesses, who testified that the settlers of Aroostook complained bitterly of the oppression of the officers and subjects of the British provinces who had forcibly taken their property "to the last cow." William Dalton, who for three years had resided on the Aroostook "thirty miles within the line on the American side," testified that the constables and officers of New Brunswick, with "precepts" and under pretense of collecting debts, had been in the habit of carrying from his settlement various kinds of property which was sold at auction at Vernt or Fredericton; and he stated that as a result of these disturbances the inhabitants of the settlement, afraid to sleep in their own houses, had spent the night on the banks of the river and in the woods and had "kept watch night and day as is customary in Indian warfare." Another witness, John Baker, testified that he had been arrested and taken from his bed at night through the agency of forty-five men in an armed barge, had been confined in a filthy and unhealthy jail, and had been sentenced to a term of imprisonment and a fine of £150.[29]

Clay, although he abstained from particular comments, regarded the proceedings as incompatible with American rights and at variance with the arrangement for mutual forbearance and moderation. He requested "such explanations as the occasion calls for." Following a prompt and courteous reply from Vaughan, he sent L. B. Barrell to obtain accurate information concerning the origin of the settlements in the disputed territory and the incidents of the recent disturbance. On February 20, 1828, he submitted Barrell's report to Vaughan with the statement that, although it indicated some misrepresentation in the earlier accounts of the disturbances, it "disclosed some transactions which the President has seen with regret." He concurred with Vaughan in the regret that collisions of authority had resulted from the long delay in the final adjustment of the boundary. He also concurred in the conclusion that vigilance of the authorities was necessary to remove misapprehension and to control misconduct arising therefrom until the experiment of arbitration could be tried. At the same time, he courteously expressed his dissent to Vaughan's conclusion that pending the adjustment of the controversy the sovereignty and jurisdiction of the disputed territory should remain with Great Britain (who had constructive possession of the uninhabited waste before 1783).

He asserted that grants of lands made by the government of New Brunswick in 1790 to intruders within the border territory of Massachusetts, at Madawaska, had "no color of authority" and could not affect the rights of the United States under the treaty of 1783. Although he admitted that New Brunswick subsequent to 1790 had occasionally exercised jurisdiction over this settlement, he stated that in 1820 the inhabitants had been enumerated in the census as a part of the population of the United States. Declaring that the jurisdiction of New Brunswick certainly could not be rightfully extended over John Baker and his neighbors who had settled on waste lands outside of the Madawaska settlement, and that Baker's arrest and confinement at Fredericton could not be justified, he demanded immediate liberation of Baker and full indemnity for injuries in the arrest and detention.

He also stated that the President could not view with satisfaction the pretension of British colonial authorities to exercise jurisdiction over the American settlement on the Aroostook which had been made about 1822, three or four years before the neighboring colonial authorities undertook to issue civil process against them.

Unable to reconcile the recent colonial acts with the recent arrangement for mutual forbearance, he protested against any exercise of any acts of exclusive jurisdiction on the Madawaska, the Aroostook, or any part of the disputed territory before the final settlement of that question.[30]

The British government in its reply to the American demand, stated that Baker had resided in New Brunswick and Canada from 1816 to 1820, that at the Madawaska settlement (to which he moved in 1820) he had lived on land granted by New Brunswick, and that as late as 1825 he had applied to the British authorities for enforcement of British laws. Apparently, the colonial authorities continued to retain him in jail beyond the period of his sentence, notwithstanding the repeated American demands for his release.[31]

In May, 1828, in response to the reply from Vaughan, Clay found occasion to explain more fully his dissent concerning the British opinion that, pending adjustment of the boundary dispute, the sovereignty and jurisdiction of the disputed territory rested with Great Britain. Concerning the recent action in the case of misconduct charged against John Baker, he suggested that, under the circumstances relating to the disputed claims and the pledge of mutual forbearance, a friendly representation to the American government with a request for proper redress would have been more conformable to good neighborhood. In view of the long delay in executing treaty provisions concerning the boundary, and uncertain when a decision for adjustment of the dispute might be reached, he would not agree to any British advantage which might tend to strengthen British claims or to invalidate American rights. In conclusion, he stated that he was charged again to protest against the exercise of every act of exclusive jurisdiction by the government of New Brunswick and to announce that the latter would be responsible for all the consequences of its acts.[32]

In May, 1829, arose a new phase of the animated correspondence. In reply to Vaughan's protest against any American occupation of Mars Hill as a military station, the purpose of which was indicated by American construction of a road across Maine, Secretary Van Buren wrote that he could not acquiesce in the supposition that the United States or Maine ceased to have jurisdiction in all the territory north of the westerly line from Mars Hill, to which the British agent had thought proper to lay claim in the proceedings before the commissioners.[33]

Meanwhile the American and British governments had selected for arbiter (under the treaty of 1827) the King of the Netherlands, who consented to serve and for whom both parties promptly began the arduous task of collecting evidence.[34]

The able American statement for presentation to the arbitrator was prepared by Gallatin, with whom was associated William Pitt Preble of Maine, in a labor of almost two years. It emphasized the evident fact that the provision of the treaty of 1783 concerning the northeast boundary originated in the purpose to continue the colonial boundary established before the Revolution—by the ancient English grant of Nova Scotia to Sir William Alexander in 1621, and by later grants, as modified by changes in the southern boundary of the province of Quebec (along the highlands or watershed south of the St. Lawrence), the British royal proclamation of October 7, 1763, and the Quebec Act of 1774. It presented arguments which were doubtless justified by the intentions of the commissioners of 1783. As later evidence it submitted the fact that the British government in 1784 (and thereafter) stated that the newly-created province of New Brunswick was "bounded on the westward by the mouth of the River Saint Croix, by the river to its source, and by a line drawn due north from thence to the southern boundary of our province of Quebec to the northward by said boundary as far as the western extremity of the Bay des Chaleurs." It also submitted many maps of the period 1763–83 showing the highlands forming the southern boundary of Quebec and the line from the source of that St. Croix northward, crossing the St. John and terminating at the highlands at the northwest angle of Nova Scotia. Concerning the Connecticut, it maintained that of the four head branches which had sources in the highlands the most westerly north of the forty-fifth parallel (according to fair inference) was the one intended. Concerning that part of the boundary along the parallel of 45°, which had been surveyed and marked between 1771 and 1774 as the boundary between New York and Quebec, and had since been the basis of land grants and jurisdiction, it submitted the suggestion that the intent and spirit of the treaty of Ghent was to except from the provision for survey the part of the boundary which had already been run and marked.[35]

The British statement, based upon an ingenious quibble concerning the difference between the Bay of Fundy and the Atlantic Ocean, contended that the northwest angle was at or near Mars Hill south of the St. John, that the highlands were located from that point westward to the Connecticut, that the American commissioners in 1782–83 had never claimed any territory north of the St. John, that Madawaska was never included in the colony of Massachusetts Bay, and that Great Britain had held uncontested *de facto* jurisdiction in it from 1783 to 1814. As head of the Connecticut it contended for the spring-head of the most northwestern water tributary to Connecticut Lake, and it contended for a survey to correct the line of the parallel of 45°.[36]

On January 10, 1831, the arbitrator, King William, rendered an award. Impressed by topographical difficulties, and declaring that the provision of the treaty was "inexplicable and impractical," he designated as a convenient boundary an arbitrary compromise line north from the source of the St. Croix to the middle of the St. John, thence (westward) the St. John, the St. Francis to the source of its southwesternmost branch, thence a line due west to the line claimed by the United States, thence to the northwesternmost source of the Connecticut (on the most northwest tributary of the northernmost of the three lakes, the last of which was called Connecticut Lake), and west of the Connecticut the parallel of 45° as determined by an accurate survey (except that a deviation should be made at Rouse's Point in order to include in American territory the American fort there). By this decision the United States was given 7,908 square miles of the 12,027 square miles in dispute.

Against the award the American minister (Preble) at the Hague, without instructions, promptly protested (on June 12) on the ground that the line of convenience recommended was a departure from powers delegated to determine the line according to the treaty of 1783.

President Jackson was inclined to accept the award and later regretted that he had not done so; but, on December 7, 1831, apparently influenced by the dissatisfaction of Maine and Massachusetts, he finally decided to submit the question of acceptance to the Senate.[37]

In discussing with Van Buren (the newly appointed minister to Great Britain) the question whether the American government would decide to abide by the award, Secretary Livingston based his arguments upon considerations both of right and of expediency. Although he desired to avoid any suggestion which would be indecorous or offensive to the monarch who had been chosen as arbiter, he did not doubt that, on the technical ground that the award did "not pursue the submission," the United States had "a strict right to declare that they will not be bound by the award." In considering the question of expediency, however, he especially recognized that America by refusal to comply with the award would risk its reputation for good faith. This reputation he estimated as more valuable than the one-third of the large area of bad lands claimed in Maine and New Hampshire which it would lose by accepting the decision, and by which the British would gain the advantage of a pass between New Brunswick and Canada (without any military advantage therefrom). Against the British gain he suggested that the American government could balance the gain of the valuable strategic fortress at Rouse's Point, the only military position adequate to the defense of the entrance to Lake Champlain in case of future war. If the balance should show an American loss, he proposed to change the reading by addition of the weight of the settlement of the question—because the "pendency of every question between nations is a positive evil." Contemplating the possible effect of non-acceptance of the award, with no expectation of a second submission, he said "the dispute must be renewed with all its consequences of broils from conflicting establishments in the disputed ground—a border war, ending, sooner or later, in a general one." In conclusion he said: "The President, then, is of the opinion that, although we are not strictly bound by the award, it is expedient that we should abide by it." At the same time, considering the question of the rights of Maine and New Hampshire whose territory would be ceded by agreeing to the award, and referring to the President's decision to act only upon the advice and consent of the Senate, he directed Van Buren to avoid any communication of intentions until after he learned the intentions of the British government.[38]

While considering the question of the award, preceding the new session of Congress, the administration faced new border controversy. In October, 1831, Secretary Livingston received a British complaint concerning an unauthorized American election of town officers at Madawaska within British jurisdiction, resulting in the arrest of the American leaders by authorities of New Brunswick. After an investigation he reported to the British chargé (Bankhead) that the Governor of Maine distinctly disavowed any part in authorizing or encouraging any innovation on the existing state of things in the disputed territory. As no exercise of jurisdiction had followed the recent local election, he respectfully suggested that the Lieutenant-Governor of New Brunswick might be willing to release the prisoners who had acted contrary to the understanding between the two governments, and who might be willing to pledge themselves to attempt no change in the state of things pending the final decision of the question between the two governments. Late in November he received official information that the prisoners had been released.[39]

A few days later (on December 6) the President announced that, influenced by the existing state of amicable relations and with a desire to prevent the recurrence of causes of irritation which might endanger the peace, he had recently authorized instructions to Van Buren for negotiations at London with a view to the termination of causes of collision. The opening of these negotiations were delayed, however, because of the English political situation.[40]

On December 7 the President submitted to the Senate the recent boundary award and requested its advice concerning the acceptance of the opinion of the arbiter. Two weeks later he submitted to it the official statement of the British determination to abide by the award. To these communications, in response to a Senate resolution of December 18, he later added (on January 24, 1832) a report of the Secretary of State.

In the Senate, Peleg Sprague promptly (on January 24) submitted resolutions denying the federal constitutional power to transfer territory of a state without consent of the state and also denying that the American government was obligated to accept the new line recommended by the Dutch King. He proposed, therefore, that the Senate should advise the President to open friendly negotiations to find the treaty line north of the St. John, to secure the undisturbed enjoyment of the right to the free navigation of the entire St. John, and, with consent of Maine, to grant to the British the undisturbed enjoyment of the right of free passage and transit across Maine on a convenient route between Quebec and St. John (in New Brunswick).[41]

A few days later, on February 3, the President received from William Pitt Preble, official agent of Maine, a copy of the resolutions of the Maine legislature (of January 19), protesting against the adoption of the new line recommended by the award, and authorizing active efforts with the American executive and Congress to prevent dismemberment of the state by transfer of its territory to a foreign power. These resolutions he promptly submitted to the Senate as a supplementary document. In prompt response Tazewell, chairman of the Senate Committee on Foreign Relations, advised Preble that from the standpoint of expediency and interests Maine would act more wisely by acquiescing in the award. This advice Preble forwarded to Governor Smith of Maine in a confidential letter of February 15.[42]

Secretary Livingston informed Preble that the President, anxious both to preserve the national honor and to save the rights of Maine, was ready to propose that the latter for an indemnity should cede to the United States its claim and jurisdiction over the territory north and east of the line recommended by the King of the Netherlands, thereby enabling the American government to arrange with Great Britain to terminate the boundary dispute in accord with American interests and honor. This proposal Governor Smith confidentially submitted (on February 22) to the Maine legislature, which promptly considered it in secret sessions and (early in March) approved and accepted it subject to the condition that any resulting agreement or treaty with Great Britain must be submitted to the Maine legislature for approval or rejection.

Later, the Senate submitted to the President a resolution inquiring whether the government had considered with Maine any proposition that the latter would receive a consideration (or compensation) for establishment of the boundary designated by the recent decision. In reply the President on March 29 submitted a report from the Secretary of State.[43]

Later, in May, Livingston, in coöperation with Louis McLane and Levi Woodbury, seeking to facilitate the way to end the controversy, obtained the signatures of Maine commissioners (William Pitt Preble, Ruel Williams and Nicholas Emery) to an agreement on provisional cession. This agreement, however, was regarded as ineffective for its purpose at that time and long remained unpublished. It doubtless would have encountered strong opposition from Maine authorities who, influenced by frontier conditions and difficulties, seemed very obstinate and unconciliatory.[44]

Meantime, President Jackson had anxiously awaited the final action of the Senate. On March 21, Tazewell from the Senate Committee on Foreign Relations submitted a report which, after admitting no doubt of the American right to refuse to accept the arbitral decision, recommended that the President, acting on an expedient policy to terminate a difficult and vexing question, should express to the Dutch King his assent to the award and give his consent to its execution. On June 2 the Senate began its delayed discussion on this report. Both Peleg Sprague of Maine and Henry Clay of Kentucky urged the necessity of a two-thirds vote on the question, in opposition to the earlier statement of Tazewell that a mere majority was sufficient. Clay suggested that the President had come to the Senate too soon or in a wrong character. On June 12, in the further consideration of the resolution, the Senate showed a disposition to reverse the earlier committee recommendation, which was opposed by Clay and Sprague and Webster. It killed the report by amendments. On June 16 by a substantial vote of thirty-five to eight it decided that the award was not binding and advised the President to open new negotiations with the British government. On June 21, by a vote of twenty-one to twenty, it advised the President to decline to adopt the recommendation of the arbiter; and, on June 23, by a vote of twenty-three to twenty-two, it advised the opening of new negotiations for ascertainment of the boundary according to the treaty of 1783. On July 10, by a vote of twenty-eight to seventeen, it removed the injunction of secrecy from the proceedings and debates.[45]

The President promptly authorized further consideration of the subject with the British government. On July 21, after informing the British chargé (Bankhead) that the Senate did not regard the decision of the King of the Netherlands as obligatory, Secretary Livingston proposed a new negotiation at Washington. Stating that the arbiter had abandoned his character as arbiter, and therefore that Maine had some reasonable basis for its objection to the acceptance of the award, he suggested that the two governments (even if unable to agree upon a true line by the treaty of 1783) might find means to avoid constitutional difficulty by an arrangement with Maine which was under consideration. Expressing a desire to remove all difficulties by previous settlement, he suggested the necessity, meantime, to refrain from exercise of jurisdiction beyond the boundaries actually possessed. Again, on July 31, he informed Bankhead that the American government, through a prospective arrangement with Maine, expected to have more ample power for later negotiations. Later he was able to obtain from the British government an agreement to renew the negotiations, during which each party would refrain from the extension of jurisdiction beyond boundaries of territory already in actual possession; but he was unable to obtain consent to consider the question of the navigation of the St. John in connection with that of the boundary.[46]

In the following year, on April 30, in response to an inquiry from Bankhead, Livingston reported that his anticipation had not been realized and, therefore, that he could renew negotiations only on the basis of the boundary indicated in the treaty of 1783; but he intimated the possibility of a practical modification by a change in the direction of the line from the head of the St. Croix, if necessary, in order to reach the highlands conformable to the treaty. Unwilling to agree with the British government that a new negotiation to fix the boundary as stipulated in the treaty of 1783 would be "utterly hopeless," he suggested to Vaughan that the disadvantages of previous methods to secure a settlement might be avoided by appointment of a new commission with an impartial umpire selected by some friendly sovereign. He submitted a proposal which was later explained by Secretary McLane. He proposed to select a commission of European experts to find the highlands (as described in the treaty of 1783) by fresh surveys and by direct line to connect their most eastern point (west of the northwest angle of Nova Scotia) with the source of the St. Croix. At the same time he neglected to explain the depressing news that the legislature of Maine (on March 4, 1833) had repealed its action of March 3, 1832, and had declared that no arrangement or provisional agreement or treaty relating to the boundary would have any binding force until it had been approved by the people of Maine in their primary assemblies (!).[47]

Late in May, 1833, in reply to his proposal, Livingston received a British suggestion that the time had arrived to agree upon a purely conventional line. On June 5 his successor, McLane, in response to an inquiry from Vaughan, explained that the President, in view of the unalterable attitude of Maine and the recent proceedings in the Senate, would probably not feel authorized to agree upon a conventional line without consent of Maine.[48]

Near the end of 1833, McLane encountered British misapprehensions as to certain activities in internal development in

Maine. On December 21, in reply to Vaughan's representation concerning alleged encroachments on the disputed territory by a road which Maine was constructing, he stated that, according to information from the Governor of Maine, the road was not within the territory of which the British government had ever been in actual possession since 1783 and that it was not planned to extend beyond the Aroostook to the St. John River as apprehended.[49]

Later, in March, 1834, he suggested for convenience an agreement to accept the line along the parallel of 45°, from the east side of Lake Champlain to the Connecticut, as surveyed and marked in 1771–72 by deputy surveyors of the provinces of New York and Quebec; and he renewed the President's proposal to make another effort to find the highlands designated in the treaty of 1783. If the latter should prove impracticable, he agreed that an attempt to agree upon a conventional line to end the difficulty might then be desirable; but he stated that such a method "could only be adopted with the special assent of Maine," which would be difficult to obtain so long as there was hope of ascertaining the true line.[50]

In reply to further correspondence of Vaughan concerning the possibility of executing the award of the King of the Netherlands, McLane explained that the President could not execute it without the positive consent of the Senate (by a two-thirds vote), and that the Senate by a vote of thirty-five to eight had refused to agree to the recommendation of the Senate committee in favor of consent to the execution on grounds of expediency. Through Vaughan he invited the British government to unite in a renewed effort to determine the line of the treaty of 1783.

In 1834–36, Secretary Forsyth continued the correspondence. The hope of finding a way of adjustment was constantly restricted by the attitude of Maine, which in 1835–37 was influenced by the project of a New Brunswick association to construct a railway between St. Andrews and Quebec involving exploration surveys across the disputed territory. In May–June, 1837, the situation was also complicated by the action of New Brunswick officials in arresting Ebenezer S. Greely, a Penobscot county official who was persistent in his efforts to complete the census of Madawaska.[51]

Meantime, on April 28, 1835, in reply to Vaughan, Forsyth stated that the President could not consent to clog the proposed submission of the question of boundary with the specific conditions proposed by the British government, that the St. John and Restigouche should be regarded by the commission as not Atlantic rivers within the meaning of the treaty of 1783.[52]

In July, 1835, a new phase of the boundary controversy arose in connection with collisions of jurisdiction in the disputed territory upon Indian Stream which was claimed both by Lower Canada and by New Hampshire. In reply to a British complaint of the arrest of a Canadian in the territory by a New Hampshire magistrate, and in accord with a resolution of the New Hampshire legislature, Forsyth submitted to Vaughan a request for release of Luther Parker who had been arrested by a Canadian magistrate.

In suggesting to Lieutenant-General Lord Aylmer an indulgent policy the British minister expressed doubt whether the pretensions and impatience of Maine, Massachusetts and New Hampshire could be reduced enough to enable the American and British governments to close the question of disputed boundary.[53]

In December, 1835, the British government (through Mr. Bankhead) formally withdrew its offer to accept the compromise award and proposed to divide the disputed Maine territory by accepting as the boundary the upper St. John from its intersection by the due north line from the St. Croix to its most southern source and thence a line to the head of the Connecticut.[54]

On February 29, 1836, Forsyth, after expressing regret for the continued British objection to the American proposal for appointment of a new boundary commission, rejected the British proposition to substitute for a highland boundary the upper course of the St. John River. This proposition he said "could not be accepted without disrespect to the previous decisions and just expectations of Maine." At the same time, convinced by the gravity of recent events that prompt settlement of the boundary by the establishment of a definite and indisputable line was important, he submitted the President's offer (if accepted by the British government), "to apply to the state of Maine for its assent" to a boundary at the St. John River from its source to its mouth. Undiscouraged by Bankhead's certainty that the British government would never agree, he still urged that the American government did not relinquish the hope that proper deliberation of the British cabinet might result in a more satisfactory decision.[55]

By the close of the following year the question of finding a settlement, which was seriously affected by threatened conflict on the New Brunswick frontier, became complicated by a new source of friction on the Niagara frontier.

REFERENCES

1. *Am. State Papers, For. Rels.*, VI, 666; *Ib.*, IV, 853–54; *152 U.S. Supreme Court Rps.*, p. 50; Edward Smith, *England and Am. after Independence*, p. 275; Richard Rush, *Residence at London*, pp. 73–76.
2. *8 U.S. Mins., Instrs.*, pp. 223–32; *Am. State Papers, For. Rels.*, IV, 377–78.
3. *Ib.*, 374, 854 and 381.
4. *Rps. Coms.*, 16–2 (1820–21), No. 45; *Annals of Congress*, 16–2, pp. 946–59; Benton, *Thirty Years' View*, I, 13; Richardson, *Messages . . . .*, II, 262; *Debates of Congress*, 18–2, p. 59; F. J. Turner, *The New West*, pp. 128–33; McMaster, *U.S.*, V, 23–27.
5. *Am. St. Papers, For. Rels.*, IV, 863; *10 U.S. Mins., Instrs.*, pp. 165–67, No. 72, July 29, 1823.
6. *15 G.B., Instrs.*, pp. 144–72, No. 62, Upshur to Everett, Oct. 9, 1843; *Ib.*, No. 2, Buchanan to McLane, July 12, 1845; *18 Regular-Confidential Docs., U.S. Senate*, 1841–46, pp. 27–32; *Am. St. Papers, For. Rels.*, V, 446–48.
7. Richardson, *Messages . . . .*, II, 209.
8. *Am. St. Papers, For. Rels.*, V, 463, 533–82 (Rush to Adams, Aug. 12, 1924).
9. *Ib.*, V, 553–64, and VI, 641–700; *13 G.B., Desps.*, No. 426, Rush to Adams, Mar. 26, 1825.
10. *11 U.S. Mins., Instrs.*, pp. 90–129, No. 1, June 19, 1826; *Ib.*, No. 6, Aug. 8, 1826; *56 Eng., Desps.*, No. 43, May 3, 1846; *Am. St. Papers*, VI, 644 and 646.

11. *33 Eng., Desps.*, June 19, 1826; *Ib.*, No. 17, Oct. 30; 56 Eng., *Desps.*, No. 43, May 3, 1846.
12. *Am. St. Papers, For. Rels.*, VI, 647, 680, 694; *Register of Debates in Cong.*, 20–1, p. 191.
13. *14 G.B., Instrs.*, No. 2, Aug. 1, 1831.
14. *8 U.S. Mins., Instrs.*, p. 69, May 24, 1816.
15. *4 For. Legations, Notes to,* pp. 34–36, June 7, 1828; *Ib.*, pp. 81–83, Oct. 22; MOORE, *Int. Arb's.*, I, 178.
16. *9 U.S. Mins., Instrs.*, No. 53, Jan. 5, 1822; *Ib.* (p. 113), No. 54, Feb. 6; MOORE, *Int. Arb's.*, I, 175.
17. RICHARDSON, *Messages* . . . , II, 209; MOORE, *Int. Arb's.*, I, 175, 177, 180, 182, 184, 190.
18. *Ib.*, 72–76.
19. *Ib.*, 78–80.
20. *11 British Legation, Notes from,* Sept. 4, 1818; *2 For. Legations, Notes to,* p. 340, Oct. 14; *C.A.*, Q, 175 A, *Canada, C.O. Records, N.A. Provinces, Commissioners' Rp.*, 1825 (Sept. 9).
21. *9 U.S. Mins., Instrs.*, No. 53, Jan. 5, 1822.
22. *Ib.*, pp. 376–91, No. 66, Adams to Rush, June 25, 1823; RICHARDSON, *Messages* . . . , II, 208.
23. HENRY S. BURRAGE, *Maine in the Northeastern Boundary Controversy* (1919), pp. 120–21; *3 For. Legations, Notes to,* pp. 443–51, Clay to Vaughan, Mar. 17, 1828; *Ib.*, Mar. 27, 1825.
24. *Ib.*, pp. 249–50, Clay to Vaughan, Jan. 18, 1826; *Ib.*, p. 275, June 23, 1826; *Ib.*, pp. 324–25, Jan. 18, 1827.
25. *11 U.S. Mins., Instrs.*, No. 6, Aug. 8, 1826.
26. *33 Eng., Desps.*, No. 17, Oct. 20, 1826.
27. *Am. St. Papers, For. Rels.*, VI, 643, 700–05; ADAMS, *Writings of Gallatin,* II, 398.
28. BURRAGE, *Maine in the Northeastern Boundary Controversy,* p. 121.
29. *3 For. Legations, Notes to,* pp. 403–05, Nov. 17, 1827.
30. *Ib.*, pp. 436–40, Feb. 20, 1828.
31. MOORE, *Int. Arb's.*, I, 86–87; *Br. and For. State Papers,* XV, 507, 565; *Am. St. Papers, For. Rels.*, VI, 838, 1015; *Sen. Exec. Docs.*, 20–1, No. 130.
32. *3 For. Legations, Notes to,* pp. 443–51, Mar. 17, 1828.
33. *4 For. Legations, Notes to,* pp. 179–83, May 11, 1829.
34. *Am. St. Papers, For. Rels.*, VI, 643.
35. MOORE, *Int. Arb's.*, I, 90–91, 104–06.
36. *Ib.*, 106–07, 109–12.
37. *Ib.*, 119, 134–37; *Sen. Exec. Docs.*, 22–1, No. 3; CURTIS, *Life of Webster,* II, 139.
38. *14 G.B., Instrs.*, No. 2, Aug. 1, 1831.

39. *4 For. Legations, Notes to,* pp. 437–39, Oct. 17 and 31, 1831; *Ib.,* p. 454, Nov. 28, 1831.
40. RICHARDSON, *Messages . . . ,* II, 547–48; *14 G.B., Instrs.,* pp. 12–22, No. 7, Feb. 4, 1832.
41. RICHARDSON, *Messages . . . ,* II, 560–61; *Register of Debates in Cong.,* 1831–32, VIII, Part 1, 1387, 1390.
42. BURRAGE, *Maine in the Northeastern Boundary Controversy,* pp. 192–94; RICHARDSON, *Messages . . . ,* II, 563–64; *14 G.B., Instrs.,* pp. 121–22, No. 7, Feb. 4, 1832.
43. BURRAGE, p. 195; RICHARDSON, II, 570; *Register of Debates in Cong.,* 1831–32, VIII, 1394, Apr. 2, 1832.
44. MOORE, *Int. Arb's.,* I, 138; *Sen. Exec. Docs.,* 25–2, No. 431.
45. *Register of Debates in Cong.,* 1831–32, VIII, Part 1, 1390–1411; *5 For. Legations, Notes to,* pp. 199–201, July 21, 1832.
46. *Ib.,* July 21 and 31; *Sen. Exec. Docs.,* 24–1, No. 414, p. 4; MOORE, *Int. Arb's.,* I, 138; *Br. and For. St. Papers,* XXII, 788, 795.
47. *5 For. Legations, Notes to,* pp. 103–06, Apr. 30, 1833; *Sen. Exec. Docs.,* 24–1, No. 414, p. 9; MOORE, *Int. Arb's.,* I, 139; *Br. and For. State Papers,* XXII, 818–20; ADAMS, *Writings of Gallatin,* II, 549.
48. *Sen. Exec. Docs.,* 24–1, No. 414 (see notes to Vaughan, Apr. 30, May 28 and June 5, 1833).
49. *5 For. Legations, Notes to,* pp. 156–57, Dec. 21, 1833.
50. *Ib.,* pp. 175–84, Mar. 11, 1834.
51. *Ib.,* pp. 185–91, Mar. 21, 1834; *Sen. Exec. Docs.,* 24–1, No. 414, pp. 39–40, 42–64; RICHARDSON, *Messages . . . ,* III, 358–69 (Sept. 26, 1837); *C.A.,* G, 224, Fox to Gosford, Confidential, Mar. 28, 1837.
52. *6 Br. Legation, Notes to,* pp. 15–29, Apr. 28, 1835; *19 Br. Leg., Notes from,* Jan. 10, 1838.
53. *Ib.,* Sept. 19, 1835, and Mar. 5, 1836; *C.A.,* G, 223, pp. 229–34, Vaughan to Lord Aylmer, July 29, 1835; *Ib.,* G, 224, Bankhead to Gosford, Feb. 24, 1836; *Ib.,* G, 224, Fox to Gosford, Jan. 14, 1837 (and also March 10).
54. *Sen. Exec. Docs.,* 25–2, No. 319.
55. *6 Br. Legation, Notes to,* pp. 52–55, Feb. 29, 1836; *Ib.,* pp. 55–57, March 5, 1836; *18 G.B., Notes from,* Mar. 4, 1836.

CHAPTER VIII

LAKE FRONTIER PROBLEMS OF THE CANADIAN REVOLUTION

IN the half decade before 1842 America encountered on the Niagara and the Lakes frontier new problems which for a time occupied the center of the diplomatic stage and diverted attention from negotiations for the settlement of the northeast boundary. These new problems were stimulated and precipitated by the construction of the Erie Canal, by increase of new settlements on each side of the Lakes, by the success of American democracy, and by the rise of the Canadian revolution of 1837 which attracted considerable active sympathy from Americans across the boundary.

American democracy, although it could point with pride to its success, was still regarded in Canada with doubts and suspicions which, together with the Loyalist memories of the Revolution and of the War of 1812, restricted amicable neighborhood relations and also Canadian political reforms. Among the rising generation in Canada, however, it had an influence noticed by British writers who predicted that by force of example it would "sooner or later induce the Canadians to hoist the standard of rebellion and to declare themselves independent."[1]

Influential British leaders still adhered to the principles of the colonial system. Sir H. Douglas in 1831 urged that British duty was to countervail the maritime pursuits and ambitions of the United States by fair policy and with a purpose to protect colonial trade.

At that time, apparently, the American government did not seek to annex Canada and expected only friendly neighborhood relations. When the question of fortifications was being considered in Congress in 1836, Cass, the Secretary of War, stated that under existing conditions, and when the United States was not hunting war, it seemed "altogether inexpedient to construct expensive fortifications" along the Lakes frontier, which, he said, "requires no permanent defenses."[2]

By the more illiberal British leaders and by the official Loyalist party in Canada the cause of the Canadian rebellion of 1837 was long attributed to American influence, both through the concrete examples of American success and the incidental propagation of the democratic views in connection with personal trans-border contacts and migrations. Some emphasized the early influence of a "Saddle-bag faction," a name applied to Methodist preachers who had been educated either in the United States or by American schoolmasters in Canada.

Other English writers, who possibly would have recognized American frontier influence, denied American responsibility for the rebellion. In 1838 one of these, in discussing the Canada crisis, recognized the American desire to avoid useless irritation. In 1839, in line with this opinion, a critical reviewer of Sir Francis Head's *Narrative* declared that Head had provoked and tempted the rebellion in Canada by his manner of dealing with an entirely constitutional opposition.[3]

The roots of the rebellion of 1837 may be found in a series of controversies resulting from inherent defects in the blundering British constitutional act of 1791 which divided Canada into two separate provinces and thereby prevented the coalescing of French and British stock. The rebellion was largely a result of "the unfortunate early British policy to prevent the union and coöperation of two peoples whom that policy had tied together." The foundations especially appeared in an animated contest of 1819, in the later proposed re-union bill of 1822 and in the British investigation of Canadian affairs in 1828. Starting as a struggle for popular control of the government and especially of its purse-strings, the movement of discontent finally became a struggle for responsible popular government. After 1830 it was influenced by both American Jacksonian democracy and the English reform act of 1832. Finally in March, 1837, the spirit of rebellion was precipitated by Lord

John Russell's resolutions, in the British House of Commons, rejecting the demands of Lower Canada for responsible government.

In Upper Canada, which after 1791 was ruled by leaders of the Loyalists who migrated from the United States at the close of the Revolution, the first opposition to the form and spirit of the government arose gradually from the pioneer American and British settlers who had been accustomed to more democratic conditions. After the War of 1812 it was revived, and was strengthened by division in the ranks of the Loyalists. The reform movement against the anti-democratic governing clique began to gather new momentum after 1815. It was especially stimulated by Robert Gourlay who in 1818 called a convention at York to adopt a declaration of grievances, and who later became an organizer of discontent and reform among the dissenting sects constituting a majority of the population of the province, resulting finally in a reform majority in the assembly of 1828.

Among the most prominent of the extreme radicals was William Lyon Mackenzie, an editor-printer agitator of York, whose chief political activity was to popularize reform ideas and who by 1834 (when he was elected mayor of Toronto) became a popular hero by a series of political experiences in alternating reëlections and expulsions.

In 1836, following the tactless action of the new lieutenant-governor, and after the defeat of the reform party by an official propagandist campaign charging the reform party with disloyalty, Mackenzie joined with a group of radicals to agitate for revolution. In 1837, following the news of Lord John Russell's instructions to administer the government of Lower Canada independent of appropriations by the assembly, he favored the plans of radicals to coöperate with Lower Canadian reformers and to arm in preparation for an emergency.[4]

On December 4, seizing an opportunity presented by government withdrawal of regular troops from Montreal, he organized a provisional executive to direct a revolt and to issue a call to citizens to support democratic government. In response to a suggestion of Head, he promptly began an attack on Toronto which ended in a precipitate retreat of his troops, probably numbering less than eight hundred. On December 13, with less than twenty-five men, he took refuge on Navy Island in the Niagara River, in Canadian jurisdiction, and proclaimed the establishment of a provisional government whose flag bore the emblem of twin stars and a new moon emerging from the clouds. Representing that Navy Island was the seat of government for Upper Canada, he issued a proclamation declaring in favor of free trial, free elections, free trade, free education, free navigation of the St. Lawrence, free western lands and freedom from weary prayers to lordlings—a program which he hoped would serve as a bait to catch many Americans for his army.[5]

After the dispersion of Mackenzie's forces from Toronto, the American government was embarrassed by the action of certain Americans near the Lakes frontier who finally responded to rebel appeals for sympathy and support, especially at Buffalo where enlistment in the insurgent movement was stimulated by some of the newspapers which published stirring editorials not calculated to calm misdirected sentiment, and by the arrival of Mackenzie in whose honor indiscreet admirers arranged "spread-eagle" demonstrations.

To encourage the insurgent movement, Mackenzie, acting in the name of the provisional refugee government on Navy Island, offered future grants of land to volunteers. He selected as military commander the son of General Van Rensselaer, of Albany, who aspired to be a "Sam Houston." They soon increased the insurgent military force to about six hundred men, including many Americans, and obtained military supplies from several American towns on the Lakes border.

In considering measures of defense the British authorities were embarrassed by the situation on the New Brunswick frontier which caused them to abstain from a contemplated request to the President for permission to transport troops across Maine in case of emergency need.[6]

Meantime, the American government promptly sought to observe its international duty. On December 7 the President through Secretary Forsyth requested Governor Marcy of New York, and the governors of Vermont and Michigan, promptly to arrest anyone engaged in hostile preparations against Canadian territory. He also directed district attorneys to prosecute all violators of the laws for preservation of peace. This action, although prompt, was not entirely effective in preventing the collection of volunteers and cannon. On December 28, the United States marshal reported that the armed forces under Van Rensselaer at Navy Island numbered about one thousand, and he suggested to the President that an armed force stationed along the Niagara would be absolutely necessary to prevent efforts of border Americans to aid the rebels. This suggestion he made after communication with Colonel McNab who was at Chippewa in command of a Canadian armed force of about twenty-five hundred.[7]

Near the end of the year a crisis in border relations was precipitated by the case of the *Caroline,* an American private vessel which had been dislodged from the ice and repaired for use in carrying rebel supplies from Buffalo and Schlosser to Navy Island. On December 29, by order of McNab this vessel was seized at the Schlosser wharf in American territory by a small Canadian naval force which, after a brief conflict resulting in the death of an American named Amos Durfee, allowed it to drift over the falls.

On the frontier the episode was followed by popular forms of appeals to belligerent sentiment which increased the muttering threats of war. The draped body of Durfee was displayed on the piazza of the city hall at Buffalo, his funeral was advertised by a panorama of placards illustrated with coffins, and inflammatory speeches added to the excitement of the people. On December 30, the whole frontier was in commotion. Sympathy for the insurgents increased and became more active, resulting in demands for war against England. In the *Buffalo Daily Star* of January 7 appeared a statement that "the whole frontier from Buffalo to Lake Ontario now bristles with bayonets."

Sympathizers with the insurgents became active in the spread of propaganda. "General" Sutherland, who had enlisted in the insurgent cause at Buffalo, went west to incite the people. At Detroit he obtained possession of several boats with supplies, including muskets which were taken from the jail and from a building adjoining the United States marshal's office. From Bois Blanc Island he began to issue his proclamations, but his air-castles fell when the *Anne,* commanded by the Irish-Canadian, Theller, was captured near Malden on January 10.[8]

The President, apprehensive of further complications, continued efforts to secure American observance of international duties. On January 5, 1838, he issued a proclamation warning Americans of their duty to refrain from giving aid to the Canadian rebels. To aid in prevention of any popular outbreaks or any violation of American neutrality, he promptly sent General Winfield Scott to the Niagara border where he established a military post, at Buffalo. At the same time, acting through Secretary Poinsett, of the War Department, he sent by Scott letters requesting the governors of New York and Vermont to call into the service of the United States a force of militia sufficient for defense of the frontier during the period of the Canadian internal contest.[9]

In submitting information of this action to Henry S. Fox, the British minister, Secretary Forsyth indicated his purpose to demand redress for the outrage on the *Caroline* and expressed his expectation of an explanation from the authorities of Upper Canada and of decisive precautions to prevent further outrage or aggression from that source. He declared that the President could not be answerable for the effects of the indignation which might follow another such outrage. From Fox, after some delay, he received a reply justifying the British act and enclosing a report of the Canadian government to show that it was in self-defense.

In the following May, at London, Stevenson submitted to the British government a demand for indemnity, which was acknowledged by Lord Palmerston with a promise that it would be given the consideration which it merited.

The controversy which was aroused by the British reply to the American demand for redress was a subject of diplomatic correspondence for three years, during which the excitement on each side of the border gradually subsided.[10]

Early in 1838, convinced by recent experience that existing laws were "insufficient to guard against hostile invasion from the United States into the territory of friendly and neighboring nations," the President recommended to Congress a revision of the laws, with additions which would vest in the executive full power to prevent the infliction of injuries upon a neighboring power by unauthorized and unlawful acts of American citizens or of foreign citizens within American jurisdiction. After referring to the recent "hostile though temporary invasion of territory" which had produced strong feelings of resentment, he requested appropriations for necessary increase of the militia on the frontier to guard against the recurrence of any similar acts.

Following the President's proclamation enjoining neutrality, Secretary Woodbury requested the commander of the cutter *Erie* to go to Buffalo to aid in enforcement of the laws.[11]

At Buffalo Scott acted with a moderation which did much to calm the excitement on the border. He objected to McNab's order to anchor two British schooners in American waters to intercept the passage of the *Barcelona* in which it was believed the insurgents intended to depart for the Michigan frontier; but, at the same time, he arranged to charter the *Barcelona* for his own use, and by keeping a watch on other vessels he interfered with movements hostile to the Canadian government.[12]

Meantime, efforts were made to neutralize the activities of the pro-insurgents. At Buffalo a public meeting was called to counteract the effects of the previous meetings. It declared that the safe policy to prevent the appearance of British steam frigates on the Lakes was noninterference in the affairs of Canada.

The cause of the "Patriots" was clearly on the wane by January 13. The insurgents at Navy Island, unable to obtain from the United States further supplies of men and ammunition and influenced by the increasing effectiveness of the bombardment by Canadian forces, ceased their cannonading there and evacuated the place. The American followers crossed to Grand Island where they surrendered their arms to a force of American militia, and where their American military leader (Van Rensselaer) was arrested.

Mackenzie, *en route* to Buffalo, was arrested for violation of American neutrality by enlisting Americans for hostile action against the British government in Canada. Released on heavy bail while awaiting trial, he continued his efforts to enlist American sympathy and aid until American authorities finally secured his conviction and his imprisonment in the Rochester jail for eleven months. After his release he resided in the United States until 1849, when he returned to Canada and was elected to membership in the Canadian Parliament.[13]

In March, 1838, Canadian authorities were still apprehensive of other danger spots. Governor Head, excited by the stories told by Sutherland in the Toronto jail concerning American aims in Canada, wrote Fox that almost every American arsenal from Lake Champlain to Lake Michigan had been broken open in order to enable American citizens to invade Canada. Unfortunately this exaggerated statement had some basis of truth in specific instances in northern New York.

A larger source of border trouble, however, arose from the activities of Canadian refugees who invited American popular sympathy and aid. In March, at Lockport, some of these refugees formed a Refugee Relief Association to aid the patriots in the United States. A small group of these occupied some of the American heavily-wooded Thousand Islands, from which (on May 13) they embarrassed the American government by the sudden seizure and destruction of the Canadian freight-passenger steamer *Sir Robert Peel* within American jurisdiction.

To guard against further use of American soil for illegal acts by the refugees or by their American sympathizers, the American government sent troops to Sackett's Harbor and Plattsburg and placed armed men on two steamers, one on Lake Erie and the other on Lake Ontario.[14]

Late in the spring, as a result of the border situation, the President was asked to consider the question of the necessity of a larger force on the Lakes frontier. Although he did not accept the House suggestion as to the expediency of providing for the construction of an armed steam vessel on Lake Erie, he approved a proposal to hire two steam vessels, one for Lake Erie and the other for Lake Ontario and to equip them under existing appropriations and without violation of treaty provisions.

Apparently the British authorities also had hired some extra boats and steamers, which were still retained for use on Lake Erie against apprehended filibustering invasions.

The organization of original secret lodges, sworn to aid the Canadian independence movement, continued to expand in 1838, especially in Michigan, where they coöperated under a chief commander at Detroit. Toward the end of the summer, according to rumors, a new secret association known as "Hunters' Lodges" was widely organized along the American border with purposes similar to the earlier lodges. It was unfriendly to the Canadian government. In New York state, it especially increased in activity during the political compaign which preceded the election of 1838 and resulted in the defeat of Governor William L. Marcy by William H. Seward (the Whig candidate). It received its support partly from American citizens who had toward Great Britain a hatred which had its origin in the Revolution of 1776, and partly from those who sympathized with the insurgents because they represented the weaker side in a contest which they regarded as a struggle for liberty. Its members, pledged to defend republican institutions on the North American continent and to oppose every power of royal origin, established lodges along the border from Vermont to Michigan. Both old and new organizations planned an invasion of Canada by an attack on Windsor, one in July and the other in November. In both cases, the attempt was defeated by official interference under authority of the American government.[15]

Meantime, between March and July, the British authorities had shown increasing uneasiness. On March 15 Fox sent to London a secret and confidential report that, although the crisis of immediate danger was over, the final settlement of accounts might yet lead to discussions of great hazard to the preservation of peace and that England should be ready to strike a sudden and astonishing blow at American commerce in case of war; but he hoped for peace and thought the chances for it were good. Referring to the "piratical war" which he said had been waged against Canada from the United States, he admitted that the American government, acting under defective laws, had tried to preserve neutrality; but, apprehensive of a renewal of war with worse violence in case of new political troubles in Canada, he doubted whether the Washington government could restrain the American population from rushing in mass across the frontier "to plunder and devastate" British territory, and therefore he feared that a national war would become inevitable.[16]

Early in April Lord Palmerston, evidently influenced by suspicions concerning the American preparation of the Pacific exploring expedition which later sailed under Wilkes, instructed Fox to make inquires and report concerning the movements and preparation of the American navy. In a confidential reply of May 17, Fox reported that he found no sign of activity or warlike preparation in the management of the American navy under the inefficient Secretary Dickerson, and that he could not see on the part either of the American government or of Congress any indication of a desire to strengthen or increase either the naval or military force of the country in consequence of the troubles in Canada and the "alarming crisis which resulted therefrom." "In fact," he wrote, "the supreme authorities of the United States do not appear to me to have had their eyes open, during any part of that crisis, to the imminent danger which existed from day to day, that events might occur, which in spite of the wishes and efforts of both Governments would have placed the two nations at war."

Early in the following July (July 4) Glenelg, of the Colonial Office, confidentially submitted this report to Lord Durham, who recently had been appointed governor-in-chief of the five British American provinces. On July 13 he approved the measures which Durham had adopted for defense of Canada, by distribution of regular troops along the frontier, in preference to volunteers. On July 20 he expressed to Durham satisfaction that the American government had "at length adopted active measures to prevent use of its territory for starting hostile enterprises against Canada and for evincing readiness to co-operate in expelling from Islands in St. Lawrence persons concerned in such hostile enterprises." Although the British government had under consideration the propriety of terminating or modifying the naval agreement of 1817, he recognized that any increase of the Lakes force, even if found necessary, might result in exaggerated alarm.[17]

Durham, who was a son-in-law of Earl Grey and a liberal in British politics, arrived at Quebec in the early summer of 1838 with instructions to restore peace and loyalty, to prevent rupture of peaceful relations with the United States, and to report conditions with suggestions of constructive remedial measures. He immediately took steps to conciliate the popular party in Canada. He also called deputations to discuss the union of all the provinces but found strong opposition to a confederation. To prevent the danger of border violence he sent a representative to Washington to arrange a more effective method for guarding the frontier. On a trip to Upper Canada he stopped at Niagara where at a banquet he toasted the American President. Encountering political opposition in Lower Canada and in England, he resigned on November 1, and returned to England. There, in the following February, he submitted his famous report, which condemned the provincial government acting under cliques at Quebec and Toronto and recommended the establishment of complete responsible government with provision for the union of Upper Canada and Lower Canada.

Meantime, early in November, Fox, who by friendly orders of the President had been informed of the alarming reports concerning apprehended hostile movements against Canada from American territory, suggested to Acting Secretary Vail that the danger of hostile disturbance was more serious and imminent than had been represented. In referring to the extent of the "secret combination or conspiracy," whose activity had increased recently, he estimated that forty thousand Americans were enrolled in the "criminal association" which (he said) conducted a plot by means of masonic lodges, secretly established in almost every town along the frontier" and co-operating by a complete system of secret signs and a cipher alphabet. He excitedly declared that the association had several superior lodges in the larger lake cities and also a grand central lodge (or convention of delegates) at Cleveland, that it was secretly collecting arms and warlike stores, that it had engaged no less than nine of the steamboats which plied regularly on Lake Erie and that its direct objects were to invade and conquer Upper and Lower Canada, to revolutionize their governments, and to wrest them from the rightful dominion of the British Crown. A few days later, he reported to the Canadian government that the American government seemed sincere in its desire to avoid a rupture, but that its neutrality laws and its methods of administering them were wholly insufficient for the emergency. Later, he expressed his belief that the Canadian conspirators obtained their funds from wealthy citizens of American towns with a deep and permanent interest in land speculation.[18]

The Secretary of State, although he saw in these exaggerated reports some room for fear, assured Fox (November 15) that "regular military bands from the American side" would be successfully repressed. He added in friendly tone that the American government would expect British officers in Canada to prevent trans-border violation of the territory of the United States. This temperate warning which Fox promptly forwarded to Canada with the additional note of caution that "any substantial act of retaliation on our part would risk the instant probability of a national war."

Recent events indicated need for discretion and vigilance on both sides. Colonel Worth of the American army had just seized at Ogdensburg an American vessel, the *United States* commanded by Captain Van Cleve, which carried filibuster passengers from Oswego and towed two "Patriot" schooners. He took the three vessels to Sackett's Harbor, leaving behind some of the "deluded youths" who were soon apprehended in Canada by the authorities there. On November 11, about two hundred "Hunters," organized as an expeditionary force, crossed the St. Lawrence to Canadian jurisdiction at Prescott and seized a windmill on a point of land at the edge of the river. After holding their position several days, they were defeated by a Canadian force. Later, several of the members, after a trial in which John A. Macdonald was the defense lawyer, were convicted and hanged.[19]

The Canadian government still felt the need of more effective steps to protect the long frontier. On November 25 Fox wrote the Department of State that the British authorities had considered the necessity of placing upon the boundary lakes and rivers temporarily a more extensive naval armament than was allowed by the stipulations of the convention of 1817. To this proposed temporary extra force the American government offered no objection. At the opening of navigation in the following spring it contemplated preparation for a similar temporary augmentation of its lake fleet if needed to protect against possible invasion.[20]

Meantime, on November 22, with good effect, President Van Buren issued a proclamation of warning to misguided or deluded Americans who, in defiance of the wishes of their government and without shadow of justification, had disregarded their personal and national obligations by engaging in criminal enterprises to aid the insurrection which disturbed neighboring dominions. A few days later, in his annual message of December 3, he assured Congress that he would continue to execute faithfully and fully the existing laws, leaving the legislative branch to decide whether these laws were sufficient to meet the situation on the Canadian border.[21]

American executive determination was reënforced by an opinion expressed by Justice McLean that Americans should observe their duty to keep aloof from the agitations of other governments, to exert their influence in suppressing unlawful enterprises against the peace of any foreign power.[22]

The last serious raid of the year 1838 occurred in the Detroit River, during the first week of December. It was preceded by a march of four hundred "Hunters" through the streets of Detroit shouting "Remember the *Caroline*," and its purpose was to capture Windsor, Canada. Armed men on the *Champlain* crossed from Detroit to Windsor and set fire to the steamer

Thomas. Several of the raiders were caught by the Canadians, who shot four and executed others after a trial.[23]

British plans for changes in the government of Canada, accompanied by certain unauthorized and "indiscreet" overtures of negotiations by James Buchanan (the British consul at New York) with Papineau at Albany, contributed to the reduction of Canadian discontent and to the cessation of filibustering agitation on the American side of the frontier.

Apparently, during the winter of 1838–39, all danger from the "Patriots" disappeared. To this improved situation General Scott contributed by his addresses to large gatherings of "Patriot" sympathizers. In June the chances of renewed excitement were further reduced by the trial and conviction of Mackenzie, who thereby was prevented from making agitating speeches. By the autumn of 1839 the Secretary of State felt that there was no longer any danger of acts of hostility against Canada.

The British authorities also felt that all danger was passing away. As a security against the renewal of the troubles of the preceding year, however, they owned or hired two steamers and one schooner and several barges, which were employed on Lake Ontario and the St. Lawrence River until the close of navigation.[24]

In his message of December 2, 1839, the President expressed the belief that Canadian disturbances would not again result in border contentions. He said that the misguided sympathy of American citizens for political struggles of popular rights elsewhere had "subsided into a rational conviction strongly opposed to all intermeddling with the internal affairs of neighbors," and that refugee immigrants from Canada were disposed to refrain from all attempts to endanger the peace of the country which had afforded them an asylum. He regretted that in Canada sentiments of hostility to American people and institutions had sometimes been applauded and encouraged by some of the subordinate local authorities.[25]

At the opening of 1840, the American government, influenced in part by the situation on the Maine frontier, still kept an eye on the situation on the Lakes border. It felt that the British had not yet given a satisfactory answer in regard to the invasion of the United States territory by the expedition against the *Caroline*. Incidentally its attention was attracted by various rumors of extensive British defenses on the northern frontier, which were proved to furnish no reasonable basis for apprehension.[26]

Following the decline of border irritation and the consequent diversion of Congress to other subjects, a new turn in the *Caroline* affair revived border feeling. In November, 1840, Alexander McLeod, while under the influence of liquor at an American border tavern, boasted that while acting as a deputy sheriff of Upper Canada he had killed Durfee on the *Caroline*. Arrested at Lewiston for murder and arson, he was placed in jail at Lockport to await the action of the grand jury, which in the following February indicted him for murder.

Excited Canadians, acting through the lieutenant-governor, promptly requested steps to secure McLeod's release. On December 13, Fox asked for release on the ground that the destruction of the *Caroline* was a public act under orders of the British government and that McLeod had not been a member of the party which executed the orders.

On December 26 Forsyth, stating that the President was unable to recognize the validity of the British demand for release, explained that the American government could not properly interpose in a case before the state court. He doubted the existence of any principle of international law under which offenders in an unjustifiable invasion would be entitled to impunity before legal tribunals on grounds stated by Fox.

A few days later, on December 29, Fox submitted to Forsyth a note justifying the British destruction of the "hostile, piratical" *Caroline* within American jurisdiction where American authority could not act promptly, and suggesting that McLeod's imprisonment might produce serious consequences. At London Palmerston informed Stevenson that the execution of McLeod would be the signal for war. He approved the course and language of Fox and confidentially instructed him to quit Washington and return to England in case of the conviction and execution of McLeod.[27]

In his reply of December 31 Forsyth, referring to the American demand for redress for the *Caroline* affair, suggested that further discussion of the circumstances at that time could be neither useful nor proper.

To the new crisis in Anglo-American relations which threatened to precipitate war, Congress contributed by its discussions of the correspondence concerning the arrest of McLeod which it had received from the President. Early in 1841 the House Committee on Foreign Relations (under Democrat influence) submitted a sensational report, resenting the language used by Fox, declaring that McLeod must be tried for murder and arson, and criticizing the assumptions of Great Britain in this and other controversies. This report the Whigs regarded as a deliberate attempt to produce an excited popular irritation which would embarrass the incoming President.[28]

On March 12, early in the Harrison administration, and in accord with the views of Lord Palmerston, Fox submitted to Secretary Webster a peremptory request to arrange the immediate release of McLeod and invited consideration of the "serious consequences which must ensue from a rejection of this demand," evidently referring to his instructions "to quit Washington in event of McLeod's execution." He also submitted a statement of the British refusal to admit the validity of Forsyth's doctrine that the American federal government had no right to interfere with state action in the McLeod case, and offered a suggestion that the admission of such an inconsistent doctrine would be equivalent to a recognition of the "dissolution of the Union as far as its relations with foreign powers are concerned."[29]

After consultation with the President, Webster was inclined to accept the British view that McLeod, acting under orders of his government, was not amenable to the criminal process of the state of New York, and that the duty of the American government was to secure his release, but he recognized that the prisoner could not be released except by process of law. On April 24, in a reply to Fox, he renewed the American explanation. After stating that the British government must show a strong necessity of self-defense in its action concerning the *Caro-*

line, he declared that the American government, without any desire to disturb the peace, could not admit that it did not have the will and the power to preserve its neutrality and the immunity of its territory against foreign aggression.[30]

In view of the serious situation precipitated by the McLeod case, and in accord with the policy of the President, Webster promptly arranged for Attorney General Crittenden to go to Lockport to assist the defense in obtaining counsel and evidence and also to consult with Governor Seward concerning his attitude as to a proper termination of the case and, if necessary, to suggest to the counsel the wish of the federal government that the case be removed by writ of error to the Supreme Court of the United States. He was disappointed to learn that the release was denied, that the trial was postponed and that in Europe were floating rumors of impending war for which the British government was preparing to send naval and military forces, and in which America was expected to terminate British rule in Canada.

When McLeod's case was removed to the New York supreme court, President Tyler, against the protest of Governor Seward, permitted a United States district attorney to act as the leading counsel for the defense. Later, when that court remanded the prisoner for trial, which was transferred to Utica by a change of venue, both Tyler and Webster (and also state authorities) were vigilantly active in efforts to prevent the success of reported plans of Hunters' lodges to seize and lynch the prisoner.

Webster was embarrassed by the refusal of the New York court to discharge McLeod under a writ of *habeas corpus* in accord with a formal opinion which he had expressed to Fox in the preceding April by direction of the President. Early in September he was urged to use his "utmost efforts to avert from both nations the heavy calamity of war." Already he had suggested the necessity of an act of Congress (enacted a year later, on August 29, 1842) to authorize federal judges to release, under writ of *habeas corpus* proceedings, foreign citizens imprisoned for an act committed under the commission or order or sanction of a foreign state or sovereignty under color of international law.

At one time in the discussions the President gave to Fox "the extraordinary intimation, privately and personally," that if McLeod was convicted and judicially executed he still hoped to be able to offer such explanation as might avert war. Then, in response to Fox's reminder of his instructions to quit the United States in case of McLeod's execution, he stated "in a friendly manner but firmly and resolutely" his resolve to take the responsibility of refusing a passport and of preventing Fox's departure, even by constraint if necessary, until the British government had time to reflect upon the arguments and explanations which he planned to offer. This statement caused Fox to write Lieutenant-Governor Sir Richard Jackson that the latter, during the period of such detention by force, "need not suspend execution of the measures directed by the British government." [31]

Meantime, following the British demand for the release of McLeod and notwithstanding the just and conciliatory reply of Secretary Webster, some American agitation for greater preparation for defense (especially in proposals for construction of armed steamers on Lake Erie) was reflected in the newspapers and in Congress.

In Congress, in June, 1841, the examination of the correspondence concerning McLeod precipitated vehement debates, in which earlier interest in Lakes harbor improvements at Chicago and elsewhere was partly shifted to Lakes defensive measures, such as defenses at Detroit and the construction of armed steamers on Lake Erie. Early in August Senator Woodbridge, although confident that the Americans had enough vessels to defend the Lakes in any possible emergency, urged the need of an appropriation for defense of Detroit to which he referred as "in the jaws of the Lyon." From the debates emerged a law of September 9 providing for construction of Lakes defenses. In accord with this act the President decided to construct one or more steamers. Late in November the Secretary of the Navy authorized the construction of one steamer for defense on Lake Erie—a side-wheel steamer which was finally begun at Pittsburgh in 1842 after the collapse of the war scare, and which in 1843 was transported to Erie in sections and there assembled under the name of the *Michigan,* for many years the only American naval vessel on the Lakes.[32]

In September, coincident with discussion of the approaching trial of McLeod, considerable disquietude appeared along the lake border of New York. With the news that Canadians were building strong vessels on the Lakes came reports that the strong secret organization on the American side of the Lakes was contemplating the renewal of plans to disturb the peace with Great Britain. To these reports were added the news of an attempt to blow up one of the locks on the Welland Canal at Allenburg, Canada, apprehensions of plans for an attempt upon the person of McLeod in case he was acquitted, and the rumor that popular discontent in Canada against the existing government was liable to lead to another uprising in which American preservation of absolute neutrality would be difficult.

Beneath these reports and rumors Governor Seward saw danger lurking. Late in September he enclosed to Webster a letter of Seth C. Hawley of Buffalo who, after confidential efforts to get information concerning Canadian operations, reported a "growing opinion" that there was "danger of a sudden blow from Canada"—an opinion which resulted from neighboring Canadian precautionary military and naval preparations with a view to possible necessity for suppression of internal commotions or preservation of tranquillity. Considering the situation, he suggested the adoption of means of defense without delay.[33]

Webster, recognizing the necessity of prudence, took immediate steps to prevent any further breach or irritation. In a note to General Scott he stated that unlawful attempts must be suppressed. To Governor Seward he wrote: "If we cannot repress these lawless acts, we shall ere long be engaged in an inglorious border warfare, of incursions and violations, ending in general hostilities." On September 24 he directed United States District Attorney J. A. Spencer to get the truth, to find the authors of the outrages and to prosecute.

On September 25, within the month before the trial of McLeod, President Tyler by proclamation denounced the acts of secret lodges and clubs which had been organized to aid insurgents against the Canadian government. He advised their abandonment and declared that the laws of the United States would be enforced. At the same time Webster asked Fox to explain the reported equipment of two British steam vessels at Chippewa.[34]

In October the trial of McLeod, although begun before the close of a new excitement resulting from the act of a Canadian armed band in seizing as a hostage an American citizen in Vermont, was conducted in an orderly way. It resulted in his acquittal based upon evidence to sustain the claim of an *alibi*. His release (on October 12) and his safe transfer to Canada greatly relieved the tension. His acquittal ended a serious source of international embarrassment, and smoothed the way for the friendly conferences between Webster and Ashburton which were opened at Washington a few months later.

Fox attributed the acquittal to the fortunate disappearance of two chief prosecuting witnesses who at the last hour either became frightened or were "kept out of the way by some private management between the Federal and the New York governments." Although he was pleased with the result, which he said had removed the prospect of immediate war and possibly had relieved him from the forcible detention threatened by the President, he said he had little doubt that some other cause of dispute would soon arise from Canadian neighborhood relations.[35]

After McLeod's acquittal and his safe removal to Canada, the agitation on both sides of the Lakes was gradually replaced by an atmosphere of tranquillity. On November 20 Webster urged upon Fox the importance of British cessation of further plans to increase the British force on the Lakes beyond the limit fixed by the agreement of 1817. On November 29, after referring to an unanswered inquiry of September 25 relating to the original object of the convention of 1817, he stated that the American government had not been disposed to complain of the temporary British deviation from the agreement in 1838 "under what was supposed to be a case of clear and urgent necessity for self-defense"; but he said that it could not be expected to acquiesce in continued naval preparation (beyond the limit fixed in 1817) "upon the ground of a vague and indefinite apprehension of future danger," and could not consent to any inequality in the observation of the stipulations of the agreement concerning reduced armaments.

Fox promptly replied that the temporary increase of British vessels on the Lakes was necessary to guard against hostile attack from unlawful combinations of armed men which threatened the Canadian provinces from territory under the jurisdiction of the United States, and which the efforts of the American government had not yet completely suppressed. Later, after the fear of insecurity along the frontier had decreased, he explained that the British government desired to continue the principle of reduced armament under the agreement of 1817 and had temporarily departed from that principle only because of absolute necessity resulting from the disturbed border conditions incident to the rebellion in Canada.[36]

Early in 1842 the British felt less need for increase of defensive measures. The danger of raids into Canada from American territory was ended, partly by the vigilance of the American government and partly by the severity of punishment administered to captured raiders by the Canadian authorities under a law against brigands. At Buffalo a public meeting recognized the severe efficiency of Canadian law.

Later, in Congress, representatives of the Lakes region urged the needs of inland commerce instead of Lakes defenses.

In Canadian history the chief importance of the revolutionary movement of 1837–38 was its influence in attracting British attention to the problem of Canadian government, which ultimately resulted in securing the union of the two Canadas, by a law enacted on July 24, 1840, which became effective by a proclamation of February 10, 1841, and especially proved useful as an important step toward the later Canadian confederation. The first Parliament under the union met on June 14, 1841, at Kingston.

In May, 1842, after receiving from Sir Charles Bagot information concerning new internal Canadian controversies and while considering the necessity of an early arrangement on the boundary question which Webster and Ashburton were considering at Washington, Peel suggested to Aberdeen the idea of a possible

British withdrawal from control and protection of the Canadas. He suggested a friendly separation in order to avoid the increasing ill humor and alienation which encouraged in the United States increasing sympathy for the Canadian radicals in politics. At the same time he favored the British retention of Nova Scotia and New Brunswick.[37]

In American history the chief importance of the Canadian rebellion was its influence in creating a better American public sentiment concerning the value of strict observance of the duties of neutrality, in order to avoid the danger of incidents such as the British attack upon the *Caroline* within American jurisdiction—an act of intervention which Webster and Ashburton (by exchange of notes) later informally agreed was justified only as an immediate and overwhelming necessity of national self-defense and should have been followed immediately by frank explanation and apology. Problems arising from the arrest and trial of McLeod by state authorities resulted in an act of Congress which provided for adjustment of such cases through discussion and decision of national authorities. Problems relating to the *Caroline* affair and other incidents of the rebellion were factors in the negotiation of a formal agreement on extradition as a means of checking lawless elements along the border—an agreement which was drafted by Webster and incorporated in the famous Webster-Ashburton treaty of 1842.[38]

REFERENCES

1. C. F. Arfwedson, *The U.S. and Canada,* II, 349; *Westminster Review,* July, 1827, pp. 1–31; *Frazer's,* May, 1830, pp. 389–98.
2. Sir H. Douglas, *Considerations on the Value and Importance of the Br. N. Am. Provinces; H. Reports, Exec. Docs.,* 24–1, No. 243.
3. *Quart. Rev.,* Oct., 1839, pp. 462–512; *Ib.,* Apr., 1839, pp. 426–53; *Blackwood,* June, 1849, pp. 727–41; *M.N.O., The Canadian Crisis and Lord Durham's Mission to the N. Am. Colonies,* pp. 49–56.
4. Shortt and Doughty, IV, 549; *Can. Hist. Rev.,* Mar., 1922, p. 37; *Ib.,* 1926, p. 14; *C.A.,* Q, 235, p. 342; *Ib.,* Q, 188, p. 345; *Ib.,* Q, 330, p. 99; *Ib.,* Q, 382, p. 481; Lindsay, *Life*

and Times of William Lyon Mackenzie, I, 44– ; DENT, *Story of the Upper Canada Rebellion.*

5. *C.A. Rp.* 1922–23, p. 314.
6. *H. Exec. Docs.*, 25–2, Nos. 74 and 64; *C.A.*, G, 224, Fox to Gosford, Confid., Dec. 18, 1837.
7. *Ib.*, *H. Exec. Docs.*, 25–2, No. 74; RICHARDSON, *Messages . . .*, III, 400.
8. *Ib.*, 401–02; *Buffalo Commercial Advertiser*, Jan. 23, 1838; DENT, *Upper Canada Rebellion*, II, 224; R. B. ROSS, *Patriot War* (*Detroit News*, 1890–91).
9. *Buffalo Hist. Soc. Pubs.*, VIII, 1–147 (TIFFANY, *Relation of the U.S. to the Canadian Rebellion*); *H. Exec. Docs.*, 25–2, No. 64, Jan. 5, 1838; *Exec. Docs.*, 25–2, No. 73, Jan. 8, 1838.
10. *H. Exec. Docs.*, 26–2, No. 33, p. 2; *Ib.*, No. 302; WEBSTER, *Works*, V, 119; RICHARDSON, *Messages . . .*, III, 401–04.
11. *Ib.*, III, 400–04; *Buffalo Commercial Advertiser*, Jan. 12, 1838.
12. *Patriot Letters, Jan. and Feb., 1838* (in Buffalo Hist. Library).
13. MCMASTER, *U.S.*, VI, 442; MCARTHUR, *The Canadian Rebellion of 1837* (in SHORTT and DOUGHTY (Eds.), *Canada and Its Provinces*, III, 361–83).
14. MCMASTER, *U.S.*, VI, 442; *Head's Narrative*, p. 399; *Exec. Docs.*, 25–2, Vol. 2, No. 440.
15. *Rps. Coms.*, 25–2, Vol. 4, No. 1008; VAN TYNE (Ed.), *Letters of Daniel Webster*, p. 154; *C.A. Rps.*, 1922–23, pp. 314ff.; *C.A.*, Q, Part 3, p. 484.
16. *C.A.*, G, 224, Fox to Colborne, Mar. 11 and Apr. 4, 1838; *C.A.*, G, 39, pp. 88–96.
17. *Ib.*, pp. 68–77 and 78–87, 108–12 (No. 67, July 13, 1838), and 142–48 (No. 75, July 20).
18. *19 G.B. Legation, Notes from*, Nov. 3, 1838; *C.A.*; G, 224, Fox to Colborne, Nov. 15 and 16, 1838; *Ib.*, Confid., Dec. 7, 1838; *Ib.*, Q, 413, Part 3, p. 484.
19. *6 G.B., Notes to*, Nov. 15, 1838; *C.A.*, G, 224, Confid., Nov. 16, 1838; *Ib.*, Q, 413 (C.O.), Part 1, pp. 37–40; VAN CLEVE, *Reminiscences of Early Steamboats*, p. 11; *Upper Canadian Gazette*, Extra, Nov. 16, 1838.
20. *19 G.B. Legation, Notes from*, Nov. 25, 1838; *Cong. Globe*, Mar. 1, 1839 (Appendix, p. 282).
21. RICHARDSON, *Messages . . .*, III, 482–83 and 485–87; *Exec. Docs.*, 25–3, Vol. 1, p. 34; *C.A.*, G, 224, Fox to Colborne, Confid., Dec. 7, 1838.
22. *Misc. Archives, Mem. of conversations with the Secy. of State*, 1893–98.
23. *Cong. Globe*, Mar. 1, 1839 (Appendix, p. 282).
24. *C.A.*, G, 225, Fox to Colborne, Private, Feb. 1, 1839; *Exec. Docs.*, 26–1, No. 163, *Report of Scott to Secy. Poinsett*, Mar. 23, 1840.

25. *Journal of the Senate*, 26–1, 1839–40; RICHARDSON, *Messages* . . . , III, 531–32.
26. *Toronto Examiner*, Jan. 1, 1840; *19 G.B., Notes from*, Oct. 21, 1839; *Cong. Globe*, 26–1, VIII, Appendix, p. 369 (also pp. 311–13); *H. Exec. Docs.*, 26–1, No. 63.
27. *Ib.*; NILES' *Register*, Oct. 10, 1840; *6 G.B., Notes to*, pp. 186–89, Dec. 26, 1840; RICHARDSON, Messages . . . , III, 623–24, Dec. 29; BULWER, PALMERSTON, III, 46, 49; *C.A.*, C.O. Series, 188, Vol. 169, *New Brunswick*, Fox to Maj. Gen. Sir John Harvey, Fredericton, Confidential, Mar. 12, 1841.
28. *H. Docs.*, 26–2, Vol. 2, No. 33, Dec. 28, 1840; *H. Rps.*, 26–2, No. 162, Feb. 13, 1841.
29. *G. B., Notes from*, Mar. 12, 1841; *C.A.*, C.O. Series, Vol. 169 (N.B.), Fox to Harvey, Mar. 12; *C.A.*, G, 227, Fox to Lieut.-Gov. Sir Richard Jackson, No. 21.
30. WEBSTER, *Works*, VI, 251; MCMASTER, *U.S.*, VI, 618–19.
31. *Ib.*, 616–17, 620–21; *25 Wendell*, 482; *26 Wendell*, Appendix; *20 G.B., Notes from*, Sept, 25, 1841; WEBSTER, *Works*, VI, 267; *C.A.*, G, 227, Fox to Jackson, No. 21.
32. *N.Y. Review*, July, 1841, p. 168; *Ib.*, Oct. 1841, p. 474; *Buffalo Commercial Advertiser and Journal*, Sept. 18 and Oct. 1, 1841; *Cong. Globe*, 27–1, Vol. 10, pp. 273, 278, 281, 284 and 327 (and Appendix, p. 141); *Sen. Exec. Docs.*, 27–1, No. 88; *Misc. Letters*, Sept., 1841; *U.S. Stats.*, V, 460.
33. *Misc. Letters*, Sept. 17 and 21, and later, 1841; *Sen. Exec. Docs.*, 27–1, Vol. 10, No. 8, Aug. 4, 1841; *Cong. Globe*, 27–1, Vol. 10, p. 327.
34. *32 Domestic Letters; 6 G.B., Notes to*, p. 219; *Buffalo Commercial Advertiser and Journal*, Sept. 29, 1841.
35. *C.A.*, G, 227, Fox to Jackson, No. 22, Oct. 11, 1841; *Ib.*, No. 23, Confid., Oct. 25, 1841.
36. *6 G.B., Notes to*, pp. 219, 223–34 (Nov. 29, 1841); *20 G.B., Notes from*, Nov. 30, 1841; *C.A.*, G, 228, Fox to Bagot, No. 2, Apr. 20, 1842.
37. CHARLES STUART PARKER, M.P., *Sir Robert Peel*, III, 379–82 and 388–89.
38. WEBSTER, *Works*, VI, 261, 293, 294 and 302; *Ib.*, V, 140.

CHAPTER IX

THE WEBSTER-ASHBURTON TREATY

DURING the period of the Canadian insurrection and the consequent problems of American neutrality and defense along the northern lake frontier, a desultory correspondence marked the tortuous and circuitous path of diplomacy concerning the serious problems of the northeastern boundary. It was continued with a tone which became more and more acrid until each party to the controversy recognized the necessity of a compromise adjustment to prevent threatened border conflict which, combined with other unsettled questions and complications, might precipitate war. From the devious negotiations finally emerged a friendlier attitude which found practical expression in the Webster-Ashburton treaty.

In March, 1837, Secretary Forsyth submitted to Fox a new subject of complaint which illustrated the importance of reaching some definitive arrangement (such as he had proposed in February, 1836) for prompt termination of the boundary controversy. He complained that the legislature of New Brunswick had incorporated the St. Andrews and Quebec Railroad Association, which had plans to promote the construction of a railway over a route which would encroach upon the disputed territory where the two goverments had agreed to abstain from any extension of the exercise of jurisdiction during the period of diplomatic negotiations for peaceful adjustment of the controversy. Submitting the President's declaration that the American government would regard the prosecution of the project as a "deliberate infringement of American rights and as an unwarrantable assumption of jurisdiction by the British government," he successfully urged prompt British action to suspend any further movements in execution of the project during the continuance of the pending diplomatic negotiations.[1]

Meantime, both Massachusetts and Maine urged speedy action in securing a final settlement of the boundary dispute. In March, 1837, the legislature of Maine sought a federal appropriation for defense on the northeast border.

In the following June Secretary Forsyth received from the governor of Maine a complaint that the authorities of New Brunswick had arrested and imprisoned Ebenezer Greely, a Maine census enumerator whom the authorities of Penobscot County had appointed to count the people of the Madawaska settlement. In July he instructed Stevenson, at London, to demand the release of Greely. In September, after receipt of information that Greely had been arrested a second time, he directed Stevenson to repeat the demand and to request indemnity. In January, 1838, the President submitted to the House the correspondence in the case.[2]

Early in 1838 Forsyth became interested in a British proposal to make a renewed attempt at adjustment of the boundary by a preliminary arrangement for a joint exploration survey to demonstrate whether the treaty line was practical. On March 1, by a note to Governor Kent, he sought to ascertain the wishes and views of Maine upon the expediency of an attempt at direct negotiations for the establishment of a conventional line. He received very little comfort or encouragement. Kent, who submitted the question to the legislature on March 14, saw little hope for the proposed departure from the treaty line of 1783. From the legislature, which was doubtless influenced by the recent seizure and imprisonment of Greely, he received the report that it could not expediently agree to such negotiations and that it was also unprepared to consent to the appointment of an arbiter. Consequently, he declared that Maine, which had waited with patience, could not quietly submit to a seizure of territory by yielding to the President the right to decide whether "to yield to a foreign power what is unjust." Coincidentally the Massachusetts legislature urged that the American government had no power which would authorize it to cede territory to a foreign nation.[3]

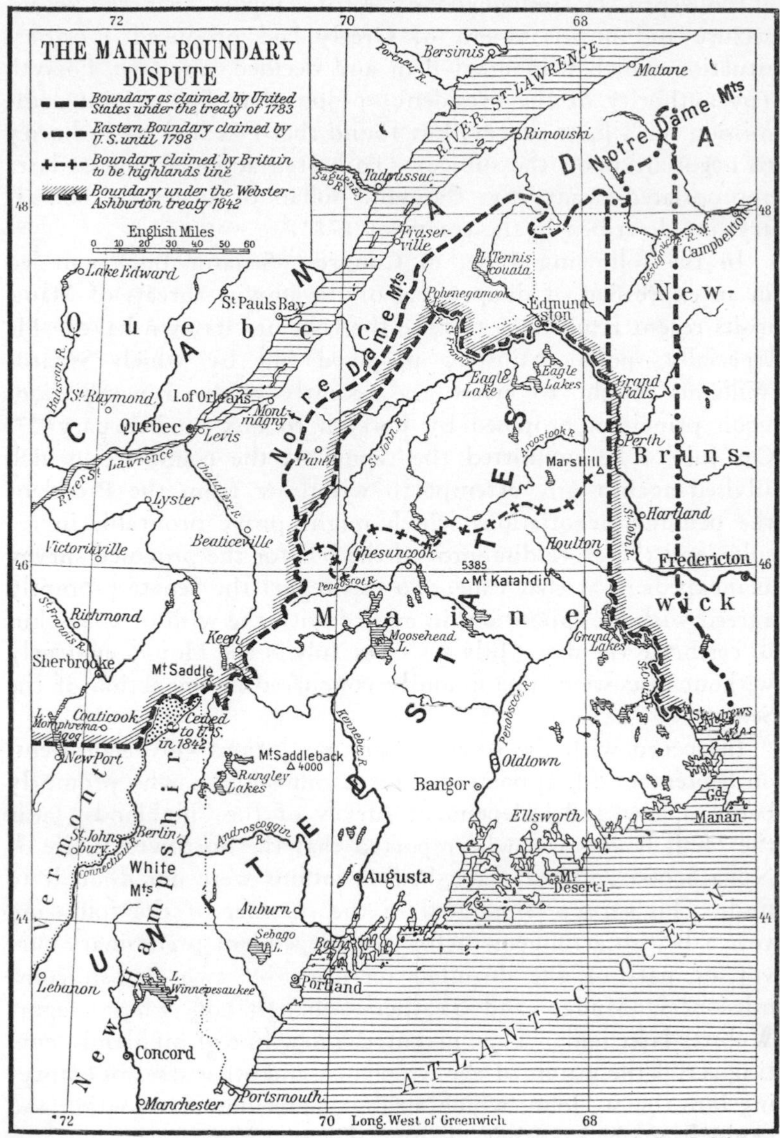

From Carl Wittke's "A History of Canada," F. S. Crofts & Co., Publishers.

On April 27, influenced by Kent's report that the recent seizure and imprisonment of Greely had produced a critical situation which demanded firm and decided language, Forsyth (by authority of the President) proposed to Fox a joint commission for a joint survey, but found that Fox had no authority to negotiate upon the subject. To hasten action Congress later appropriated twenty-five thousand dollars to survey the boundary line described in the treaty of 1783.[4]

In the following June, in Congress, Senator Buchanan led in an expression of disapproval of the unwise threats of Maine in its recent resolutions to take the law into its own hands. He especially spoke against a proposed bill by which Senator Williams sought to arrest the recently renewed negotiations upon principles proposed by Forsyth to Fox on February 27. On July 4 he submitted the report of the committee which advised against any attempt to withdraw from the President the pending negotiations which might prove profitable in results, and therefore disapproved the bill for the proposed survey as inexpedient at that time. To this report the Senate promptly agreed without opposition, in accord with the wish of Clay thus to celebrate the day (July 4). On July 7 the House, evidently without discussion, unanimously concurred in the action of the Senate.[5]

In accord with the recent Maine resolutions Governor Kent, on September 10, appointed three commissioners who promptly began a new and independent survey of the "highlands" near the Metis River, and who reported that the northwest angle of Nova Scotia and the watershed elevations were not difficult to find. This survey stimulated in the summer of the following year a British arrangement for an independent preliminary survey of part of the disputed territory by two British commissioners, Mudge and Featherstonhaugh, of whose report Webster later said: "They invented a new line of highlands, cutting across the waters of the Aroostook and other streams emptying into the St. John, which, in every precious examination and exploration, had escaped all mortal eyes."[6]

Early in 1839 arose the bloodless Aroostook war which caused great excitement in Maine and New Brunswick. This conflict originated in an act of the Maine legislature, directing certain land agents to arrest and imprison trespassers. One of these agents went to the Aroostook River with two hundred men and found three hundred New Brunswick men ready to resist. Following the capture and imprisonment of fifty of the Maine men by the New Brunswick forces, the Maine legislature retaliated by a resolution to raise eight hundred thousand dollars for a military force. It also requested United States aid, which Congress was willing to grant if necessary to resist any British armed attempt to enforce the British claim. Governor Fairfield expressed Maine's disappointment that the Washington government did not adopt a more vigorous policy to terminate the dispute which threatened to precipitate a border war.[7]

On February 26, following Fairfield's statement of the threatening conditions which had influenced the Maine government to call for large reënforcements to prevent timber depredations of New Brunswick trespassers, President Van Buren in a message to Congress admitted the right of Maine to arrest the depredations.[8]

The situation caused considerable debate in Congress. It resulted in the introduction of a bill authorizing the President to resist any British attempt to enforce by arms the British claim to exclusive jurisdiction over the disputed territory and to accept the service of volunteers in case of actual invasion. This bill was passed in the House by a vote of 201 to 6, and it was unanimously accepted in the Senate. In reply to the suggestion of Fox that this action might be regarded as a menacing act, Forsyth said there should be no such misapprehension concerning an enactment which was obviously only in answer to the threat of British provincial authorities.[9]

On March 6, following the border clash at Aroostook and in accord with the recent action of Congress, Forsyth directed the attention of Stevenson, at London, to the urgent need for prompt settlement of the Maine boundary in order to guard against further collision, and instructed him to press upon Lord Palmerston the importance of early action to avert impending calamity.

At the same time he suggested to the President the plan to

continue the embarrassing efforts to secure a settlement by negotiations in charge of a special envoy—a plan which Palmerston declined to accept. For this proposed mission he recommended Webster, who, although not appointed by Van Buren, outlined a plan for settlement which he submitted to Forsyth and which he used in the later negotiations (for a conventional line) terminating in the treaty of 1842.[10]

Meantime, the situation precipitated a lively diplomatic correspondence at Washington. On February 23, after receiving from Lieutenant-Governor Harvey of New Brunswick a complaint of Maine's "unjustifiable incursion into the Aroostook territory," Fox represented to Forsyth that the disputed territory there had been placed under the exclusive jurisdiction of British authority. Stating that the executive of New Brunswick could properly expel by force the Maine militia, he invoked American interference with Maine to prevent threatened collision. In reply (of February 25) Forsyth sustained the unmilitary action of Maine in its purpose (through its land agent) to remove trespassers from the territory, and complained of the unexpected seizure and detention of the land agent by the trespassers. As a step toward the prevention of any occasion for collision, he suggested the propriety of the prompt release of the authorized agents arrested by each side. This suggestion he justified by the assertion that the right of jurisdiction had remained in controversy. He suggested that the improvements in intercourse between Great Britain and the American continent furnished "amply sufficient reason to prevent any hasty action on the part of the Colonial Government."[11]

Fortunately the Van Buren administration arranged with Fox at Washington a memorandum agreement of February 27 for the release of the Americans from the New Brunswick jail and the voluntary withdrawal of the Maine troops from the disputed territory, leaving the question of adjustment to further diplomatic negotiations.[12] Forsyth promptly wrote a letter to Governor Fairfield urging him to accept the suggestion of the agreement. This letter he entrusted to General Winfield Scott who reached Augusta on March 5, and who strategically and tactfully proceeded to calm the excitement, thus demonstrating the value of military authority in the preservation of peace.

Following Scott's efforts, the Maine legislature, on March 23, authorized the governor first to satisfy himself that New Brunswick had abandoned all intention to occupy the disputed territory with a military force, and then to withdraw the Maine militia and to leave the land agent with only a *posse*. At the same time Scott received from the lieutenant-governor of New Brunswick the acceptance of the proposition not to seek to occupy the disputed territory with a military force during a period of expected renewal of diplomatic negotiations between the two governments. On March 25 he received a similar assurance from Governor Fairfield. By this mutual understanding the Aroostook region remained in possession of Maine and the Madawaska region in the possession of New Brunswick; but under it various complaints arose.

The situation, although somewhat relieved, was still dangerous. During a summer visit to Maine, Forsyth had opportunities to confer with officials and other leading citizens. After his return, he expressed to Fox the expectation that the Maine legislature at its meeting in the following January would instruct the state government to take military possession of the whole of the disputed territory. He doubted whether the federal government would have the power to restrain state action unless the President could announce before January an agreement with the British government on the project of a convention providing for a conclusive arrangement.[13]

Fox, considering the "temper of the American multitude," did not doubt that this calculation concerning the possible rash and unconstitutional action of Maine was well founded. On September 28, after a conversation with Forsyth, he wrote Lord Palmerston that, although he thought there was less immediate danger of serious mischief on the frontier, he did not regard Forsyth's tone and language as encouraging or satisfactory as to the prospect of peace in the ensuing winter. Confidentially, he remarked: "I never find myself able to place much confidence in Mr. Forsyth's language, excepting when he is under the immediate eye of the President." Although confident that the President would use every means at his command to preserve peace, he expressed his intention in December to urge British colonial authorities to proceed to the immediate military occupation of the Madawaska settlement and the left bank of the line of the St. John River—as a step to discourage any Maine attempt to begin an attack there. On November 3, in a confidential communication to Thompson, he urgently recommended the expediency of prompt military re-occupation of the Madawaska settlement and the valley of the upper St. John as a precautionary measure to discourage any military attempt of Maine to occupy a position which would intercept the British line of communications north of the St. John, and incidentally to prevent a collision which might result in war along the entire line westward to Detroit.

At the same time, in a confidential letter to Governor Harvey, he enclosed the American counter project of a convention for the establishment of a new joint commission for exploration and survey of the disputed territory (a counter project which he had submitted to the British government in August). Stating that the next Anglo-American diplomatic act should bear on its face the promise of final settlement of the dispute, he announced that he was favorably disposed to accept the recent American proposal to stipulate for the selection of scientific arbiters chosen by three independent sovereigns or states for eventual and final settlement of points of disagreement between the British and American commissioners.[14]

The President, considering the long experience in efforts to adjust the Maine boundary, recognized that the danger had increased with delay. Hoping to avoid another boundary controversy in which a state government might claim the right to be consulted, he sought to enter into negotiations with Great Britain to designate definitely the line of coterminous dominion from Lake Superior and the northwestern point of the Lake of the Woods before the American region bordering thereon was ready to seek statehood in the Union. To his proposition to adjust the points of difference by arbitration of a friendly power he apparently received no written reply.[15]

Near the close of the year Forsyth encountered a new phase of the Maine controversy—a question concerning observance of the temporary *modus vivendi* arrangement of February 27 relating to border jurisdiction. He received complaints that Maine, impatient with delay, was preparing to exercise jurisdiction and to establish fortifications in the disputed territory. By prompt investigation, he learned that Maine authorities planned only to counteract reported British military plans in the disputed territory. In reply to the British contention he submitted a denial based upon three statements: (1) that the territory contiguous to the mouth of the Fish River, on either side of the St. John, could not properly be considered a part of the British Madawaska settlement; (2) that no restriction had been placed on the maintenance of a small civil *posse* (armed or unarmed) under a land agent to prevent further timber depredations of trespassers in the disputed territory; and (3) that the American completion of the construction of a useful road (begun in 1826) to the Aroostook and thence to the mouth of the Fish River was no new project conflicting with any existing arrangement.

Nearly a month later, on January 16, 1840, he informed Fox that any British attempt to extend the civil or military jurisdiction of the original Madawaska settlements into territory wholly unconnected therewith would be regarded as a bold infraction of existing arrangements. Ten days later he was assured, by the reply of Fox, that the British authorities had no intention to infringe the terms of the provisional agreements. Early in March he incidentally gave Fox the impression that neither the President nor Congress desired war and that Congress might delay action by prolonged discussions designed to give time for the cooling of the rash attitude of the Maine legislature. On March 25, he explained that the American refusal to admit the British pretension to extend temporary jurisdiction to the Fish River was partly based upon the wish to avoid any concession which later might be interpreted as an equivalent to a decision on the merits of the whole controversy in favor of Great Britain.[16]

Meantime, Forsyth received from the governor of Maine a vigorous declaration of the Maine legislature (approved by the governor on March 18) that, unless the British government should make an early and satisfactory proposal for immediate adjustment of the dispute, the American government should take military possession of the disputed territory and protect Maine in the extension of its authority or that, in case the American government failed to act, Maine must assume the defense of the honor of the state and the nation by expulsion of British troops from territory claimed by Maine. This declaration, and some recent diplomatic correspondence, the President submitted to the Senate Committee on Foreign Relations.

On April 14, Buchanan, the chairman of the Senate committee, reported as the policy of the administration the firm determination to maintain the territorial rights of Maine in an amicable spirit even if the conduct of the British government should make war inevitable. In the following July Congress authorized the appointment of American commissioners to aid in the establishment of a suitable boundary. Promptly appointed by the President, these commissioners reached the region of their proposed operations (north of the St. John) in September, but encountering early snows, they accomplished little. They submitted their report to Secretary Forsyth on January 6, 1841 (and also supplemental reports to Secretary Webster early in 1842).[17]

On August 13, 1840, during a political campaign and following several projects and counter-projects for settlement of the dispute, and especially in reply to Fox's proposal for two commissions (one to survey and the other to arbitrate), Secretary Forsyth submitted a draft of a treaty conceding much to Great Britain but risking British disapproval by providing for the appointment by Maine (at its option) of two commissioners, to be associated with an international board of commissioners, with a view to consideration and settlement of proposals for the establishment of a conventional line. This proposal Fox referred to his government.

Palmerston objected to the preamble of the proposed draft and also opposed the proposal that the commissioners of survey should meet at Boston which he regarded as an inconvenient place (in comparison with Quebec). He also refused to agree to the proposal tending to introduce Maine as a party to the negotiations, and insisted that the survey should begin at the head of the Connecticut River instead of the eastern point proposed by Forsyth. Therefore, probably in accord with Van Buren's wishes, he postponed further efforts until after the close of the Van Buren administration.[18]

Further negotiations of Forsyth with the British minister were inconclusive and were doubtless affected adversely by the strained relations resulting from other controversies.

In 1841 the condition of Anglo-American relations concerning border problems, and also problems elsewhere, indicated the necessity for early peaceable adjustment to prevent the danger of a precipitation of war which might result from irritating subjects of dispute. The crisis in the northeast boundary issue was complicated by the unsettled question concerning the British destruction of the *Caroline* and by the incidental issue resulting from the arrest of McLeod.

With a desire to adjust the difficult questions of dispute, Daniel Webster accepted the office of Secretary of State by appointment of President Harrison, and following the latter's death he remained in the cabinet of Tyler after all his colleagues had resigned. For his new duties he was well equipped by his political experience and prestige and by a recent visit to England (in the summer of 1839) where he met many leading men —including Ashburton with whom he later conducted the negotiations for the famous treaty which bears their names.[19]

As early as 1839 Webster had decided that a compromise, without further public discussion of the old arguments, was necessary to a successful conciliatory adjustment of the persistent boundary dispute. Therefore, he favored a conventional line to which he said the consent of Maine should be obtained. In 1841, before he reopened negotiations with this purpose in view, he had little basis for hope that Maine would agree. He knew that the governor of Maine had recently indicated to the legislature that he saw no evidence that Maine was prepared to withdraw from its position on the boundary, and that in this opinion the legislature had promptly concurred.

Early in June, he opened negotiations to regulate temporary

jurisdiction over the disputed territory, and in July he verbally informed Fox that he would not object to the British proposal to station a British force north of the St. John—a liberal concession by which Fox was very favorably impressed.[20]

In England Palmerston was aggressively insistent in pressing upon the Whig ministry his views of foreign policy. On July 19, after considering recent official correspondence of Lord Sydenham and Fox relating to the apprehension of acts of aggression by Maine, he urged the necessity of some amended arrangement to relieve the inconvenience and danger of the existing condition, and especially to press the expediency of withdrawal of the Maine civil *posse* from the post at the mouth of Fish River and an arrangement for provisional occupation by regular troops of the two governments—the British in the valley of the St. John along the northern banks, and the Americans in the valley of the Aroostook. Early in August Sydenham, in writing Fox of his approval of the plan to maintain border tranquillity through forces responsible to the two central governments, did not feel authorized to sanction or recommend Webster's proposal for American retention of the blockhouse at the mouth of Fish River, south of the St. John. He feared that acceptance of this condition would debar British forces of the Madawaska from the necessary active interposition south of the St. John as previously authorized. He concluded that, unless otherwise instructed, he would "take such measures as may appear necessary to check any further encroachments of Maine even at the hazard of collision." [21]

Early in September, 1841, after submitting Sydenham's views to the President, Webster sought to correct misapprehension of motives by sending to Fox a communication in which he said the American national protective forces (which replaced the local armed forces) would not interfere in any question of civil jurisdiction south of the St. John. At the same time he suggested that "although neither government accepted the award of the King of the Netherlands, yet the boundary recommended by him might be worthy of regard as a limit of the temporary possession held by the two governments." To this Fox replied that the British authorities could not consent to relinquish the exercise of provisional British jurisdiction south of the St. John if necessary to protect the inhabitants in settlements which were regarded as part of the Madawaska settlements.[22]

Meantime, on August 24, Palmerston explained to Fox that the British government still adhered to the British draft which Fox had presented to Forsyth on July 28, 1840, and that it regarded as inadmissible several propositions of Forsyth's subsequent counter-draft of August, 1840, which at that time had caused him to decide to postpone further steps in the proposed treaty negotiations until after the inauguration of Van Buren's successor. Now, however, he was willing to resume negotiations. He especially urged that the question at issue should be based upon the treaty of 1783 instead of the treaty of Ghent, that the commissioners should start from Quebec because of its nearness to the western end of the disputed territory (at the head of the Connecticut River) at which the British government proposed that the survey should begin, that the commission should not be required to examine the documents and maps in the public archives at Washington and London, and that Maine should not be introduced as a party to the international negotiation. Stating that the British government was ready to negotiate with the American government for a conventional line, he instructed Fox to propose to Webster arbitration by a commission of experts to be named by the kings of Prussia, Sardinia and Saxony.[23]

The Washington government under President Tyler was considerably amused by this last proposal of Lord Palmerston, submitted only a few days before the latter's retirement with the Whig ministry—a proposal which provided for the settlement of the long dispute of fifty-eight years by a mixed commission, or (in case the latter failed) by three expert scientists, foreign professors, named by three kings. Secretary Webster, and also Sir Robert Peel, wondered how citizens of Maine might regard the visit of the learned foreign professors to the wilds of the disputed region and their subsequent solemn cogitations in Europe (!).[24]

Later, in the summer of 1841, Webster informed Fox of his willingness to attempt a settlement on the basis of a conventional line, although he knew the consent of Maine would be difficult to obtain. Late in 1841, following the negotiations with Lord Aberdeen through Edward Everett at London, he was notified that the British government had decided to send the well-known Lord Ashburton (Alexander Baring) to Washington as a special minister to settle the boundary controversy and all other subjects of difference which he wished to see settled. He was pleased with the selection.

Ashburton, through business and personal relations, had long been interested in American affairs. When a very young man he had resided in the United States as a manager of the American affairs of his father's financial house. At Philadelphia in 1796 he had heard the debates in Congress on the Jay treaty, and in 1798 he had married a daughter of Senator William Bingham of Pennsylvania. After his promotion to the head of the Baring firm in 1810, he had exerted his influence to prevent the War of 1812.[25]

Seeking to establish conditions favorable to the negotiation, Webster tactfully prepared the way for the coöperation of Maine authorities in securing previous consent of Maine and Massachusetts to an international agreement for a conventional line—a new plan to whose success he later attributed the fortunate result of the whole negotiation. On February 2, 1842, following the arrival of Everett's dispatch of December 31 announcing Aberdeen's proposal, he wrote Senator Reuel Williams of Maine a letter requesting him to sound the governor of Maine on the plan to select Maine commissioners to participate in the discussions and conclusions incident to negotiations. Receiving an encouraging reply, he awaited the arrival of Ashburton for further consultation.[26]

Webster's course in the later negotiations was influenced by a private letter of Jared Sparks (dated February 15) which he received on February 21, and with which was enclosed a map of Maine showing in black the location of a famous "red line" of the old map which Sparks had seen in the geographical department of the *Archives des Affaires Étrangeres* in Paris. Finding that the line on this map seemed practically to sustain the British claim to all territory drained by the St. John and its branches, he seized an opportunity to use this information in preparing the way for the coöperation of Maine in the proposed compromise settlement by an arrangement for some compensation or other equivalent. Although he did not doubt the authority of the American government to settle the question by compromise, or in any other way, he suggested that, under the existing conditions, "it will not be prudent to stir in the direction of compromise without the consent of Maine." Through the two Maine senators to whom he disclosed his views he suggested the expediency of inviting Maine to send agents to participate in the discussions and to agree to the result of the negotiations with Lord Ashburton.[27]

On April 11, five days after the reception of Lord Ashburton by President Tyler at Washington, Webster wrote Governor Fairfield concerning his plan. Stating that the President desired the coöperation of Maine and Massachusetts in efforts to terminate the controversy which had been too long continued, he submitted the proposal that these states appoint commissioners to confer with the American government upon a conventional line, by agreement with equivalents. Thus he influenced Governor Fairfield to call an extra session of the legislature, which convened on May 18. On May 14, in company with Jeremiah Mason and Peleg Sprague, he met Sparks at Boston and requested him to go to Augusta on a confidential mission to impress upon Governor Fairfield that the proposed commissioners should be appointed with full and unrestricted powers. He also informed him that Judge Sprague would go to communicate with some principal men of the legislature.

Sparks arrived at Augusta coincidentally with the assembling of the legislature, to which Governor Fairfield promptly submitted Webster's method of settlement with his approval. On May 19 he reported the probable partial success of his mission. He stated that Maine apparently would accept no money from the British government, but would want reasonable equivalents in the privilege of the navigation of the St. John and the islands at the mouth of the St. Croix, and would also want the United States to pay all the state expenses incurred in defending the territory.[28]

Influenced by Fairfield's attitude and by the views of Webster's representatives at Augusta (including Sprague, Senator Alfred Smith and Professor Sparks), the legislature on May 26 by a vote of 177 to 11 agreed to a report of a joint committee, which resolved to appoint four commissioners to confer as suggested and (by their unanimous approval) "to give the consent of the state to any conventional line . . . [with equivalents] consistent with the honor and interests of the state." This decision Governor Fairfield forwarded to Webster on May 27 with the explanation that Maine, as an evidence of its desire to preserve the peace of the Union, had accepted the invitation to aid in the proposed agreement.[29]

Meantime, Ashburton had been busy in studying the situation. In a hopeful letter of April 16 to Governor Sir Charles Bagot he announced that his reception had been favorable and that the American government seemed disposed to listen to proposals which had often been rejected (including a provision for extradition). He recognized that the chief difficulty of his task would be "to deal with a critical and jealous public." He promptly began efforts to obtain the opinions of the leading colonial authorities. He especially took steps to prepare New Brunswick for a coöperative attitude toward negotiations for an "equitable adjustment" in order to prevent future disturbance. In a private and confidential letter to Sir William M. Colebrooke, who was instructed to forward a copy to Governor Bagot, he stated that his negotiations would be wholly with the federal government but would be aided by coöperation of the governors of Maine and Massachusetts with Secretary Webster. He asked advice and information concerning the narrow strip west of the lower St. John River, the cession of which Maine had proposed. He particularly sought the relative value of the strip compared to equivalents for which it might be exchanged, and how far south of the St. John the strip could be spared. Referring to Webster's statement of Maine's desire to acquire by exchange the island of Campo Bello in Passamaquoddy Bay in order to secure a free harbor at the mouth of the St. John, he suggested that the island was almost indispensable to give New Brunswick a protected entrance to the Bay and to the harbor of St. Andrews.

This correspondence he continued in May and concluded in August. He found that Colebrooke preferred to give to the Americans "a money compensation for land released by them under the award of 1831" and that he suggested that Massachusetts and Maine would probably be willing to accept a compensation of $1,000,000 to $2,500,000. Early in June he received official notice that Colebrooke, following the favorable action of the Maine legislature, had sent two representatives to furnish information which might be desired, and had submitted a suggestion that New Brunswick offered no objection to granting to Americans free navigation of the St. John for timber and other produce as a concession in exchange for reciprocal advantages in the exportation of New Brunswick produce to the United States.[30]

On June 12, before the beginning of the official negotiations of Webster with Ashburton, the four Maine commissioners arrived at Washington. They and the three Massachusetts commissioners were in correspondence with the government during the whole period of the Webster-Ashburton discussion. Although at first they were inclined to oppose any considerable loss of territory claimed by Maine, they were finally influenced to approve a compromise line at the St. John, by which the United States received less territory (over eight hundred square miles less) than it would have received by the Dutch award of 1831. A large factor in the determination of their approval was their inspection of the map upon which Sparks had indicated the boundary line marked by Franklin on the map deposited in the French archives—the line westward from the source of the St. Croix via the watershed south of the St. John and north of the Penobscot and Kennebec. Another factor was a compensating treaty provision which furnished a convenient justification for their acquiescence.

Following preliminary informal conferences at Washington between Webster and Ashburton, the latter took a more formal step toward the opening of negotiations by submitting to Webster a note of June 13. In this note he expressed his conclusion that, in approaching negotiations for an amicable settlement, no advantage would be gained by reverting to the interminable discussion of the grounds of the controversy. He said that the only remaining alternative with any hope of success was a compromise solution of the otherwise apparently insurmountable difficulty. Although he abstained from opening any general argument, he offered some observations in refutation of the misleading public statements to the effect that the British had begun the boundary controversy in 1814 with motives of interest and expediency in obtaining territory needed to establish direct overland connection between Quebec and the British maritime provinces. In conclusion, after admitting that considerations of policy and expedience had prompted in some measure the perseverance in maintaining a position determined by justice and equity, he said that the disputed territory which Great Britain expected to obtain by any amicable settlement was worthless for any purpose of habitation or cultivation and that its only obvious use was to connect the British provinces. Except for the latter he declared that the British government long since would have willingly sacrificed the territory to its neighbor country with which it desired to maintain the most perfect harmony and good will.[31]

After informal "trackless" conferences, Webster submitted a note of Friday, June 17, stating that he was authorized to treat for a conventional line. In the first formal conference of the next day, and in accord with his plan of 1839 to force Great Britain to take a definite position, he requested Ashburton to prepare a formal statement of the British views and expectations.

On June 21 Ashburton replied that the British aim in plans to trace a new line was to get a convenient boundary without any effort to drive a bargain and with no expectation of any undue advantage. Especially desiring a boundary which would prevent collision and dispute, and give to the British colonies an "unobstructed communication and connection with each other," he proposed the St. John from a point north of the St. Croix; but he suggested one exception which would include in the British Madawaska territory the scattered British settlements south of the St. John, which he said were naturally a part of a united British community. For this compromise line he offered (as a concession) to accept the old survey of 1774 along the parallel of 45°, and also suggested a possible arrangement with New Brunswick for the free navigation of the St. John to provide access to the sea for the lumber and other forest products of the Aroostook valley and the southern borders of the St. John.[32]

Ashburton's note and a copy of Spark's map Webster submitted to the Maine commissioners. From them he received a written reply of June 29, uncompromisingly refusing to relinquish territory south and west of the St. John but proposing a new line.

A line similar to this proposed new line Webster suggested to Ashburton in a note of July 8. After expressing the President's appreciation of Ashburton's motives in undertaking the mission and accepting his statement in denial of imputations of British bad faith concerning the provision of the treaty of 1783, he asserted that the American government would never relinquish the territory south of the St. John west of the north line from the St. Croix—at least not without a British cession of all or part of the strip between the north line and the lower St. John as an equivalent. He suggested that experience had shown the propriety of using rivers as boundaries when their courses suited the purpose. In considering the question of what branch of the upper St. John was most suitable for a convenient boundary he proposed the Madawaska, which had the same general course as the lower St. John and might conveniently be supplemented by the Temiscouata Lake to the highlands south of the St. Lawrence drainage area. Recognizing, however, the propriety of the British wish to exercise sovereignty over the accustomed or most convenient route of communication between Canada and New Brunswick, he was willing to agree upon a line farther south. Therefore, partially abandoning his principle of preference for a river boundary, he proposed that at a point on the St. John, three miles west of the mouth of the Madawaska, a direct line should be run to the outlet of Long Lake, thence westerly by direct line to the point at which the St. Francis emptied into Lake Pohenagamoot, and thence in the same direct line to the highlands (dividing the Du Loup from the St. Francis) along which the route to the head of the Connecticut might be determined by further conference. The proposal as to American navigation of the lower St. John he regarded as a just and natural partial equivalent to Maine and Massachusetts for relinquishment of lands north of the river. He suggested, however, that the concession as to the strip of territory along the parallel of 45° (although of value to New Hampshire, Vermont and New York and to the United States) was of no particular interest to the states of Maine and Massachusetts, which, therefore, might expect that the value of it should be paid to them.[33]

Discouraged by the uncompromising views of Maine, Ashburton contemplated withdrawal from further negotiations. In deciding to continue he was influenced largely by the persuasions of President Tyler. In an able, frank reply of July 11, while maintaining proper courtesy and dignity, he did not conceal his disappointment. He even showed some irritation in considering controversial details, whose endless and fruitless arguments he had hoped to escape but which he felt compelled to notice in order to prevent any construction of disrespect. He regretted the renewal of old arguments so often advanced and refuted in the long period of controversy. Referring somewhat humorously to one "apparently new discovery" of the Maine commissioners in shifting the long lost northwest angle of Nova Scotia to the Temiscouata Lake at the head of the Madawaska, he said: "If this new discovery leads us to no other inference we can hardly fail to derive from it the conviction that all the ingenuity applied to unravel this mystery leaves us equally in the dark." He insisted that to refer to the disputed territory as the indisputable possession of one party, to be yielded only as a concession for equivalents, was unfair; and he declared that, in case of the failure of efforts at amicable compromise, he must claim that Great Britain, until the final settlement of the question, retained a right to every part of the territory in dispute. He suggested that only his desire to shorten the discussion prevented him from submitting treaty proofs that the "highlands" contemplated in the negotiations of 1783 were those at the heads of the Penobscot, Kennebec and other rivers west of the St. Croix.

In reply to Webster's proposition, he explained that he had "no power to give up" the narrow strip between the St. Croix north line and the lower St. John and he frankly stated that the new proposal for an arbitrary direct line from the St. John three miles west of the Madawaska to Long Lake and thence to Lake Pohenagamoot and thence to the highlands was inadmissible. The latter he regarded as nonconciliatory, giving Great Britain less than the award of the arbiter, and denying an equitable claim to a barren strip above the upper St. John which was "wanted for no other purpose than as a boundary." Appealing to Webster's candor, he said, "Any convention which I sign must be for a division of that which is in doubt and dispute. With any arrangements between the state of Maine and the general government I have nothing to do." Referring to the unnecessarily slow progress in the negotiations, he repeated a previous suggestion that the chances of success might be improved by substitution of conference for correspondence and by the avoidance of doubts and distrusts.[34]

In the several conferences which promptly followed Ashburton's frank statement the negotiators successfully reached an agreement on the boundary: the upper St. John to the St. Francis, the latter to Lake Pohenagamoot, thence an arbitrary direct southwest line to a point near the southwest branch of the St. John, thence a line via the crest of the hills to the northwest source of the Connecticut (Hall's Stream), and the old survey line of the parallel of 45° to the St. Lawrence.[35]

After describing the line of the northeast boundary, Webster suggested that the disputed boundary in Lake Superior might be adjusted "to leave a disputed island within the United States." In reply Ashburton agreed to concede to the United States St. George's Island in the St. Mary's River (in accord with the earlier views of Porter) on condition that the American government agree to grant free and open navigation of certain

American channels at the mouth of the St. Clair River and at Upper Long Sault Island and Barnhart's Island in the St. Lawrence. This condition Webster conceded on condition of a reciprocal freedom of passage through the Canadian channel at Bois Blanc Island at the mouth of the Detroit River. To the latter Ashburton assented. Webster also proposed that the line north of Isle Royale at the western end of Lake Superior should run to the mouth of the Pigeon and that the water communications and portages from that point through the wild region to the Lake of the Woods should be made a common highway for use of the citizens of each country. To this Ashburton also agreed, although on July 16 he had proposed a line beginning at a point six miles south of the mouth of the Pigeon and following the grand portage route to Lac la Pluie.[36]

Meantime, on July 15, Webster tactfully returned to the more difficult task of negotiating with New England neighbors under an extra-constitutional arrangement. He submitted to Maine and Massachusetts a suggested boundary (with possible use of the St. John as an equivalent for territory relinquished by the United States) which he thought Ashburton would accept; and he proposed that Maine and Massachusetts, if their commissioners assented, would receive from the United States $250,000 and payment for expenses due to maintenance of civil *posse* and for cost of a survey. On July 20 the Massachusetts commissioners yielded their consent, with a request that the compensation to Massachusetts be increased to $150,000. On July 22 the Maine commissioners, although not inclined to accept, agreed to waive their objections if the United States Senate should advise and consent to the ratification of the treaty.[37]

On July 27, as a result of the agreements of the conferences with Ashburton and the favorable replies of the Maine and Massachusetts commissioners, Webster submitted to Ashburton a memorandum note formally proposing the line of division in accord with the informal conference settlements. Two days later he received the approval of Ashburton who suggested the preparation of the final draft of the treaty by the final consideration of each article and also recommended the completion of the delineation of the boundary on the excellent charts which had already been prepared.[38]

The final draft of the treaty contained the northeast boundary provision as described in Webster's memorandum. The compensating provisions for loss of territory in Maine were the five British agreements: (1) to open the St. John to the sea for free transportation of all forest products from the Maine territory in its drainage area; (2) to waive all claim to Rouse's Point on Lake Champlain; (3) to permit the United States to retain all the narrow triangular strip north of 45° which the American government had claimed under an early incorrect survey completed in 1774 and upon which it had later built the fort at Rouse's Point; (4) to consent to a division, between Maine and Massachusetts, of a "disputed territory fund" which New Brunswick authorities had collected for timber cut in the disputed area claimed by Maine; and (5) to consent to an American payment of $150,000 to Maine and $150,000 to Massachusetts "on account of their assent to the line of boundary" and in consideration of conditions and equivalents received from Great Britain besides a refund of the expense of protection and for survey of the territory in 1838.

To the latter provision, introducing irregular terms of agreement between the American government and the commonwealth commissioners, Ashburton agreed only after the earnest persuasion of Webster, and after the assurance that Great Britain would incur no responsibility by it. For some time after the conclusion of the treaty, the "disputed territory fund" was a subject of controversy, which Secretary Buchanan finally (in 1846) arranged to adjust by two agents (one for Maine and the other for Massachusetts) who were sent to New Brunswick through the coöperation of the British minister at Washington.[39]

In accord with the agreements reached in the negotiations the treaty also provided for final settlement of the portion of the lake and land boundary from the communication between Lake Huron and Lake Superior (Sault Ste. Marie) westward through Lake Superior and thence through the wild region to the northwestern point of the Lake of the Woods, upon which

Porter and Barclay had failed to reach an agreement in 1826–27.[40]

Another provision of the treaty was an extradition article suggested by Senator Woodbridge of Michigan. It was inserted probably with special consideration to the increasing necessities resulting from increasing neighborhood relations along the American-Canadian border—necessities illustrated by the recent disorders along the Canadian frontier, including the activities of the "Hunters' Lodges." According to President Tyler's explanation to the Senate, this provision was incorporated especially to facilitate the apprehension of criminals who by easy passage of the boundary along the expanding frontier had often escaped justice and had thereby instigated the unprincipled and reckless to commit other crimes which often disturbed the peace and good neighborhood of the border. It stipulated for extradition on charges of murder or attempted murder, piracy, arson, robbery, forgery or utterance of forged paper—an extension of the provision of the Jay treaty, which had included only murder and forgery. By the careful and specific enumeration of extraditable crimes it sought "to exclude all political offenses or criminal charges arising from wars or intestine commotions." Naturally, in accord with British and Canadian views, it contained no provision for American recovery of fugitive slaves and deserters, a subject upon which Secretary Clay had proposed negotiations in 1826–28 but upon which he found the British unwilling to treat.

Unfortunately, the legislation which Congress enacted (on August 12, 1848) to facilitate the execution of the treaty was not specific enough to avoid future controversy concerning requests for the return of fugitive criminals, including questions of distinction between murder and manslaughter and whether the place of murder should be determined by the place of death.[41]

Incidental to the treaty negotiations were several subjects of controversy which Ashburton suggested were of a nature not susceptible of settlement by treaty or convention. Concerning the American complaint of British violation of American territorial jurisdiction in the *Caroline* affair, for which the

British government had offered no apology, Webster could only obtain from Ashburton the assurance (of July 28) that in the violation of courtesy "in the hurried execution of the necessary service" the British authorities intended no slight to American authority, and an expression of his regret that no immediate explanation and apology had been made for the British action in the temporary suspension of the paramount obligation of respect for the territory of a neighbor. Apparently he was satisfied with the explanation, with the expression of "regret that the event should have disturbed the harmony" which the British government "wished to maintain with the American people and government," and with the assurance that the British government "far from thinking that an event of this kind should be lightly risked, would unfeignedly deprecate its recurrence." In his reply of August 6 he stated that the President, satisfied with the conciliatory spirit of Ashburton's note, would cease to press the complaint of violation of territory. He doubtless was in full accord with Ashburton's closing sentence: "I trust, Sir, I may now be permitted to hope that all feelings of resentment resulting from these truly unfortunate events may be buried in oblivion, and that they may be succeeded by those of harmony and friendship which it is certainly the interest and I also believe the inclination of all to promote." [42]

In reply to a question of Ashburton, and after expressing regret that the release of McLeod was so long delayed, Webster stated that the subject of the enactment of legislation to expedite proceedings in such cases had been submitted to Congress, and he added the assurance that the American government "holds itself not only fully disposed, but fully competent, to carry into practice every principle which it avows or acknowledges, and to fulfil every duty and obligation which it owes to foreign Governments, their citizens, or subjects." [43]

On August 8, in connection with the negotiations to settle problems of the American-Canadian border, Webster incidentally obtained an opportunity to present an important definite statement on the subject of impressment—presenting arguments which Ashburton characterized as "very ingenious." In a brief friendly reply of August 9 Ashburton explained that he did not consider impressment as an existing subject of difference, as the practice had "wholly ceased" and could not be resumed under existing British laws and regulations. Referring to the fact that America, receiving many emigrants who were useful in the gradual advance of the American frontier, naturally held a doctrine of allegiance opposite that held by Great Britain, he suggested that any consideration of this subject should be calm and deliberate, without unnecessary abstract speculation.[44]

The treaty was signed on August 9 and submitted to the Senate two days later. On August 16, feeling that the object of his mission had been "satisfactorily terminated," Ashburton was preparing for a hasty departure to New York where some of his American admirers honored him by a dinner on September 1.[45]

After considerable debate which was closed by an opposing partisan speech of Buchanan, the Senate on August 20 by a vote of thirty-nine to nine consented to ratification. The opponents were Williams of Maine, Smith of Connecticut, Buchanan and Sturgeon of Pennsylvania, Allen of Ohio, Benton and Linn of Missouri, Bagby of Alabama, and Conrad of Louisiana—all Democrats except Conrad. Their opposition was chiefly political, resulting from "the isolation of Tyler and the anomalous position of Webster."[46]

In connection with the Senate debates Webster was embarrassed by the disclosure (to the public) of information concerning the red line map—a disclosure which occurred through a speech of William C. Rives, Chairman of the Committee on Foreign Relations, in secret session. Following the disclosure he (and also Sparks) was unfairly criticized in England and in Canada, especially by the press, for withholding information of the map in connection with the negotiations with Ashburton. He properly replied that his conviction concerning the American claim was founded on the terms of the treaty of 1783—which, even by the admission of Aberdeen, sustained American rights.

In his course of conduct Webster was justified by diplomatic usage, and also by the successful peaceful adjustment of a serious problem which, if it had remained unsettled, would have threatened the precipitation of war. He was also sustained by American public opinion which seemed satisfied to terminate a boundary controversy by compromise and to approve the liberal American policy which enabled Great Britain to obtain a shorter route for the establishment of improved communication between New Brunswick and Quebec.[47]

In Maine, and also in Massachusetts, Webster was severely criticized by Democrat leaders, including editors of the press. He was blamed for remaining in the Tyler cabinet, for loss of Maine territory by terms of the treaty, and for failure to negotiate for settlement of the Oregon question. On September 30 he ably defended himself in a speech at Faneuil Hall. In March, 1843, in a friendly letter to Sparks, he expressed his satisfaction with the procedure in the negotiations. Three years later, provoked by attacks upon the provision for a compromise line at the northeast, he spoke for two days (April 6–7) in the Senate in defense of the treaty.[48]

Webster was unjustly criticized for a sin of omission in failing to adjust the Oregon boundary. In the list of subjects for adjustment he had expected to include this question, upon which Lord Ashburton had specific and detailed instructions; but, after a conference, he found that Ashburton, apprehensive that discussion of the additional question might endanger or impede the settlement of the more important question, had decided not to press for negotiations on the Oregon problem.[49]

REFERENCES

1. *6 Brit. Legation, Notes to,* pp. 66–67, March 23, 1837; RICHARDSON, *Messages . . . ,* III, 367–69; *C.A.,* C.O. Series, 188, Vol. 164 (N.B.), Fox to Archibald Campbell, Confid., Mar. 28, 1837.
2. *Ib.,* Fox to Harvey, Confid., July 24, 1837; *Sen. Docs.,* 24–1, Vol. 3, No. 267; RICHARDSON, *Messages . . . ,* III, 405–12.
3. *Sen. Docs.,* 25–2, Vol. 4, No. 319, March 20, 1838; *Ib.,* No. 424 (May 7); *Ib.,* Vol. 5, No. 431 (May 10); *Ib.,* Vol. 6, No. 502; *H. Docs.,* 25–2, No. 354 (Apr. 28).

4. *Sen. Docs.*, 25–2, Vol. 5, No. 451, May 19, 1838; *6 Brit. Legation, Notes to*, pp. 94–95, Apr. 27, 1838.
5. *Cong. Globe*, 25–2, VI, Appendix, 384–85, 386, and 396–98, June 18, 1838; *Sen. Docs.*, 25–2, No. 502, pp. 1–16.
6. *Ib.*, 26–1, No. 107, p. 56; GALLATIN, *The Right of the U.S. to the Northeast Boundary*, pp. 150–52; WEBSTER, *Works*, V, 91–92.
7. EDWARD SMITH, *England and Am. since Independence;* BURRAGE, *Maine and the Northeast Boundary*, pp. 256–57, 264.
8. RICHARDSON, *Messages* . . . , III, 516–20, 521–27.
9. *Ib.; 14 G.B., Instrs.*, pp. 287–89, No. 52, Mar. 6, 1839.
10. *Ib.;* CURTIS, *Life of Webster*, II, 3; VAN TYNE, *Letters of Webster*, p. 215.
11. *19 Br. Leg., Notes from*, Feb. 23, 1839; *6 G.B. Leg., Notes to*, pp. 100–04 (Feb. 25), and 104–06 (Feb. 27).
12. *Ib.*, pp. 104–06, Feb. 27, 1839.
13. RICHARDSON, *Messages* . . . , III, 530–31; *C.A.*, G, 225, pp. 352–58, Fox to Thompson, Nov. 3, 1839, inclosing (pp. 359–83) a copy of Fox's dispatch (No. 41 of Sept. 28) to Palmerston.
14. *Ib.*, pp. 352–58, Fox to C. P. Thompson, Nov. 3, 1839; *Ib.*, Fox to Harvey, Confid., Nov 2, 1839.
15. RICHARDSON, *Messages* . . . , III, 531, 604.
16. *6 Br. Leg., Notes to*, pp. 140–44, Dec. 24, 1839; *Ib.*, pp. 145–48, Jan. 16, 1840; *Ib.*, pp. 160–67 (Mar. 25); RICHARDSON, *Messages* . . . , III, 568–71 (Jan. 29, 1840) and 574–78 (Mar. 9); *C.A.*, G, 226, Confid., Fox to Thompson, Mar. 10, 1840; *C.A.*, G, 251, pp. 67–68 and 25–26, Fox to Sir J. Harvey, Mar. 19 and 28, 1840.
17. *Compilation of Reports of (Senate) Committee on For. Rels.*, V, 601; RICHARDSON, *Messages* . . . , III, 629–39; *Ib.*, IV, 92–99, 113–41.
18. *Ib.*, III, 582–85, 595–99; *6 Br. Leg., Notes to*, pp. 173–85, Aug. 13, 1840; *Sen. Docs.*, 29–1, Vol. 5, No. 274, pp. 3–20; *C.A.*, G, 227, Fox to Sydenham, No. 10, July 27, 1841 (also G, 255).
19. MCMASTER, *U.S.*, VII, 271–73.
20. *N. Am. Rev.*, Apr., 1843 (SPARKS); *C.A.*, G, 227, Fox to Sydenham, No. 10, July 27, 1841.
21. *20 Br. Leg., Notes from* (inclosures).
22. *6 Br. Leg., Notes to*, pp. 213–15, Sept. 4, 1841; *Ib.*, Sept. 6.
23. *20 Br. Leg., Notes from* (inclosure: No. 23, Palmerston to Fox, Aug. 24, 1841).
24. WEBSTER, *Works*, V, 95–96.
25. *Ib.*, V, 97; *Ib.*, VI, 270; WEBSTER'S *Diplomatic and Official Papers*, p. 33, Dec. 31, 1841.
26. H. B. ADAMS, *Life and Writings of Jared Sparks*, p. 403 (Webster to Sparks, Mar. 11, 1843); VAN TYNE, *Letters of Webster*, p. 256; REEVES, *Diplomacy under Tyler and Polk*, p. 41.

27. *Misc. Letters,* Jan.–Feb., 1842; VAN TYNE, *Letters of Webster,* pp. 248–49.
28. WEBSTER, *Works,* V, 98–99; *Ib.,* VI, 272–75; *Misc. Letters,* May, 1842; H. B. ADAMS, *Life and Writings of Jared Sparks,* II, 393–418.
29. *Misc. Letters,* May, 1842.
30. *C.A.,* C.O. Series, 188, Vol. 170, N.B., *Despatches to Lieut.-Gov.,* pp. 1–13, Ashburton to Wm. M. Colebrooke, Apr. 28, 1842; *Ib.,* May 17, 24 and 29 and Aug. 9, 1842.
31. RICHARDSON, *Messages . . . ,* IV, 163–64; *21 G.B., Notes from,* June 13, 1842.
32. *Cong. Globe,* 27–3, p. 5; *H. Exec. Docs.,* 27–3, Vol. 2, pp. 31–34; *21 G.B., Notes* [*from*], June 21, 1842.
33. *Cong. Globe,* 27–3, p. 14; 6 *G.B., Notes to,* pp. 227–39, July 8, 1842.
34. CURTIS, *Webster,* II, 105; *21 G.B., Notes* [*from*], July 11, 1842; *Cong. Globe,* 27–3, p. 9.
35. WEBSTER, *Works,* VI, 276–89.
36. *Ib.,* VI, 281, 284; WEBSTER, *Private Corres.,* II, 140; *21 G.B., Notes* [*from*], July 16, 1842; *Ib.,* July 29.
37. *H. Exec. Docs.,* 27–3, Vol. 2, pp. 70–78, 90–97; WEBSTER, *Works,* VI, 276–97.
38. *Ib.,* VI, 282–89; *H. Exec. Docs.,* 27–3, Vol. 2, pp. 55–59; *21 G.B., Notes* [*from*], July 29, 1842.
39. WEBSTER, *Works,* VI, 282–88; *C.A.,* G, 260, Colebrooke to Ashburton, Sept. 1, 1842; *C.A.,* C.O. Series, 188, Vol. 171 (N.B.), Fox to Colebrooke, Mar. 6, 1843; *Ib.,* Vol. 172, Pakenham to Colebrooke, Mar. 14, 1844 (18 pp.), and also June 10 and Nov. 15, 1844, and Mar. 15, 1845; *Ib.,* Vol. 174, Sept. 1, 1846.
40. WEBSTER, *Works,* VI, 289; *21 G.B., Notes* [*from*], Aug. 9, 1842; MOORE, *Int. Arb's.,* I, 162–94.
41. RICHARDSON, *Messages . . . ,* IV, 168–69; *C.A.,* G, 225, Fox to Colborne, Aug. 30, 1839; *6 Br. Leg., Notes to,* March 20, 1839; WEBSTER, *Works,* V, 78–150; *Cong. Globe, Senate,* Apr. 6–7, 1846; *Library of Congress, Film Photos of Cor. from Br. Min. Washington to Gov.-in-Chief Canada,* Vols. 7, 8, 9 and 15 *passim* (especially Lyons to Sir Edmund Head, July 6 and 23, 1859); *C.A.,* G, *Gov. Genl's Letter Book, 1864–66 and 1866–67; C.A.,* G, 236, *passim* (also see G, 1178, Thornton to Young, No. 29, Nov, 27, 1869); *12 U.S. Mins., Instrs.,* pp. 122–25, No. 3, June 13, 1828.
42. *6 Br. Leg., Notes to,* pp. 246–47, July 27, 1842; *Ib.,* pp. 259–61, Aug. 6; *21 G.B., Notes* [*from*], July 28.
43. *6 Br. Leg., Notes to,* pp. 259–61, Aug. 6, 1842.
44. *21 G.B., Notes to,* Aug. 9, 1842; WEBSTER, *Works,* VI, 289.
45. *N. Am. Rev.,* Apr., 1843 (SPARKS); WEBSTER, *Works,* VI, 270;

Br. and For. State Papers, XXX, 136; *H. Exec. Docs.,* 27–3, No. 2, p. 31.

46. RICHARDSON, *Messages . . . ,* IV, 162–65; *Cong. Globe,* 27–3, Appendix, pp. 7, 16, 27–28, 49–56, 59–62, 101–10; REEVES, *Am. Diplomacy under Tyler and Polk,* p. 57.
47. *N. Am. Rev.,* Apr., 1843 (SPARKS); H. B. ADAMS, *Life and Writings of Jared Sparks,* II, 403, 407.
48. *Ib.,* 403; WEBSTER, *Works,* V, 78.
49. *21 G.B., Notes [from],* Nov. 15, 1842.

CHAPTER X

THE NORTHWEST BOUNDARY: THE OREGON QUESTION

AFTER the adjustment of the northeast boundary, the American government recognized that it must soon find a solution for the Oregon boundary controversy, which had its origin in the early interest of Americans on the coast of the Pacific Northwest in connection with their interests in the China trade, and the settlement of which had been postponed since 1818 by temporary Anglo-American agreements for joint occupation. It had observed within the previous decade the increasing eastern popular interest in the Oregon country, an interest recently reflected in expressions in Congress. It recognized that the course of recent events had increased the importance of a permanent boundary adjustment which would satisfy the needs of recent American settlers in the region and stimulate the recent movement for an increase of settlements.

American emigration to Oregon, first encouraged and stimulated in 1829 by the activities of Hall J. Kelley (a New England school-teacher) in collecting and distributing information concerning the country, had begun by 1835–36. In 1832 Nathaniel J. Wyeth of Cambridge, Massachusetts, using the knowledge of routes obtained from earlier expeditions and from information of trappers, and starting from a point on the short railroad west of Baltimore, led a small party of twenty-one persons on an overland trip to Oregon which proved that the short route via Fort Hall was "an easy road, practicable even for wagons." In 1834 he led a second expedition to which was attached Methodist missionaries who located on the Willamette. The missionaries began the work of real colonization. In 1836 other missions were founded by a group of Presbyterian mission workers, including Samuel Parker, H. H. Spalding and Marcus Whitman. Spalding and Whitman, newly married, and accompanied by their wives, had traveled from Pittsburgh to Walla-Walla by wagon in four months. In the same year President Jackson sent to Oregon an agent, W. A. Slocum, whose report of December 1837 contributed to the stimulation of migration to the region.[1]

Other information contributed to raise the question whether joint-occupation was satisfactory from the standpoint of American interests. Secretary Forsyth in a report of December 23, 1837, to President Van Buren, stated that according to information recently received the Hudson's Bay Company had a steamboat on the Columbia and had erected a sawmill there, and that its operations included the cutting of timber on territory claimed by the United States and the shipment of it to the Sandwich Islands in considerable quantities.[2]

In October 1837, following a preliminary report of Slocum on his trip to the Pacific coast, Senator Lewis F. Linn of Missouri induced the Senate to request the President to submit any correspondence concerning the occupation or status of the Oregon country. Later, on February 13, 1838, he submitted a bill proposing to organize the territory and to extend to it other acts of American jurisdiction by establishing a port of entry and revenue laws and military defense, and by land grants. In this policy he was strongly supported by James Buchanan who declared that the American claim to Oregon should be pushed or abandoned. In June he submitted an exhaustive committee report favoring the use of the army and navy for protection of American settlers. In January 1839 he presented a petition (of March 1838) from the Oregon missionaries and settlers on the Willamette who, recognizing that the feeling of dependence on the Hudson's Bay Company was only temporary, requested Congress speedily to extend its jurisdiction over Oregon. Congress, although it considered the subject in connection with other reports within the next year, enacted no legislation concerning it.[3]

Early in 1840 the Van Buren administration was somewhat apprehensive of British activities in Oregon. On May 6 Forsyth instructed Stevenson to inquire at London in regard to the authenticity of an incidental statement that the British government had granted to the Hudson's Bay Company a large and valuable tract of land south of the Strait de Fuca, and that the company was making sales from it to individuals.[4]

In December 1841, when the estimated number of American immigrants was about 400, Senator Linn, seeking to encourage American settlements, introduced a bill to provide a line of forts along the trail from Missouri to Oregon and grants of land to all male immigrants of the age of eighteen years or more. This bill was strongly opposed, principally on the ground that its purpose, to allure settlers by land grants, would be a breach of the convention of 1827. Although it did not pass the Senate until January 1843 and failed in the House, it probably was a factor in stimulating the increase of immigration, which furnished a reason for the termination of joint-occupation and the adjustment of the boundary question in order to prevent possible friction and to prepare the way for local self-government on the lower Columbia.

Awakened to the importance of a safe land route to Oregon, the Tyler administration early in 1842 employed Lieutenant John C. Frémont under the War Department to survey a route which Senator Benton had long desired to aid American emigration to that region. Frémont promptly engaged Kit Carson as a guide and early in August discovered at the head of the Platte an important pass (South Pass) which with other explorations encouraged the earnest march of pioneers toward the Willamette.

In the spring of 1842, immediately following Frémont's appointment and the appointment of Elijah White as an Indian agent in Oregon, increasing popular attention in the emigration movement was especially illustrated by the organization of an emigrant party at Elm Grove near the Big Bend of the Missouri. This party, which was led first by White and later by Lansford W. Hastings, reached the Willamette Valley in September. A portion of the party (about fifty) accompanied Hastings to California in the following spring.[5]

On the arrival of Ashburton at Washington to negotiate with Webster a settlement of the Northeast boundary dispute,

Linn's bill was put aside with the expectation that the Oregon question would also soon be settled by negotiation. After the settlement of the Northeast question, much public agitation was aroused by the failure to include the Northwest question in the negotiations. This contributed to a growing American inclination to terminate the Oregon controversy and to adopt measures for immediate occupation of the Oregon country by American troops.

In the desire for adjustment the British shared. In October 1842, following the ratification of the Webster-Ashburton treaty, Aberdeen in his instructions to Fox at Washington suggested that the time was auspicious to attempt the settlement of the only remaining subject of territorial difference—and one which might later endanger the good understanding, and possibly the mutual peace, of nations who "ought never to be at variance with each other." He proposed that Webster should induce the President to authorize instructions to the American minister at London to negotiate upon the subject, and he gave assurance that the British government was prepared to proceed with the negotiations for adjustment "on a basis of equitable compromise."

In November 1842, after reading an extract of Aberdeen's instructions, Webster stated that the President concurred entirely in the expediency of immediate negotiation on the subject, that he had already planned to express this opinion in his message to Congress, and that in accord with the President's views he would soon instruct the American minister at London on the subject. Tyler, in his message of December, informed Congress that he would urge on England the necessity of an early settlement of the question, but he did not mention the recent British pressing overture for negotiations. With plans to send Webster on a special mission to London, he postponed instructions while awaiting a special appropriation which the House Committee finally refused to recommend.[6]

At the close of the year 1842, possibly influenced by Whitman's famous ride from Oregon to the East, and seeking to hasten negotiations by which to encourage and protect American settlement in Oregon, Senator Linn renewed his bill for land grants and forts and extension of American jurisdiction—a bill which was strongly opposed and which precipitated an interesting debate (in January 1843). Among those who opposed were Dickerson (of New Jersey) and McDuffie (of South Carolina) who said that distant and isolated Oregon could never become more than a colony, and also Calhoun who favored a policy of "masterly inactivity" which would leave to time the settlement of the Oregon boundary. Others, including Benton and Linn, advocated the maintenance of American claims at any risk. The bill finally passed the Senate on February 3, 1843 by a vote of 24 to 22; but, in the House, on February 16, Adams reported from the Committee on Foreign Affairs a recommendation against it. Its failure, which was soon followed by a significant advance of settlers from the Big Bend of the Missouri to the valley of the Willamette, resulted in various public meetings, including a Cincinnati convention of delegates from six states (in July, 1843) which proposed to add strength to the popular agitation.[7]

The necessity of providing a government for the steadily increasing Oregon settlements was becoming a very practical question. Already, early in 1841, the settlers on the Willamette called a meeting which took the first step in a movement toward self-government. In May 1843 they decided to organize a government. In a convention of the following July they adopted a constitution for a spontaneous provisional frontier government which was to continue until the Washington government could decide to extend its jurisdiction, and which threatened to reduce the benevolent but despotic influence of Dr. John McLoughlin (the factor of the Hudson's Bay Company) at Fort Vancouver on the Columbia. This action, and the wider movement for re-occupation or re-annexation which followed in 1843–44, aroused the interest of both American and British governments, which were already considering the question of renewed negotiations to settle the Oregon boundary dispute.

Meantime, the American government had been apprehensive of the recent occupation of the Sandwich Islands by a British naval officer acting in the name of Great Britain. This apprehensiveness was allayed by a British explanation (on June 25) to Upshur that the act was entirely unauthorized and that the British government had no purpose to seek to establish in the islands a paramount British influence at the expense of the influence enjoyed by others.[8]

President Tyler was criticized for delay in negotiations which were urged as necessary for protection of the rights of the American settlers. In Congress efforts were made to hasten action. In October, 1843, Senator David R. Atchison (Linn's successor) introduced a new Oregon bill to authorize occupation from 42° to 54°40′, and to encourage settlement by construction of blockhouses or forts on the Oregon trail and at the mouth of the Columbia and by land grants of 640 acres to each settler. As a logical supplement to this bill, Senator Semple offered a resolution requesting the President to submit to the British government the one-year notice required by the convention of 1827. This resolution was rejected because of the feeling that it might embarrass negotiations for settlement of the boundary issue.

In beginning the new negotiations on American claims to Oregon, negotiations which were initiated by Aberdeen of the British government, President Tyler followed the course of compromise adopted by his predecessors. Secretary Webster had been inclined to yield to British wishes in Oregon in consideration of British acquiescence in America's acquisition of territory in California. His successor, Upshur, in reply to Aberdeen's renewed instructions (of August 18, 1843) offering to negotiate either with Edward Everett at London or (through Fox) with the Department of State at Washington, chose negotiations at Washington and indicated his willingness to compromise by accepting the line of 49°. In his instructions of October 9 to Everett, he fully reviewed the bases of American claims on the Northwest Coast, and the efforts at adjustment in 1823–24. After denying that Spain by the Nootka Sound Convention of 1790 had ceded to Great Britain any territorial rights, he clearly indicated the administration policy of compromise. "The offer of the 49th parallel of latitude, although it has once been rejected," said he, "may be again tendered, together with the right of navigating the Columbia upon equitable terms. Beyond this the President is not prepared to go. Nevertheless, you may propose or receive, subject to the approval of this government, any other terms of compromise which in the progress of your discussions may appear to promise a satisfactory adjustment."

President Tyler, in his annual message of December, 1843, announced to Congress that the American government by new instructions would resort to every proper expedient "to bring the negotiation now in progress of resumption to a speedy and happy termination," but that nothing would be done to compromise the rights or honor of the United States. At the same time he repeated previous recommendations for establishment of military posts to protect hardy adventurers from hostile Indian tribes on the line of travel to Oregon.[9]

Late in 1843, the British government entrusted the proposed negotiations to Pakenham who had recently succeeded Fox as British minister at Washington, and who promptly (late in February) sought an interview with Upshur. After some delay resulting (in part) from the death of Upshur, the negotiations (which had remained as Gallatin left them in 1827) were finally resumed in August, 1844 by Secretary Calhoun who recently in the Senate (in January 1843) had favored a policy of "wise and masterly inactivity," but who now acted upon the order of the anxious President Tyler.[10]

Calhoun declined Pakenham's offer to agree upon a boundary at 49° from the Rockies to the northeast branch of the Columbia and thence down the Columbia to the Pacific, with provisions for American free navigation of the river and ownership of some territory at the entrance of the Strait of Juan de Fuca and the choice of a port or ports south of 49° on the mainland or on Vancouver Island. Later, he refused Pakenham's offer (of January 15, 1845) to arbitrate, and stated the President's belief that a settlement could be reached by direct negotiations.

In February, 1845, just before the inauguration of Polk as his successor, and in reply to a recent request of the Senate for information concerning progress in the Oregon negotiations, President Tyler stated that discussions had been conducted in a friendly spirit; but his administration closed without any progress toward adjustment of the issue.[11]

Meantime, in connection with the presidential nominations and campaign of 1844, the Oregon question had become a chief issue. James K. Polk was nominated at Baltimore by the Democrat convention which declared the American right to all of Oregon (in order to satisfy the Democrats of the middle Northwest). In his successful campaign for election he approved the popular cry of "54°40′ or fight." In accord with the decided stand of the campaign slogan, he confidently asserted in his inaugural address (of March 4, 1845) that the United States had a clear and unquestionable title to all of Oregon and should extend American jurisdiction to it for the benefit of American settlers there.

In considering this unofficial assertion of Polk the British ministry spoke in a similarly defiant tone, but Lord Aberdeen explained (in the House of Lords on April 4) that it should not be regarded as having the same importance as an official executive document presented to Congress. In the Commons Sir Robert Peel referred to it with an expression of regret for the indiscretion, and with a calm assurance of British readiness to maintain British rights if invaded.

Promptly thereafter, Aberdeen approved initial efforts in a difficult task to prepare the British cabinet and the British public for concession on the Oregon question. These efforts began with the publication of an editorial article in the columns of the Opposition newspaper, the *London Examiner,* on April 26, prepared by Nassau W. Senior, a British economist, who in the collection of data was aided by Edward Everett, the American minister at London. They were soon continued by an elaborated article in the *Edinburgh Review,* the principal organ of the Whig party and later by an editorial in the *Times* which was regarded as inspired by the Foreign Office and which was followed by an article in the *Quarterly Review.*[12]

Later, in finding a practical way of escape from earlier radical and uncompromising policy, and a practical course for conduct of negotiations with the friendly and moderate Aberdeen, President Polk was aided by two able and experienced

American public men of discretion and moderation. One was the Secretary of State, James Buchanan, who between his periods of service with the House and the Senate of the United States had been the American minister to Russia (1832–34). The other was the American minister to England, Louis McLane, who after service in both houses of Congress had successively served as minister to England (1829–31), Secretary of the Treasury (1831–33), and Secretary of State (1833–34).

On July 12, 1845, Secretary Buchanan, in resuming with Pakenham the negotiations at the point reached in the previous September under his predecessor (who had declined the British proposal), explained to the British minister that the American title to the part of Oregon between the Columbia and 54°40′ was recorded in the Florida Treaty of 1819 with Spain, who (before the treaty) had a good title to all the territory "as against Great Britain." The British claims under the Nootka Sound Convention of 1790, which were not mentioned in the negotiations of 1818, he regarded as without foundation. The American title to the valley of the Columbia he declared was older than the treaty of 1819 and independent of its provisions. He stated, however, that the President, finding himself "embarrassed if not committed by the acts of his predecessors" (Monroe and Adams) in favor of friendly compromise, had instructed him to propose in the interest of peace and harmony a division of the territory at the parallel of 49° from the Rockies to the Pacific and to offer to Great Britain free ports on Vancouver's Island south of this parallel.[13]

At the same time, he sent to McLane at London (for his information) a carefully prepared historical sketch of previous propositions which had been rejected, beginning with 1818. He also submitted an explanation of Polk's decision not to concede the privilege of the navigation of the Columbia, which he thought would be a perpetual source of strife and collision between citizens of the two nations. He intimated that the only possible concession which could be made south of 49° (for adequate equivalent) was that of the small cape of Vancouver's Island which would be of no importance to the United States and was of considerable value to Great Britain. After expressing the President's conclusion that he could with no dishonor pursue the course adopted by his Revolutionary predecessor (Monroe) and consistently accepted by all succeeding administrations, he instructed McLane to enforce upon the British the compromise proposition which he offered only in the interest of consistency with previous policy. He added the consoling declaration that the President in case his proposition should be rejected would be "relieved from the embarrassment in which he has been involved by the acts, offers and declarations of his predecessors." "Afterwards," said he, "if the difficulty can only be resolved by the sword, we may then appeal, with confidence, to the world for the equity and justice of our cause, and may anticipate the smiles of Heaven upon the right." [14]

This friendly and liberal proposition, which he approved on the bases of the principles of consistency of policy and continuity of the established cis-Rocky boundary and in the interest of peace, he withdrew on August 30 by a note to Pakenham by direct order of the President, following the invitation of the British minister to consider another proposal (of July 29) "more consistent with fairness and equity and with the expectations of the British Government." He especially resented the action of Pakenham in rejecting his proposition without even a reference to his own Government, although apparently he was pleased with the effect of the British rejection in relieving the President from the embarrassment in which he had been placed by the acts of his predecessors. In his reply he ventured to assert that "to Spain and the United States belongs all the merit of the discovery of the northwest coast of America south of the Russian line," and he added that the "Spanish American title now held by the United States, embracing the whole territory between the parallels of 42° and 54°40′, is the best title in existence to this entire region." [15]

The British government, contemplating the probability of a call to maintain the national honor, had already considered the possibilities of war. On September 7, 1844, during the excitement of the American presidential campaign, Peel had submitted to Lord Stanley a confidential communication in which he stated that any great expenditure on military land defenses as a protective measure against the hostile disposition of the Americans would be a loss "so far as the Canadian policy is concerned." He favored dignified efforts to secure mutual adherence to the letter and spirit of engagements concerning the amount of armaments; but he added that the British government, if it could not get satisfaction, had no alternative except counter-armament. On August 12, 1845, Stanley, after receiving from Lord Metcalfe "a very wild letter on the chances of war with the United States," expressed to Peel the opinion that in case of war the British "operations on the Canadian frontier must be purely defensive." This opinion was contrary to that of Metcalfe and also to the earlier expensive plan formulated by Wellington in 1826.[16]

At the end of August, against Buchanan's desire to avoid strong measures (which might lead to war), the President decided to reaffirm the Monroe doctrine against European colonization or interference on the continent of North America. In October, in connection with the preparation of his first annual message he obtained approval of his cabinet for a proposed clause relating to the Oregon question and the Monroe doctrine. In his message of December he deprecated the early attempts at compromise of the Oregon boundary, and boldly rejoiced that a compromise line was impossible. Standing firmly on his party platform he recommended various measures incident to the uncompromising assertion of the claim to all of Oregon. After reviewing the Oregon controversy, and while claiming that he was still desirous of peace, he advised Congress to give the notice necessary for termination of joint occupation. He also recommended legislation to provide for extension of jurisdiction and for proper defense of the route of emigration.[17]

By December 13, 1845, probably influenced by the view of Secretary Buchanan, Polk began to prepare the way for renewal of negotiations by a suggestion that he might submit to the Senate for its previous advice any proposal of Pakenham to offer with the Strait of Fuca an equivalent of free ports north of 49°. Buchanan recognized that the Oregon question was approaching a crisis which "might involve the issue of peace or war." He instructed McLane that any new movement toward adjustment must originate with the British government, which, according to reports, was "making extensive warlike preparations" (possibly not connected with the Oregon question). He also explained that the President, before making a final decision on any new British proposition, would submit it to the Senate for the previous advice of that body which must share the responsibility.[18]

Preceding Polk's decision to submit to the Senate (for its previous advice) any new British proposition, and, apparently in accord with an understanding with the administration, Senator Cass (on December 9) offered a motion looking toward defensive measures. He soon followed it (on December 15) with a speech of "foaming patriotism," in which he raised the "storm signal" of an approaching crisis indicative of possible war. Three days later, Senator Allen of the Senate Committee on Foreign Affairs submitted a joint resolution in favor of terminating the convention of 1827—a resolution which was opposed by Calhoun and Webster, who favored time for sober reflection. On December 29, Hannegan introduced resolutions declaring that the American government had no power to transfer its soil and that the title to the territory between 42° and 54°40′ was not open to compromise. In the House, similar resolutions were proposed. Several leaders of the middle West, possibly influenced by the annoyances resulting from British colonial commercial policy, restlessly demanded that the administration should stand on its platform and fulfill the pledge to hold all of Oregon, which was regarded as a key to the Pacific and the East.[19]

On December 29, 1845, Buchanan declined a British offer to refer to a friendly power the question of an "equitable division" of the territory. This refusal he said was justified on the ground that acceptance would have been regarded an admission that the President had erred in asserting the American title to all the territory. Late in the following January, he regarded as equally objectionable Pakenham's modified proposition for arbitration of "the question of title in either of the two powers to the whole territory," a proposition which also provided for possible division of the territory by the arbiter "according to a just appreciation of the claims of each" party. In his instruction to McLane, after commenting upon the objections and upon the increasing intensity of public opinion in favor of the President's policy of asserting a right to all of Oregon, he declared the President's fixed determination not to place in jeopardy the American claim to territory on the Northwest Coast by referring it to the decision of any individual, whether sovereigns, citizens or subjects. Suggesting that the Senate might advise the President not to insist upon the full extent of the American rights, he said that the American government "could never place it in the power of any arbitrator to deprive us of a foot of the soil on the continent south of the 49th parallel of latitude, and of the valuable harbors of Puget's Sound." Cautiously seeking the British ultimatum he significantly added: "If the British Government intends to make a proposition to this Government, they have not an hour to lose, if they desire a peaceful termination of this controversy." In concluding he declared: "The President will accept nothing less than the whole territory, unless the Senate should otherwise determine." [20]

That war was expected by Great Britain was shown by the correspondence between London and Canada concerning measures of defense. On February 3, 1846, in replying to Cathcart's recent letters concerning the defense of Canada, Gladstone confidentially requested him to consider the general views of Stanley's confidential dispatch of September 15, 1845, to Lord Metcalfe and, acting under those views, to use any means in his power to expedite the works on the canals of the St. Lawrence and on the Welland Canal in order to open communication between the sea and the Lakes, and also to submit to the provincial legislatures a measure for prompt levy and organization of an adequate militia force (30,000) in case of war. Under the stimulation of the situation which seemed to threaten interruption in amicable relations with Canada, he also considered the question of better mail connection, especially a proposed post-road from Halifax to the St. Lawrence at a point 207 miles below Quebec.[21]

On February 3 McLane reported that Aberdeen, without abandoning his hope to preserve peace, felt obliged to withdraw his previous opposition against preparations which others had regarded as necessary for protection and defense of the Canadas and for offensive operations of war in the contingency. Later, however, on March 17, he explained to Buchanan that Aberdeen in his friendly interview on this subject evidently had no purpose of menace.[22]

Meantime, by February, McLane suggested to Buchanan that Aberdeen, anxious for peace and a good understanding and embarrassed by the situation arising from President Polk's determined attitude, would probably agree to 49°. He stated that both parties in England strongly disapproved Pakenham's rejection of the American proposition without submitting it to his government. Confident that, "without any improper commitment of the President," he could informally and personally lead the way to renewal of negotiations at Washington on the American basis offered in the preceding July, "with some modifications not inconsistent . . . with our national honor," he tactfully expressed a wish that he could officially know whether the proposition would be acceptable at Washington. "I would not be unwilling," said he, "to urge a final adjustment . . . according to that proposition, but conceding to the Hudson Bay Company a continuance of the privileges of joint occupation, including the navigation of the Columbia for a period of seven or ten years or longer. I would be willing to assume the responsibility of an adjustment by extending the boundary to the Pacific by the 49th parallel and the Strait of Fuca with free ports to both nations; or by extending the free navigation of the Columbia for a longer period, provided similar advantages upon the St. Lawrence could thereby be secured to the United States."[23]

On February 4, Buchanan rejected Pakenham's renewed proposal of arbitration, indicating among his reasons his belief that the national territorial rights in such a large and important contiguous area (nearly thirteen degrees of latitude along the Pacific Coast) were not a proper subject of arbitration. After explaining the President's refusal to adopt any measure which would transfer from the American government and people the control of American title to territory, he suggested that the two nations ought to be able or willing to do each other justice without the interposition of an arbitrator. On February 26, transmitting to McLane a copy of the reply to Pakenham, he suggested the "other powerful reasons" against the proposed treaty arbitration: (1) the probability that the constitutional majority of the Senate necessary for its approval for ratification could not be obtained, and that rejection by the Senate would involve the question in far greater embarrassments and render adjustment more difficult; (2) the dangerous post-ratification delays in the process toward final termination of the controversy, delays which would probably postpone the final award for several years during which the swelling tide of emigration would constantly increase the danger of collisions in the territory; (3) and the difficulty of selecting suitable arbitrators, whether from the sovereigns of Europe or from individuals. At the same time, referring to Aberdeen's complaint of the terms and manner in which he had declined Pakenham's first proposal of arbitration, and to the British apprehension that the President had determined to discourage any new proposition on the basis of compromise, he stated that the President had always been ready to receive and to treat with the utmost respect any British official proposal for compromise.

Expressing the President's regret that Aberdeen had determined to withdraw his opposition to British preparation of armaments "founded upon the contingency of war with the United States," he asserted that a British naval demonstration on the American coasts would not intimidate the American people, but would arouse the national indignation to a degree which would "render any compromise of the question entirely hopeless."

Concerning McLane's confident opinion that he could probably lead the British government to renew negotiations on a satisfactory basis, Buchanan frankly stated that the President, whose own opinion remained unchanged, recognized the constitutional responsibilities of the Senate as a portion of the treaty making power and also as a part of the war-making power, and would submit to that body for its previous advice any British proposition not inconsistent with American national rights and honor. He suggested that, judging from recent proceedings in that body, the Senate would probably consider favorably a special proposition to adjust the Oregon question on the parallel of 49°. Concerning the question of a "continuance of the privileges of the Hudson's Bay Company" for a limited period he distinctly stated that he could not agree to any concession which would deprive the American government of the power to establish territorial government and to make grants of land south of 49°. He also frankly asserted that the President, desiring to avoid any concession from which might arise new difficulties and which might "become a perpetual cause of strife and collision," could not agree to submit any proposition which contemplated an American concession of a perpetual British right to navigate the Columbia—not even if the British should offer as an equivalent the free navigation of the St. Lawrence, which (he said) had become "comparatively valueless in consequence of the construction of railroads and canals leading to the harbors of New York and Boston." Only with some reluctance would he consent to submit a proposition to surrender the cape of Vancouver Island, by accepting the water boundary of the Strait of Fuca as a modification of the western end of the line of 49°, without the previous proposition of free ports but with a distinct understanding that the Strait is an arm of the sea.[24]

Meantime, on February 25, McLane had an interview with Aberdeen which furnished the basis of a long dispatch of March 3 concerning the embarrassing situation and the possibilities of future negotiations. Apparently his chief purpose was to coöperate with Buchanan in preparing the President to encourage further negotiations for a compromise. He doubted whether Aberdeen would accept without modification the partition proposition offered by Gallatin in 1826–27, but thought he would favor an equitable partition to save the honor of each country. He guessed that he would probably assent to nothing better than the extension of the line of 49° to the Strait of Fuca and the middle of the Strait to the Pacific, with the free navigation of the Columbia if the latter should prove to be navigable to 49°; but he reported Aberdeen's declaration that under no circumstances would he agree to treat of the navigation of the St. Lawrence in connection with that of the Columbia. Unwilling to believe that the British government "at the certain consequence of war" would insist upon the navigation of the Columbia for a longer period than was required for the reasonable accommodation of the rights of the Hudson's Bay Company which had grown up during joint occupancy, he hoped that the American government might be able to offer a reasonable concession for ten or fifteen years without any sacrifice of American rights or honor. He concluded his dispatches with an expression of regret that, in the face of the universal British disposition to sustain the British claims, so many American writers (such as "one of the contributors to the last *North American Review*") diligently refuted the rights asserted by the American government—thus encouraging unreasonable foreign demands which might lead to war.

On March 17, following another friendly interview with Aberdeen and still hopeful of future renewal of negotiations upon satisfactory terms, he assured Buchanan that "next to just and honest dispositions on both sides the best hope of an amicable adjustment . . . will consist in keeping the negotiation as much as possible in the hands of those to whom the Constitution confines it; and certainly to discourage speculations in the public press, and especially in one so closely connected with the Government as the *Union*." Again, referring to the importance of dignified moderation and reserve (such as that shown by Aberdeen and the British ministry), he wrote: "It has been . . . our misfortune in the United States, in the conduct of the Oregon question, to have more negotiators out of office [not official] than are to be found officially engaged in its management; and it will be fortunate for the peace of the two countries, if those who are so indefatigable in gratuitously enlightening the public, in newspaper essays and in individual correspondence, be not found in the end to be the most efficient promoters of a catastrophe that all good and wise men deprecate." [25] Later he suggested that American division of opinion, and especially the opposition of Senators against the executive policy, was liable to defeat the efforts to preserve peace and had already influenced the determination of the British government to postpone further steps toward negotiations of the Oregon question until after the final decision of Congress upon the resolutions of notice to terminate joint-occupation.[26]

Early in April, McLane reported that Peel had declined to submit to the House of Commons any official diplomatic correspondence on uncompleted negotiations relative to Oregon except that which had already been made public by the American government.[27]

Meantime, the prospects of peaceful solution had clearly improved. To this improvement, Congress contributed by its tendency toward a more moderate tone. On March 4 and 5, Senator Haywood, after consultation with the President to prepare the way for a compromise, maintained that neither Polk nor the Baltimore platform had claimed territory between 49° and 54°40′ and, therefore, that the acceptance of 49° would not be inconsistent. Both Webster and Calhoun said the people were beginning to regard 49° as the best basis of compromise. Over a month later, on April 16, after long debates, the Senate by a vote of 40 to 16 approved a mild and dignified resolution authorizing the President "in his discretion" to give the necessary year's notice to terminate the convention of joint occupation—a resolution similar to one which had been approved by the House on February 9. The result was the passage of a joint resolution of April 23 which was promptly approved by the President on April 27.[28]

Secretary Buchanan felt that the way had now been prepared for a new British proposal. Already, on March 28, referring to Aberdeen's statement that one possible alternative in renewing negotiations was to offer a proposition through McLane, he had written the latter: "You are authorized to receive and transmit to this Department any proposition made by him; but in no event will the President consent to transfer the negotiation to London." A month later, on April 28, by authority of the President, he forwarded to McLane the notice to terminate the treaty, submitting with it instructions to deliver it with due formality. Incidentally he mentioned the President's opinion that the controversy might have been adjusted more speedily and upon better terms to the United States if Congress had adopted a naked resolution in the previous December. He repeated the earlier declaration that the President, without initiating further negotiations by distinct invitation, was prepared to receive with respect any British proposal for compromise of the Oregon question. He said the first proposal clearly should proceed from the British government.[29] Fortunately there was no longer any serious danger of rupture, and probably there had been little danger since February.

Coincidently (April 28), at London, McLane, who had lamented the delay of the action of the Senate and the opposition to the notice which he thought would accelerate and facilitate negotiations for settlement of the question, had an interview with Aberdeen concerning the probable nature of the contemplated new British proposition for reopening negotiations. In a dispatch (of May 3) reporting the chief points discussed he said Aberdeen still maintained the right to consider as a basis or starting point the offers of 1826 and 1827 (which, after rejection, had been withdrawn) and had suggested that some further concessions might be added as a *salvo* to national honor and pride.

Apparently the chief point of discussion was the question of British navigation of the Columbia which Gallatin had offered in his proposition of two decades earlier. McLean contended that, as a result of the recent American emigration movement to Oregon, the British could not with justice long insist upon this earlier right, even if the upper branches of the river should be navigable from 49° to the main stem (which was not navigable to the ocean without the use of portages).[30]

On May 15, McLane received Buchanan's instructions concerning the notice to abrogate the convention of joint-occupation. Following a long conference with Aberdeen concerning the resumption of negotiations for amicable adjustment by partition of the territory in dispute, he promptly reported (on May 18) that the British instruction to Pakenham would probably contain a proposition for the line of 49° and the Strait of Fuca, for perpetual titles to British citizens occupying lands south of that line (in American jurisdiction) and for free navigation of the Columbia under American sovereignty (without any concession as to the navigation of the St. Lawrence). Although he had discouraged any expectation that it would be accepted by the President or approved by the Senate, he suggested that the British government was relying upon its acceptance by the Senate. He recognized that, since the publication of the President's message and the subsequent discussion in the Senate, future negotiations could not be conducted without reference to the opinions of members of the Senate; and, therefore, he suggested the importance of securing the previous consent of the Senate to any modification which the President might think proper to propose to Pakenham's offer. He stated his belief that, if the proposed boundary was acceptable, the British demand of a right to free navigation of the Columbia "could be compromised upon a point of time." He significantly suggested that the American government probably could not expect to receive better terms from the prospective new British ministry.

Later (on June 3) following the news of the beginning of the Mexican War and in commenting upon the British attitude and apprehensions, he suggested that the existence of the war and the feeling which it excited in England would "make it much more difficult if not impossible to obtain any material modification of the offer recently submitted through Mr. Pakenham." He also regretted to find an increasing "probability of an early change of ministry." He seemed somewhat apprehensive of British shipments of war materials which he believed were sent to Canada with a view to the possible necessity of defensive operations against the United States.[31]

The negotiations to find a way to solve the difficulty resulting from Pakenham's rejection of Polk's offer of 49°, and from Polk's refusal to renew the offer, finally resulted in an arrangement for British initiative in a new proposal. Under Aberdeen's instructions to Pakenham, issued after receipt of Polk's notice of the abrogation of the convention of 1827 and received at Washington just after the vote of the Commons to repeal the British corn laws, negotiations on the Oregon question were renewed at Washington on June 6—after the resignation of the Peel ministry and the retirement of Aberdeen from office.

They proposed to agree upon a boundary at 49° to the water channel south of Vancouver Island, and thence through the Strait of San Juan de Fuca to the Pacific, and with reservations of free navigation of the Columbia.[32]

On June 10, after consultation with the Cabinet, and trusting to the exertions of Benton and the Whigs to relieve him from an embarrassing situation, Polk confidently submitted to the Senate the situation and asked its previous advice concerning negotiations on the terms proposed by the British government. Thus, warning the Senate that rejection might result in war, he shifted the responsibility for his change of policy and at the same time declared that his views had not changed since the date of his annual message. On June 12, the Senate by a vote of 37 to 12 (after brief debate of two days) advised acceptance of the terms, with the understanding that the right of the Hudson's Bay Company to navigate the Columbia would expire on May 30, 1859 (the limit of its license to trade with the Indians of the Northwest coast). Three days later, on June 15, Buchanan signed with Pakenham a treaty similar to that which Aberdeen had outlined to McLane, agreeing to the line of 49° and the Strait of Fuca and conceding to Great Britain free navigation of the Columbia.[33]

This treaty, to which the Senate promptly gave its assent on June 18 by a vote of 41 to 14, was mutually ratified by the two governments on July 17. Thus, a serious boundary controversy, which threatened to precipitate war, was peacefully adjusted by a reasonable compromise which established a logical line of division—probably the most logical that geographers and statesmen and politicians could have planned. The American government "for the sake of peace consented to a deflection from the parallel of 49° so as to leave Vancouver's Island undivided to Great Britain."[34]

To those who desired a line farther north Benton stated that the line of 49° had been favored by Jefferson and four later presidents, and that it marked the northern limit of the best land. He added that in his opinion Vancouver Island was one of the most worthless of the thousand worthless islands of the Northwest coast archipelago and that he would not accept it as a present. In direct opposition to this opinion, American officials in 1855, after making a reconnaissance of Oregon, reported that the island was the key to the Northwest coast and should belong to the United States. In the decade after 1846 occasionally appeared other evidence of a lingering American hope of acquiring, by accretion and assimilation, additional territory beyond the established northern boundary.[35]

The further development of Oregon was encouraged by new immigration, by the establishment of a temporary territorial government in 1848 and by a project of a railroad from Lake Michigan to the Columbia River.[36]

Either from the carelessness of the treaty negotiators or from their lack of geographic knowledge, a new Anglo-American difference of opinion arose in regard to the exact location of the water boundary east of the southern end of Vancouver Island, southward from the parallel of 49° in the middle of the Gulf of Georgia to the Strait of Juan de Fuca, resulting in conflict of jurisdiction on San Juan Island, between Haro channel, upon which Americans had begun to settle in 1854–56, and Rosario Strait. The dispute began in 1854 by the seizure and sale of certain ships of the Hudson's Bay Company which had failed to pay taxes levied by local authorities of Washington Territory. Following a protest from Governor Douglas of Vancouver Island, and with a desire to seek a peaceful situation, President Pierce in 1856 arranged with the British government to settle the question by appointment of two commissioners, one American and one British. These commissioners, who met at Esquimalt in June, 1857, reached opposing conclusions and could agree on nothing except to disagree.[37]

In 1859, following new immigrations and increasing settlements along the water boundary, arose a new and more serious local dispute in regard to jurisdiction on San Juan Island, resulting in a temporary American military occupation of the island by rash orders of Brigadier General Harney (without orders from Washington) and also in a consequent British establishment of a rival camp. With a desire to relieve the serious situation, President Buchanan sent to the region General Winfield Scott who removed the American troops from the island and arranged for a joint occupation (to begin March 30, 1860) to secure observance of the spirit of the earlier Marcy-Crampton precautionary arrangement for abstention of acts of force which might provoke conflict before the governments could settle the question by treaty.[38] In December, 1859, he explained to Congress the satisfactory changes in the situation.[39]

At the same time the President recognized that the question of title might seriously threaten friendly relations unless adjusted without long delay. Disappointed by Lord John Russell's objectionable and re-affirmed declaration that the British government would accept no settlement which did not provide for reservation of San Juan to the British,[40] and hoping that American rights could be established by friendly discussion and without further collision,[41] he directed Secretary Cass to issue the counter declaration that the United States under all circumstances would maintain its right to the island until the determination of the question of title by some amicable arrangement between the parties to the dispute.[42]

Meantime, another source of border controversy influenced the discussion of the San Juan question. The American gold hunters who migrated to the Fraser River region in 1857–58 complained of various exactions at Vancouver Island and for a time their threats of insubordination to the British authorities there furnished Governor Douglas some cause for alarm.[43] To relieve these new sources of irritation, the American government appealed to the London government to prevent Governor Douglas' proposed exclusion of Americans from navigation of the Fraser River and the mines of New Caledonia (later British Columbia)[44] and (in August, 1858) also sent John Nugent to Vancouver Island as an agent to infuse among the Americans temporarily resident in the vicinity a spirit of subordination to the colonial British authorities and to seek to obtain from the governor the abrogation or abatement of the rigorous exactions by which the Americans had been irritated.[45] Although by 1859 the larger number of dissatisfied American immigrants to the new British gold region had returned to California and Oregon, possibly over 3,000 remained as prospectors or residents. They established in British Columbia an American influence which doubtless stimulated the later agitation for American annexation of British Columbia to the United States.

Another subject of controversy in the fifties, and in the early sixties, was the possessory rights and claims of the Hudson's Bay Company and its accessory, Puget Sound Agricultural Company, under the treaty of 1846. Soon after the conclusion of the treaty both companies began to complain of invasion of their rights, resulting in uncompleted negotiations between 1848 and 1850 for disposition of their interests. In 1854 their extraordinary claims to trade with the Indians of Oregon and Washington territories were denied by Secretary Marcy.[46] After nearly another decade of controversy, a final settlement of all their rights and claims was satisfactorily arranged by a treaty of July, 1863, which provided for appointment of a commission and an arbitrator or umpire. This commission (Alex. S. Johnson of New York and Sir John Rose of Canada) met at Washington in January, 1865, and promptly selected an umpire (Benjamin R. Curtis). Four years later, September 10, 1869, it submitted its award, deciding that the American government should pay $450,000 to the Hudson's Bay Company and $200,000 to the Puget Sound Agricultural Company for the transfer and release of all rights and claims.[47]

REFERENCES

1. *Sen. Docs.*, 25–2, Vol. 1, No. 24.
2. RICHARDSON (ed.), *Messages and Papers*, III, 398.
3. *Sen. Docs.*, 25–2, Vol. 1, No. 24; *Senate Journal*, October 16, 1837; *Exec. Docs.*, 25–2, Vol. 2, No. 43.
4. *15 G.B., Instrs.*, pp. 3–4, No. 74, May 6, 1840.
5. *Cong. Globe*, 27–3, 240; MCMASTER, *U.S.*, VII, pp. 286–88.
6. *21 G.B., Notes [from]*, Nov. 14, 1842; *6 G.B., Notes to*, p. 278, Nov. 25, 1842; RICHARDSON (ed.), *Messages and Papers*, IV, 196; *Sen. Docs.*, 29–1, No. 1, pp. 139–40.
7. *Cong. Globe*, 27–2, p. 736, and 27–3, *passim* (Appendix, pp. 38, 110–12 and 149–55).
8. *21 G.B., Notes [from]*, Fox to Upshur, June 25, 1843.
9. *15 G.B., Instrs.*, No. 2, July 12, 1845; *18 Regular-Confidential Docs., U.S. Senate*, pp. 27–32; RICHARDSON, *Messages and Papers*, IV, 258.

10. *Exec. Docs.*, 29–1, No. 2, p. 141; Calhoun's *Works*, IV, 238.
11. McMaster, *U.S.*, VII, pp. 303–304, 408.
12. *Ib.*, pp. 350, 408–09; *Van Buren Papers;* Hansard, *Parliamentary Debates*, LXXIX, 115–23, 178–99; *London Examiner*, Apr. 26, 1845; *Washington Daily Union*, May 29; *Edinburgh Rev.*, July, 1845, pp. 238–65; Everett Mss., Mass. Hist. Soc.; *Quart. Rev.*, March, 1846; *Times*, Jan. 3, 1846.
13. *7 G.B., Notes to,* pp. 76–89, July 12, 1845; *Ib.*, pp. 89–121, Aug. 30, 1845; *15 G.B., Instrs.*, No. 2, July 12, 1845; *18 Regular-Confidential Docs., U. S. Senate*, pp. 27–32.
14. *15 G.B., Instrs.*, pp. 271–81, No. 2, Buchanan to McLane, July 12, 1845.
15. *7 G.B., Notes to,* pp. 89–121, Aug. 30, 1845; *Polk's Diary*, Aug. 30, 1845.
16. Charles Stuart Parker, *Sir Robert Peel*, Vol. 3, pp. 195 and 216.
17. Polk's *Diary*, Oct. 24, 25, 27 and 29, 1845.
18. *Ib.*, Dec. 23, 1845; *15 G.B., Instrs.*, pp. 283–85, No. 20, Dec. 13, 1845.
19. *Cong. Globe*, 29–1, pp. 197, 239–48 and 834.
20. *15 G.B., Instrs.*, p. 285, No. 21, Dec. 29, 1845; *Ib.*, pp. 296–99, No. 22, Jan. 29, 1846.
21. *C.A.*, G, 123, pp. 204–07, 209–17, 227–46, 247–57; *56 England, Despatches*, No. 34, Feb. 3, 1846.
22. *Ib.*, No. 36, Mar. 17, 1846.
23. *Ib.*, No. 34, Feb. 3, 1846.
24. *7 G.B., Notes to,* pp. 130–34, Feb. 4, 1846; *15 G.B., Instrs*, pp. 299–307, No. 23, Feb. 26, 1846.
25. *56 England, Despatches* (No. 35), Mar. 3, and (No. 36), Mar. 17, 1846.
26. *Ib.*, No. 37, Apr. 3, 1846.
27. *Ib.*
28. *Cong. Globe*, 29–1, p. 349; *Niles' Register*, LXX, 394.
29. *15 G.B., Instrs.*, pp. 308–09, No. 26, Mar. 20, 1846; *Ib.*, pp. 292–94, No. 38, Apr. 28, 1846; *Niles' Register*, CXX, 394.
30. *56 England, Despatches*, No. 43, May 3, 1846.
31. *Ib.* (No. 44), May 18, and (No. 54), Apr. 3, 1846.
32. *Ib.*, No. 44, May 18, 1846; *Cong. Globe*, 29–1, Appendix, p. 1170.
33. Richardson (ed.), *Messages and Papers*, IV, 449; *15 G.B., Instrs.*, pp. 312–13, No. 34, June 13, 1846; *Journal of Senate; Cong. Globe*, 29–1, Appendix, p. 1168; *Sen. Docs.*, 29–1, Nos. 476 and 489.
34. *Ib.;* also, *17 G.B., Instrs.*, pp. 229–54, No. 209, Oct. 20, 1859; *Washington Chronicle*, Jan. 28, 1868 (article by R. J. Walker).
35. Sumner's *Works*, Vol. 12; *Cong. Globe*, 32–2, Jan. 10 (Appendix) and Jan. 15, 1853.

36. *Reports Committees,* 30–1, Vol. 3, No. 733; *House Reports Committees,* 31–1; No. 439.
37. *7 G.B., Notes to,* p. 436, July 22, 1854; *Ib.,* pp. 485–86, July 17, 1855; *17 G.B., Instrs.,* pp. 229–54, No. 195, Sept. 22, 1859; *Sen. Docs.,* 40–2, No. 20; BANCROFT, *History of British Columbia.*
38. *17 G.B., Instrs.,* p. 221, No. 196, Sept. 24, 1859; *Ib.,* p. 330, No. 262, June 8, 1860; *Amer. State Papers, Exec. Docs.,* 36–1, No. 65, pp. 28ff; *Sen. Exec. Docs.,* 35–2, Vol. 10, No. 29; *H. Exec. Docs.,* 35–2, No. 111, Mar. 3, 1859.
39. RICHARDSON (ed.), *Messages and Papers,* V, 561–63.
40. *17 G.B., Instrs.,* pp. 229–54, No. 209, Oct. 20, 1859.
41. *8 G.B., Notes to,* pp. 262–64, Oct. 22, 1859.
42. *17 G.B., Instrs.,* pp. 269–74, No. 231, Feb. 4, 1860; *39 G.B., Notes* [*from*], No. 123, Dec. 16, 1859.
43. E. D. BRANCH, *Westward,* pp. 503, 505; *Sen. Exec. Docs.,* 35–2, Vol. 10, pp. 1–30, No. 29, Jan. 29, 1859 (Nugent's report of Jan. 8).
44. *17 G.B., Instrs.,* pp. 108–09, No. 108, May 24, 1858.
45. *Sen. Exec. Docs.,* 35–2, Vol. 10, No. 29.
46. *7 G.B., Notes to,* pp. 416–17, Apr. 22, 1854.
47. MALLOY, *Treaties and Conventions,* Vol. 1, pp. 688–91; J. B. MOORE, *International Arbitrations,* Vol. 1, pp. 237–70; RICHARDSON (ed.), *Messages and Papers,* VII, 35.

CHAPTER XI

THE RECIPROCITY TREATY OF 1854

THE Reciprocity Treaty of 1854 originated in the proposals of Canada following Peel's adoption of a new colonial policy which during the Oregon negotiations was mentioned by Aberdeen as a concession to the United States. Originating in Canadian efforts to find a means to avoid trade losses resulting from changes in British economic policy, it was accepted by the American government as a convenient way to secure an adjustment of American northeast fishery rights, to meet the demands of the growing western trade and the expectations of eastern manufacturers, and possibly to cultivate a growing desire for closer future political relations. It was an interesting American-Canadian experiment which followed almost a decade of preparatory consideration and was terminated after scarcely more than a decade of trial.

The question of the fisheries which after 1850 furnished Canada a convenient make-weight in its plans for trade had become a subject of controversy under the operation of the Nova Scotia "Hovering Act" of 1836, which by various regulations and penalties sought to prevent the hovering of vessels within three miles of the coasts and harbors. It had become more prominent after 1839 as a result of Nova Scotian policy to exclude American fishermen from all bays, and even from all waters within lines drawn from headland to headland and to deny them all privileges of traffic in the British colonial ports. By February, 1841, its scope was extended by the threat to close the Strait of Canso which had been used as a free passage to the St. Lawrence since 1783. In 1845, after a wearisome correspondence, the headland interpretation was relaxed for the Bay of Fundy,[1] influencing the United States (in 1846) to reduce the duties on imports of colonial fish and to permit the entrance free in bond.[2]

A prominent influence in the development of trade and trade policy was the opening of railway connection, in 1842, across New York from Albany to Buffalo (parallel to the Erie Canal) and eastward from Albany to Boston, and the later increase of railway communication between the Atlantic and the Lakes and in the old American Northwest, stimulating Canadian responses in canal and railway construction and requests for trade reciprocity.[3]

Following the opening of the railway to Buffalo, which stimulated a House resolution (of April, 1842) requesting the President to open negotiations for an equitable conventional arrangement for trade with Canada,[4] the British Parliament enacted the Canadian corn law of 1843 which favored the St. Lawrence route for shipments of wheat and other western commerce, encouraged efforts to complete the Canadian canal system and stimulated a temporary boom in business at Montreal.[5] This economic advantage it terminated in 1846 by a reversal of policy against the wishes of Canadian commercial interests.[6]

In 1845, Canada unsuccessfully proposed to the British government an imposition of new differential duties on Canadian imports through American territory or a policy to encourage traffic shipments by sea to the St. Lawrence in order to divert them from the route via New York and other American ports.[7] In May, 1846, following protests against Peel's policy of repeal of the colonial preferential duties, it successfully submitted a request to open negotiations for a reciprocal trade arrangement with the United States. By this request it took the first official step toward the new reciprocity movement.[8] Taking prompt advantage of its larger fiscal independence it prepared to abolish differential duties, thereby causing the American Congress to enact a responsive law which permitted the transit of Canadian goods across American territory in bond free of duty (and which incidentally contributed to the diversion of Canadian commerce from the St. Lawrence route to American seaboard ports).[9] At the same time it proposed to the British government to extend American navigation transit on the St. Lawrence below Montreal to Sorel and thence up the Richelieu to Lake Champlain—a privilege which the British Privy Council granted temporarily with a proviso that it must not be claimed later as a right.[10]

In July, 1846, Pakenham received Aberdeen's instructions to open reciprocity negotiations at Washington. After awaiting the result of the Senate debates on the Walker tariff and after obtaining certain data from Canada, he discussed the subject with Walker who regarded it with favor, but action was delayed.[11] In Canada, in 1847, he was aided by the legislative reduction of duties on American imports and by a reciprocity resolution of W. H. Merritt[12] who in 1848 appeared before committees of Congress to urge the adoption of his proposed policy.[13]

Congress was divided on the question. In July, 1848, the House approved a bill for reciprocal free trade in certain articles of natural production; but the Senate tabled it, chiefly on the grounds of its narrow scope, its restriction on the revenue power of the House, and its failure to provide for navigation of the St. Lawrence and for free fishery rights on the coasts of the maritime colonies. The delay in the Senate resulted in an increase of annexation sentiment on the St. Lawrence.[14]

In connection with the consideration of reciprocity in Congress, Canada (through Lord Elgin) sought the views of the British colonial office, which it found favorable.[15] Before the close of 1848 it sought other facilities for freedom of trade: the repeal of the navigation laws and the opening of the free navigation of the St. Lawrence (as a means to attract American grain to Montreal).[16] During the year it coöperated in extending courtesies to the American government by granting requests for passage of American revenue vessels on the St. Lawrence between the Lakes and the ocean.[17]

Early in 1849, the Senate again failed to approve the reciprocity bill, and thereby caused much disappointment in Canada. Possibly it was influenced by the views of Israel DeWolf Andrews, the American consul at St. John, New Brunswick, who was called to Washington for consultation and who advocated a wider measure of reciprocity [18] which would include the free navigation of the St. Lawrence and other larger rivers [19] and the abolition of the New Brunswick export tax on lumber descending the St. John.[20]

At the beginning of the new Whig administration at Washington, the British government showed an increased interest in Canadian-American trade relations. Influenced by Canadian conditions which threatened internal political trouble, and especially by Lord Elgin's warning that the end of British colonial rule in British America might be near, it submitted to Secretary Clayton an invitation to reconsider the question of reciprocity and suggested the hope that an attempt to negotiate a reciprocity treaty might be more successful than legislative action. Following the delivery of this invitation by Crampton, Canada made a friendly homeopathic legislative gesture to which the American government failed to respond—probably because it awaited some assurance of equivalents such as the navigation of the St. Lawrence.[21]

Later, in April, Crampton reported to Palmerston that the uneasy state of political feeling in Canada had resulted in irresponsible predictions of speedy American annexation; but he was confident that the President was determined to prevent the execution of any frontier schemes of violence from American territory.[22] In June, greatly concerned over the continued depression and the consequent discontent in Canada, he reported that a trade arrangement with the United States was vitally necessary. At the same time, he submitted to Clayton a Canadian reciprocity memorandum prepared by W. H. Merritt.

To the latter Clayton promptly replied that the proposed attempt to regulate tariffs by treaty was impracticable, and in conflict with the financial policy of the President. He stated that the American government would not consider any reciprocity arrangement unless it was applicable to all the British North American provinces, and he inquired whether free navigation of the St. Lawrence would be conceded. By declining to negotiate, he incurred the displeasure of the colonial authorities, who later expressed it by a demand for a British armed force to restrict American fishing on the colonial coasts.[23]

Meantime the economic and political situation in lower Canada had continued to grow steadily worse, resulting in an increase of sentiment in favor of annexation to the United States which had prospered by the diversion of western traffic from Montreal to American ports. Efforts to secure prompt remedial British action were unsuccessful.[24] Organized efforts to adopt a remedial program and to counteract the annexation agitation were disappointing in their results.[25] The British act repealing the navigation laws, completing Canadian control of its trade and customs dues, became operative too late to relieve the situation for the current season.[26] Elgin, who continued to urge upon Great Britain the desperate demands of the commercial interests for further trade negotiations with Washington, recognized (by July) the danger of an early severance of the Canadian imperial connection.[27] In this apprehension he was probably justified by his recent experience (in April) with a disorderly mob at Montreal [28] and by the annexation movement on the St. Lawrence [29] which later reached a climax in the famous manifesto of October 10 [30] and met some border frontier encouragement.[31] In England, opinion on the Canadian problem was divided, some favoring separation as a remedy and others advocating imperial measures to strengthen the colonial attachment.[32]

By the close of 1849 the Canadian annexation movement and the contagion of unrest was weakened by a counter-manifesto issued by government leaders at Montreal.[33] In Ontario it was almost universally condemned, and its growth was especially restricted by the warning advice of W. L. Mackenzie and the editorials of George Brown in the *Toronto Globe*.[34] It declined everywhere in the early part of 1850 and collapsed before the close of the year, partly as a result of improvement in economic conditions,[35] and partly because it received no encouragement from the American government and was regarded with apparent indifference by American public opinion.[36]

In the latter part of 1849 the American government had a special avenue of information in regard to the Canadian situation. In July it appointed Israel D. Andrews as a special agent to visit the British provinces and to collect data, especially upon their present and prospective relations, commercial and political, with the United States. Between July and December it received from him several private notes concerning the depression and discontent and the consequent sentiment in favor of reciprocal free trade or annexation.[37] In December, it received from him an extensive report. Thereafter it retained his services as a special agent until July, 1850, when he presented his bill for his salary and expenses.[38]

Andrews, in his report, urged a general comprehensive adjustment with a view to the interests of all the British North American colonies and including both the Atlantic and Pacific fisheries and the navigation of the St. Lawrence. He mentioned as obstacles to further negotiation the hesitation of Canada to join the lower colonies in a general plan, the feeling in the West against proposed Canadian restrictive measures as to the Welland Canal, the opposition in Nova Scotia and Newfoundland against American participation in the sea and coast fisheries, and the refusal of the British government to include Newfoundland in the proposed plans of adjustment.

The British government, influenced by Elgin's reports of the situation and his protests against British assumptions that Canadian separation was ultimately inevitable, finally groped its way toward a solution. Late in 1849 it appointed Sir Henry Lytton Bulwer to conduct reciprocity negotiations with Clayton. It authorized concessions concerning American fishing in colonial waters in return for American free admission of all fish from the British North American possessions, and also offered to concede the free navigation of the St. Lawrence (and its canals) and to forego the British right to navigate the Columbia River.

In January, 1850, at Washington, Bulwer promptly opened negotiations by a note which was promptly followed by consideration of a House reciprocity bill to which Senator Douglas and others sought to add a concession clause on free navigation of the St. Lawrence. In March, in response to a House inquiry (through Clayton) he stated that after the completion of the desired concurrent legislation on reciprocal trade, by action of Congress, the British government (on application of the American government) would promptly consent to open the St. Lawrence and the adjoining canals by a special convention (which he regarded as the suitable way to reach agreement upon an imperial question).[39]

In the Senate, in April, Douglas submitted petitions indicating that free navigation of the St. Lawrence was urged primarily upon the ground of expensive delays in transportation via the New York canals which were crowded beyond their capacity. In reply to Seward's apparent opposition to the St. Lawrence clause, he stated that the additional route of navigation was needed to provide for the increasing trade of the Northwest and that it was not expected to diminish the trade of New York.[40] In the House, in May, Buel of Michigan expressed the opinion that no reciprocity was possible without provision for free navigation of the St. Lawrence. The latter the House committee regarded as a "natural right," but it recommended purchase of the right by some equivalent in case the British remained unmoved by American "natural right" arguments.[41] Although the President (on May 7) submitted the whole subject to the consideration of Congress and furnished full information concerning recent negotiations, both houses postponed the subject, possibly influenced by the strong opposition and by strained Anglo-American relations resulting from rivalry in Central America.[42] On September 14, Secretary Webster suggested to Bulwer that the reciprocity bill seemed more advantageous to Canada.[43]

In the next session, finding that the reciprocity proposal still encountered strong opposition, Congress again failed to reach a vote upon the subject, resulting in a renewal of Canadian disappointment. The House apparently was unaffected by the Canadian attempt to hasten action by a threat of retaliatory legislation. The Senate, by detour, avoided a special order by which Douglas sought to obtain consideration.[44]

On the question of conceding the navigation of the St. Lawrence, the Canadian government apparently was more liberal than the British government. In March, 1851, it was asked by the Colonial Office to explain its recent action in granting (as a special exception) permission for passage of an American vessel, the *Minnesota*, from Lake Superior to Quebec with a cargo of copper.[45]

At the same time, both Elgin and Bulwer were disturbed by Canadian threats to adopt plans of retaliation to hasten American action on trade reciprocity. In March, and again in June, with a desire to relieve Canadian disappointment and dissatisfaction which threatened to result in friction, Bulwer urged upon Webster the necessity of early negotiations for an understanding on a treaty of commercial reciprocity and stated that the British government was willing to open the St. Lawrence and canals and also to open the coast fisheries with conditions.[46]

The American government still hesitated to adopt a policy of action on the question of trade reciprocity. It was told by Andrews that either the refusal or acceptance of reciprocity would result in annexation, immediate or deferred. By others it was advised to accept with non-participation in political propagandism.[47] It encountered difference of opinion as to the best method to regulate trade with Canada. In December the President expressed the opinion that reciprocal legislation was preferable to a treaty. The proposition to combine questions of river navigation and coast fisheries with a trade arrangement was still under discussion.[48]

Early in 1852 Canada sought a new means to encourage in Congress a more favorable attitude toward a trade agreement. In February Hincks submitted to Elgin a recommendation that the British government should grant immediately a concession of the navigation of the St. Lawrence pending the decision on reciprocal trade. In the following May, disappointed by an adverse British decision based upon Malmesbury's opinion that "further concession without countervailing advantages would be unwise and impolitic," he unsuccessfully repeated his recommendation, at London, and urged it as a means to allay Canadian discontent. In the following September, although he still favored his proposed liberal unilateral concession to allay increasing irritation, he finally decided to favor the adoption of anti-American retaliatory measures which Crampton and the British government regarded as inexpedient and impolitic because they might prevent prospective reciprocity legislation in Congress.[49]

Meantime, by the summer of 1852, the question of the fisheries had reached a point of serious controversy which made it an influential factor in the later negotiations. The British interpretation of the wording of the treaty of 1818 threatened injury to Americans who at certain seasons had fished for herring and mackerel in the bays and inlets of Nova Scotia and Cape Breton and Prince Edward Island (and often within the three-mile limit). In June, 1851, officials of Canada and Nova Scotia had agreed to coöperate in providing vessels to protect the fisheries from American incursions. Later they requested the British government to aid in enforcing the treaty provisions, resulting finally in a thorough patrol of July, 1852, which the Americans called an armed raid. Evidently, and possibly with some sense of native humor, they sought to use the fisheries as a make-weight in plans to secure reciprocity in trade, whose final achievement Sir John Macdonald later attributed chiefly to "the vigorous protection of the fisheries which preceded it."[50]

Early in July, 1852, the Fillmore administration received a report that, at the urgent request of the colonists and without previous notice to the American government, the British government had sent a fleet of nineteen armed cruisers to protect rights claimed by the colonists but previously "neglected." On July 17 Webster invited Crampton to a conference at Boston and suggested that until after the conference no seizures should be made. Eight days later in a speech at Marshfield he said that American fishermen's rights would be protected. Meantime, in the Senate the British action, which was regarded as an unwise strategic policy to enforce favorable treatment of reciprocity by threats, precipitated a lengthy debate in which the danger of collision was generally recognized.

On August 2, in reply to a request (of July 23) of the Senate, the President submitted the correspondence relating to seizures or detention of American fishing vessels. Coincidently with the purpose of protecting American fishing rights, he sent to the fishing grounds an American steam frigate under the command of Commodore M. C. Perry; but this action was too late to prevent the loss of the American mackerel fishing for the season. Thereafter rival fleets, with instructions based on opposite conclusions, continued to patrol the coast.[51]

Contemplated negotiations for an arrangement to adjust the fishery question in connection with the British proposals for commercial intercourse were postponed, first by the illness of Secretary Webster and later by his death, on October 24.[52] In December, Webster's successor, Secretary Edward Everett, initiated with Crampton negotiations for which he found that circumstances were unfavorable. Coincidently, on December 4, he instructed Ingersoll, the American chargé at London, that the President wished to continue the negotiations concerning fisheries and commercial reciprocity for which Webster had prepared to negotiate with Crampton, but that he was of the opinion that the two subjects should not be combined in one treaty.[53]

Meantime, on August 19, Andrews had submitted to the Secretary of the Treasury a historical report relating to the navigation of the St. John, which became an additional subject of discussion in the later negotiations.

By the close of 1852 the Washington administration had not yet reached a decision on the question of reciprocity. In his message of December 6, President Fillmore avoided any commitment on a policy of reciprocity, although he commended the principle and had informed Crampton of his desire to settle all commercial questions before the close of his administration. After contrasting the illiberal Canadian fishery policy with the liberal American policy toward admission of colonial fish under the tariff act of 1846, he suggested that as the British wished for freer commercial intercourse, the time was favorable for a reconsideration of the question of the fisheries with a view to placing them on a more liberal footing of reciprocal privilege. He thought, however, that the two subjects should be embraced in separate conventions. Although he said that these conventions might be concluded before spring if an agreement should be found practical, he was still influenced by the fact that he had been an advocate of the protective policy of 1842. He restrained Secretary Everett's tendency toward greater freedom of trade with Canada, and he especially sought to exclude coal from the free list.[54]

On February 7, 1853, near the close of his administration, the

President submitted to both houses of Congress an elaborate special report and also a report from Secretary Everett on the status of pending negotiations on reciprocal intercourse and navigation of the St. Lawrence and canals. He also urged the necessity of adjustment of the fisheries, recommending an act admitting fish free of duty on condition that American fishermen be admitted to full participation in the provincial fisheries.[55]

Meantime, Congress had renewed consideration of the subject. In the House Seymour of New York submitted a committee report recommending reciprocal trade—a policy which was opposed by the Vermont legislature. Coincidently, on February 5, Senator Davis of Massachusetts introduced a bill for common reciprocal fishing rights. This bill, following its favorable report from the committee, was strongly opposed by Senator Mallory of Florida on the constitutional ground that the federal government could not grant to a foreign power fishery rights within the water jurisdiction of a state. Even after a proposed amendment to limit the reciprocal fishing rights to the coast north of 40° it failed to pass. In the House a similar bill failed, as also did a bill of Seymour proposing to combine the questions of fishery rights and navigation with trade reciprocity in an enumerated list of articles. Thus the question, complicated by friction on the fishery coast, remained for consideration of the next administration.[56]

President Pierce recognized that the unsettled Canadian questions were full of danger. Although as a protectionist he was opposed to the free admission of Canadians to American markets, he decided to negotiate for a treaty of reciprocity which (if concluded) he believed would gradually and peacefully result in the settlement of the Canadian questions by relations conducive to a development into annexation. From the beginning he and Secretary Marcy foresaw that the chief obstacles to such a treaty would be presented by the British colonies, each of which had interests different from the others. Probably in the later negotiations they were also influenced by a long letter which Andrews wrote to Marcy on May 3, concerning a conversation with the British minister Crampton, on the question of greater independence for the British provinces, the idea of the American "continental system," and a possible change in the political sympathies of the colonists.[57]

The President was alert in providing a protective patrol force off the British American fishery coasts. Early in July, he concentrated at Portsmouth, New Hampshire, a small naval force under Commodore W. B. Shubrick to cruise in the seas and bays frequented by American fishermen, and to remonstrate firmly against any British attempt to deprive American citizens of their just rights, but not to resort to violence except in self-defense. In this action he had a double incidental purpose: (1) to quiet the American public mind which was apprehensive of the purpose of the British patrol fleet and (2) to prevent collision which might result from possible warlike acts of private armed vessels of American fishermen who threatened to defend their rights by self-help.

After several interviews with Secretary Marcy, Crampton recognized that the situation might become even more critical by a collision of rival naval forces on the fishing coasts. Therefore, he visited Halifax to suggest to Sir George Seymour the wisdom of discretion concerning seizure of American vessels and to advise against any impolitic action concerning American fishing privileges during pending negotiations.[58]

Late in July, seeking a convenient and comfortable place for the discussion of a *projet* of a treaty which would include provisions for both reciprocity and fisheries, Secretary Marcy went to Berkeley Springs, Virginia, with Crampton who had just returned from the trip to Halifax. There, on August 1, he and Crampton resumed negotiations by comparing two sketches of a convention, one prepared by Everett and President Fillmore and the other by the British government. In considering an article on a list of natural productions (suitable for reciprocal free trade), which had been a great difficulty in the negotiations, Marcy objected to the inclusion of coal, metals, skins, pelts and tails, which Crampton had urged. He especially opposed the insertion of coal which he thought would encounter the strenuous objections of Pennsylvania, Maryland and Virginia. After coal, the two remaining obstacles to the immediate conclusion of a treaty were the British proposals for removal of the American bounties to fishermen and for adoption of American registry of British-built ships when acquired by American citizens (as American-built ships were registered by Great Britain after their acquisition by British citizens). Marcy proposed the admission of unrefined sugar, to which Crampton strenuously objected. In considering the question of fishing reciprocity he proposed to exempt Florida and to extend the principle to the Pacific coast, to which Crampton offered no serious objections (although he declined to assent without further instructions). In his later consideration of the *projet* he was aided by data furnished by Andrews who arrived after the conference of August 3. He was also aided by the counsel of Everett, contained in a dispatch of August 15 from London.[59]

On September 1, at Washington, Marcy submitted to Crampton a matured *projet* which he expected to serve as a basis for the proposed treaty. In this he mentioned only reciprocal fishing rights along the coasts of the Atlantic and the Pacific (including Newfoundland and excluding Florida), commercial reciprocity in enumerated articles of produce of each country, American navigation of the St. Lawrence and Canadian canals and the St. John, and free export of Maine timber and lumber floated down the St. John for shipment to the United States via New Brunswick. In the free list of articles he included furs, rice, tar, pitch, and turpentine. He omitted manufactures, coal, tobacco, and unrefined sugar. This matured *projet* was kept quiet.[60]

At this point in the negotiations President Pierce, in order to negotiate a treaty satisfactorily to all concerned, felt the need of further information concerning the Canadian provinces, especially concerning their trade and commerce and political feeling, and "the exact state of their relations with Great Britain and this country." To secure this information he appointed as a special agent the experienced Andrews who, by a period of residence in the British colonies, had become acquainted with colonial officials and conditions of trade. In official instructions of September 12, after referring to the divided opinion of the Canadian provinces on the question of reciprocal trade and the fisheries, Marcy stressed the American desire that the treaty would be acceptable to all the colonies, that it would prove satisfactory in settling the various conflicting questions at issue and that it would serve "to stimulate and extend an increased regard and interest for this country and its institutions." In concluding he said: "You will, therefore, in a proper manner confer with the most influential men in the colonies to express the interest this Government has in their advancement and its wish to tighten the bonds which unite the two countries." [61]

While Andrews was performing with discretion the delicate duties in the British colonies, the negotiations for conclusion of a treaty at Washington were delayed, partly by British diversion of attention to threatening relations with Russia, and partly by the indolent habits of the affable Mr. Crampton who was not regarded by Buchanan as a proper representative of Great Britain.

In January, 1854, Marcy regarded the situation as serious. This opinion he based partly upon decreased interest in the provinces and partly upon information from Crampton that Lord Clarendon had rejected the American propositions concerning free use of the St. John and the exception of Florida from the reciprocal fisheries and the addition of the Pacific coast thereto, and that the British government would probably insist on registry of colonial-built vessels as a *sine qua non* but had made no proposals. He promptly directed Andrews to return to the lower colonies to remove the growing indifference and other obstacles to the success of the treaty. On March 11, in vigorous instructions to Buchanan, he complained of the long delay and insisted that, in case treaty negotiations should fail, the British government should consent to abandon its pretension to exclude American fishermen from the open bays of the British North American coasts. This British concession he urged as necessary, in order to prevent collision on the fishing grounds where Americans recently had been more attracted by mackerel and herring than by codfish. The claim of American fishermen to the right to take fish in the open bays he said the American government would "feel bound to maintain at any hazard."

"As soon as it is ascertained that the difficulties concerning the fisheries cannot be arranged by negotiation," said he, "this Government will prepare to sustain our fishermen in the assertion of all their rights." In a private letter to Buchanan, written on the following day, he added: "If the negotiation falls through and England insists on excluding us from the open bays, there will be trouble."[62]

Meantime Andrews, in his efforts to influence the British maritime provinces in favor of the treaty, had encountered difficult problems. He especially found difficulty in Nova Scotia, whose leaders feared that provincial interests might be sacrificed by weak British concessions, and whose hostility to the United States had been reflected in resolutions adopted by citizens of Halifax in September, 1852. In a private dispatch of March 31, 1854, from St. John, he stated that the colonies had received no official information from Crampton concerning the British negotiations or the views and intentions of the British government and that, following some increase of prosperity since 1850, they were less inclined to make concessions. On April 3, in a rather gloomy confidential report to Marcy, he suggested that, in order to silence opposition and to promote a favorable attitude in public opinion, he should have at his command a considerable secret service fund.

To this financial suggestion Marcy replied (on April 10): "I have always been distrustful of attempts to change public opinion of any community by such means as you refer to. We cannot purchase by concession all that each colony may demand." Five days later, however, after consultation with the President who recognized the importance of the mission and a duty to aid it by all proper means, and after learning from Crampton that the condition of European affairs made Great Britain immediately anxious to avoid difficulty with the United States as to Canada, he sent fresh instructions authorizing Andrews to issue drafts on the Department for amounts aggregating not more than five thousand dollars, for which he was required to render an account either in the ordinary way or confidentially to the President. On the basis of recent conferences with Crampton, who had received enlarged powers in regard to the pending negotiations and who was planning efforts to induce the provinces to acquiesce in a proper arrangement, he said: "We should probably be able to make a satisfactory arrangement with the home government were it not for the embarrassments thrown in the way by the provinces." In concluding, he added: "Whatever is done must be done promptly—for the fishery season will soon come, and with it the apprehended difficulties." [63]

Encouraged and stimulated by the evidence of confidence in his mission, Andrews acted promptly and with diligence in further efforts to mold public opinion in the lower or Atlantic provinces, which Hincks (in an interview with Andrews at New York in February) had admitted were "beyond the power of either himself or Mr. Crampton," and whose opposition Lord Clarendon considered so formidable that he "refused to go on" unless it could be withdrawn. In his expenditures of the next few weeks (the latter part of April and the larger part of May) he far exceeded the amount placed to his credit for extraordinary expenses. Among the items of expense mentioned in his statements to the Department were the following: special services of confidential and secret agents (at Halifax, in the country districts and elsewhere); special messengers to Prince Edward Island, Newfoundland; telegraphic messages; necessary information from public departments; preparation and publication of editorial articles in newspapers; dinner parties and coach hire; "certain purposes of a government and legislative character"; contribution to election expenses of a government candidate, etc. ($3,900); payments "to officials and to others for whom it was not proper to ask for vouchers" ($11,051), including payments for purposes of a delicate nature at Washington ($3,000).

On May 13, in a "Private and Confidential" dispatch from Montreal, and while planning for an early intercolonial convention which he hoped would meet at New York in preference to Montreal, he stated that an opposition party in Nova Scotia had opposed the surrender of the fisheries on any terms and that some of its members had threatened him with personal violence. After reporting that the struggle in Nova Scotia was severe but that the result was probably successful, he added: "I found it necessary to disburse money very liberally and shall probably require a larger sum than I asked for at the outset." Referring to the New Brunswick opposition, whose members were no less determined (although more quiet) than those of the Nova Scotia opposition, he reported that he had taken such measures as the circumstances required "to moderate the opposition and keep the public mind in a quiet state." Concluding that the colonies were "now in a favorable mood," he suggested that the "present favorable opportunity for effecting a treaty" was one which might not again occur.[64]

For expenses in excess of the amount authorized, part of which were paid from funds which he borrowed at Washington, Andrews later requested reimbursement, claiming that he had spent nothing recklessly. As to the wisdom of his management, he said: "I unhesitatingly declare that the expenditure saved the treaty." He was unable to secure the approval of Marcy for all his bills, part of which remained unpaid at his death. In 1858 his bills against the government amounted to $66,797.32, against which were total credits of $14,012.38, leaving a claim for a balance of $52,784.94.[65]

Andrews rendered valuable service in preparing the way for the mission of Lord Elgin to Washington to complete the negotiation of the treaty. As early as February, 1854, he had suggested to Hincks at New York that either Lord Elgin or Crampton should be given full authority to complete the treaty. Thereafter, by correspondence, he kept in close touch with Hincks who was in London at the period of Lord Elgin's visit there. As early as May 4, after a conference at Fredericton with Sir Edmund Head (the Governor of New Brunswick) who had received private news from London, he wrote Marcy that Lord Elgin was expected to return soon with fresh instructions on colonial questions and would probably go to Washington to see the President and the Secretary of State. In his dispatch of May 19 (from Eastport, Maine) he informed Marcy that delegates from the maritime provinces were preparing to go to New York to consult with Crampton and with Elgin (who was just returning from his trip to London).[66]

On May 26, four days before the passage of the famous Kansas-Nebraska bill, Lord Elgin arrived at Washington with his suite which included Hincks, Captain Hamilton (aide-de-camp), and Laurence Oliphant (private secretary). For the next ten days he and Marcy were busy in considering points of difference on the treaty. He found that the President and Marcy, who strongly expressed a desire to complete the proposed treaty, were rather doubtful whether they could obtain the approval of the Senate in which they expected a large opposition, chiefly Democrats—and especially Southern Democrats who had been somewhat apprehensive of the strength of the annexation movement in Canada. He also found that Marcy feared some opposition from Virginia, Maryland and Pennsylvania against inclusion of free coal. He promptly utilized the polite and convivial methods of diplomacy to overcome the opposition. At various hospitable festivities, including a dinner given by Robert Toombs, he cultivated the acquaintance of opposition Democrats who soon ceased to feel any restraint in his presence and were much delighted with his brilliant repartee and racy anecdotes. According to Oliphant, he was well supported by Crampton, who in honor of the Queen's birthday gave a ball at which (according to a press statement) the fisheries question was settled by the guests after they had "partaken freely of the bait so liberally provided by the noble host." After over a week of festivities, "irrigated" by champagne, he informed Marcy that he could assure the President that the Senate would favor the treaty. Three days later (June 5), at midnight, he and the venerable Marcy signed the completed document.[67]

The treaty contained provisions similar to Marcy's protocol of September 1, 1853, except that it limited reciprocal fishing rights to the Atlantic coast waters north of 36°, conceded to the British a concession of free navigation of Lake Michigan for American use of the St. Lawrence and connecting canals and the St. John, and made small changes in the schedule of free articles (omitting flax and hemp and tow, and adding fish products, eggs, slate, coal, unmanufactured tobacco and rags). It allowed American commercial and fishing vessels freely to enter every Canadian port and to send their cargoes in bond to the United States, but it did not grant the use of the "salmon and shad fisheries and fisheries in the rivers and mouths of rivers." To settle disputes concerning places (in rivers) reserved from the common rights of fishing, it provided for commissioners and an umpire. After a period of ten years it was terminable by either party by a notice of twelve months. Although its free list contained no manufactures, the American government expected the Canadian government to adopt a liberal commercial policy in accord with the assurance or prediction given by the British minister at Washington on June 24, 1851. In this it was disappointed by the rise of a Canadian policy of protection. Besides the conditional concession of free navigation of Lake Michigan, the American government agreed "to urge upon state governments" to secure to British subjects the use of the several state canals on terms of equality with inhabitants of the United States.[68]

On June 19 the President submitted the treaty to the Senate which approved it on August 2 by a vote of thirty-two to eleven. In this approval appeared a felicitous coöperation of adverse political and sectional elements. Southern leaders such as Mason and Toombs, rejecting alarming appeals to proslavery prejudices which were uttered in secret sessions of the Senate, coöperated with Northern leaders such as Douglas and Seward.

The question of the motives of senators in their approval was later a subject of discussion. Many regarded reciprocity as a preparation for more intimate relations, and even as a step toward political union. The Southern senators who favored the treaty probably were influenced by the inclusion of rice, pitch, tar, turpentine and unmanufactured tobacco on the free list. Possibly some were especially influenced by explanatory statements that the motive in negotiating the treaty was to allay Canadian discontent and thereby to prevent or postpone annexation of Canada to the United States. A writer in the *North American Review,* however, after referring to the question of annexation which arose in informal discussions of members of Congress during the progress of the debate on the treaty, stated that both Americans and the English "seem to consider that the Canadas will ultimately be annexed to the United States." That many held this view is probably true.[69]

Later, in referring to the taunts of opponents of the treaty that "it had been floated through on champagne," Oliphant said: "Without altogether admitting this, there can be no doubt that, in the hands of a skillful diplomatist, that beverage is not without its value." [70]

On August 5 the President signed an act of Congress authorizing him to make the terms of the treaty effective by proclamation following the reception of satisfactory evidence of legislation by the British and provincial parliaments to give full effect to its provisions. Following his ratification on August 9 and the exchange of ratifications on September 9, he proclaimed the treaty on September 11.

Within the next year the treaty was accepted by all the British American provinces except British Columbia. Apparently Nova Scotia, which (in February, 1853) had unsuccessfully asserted the right to be consulted in the negotiation of the treaty, offered the chief opposition. It eventually enacted the necessary legislation to make the treaty effective, but not without spirited protests from a respectable minority of the assembly. On April 3, 1855, the assembly agreed to a resolution recommending the appointment of a competent Canadian representative to protect British colonial interests in the United States consequent upon the operation of the new treaty.[71]

On May 16, 1855, after the arrival of information of the required favorable action by the provincial legislatures of Canada, Prince Edward Island, and Nova Scotia, the President issued the formal proclamation making the benefits of the treaty effective for those provinces. On December 12, following the favorable action of Newfoundland in the previous July, he issued an additional proclamation making the terms of the treaty effective for that island province.

Meantime, on July 2, in accord with a provision of an act of March 3, 1845 (Section 7), the President by proclamation extended the privileges of exportation of merchandise in bond to the border ports of Rouse's Point, Cape Vincent, Suspension Bridge and Dunkirk in New York, of Swanton, Alburg and Island Pond in Vermont, of Toledo in Ohio, of Chicago in Illinois, of Milwaukee in Wisconsin, of Michilimackinac in Michigan, of Eastport in Maine, and of Pembina in the Territory of Minnesota.[72]

The only delay in making the provisions of the treaty effective arose in connection with the fisheries. In June, 1857, and again in November, 1859, Secretary Cass, in notes to the British minister at Washington, complained of the delay of the British commissioner in the duty of coöperation to conclude the business of the joint commission appointed under Article 1 of the treaty. This delay resulted in some Canadian irritation concerning "encroachments of American fishermen in Canadian waters" and exposed the American commissioner to some "unmerited censure." [73]

The new treaty, which was completed amidst such warm social amenities, inaugurated a period of a half decade of smooth and friendly relations. Excepting the border irritations on the British Columbia boundary, these friendly relations were ruffled only by British plans of recruiting in the United States for the Crimean War in 1855 by undisguised enlistment of Americans through a military depot at Halifax to which their transportation from certain American cities was supervised by provincial authorities, apparently with the coöperation of British consuls in the United States and the British minister at Washington (Crampton), whose recall the American government consequently demanded in 1856 on the ground that they were deeply implicated in the infringement of the American neutrality law.[74]

To American shippers the treaty proved useful by its result in relieving the tension concerning the fisheries and in increasing the tendency toward reasonable railway rates to the Atlantic seaboard as a strategic means to capture shipping traffic which otherwise might have been diverted to the St. Lawrence waterway. Although it increased American trade with Canada, and thereby benefited both parties, it was of larger benefit to the export trade of Canada than to that of the United States. Although at first it was regarded as satisfactory to both parties, it gradually became more favorable to Canada.

According to American economists the great defect of the treaty was the lack of any express stipulation concerning Canadian admission of American manufactures—a defect which could have been remedied by subsequent arrangement if the desire for reciprocal trade relations had remained as strong as in 1854.

In 1859 Canada, by a change in its financial policy, unintentionally prepared the way for the later termination of the treaty. Facing an exhausted exchequer, and influenced by the necessity of securing increasing revenues to meet the increasing expenses of its continued policy of internal development, it adopted the views of A. T. Galt in favor of the promotion of a protective tariff policy. It began to adopt an increase of tariffs on articles not included in the treaty—an increase which the American government regarded as a violation of the spirit of the treaty. In reply to the British attempt to prevent tariffs which were in conflict with the spirit of the treaty, it affirmed (in 1859) the right of the provincial government to regulate its own tariffs without interference.[75]

In its new tariff policy Canada was influenced in part by the problems of transportation. In favoring the treaty, it had expected a larger deflection of the transportation of the products (grain, pork and beef) of the American Middle Northwest to the sea via the Canadian canals and the St. Lawrence, a deflection which would have increased Canadian prosperity and content. In this it was disappointed by the preference of shippers for the continued use of the Erie Canal and American railways to New York where freight rates to Europe were lower than the rates at Quebec or Montreal.

However, by 1859, Canada recovered part of the trade which since 1846 had been diverted to American routes. From a carrier which limited itself to the commodities required for its own use, it became a considerable carrier for the United States. By 1860, by new railroads partly political in purpose, it was competing for the important commerce of the Lakes and the Mississippi. Apparently it was favored by an increasing amount of western traffic carried eastward by Canadian railroads for transshipment in bond through American territory to American territory to American Atlantic ports. Israel T. Hatch, of New York, in a report of March 28, 1860, stated that under the treaty it was getting the benefits of a union with the United States without formal annexation, which he said no longer had many advocates on either side of the line. Declaring that Canada had used each concession as a vantage ground, he urged that the American government had a duty to protect American enterprises from foreign aggression (!).[76]

For the changed Canadian policy of 1859, which was largely influenced by the continued development of internal improvements, the commercial interests of the lower St. Lawrence region were largely responsible. They planned tariffs to encourage importations via the St. Lawrence to injure the trade of New York and the West. These tariffs encountered considerable opposition in Upper Canada which, in order to escape the increased duty on leading articles previously purchased across the border, was forced to import via the St. Lawrence.[77]

In 1860 Canada adopted other strategic acts or methods concerning which the Committee on Commerce in Congress later complained (1862). In order to encourage greater use of the lower St. Lawrence by American vessels, it enacted a law allowing to vessels and goods which had passed through the Welland Canal a rebate of ninety per cent when they entered the St. Lawrence Canal or any Canadian port. In order to encourage rapid settlement of remote territory, it established at Sault Ste. Marie a free port extending a thousand miles along the shores of Lakes Huron and Superior and tempting American settlers and mariners to evade customs duties. It also established another great free port at Gaspé on the St. Lawrence with a frontage of twelve hundred miles.[78]

By 1860, in the face of recent increased business relations between Canada and the United States, and recent increase of American lake and ocean shipping, an American movement against the treaty of 1854 was started with a view to its early termination on the ground of general dissatisfaction with it south of the boundary. Apparently this movement was begun in New York; and as early as February, 1859 the question was debated in Congress. Influenced by the Canadian acts and by the construction of the Grand Trunk Railway, the New York legislature urged regulations which would render trade "reciprocally beneficial and satisfactory, as was intended and expressed by the treaty."

In the West the anti-treaty movement encountered considerable criticism. In May, 1860, a committee of the Chicago Board of Trade, stating that the treaty had been beneficial, complained that the opposition movement was originated and "fostered by railway monopolies to force trade over their routes to the seaboard" and expressed opposition to any partial legislation or government action to force the trade of the West and Northwest to Atlantic ports over any particular route. James W. Taylor, of Minnesota, in a report of May 2, 1860, stated that American sentiment west of Buffalo was entirely opposed to abrogation of the treaty. He declared that the attack on the reciprocity policy could be traced exclusively to shipping interests of New York and Philadelphia and the lines of transportation between those cities and the West, and that the purpose was to prevent the deflection of the western commerce to the St. Lawrence and the Grand Trunk Railway.

At the same time a Canadian select committee (of the legislative assembly) was appointed to inquire into the causes which had directed the trade of the West through the United States via the Hudson and the port of New York and the mode of regaining it.[79]

Later Hatch and Taylor, who were appointed by the American government to inquire carefully into the operation of the treaty, reported against its continuation under existing Canadian laws and regulations. They advocated a complete zollverein, or commercial treaty, as the best solution.

Convinced that Canada had violated the spirit of the treaty by the increase of its duties on manufactured articles in order to protect the growing competitive manufacturing interests in Canada, and seeking to retaliate for Canadian exaction of canal tolls from American vessels, the American Congress showed an increasing opposition to the treaty. Finally, in 1865, stimulated by a pressing need for more revenue, and influenced by new sources of friction and agitation in the Civil War period, it reached a decision to authorize the American government to give the required notice to abrogate the treaty.[80]

REFERENCES

1. J. B. Moore, *Int. Arb's.*, I, 710–11; Sidney Webster, *Can. Reciprocity Treaty of 1845; 15 G.B., Instrs.*, pp. 17–21, No. 89, Feb. 20, 1841.
2. Richardson, *Messages . . .* , V, 164.
3. Skelton, *The Railway Builders*, pp. 33–34; *C.A.*, G, 141, *Canada*, pp. 274–81; A. T. Galt, *Canada in 1849 and 1859*, p. 26; Shortt and Doughty, X, 544.
4. *9 Cong. Globe*, 27–2, pp. 422, 442, Apr. 14 and 25, 1842; *H. Rps.*, 32–2, No. 4, Feb. 11, 1853.
5. C. D. Allin and George M. Jones, *Annexation, Preferential Trade and Reciprocity*, pp. 11–12.
6. C. C. Tansill, *The Can. Reciprocity Treaty of 1854;* Thomas C. Keefer, *Eighty Years of Progress of Br. N.A.;* R. H. Bonnycastle, *Canada and the Canadians in 1846*, pp. 290–92; D. A. McGibbon, *Railway Rates and the Canadian Railway Commission (1917)*, p. 13; Edward Porritt, *Sixty Years of Protection in Canada*, 1846–1907, pp. 45–47; *C.A.*, G, *Governor Generals' Letter Books*, p. 406; Allin and Jones, pp. 12–17.
7. *C.A.*, G, 123, *Instrs. for C.O.*, pp. 155–73, Feb. 3, 1846; *Ib.*, pp. 365–87, Mar. 3, 1846.
8. *C.A.*, G, 125; *C.A.*, G, 133, *Canada*, pp. 298–316; *Rps. Coms.*, 32–2, No. 4, p. 53; *Exec. Docs.*, 31–1, No. 64; Shortt and Doughty, *Canada*, V, 236–37.
9. *7 G.B., Notes to*, pp. 18–19, June 10, 1844; *3 Drafts of Treaties, U.S. and G.B.* (Br. Mem. of Apr. 27, 1874); Shortt and Doughty, IX, 373; Richardson, V, 326–27; *U. S. Stats.*, IX, 512; *H. Exec. Docs.*, 36–1, Vol. 13, No. 96, June 16, 1860; Allin and Jones, pp. 18–19, 24–29; *Can. Hist. Rev.*, VII, 1926, p. 10; *105 Hansard*, p. 71, June 15, 1848; *Quebec Gazette*, Jan. 8, 1849; A. T. Galt, *Canada in 1849 and 1859*.
10. *C.A.*, G, 127, pp. 252–54, No. 38, Grey to Elgin, Mar. 19, 1847; *Ib.*, pp. 256–79 (inclosures); *Ib.*, 322–64, Rp. of Nov. 14, 1846, to the Lords of the Com. of the P.C. for Trade.
11. *C.A.*, G, 125, No. 94, Gladstone to Cathcart, June 27, 1846; *C.A.*, G, 128, No. 91, Grey to Elgin, June 22, 1847.

12. HAYNES, *Reciprocity Treaty with Canada*, p. 12; SHORTT and DOUGHTY, V, 237; *H. Exec. Docs.*, 31–1, No. 64.
13. *C.A.*, G, 133, p. 298; *C.A.*, G, 131, Grey to Elgin, June 9, 1848; *H. Exec. Docs.*, 31–1, No. 64, pp. 89–94; SHORTT and DOUGHTY, V, 237.
14. I. D. ANDREWS, *Reciprocity and Fishery Treaty* (1862); *Cong. Globe*, 30–1, pp. 723, 923; *Ib.*, 30–2, pp. 182–86; *Ib.*, 38–3, Part 1, p. 210; *C.A.*, G, 133, p. 298; *H. Exec. Docs.*, 31–1, No. 64; *Can. Hist. Rev.*, VII, 1926, p. 11; ALLIN and JONES, pp. 19–20.
15. *C.A.*, G, 132, pp. 313–20, Grey to Elgin, Aug. 10 and Dec. 21, 1848 (No. 303).
16. SHORTT and DOUGHTY, V, 224, 227, 229 and 237; *Can. Hist. Rev.*, VII, p. 11.
17. *25 G.B., Notes from; C.A.*, G, 132, pp. 227–28, Grey to Elgin, No. 90, Oct. 24, 1848 (in reply to Elgin's No. 124 of Sept. 13).
18. *Cong. Globe*, 30–2, pp. 46, 62, 182–86; *C.A.*, C.O. Series, 188, Vol. 177 (N.B.), Crampton to Sir Edmund Head, Mar. 12, 1849 (12 pp); *C.A.*, G, 133, No. 354, Grey to Elgin, Mar. 31, 1849; SHORTT and DOUGHTY, V, 237.
19. *Ib.*, V, 230; I. D. ANDREWS, *Reciprocity and Fishery Treaty; Reciprocity Negotiations*, 1848–54, p. 1 (Private), No. 44, Andrews to Buchanan, Nov. 1, 1848.
20. *15 G.B., Instrs.*, pp. 194–95, No. 87, May 16, 1844.
21. *C.A.*, C.O. Series, 188, Vol. 177 (N.B.), Crampton to Head, Mar. 12, 1849; SIDNEY WEBSTER, *Can. Reciprocity Treaty;* T. WALROND, *Letters and Journals of Lord Elgin*, pp. 100–04; *H. Exec. Docs.*, 31–1, No. 64, p. 3; *C.A.*, G, 133, pp. 288 and 298–316, Enclosure in Grey to Elgin, Apr. 28, 1849; *7 G.B., Notes to,* pp. 234–35, Clayton to Bulwer, Mar. 26, 1850.
22. *C.A.*, G, 133, pp. 284–86 (Confidential), Grey to Elgin, Apr. 27, 1849.
23. RICHARDSON, V, 44; *H. Exec. Docs.*, 31–1, No. 64, p. 33; *6 Rp. Book*, pp. 303–04, Taylor to H. R., May 7, 1850.
24. *Quebec Gazette*, Jan. 8, 1849; WALROND, *Letters and Journals of Elgin*, pp. 60 and 70; ALLIN and JONES, pp. 25 and 45.
25. *Ib.*, pp. 53–67.
26. *Ib.*, p. 36; A. T. GALT, *Canada in 1849 and 1859*, p. 6.
27. WALROND, *Letters and Journals of Elgin*, p. 113.
28. *Ib.*, pp. 70–86; ALLIN and JONES, pp. 53–67.
29. SHORTT and DOUGHTY, V, 234; *9 De Bow's Rev.*, pp. 397–412, Oct., 1850.
30. ALLIN and JONES, pp. 99, 102, 106–14, 385–90; *67 Blackwood*, pp. 249–67, Feb., 1850.
31. *Burlington Daily Sentinel*, Oct. 22 and 31, and Nov. 6, 1849.

32. 66 *Blackwood,* pp. 471–85, Oct., 1849; 67 *Blackwood,* pp. 249–67, Feb., 1850.
33. ALLIN and JONES, pp. 144–61.
34. *Ib.*, pp. 209–65 (also pp. 89 and 98).
35. *Ib.*, p. 115; SHORTT and DOUGHTY, V, 234.
36. ALLIN and JONES, pp. 374–84.
37. *1 Spl. Missions,* pp. 275–78; *16* and *17 Spl. Agents,* 1849; I. D. ANDREWS, *Desps.*, Nos. 2, 3, 4, 7.
38. *C.A.*, G, 136, pp. 47–48, No. 49, Grey to Elgin, Jan. 9, 1850; Package of Misc. Letters on claims of I. D. Andrews for compensation as special agent, 1847–54.
39. WALROND, *Letters and Journals of Elgin,* p. 112; *Clayton Papers,* VIII; *C.A.*, G, 136, pp. 467–70, 307, 310–12, 318–29, 336–40 and 485–88 (Nos. 37, 481 and 483, Feb. 18, Mar. 2, Apr. 4, Apr. 16, and May 15, 1850); *27 Brit. Leg., Notes from,* Mar. 27, 1850; RICHARDSON, V, 44–45; *H. Exec. Docs.*, 31–1, No. 64, p. 36.
40. *Cong. Globe,* Apr. 11, 1850, pp. 701–02.
41. *Ib.*, May 2, 1850, pp. 893–94 and 923; *H. Rps.*, 31–1, II, No. 295; *Can. Hist. Rev.*, VII, 1926, p. 11.
42. *6 Rp. Book,* pp. 303–04; RICHARDSON, V, 44–45; *H. Rps.*, 32–2, No. 4, pp. 51–52; *H. Exec. Docs.*, 31–1, No. 64; *H. Rps.*, 31–1, II, No. 295, May 2, 1850; *Cong. Globe,* 31–1, pp. 1008–10; *C.A.*, G, 136, pp. 536–37, No. 86, Bulwer to Palmerston, May 20, 1850.
43. *7 G.B., Notes to,* p. 262, Sept. 14, 1850.
44. *Cong. Globe,* 31–2, pp. 22, 203 and 293–96; *Sen. Exec. Docs.*, 31–2, No. 1, p. 86.
45. *C.A.*, G, 138, pp. 276–81, No. 572.
46. ANDREWS, *Reciprocity and Fisheries Treaty,* p. 55; *Sen. Exec. Docs.*, 32–1, No. 1, pp. 83–84, 89–90.
47. *74 N. Am. Rev.*, Jan., 1852, pp. 168–97; *Ib.*, Apr., 1852, pp. 261–79.
48. RICHARDSON, V, 118–19; *For. Rels., 1873,* Part 3, p. 293; *Treaty of Washington Papers,* 1871.
49. *C.A.*, G, 141, No. 17, No. 23 (May 14), and No. 40 (pp. 274–81, enclosure in J. S. Pakington to Elgin, June 30, 1852); *C.A.*, G, 462, Feb. 20, 1852; *C.A.*, G, 407A, No. 80 (Confidential), Elgin to Pakington, Sept. 23, 1852; *C.A.*, G, 142, Instructions of Pakington to Elgin, Oct. 30, 1852.
50. *C.A.*, C.O. Series, 188, Vol. 180 (N.B.), Crampton to Head, Confid., July 20, 1852; *Can. Sessional Papers,* 1872, No. 18.
51. *29 Cong. Globe,* 32–1, July 23, 1852, and pp. 898, 1893 and 1897; *H. Exec. Docs.*, 32–1, No. 120, pp. 107–08; *Sen. Exec. Docs.*, 32–2, No. 22, pp. 444–45; *Ib.*, 32–1, Vol. 10, No. 100, Aug. 2, 1852, p. 1.

52. *Ib., 33-Spl.* No. 3, pp. 2–4, 9–10.
53. *Ib.*
54. *Sen. Exec. Docs.*, 32–1, XI, No. 112, Aug. 25, 1852; RICHARDSON, V, 164.
55. *Ib.*, 188; SIDNEY WEBSTER, *Can. Reciprocity Treaty; H. Exec. Docs.*, 32–2, Vol. 4, No. 40, Feb. 7, 1853; *Ib.*, Vol. 3, No. 23, Jan. 15, 1853.
56. *H. Misc. Docs.*, 32–2, Vol. 1, No. 19, Jan. 20, 1853; *Cong. Globe*, 32–2, pp. 198, 567–68, 582, 777, 953, 956–57; *H. Rps.*, 32–2, No. 4; *Rp. Book*, Vol. 6, p. 492; *Sen. Exec. Docs., 33-Spl.*; CURTIS, *Life of Webster*, pp. 246–49.
57. SIDNEY WEBSTER, *Can. Reciprocity Treaty.*
58. *H. Exec. Docs.*, 33–1, No. 21, pp. 3–7; *Marcy Papers*, Vol. 39.
59. *Ib., Marcy Papers, Diary*, pp. 1–12.
60. *U. S. For. Rels., 1873*, Part 2, p. 296.
61. *Sen. Exec. Docs.*, 31–2, No. 23; *3 Spl. Missions*, pp. 109–13; *Pierce Papers*, Vol. 4.
62. TANSILL, *The Canadian Reciprocity Treaty of 1854*, pp. 62–66; *Am. Hist. Rev.*, Oct., 1919, pp. 36–67; *16 G.B., Instrs.*, pp. 274–83, No. 29, Mar. 11, 1854; *Marcy Papers*, Vol. 48; *Ib., Private Letter Book*, Mar. 12, 1854.
63. *H. Exec. Docs.*, 32–2, No. 53, pp. 450–51; *Andrews Papers; Marcy Papers*, Vol. 49, p. 68, Apr. 10, 1854; *3 Spl. Missions* [*Instrs.*], p. 36, Confidential, Apr. 15, 1854.
64. *Pierce Papers*, Vol. 4; *Andrews Papers.*
65. *Ib.*
66. *Marcy Papers*, Vol. 1.
67. *Ib.*; LAWRENCE OLIPHANT, *Episodes in a Life of Adventure*, pp. 51–52.
68. *Sen. Exec. Docs.*, 32–1, No. 1, p. 89; P. BARRY, *International Trade of the U.S. and Eng. and the U.S. and Canada* (1858); MALLOY, I, 671.
69. *N. Am. Rev.*, LXXIX, 483; *Ib.*, Oct., 1854, pp. 464–85; *Cong. Globe*, 38–2, 1864–65, Part 1, pp. 210 and 230.
70. OLIPHANT, *Episodes in a Life of Adventure*, pp. 36–46.
71. *Can. Hist. Rev.*, VII, 27–30.
72. TANSILL, pp. 77–80; RICHARDSON, V, 327.
73. *8 G.B., Notes to*, pp. 265–66.
74. *16 G.B., Instrs.*, pp. 499–526, No. 14, Marcy to Dallas, May 27, 1856.
75. *C.A.*, G, 157, pp. 32–35; Sir E. W. WATKINS, *Canada and the States*, p. 396; A. T. GALT, *Canada in 1849 and 1859*, p. 31; *State Dept. Pamphs., Rp. Com. on Commerce*, Feb 5, 1862.
76. *H. Exec. Docs.*, 36–1, Vol. 13, No. 96, June 13, 1860; *C.A.*, G, 239, pp. 31–63.

77. *H. Rps.*, 38–1, Vol. 1, No. 39, Apr. 1, 1864; SIDNEY WEBSTER, *Can. Reciprocity Treaty of 1854*.
78. *Rps. Coms.*, 37–2, Vol. 3; *Cong. Globe*, 38–2, Part 1, p. 230; *Rp. Com. on Commerce*, Feb. 5, 1862; *Rp. of Min. of Finance* (GALT) *on the Reciprocity Treaty, 1862;* E. H. DERBY, *Preliminary Report on the Treaty of Reciprocity* (*1866*), p. 26.
79. *C.A.*, G, 235, Napier to Sir Edmund Head, Feb. 28, 1859; *H. Misc. Docs.*, 36–1, Vol. 6, No. 89, May 28, 1860; *Archives Publiques*, 1914–15, *Catalogue des Brochures* (by N. FEE), p. 289, No. 2353.
80. *C.A.*, G, 229, Lyons to Gov. Gen. Head, Oct. 6 and 17 and Dec. 18, 1859 and July 10, 1860; *H. Rps.*, 38–1, No. 39; *H. Exec. Docs.*, 39–1, Vol. 1, part 1, p. 111; *Cong. Globe*, 36–1, Part 2, p. 1357; CHALFANT ROBINSON, *A Hist. of Two Reciprocity Treaties*, pp. 66–67.

CHAPTER XII

BORDER PROBLEMS OF THE CIVIL WAR PERIOD

THE American Civil War, whose problems involved serious controversy with Great Britain and taught Canada the importance of a strong central government, precipitated along the American-Canadian frontier several questions affecting the routing of regular relations, and also policies concerning future relations. It produced conditions which severely damaged the happy relations established by Bagot and Elgin and obscured for several years the Anglo-American international harmony and cordiality which had been reached in 1860.

Notwithstanding the San Juan boundary controversy of the Northwest and the Canadian tariff policy at the Northeast, the American government on the eve of the Civil War recognized a cordiality of Anglo-American relations which was illustrated by the incidents of the visit of the Prince of Wales to the United States in 1860. At the opening of the war, it found evidence of Canadian sympathy with the cause of the Union. This it saw especially in the large number of Canadians who joined the Union army early in the war. Later it saw new evidence in the correspondence concerning the cases of British citizens in the American army in 1863 and especially in May and June, 1864.[1]

Early in the war it became suspicious of the British imperial neutrality policy which seemed to indicate sympathy with the secession movement of the Confederates. It also resented the unjustified British expectations of a permanent division of the American federal Union into "disunited states." Later, in the Confederate operations in Canadian territory and outrageous Confederate raids across the border, it found a basis for special grievances against Canada, resulting in some feeling of hostility which possibly contributed an impetus to the later Fenian movement against Canada.

Unfortunately, William H. Seward, who directed the American Department of State in the Civil War period, had previously expressed opinions which caused Lord Russell, of the British Foreign Office, to regard him as an undisguised Anglophobe and to suspect him of reckless, chauvinistic designs to annex Canada, possibly by war. His latest expression on annexation had appeared in a press report in 1860. This had attracted the attention of Russell, and had produced in his mind suspicions which Adams sought to dispel near the close of 1861 by the explanation that his chief's statements had been essentially speculative—that they had referred to the probable course of future events without in any way involving the adoption of a distinct line of aggressive policy to hasten annexation.[2]

Early in the war Seward was determined to prevent suspected plans of the Confederates to obtain sympathy or aid in Canada. On April 13, he appointed a special confidential agent to correct any erroneous Canadian views concerning the American problem of secession; but five days later he cancelled the appointment on the ground that the usefulness of the mission had been annulled by the announcement of it in the public journals. On May 1, he complained to Lord Lyons that the Confederates had bought the *Peerless* at Toronto and that, under regular British papers, they were taking it from Lake Ontario to the ocean for use as a privateer. Finding that, in view of the uncertainties of the case, Lyons could not agree to recommend detention, he declared that the American government could "not tolerate the fitting out and delivery of piratical vessels on the St. Lawrence," and he threatened to direct American seizure and detention of the vessel "under whatever flag or paper" if evidence indicated plans for delivery to the American insurgents. In the face of the opposition of Lyons, who "verbally protested unequivocally and without reservation," he promptly gave the conditional instructions for the seizure and detention.[3]

Later, American relations with Canada were affected by the precipitancy of the British declaration of neutrality (of May 13) which recognized the Confederates as belligerents and seemed to deny American sovereignty over the Confederate states.[4]

By June, 1861, questions relating to the Reciprocity Treaty of 1854 were subjects of considerations at Washington, but extended discussion on the treaty and tariff policy was wisely avoided. Throughout the year and in the following year, the American government had reason to recognize advantages arising from the treaty provisions of 1854. At a time when the Mississippi was interrupted by insurrection the Northwest especially recognized the value of free navigation of the St. Lawrence. At the same time, and probably throughout the period of the war, America was greatly benefited by the large increase of imports from Canada, especially by import of wool for blankets and of horses for army service.[5]

Before the close of 1861 both the American and the British governments were somewhat apprehensive of possible enlargement of armaments on the border. In September, in reply to the British inquiry whether the American naval force on the Lakes above Niagara Falls was in excess of the limit stipulated by the arrangement of 1817, Seward stated that the *Michigan* (of fifty-two tons) was the only American vessel on the Lakes, that it was used exclusively for recruiting purposes and for artillery practice for newly recruited seamen, and that he did not consider its retention as a violation of the agreement of 1817. On October 10, apparently influenced by information that the British were sending troops for defense of Canada, he sent to governors of the border states a circular in which he spoke of the need of defenses for the Lakes. By this statement he drew from Canadian newspapers a reply that border fortifications would be a menace to Canada.

Soon thereafter Seward received a statement of Canadian complaint in regard to American violation of Canadian territory by a small party of unarmed American soldiers, who crossed the boundary to persuade some deserters to return.[6]

Late in 1861, following the British demands in regard to the *Trent* affair, Canadians became apprehensive of possible war and consequent invasion. In this expectation of war, which resulted in a decrease of Canadian sympathy for the Union cause, they were justified by the seriousness of the situation. At London Adams reported the signs of impending war. On December 12 he expected the early termination of his mission. On December 19 he obtained an unofficial interview with Lord Russell, with a purpose to ascertain whether war was inevitable. Fortunately, in the full and frank conversation of the interview, in which his chief object evidently was to correct the impression that the American government was determined upon a hostile attitude or a policy of conquest, he obtained from Russell an explanation (of recent British measures) which suggested to him the possibility of a satisfactory adjustment of the dangerous situation.[7]

Early in January, 1862, following the excitement resulting from the *Trent* affair, Seward took occasion to correct certain British "misapprehensions" in regard to his aggressive policy concerning Canada. Apparently he was somewhat successful. In the same month, after the *Persia* of the Montreal Ocean Steamship Company had been unable to enter the St. Lawrence and sought to transfer its cargo to its destination via American territory, he courteously volunteered permission for the landing of British troops and military stores at Portland, Maine, *en route* to Canada via the Grand Trunk Railway. Early in March he announced that a recent passport regulation had been rescinded. Later, after criticizing a reported indiscretion of Russell, he expressed a hope for better Anglo-American relations.[8]

Psychological effects of the excitement concerning the *Trent* affair appeared in American popular agitation early in 1862 for defensive preparedness measures on the northern frontier to neutralize British advantages there. Requests for the establishment of naval stations on the Lakes were later followed by proposals for Lakes harbor defenses, and later by petitions for military (and commercial) canals to connect the Lakes with the Mississippi and the Hudson.[9] To these Congress responded by various committee reports and discussions,[10] but it was not convinced of the military necessity of the measures which doubtless were proposed chiefly with a view to promote the interests of western commerce.[11]

After the adjustment of the *Trent* affair, the British government (while disclaiming any right or desire to interfere in Canadian party politics) was inclined to place upon Canada the responsibility of providing for its own protection. In August, 1862, Newcastle urged upon Governor-General Monck the importance of prompt resumption of measures for some better Canadian military organization. He especially emphasized the importance of measures of necessary preparation for self-defense, stating that the importance was greatly increased by the recent first appearance of a large standing army on the American continent and by the unsettled condition of the neighboring states.[12]

American-Canadian relations in 1862–63 were affected by British policy concerning Confederate use of British ports, which was determined by Palmerston's interpretation of the old British enlistment act of 1819 and Russell's desire to favor the preservation of British shipbuilding interests. The British government permitted the Confederate naval agent, James D. Bullock, to build or buy in British ports vessels which were later equipped to cruise against American commerce. From the British port of Liverpool it permitted the departure of four such vessels, although it had evidence of their purpose. By May, 1863, however, it was learning to be more vigilant as shown by the prompt action of Lord Lyons in investigating reports that Confederates were fitting out vessels at Vancouver Island to cruise against American commerce.

On July 11, after the tide of the Civil War had clearly turned in favor of the Union cause, Seward began to speak in a more decided tone his warnings against the British policy concerning Confederate use of British ports. On September 2, expressing to Adams his views concerning the painful condition of Anglo-American relations, he urged that the two nations should not be left to drift toward absolute alienation. He declared that the American government, with a desire for amicable relations, was engaged in the duty of averting foreign war.

Already, Adams was speaking in a decisive tone at London, illustrated by his presentation of American claims for depredations committed by the *Alabama* and the *Florida*. On September 5, when several Confederate ironclads were under construction by the Lairds in the Mersey, and after unsuccessful American efforts to induce the British government to interfere to prevent plans for the early departure of one of them, he expressed to Russell his regret concerning the unfavorable British decision and significantly added a hint of war which might result from British policy. Three days later he was rewarded by a favorable response. The British government decided to detain all the Confederate ironclads, but it refused to assume any responsibility for the damages committed by the cruisers which it had previously allowed to depart.[13]

Later, beginning before the close of 1863, American relations with Canada were affected by Confederate activities in Canada with plans of offensive trans-border operations which threatened to create embarrassing international complications. On November 11, 1863, the American government received through Lord Lyons from Governor-General Monck a telegraphic report of a rumored Confederate plot under the direction of Lieutenant Minor for a contemplated expedition to capture steamers on Lake Erie, to release Confederate prisoners at Johnson's Island, and to attack Buffalo. It promptly sent General Dix to the frontier and Preston King to confer with Monck with a view to coöperative understanding of the authorities on each side of the border. It also ordered the *Michigan* to anchor off Johnson's Island. Aided by the coöperation of Canadian authorities, including a warning by Lord Monck, it established along the frontier a close watch to prevent the execution of the Confederate plans. Fortunately it found that Monck's warning was effective, making the frontier demonstration unnecessary.[14]

In December the American government was offended by the seizure of the American steamer *Chesapeake* on the high seas, between New York and Portland, by fourteen men for whose acts the Confederate government at Richmond at first assumed responsibility. Following the recapture of the vessel in the harbor of Sambro (Nova Scotia) by an American naval commander who delivered it to the British authorities at Halifax, the Washington authorities demanded the delivery of the fourteen men for trial in the United States. The insurgent government at Richmond sent J. P. Holcombe to defend the men and to claim the vessel on the ground that citizens of the Confederacy, which Great Britain had recognized as a belligerent, had a legal right, during war, to make captures (even if they had no commission). In the following April, however, it acknowledged its error and disclaimed the seizure. Meantime, Holcombe, on his arrival at Halifax, in March, found that the case was already decided. After enjoying the hospitality of Confederate sympathizers at Halifax, he went to Niagara to coöperate with C. C. Clay and other Confederates in plans for operations across the border.[15]

In view of the situation, the American government was probably justified in authorizing stricter regulations for vessels departing from New York. Through the Collector of Customs at New York it exacted from export merchants new and onerous bonds as security that the flour and provisions exported to Newfoundland would not ultimately reach the insurgent enemies of the United States. Early in January, 1864, in response to a complaint of the British consul, Seward took occasion to refresh Lord Lyons' recollection of certain embarrassing circumstances which might explain the reason for the new regulation. He especially referred to an unsuccessful piratical attempt to make war on the United States from British provinces on the shores of the Lakes and the St. Lawrence, and to the more recent seizure of the *Chesapeake* on the high seas by "a band of pirates." He also mentioned several other causes of American complaint: the recent shipment of one thousand rifles from New York to Halifax in violation of military regulations, the recently discovered plans of Confederate "pirates" at Halifax to capture other American steamers between New York and Halifax, the plans of "neutral passengers" to carry forbidden and treasonable mails to the insurgents and the plans of "neutral merchants" to carry war supplies. He declared that these proceedings tended "to involve the British provinces and the United States in a border war which would be calamitous to both countries," and that the American practice of vigilance was necessary to prevent the conveyance of information and war materials through the British provinces to the insurgents "to sustain and prolong an inexcusable domestic insurrection." [16]

Later, in 1864, the watchful Lord Monck actively sought to relieve American anxiety concerning the increasing number of Confederates in Canada and the purpose of certain suspicious-looking vessels in Canadian waters. On March 19, after prompt steps to detain certain vessels which were suspected of plans to attack American trading vessels on the Lakes, he wrote the Duke of Newcastle that Great Britain was "bound to take stringent precautions that her harbors shall not be used for the preparation of expeditions hostile to the lake trade of the United States," which by the stipulations of 1817 had on the Lakes no adequate defensive force. For this purpose he suggested as a measure for enforcement of commercial police a temporary transfer of five small vessels to the Lakes. These, however, were not sent, and fortunately were not needed at that time. Possibly the British government doubted the wisdom of any temporary frontier preparation which the American government might misconstrue as a menace.[17]

Meantime, Seward had found himself somewhat embarrassed by the publication of certain expressions (concerning the British failure to observe strict neutrality) which he had used in his instructions to Adams in July, 1863, and which by later incorporation into the President's message had encountered the criticism of the British government and members of Parliament on the ground that they were regarded as "disrespectful and menacing." On March 2, he explained that no menace had been intended, but he asserted that the President had a duty to furnish information to Congress on whom the government depended.[18]

Early in April, 1864, possibly influenced by Confederate activities in Canada, the American government began at Black Rock (near Buffalo) the construction of several side-screw revenue cutters for service on Lake Erie; but Seward explained to Lord Lyons that the cutters formed no part of the American naval force and were intended exclusively for prevention of smuggling.[19]

Coincident with the beginning of the construction of the cutters appeared the beginning of an agitation to terminate certain treaties. On June 1, a committee report of the House advised abrogation of the Reciprocity Treaty—a subject which was finally postponed by the House on May 26 by a vote of 77 to 72. On May 25, after discussing the inequalities of this treaty, R. P. Spalding of Ohio turned to consider the inequalities of the agreement of 1817, which (he said) restricted American plans for military canals to connect the Lakes with other American waters and prevented American construction of a naval depot or navy yard on the American coast of one of the Lakes. On June 13 he introduced a joint resolution authorizing and directing the President to give the required notice to terminate the agreement, which he said was intended as only a temporary arrangement. This resolution, which was adopted by the House, was not considered by the Senate.[20]

In the following August, in reply to a statement of Lord Lyons that the British government would view the abrogation of the agreement of 1817 with regret and alarm, Seward offered assurance that the American government at that time had no intentions to abrogate.[21]

Meantime, the American government was suspicious of the plans and activities of Jacob Thompson and Clement C. Clay, whom Jefferson Davis (on April 27, 1864) had sent to Canada as special secret service agents to execute oral instructions by which Canada was to be used as a base of operations for aiding disruption between the American East and West during the approaching election, and who had been given bills of exchange for nine hundred thousand dollars to finance their operations. That these suspicions were justified Thompson furnished ample evidence in his reports to Richmond. In conferences with disaffected Americans he encouraged the organization of insurrection against the Washington government. Among the various terrorizing enterprises which he planned was a release of Confederate prisoners who were expected to aid in offensive operations from Canada. Incidental to this were plans to capture lake steamers, and to start fires in northern cities. In July he reported from Windsor that he had sixty escaped prisoners who were ready for any enterprise. He expected to begin after the middle of August certain "work" in which he said much caution would be necessary.[22]

In July, seeking to embarrass President Lincoln and to aid in anti-administration efforts to prevent his reëlection, Thompson and Clay decided to stimulate peace meetings in the northern states and to open a correspondence looking toward peace negotiations. In this plan, in which they were aided by J. P. Holcombe and G. N. Sanders, they sought to induce Lincoln to take the initiative in a conference which might be interpreted as a recognition of the official status of the Confederate government; but although they led Horace Greeley on a rainbow chase to Niagara, they were unable to entangle Lincoln who terminated their peace comedy by sending Colonel John Hay to verify his belief that they had no authority to open peace negotiations.[23]

In the same month, influenced by rumors of Confederate plans to destroy lake cities, the American government placed a restriction upon export of materials of war from New York to the British colonies. In reply to the British arguments against the restrictions it submitted the American claim that a nation at war has the legal right to prevent the exportation of war materials which, by use of the insurgent enemies, might endanger the public safety. Among its trade restrictions it had included a prohibition on the export of anthracite coal, to prevent Confederate blockade runners from obtaining it. Finding that this prohibition threatened to result in great losses to Canadian manufactures, it considerately withdrew the prohibition along the interior Canadian frontier on condition that Canada would prevent reëxport from any Canadian port. Soon thereafter, however, irritated by recent non-neutral operations from across the border, Seward rebuked Canada by adoption of a passport system which was not rescinded for Canada until March, 1865, and not finally withdrawn until May, 1865.[24]

On August 9, Seward, in a note to Lyons, complained of

reported Confederate projects in Canada. About the same time Lyons complained of the nefarious practices of crimps and other unscrupulous men, at Buffalo and elsewhere, to secure Canadian recruits for the American army. These discords, however, were succeeded by acts of international accord. In September Adams obtained Lord Russell's consent to an American proposal relating to consular arrangements with Canada.

Later, American complaints became more serious. In September and October Seward was aroused by events which threatened to produce a crisis on the Lakes. He first learned that Confederates from Canada, with plans to seize the United States armed steamer *Michigan* at Sandusky, had captured the steamer *Philo Parsons* on Lake Erie on September 19, that they had unfurled the Confederate flag upon it, and (after failure of their plans) had left it in a sinking condition at Sandwich in the Detroit River. After preparing a statement of this affair, he received the news that twenty-five desperate men, commanded by Lieutenant Bennett H. Young of the Confederate army (and apparently under instructions from Clay), had made a raid upon St. Albans, Vermont, and had escaped by returning to Canada on stolen horses. Although he recognized that the Canadian executive authorities had coöperated faithfully with the American authorities, he and others felt that Canada was responsible for the dangerous conduct of its Confederate guests. This feeling was not mollified by the later acceptance of responsibility by the Confederate authorities at Richmond, who stated that the raid had been authorized by instructions of June 16, 1864.[25]

A few days after the news of the St. Albans raid, and immediately before the presidential election, appeared alarming rumors and false reports which added to the excitement. One of these, a report from Toronto that one hundred Confederates had left there for a raid across the Detroit River, disturbed the Sunday church services at Detroit, on October 30. Others relating to Confederate plots to start fires in the principal northern cities on election day, early in November, caused the American government to authorize precautionary measures, resulting in orders to General Butler and General J. R. Hawley to place seven thousand men upon lake steamers ready for quick service at any point if needed to prevent Confederate attempts to execute rumored plots.[26]

Whatever were their preëlection plans, the Confederates saw in the results of the election the approaching doom of their cause, and they produced no further serious trouble on the northern frontier. Although Holcombe (who returned to Richmond by November 16) advised further encouragement of disaffection in the North with a view to the separation of the Northwest from the Union, the Confederate government made no favorable response and apparently in its later plans sought chiefly to involve the American government in foreign difficulties elsewhere. Thompson, although he still had a considerable part of the funds appropriated for his use, wrote Benjamin on December 3 (from Toronto) that he was not anxious to continue his operations from Canada in the face of the strict detective surveillance which appeared at every corner. On the basis of this suggestion, which did not reach Richmond until February 13, he was finally recalled.[27]

After careful consideration of the frontier excitement resulting from the Confederate capture of the *Philo Parsons* the American government decided that a temporary increase of "observing force" in that quarter was necessary. Seward explained that this proposed action was only in self-defense, and that it was necessary to meet conditions not anticipated in 1817. Finally, after discussions with the British representative at Washington, he decided to give to Lord Russell the notice necessary to legalize the increase of Lakes naval armament required for prompt action to prevent situations which might result in ultimate conflict upon the Canadian borders.[28]

In his instructions of October 24, after referring to the increasing instances of the use of neighboring British possessions as bases for hostile and felonious activities of the insurgents against American territory, and after repeating a request for efforts to remedy the insufficiency of the old British neutrality act, Seward expressed to Adams his conviction that peace could not be reliably maintained upon the border without the adoption of more effective measures for that purpose and, with no purpose of hostility, directed him to give the required notice to enable the American government in the existing exigency to feel at liberty to increase its naval armament upon the Lakes. After referring to the American right to expect fulfillment of the obligations of good neighborhood, and after suggesting the possibility of future British provincial political agitations and the consequent importance of establishing safe precedents which would avoid the possible danger of trans-border provocations, he asked: "Would it not be wise to establish a proper system of repression now, which would prove a rock of safety for both countries hereafter?" The substance of these instructions Adams promptly submitted to Lord Russell.[29]

Seward, although apparently he found no fault with the attitude of the Canadian authorities in their attempts to preserve neutrality, recognized some basis for American popular feeling. On November 3, after Governor Monck had taken offense at the General Dix military order to pursue across the boundary any offenders such as the raiders against St. Albans, and after the later Canadian objection to the offensive tone of some American newspapers, he wrote Lord Lyons that "indignant complaints by newspapers . . . as well as hasty popular proceedings for self defense and retaliation are among the consequences which must be expected to occur when unprovoked aggressions from Canada no longer allow [American] citizens to navigate the intervening waters with safety, or rest at home with confidence of security."[30]

On December 7, after further correspondence concerning the recent Confederate activities from the neighboring British possessions, and following alarming rumors of plans for renewed activities, Seward wrote Adams that the danger of these operations from Canada, which engaged the watchfulness of General Dix, might necessitate the organization of border defenses. On December 13 he sent to Adams a copy of an alarming report of Major-General Dix which he said reflected the apprehensions of imminent danger of enemy invasion from the British American provinces and foreshadowed the possible necessity of organized defense and consequent interruptions of commercial and social intercourse between the United States and the provinces.

On the following day, after reception of telegraphic information from Montreal that the participants in the St. Albans raid had been set free and were at large near the American border, he wrote Adams of the popular passion aroused by the news and instructed him to ask the British government whether it had any plans for provincial measures to prevent the departure of Confederate forces for invasion across the border. On December 19 he wrote that complications had increased—both by the Canadian release of the St. Albans raiders on the testimony of Lieutenant Bennett H. Young that he had commanded the raid as a commissioned Confederate officer, and by the American House resolution proposing to give the required notice to end the Reciprocity Treaty. He might have added that the official situation was somewhat complicated by injudicious speeches of federal-soldier members of the Fenians.[31]

Meantime, in December, influenced by the Confederate operations from Canada, Congress engaged in excited debates which after publication in the London press created considerable alarm in the British Parliament, threatening to result in angry British debates which Palmerston sought to prevent. Senator Chandler of Michigan proposed to authorize a defensive military force on the northern frontier. Senator Sherman proposed to authorize the President to place a necessary naval force upon the Lakes. The House approved a bill to terminate the Reciprocity Treaty.

At the same time, by order of the State Department, all non-immigrant travelers from Canada to the United States were required to obtain passports from American consuls.[32]

Both in the United States and in Canada, near the close of the year, the attitude of the press (and also of Congress and the Washington government) was interpreted as indicating the danger of a crisis.[33]

Early in 1865, while border feeling was gradually becoming less aggressive, and even after Canada enacted a law of February 6 to repress outrages in violation of the peace on the frontier, Congress seemed to be growing more aggressive. By its activity it produced in England an undercurrent of much restlessness and distrust which increased the fear of possible war for conquest of Canada. It also evidently contributed to a Canadian feeling of danger which was expressed in proposals for the establishment of direct communication between Montreal and Lake Huron via the Ottawa and French rivers and Lake Nipissing. In January, it particularly offended Canada by its approval of a resolution authorizing and requesting the President to give the required notice for unconditional abrogation of the Reciprocity Treaty of 1854 resulting in its termination in March, 1866. In this action, ignoring the heavy demand for importation of horses, meat, wool, lumber and fish from the British North American provinces, it accepted (by large majorities) the arguments of the growing abrogation movement, which had originated largely from opposition to Canadian policy concerning canals and duties on manufactures, and which was especially strengthened by the American coal and fish and lumber interests. Incident to this abrogation policy, W. P. Fessenden (of Maine) submitted to the House the question of a change in the law on bonded transit of goods through Canada between different points in the United States.[34]

A few days later the Senate approved a resolution confirming the executive notice of October 24 for termination of the agreement of 1817 concerning reduced armaments on the Lakes—a notice which Adams had delivered to Lord Russell on November 23. In the discussion of the subject, Senator Davis stated that the Committee was unanimous in the opinion that the act of the President in giving the notice was without authority, and, therefore, ineffective and inoperative until confirmed by action of Congress. He also stated that the expediency and propriety of terminating the agreement was indicated by the altered condition of Canada resulting from construction of its ship canals. Some advocates of the legislative sanction of the executive notice for abrogation hoped that the President would institute proceedings to renew the arrangement.[35]

Before the end of January, after receiving Adams' report of a satisfactory conference with Earl Russell, Seward spoke in a more hopeful tone. On January 26, he freely confessed that the recent action of the British government in relation to the "Canadian outrages" was just and fair, and that the provincial authorities with their hands thus strengthened had begun to act with energy in the spirit of the British instructions. The latter he hoped might result in the surrender of the "St. Albans and *Philo Parsons* felons" in compliance with the American requisition, and also in a restoration of the treasure which they had purloined.[36]

A few days later (February 2), following news of restrictive measures in agitation at Washington against Canada, and also following the news of the closing of the last Confederate port, Adams reported from London a British undertone of apprehension of an American determined spirit of enmity which, after a possible conciliation between Federals and Confederates, might result in an American declaration of war against Great Britain and an advance of the joint American armies into Canada. Later he reported that the Confederates sought to encourage this apprehension by erroneous statements concerning the nature of the Hampton Roads Conference of February 3 between Lincoln (and Seward) and the Confederate commissioners.[37]

Coincidently, however, appeared new evidence of friendly changes in British policy. On February 6, at the recommendation of the British government, Canada enacted a law to repress frontier outrages which were in violation of peace. On February 13, at London, Lord Russell notified Mason, Slidell and Mann of the complaints that Confederate agents sought to involve Great Britain in foreign complications. Referring to the seizure of the *Philo Parsons* and the plan to capture the *Michigan*, and the raid into Vermont, he stated that the "so-called Confederate States," by assuming responsibility for such acts under the guise of belligerent operations, showed a gross disregard of British neutrality and a desire to involve the British government in hostilities with a coterminous power. In conclusion, he sought a promise that such practices would cease and be entirely abandoned for the future. A copy of this notice he sent through Seward for delivery through Grant's lines to Judah P. Benjamin at Richmond.

Benjamin, who on March 14 diplomatically declined to receive Russell's note, had already decided to stop operations in Canada. On March 1, he had recalled Thompson in accord with the latter's expression of his indifferent attitude toward the continuation of his operations from Canada in the face of the strict detective watch upon his movements. Clay returned to the Confederacy just before the close of the war. Apparently Sanders (or Saunders) remained in Canada until the summer of 1865 when an effort to kidnap him resulted in the arrest and trial of the persons who attempted the capture, and whose continued detention in the Montreal jail after the jury failed to agree was a subject of some correspondence with Seward.[38]

Probably the final purpose of the Confederate agents in Canada was connected with the final Confederate attempt at negotiations in Europe. In a confidential note of March 1 Seward enclosed to Adams the contents of a cipher of February 13, from a Confederate in Canada to Jefferson Davis, concerning an attempt of Thompson and Clay to get British and French terms for assistance and recognition.

Meantime, on February 13, in connection with an announcement of the recent vigorous peace efforts of Confederate commissioners at Hampton Roads, Seward had sent Adams a copy of the joint resolution of Congress (of February 9) to terminate the agreement of 1817 which had so long restricted naval forces on the Lakes. In submitting to Lord Russell the information Adams expressed the hope that there would be no necessity to resort to extraordinary permanent measures of precaution. Regarding armaments as expensive and useless, serving in troubled times to breed mutual suspicions, he expressed the wish to continue the policy of mutual full reliance on good faith. He agreed with Russell that the reduction of armaments on the Lakes had been beneficial and also stated that, fortunately, the contemplated increase was unnecessary since the end of the American scare. Thus, at the suggestion of Lord Russell, steps were later taken to continue the policy of practical disarmament.[39]

On February 21, in reply to Adams' reports (of February 2) of British apprehensions of future American policy, Seward wrote that the American government, although it had many just causes of war against Great Britain, had acted in moderation. He said that it had maintained free trade and intercourse with British subjects in Canada until its northern frontier had become unsafe by acts of plunderers and incendiaries who had found shelter and protection in the British provinces, and that it now limited its restrictive action to the discontinuance of reciprocal trade and the imposition of some restraints on intercourse, "reserving the power to relax or increase them, as the course of Canada and the British government should become friendly or grow more hostile and injurious." If the moderation thus practiced was regarded by the British as an indication of determined enmity, he doubted whether the impression could be corrected. "We are not able," said he, "to endure more patiently or more meekly than we have endured injuries from that quarter. Relaxation on our part, without receiving any guarantees from Canada, would expose us to new aggressions." Four days earlier, in a written reply to a note of Bruce submitting a British proposal for a renewal or modified extension of the expiring Reciprocity Treaty of 1854, he repeated his previous verbal explanations that the President was not encouraged by public sentiment to direct the opening of negotiations, and that he had recently confirmed his belief that Congress preferred to treat the questions of commerce and national finances directly instead of by approach through diplomatic agreement.[40]

On March 8–10, following a fuller report from Adams, Seward made further efforts to remove the grounds of continued British apprehension and suspicion that the United States might inaugurate against Great Britain a war in which Canada would be the objective point. On March 8, coincident with a decision to stop the passport system on the northern frontier, he practically withdrew his recent notice to terminate the agreement of 1817 by expressing a hope that under changed circumstances the danger of insurgent incursions from Canadian territory had disappeared. Later, he removed all British doubts concerning the meaning of his note by stating that his purpose was to withdraw the previous note of abrogation.

On March 9, he authorized Mr. Burnley to explain to Lord Russell that, even if there had been no disturbance of friendly relations with Canada or Great Britain, the American government could not agree to continue the Reciprocity Treaty of 1854 beyond the appointed period of ten years without a thorough revision which would necessarily involve a submission of the whole subject to the Senate and also to the House. He stated that the American government, after an expected early recognition of full American authority over all the territory of the United States, and if agreeable to Congress, would "cheerfully enter into negotiations with a view to ascertain whether a just, fair and equal reciprocity in trade can be established between the United States and Canada."[41]

At the same time he sent conciliatory instructions. On March 10, after a reminder that he did not assume to speak for the Senate or for Congress, he said: "Perhaps it is not improper to add that in no case does this government contemplate war against Great Britain, whether for Canada or any other object." Early in the following month, after receiving from Adams a report of the debate of February 13 in Parliament upon the question of appropriation for defense of Canada, he suggested that a cheap and easy way by which the British could render that important dependency of the crown entirely secure for an indefinite period was by the practice of simple justice towards the United States.[42]

On March 14, in order to secure promptness of action concerning further operations of the insurgents and their abettors in Nova Scotia, Seward agreed to comply with Burnley's wish that he instruct the American consul at Halifax to notify the Governor-General directly of any information which might facilitate prompt action by the British authorities in the prevention of hostile proceedings. He insisted, however, that, notwithstanding the neutral friendly attitude of the governor and judges of Nova Scotia, restrictions on trade and intercourse were still necessary because of the connection of Halifax merchants with the transshipment of war materials by blockade runners to the insurgents, and because of the use of Halifax as a rendezvous for Confederate cruisers and as a postal and dispatch station between the insurgents at Richmond and their emissaries in Europe.

Later efforts to induce Congress to prevent the termination of the Reciprocity Treaty, or to authorize a new one, were unsuccessful. A. J. Galt, and three other Canadian delegates, arrived at Washington on January 24, 1866, for conferences on plans for renewal, but after two weeks returned discouraged.

Apparently Congress was opposed to any form of renewal. Probably its feeling was expressed by Senator Morrill in his statement that the Americans, having been deluded by a treaty which had been "extorted by an armed raid" on American fishermen in 1852, were too old to be deluded again by yielding to a growl. To the commission of Canadian representatives it gave no encouragement of any prospective change of mind. In reply to their proposal to put trade upon a better footing and to neutralize the canals and other waters, Morrill said: "That will have to be postponed until you, gentlemen, assume your seats *here*."[43]

On February 17, 1866, in reply to a British proposal to extend or renew the reciprocity treaty, Seward reported that the President by inquiries had been convinced that the lack of harmony of public sentiment concerning the extension of the treaty would not justify or encourage the opening of negotiations on the subject, and that he had been confirmed in his belief that Congress preferred to treat directly on the subject, without diplomatic approach. He suggested, therefore, that all communications upon the subject should be submitted to the consideration of the proper committees of Congress.

A few days later Morrill reported a bill to regulate trade with British North America, but with no provision for trade reciprocity. Over three months later he expressed to Bruce a disposition to reduce the duty on fish if the British colonial authorities would agree to reduce the duty on American fishing vessels to fifty cents (for license fee).[44]

The determined American refusal to consider Canadian proposals for a renewal of the treaty on more favorable terms resulted in a Canadian feeling of resentment. This resentment was only partly allayed by an act of Congress (of 1866) which (under pressure of Americans interested in Canadian railway lines) authorized the Secretary of the Treasury to permit the passage of Canadian goods in sealed cars through American territory from one point in Canada to another, without payment of duties. It resulted in an unfriendly Canadian disposition to claim the right to exclude American citizens from the navigation of the St. Lawrence to the ocean (which Americans regarded as a "natural right"), and led to American apprehensions of a repetition of Canadian "unneighborly acts" toward American fishermen. In 1870, after considering the Canadian attitude, President Grant recommended to Congress that it should confer upon the executive the power to suspend by proclamation the operation of the laws authorizing the transit of merchandise in bond across American territory to Canada, and, if necessary, also to suspend the laws which permitted Canadian vessels to enter American waters.[45]

Although irritated by the American abrogation of the treaty, Canada continued to permit the privileges granted to the United States under it. It allowed the St. Lawrence and Canadian canals to remain open to American commerce. It admitted free of duty practically all the articles which were free by treaty. Although it threatened to be less liberal concerning the fisheries, it adopted liberal temporary regulations in deference to the advice of the Colonial Office. It unwillingly continued the freedom of the shore fisheries by adoption of a license system under which full fishery privileges were granted to American schooners by payment of an annual fee.

In 1870, following the gradual increase of the annual license fee to a sum which the Americans regarded as prohibitive and refused to pay, the British government discontinued the license system for the fisheries and practically reënacted the Nova Scotian statute of 1836, with increased stringency of regulations and penalties. At the same time, it generously announced its intention not to exclude American fishermen from the body of the Bay of Fundy, nor to insist on prohibition from entrance to other bays except when there was reason to apprehend some substantial invasion of British rights, nor to prevent American vessels from navigating the Gut of Canso without injury to colonial fishermen and without other improper purposes. Following the increasing violence of fishermen's quarrels, the Governor-General issued a questionable order prohibiting foreign fishermen from fishing in Canadian waters. This order, which was difficult to enforce, resulted in a new Dominion expense for cruisers to patrol Nova Scotian waters to prevent American purchase of bait and supplies in open violation of the law.

The threatening situation was an important subject in the negotiations of 1871.[46]

Meantime, for several years, the Irish Fenian movement in the United States, partly a resultant of the war period, had threatened to disturb border relations. In May, 1865, rumors and apprehensions of a Fenian scheme to invade Canada caused an interruption of Canadian trade through the Welland Canal and on the Lakes and stimulated the Canadian government to begin active preparation for defense. Over a year later, following the abortive Fenian invasion (of June 1–3, 1866) at Fort Erie on the Niagara, the American government, with a view to prevent further invasions, sent the *Michigan* and a revenue cutter to patrol the Niagara River and placed General Berry with thirteen companies to patrol other parts of the frontier. On June 6 President Johnson issued a proclamation ordering strict enforcement of the neutrality laws, and resulting in effective action.

In Congress appeared some evidences of sympathy with the anti-British movement. On July 26, 1866, a few weeks after the Fenian movement had reached its American climax in an abortive invasion from New York and from Vermont, the American House of Representatives unanimously approved a bill which proposed a modification of the neutrality laws to permit the sailing of war vessels and the organization of military expeditions against a friendly power.[47]

The Canadian government contemplated the possible need of further precautionary measures against possible Fenian attempts at invasion. In August, 1866, it proposed the use of two steamers as temporary gunboats on Lake Erie and Lake Huron as an emergency measure. Later Canadian apprehension of further Fenian activities appeared in connection with the Fenian trials at Toronto and the anti-Fenian demonstrations which were subjects of correspondence between Seward and the British legation at Washington.[48]

On June 27, 1868, when Canada was again apprehensive of further Fenian attempts at invasion, Seward received from Sir Edward Thornton a confidential presentation of Monck for a grant of permission, if necessary as a defensive measure, to pass

British armed vessels or military transports through certain waters of Lake Champlain without delay from the American customs authorities. This request for what he regarded as a dangerous concession he declined to recommend. His refusal he sought to justify by the erroneous statement that Vermont and New York had jurisdiction over Lake Champlain. He stated that even the announcement of such a proposal, for use of American waters for hostile purpose against the Fenians, would create a bad popular impression. He expressed his conviction, however, that the proposed concession would not be required—that Fenians in the United States had neither the power nor the intention to attempt any aggression on Canada at that time.

Nearly two years thereafter, in March, 1870, appeared new Fenian plans for an invasion of Canada. The American government kept the *Michigan* ready for service on Lake Erie. Canada, after defeating an attempted raid in May, arrested the Fenian leader, John O'Neil, who was tried and convicted, but pardoned. Farther east, in the summer of 1870, it frustrated an attempted invasion of five hundred men from Vermont.[49]

Later, in the fall of 1871, in response to Canadian apprehension of possible Fenian plans for a raid into the Red River country (Manitoba) to which O'Neil had turned his attention, the American government promptly adopted precautionary measures. It especially ordered General Hancock to reënforce the American military post at Pembina near the Hudson's Bay Company fort which the Fenians temporarily captured on October 5. Its efforts were successful in preventing any other contemplated raid, but it was unable to prevent the effect of the previous raids in renewing the old Canadian hostility which proved useful in the cause of Canadian confederation.[50]

In 1868, in connection with the Fenian movement and diplomatic discussions concerning American claims for damages resulting from British neutral policy in the American Civil War, questions as to the rights of naturalized citizens became prominent and soon resulted in a naturalization protocol. Later, the American government sought to obtain a more satisfactory settlement of the naturalization question, which was regarded as a preliminary to the settlement of the San Juan controversy.

On June 10, 1869, in a private interview with Lord Clarendon, Motley stated that the American government was ready to convert the naturalization protocol into a treaty whenever the necessary legislation was completed by Parliament.[51] Successful in his efforts, he was able to conclude a satisfactory convention which was signed on May 13, 1870. This convention for the regulation of the citizenship of emigrants from either country by naturalization or by renunciation of naturalization was later supplemented (on February 23, 1871) by a convention which stipulated the manner of declaring renunciation.[52]

Meantime, within the decade after 1861, new international problems had arisen along the unfortified frontier west of Lake Superior and the new State of Minnesota. The most important of these was the problem of border Indian relations. This was a subject of considerable Anglo-American correspondence, which originated in 1862 in connection with an Indian massacre in Minnesota and a flight of part of the Sioux tribe to Canada where it was assigned to a Canadian reservation near the international border. With it was associated the problem of military opening and protection of an immigrant road from the new State of Minnesota to new mining camps in Montana including incidental questions of control of predatory Indians along the route and across the Canadian boundary.[53]

In seeking a solution of this problem the American government became more active in 1867. Impressed with the need of a system of frontier military posts, Secretary Seward especially sought British coöperation in a policy to protect the road from Fort Abercrombie to the region beyond Fort Benton—a policy which he regarded as "essential to the progress of civilization on this continent." [54]

Farther east, in 1870, arose a question of the observance of neutrality in connection with the insurrection led by Riel in the Red River region. In May, Secretary Fish requested Governor Baldwin of Michigan to refuse the use of the Sault Ste. Marie Canal to British-Canadian steamers engaged in the transportation of war materials or troops. Subsequently, however, he authorized the westward passage of the *Chicora,* after he was assured that it formed no part of a military expedition.[55]

Later, as a result of increasing frontier settlements, and following the Canadian peaceful acquisition of the jurisdictional rights of the Hudson's Bay Company and the Canadian military suppression of Riel's rebellion, the American government encountered another problem concerning the border of the Middle Northwest. In November, 1870, following suggestions of a possible error in the boundary line from the Lake of the Woods to the Rocky Mountains, Secretary Fish invited the British government to coöperate in steps to locate the exact line of 49° near Pembina. This invitation resulted in an early and satisfactory adjustment, by locating the line north of Pembina. The entire line west of the Lake of the Woods was not determined until 1877.[56]

In the farther Northwest, following the American acquisition of Alaska in 1867, arose a new problem resulting from new contacts with the great British trading company there. Early in February, 1869, the American government, through instructions to Reverdy Johnson, complained of encroachments of the Hudson's Bay Company upon Alaskan territory. Two months later, after learning that the Company probably would not withdraw its posts from the Yukon before the next spring, it urged a reasonable effort for earlier withdrawal. Early in December, while awaiting action on the Yukon, it received from the Hudson's Bay and Puget Sound companies deeds of transfer and release of their possessory rights south of 49° and the Strait of Fuca. This transfer was hastened by Sir John Rose, the later useful agent in initiating Anglo-American negotiations for peaceful settlement of serious controversy which for a time threatened to result in an American demand for withdrawal of the British flag from Canada.[57]

REFERENCES

1. *The Evening Citizen* (Ottawa), July 24, 1934; T. D'Arcy McGee, *Speeches and Addresses; C.A.*, G, 231, pp. 142–48, May 22, 1863; *Ib.*, Dec. 8; *Ib.*, G, 232, Apr. 8, 1864; *Ib.*, G, 233, Aug. 15, 1864 (also Aug. 23 and 25).
2. *78 G.B., Desps.*, No. 93, Dec. 20, 1861.

3. *21 Special Agents,* Seward to Ashnum, Apr. 18, 1861; *C.A.,* G, 229, *Canada,* pp. 50–64, May 2, 1861.
4. *17 G.B., Instrs.,* pp. 438–39, June 21, 1861.
5. *C.A.,* G, 230, pp. 43–44 and 64; *Ib.,* 239, *Canada,* pp. 180–82, Confid., No. 20, June 11, 1861; *H. Exec. Docs.,* 37–2, Vol. 10, No. 146, p. 26, June 20, 1862; *H. Rps.,* 37–2, Vol. 3, No. 2, Feb. 15, 1862.
6. *C.A.,* G, 229, *Canada,* pp. 113–15 and 129–31; *42 G.B., Notes from; 9 G.B., Notes to; Misc. Letters,* Sept. 10, 1861.
7. *78 G.B., Desps.,* No. 88, Dec. 12, 1861.
8. *Ib.,* No. 93, Dec. 20, 1861; *Phila. Press,* Jan. 8, 1862; *18 G.B., Instrs.,* p. 96, No. 162, Jan. 8, 1862; *Ib.,* p. 111, No. 178, Feb. 4, 1862; *Ib.,* p. 156, No. 218, Apr. 1, 1862; *C.A.,* G, *Gov.-Genl's Letter Book, 1861–63,* Jan. 23, 1862; *C.A.,* C.O. Series, 188, Vol. 189, Lyons to A. A. Gordon, Confid., Jan. 20, 1862; *Ib.,* Lyons to Gordon, March 7 (and Lyons to Monck, Jan. 28).
9. *Sen. Rps. Coms.,* 37–2, No. 22, Mar. 10, 1862; *Ib.,* No. 23; *Sen. Misc. Docs.,* 37–2, Nos. 19, 27, 31, 33, 43 and 44; *C.A.,* G, 230, *Canada,* pp. 43–44 and 64; *Ib.,* Lyons to Monck, Feb. 20, 1862; Callahan, *Neutrality of the Am. Lakes,* pp. 142–43.
10. *Ib.,* pp. 16 and 141–43; W. H. Russell, *Canada and Its Defenses, Conditions and Resources; Cong. Globe,* 38–1, May 25, 1862.
11. *9 G.B., Notes* to, p. 563, Apr. 21, 1863; *C.A.,* G, *Cor. with Gov.-Genl.'s Secy.,* Lyons to Monck, Apr. 25, 1863; *57 Cong. Globe.*
12. *C.A.,* G, 168, *Canada,* pp. 230–36, No. 163, Aug. 21, 1862.
13. *10 G.B., Notes to,* pp. 27–28, May 18, 1863; *18 G.B., Instrs.,* pp. 589–91, No. 691, Sept. 2; Adams, *Treaty of Washington,* p. 67.
14. Callahan, *Diplomatic History of the Southern Confederacy,* Chap. X; *Naval War Records,* 1°, Vol. 2, No. 36; *H. Docs.,* 54–1, Vol. 41.
15. Callahan, *Dip. Hist. of the So. Confederacy,* pp. 223–25.
16. *10 G.B., Notes to,* pp. 461–64, Jan. 7, 1864.
17. *62 G.B., Notes from;* Callahan, *Neutrality of the Am. Lakes,* pp. 146–47; *Toronto Weekly Leader,* Dec. 30, 1864.
18. *19 G.B., Instrs.,* pp. 214–18, No. 859, Mar. 2, 1854.
19. *63 G.B., Notes from; 64 Domestic Letters,* Seward to Chase, May 7, 1864; *11 G.B., Notes to,* p. 222, May 11.
20. *H. Rps.,* 38–1, Vol. 1, No. 39, Apr. 1, 1864; *Cong. Globe,* Vol. 58, 38–1, pp. 9, 19, 1387, 2333–38, 2364–71, 2454–56, 2476–83 and 2502–09.
21. *67 G.B., Notes from,* Aug. 4, 1864; *11 G.B., Notes to,* p. 558.
22. Callahan, *Dip. Hist. of the So. Confederacy,* pp. 225–26.
23. *Ib.,* pp. 229–31.
24. *11 G.B., Notes to,* p. 573, Aug. 8, 1864; *C.A.,* G, 232, pp. 252–

54, and 255–57, Monck to Lord Lyons, May 3, 1864; *Ib.*, G, 233, *Canada*, p. 172, Aug. 27 (and Aug. 22); *Ib.*, G, 236, June 9, 1865; *2 Southern Rev.*, Oct., 1867, pp. 449–61.

25. *C.A.*, G, 233, pp. 64–110, 119–27 and 149–60; *G.B.*, *Desps.*, No. 787, Sept. 22, 1864; *19 G.B.*, *Instrs.*, p. 475, No. 1115, Oct. 7, 1864; *Ib.*, pp. 491–503, No. 1136, Oct. 24; *N. Y. Times*, Jan. 1, and Feb. 19, 1865; CALLAHAN, *Dip. Hist. of the So. Confederacy*, p. 235.
26. *Ib.*, pp. 235–36; *C.A.*, G, 234, pp. 17–18 and 21–22, Burnley to Monck, Nov. 7 and Nov. 11, 1864.
27. *N. Y. Herald*, July 24 and 25, 1872; *London Times*, Dec. 19, 1864; *Naval War Records*, 1°, Vol. III, No. 379, p. 714.
28. *12 G.B.*, *Notes to*, p. 185, Sept. 26, 1864; *Ib.*, p. 203, Oct. 1; *19 G.B.*, *Instrs.*, pp. 491–503, No. 1136, Oct. 24, 1864; *88 G.B.*, *Desps.*, inclosure of Adams to Russell, Nov. 23, 1864.
29. *19 G.B.*, *Instrs.*, No. 1136, Oct. 24, 1864; *C.A.*, G, 176, *Canada*, pp. 218–24 (Carnarvon to Monck, No. 21, Aug. 4, 1866); *88 G.B.*, *Desps.*, Nov. 23, 1864.
30. *72 G.B.*, *Notes from*, Oct. 29, 1864; *12 G.B.*, *Notes to*, p. 346.
31. *19 G.B.*, *Instrs.*, p. 541, No. 1186, Dec. 7 and 13, 1864; *Ib.*, pp. 544–45, No. 1190, Dec. 14; *Ib.*, pp. 549–54, No. 1194, Dec. 19; *C.A.*, G, 234, pp. 139–40, Burnley to Monck, Dec. 14; *Ib.*, G, 235, pp. 211–12, Dec. 22, 1864; *Ib.*, Jan. 25, 1865; *Toronto Weekly Leader*, Oct. 28, Nov. 4; *Detroit Free Press*, Nov. 4; *Sen. Docs.*, 38–2, Vol. 1, No. 2, Dec. 8; *Corres. rel. to Fenians and the Rebellion in the Southern States.*
32. *Sen. Misc. Docs.*, 38–2, Vol. 8, No. 5; *67 Cong. Globe*, 38–2, Part 1, p. 57, Dec. 19, 1864; *19 G.B.*, pp. 549–51, No. 1194, Dec. 19, 1864; *C.A.*, C.O. Series, 188, Vol. 193 (N.B.), Burnley to Gordon.
33. *Toronto Leader*, Dec. 16, 1864.
34. *Parl. Debates*, Vols. 177 and 178, Mar. 13 and 23; *88 G.B.*, *Desps.*, No. 870, Feb. 9, 1865; *Montreal Gazette*, Mar. 14; HAYNES, *Reciprocity Treaty of 1854; Cong. Globe*, 38–1, 1863–64, pp. 9, 19, 1371, 1387, 2298, 2333, 2452, 2476, 2482, 2502, 2508; *Ib.*, 38–2, Part 1, pp. 31–35, 204–38, 265, 267, 276–77, 291; *Cong. Digest*, May, 1933, pp. 130–32; *H. Exec. Docs.*, 38–2, Vol. 8, No. 28.
35. *67 Cong. Globe*, 38–2, 1864–65, Part 1, pp. 311–16.
36. *20 G.B.*, *Instrs.*, pp. 26–27, No. 1247, Jan. 26, 1865.
37. *88 G.B.*, *Desps.*, No. 868, Feb. 2, 1865; *Ib.*, No. 870, Feb. 9; CALLAHAN, *Neutrality of the Am. Lakes.*
38. *75 G.B.*, *Notes to; Canada Gazette*, Feb. 6, 1865; *88 G.B.*, *Desps.*, Nos. 874 and 879, Feb. 10 and 16; *Ib.*, Feb. 16 (Inclosure, Russell to Adams, Feb. 15); J. B. JONES, *Diary*, Mar. 24 and 27; *Mason Papers*, Benjamin to Mason, No. 40, March 25; *N. Y.*

Herald, July 24, 1872; *20 G.B., Instrs.*, p. 75; *C.A.*, G, 236, Bruce to Lieut. Gen. Sir John Michel, Private, Dec. 21, 1865.

39. *Ib.*, pp. 51–52, No. 1263, Feb. 13, 1865; *Ib.*, p. 55, No. 1269, Feb. 13; Callahan, *Neutrality of the Am. Lakes*, pp. 159–63.
40. *81 Br. Legation*, Feb. 16, 1865; *20 G.B.*, pp. 62–67, No. 1274, Feb. 21.
41. *Ib.*, pp. 89–90, No. 1289, Mar. 8; *Ib.*, No. 1290, Mar. 8; *Ib.*, No. 1296, Mar. 10; *C.A.*, G, 235, pp. 158–59, March 8; *National Intelligencer*, Mar 9; *13 G.B., Notes to*, p. 189, Mar. 20; *Ib.*, p. 358, June 16; *Ib.*, p. 438, Nov. 4.
42. *20 G.B.*, pp. 147–48, No. 1328, Apr. 4, 1865.
43. *13 G.B., Notes to*, pp. 169–71, Mar. 14, 1865; *Cong. Globe*, Mar. 6, 7, 9, 12, 1866 (see p. 1210); Watkins, *Canada and the U.S.*, pp. 405–18 and 425.
44. *81 Br. Legation*, Feb. 16, 1866; *13 G.B., Notes to*, pp. 525–26, Feb. 17; *C.A.*, G, 237, pp. 55–57, Bruce to Monck, Feb. 21, 1866 (and Mar. 2); *Ib.*, June 4, 1866; *Ib.*, G, 239, pp. 180–82, Bruce to Monck, Confid., June 11, 1867.
45. *Ib.*, G, 239, Bruce to Jno. Michel, Feb. 9, 1867; *Ib.*, G, 159, Thornton to Young, No. 25, May 25, 1870; *19 Cong. Record*, 50–1, Part 8, p. 7205, Aug. 3, 1888; Richardson, VII, 104.
46. Shortt and Doughty, *Canada and Its Provinces*, IX, 129; *20 G.B., Instrs.*, pp. 446–49, No. 1737, Apr. 10, 1866; *For. Rels.*, *1870*, pp. 408, 414, 419–21.
47. *78 G.B., Notes from*, May 19, 1865; Richardson, VI, 433; *H. Exec. Docs.*, 40–1, No. 9, Mar. 20, 1867; *Cong. Globe*, 39–1, p. 493.
48. *C.A.*, G, 176, *Canada*, pp. 218–24, Carnarvon to Monck, No. 21, Aug. 4, 1866; *C.A.*, G, 237, pp. 130–32, Bruce to Monck; *21 G.B., Instrs.*, p. 96, No. 1868, Oct. 30, 1866.
49. *F.O.*, 5/1344; *C.A.*, G, 239, *Canada*, pp. 185–87, Thornton to Monck, Confid., No. 24, June 27, 1868; *Ib.*, G, 573A, 696, pp. 86– , Thornton to Sir John Young, Dec. 4, 1868 (and Dec. 22); *Ib.*, G, 161, #1485, Thornton to Young, No. 26, May 25, 1870; *Misc. Letters*, Mar. 7 and 10, 1870.
50. *15 G.B., Notes to*, pp. 353 and 364, Sept. 23 and Oct. 6, 1871; *Ib.*, p. 424, Jan. 9, 1872.
51. Adams, *C. F. Adams*, p. 357; *21 G.B., Instrs.*, p. 576, No. 3, May 15, 1869; *22 G.B., Instrs.*, pp. 193–205, No. 151, Feb. 15, 1870; *Sen. Exec. Docs.*, 41–2, No. 114; *Sen. Docs.*, 41–3, No. 11; *99 G.B., Desps.*, No. 8, June 12, 1869.
52. *22 G.B., Instrs.*, pp. 255–56, No. 203, May 27, 1870; Malloy, *Treaties of the U.S.*, I, 698–99.
53. *9 G.B., Notes to*, pp. 406–07, Jan. 12, 1863; *11 G.B., Notes to*, p. 123, Apr. 6, 1864; *For. Rels.*, *1863*, pp. 551 and 610, May 23 and July 25; *C.A.*, G, 231, Lyons to Monck, Jan. 12, June 6 and

July 25, 1863; also see G, 237, pp. 233–34, Bruce to John Michel, Dec. 24, 1866.

54. *For. Rels., 1867*, Vol. 1, p. 68, Mar. 21; *21 G.B., Instrs.*, pp. 173–76, No. 1946, Mar. 21, 1867; *102 G.B., Desps.*, No. 1354, Apr. 15.

55. *Sen. Exec. Docs.*, 41–2, Vol. 2, No. 88, May 21, 1870.

56. *15 G.B., Notes to*, p. 161, Nov. 7, 1870; *22 G.B., Instrs.*, p. 289, No. 245, Aug. 15, 1870; *Sen. Exec. Docs.*, 44–2, No. 41; *C.A.*, G, 200, #1569, pp. 186–90, Thornton to John Young, Confid., No. 36, July 21, 1870; *Ib.*, G Series, Sept. 10, 1873; *Rp. U. S. Commissioner* (Washington, 1878), pp. 22–27.

57. *21 G.B., Instrs.*, p. 516, No. 73, Feb. 6, 1869; *22 G.B., Instrs.*, p. 28, No. 44, Aug. 10; *Ib.*, p. 143, No. 106, Dec. 3; *Ib.*, p. 112, Tel., Nov. 6.

CHAPTER XIII

ANNEXATION AGITATION AND CANADIAN DESTINY, 1861–71

THROUGHOUT the period of the American Civil War, and also for the half decade immediately following, the American government was confronted with British American political situations which suggested to it opportunities for early territorial annexation, the possibility of which already had been contemplated in connection with the discussions on the policy of trade reciprocity. In the half decade after 1865, in seeking adjustment of the Anglo-American international controversies arising in the period of the war, its largest subject of consideration was the problem of the destiny of Canada—especially the problem of the destiny of the great Canadian Northwest which was so largely affected by the results of the American westward movement and by the evolution of American and Canadian policies after the negotiation of the Oregon treaty.

Over a decade before the Civil War British writers and political leaders considered Canadian destiny with uncertainty. After the British repeal of the corn laws they had premonitions and apprehensions that the American expansion spirit might turn northward. Long after 1849 they recognized that Canada might find in American annexation a promise of the realization of its larger interests.[1]

In the early fifties, as the quasi-national union between Canada and the United States was growing closer, many believed that the majority in discontented Canada desired annexation to England's growing rival, who was already seeking the control of the Asiatic trade, and who might easily control all North America by the construction of Whitney's proposed railroad across the continent and the termination of English colonial government in Canada. To counteract American influences, Captain F. A. Wilson urged a scheme for the construction of a continental road across Canada as the only remedy that would relieve the distress of Great Britain and Canada. In considering the condition of affairs in Europe early in 1854, British leaders realized that Canada was a hostage by which the United States could command its own security.[2]

At the same time Seward and others, considering the possible necessity of seeking a territorial counterpoise to Southern plans to acquire Cuba, contemplated the future American acquisition of Alaska and Canada. Others proposed to hasten the operation of destiny for Canada by Irish invasion or by American open negotiations with England for annexation.[3]

Possibly the Pierce-Marcy administration expected the Reciprocity Treaty of 1854 to result in the gradual, quiet, peaceful settlement of the Canadian question, by the growth of close relations which would develop into annexation. If so, its successor, confronted by increasing Canadian tariffs and new transportation strategy to divert more western trade to Montreal and Quebec, found little basis for such expectations. In the face of this change of situation, however, several prominent Americans still had lingering hopes supported by convictions of expediency. In February, 1859, in opposing the proposed purchase of Cuba for military reasons, Senator Hale of Maine suggested that there was much more military reason for annexation of Canada because of the strategic position of the St. Lawrence River.[4]

In 1857–60, new conditions along the international border at the Pacific Northwest and west of Lake Superior encouraged annexation sentiment and threatened to complicate American relations with Canada and Great Britain.

At the Pacific, in 1858, the large American immigration to the Fraser River gold regions led to conflict and danger of collision with the British authorities at Vancouver Island, who feared American seizure of the British colonies. John Nugent, whom the American government sent as special agent to urge subordination of the Americans to the British colonial authorities and to endeavor to secure from Governor Douglas of

Vancouver the abrogation of the rigorous system of exactions, reported that although the Americans had entered the colonies with no marauding propensities the ultimate accession of both Vancouver and British Columbia to the American possessions was scarcely problematical. Later, in 1867, as the result of an agitation in Vancouver in favor of annexation to the United States, the island was united with the mainland to form the province of British Columbia whose integration between interior and coast was largely influenced by the famous Cariboo trail of the gold hunters.[5]

Coincidently, American relations with the British authorities north of Juan de Fuca Strait were affected by the unsettled controversy in regard to the water boundary south of the parallel of 49° in the Gulf of Georgia.[6]

In the neighboring eastward region, during the Civil War, appeared a new American advance along the border south of the boundary, a significant event which pointed to the increase of American influence along the entire boundary west of the Lakes. Early in 1861, an eastward migrating movement from the Pacific coast rapidly filled Walla Walla with miners *en route* to Idaho where Lewiston soon originated as an outfitting point for pack trains to a new mining region. In 1863 a new movement advanced into the Boise basin of southern Idaho and into Montana. By 1864 Walla Walla was connected with the east by a road from St. Paul.[7]

Farther east, in the vast fertile region drained by the Saskatchewan and the Red rivers, and especially in the Red River Valley north of the new American commonwealth of Minnesota, appeared other new border influences, resulting from the disappointed efforts of the Winnipeg region to induce Canada to adopt a westward expansion policy and also from the stimulation of the awakening touch of neighboring American industry.

In the late fifties Sir Edward Bulwer-Lytton, the British Colonial Secretary, had proclaimed a policy of continuous British colonies from Lake Superior to the Pacific, but this policy was opposed by Lower Canada. Later, finding that the Canadian government declined to institute court proceedings to determine the validity of the charter of the Hudson's Bay Company or to undertake to extend Canadian political institutions and jurisdiction, he decided that annexation of the Winnipeg basin to Canada was impracticable and that the exclusive occupation of the Hudson's Bay Company could be removed only by organizing a separate colony.[8]

Meantime Selkirk south of Lake Winnipeg felt the influence of an increasing ox-cart trade with St. Paul, a considerable immigration of settlers from Minnesota and the opening of a weekly trans-border mail (by 1861). By 1860 the *Nor-Wester*, a Red River newspaper, voiced the strong feeling of the region in favor of annexation to the United States. Influenced by such expression, Senator Seward, in September, 1860, in a speech at St. Paul, suggested that Canadians were building states which would later join the American Union.[9]

While the British authorities remained indifferent to the Red River cries, and while some of the people of the eastern provinces preferred to contemplate the possibility of a plan for expansion into Maine which stood like an entering wedge between Canada and New Brunswick, American influence from Minnesota continued to operate across the boundary into British territory. By the middle of 1862 there were renewed expressions of discontent at Selkirk and threats of annexation to the United States.[10]

Meantime, the Canadian government was preparing to take an important step toward a policy of westward expansion to the Pacific. In April, 1862, with a view to the establishment of road and telegraphic communication between Canada and the gold regions of British Columbia, it proposed to establish steam communication on Lake Superior and to open roads from Fort William in the direction of the Red River, and to rely upon the Hudson's Bay Company to continue the work through its territory. In June the Colonial Office stated that the British government would coöperate in any well-devised scheme of communication. It especially directed attention to the facilities for acquisition of land announced by the Hudson's Bay Company as an inducement to settlers in the Red River region.[11]

After the crisis of the American Civil War in the summer of

1863, when disintegrating secession was rapidly losing, the British recognized the possibility of postbellum American expansion into disunited Canada. Eastern Canadians, contemplating the complications which might result from foreign questions, suggested that England, if it should become involved in war with the United States, should consent to establish the neutrality of Canada, whose material interests were largely dependent upon the northern part of the United States. Later, in 1864, the Canadian government recognized increasing danger in the unhealthy border excitement which was caused by Confederate operations across the border from Canada and which resulted in considerable popular agitation for annexation.[12]

In considering the condition of affairs Canada was stimulated to take steps for a confederation. On October 10, 1864, delegates from the British North American provinces assembled in conference and agreed to resolutions which formed the basis of the later Act of Union. In January, 1865, they submitted their resolutions to the Legislative Assembly of Canada. The Assembly, after debating them from February 3 until March 14, agreed by large majorities to ask the Queen to submit the plan to the British Parliament. In the debates, leading members urged the necessity of the proposed confederation as a measure to counteract the American ambition for acquisition. On February 9 Thomas D'Arcy McGee said that the Monroe Doctrine in popular paraphrase had become a policy of continental expansion. Recalling the recent American notice to abrogate treaties, the vast increase of the American armies, the gravitation of the Canadian trade from the region west of Kingston across the Lakes to New York and the trade of New Brunswick and Nova Scotia to Portland and Boston, and the previous American territorial extensions, he urged that Canadian confederation was the only way to prevent the risk of the absorption of Canada by the "spirit of universal democracy" in the United States.[13]

The later decision of Parliament in favor of confederation, by the passage of the North American Act and the authorization of a guarantee of a Canadian loan of three million dollars for the construction of the long-desired intercolonial railway, was largely influenced by the American expression of annexation sentiment which attracted attention in England.[14] The act received the royal assent on March 29, 1867. It became operative on July 1, which was thereafter celebrated as "Dominion Day."

The United States emerged from the Civil War with an optimistic consciousness and courageous confidence born of experience, and with temptations to practice strategic diplomacy. Confronted by grave foreign complications, the American government did not seek to evade or postpone the settlement of accounts. It began at once to rid the continent of the most prominent sources of future troubles. It was determined to secure indemnity from England for damages to American commerce committed by English-built Confederate cruisers during the war. For a half decade, therefore, influenced by the coincident negotiations for British settlement of the famous *Alabama* claims and by Canadian plans for consolidation of the eastern provinces of British America, and also stimulated by consideration of possible future border difficulties and future American interests, it contemplated a policy of annexation of all British North America as compensation for American claims for British violations of neutrality. By expressions of this policy it stimulated and strengthened the Canadian counter-policy of confederation and of transcontinental railway communication eastward to the Atlantic coast of Nova Scotia, and westward to the Pacific coast of British Columbia.

The new policy of hastening and compelling the annexation of Canada, which was foreseen in the non-renewal of the Reciprocity Treaty and the associated expectations of Canadian application for annexation for commercial reasons, was clearly formulated before the close of 1866. It appeared in urgent requests for the construction of the Northern Pacific Railway as a valuable political measure in relation to Canada, in special reports on commercial relations, and in House and Senate resolutions.

In an interesting report of June 6, from St. Paul, James W. Taylor (a special agent) referred to the slow but sure Americanization of the Red River region and predicted a much more rapid Americanization of the Saskatchewan region by the camps of the treasure-seekers from newly organized Montana Territory. Stating that overtures should be made for the union of the United States and British America, he proposed in detail a plan which provided organization of states, construction of canals and railways, payment of Canadian debts, and surveys of public lands. "The United States may interpose with the requisite guarantees," said he, "and if so why shall we not combine to extend an American union to the Arctic circle?" He concluded as follows:

> I cannot resist the conclusion that events have presented to the people of the government of the United States the opportunity—let me rather say, have developed the duty—of interposing by an overture to the people of the English colonies on this continent, upon the fullest consultation with Great Britain, to unite their fortunes with the United States.[15]

On July 2 Banks, Chairman of the Committee on Foreign Affairs, reported a resolution suggesting that, when the Department of State should be informed officially that Great Britain and the several British provinces in Canada accepted the proposition of annexation, the President should declare by proclamation that Nova Scotia, New Brunswick, Lower Canada, Upper Canada, and the territories of Selkirk, Saskatchewan, and of Columbia should be admitted to the United States as states and territories.[16]

Meantime, in June, after Russell refused to arbitrate the *Alabama* claims many members of Congress were disposed to favor the Fenians who for several months had threatened to carry the green flag into Canada. In the House appeared several pro-Fenian resolutions which were referred to the Committee on Foreign Affairs by a vote of eighty-seven yeas against thirty-five nays (with sixty-one not voting). Six weeks later, in a report on the resolutions, Banks stated that the American government had been too strict in enforcing neutrality laws against Fenian invasion of Canada. A subsequent bill to modify the neutrality laws, so as to permit the preparations of warships and military expeditions against friendly powers, received the unanimous vote of the House

(123 yeas and 63 not voting), but in the Senate it was referred to the Committee on Foreign Relations, which failed to report it.[17]

Early in July, expecting the early beginning of French withdrawal from Mexico and the consequent security of American political interest there, Seward instructed Adams that "under the influence of these cheerful expectations" the American people would naturally be expected to fix attention on discussion of the adjustment of grave subjects in relations with Great Britain.[18]

In the same month, after the publication of Taylor's trade reports and plans, he was requested by the House and the Senate to furnish further information needed in reaching a conclusion concerning the best policy to apply in relations with Canada. Six months later, in response to the Senate's request, he submitted a new report prepared for him by E. H. Derby, special agent to Canada, who had recently advocated a new treaty of reciprocity on the ground that the United States could seek annexation to better advantage after it had paid its debts and after England had paid its indemnity claims.

Derby still favored a policy of conciliation instead of retaliation. In his report to Seward he suggested that Great Britain, if it desired to propitiate the United States, might easily find a peaceful solution to the question of American claims by an offer to cede a portion of its remote territories, especially Vancouver Island and British Columbia, so important to American interests on the Pacific coasts and settled in a great part by American citizens. Possibly he knew that Seward had just received from Victoria, Vancouver Island, a petition requesting the annexation of British Columbia, whose slow growth was noticeable in painful contrast to the rapid progress of California and Oregon. Submitting a plan for the annexation of the Canadian provinces to the United States, and indicating the economic, political, and international advantages of such a continental union which would effectively remove all neighborhood difficulties and ensure future pacific relations with Great Britain, he suggested that England should wisely and magnanimously take the initiative in the achievement of the union. Mentioning in contrast the previous policy of England he said: "While she consolidates provinces and fortifies Halifax and Victoria, or at Esquimalt harbor, can she wonder that the United States seeks alliance with Russia?" [19]

The intimation that consolidation of the provinces of British America would cause the United States to seek closer cooperation with Russia was significant. It reflected the strong American opposition to the evident purpose of the recent Canadian movement. Later, on March 27, 1867, the House, without opposition, approved a resolution from the Committee on Foreign Affairs expressing American solicitude concerning the proposed Canadian confederation which was to be formed without the consent of the people of the provinces to be confederated, and which would probably increase the embarrassment already existing between the United States and Great Britain. Three days later a counter-movement against the future extension of the confederation westward from the Lakes to the Pacific was inaugurated by the treaty for the transfer of Alaska to the United States.

The chief motives in the American acquisition of Alaska, territory which was regarded as unproductive, seem clear. Russia in deciding to retire from America expected England to retire also. It hoped that the cession might ultimately lead to the expulsion of England from the Pacific. Seward, in an interview soon after the purchase, stated that the American purpose was to prevent the possible extension of England's coast line on the Pacific, to strengthen American influence in British Columbia, and to hasten the destiny of Canada to form a political union with the United States that would result in the development of its resources and the removal of causes of irritation between England and the United States. Possibly, as Senator Ingalls later asserted, the acquisition at that time was regarded as a step (under the Monroe Doctrine) toward the "unification of this continent under American domination." [20]

Many who approved the policy of acquiring Alaska were largely influenced by the expectation that it was a step toward the peaceful absorption of Canada by a natural process of accretion, beginning with a "necessary annexation of overtaxed British Columbia." Senator Sumner, in his speech on the Alaska treaty, on April 7, 1867, said: "The present treaty is a visible step in the occupation of the whole North American continent." This view was accepted by many of the leading newspapers.[21]

The Alaska treaty was particularly regarded as a direct step toward termination of British title on the Northwest coast, as a necessary initiatory step to close the gap between Washington Territory and 54°40′ by a reasonable proposition for purchase. That British Columbia might desire to join the United States was philosophically admitted by the *London Times,* and was also recognized by members of the British Parliament, who urged that Great Britain must build a railroad across the continent to preserve its Pacific possessions and to retain its influence in the Pacific Ocean.[22]

In November, 1867, Major-General Halleck, reporting (from San Francisco) the "anomalous" condition which had existed since 1869 at San Juan Island in the Haro Archipelago on the Washington Territory frontier, suggested that the conflict of authority there should be terminated by annexation of all British territory west of the Rockies. This policy he justified as a measure which (without injury to Great Britain) would increase American coastwise trade, prevent future sources of border irritation, and benefit British Columbia by increase of immigration and stimulation of industry.

About the same time, in an article in the *Washington Chronicle,* R. J. Walker stated that the territory between 49° and 54°40′ which had been abandoned in 1846 must ultimately gravitate back to the United States. Later, in 1868, in a talk with Banks during the House debates on the appropriation for the Alaska purchase, he declared that he had always regarded the acquisition of Alaska as a measure of the highest importance, particularly in connection with the acquisition of British Columbia and the prevention of European possessions on the Pacific coast.[23]

In 1867–68, following the American negotiations for acquisition of the Danish West Indies, Walker suggested to Seward a further step toward "hemming in" the Canadian possessions of Great Britain. Declaring that the North American confederacy in Canada was conceived in hostility to the United States, he suggested as a counter flank movement, on the northeast, the purchase of Greenland, with the hope that it might greatly increase Canada's inducements "peacefully and cheerfully to become a part of the American Union." [24]

For a time the success of the Canadian confederation hung in the balance. In the eastern provinces, except in Nova Scotia, there was a growing aspiration for self-reliance, union, and nationality. Admitting that Canadian "sympathies might in time ripen into political connection," Canadian leaders urged immediate commercial union and self-reliance as a political necessity to prevent the success of the "starvation policy" which they said Seward had adopted in order to drive the provinces to seek annexation. They recognized the necessity of conciliation in Nova Scotia, where the commercial effects of the repeal of the Reciprocity Treaty had resulted in much opposition to the confederation and in a demand at Halifax (in 1867) for permission to secede. In 1869 the Dominion government was successful in reconciling the maritime province by a promise to pay a subsidy of $82,698 a year for ten years as compensation for certain losses of revenue. Various causes combined to strengthen the bonds of the confederation and to substitute a sentiment of nationality for the sentiment of annexation to the United States.[25]

Meantime, Canada was preparing for western expansion as a counter movement to American northern expansion on the Pacific Coast. Stimulated by recent American policy, it adopted a determined Anglo-Canadian policy to complete the scheme for the confederation of the British colonies from sea to sea, including also the territory of the Hudson's Bay Company.[26]

The greatest event in the first session of the Dominion Parliament, which was opened at Ottawa November 7, 1867, was the movement started by Honorable William McDougall for annexation of the Canadian Northwest over which the Hudson's Bay Company had so long been a sovereign power in disguise. As a result the imperial government was asked to transfer to the Dominion government the jurisdiction over all those vast territories, in order to forestall any attempt to annex them to the United States. In making the request, the Canadians were motivated by the feeling that the increasing American growth on the frontier and on the Pacific coast must be met by Canadian western colonization and by the opening of Canadian roads across the continent.

This Canadian movement met with some opposition in the United States. It was especially opposed in Minnesota where the proposition that England should transfer to the Dominion (by an order in council) all the territory between Minnesota and Alaska ("settled largely from the United States") was regarded as an "unwarranted interference with the principles of self-government."

In December, 1867, and again in January, 1868, Senator Ramsey, who had had an active part in the development of Minnesota, offered to the Senate a resolution directing the Committee on Foreign Relations to inquire into the expediency of negotiating with the Dominion a treaty of reciprocity with a clause providing that Canada with the consent of Great Britain should cede to the United States the districts of North America west of 90° longitude, on condition that the United States pay six million dollars to the Hudson's Bay Company, assume the public debt of British Columbia to the amount of two million dollars to aid in the construction of a northern Pacific railway from Lake Superior to Puget Sound, and agree to organize the region into not less than three territories with the laws and rights of Montana as far as they could be made applicable. This resolution provided for a duty of only five per cent *ad valorem* on the exclusive products and manufactures of each country, the assimilation of excise duties by concurrent legislation, the navigation of the St. Lawrence, freedom of the Atlantic coast fisheries, and a common system of laws regulating copyrights and patents and postage. A few weeks later (on March 6) the Minnesota legislature sent to Congress a memorial which, after requesting the ratification of the Alaska treaty, and after opposing the transfer of the Hudson's Bay territories to Canada, closed with a resolution expressing a desire for assurance "that the cession of northwest British America to the United States, accompanied by the construction of a northern Pacific railway, are regarded by Great Britain and Canada as satisfactory provisions of a treaty which shall remove all grounds of controversy between the respective countries."[27]

Later, in 1868, in connection with the study of the Canadian problem, the expediency of negotiating a new reciprocity arrangement with Canada was still under consideration. In response to an earlier House resolution Hatch submitted a supplemental report upon the subject in January, 1869.[28]

By the close of 1868, and during the year 1869, there was a growing sentiment that the annexation of British America was the best solution of the various irritating international problems. Prominent newspapers suggested that England, to secure a new and real friendship with America, should promptly and frankly tender to the United States, in full satisfaction of all claims, "the relinquishment of her sovereignty on this continent." Chandler in an aggressive speech declared that American acquisition of all British possessions in North America, by British peaceful surrender for settlement of American claims, was a national necessity.[29]

In the debate on the Johnson-Clarendon convention, in the executive session of the Senate, on April 13, 1869, was dimly outlined the policy of closely associating the question of Canadian independence with the question of settlement of claims. In opposition to the treaty Senator Sumner made a vigorous and famous speech, publicly characterized by Goldwin Smith as an oratorical effort which rendered renewal of negotiations almost impossible. He desired the peaceful acquisition of Canada, the first step toward which was the withdrawal of England from this hemisphere in accord with a logical development of the Monroe Doctrine and the doctrine of manifest destiny. He believed that the time for the fulfillment of Cobden's prophecy was at hand—that the British possessions could be peacefully annexed "by the voluntary act of England and with the cordial consent of the colonists." With the expectation of carrying out his plans, in shaping the destiny of a hemisphere by annexing the "whole zone from Newfoundland to Vancouver," he secured the appointment of his friend Motley as minister to England and endeavored to usurp the functions of the Department of State. Later, on September 22, in a speech which he delivered in Massachusetts, he said that the future voluntary union of Canada with the United States, on the principle of the consent of the governed, was an appointed destiny.[30]

After the rejection of the Johnson-Clarendon treaty by a Senate vote of fifty-four to one, many farsighted statesmen believed that the greatest menace to American peace with Great Britain was the British maintenance of a neighboring colonial dependency which it regarded as a source of weakness, especially in the existing state of international affairs. This belief was not without foundation. On December 18, 1869, the *London Times,* which was supposed to be inspired by the British government, stated that England should not oppose any deliberate conclusion by the colonies in favor of the convenience of annexation to the American Union. In explanation, it added that "the mother country has become the dependency of the colonies." This view of the situation was reenforced by recent events.[31]

After the rejection of the treaty, the Grant administration took occasion to ascertain whether the territorial method of settling claims would be satisfactory to England. On June 9, 1869, after suggesting that the American claims were too large for a money settlement, Fish sounded Thornton on the question of ceding Canada. He received the reply that England, although it did not wish to keep Canada, "could not part with it without the consent of the population." [32]

About the same time Fish sent to Motley the President's suggestion of the wisdom of adopting a brief interval of abstinence of discussion concerning American claims, while awaiting the subsidence of violent emotions and of public manifestations of excited feeling. This suggestion, with an explanation of the causes of the Senate's refusal to give its advice and consent to the draft treaty (which unfortunately had been published by accident before the Senate's unfavorable action), Motley submitted to Lord Clarendon in an interview which he regarded as private and confidential. Expressing his sense of the gravity of the situation, he stated the President's opinion that the Senate's almost unanimous rejection, which had been foreshadowed in strenuous expressions of popular disapprobation, did not imply discourtesy to the British government but a wish for peace and honest friendship and for a healing of wounds which must first be probed. From Clarendon, who welcomed the suggestion of the brief interval of abstinence, he received an energetic expression concerning "the horror of war or even permanent alienation between the two branches of the Anglo-Saxon race."

Later, Secretary Fish, influenced by the attitude of Motley in assuming to present at London the views of Senator Sumner, decided to transfer to Washington the negotiations concerning the national claims against Great Britain, and later he also recalled Motley. In this decision he was encouraged by the co-operation of John Rose of Canada who, by arrangement of Caleb Cushing, arrived at Washington from Ottawa and dined with Fish on July 9. He suggested to Rose that, after the subsidence of the excitement, a settlement might be reached if Great Britain should send to Washington some person of high rank to express some kind word of regret. He outlined a plan which later was practically followed. Immediately after the informal conference, while Rose went to England to confer with leading public men, Fish and Thornton at Washington unsuccessfully endeavored to find a basis for agreement. Finally, on September 25, Fish instructed Motley to notify Clarendon of the President's hope that the British government would be willing to conduct future discussions at Washington.[33]

In the following November, at a Cabinet meeting, President Grant suggested the possibility of a withdrawal of England from Canada and expressed a desire to postpone the adjustment of claims until England was ready to withdraw.[34]

Later American policy concerning British America was influenced by British adoption of a new policy concerning the Canadian Northwest over which the Hudson's Bay Company had so long exercised authority.

In 1869, the British government induced the Hudson's Bay

Company to agree to transfer to the Dominion its territorial rights for £300,000 and one-twentieth of the lands surveyed for settlement by the government for the next twenty years, and with the privilege of retaining its posts and special facilities for trade. As a result of the subsequent transfer of territory and jurisdiction, which was authorized by a British Order in Council of June 24, 1870, and which followed other acts of British preparation for Canadian self-reliance, the Dominion encountered a new frontier problem. In the Selkirk Red River country, it found considerable opposition to the prospective change of government. The people, who were chiefly half-breeds, vigorously protested against the general demeanor and activities of the Canadian subordinates who were sent to build roads and survey the lands for settlement. Some who dreamed of a Red River republic, and others who were determined to secure for that region annexation to the United States to which it was commercially attached by heavy cart traffic with St. Paul and by steamer traffic on the Red River, were strenuously opposed to the policy by which they were to become a colony of a colony. Under the leadership of Louis Riel, a youthful half-breed, they rose in rebellion and refused to receive the new governor, William McDougall, who had journeyed from Canada through the United States on his way to assume the government. In November they seized Fort Garry and the treasure of the Hudson's Bay Company and proclaimed the independence of the settlement. After some time for deliberation, however, they sent to Ottawa to ascertain the terms of union and decided to submit without resistance. When the Canadian military expedition arrived at Red River in August, 1870, after a long march along the northern border of Lake Superior,[35] Riel had fled to the United States. The new government was inaugurated, and the district received the name of Manitoba. After the failure of the rebellion many of the half-breeds, unwilling to submit to the new authority, sullenly withdrew to the farther West, seeking fuller freedom along the shores of the Saskatchewan; but their places were rapidly filled by pioneers from the East (and from Europe) who came on American railroads to Minnesota and there transferred to canvas-covered wagons for the remainder of the distance to the exhaustless wheat lands.

Meantime, in December, 1869, before the completion of arrangements for extension of Dominion authority over the Canadian Northwest, the Grant administration decided to investigate the situation on the northwest border. Secretary Fish, who had succeeded Seward, sent James W. Taylor to the Red River region on a special and strictly confidential mission to secure information upon the following subjects: (1) full details of the revolt against the Canadian confederation and the expulsion of McDougall; (2) the geographical features and commercial affinities of the Selkirk, Saskatchewan, and Columbia districts; (3) the character and disposition of the population; (4) the existing routes of commerce between Canada and the United States; (5) the political relations of the several British possessions between Minnesota and Alaska; (6) the general question of the commercial and political relations between Canada and the several provinces. Five weeks later, Taylor's report (of fifty-two pages) was submitted to the Senate.[36]

Coincidently, both in December, 1869, and in January, 1870, Fish in his conversations with Thornton urged the entire withdrawal of Great Britain from Canada as a basis for the immediate settlement of the *Alabama* claims. He received the reply that, although the Canadians did not desire it, the British were ready to let them go whenever they wished to do so. On January 14, he informally called Thornton's attention to the original copy of a paper, which had recently appeared in the newspapers, purporting to be a memorial from the inhabitants of British Columbia and urging the transfer of the colony to the United States. At the same time he suggested that possibly the desire indicated by the petition, together with the troubles in the Red River or Selkirk settlement and the strong opposition of the maritime provinces against the confederation, might cause the British government "to consider whether the time was not near when the future relation of the colonies to Great Britain must be contemplated with reference to these manifestations of restlessness, and to some extent, of dissatisfaction with their present condition."

Of his informal conversation with Thornton he promptly wrote Motley, on the same day. He added that the recent accounts of the disturbance in the Red River settlement, consequent on the proposed transfer of the Hudson's Bay Company rights to Canada, indicated a more extended and deeper feeling of discontent than the British authorities in Canada were inclined to admit. He especially expressed the American anxiety concerning the possible effect which any actual conflict of force in the region might have upon the Indians, who were liable to become involved and might produce complications by their failure to observe the limits of an imaginary boundary. He also mentioned a recent confidential communication from Winnipeg reporting that Governor MacTavish planned to submit to the Hudson's Bay Company office in London the question of its interest to favor annexation of that region to the United States—a subject of consideration which Fish said should be discreetly encouraged without compromitting the government in any respect. He also referred incidentally to the annexation movement in British Columbia, and to the anti-Dominion attitude in the maritime provinces.[37]

In his instructions to Motley, after referring to the practical arguments in favor of the early independence of British American colonies (including the avoidance of dangers of border strife and of border Indian war), he wrote:

> You will exercise your discretion . . . availing yourself of every opportunity to obtain information as to the real sentiments of the British government on the question of the separation of the colonies from the mother country and, when opportunity offers, indicating the facts which seem to make such separation a necessity.[38]

Early in February he received from Motley authentic information that MacTavish had not acted upon the expressed intention and had not even made any allusion to it in his letters to London. Later in February he also received from Motley a clipping from the *Pall Mall Gazette*, containing a brief account of the presentation of a monster petition in favor of maintaining existing relations between England and the colonies—a petition which seemed to indicate the attitude of the government.

Early in March Fish received a confidential dispatch (of February 21) which furnished more authoritative information of British policy, obtained by Motley in an informal and intimate interview of February 19 with Clarendon. At this interview Motley introduced the question of annexation through a discussion of the Red River insurrection and suggestions of possible international dangers which might spring from Indian hostilities on the borders, and which might result in the precipitation of an unintentional and undesired international conflict. On the general subject of independence and annexation of British colonies he expressed his conviction that such changes would follow in the natural course of events on the American continent. From Clarendon, who expressed no dissent from these views and contemplated such a future without regret, and whom he regarded as rather unsympathetic with the recently agitated pro-colonial feeling, he elicited the statement that the British government would never of its own initiative throw off the colonists and that it would never use force to retain them whenever they decided to assert their independence, but that it would deprecate any American attempts at conquest or violent annexation of Canadian territories.[39]

In March, 1870, on the eve of the Franco-Prussian War, Fish again urged that the American provinces were a menace of danger to Great Britain and that their independence would remove the cause of irritation and possible complication which existed especially in times of Fenian activity. Thornton, considering the contingencies of possible European wars in which England might be involved, replied that Great Britain could not inaugurate a separation, but was "willing and even desirous to have one."

Later, the question of negotiations for annexation was introduced in the Senate. On April 22 Senator Chandler submitted a resolution requesting the President to send agents to Red River Settlement to treat with the inhabitants for its annexation. Later, on May 19, Senator Pomeroy offered a resolution requesting the President, if expedient, to open negotiations with Great Britain in order to ascertain whether the union of the British North American provinces with the United States could be accomplished upon terms equally advantageous and honorable to Great Britain, the British provinces, and the United States.[40]

Fish, although he had gradually drifted from Sumner's policy and never again urged withdrawal, had occasion to refer to the subject in subsequent conversations with Thornton. In September, 1870, on the day that the German army invested Paris, he intimated to Thornton that the independence of Canada was the proper solution of the fishery disputes. Thornton, after repeating what he had said before, significantly added:

> "It is impossible to connect the question of Canadian independence with the *Alabama* claims—not even to the extent of providing for the reference of the question of independence to a vote of the people of the Dominion."

Although in subsequent negotiations Fish dropped Canada from the discussion, the President was still under the influence of the view held by Sumner, that the settlement of money claims should be combined with a movement in the direction of the withdrawal of the British flag from the North American continent. In suggesting to Fish instructions for a minister to replace Motley at London, he proposed an attempt at negotiation of the *Alabama* claims upon a basis of payment of actual losses, revision of the principles of international law, and "the submission to the voters of the Dominion of the question of independence." His expectations of early annexation were not shared by Fish who, however, did not doubt eventual annexation.

Near the close of 1870 a series of events contributed to hasten the negotiations for the adjustment of the *Alabama* claims. About the middle of November, over two months after the Prussian defeat of Napoleon at Sedan, Fish received from Constantin Catacazy, the Russian minister, a suggestion that the condition of European affairs indicated that the time was opportune to press for an immediate settlement. On November 20, he mentioned this suggestion to Thornton and (in reply to the latter's inquiry) stated a basis of settlement which omitted any mention of Canada.

Two weeks later Grant in his annual message, after expressing regret that the British attitude had resulted in a failure of efforts to adjust claims, recommended the authorization of the appointment of an American commission to take proof of all private claims with a view to their settlement by the American government, in accord with Fish's proposal that the government should assume "responsible control of all demands against Great Britain." After a half-paragraph reference to the *Alabama* claims, he devoted several paragraphs to Canada which presented problems closely associated with future American development. With no attempt at diplomatic dodges, he protested against Canadian harsh treatment of American fishermen and proposed to retaliate by suspension of free transit of goods, and by more extreme measures if necessary. He also complained of the unfriendly disposition of Canada as manifested in the maintenance of an inconsistent claim of a right to exclude American citizens from the navigation of the St. Lawrence to the sea. In another connection, contemplating future American acquisitions in the Caribbean and the Pacific and the "not far distant" cessation of European political connection with the American continent, he suggested that the annexations might include "perhaps Canada if she is amiable, or if she is troublesome and ungracious." [41]

On December 6, when France was rapidly succumbing to the rising power of Germany, this "menacing" message appeared in the London papers and visibly quickened the speed of negotiations for a peaceful Anglo-American settlement. From Sir John Rose, who had served on the commission for the settlement of the claims of the Hudson's Bay Company, Fish had already received an intimation that the British Cabinet was "disposed to enter into negotiations." The note in which this intimation appeared he read to the Cabinet on December 9.

Exactly one month later, Mr. Rose reached Washington on a confidential mission to ascertain unofficially whether the American government would agree to attempt to settle all pending questions by a joint commission. In an after-dinner talk at the home of Mr. Fish he prepared the way for referring all questions to such a commission, which should adjudicate them or arrange by treaty for such adjudication. Finally, after considering the American view that the negotiation of a treaty for such a commission would be useless unless it contained a statement that the British government admitted liability for the *Alabama* claims, and also the British decision not to take the initiative on the *Alabama* claims, he submitted the practical suggestion that the British government could propose a commission to settle the Canadian questions and that the American government could accept on condition that the *Alabama* claims be included. To this proposal he obtained the consent of Fish. On January 11, 1871, coincident with Senator Stewart's statement that Canada could not long live without annexation, he submitted a confidential memorandum of a plan for the "full and final adjustment" of the various questions of difference in order to secure the rights and interests of both nations and the "foundation of lasting bonds of amity." [42]

In considering the success of the plan it was important to know the attitude of Sumner, whose friend Motley had recently been recalled from London. Therefore, on January 15, after a conference with Senator Conkling and General Schenk (the newly appointed successor to Motley), Fish called on Sumner "to ask his opinion and advice" and above all to secure his approval of the proposed plan. After two days' reflection, Sumner submitted his written reply in the form of an ultimatum based upon the policy of Canadian independence. Referring to Mr. Rose's idea that "all questions and sources of irritation between England and the United States should be removed absolutely and forever that we may be at peace really and good neighbors," he said:

> Nothing could be better than this initial idea. It should be the starting-point. The greatest trouble, if not peril, being a constant source of anxiety, is from Fenianism, which is excited by the proximity of the British flag in Canada. Therefore the withdrawal of the British flag cannot be abandoned as a condition or preliminary of such a settlement as is now proposed. To make the settlement complete the withdrawal should be from this hemisphere including provinces and islands.[43]

The administration determined to ignore this ultimatum and to shape its foreign policy without further reference to Sumner. After consulting with Sumner's colleagues, and after taking other precautions to enable him to feel sure that the Senate was ripe for revolt against Sumner's domination, Fish invited Rose to his house (on January 24) and informed him that the United States would enter on the proposed negotiations. He showed to him in confidence Sumner's "flag withdrawal" ultimatum which doubtless had an important influence in the negotiations that followed; but he stated clearly that, if Great Britain should send commissioners to treat on the basis agreed upon (to arrange a treaty which would refer adjudication of claims to arbitral tribunals), the administration would spare no effort "to secure a favorable result even if it involved a conflict with the chairman on foreign relations in the Senate."[44]

Events now moved rapidly. On February 1, by aid of the submarine telegraph cable, Rose and Thornton were able to report that the Liberal Gladstone ministry accepted the American proposal to include the *Alabama* claims, and that it was ready to send a special mission to treat on all questions at issue, including all claims arising from acts committed in the Civil War. In another week President Grant named five commissioners, whose appointments were at once confirmed by the Senate. On February 27 the joint high commission organized in Washington. On May 3 it substantially terminated its difficult negotiations (which are treated in a separate chapter). On May 8 the treaty was signed. Two days later it was submitted to the Senate. There it was promptly referred to the Committee on Foreign Relations, from the chairmanship of which Sumner had been displaced in March. On May 11, by a leakage, it was published in the *New York Tribune*. On May 24 it was approved by the Senate, Sumner casting his vote for it.[45]

The successful completion of the treaty providing for the peaceful settlement of all chief difficulties without British flag withdrawal, was doubtless a surprise to the Russian government. The Russian minister, Catacazy, had used methods at variance with diplomatic practice to defer or to prevent a peaceful adjustment with England. He had attempted to prejudice and defeat the negotiations of the Anglo-American joint high commission. In the spring of 1871, he continued his methods of interference to prevent the successful execution of the provisions of the completed treaty. The logical result was an American request for his recall, to which Russia finally acceded, and which was followed by the recall of Curtin, the American minister at St. Petersburg.[46]

After some hesitation, accompanied by some controversy with the British government concerning the concessions which it was requested to make for the benefit of the British empire, the Canadian government in 1872 finally agreed (in the interest of the empire) to secure the enactment of measures to make the treaty effective, on condition of a British guarantee for a Canadian loan to aid the construction of a proposed Canadian Pacific railway and the enlargement and extension of Canadian canals.[47] By the promise to construct this transcontinental railway, conceived as a project to frustrate the threatened exclusion of the Dominion from the Pacific coast, it had enticed British Columbia into the confederation in 1871, thereby obtaining control of a strategic territorial position of the greatest importance and significance in connection with the destiny of Canada and the later development of the British empire.[48] It shared largely in the beneficial results of the treaty, although it felt that its influence in the negotiations had been restricted by the pressure and precedence of American and British imperial interests and by the cautious policy of the British members of the commission.

REFERENCES

1. Israel Buchanan, *Relations of the Industry of Canada with the Mother Country* (1864).
2. *N. Am. Rev.*, Jan., 1852, and Oct., 1854; *De Bow's Rev.*, Oct., 1852; F. A. Wilson and A. B. Richardson, *Britain Redeemed and Canada Preserved* (1850); *Cong. Globe*, 32–1, Appendix, Jan. 3, 1853; *3 Spl. Missions*, p. 36, Marcy to Andrews, Apr. 15, 1854.
3. *N. Y. Times*, Mar. 27, 1854; *N. Y. Herald*, Mar. 28, Apr. 7, 29 and 30, and May 22, 1854; *London Times*, Apr. 18, 1854.
4. *N. Am. Rev.*, Oct., 1854; F. E. Haynes, *Reciprocity Treaty with Canada* (*Am. Econ. Assoc. Pubs.*, Nov., 1892); *H. Exec. Docs.*, 39–2, Vol. 11, No. 78, Feb. 6, 1867; *31 Cong. Globe*, p. 126, and Appendix, pp. 97–100 (Jan. 25, 1853); *48 Cong. Globe*, p. 904, Feb. 9, 1859.

5. *Frazer's Mag.*, Oct., 1858; *Sen. Exec. Docs.*, 35–2, Vol. 10, No. 29, Jan. 29, 1859; C. D. ROBERTS, *Hist. of Canada*, p. 334.
6. *Sen. Exec. Docs.*, 35–2, Vol. 10, No. 29; *H. Exec. Docs.*, No. 111, Mar. 3, 1859.
7. *Oregon Hist. Quart.*, Vol. 17 (Apr., 1926), pp. 105–13 (D. E. CLARK, *The Movement of the Far West during the Decade of the Sixties*).
8. *H. Exec. Docs.*, 37–2, Vol. 10, No. 146, June 20, 1862 (*Taylor Rp.*), p. 45.
9. E. D. NEILL, *Hist. of Minn.*
10. *H. Exec. Docs.*, 37–2, Vol. 10, No. 146, pp. 38, 43, 45; E. H. DERBY, *Relations of the U.S. and the Br. Provinces*, Jan., 1867.
11. *C.A.*, G, 168, *Canada*, pp. 2–11.
12. *London Times*, Sept. 14, 1863, and July 1, 1864; BUCHANAN, *Relations of the Industry of Canada and the Mother Country.*
13. ROBERTS, *Hist. of Canada* (Chap. 22); E. W. WATKINS, M.P., *Canada and the States*, 1851–86.
14. *London Times*, Sept. 18, 1866.
15. *N. Y. Times*, May 21 and 24, and July 22, 1865; *Ib.*, May 11, 1866; *Nation*, Aug. 3, 1866; *Chicago Tribune*, Jan. 6, 1866; *Cong. Globe*, 39–1, Appendix, p. 195 (Apr. 25, 1866); WATKINS, *Canada and the States*, p. 425; *H. Exec. Docs.*, 39–1, Vol. 12, No. 128 (June 12, 1866).
16. *Cong. Globe*, 39–1, p. 3548.
17. *Ib.*, June 11 (p. 3085), and July 26, 1866 (pp. 4193–97); *H. Rps.*, 39–1, Vol. 1, No. 100, July 25, 1866.
18. *20 G.B., Instrs.*, pp. 507–08, No. 1798, July 7, 1866.
19. E. H. DERBY, *Preliminary Rp. on a Treaty of Reciprocity* (1866), p. 20; DERBY, *Rp. on Rel. of the U.S. to the Brit. Provinces* (Jan., 1867).
20. *Am. An. Cyc.*, 1867, p. 275; *H. Exec. Docs.*, 40–2, No. 177, p. 130, Feb. 27, 1868; *Dip. Cor.*, 1867, p. 390; *N. Y. Sun*, Jan. 29, 1893; *Colburn's Mo. Mag.*, June, 1867, pp. 247–48; *64 Cong. Record*, 48–1, p. 566.
21. *H. Exec. Docs.*, 40–2, No. 177; CHARLES SUMNER, *Works*, Vol. 11, p. 222; *N. Y. Times*, Apr. 11 (Monroe doc.) and 19, 1867; *London Times*, Apr. 1, 10 and 21, May 1, and June 23, 1867; *Colburn's New Mo. Mag.*, June, 1867, pp. 247–48; *Every Saturday*, May 4, 1867, pp. 563–64.
22. *St. Louis Times*, Apr. 10, 1867; *Phila. No. Am. Gazette*, Apr. 12; *Pacific Tribune*, Aug. 31; *H. Exec. Docs.*, 40–2, No. 177, p. 118; *Parl. Debates*, June 9, 1868; *Cong. Globe*, 40–2, pp. 386–88 (Banks's speech of June 30, 1868).
23. *State Dept. Pamphs.*, *U.S. Dipl. Questions*, II; *Misc. Letters*, Jan., 1868 (Part 2), *H. Rps.*, 40–3, Vol. 1, No. 35.

24. Benjamin Mills Pierce, *Rp. on Resources of Greenland and Iceland,* 1868.
25. R. G. Haliburton, *International Trade Our Only Safeguard* (Ottawa, 1868).
26. *London Times,* Apr. 16, 1867; *Colburn's New Mo. Mag.,* June, 1867, pp. 250–52.
27. *Sen. Misc. Docs.,* 40–2, Vol. 1, No. 4, Dec. 9, 1867; *Ib.,* No. 22, Jan. 31, 1868; *Ib.,* No. 68, Mar. 31, 1868.
28. *H. Exec. Docs.,* 40–3, Vol. 9, No. 36, p. 21.
29. *N. Y. Herald,* Feb. 3, 1869; *N. Y. Tribune,* Feb. 22, and Apr. 7; *N. Y. Times,* Mar. 30, Apr. 13 and 22, and Aug. 28, 1869.
30. E. L. Pierce, *Memoir and Letters of Charles Sumner,* IV, 409, *et seq.* (Sumner to Motley, June 15, 1869); Sumner, *Works,* XII, *Prophetic Voices.*
31. *Sen. Exec. Docs.,* 41–2, Vol. 2, No. 90, May 23, 1870; *Ib.,* No. 75, Mar. 30; *Contemp. Rev.,* March, 1873 (Arthur Mills).
32. C. F. Adams, *Before and After the Treaty of Washington,* pp. 106, *et seq.;* Pierce, *Sumner,* IV, 409 (Sumner to Motley, June 11, 1869).
33. *99 G.B., Desps.,* No. 8, June 12, 1869; *Ib.,* No. 65, July 30; *22 G.B., Instrs.,* No. 75, Oct. 11; *Ib.* (pp. 50–83), No. 70, Sept. 25; *Ib.* (pp. 83–84), No. 71, Sept. 25; *Ib.,* pp. 97–98, No. 119, Dec. 22, 1869; J. C. B. Davis, *Mr. Fish and the* Alabama *Claims,* p. 45; *Sen. Exec. Docs.,* 41–3, No. 11, 1871.
34. *Ib.,* 41–2, Vol. 3, No. 114, July 13, 1870.
35. *Ib.,* 41–2, No. 88, May 21, 1870.
36. *3 Spl. Missions,* p. 208; *Sen. Exec. Docs.,* 41–2, No. 33, Feb. 2, 1870.
37. *22 G.B., Instrs.,* pp. 163–68, No. 129, Jan. 14, 1870; *Sen. Exec. Docs.,* 41–2, Vol. 3, No. 114, July 13, 1870.
38. *Ib.; 22 G.B., Instrs.,* pp. 163–68, No. 129, Jan. 14, 1870.
39. *101 G.B., Desps.,* No. 232, Feb. 2, 1870; *102 G.B., Desps.,* No. 248, Feb. 17, 1870.
40. *Ib.,* Confidential, Feb. 21, 1870; *Sen. Misc. Docs.,* 41–2, No. 140; *C.A.,* G, 147, #1417, No. 14, Thornton to John Young, Apr. 23, 1870.
41. Richardson, VII, 102–06; *Scribner's Mo.,* Feb., 1870, p. 450.
42. J. B. Moore, *Int. Arb's.,* I, 521–23; J. C. B. Davis, *Mr. Fish and the* Alabama *Claims,* p. 59.
43. *Ib.;* Sumner, *Works,* XIII, 385; Moore, *Int. Arb's.,* I, 525–26; C. F. Adams, *Treaty of Washington,* p. 141; *Nation,* Feb. 23, 1871; *N. Y. Times,* Jan. 9, 1871; *N. Am. Rev.,* July–Aug., 1878 (see p. 61); *N. Y. Herald,* Jan. 4, 1878 (J. C. B. Davis).
44. Moore, *Int. Arb's.,* I, 528–30.
45. *N. Y. Tribune,* May 11, 1871.
46. *Sen. Exec. Docs.,* 42–2, Vol. 1, No. 5 (Dec. 7, 1871), p. 12;

22 G.B., Instrs., p. 558, No. 68, Oct. 11, 1871; *2 Turkey, Instrs.*, p. 358; *Rus., Instrs.*, No. 110, Nov. 16, 1871; *24 Rus., Desps.*, Nos. 188 and 190, June and July 1, 1872; *N. Y. World*, Nov. 29, 1870; *N. Y. Times*, Jan. 5, 17 and 29, 1872; *N. Y. Tribune*, Jan. 15, 1872.

47. *Contemp. Rev.*, Vol. 21, March, 1873; *Messages, Despatches, and Minutes of the Privy Council* (1872); *State Dept. Pamphlets*, No. 8486.

48. *N. Am. Rev.*, Apr., 1883 (P. BENDER); *Sen. Rps.*, 51–1, Part 2, No. 1530, July 2, 1890, p. 889; *Can. Law Rev.*, Sept., 1902, pp. 525–37 (HODGKINS).

CHAPTER XIV

NEGOTIATIONS OF THE TREATY OF 1871

IN the negotiations by which the British sought peaceful methods for adjustment of the famous *Alabama* claims, and which resulted in the treaty of 1871, the American government discovered that Canada was primarily interested in the adjustment of questions directly affecting American-Canadian relations in which it had an immediate concern, chiefly the questions of reciprocity.

In the initiation of these negotiations the Canadian government had contributed suggestions indicating that it especially sought to restore the Reciprocity Treaty.

This was in accord with its earlier unsuccessful efforts, since the close of the American Civil War. Late in July, 1865, Galt and Howland had gone to Washington on a mission to secure renewal of the treaty before its expiration under the notice. From Sir Frederick Bruce they learned that Seward had recently said that any application for renewal of negotiations on trade reciprocity would be refused. From Secretary McCulloch of the Treasury they elicited a similar statement. After their return, they opened a confidential correspondence with Mr. Wells, chairman of the United States Revenue Commission. At the suggestion of Wells and Mr. Derby, Galt again went to Washington. There he saw McCulloch, who, in the presence of Mr. Morrill, stated that whatever was done in regard to the treaty must be by legislation originating in the House. He then saw Secretary Seward who informed him that, with the existing attitude of Congress, no new treaty could be made, and that under existing relations with Great Britain the American government was indisposed at that time to enter into new treaty obligations.[1]

Later, in January, 1866, after a New York conference with representatives of New Brunswick and Nova Scotia and Newfoundland, Galt and Howland had returned to Washington to interview the House Committee of Ways and Means. After conferences of January 24 to February 6, their negotiations had failed. From Morrill, who had led in the questions and discussions, they had received (on February 5) a memorandum stating that the Committee was ready to recommend a law for continuance of some of the measures in the reciprocal treaty: (1) the conditional use of Lake Michigan; (2) mutual free transit under bond on condition of the abolition of provincial free ports; (3) repeal of bounties given to American fishermen, and an agreement as to duties on fish, on condition of the continuance of all rights of fishing near the shore; (4) mutually free admission of a proposed list of articles (including millstones and grindstones, rags and unground gypsum) for free navigation of the St. Lawrence and Canadian canals and the privilege of the inshore fisheries. In reply Galt announced his disappointment.

The Canadians had wanted to remove American restrictions on the coasting trade. They had especially desired free trade and navigation of international waters and a continuation of the Canadian free ports at Sault Ste. Marie and Gaspé.[2]

Later, after the abrogation of the Reciprocity Treaty, the Canadian government had hesitated to adopt a retaliatory policy. In April, 1868, however, Sir John Rose, Canadian finance minister, stated that it might be compelled to adopt a new policy; and soon thereafter R. G. Haliburton, perplexed by the "inscrutable" American policy, advocated a Canadian policy of intercolonial trade as the only way to prevent America from starving Nova Scotia into annexation.

The New Dominion Parliament, in its first tariff law, inserted a standing offer of reciprocity, which was retained in its tariff act of 1870, and later repeated in modified form. In 1869 Sir John Rose went to Washington to secure reciprocity, but failed.[3]

In the expectations of a renewal of a reciprocity policy, Canada was probably encouraged by the official reports of certain American special agents of the Treasury. In 1866 Derby had advocated negotiation of a new reciprocity treaty. Considering the geographic disadvantages of Canada, he had recommended American liberality in the encouragement of friendly relations, but he had suggested that intercourse with the Dominion by concurrent legislation was made impossible by British colonial sectionalism. In a later report of March, 1868, George W. Brego had recommended the encouragement of reciprocal trade with a continuation of the open navigation of the St. Lawrence and efforts to end the ill-feeling concerning the fisheries. Later, in January, 1871, J. N. Larned declared that Canada was mistaken in its recent belief that American policy aimed at coercion. In case Canada should not decide upon a political union, he was inclined to favor an American zollverein or commercial union —a plan which had been advocated as the "natural policy of Canada" in 1864 by Israel Buchanan, an irreconcilable opponent of the principles of George Brown of Toronto.[4]

To secure restoration of reciprocity the Canadians had planned to exercise pressure in connection with negotiations concerning the fisheries. In accord with the policy of the Colonial Office, however, they had continued the freedom of the shore fisheries to American vessels on the basis of an annual license fee, which the owners of many American vessels refused to pay. By 1870, the Dominion government was convinced that a system of steadily increasing license fees had proved ineffectual in its purpose to prevent trespass—that it had resulted in a large decrease in the number of licenses and an increase in evasions. Therefore, after a brief trial of marine police on the fishing ground (in 1869), it decided to abolish the license system. This decision which Thornton submitted to Fish on April 29, 1870, was soon followed by the news that British cruisers and Canadian revenue vessels had seized twelve American fishing ships.

The Canadian government, by urging upon Great Britain the expediency of intervention on the fishing coasts influenced the British decision to appoint a joint commission.[5]

In discussing the fisheries situation Fish stated that the British headland doctrine was without foundation. He declared that the American government could not acquiesce in the British assumption and assertion of the right to exclude American fishermen from the open ports of the Dominion to prevent them from purchasing bait and other supplies, and to prevent them from transshipment of their fish in bond under color of the provisions of 1818. He stated that whether the terms of the convention of 1818 were fairly applicable to the troublesome mackerel fishery, which had come into existence since the negotiation of that convention, was a subject for consideration.[6]

Meantime, early in 1870, Fish announced to Thornton his regret that the House was decidedly opposed to the plans for commercial relations submitted by John Rose in the previous July, and, therefore, that any immediate attempt to negotiate a convention founded upon the proposals of Rose and himself would be quite useless. He added, however, that certain western members, whose constituents were opposed to certain combinations controlling communication between the West and the sea, had suggested that they might be able to carry through Congress an agreement for negotiation upon certain reciprocal terms. Apparently seeking to prepare the way for formal negotiations, he confidentially requested Thornton to inquire whether the Canadian government would grant the free navigation of the Welland Canal and the St. Lawrence, and whether it would agree to put the canal in a proper state for navigation in return for a considerable reduction of American import duties on lumber, salt, fish and coal, or a possible abolition of all duties on the first three articles.

To this request Thornton promptly responded with unsatisfactory results. Later, on February 25, stimulated by further inquiries from Fish, he earnestly pressed the Canadian minister for a more definite reply. He urged that a plain rejection was less liable to offend than a mere refusal to offer an opinion upon the suggestion submitted. Finally, on March 17, he reported that the Canadian government considered the free importation of fish as the only satisfactory part of the proposal and that it especially regretted the omission of products of the most populous sections of the Dominion.

Soon thereafter, in a confidential memorandum of July 12, the British government submitted as a basis for negotiations a Canadian proposal to restore the United States to the enjoyment of the fisheries as under the treaty of 1854 and to the navigation of the inland waters of Canada in return for a satisfactory reciprocity treaty and permission for Canadian navigation of American inland waters, and also to agree to enlarge and improve the access to the ocean in return for assurance of the permanency of the arrangement for reciprocity. The proposal also contemplated the mutual opening of the coasting trade, reciprocal patent and copyright laws and free transit trade, extension of the provisions of extradition treaties and a readjustment of the Canadian excise duty.

On July 27, in compliance with the request of Canada, the British government decided to propose to the American government the appointment of a commission to settle questions of dispute concerning the geographical limits of the exclusive fishing rights of Canada under the treaty of 1818.[7]

President Grant, in his message of December 5, 1870, complained of the "unneighborly" and unfriendly course of Canadian authorities toward American fishermen and proposed to retaliate by suspension of the operation of the laws concerning transit in bond. He also complained of a similarly unfriendly disposition to maintain a claim of right to exclude American citizens from the navigation of the St. Lawrence which furnished a natural outlet to the ocean for eight states. Reviving the old American claim to the natural right to enjoy the navigation of the river to the sea, subject to reasonable police regulations by the British government or by mutual agreement, he added the hope that the British government would "see the justice of abandoning the narrow and inconsistent claim to which her Canadian Provinces have urged her adherence."

In Canada this message elicited considerable criticism. One writer characterized it as "menacing," especially resenting its intimations concerning Canadian "semi-independence" and irresponsibility. He declared that it would prepare Canada to redouble its efforts to complete an improved system of railway and canal communication from the Northwest to the Atlantic coast.[8]

Meantime, after a brief experiment in retaliation in 1870 by imposition of duties on coal, salt and breadstuffs, Canada was ready to abandon the policy by new negotiations. It especially sought to press its advantage in the shore fisheries and in water transportation facilities with a view to the purchase of admission to the American markets by reciprocal freedom of trade. By suggestion of a conference to determine the exact rights of each country in the shore fisheries it originated a plan for negotiations which was later widened to provide for settlement of the irritating *Alabama* claims.[9] In submitting this suggestion, it was probably influenced largely by important domestic problems which had recently occupied considerable attention: the completion of the Intercolonial Railway to connect Quebec with the maritime provinces, the establishment or a provincial government for the Red River region and terms for admission of British Columbia and Prince Edward Island into the confederation.[10]

Influenced partly by Canadian suggestions, partly by the condition of European affairs, and partly by President Grant's "menacing" message, the British government was finally induced to quicken its speed toward completion of negotiations for peaceful settlement of all Anglo-American questions, both British and Canadian. To open the way it accepted the exploratory investigation service of Sir John Rose who, by a confidential and unofficial conference with Secretary Fish at Washington on January 9, 1871, prepared the way for reference of all controversial questions to a joint commission authorized to adjudicate them or to arrange for such judication by a treaty.

On February 3, 1871, Secretary Fish officially accepted the final British proposal concerning the scope of negotiations by the proposed joint high commission of five American and five British representatives. President Grant promptly appointed the American members: Secretary Fish, Robert C. Schenck (the American minister to Great Britain), Justice Samuel Nelson of the Supreme Court, Ebenezer R. Hoar of Massachusetts, and George H. Williams of Oregon. The British government appointed Earl de Grey and Ripon (President of the British Privy Council), Sir Stafford H. Northcote, M.P., Sir Edward Thornton (the British minister at Washington), Sir John A.

Macdonald of the Canadian government, and Montague Barnard (professor of international law at Oxford).

In his memorandum letter of February 22, 1871, to the other American commissioners, Secretary Fish indicated that the subjects for discussion would include:

(1) Fisheries;

(2) Navigation of the St. Lawrence;

(3) Reciprocal trade between the United States and Canada;

(4) Northwest water boundary and San Juan Island;

(5) The claims of the United States against Great Britain on account of acts committed by rebel cruisers;

(6) Claims of British subjects against the United States for losses and injuries arising out of acts committed during the recent American Civil War.[11]

The commission convened at Washington on February 27, and closed its work on May 6 after thirty-seven long sittings. Secretary Fish, whom the British members gracefully proposed for chairman, modestly expressed his wish that in order to avoid unnecessary formality no chairman should be named. By mutual agreement, in order that the discussions might be more unrestrained, the protocols of the meetings (except the final one) were informal.[12]

The negotiations encountered many difficulties which resulted in prolonged discussions. On the *Alabama* claims, concerning which discussions were begun on March 8, agreement was not reached until April 13 (Articles I–XI of the treaty). On private claims of citizens of each country against the government of the other for the period of the Civil War (discussed from April 13, 1861, to April 9, 1865) agreement was reached on April 15 (Articles XII–XVII). On the fisheries, after prolonged discussion, agreement was practically completed on April 22 (Articles XVIII–XXV). Agreement was reached on the northwest water boundary on the same day (Articles XXXIV–XLII). On May 3 the labors of negotiations were substantially terminated; and on May 4 the protocol of the conference was approved. The conference adjourned on May 6 and its members signed the treaty on May 8.[13]

From the beginning of the conference the Americans offered

no encouragement to the Canadian plan for trade reciprocity. On March 5 Macdonald in a private and confidential letter to Charles Tupper reported that a leading American statesman had informed Lord de Grey that the United States must have the inshore fisheries, and was willing to pay for them, but that Congress probably would not sanction a renewal of the Reciprocity Treaty of 1854. Having considered no equivalent except enlarged commercial intercourse, he had promptly expressed to Lord de Grey the opinion that Canada, with its prospective increase of population and with a desire to improve its position as a maritime power, would not agree to surrender forever the fishery rights for any compensation however great, but might consent to a surrender for a term of years.

At the conference of March 6th American commissioners declined the British proposal to restore in principle the Reciprocity Treaty of 1854 with provisions for reciprocal opening of the coasting trade and the navigation of the St. Lawrence and Canadian canals. Secretary Fish inquired through Thornton whether the Canadian government would grant the free navigation of the Welland Canal and the St. Lawrence and put the canals in a proper state for navigation, in return for a considerable American reduction in import duties on lumber, salt, fish and coal (or a possible abolition of all duties on the first three articles). On March 17, in a private and confidential letter, Thornton replied that the Canadian government regarded free importation of fish as the only satisfactory part of the proposal and regretted the omission of products of the most populous sections of the Dominion.

On March 18 the American commissioners declined to consider the question of reciprocal opening of the coasting trade of the Lakes, but agreed to the British proposal to consider the question of transshipment and the question of transit of goods in bond through American and Canadian territory. They also declined the British proposal to consider the question of reciprocal registration of vessels.[14]

On March 21 Macdonald reported to Tupper that the discussion was unsatisfactory and unpromising, and that he had nearly made up his mind that the Americans wanted everything and would give nothing. He was pleased, however, that Lord de Grey had notified Fish that any fishery treaty must be ratified by Canada. Referring to the inquiry of Fish as to whether the treaty would also be subject to ratification by Prince Edward Island and Newfoundland, he expressed his opinion that if any satisfactory treaty should be reached it should be limited to the Dominion of Canada, "so that if Prince Edward Island and Newfoundland desire the advantages . . . they must come into the Confederation." To his British colleagues he insisted that agreement on any terms would probably be exceedingly unwise if acceptance by Canada was not reasonable.

In a long telegram of March 22 he indicated that his position concerning the fisheries was exceedingly embarrassing. In the separate caucuses with his colleagues he was continually pressed to yield. Finally, with a feeling that he had been too disagreeable, he consented to a British proposal to accept free coal, salt, fish and lumber and the American coasting trade in exchange for the fisheries.

The request for the coasting trade, by which Macdonald hoped that Canada would absorb all coastwise trade on the Lakes and the North Atlantic coast, Fish promptly declined as had been expected. For the Americans he then made a counter proposition, offering free coal, free salt and free fish (mackerel, herring and cod), and also free lumber after July 1, 1876, and claiming mutual free fishing in the Lakes and the St. Lawrence.[15]

On March 25, preceding the usual official conference, Macdonald submitted to Lord de Grey a distinct opinion of the Canadian government with a request that it should be regarded as a formal statement of his non-concurrence in the proposition concerning the fisheries. Then, presenting Tupper's private opinion that the Canadian Council "might agree to the four articles free with a substantial money consideration," he significantly hinted to Lord de Grey that "compensation must come from either the United States or England." By this suggestion he intended to introduce a foundation for a later demand upon the British government for full compensation for any sacrifices which Canada might be requested to make for the benefit of the empire.

In the conference which followed, Lord de Grey stated that he was ready to recommend a grant of the inshore fisheries for a term of years "in exchange for the four free articles" (coal, salt, lumber and fish). To this Macdonald objected on the ground that according to the Canadian view the consideration was not adequate. He expected the American Congress to repeal the duties on coal and salt at its session of the following December (in accord with the American demands), and he asserted that Americans would continue to purchase mackerel at any price. He also thought that Canadian lumber would continue to find a steady sale. Therefore, he suggested that as an equivalent for the inshore fisheries the Americans should make a substantial payment in money to supplement the proposed free admission of the four Canadian products.[16]

On March 27, at the British caucus conference, Macdonald submitted to his colleagues a formal written statement that the Canadian Parliament would reject the treaty. To this Lord de Grey objected, suggesting that the logical sequence of such an official statement was a candid notice to the American commissioners that negotiations as to fisheries were at an end. After considerable discussion, Sir John explained that he had not said that he would refuse to justify or defend any such treaty, and he agreed to modify his expressions as to the anticipated action of the Canadian Parliament.[17]

Meantime, other questions had been discussed. On March 23, the American commissioners agreed that any reciprocal arrangement on the transit question should be "for the period for which the fishery articles should be in force." Four days later they proposed to consider the subject of the New Brunswick export duties on American lumber floated down the St. John for shipment to the United States. In reply they received a British offer to urge upon New Brunswick the cessation of such duties.[18]

Meantime, also, questions relating to navigation were under discussion. In reply to the British suggestion that free navigation of Lake Michigan would be regarded as an equivalent for the concession of free navigation of the St. Lawrence, and that some equivalent should be given for the Canadian surrender of the right to control the tolls for use of the Canadian canals, the Americans stated that they were not disposed to make any concessions unless conditional upon adequate enlargement of the Welland Canal. Asserting the previous claim to the natural right to navigate the St. Lawrence, they could not concede the navigation of Lake Michigan as an equivalent. They regarded the proposed concession of the navigation of Lake Michigan and certain American canals (Sault Ste. Marie and St. Clair Flats) as more than an equivalent for the requested concessions as to Canadian canals.

In connection with a reciprocal arrangement as to transit and transshipment, the Americans proposed that Canada should agree (1) to enlarge the Welland and St. Lawrence canals, (2) to charge no discriminating tolls, and (3) to limit tolls to rates required for cost of maintenance and repayment of the cost of construction. These proposals the British commissioners declined, but they later mentioned Canadian plans to enlarge the capacity of the canals.

In the discussions with Fish, Macdonald claimed the British right to navigate Lake Champlain and to use all the channels through the St. Clair Flats. Concerning the suggestion that Canada should agree to deepen its canals to fourteen feet, and agree to a fair toll he stated that the question of the canal enlargement and tolls should be left to the judgment of the Canadian government which had as good right as New York to make a profit from its canals. He suggested, also, that Canada, in preference to the use of the American Sault Ste. Marie Canal, might decide to construct its own canal on its side of the boundary, at an estimated cost of $550,000.[19]

On March 29, in an informal conversation with Lord de Grey on the *Alabama* question, Fish suggested that because of the feeling in the West concerning the exaggerated importance of arrangement for free navigation, the treaty might encounter considerable opposition in the Senate unless Canada made some concession as to the canals—a suggestion which Macdonald interpreted as a method used to frighten Lord de Grey. He was willing to accept the navigation of the St. Lawrence for that of Lake Michigan and Lake Champlain, and the use of the Welland and St. Lawrence canals as an equivalent for the use of the Sault Ste. Marie and the St. Clair Flats canals. He also desired a permanent arrangement for a bonding system. Notwithstanding the American policy concerning coasting trade, he was willing to grant to British vessels the right to carry (in bond) between American ports on the lakes, where land transport intervened, upon condition that the British granted a similar privilege to American vessels, and upon condition that no export duty be charged upon American lumber at St. John (New Brunswick) nor upon the products of either country when shipped from the other.[20]

On the following morning Macdonald had "another scrimmage" with his colleagues. He stated that the proposed American relaxation of the coasting trade was not an equivalent for the Canadian canals which Canada desired to control until it could obtain free trade in exchange for free transit. When his colleagues argued that Canada would never resort to discriminating tolls and, therefore, had no reason for returning the power with a view to using it like the threatening crack of a whip, he replied that Canada had exclusive ownership of its canals and a right to do what it liked with its own—the same right exercised by New York in regard to its canals.

He especially regretted the delay in the settlement of the *Alabama* question which had forced a premature discussion of the fisheries (to occupy the time) and which also had rendered more difficult the adjustment of Canadian questions. In his private report to Tupper he expressed great disappointment at the course of the British commissioners, whom he thought were too much influenced by the desire "to go home to England with a treaty in their pockets, settling everything no matter at what cost to Canada." Feeling that Canada was clearly right and "must throw the responsibility on England," he stated that a declaration of the imperial Parliament against the Canadian policy and acts would "greatly prejudice the idea of British connection, as British protection will have proved itself a farce." [21]

The adjustment of the controversy concerning the northwest

water boundary east of Vancouver Island and south of 49° to the Fuca Strait (involving the ownership of San Juan Island) encountered comparatively little difficulty. Macdonald, although he had said the question "presented more difficulties than all the other cases put together," decided (by April 5) that it was less important than he had first thought. To his colleagues he privately suggested that joint occupation of San Juan Island should be continued for twenty-five years, with a guard reduced from one hundred men to ten for each party. In favor of this plan he proposed to say, jocularly, to the American commissioners that before the end of the quarter century "the infallible destiny of absorption, which they all believe awaits us, will have settled the difficulty."

A few days later, Fish stated to Lord de Grey that the American government would agree to submit the San Juan controversy to arbitration only in case of the previous satisfactory settlement of the *Alabama* and fishery questions. On April 22, after agreement on the *Alabama* claims and on private claims, the commissioners agreed to submit the controversy question to arbitration by the Emperor of Germany and to accept his award as absolutely "final and conclusive" (an award which in October, 1872, was announced in favor of the American contention).[22]

Meantime, questions relating to navigation remained unsettled. On April 22, after again rejecting the British proposal to accept navigation of Lake Michigan as an equivalent for navigation of the St. Lawrence, the Americans agreed to consider the new British proposal to grant the use of the St. Lawrence on condition that the Americans agree to open certain rivers originating in British territory and flowing through Alaska to the sea—a proposal which was later accepted. They also agreed to concede to Canada the navigation of Lake Michigan for ten years, and to accept therefor the British proposal concerning the form of the arrangement for reciprocal use of border canals, but limiting the American canals to those "connected with the navigation of the lakes or rivers traversed by or contiguous to the boundary line between the British and American possessions" (*i.e.*, canals directly connecting the

Lakes). They also obtained an agreement that the transshipment arrangement should be made dependent upon the non-existence of discriminating tolls or regulations on the Canadian canals, and also upon the abolition of the New Brunswick export duty on American lumber intended for the United States, and that the right of carrying should be made dependent upon mutual non-imposition of export duties on the goods passing in transit.[23]

In the final form of the treaty several concessions were granted conditionally. While conceding directly the use of the St. Clair Flats Canal, the American government obligated itself only to urge upon the state governments to secure to British citizens the use of the several state canals connected with the navigation of the lakes or rivers traversed by or contiguous to the international boundary line. Likewise the British government obligated itself (1) only to urge upon the government of the Dominion of Canada to secure to American citizens the use of the Welland, St. Lawrence and other canals of the Dominion, (2) only to urge the Parliament of Canada and the legislatures of the other colonies not to impose any export duties on American goods or merchandise in transshipment under Article XXX, and (3) also only to urge upon the Parliament of Canada and the legislature of New Brunswick that no export duty or other duty be levied on lumber or timber cut in Maine territory watered by the St. John and its tributaries and floated down the St. John to the sea and thence shipped to the United States.[24]

To the article relating to transshipment (Article XXX), and to the related article on abolition of the New Brunswick export duty on American lumber and timber floated down the St. John, the commissioners finally agreed on May 3, on the basis of previous agreement concerning conditions. The article on transshipment provided that for ten years the citizens of each country might carry in the vessels of their country, without payment of duty, goods or wares or merchandise from one port or place to another within the territory of the other along the St. Lawrence and Great Lakes frontier, or within other territory of the British North American possessions, provided a part of the transportation was through their own territory by land carriage and in bond.

To the article on transit in bond (Article XXIX) the commissioners also agreed on May 3. This article provided for conveyance in transit of imports and exports of either country across the territory of the other for a period of ten years, without payment of duties, subject to the rules and regulations prescribed by the government of the territory for protection of the revenue. This article was based upon a recognition of the geographic conditions which determined the transit dependence of Ontario and Quebec upon the United States for access to the sea, especially during the long winter seasons. By provision of the treaty the American government was authorized to suspend the right of transit if the Dominion of Canada failed to establish the required exemption from export duties, or if it failed to open its canals to Americans on equal terms, or if it and New Brunswick failed to free from all duties the American lumber and timber cut on the St. John in Maine and floated down that river through New Brunswick for export to the United States.[25]

Meantime, since the beginning of April, the discussion of the question of the fisheries had alternated with the discussion of other questions. On April 5 Macdonald had written Tupper that the home government had supported his view concerning the inadequacy of the compensation for the inshore fisheries, and had stated that there should be a substantial money payment and a repeal of the American duty on timber. When asked by his colleagues whether he had a definite proposition, he replied that as the question was a commercial one, he had decided to consult the Canadian Council which had members better qualified to understand the money value of the proposed fishery concession for twelve years. To Lord de Grey's observation that political consideration weighed more than the question of a commercial equivalent, he replied that he could not suppose that friendly relations with the United States were endangered by the maintenance of an undisputed right.

A few days later, at a private interview, Lord de Grey informed Fish that the American terms offered were inadequate compensation for the right to enjoy in perpetuity the inshore fisheries, and must be supplemented by a money payment. He received the reply that a tariff arrangement with a money consideration would be difficult, and a suggestion that the compensation should be limited to a money payment of $1,000,000 (which was rejected). When he reported this conversation to his colleagues in caucus, Macdonald precipitated a warm discussion by submitting a telegram from Tupper offering to take "$150,000 per annum and $50,000 additional until lumber was free"—an offer which his colleagues could not regard as serious.

Soon thereafter Fish, at another meeting with Lord de Grey, after repeating his feeling concerning the difficulty as to a proposed tariff arrangement and his pleasure that it had not been accepted, again proposed a money consideration, the amount to be determined by the decision of an impartial arbitrator. Although he did not refuse Lord de Grey's suggested inclusion of free fish, he again referred to the difficulty of commingling a question of tariff with a money consideration.[26]

On April 15, at a caucus with his British colleagues, Lord de Grey stated that the time had arrived for a practical conclusion as to acceptance of Fish's offer to submit to arbitration the question of a money compensation for the inshore fisheries. Macdonald objected. He stated that Canada should be the judge of the value of its own property, that it would insist upon fixing its own price, and that it would claim the right to remain in exclusive possession of the fisheries if it could not get a satisfactory equivalent. He significantly declared that the origin and basis of the commission was the Canadian proposition to ascertain in a friendly way the extent of the respective rights of Canada and the United States in the fisheries. He precipitated a warm discussion by the announcement that Canada, under the provisions of the British North American Act of 1867, would insist upon its exclusive right of dealing with the fisheries.

At a later caucus, on the same day, Macdonald objected to the form of a telegraphic dispatch to London, and especially to the assertion that the settlement of the fisheries was necessary to the continuance of the other negotiations, and he insisted that he still adhered to the proposition for free admission of coal, salt, fish and lumber into the United States. At the same time he warned Lord de Grey that if a lease of the fisheries without adequate compensation was necessary for England's purposes, Canada would ask England for compensation. For this warning he found his opportunity in Lord de Grey's private offer to ask the London government whether it would be willing to pay to Canada a sum of money to extinguish the Fenian claims to which the Americans had objected on the ground that they had not been included in the subjects designated for consideration of the commission. He suggested that a guarantee ("a mere pledge of credit") for railways was "a preferable mode of aiding Canada in any money arrangement for any purpose that might be made," and he also stated that a guarantee for a Canadian Pacific railway would be a matter of imperial interest.[27]

In connection with the unpleasant discussion with his colleagues, Macdonald especially resented the attempt of Lord de Grey to lecture him upon his duty as a British commissioner. On the next day he received an after-church call from his colleague, who frankly and fully and forcefully discussed with him the gravity of the situation. He was told that "the failure in the settlement of the fishery question would involve the complete disruption of the negotiations." He was authorized to inform the Canadian government that the British government in its instructions had mingled the principal subjects of reference (the *Alabama* claims, the fisheries and the San Juan) so that the commissioners could not agree upon the settlement of one without the others. He was asked to warn the Canadian government of the responsibility involved in the rejection of a reasonable compromise such as an agreement for free fishing for a short period of ten years, after which the question would no longer be involved with other questions.[28]

In reply Macdonald stated that the Canadian government was not responsible for the commingling of the various subjects of difference, nor for the consequential situation in which it was asked against its will to enter into an arrangement unsatisfactory to the Canadian people. He contended that the right to the inshore fisheries, which Canada was asked to sacrifice, was not a matter of difference or controversy between the two countries. He urged that, notwithstanding any bullying attitude of the American commissioners, the American government could not properly object if Canada declined to sell or lease its fishery rights, and that it could not be expected to countenance any lawless proceedings or hostile action threatened by the Gloucester fishermen. Furthermore, increasingly heated by his combative arguments, he warned his colleague that the Canadian annexation party, if it considered England unwilling to protect undoubted Canadian rights, might gain strength enough to imperil connection with the mother country, or even to accomplish a separation which would inevitably result in annexation to the United States. At the close of the animated conversation he received from Lord de Grey the confidential assurance that the British government would consent to pay to Canada a sum of money in payment of the Fenian claims if the United States refused to pay them, and if all other matters were settled. He immediately wrote to Sir George Cartier a private and confidential letter in which he presented a full summary of the conference. He also wrote to Tupper a brief letter in which he said: "I find it absolutely necessary to hold my position with firmness." [29]

On April 17, following an informal meeting between Lord de Grey and Secretary Fish, Macdonald renewed his opposition in a caucus with his colleagues. At this caucus Lord de Grey stated that the questions of the *Alabama* claims had been arranged and that Fish had intimated the American intention to submit the San Juan controversy to arbitration after the settlement of the other questions. Therefore, he suggested the provisional continuation of negotiations concerning details of the treaty article on the fisheries while awaiting a cable message of instructions from London, and with the assumption that the British government had given its consent to the principle of arbitration proposed by Fish. Macdonald, who found himself alone in opposing the suggestion, repeated his previous statement of his belief that Canada would not ratify the arrangement. To this he added the statement that he ought either to absent himself from the conference or openly to inform the American members of his belief, and also of his doubts concerning sanction by the British Parliament. By this statement, which Lord de Grey regarded as very grave and as involving serious responsibility, he induced his colleagues to postpone action.[80]

At the joint conference which followed Lord de Grey reported that his government had concluded that the American offer of free admission of coal, salt, fish and lumber was not an adequate equivalent for the fisheries, and proposed an additional payment of money. To this Fish replied that the American government formally withdrew its previous offer and was not prepared to make an additional money grant—an official statement of what he had already told Lord de Grey at an informal interview with him alone. He then reverted to the proposal of a money consideration to be determined by impartial arbitration, preferably with no time limit.

In a confidential letter of April 18 Macdonald stated his belief that a change of feeling at Washington had resulted from the Canadian repeal of the coal and salt duties, and from the consequent pressure of American coal and salt interests to prevent similar action by Congress. Annoyed by the low value placed upon the fisheries by the American commissioners, he said: "They found that our English friends were so squeezeable in nature that their audacity has grown beyond all bounds." [81]

After the arrival of the British cable message authorizing arbitration of the value of the fisheries, Macdonald contemplated resignation of his commission. Fortunately, however, he refrained from such rash action, although he reserved to himself the right of ulterior action. Feeling that the British government, with its "craven desire" to settle all matters, might be forced to offer a substantial compensation to the Dominion of Canada in order to induce its government to consent to the treaty, he continued a policy of protest with a sense of his "duty to remove as many obstacles as possible." He was successful in reducing the period of the lease of the fisheries from twenty-five to ten years, in removing a restriction of free admission of fish, and in securing free admission of fish oil; but he accomplished little by his efforts against the American pressure for concession of free navigation of the St. Lawrence (ascending and descending) and of the Canadian canals.[32]

By the final conference agreement the fisheries were placed on an independent footing, no longer a convenient weapon or menace which might be used to induce the American government to revive the Reciprocity Treaty.

By Article XVIII of the new treaty, the American citizens (in addition to previous liberties under the treaty of 1818) secured for ten years "the liberty to take fish of every kind (except shell-fish) on the sea coasts and shores, and in the bays and harbors and creeks, of the provinces of Quebec, Nova Scotia, and New Brunswick, and the colony of Prince Edward Island, and of the several Islands adjacent, without being restricted to any distance from the shore, with permission to land upon the said coasts and shores and islands, and also upon the Magdalen Islands, for the purpose of drying their nets and curing their fish, provided that in so doing they did not interfere with the rights of private property, or with British fishermen in the peaceful use of any part of said coasts in their occupancy for the same purpose." This liberty applied only to the sea fishery. It did not extend to the salmon and shad fisheries, and the other fisheries in rivers and mouths of rivers (which were reserved exclusively for British fishermen).

By Article XIX British citizens were conceded the same liberty "on the eastern sea coasts and shores of the United States north of the thirty-ninth degree of north latitude."

By Article XXII, the American government agreed to make compensation for any excess in value of fishing privileges accorded to Americans, the amount to be determined by special commissioners who were to be selected for that purpose and who were required to meet at Halifax.

The treaty specified that the provisions of the article relating to fisheries, so far as applicable, were extendable to Newfoundland by legislative enactments of Great Britain and Newfoundland and the United States for making the articles effective.[33]

On April 28 Macdonald accepted Lord de Grey's statement that the British government had saved the rights of Canada by reserving to it the ultimate decision involved in the question of enacting legislation necessary to make the fisheries articles effective. However, he still complained that the original object of the commission as proposed by Canada (to settle disputes as to geographical limits of exclusive fishing rights under the treaty of 1818) had been "altogether ignored" in the later negotiations, and that the British instructions to the British commissioners concerning the fisheries were without the consent of Canada and against its solemn protest. He did not see how the proposed arbitrators could determine the value of the fisheries until after their extent was determined; but he recognized that Canada, if it declined to sanction the treaty, must bear the *onus* of publicly repudiating the terms which his colleagues had accepted against his advice, and that thereby it would encourage a Canadian public opinion injurious to Canadian relations with Great Britain and advantageous to the United States.[34]

In a series of conference discussions concerning the expediency of a provisional arrangement to prevent danger of conflict in the fisheries in the ensuing season, Macdonald invariably stated that he was unable to suggest any method to solve the difficulty. On April 29 he reported to Tupper a decision on an arrangement to which he objected, and which he said Canada would refuse. "Sir Edward Thornton, as British Ambassador," said he, "is to write a humbugging note to Mr. Fish stating that if the Treaty is ratified by the Senate Her Majesty's Government will undertake for itself, and urge on the Governments of Canada and Newfoundland and Prince Edward Island, the making of such regulations for the opening of the inshore fisheries during the present season as may not be inconsistent with the present state of the law, such regulations to take effect as soon as the United States Government shall have opened the American market to our fish in accordance with the proposed Treaty."[35]

Several times, when disappointed by what he regarded as a sacrifice of Canadian interests, Macdonald had "hinted at severing" himself from the commission. Each time he encountered a unanimous protest from his colleagues, who declared that such action would probably prevent the confirmation of the treaty by the Senate. Several times he received from the tactful Lord de Grey an apologetic explanation that England's policy in Europe was largely affected by the apprehension that unsettled Anglo-American questions might cause the American government to coöperate with Russia in any possible European war, and that England's apparent want of firmness of action concerning European complications was due to the dread of a possible attack in the rear by the United States. Finally, recognizing his duty as an officer acting directly under the imperial government, he ignored the advice of the Canadian government that he should withdraw from the commission.[36]

On May 5, two days after the labors of negotiation were substantially terminated and after the commission had agreed to the formal protocol containing a condensed statement of the proceedings, Macdonald repeated to Lord de Grey his opinion that the arrangements concerning the fisheries were "decidedly injurious to Canada whose interests had been sacrificed, or made altogether of secondary consideration, for the sake of getting a settlement of the *Alabama* and San Juan matters." Repeating his opinion that the Canadian Parliament would not sanction the arrangement, and reiterating his earlier arguments, he intimated that he might decide not to sign the treaty. He was urged by his colleague to consider the importance of his signature, which was regarded as necessary to prevent the risk of rejection of the "fair and honorable" treaty by the Senate, and as a responsible duty resulting from his position as a joint member of the Joint High Commission under orders of the British imperial government.[37]

Two subjects submitted by the British for treaty adjustment the Americans declined to admit. One was the question of a survey of the boundary line between the Lake of the Woods and the Rockies, to which the President had referred in his recent message (of December 5, 1870) to Congress, and which he regarded as a subject for administrative action without a treaty provision. It included a question of the boundary at

Pembina which, by the survey of an American corps of engineers in the previous April, was found to be in American territory, although previously regarded as within British jurisdiction. The other subject was the question of Canadian claims for injuries resulting from the Fenian raids which the Americans declined to consider, on the ground of lack of authority. These claims had not been contemplated at the time of the creation of the commission and were not regarded as proper.[38]

On May 6, 1871, the conference adjourned. Two days later all members signed the treaty, which was promptly approved by the American Senate on May 24, ratified by the President on May 25, and proclaimed on July 4, seventeen days after exchange of ratifications.

In America the importance of the treaty was more highly regarded than in Canada. Caleb Cushing later referred to it as "one of the most notable and interesting of all the great diplomatic acts of the present age." It marked the success of a purpose to provide for the amicable settlement of all causes of difference between the two countries. It provided for commissions of arbitration to settle the question of British obligations of neutrality in the American Civil War and American-Canadian controversies concerning the San Juan boundary and the northeastern fisheries. It also contained agreements on certain American-Canadian neighborhood questions, such as transshipment, bonded transit, and navigation of waters connecting the Lakes with the sea. By it the Americans obtained a perpetual right to the free navigation of the St. Lawrence, for which the American government granted to Canada the right to navigate certain Alaskan rivers from Canadian territory to the sea.[39]

In June, 1871, Sir John Rose regretted to see that the tone of the Canadian press toward the treaty indicated the possibility of an issue between Canada and England. In a confidential communication (of June 8) from London to Macdonald, he presented the English view that the treaty was the best that could have been negotiated with a view to the interests of Canada, and that England had made greater sacrifices than

Canada to whom the restoration of friendly Anglo-American feeling was an object of no small importance. He doubted whether the British government desired to force anything on Canada.[40]

In urging the Canadian Parliament to pass the acts necessary to give effect to the treaty, the Earl of Kimberley (the British Colonial Secretary) expressed confidence that the Canadian people would receive advantages commensurate with the concessions which they were asked to make. In reply Lord Lisgar reflected the disappointment of Canada, resulting from failure to secure a renewal of the Reciprocity Treaty and a consideration of its claims to damages for raids of Fenians. He especially stated that Canada resented the settlement of the fisheries question by abandonment of Canadian exclusive "territorial rights of great value" contrary to the wishes of the Canadian government which claimed the right to name the proper equivalent for the inshore fisheries, and which also emphatically disclaimed "the imputation of desiring to imperil the peace of the whole empire in order to force the American government to change its commercial policy."

After some controversy, the Dominion Privy Council (on January 20, 1872) admitted the unprofitableness of prolonged controversial discussion on points of difference, although it still adhered to its previous objections. As a means of surmounting the difficulties in obtaining the consent of the Canadian Parliament to the measures necessary to give effect to the treaty, it suggested an imperial guarantee for a Canadian loan not to exceed £4,000,000 to aid in constructing a railroad to the Pacific and in enlarging the Canadian canals. In response to this the British government agreed to propose a guarantee of a Canadian loan of £2,500,000 as soon as the treaty should take effect. This modified proposition the Canadian Privy Council accepted, on April 15, in accord with a feeling of "duty in the interests of both Canada and the empire at large." In the face of a strong popular opposition, the Canadian Parliament accepted the provisions of the treaty, as soundly urged by Macdonald. Recognizing Canadian internal weakness involving a possible secession of British Columbia and a possible attempt of Quebec to establish a hostile state, and feeling that Canadian independence might involve a danger from the material temptations which the United States could offer, it decided to accept a limited subordination to Great Britain as a temporary safeguard for a period of preparation for Canadian autonomy.[41]

Later, the maritime provinces also enacted appropriate legislation for carrying the treaty into effect.

In connection with the consideration of the execution of the treaty, several provisions were later subjects of discussion. Among these were the American claims for the St. Albans raid of Confederates from Canada which, during the negotiations of the Joint High Commission, had been mentioned frequently as within the intent of the negotiations concerning claims. In December, 1871, Lord Granville, apprehensive that they might prejudice Canadian action on the treaty) suggested that they should not be presented before the claims commission. In reply, Fish declined to withdraw them. A few days later, however, he agreed to delay the claims to help the situation between Great Britain and the Dominion.[42]

On January 12, 1873, at Washington, Sir Edward Thornton wrote Macdonald concerning certain whispered rumors of prospective opposition to the American House bill for carrying into effect the treaty articles relating to Canada. He had just received a call from Senator Morrill who stated his opposition on the ground of the Canadian practice of granting to Canadian vessels, upon entering a Canadian port, a rebate of 90% of the Canadian canal dues paid *en route,* and of requiring full dues from American vessels carrying their cargoes through the Canadian canals to American ports (!). Apparently, several members of the Senate had severely criticized Fish for his failure to settle these questions in the negotiations of 1871.

By act approved March 1, 1873, Congress authorized the operation of the transshipment arrangement (under Article XXX of the treaty) subject to agreement between the British and American governments upon administrative rules and regulations. In the following July the American government considered a Canadian suggestion of some modification of American regulations for transit of goods.

Over a year later, July 12, 1874, Fish had occasion to inquire concerning the practical working of the recently proclaimed Canadian coasting laws relating to foreign vessels in Canadian ports, the announcement of which had raised doubts and apprehensions as to the rights of American vessels in those ports. Later, he raised a question concerning the status of Labrador. In May, 1875, after ascertaining that Labrador was politically a part of Newfoundland, the American Treasury Department decided that fish importations therefrom should be exempted from duty.[43]

Meantime, the discussion of the question of trade reciprocity, upon which no agreement had been reached in the negotiations of 1871, had been renewed by Canada.

REFERENCES

1. *Sir John A. Macdonald Papers, Reciprocity, 1865–66* (Confidential Memorandum, Aug. 3, 1865).
2. *Ib.; 8 Can. Mag.*, May, 1897, pp. 424–29 (A. H. U. COLQUHOUN, *Reciprocity Trips to Washington*).
3. SHORTT and DOUGHTY, *Canada and Its Provinces*, IX, 129; *H. Exec. Docs.*, 40–2, Vol. 15, Part 2, No. 240, Mar. 30 (and May 14), 1868; R. G. HALIBURTON, *Intercolonial Trade.*
4. E. H. DERBY, *Preliminary Rp. on a Treaty of Reciprocity; H. Exec. Docs.*, 40–2, Vol. 15, No. 240, p. 16; *Ib.*, 41–3, Vol. 8, Feb. 3, 1871; ISRAEL BUCHANAN, *Relations of the Industry of Canada with the Mother Country and with the U.S.* (Montreal, 1864); also see *C.A.*, G, 239, #504, pp. 180–82, Bruce to Monck, Confid, June 11, 1867.
5. *C.A.*, G, 200, #1617, Thornton to Young, Confid., No. 45, Sept. 12, 1870; *21 Contemp. Rev.*, March, 1873, pp. 597–615 (ARTHUR MILLS); SHORTT and DOUGHTY, *Canada and Its Provinces*, IX, 129; *Treaty of Washington Papers, 1871*, Confid. Mem. (for use of the commissioners of the U.S. in the Am.-Br. Joint High Commission), p. 25.
6. *Ib.*, p. 27.
7. *C.A.*, G, 116, #1314, Thornton to Young, Feb. 10, 1870 (Private and Confid.); *Ib.*, G, 122, #1354, Thornton to Young, Confid., No. 5, Feb. 25, 1870; *Treaty of Washington Papers, 1871* (IV, *Reciprocal Trade*, May 17, 1870; and III, *Navigation of the St. Lawrence*); *22 G.B., Instrs.*, pp. 163–68, Jan. 14, 1870; *Macdonald Papers*, I, 67 (To Lord de Grey, Apr. 28, 1871).

8. RICHARDSON, *Messages*, VII, 102–06; *Review of Grant's Message* (Ottawa, Dec. 12, 1870, 64 pp.).
9. SHORTT and DOUGHTY, *Canada and Its Provinces*, IX, 125, 129; *Treaty of Washington Papers, 1871.*
10. SHORTT and DOUGHTY, IX.
11. *Treaty of Washington Papers, 1871.*
12. *Macdonald Papers, Washington Treaty, 1871,* Vol. 1, p. 67 (To Cartier, Private and Confid., May 6, 1871).
13. *Messages, Papers and Minutes of the Privy Council, relating to the Treaty of Washington* (Ottawa, 1872).
14. *Macdonald Papers, Washington Treaty, 1871,* Vol. 1 (March 15, 1871); *Treaty of Washington Papers, 1871, Protocol of Conferences.*
15. *Macdonald Papers, Treaty of Washington, 1871,* Vol. 1 (To Tupper, Mar. 21 and March 29).
16. *Ib.* (To Tupper, Mar. 29, and to Earl de Grey and Ripon, March 25, 1871).
17. *Ib.* (To Tupper, Mar. 25, 1871).
18. *Treaty of Washington Papers, 1871, Protocol.*
19. *Ib.*; *Macdonald Papers, Washington Treaty, 1871,* Vol. 1 (To Tupper, Mar. 29).
20. *Ib.* (To Tupper, Private, Apr. 1, 1871).
21. *Ib.*
22. *Ib.*, pp. 27 and 30 (To Tupper, Private and Confid., Apr. 5 and Apr. 16, 1870); *Treaty of Washington Papers, 1871, Articles;* MALLOY, *Treaties*, I, 716–17.
23. *Treaty of Washington Papers, 1871, Protocol; C.A.*, G, Dufferin to Thornton, No. 39, Sept. 25, 1873 (also Jan. 12, 1875).
24. *Treaty of Washington Papers, 1871, Protocol.*
25. *Ib.*
26. *Macdonald Papers, Washington Treaty, 1871,* Vol. 1, pp. 25–26 and 28–32 (To Tupper, Private and Confid., Apr. 5 and 16).
27. *Ib.*, pp. 31 to 33 (To Tupper, Private and Confid., Apr. 16, 1871).
28. *Ib.*, p. 34 (To Tupper, Apr. 16, 1871); *Ib.*, pp. 38–40 (To Cartier, Private and Confid., Apr. 16, 1871).
29. *Ib.*, pp. 38–41 (To Cartier, Apr. 16, 1871).
30. *Ib.*, pp. 43–48 (To Tupper, Private and Confid., Apr. 18, 1871).
31. *Ib.*, pp. 43–48.
32. *Ib.*, pp. 54–55 (To Tupper, Private and Confid., Apr. 27, 1871).
33. *Messages, Despatches and Minutes of the Privy Council, relating to the Treaty of Washington* (Ottawa, 1872); MALLOY, *Treaties*, I, 708–10.
34. *Macdonald Papers, Washington Treaty,* Vol. 1, pp. 65–67 (To De Grey, Apr. 28, 1871).
35. *Ib.*, pp. 58–60 (To Tupper, Private and Confid., Apr. 29, 1871).
36. *Ib.*, pp. 61–62 (To Tupper, Apr. 29).

37. *Ib.*, pp. 67–68 (To Cartier, Private and Confid., May 6, 1871); *Ib.*, p. 75 (De Grey to Macdonald, Private, May 6, 1871).
38. *Treaty of Washington Papers, 1871, Protocol of Conferences;* RICHARDSON, *Messages*, VII, 102; *Messages, Despatches and Minutes of the Privy Council, relating to the Treaty of Washington* (Ottawa, 1872); MOORE, *Int. Arb's.*, I, 686–87; *For. Rels., 1873*, Part 3, p. 398.
39. CALEB CUSHING, *The Treaty of Washington.*
40. *Macdonald Papers, Washington Treaty, 1871*, Vol. 1, pp. 481–98 (From Sir John Rose, June 8, 1871).
41. *Messages, Despatches and Minutes of the Privy Council, relating to the Treaty of Washington* (Ottawa, 1872); SHORTT and DOUGHTY, IX, 130; *8 Can. Mo. and Nat. Rev.*, Nov. 1875, pp. 428–32 (FISHER).
42. *22 G.B., Instrs.*, pp. 591–92, No. 107 (To Schenck), Dec. 18, 1871; *23 G.B., Instrs.*, p. 4, No. 119, Jan. 8, 1872; *Ib.*, p. 42, Tel., Mar. 1, 1872.
43. *Macdonald Papers, Washington Treaty, 1871*, Vol. 1, pp. 588–94 (From Thornton (Private), Jan. 12, and Feb. 1, 1871); *Cong. Record*, Jan. 14 to Mar. 4, 1873, *passim; 16 G.B., Notes to*, pp. 162, 216–17 and 383–85, Fish to Thornton, July 22 and Sept. 30, 1873, and June 12, 1874; *Ib.*, pp. 387, 406 and 568, June 19 and July 27, 1874 and May 28, 1875.

CHAPTER XV

NEW PROBLEMS OF RECIPROCITY AND FISHERIES, 1872–89

FOR almost two decades after 1871 the American government in its Canadian relations was chiefly troubled by questions concerning the northeastern fisheries which Canada sought to use as a counterweight to secure reciprocal trade concessions. Coincidently it declined to respond to the persistent efforts of Canada to secure a renewal of the Reciprocity Treaty. In this policy it probably was influenced largely by the fact that Canada possessed no treaty-making powers except through the British government.[1]

In 1874, the Canadian government initiated renewed reciprocity negotiations by sending George Brown to Washington as joint plenipotentiary to coöperate with Sir Edward Thornton in arranging a treaty of fisheries, commerce and navigation, which was expected to combine fishery rights with trade agreements for natural products and for many manufactured articles. In an interview of March 28, these representatives informed Secretary Fish that the British government was prepared to accept a renewal of the treaty of 1854 as a substitute for the fishery arbitration provision of 1871—a provision for an uncertain money payment which was expected to prove irritating.

In reply, although he declined to make a proposition, Fish suggested an enlargement of the scope of the treaty. As topics for discussion be suggested (1) the enlargement of the Canadian canals and (2) the addition of certain classes of manufactures to the free list. He received assurance that the Canadian government would heartily assent to any mutually advantageous trade measure, provided it was not seriously prejudicial to existing Canadian industrial interests.[2]

On April 27, Thornton and Brown, in accord with their promise, submitted to Fish a memorandum on American-Canadian commercial relations, which was practically prepared by Brown alone. As one proof of the probable value to the United States of the earlier partial reciprocity in the decade before 1866, they cited the increase of Canadian foreign bonded traffic across the United States since 1868. Stating that Canada in seeking reciprocity was actuated by considerations of common interests and mutual friendliness and good will, and the value of near markets, they proposed a new treaty for a term of twenty-one years. Besides provision for mutual free admission of a list of specified articles, they proposed that it should include the following concessions: American enjoyment of the Canadian coast fisheries without compensation; reciprocal enjoyment of the coasting trade; enlargement of the Canadian canals at Canadian expense; mutual use of Canadian and American canals with right of transshipment of cargo at canal terminals; free navigation of Lake Michigan by Canadian vessels; arrangement for mutual registration of vessels; joint commissions for improvement of the navigation of the St. Clair and Detroit rivers and Lake St. Clair, for erection and proper regulation of necessary lighthouses on the Great Lakes common to both countries, and to promote the propagation and protection of fish in the common inland water; reciprocal patent laws; and coöperation in methods of preventing illicit trade.

Later, in June, the British proposals were submitted in another memorandum in the form of a treaty draft, with some changes and some additions. The latter included provisions as to copyright, transit trade, extradition, "certain articles of manufacture," Canadian adjustment of excise duties on spirits and beer and tobacco, Canadian construction of a free canal from Caughnawaga on the St. Lawrence to Lake Champlain on condition that the American government or New York State would construct a free canal from Whitehall to Troy, and transshipment under the flags of both nations on the Lakes and other border waters.[8]

On June 15, following an interview of the previous Saturday, Fish submitted to Thornton a copy of a proposed substitute clause by which he agreed to urge the New York government to enlarge the existing canal from Lake Champlain (Whitehall) to Albany and also to urge the governments of New York and Michigan to secure to the inhabitants of Canada the use of the Erie, Whitehall and Sault Ste. Marie canals on terms of equality with the United States.[4]

The tentative unsigned British draft, with a few slight changes, Fish submitted to the President with a statement of the extent of his agreement with it. On June 18 (near the close of the session of Congress) the President promptly submitted it to the Senate with a special message requesting its advice. He expressed his opinion that the proposed treaty contained many commendable features. Apparently, he was especially pleased with the provision which proposed to dispense with the fishery arbitration clause of the treaty of 1871.[5]

In July, following the Senate's decision to postpone the subject "to the next session of Congress," Fish received from the British legation a note implying expected consideration by the Senate in December. On July 18, in order to avoid the possibility of misapprehension, he stated that the Senate had given no such assurances.

In the following session the Senate delayed action and failed to give its assent. In its non-action, it was probably influenced largely by the feeling that the proposed arrangement was too favorable to Canada—a feeling which probably was not materially decreased by the presence of a Canadian "confidential mission" at Washington to influence public opinion in favor of the treaty. By a resolution of February 3, 1875, it declared the inexpediency of a recommendation of negotiations for reciprocal trade relations.[6]

In a speech in the Senate on February 3 Senator Morrill expressed the bases of opposition to the project. He included the objections that the President had no power to interfere with the prerogative of the House to originate revenue bills, and that such an arrangement would postpone peaceful annexation which he regarded as desirable for the convenience and prosperity of both countries. With a reminder of the disappointing results of the treaty of 1854 he said: "Let us not be deceived by the present commercial caresses of our Canadian friends. . . . They seem to think we ought to discover that annexation is but a little way off from reciprocity, but this bait is growing stale." He asserted that American policy was neither to force or unduly hasten annexation, nor to bar or retard it, by a reciprocity treaty. Confident of American advantages from physical conditions, he said: "Geographical barriers must forever compel the people of British Columbia, Manitoba, Saskatchewan, New Brunswick, Nova Scotia, Newfoundland and Labrador to seek and to prefer commercial relations with the United States with or without reciprocity." He especially contended that Great Britain, by its back-door commercial connection with Canada which felt bound to consult the imperial interests, was the chief obstacle to the proposed reciprocity arrangement. In explanation he added: "It is an unequal commercial triangle which cannot be squared. Our manufacturers do not wish to meet Great Britain when they are nominally invited to meet Canada, or to live with Leah when they only love Rachel." [7]

Canada complained of the rejection of a treaty which was the culmination of its efforts. One Canadian writer, complaining that treaty-making had unmade Canada, expressed a dislike for the diplomatic air at Washington where the self-sufficient British foreigner was bewildered by frolic and delicate attentions, "listening to the voice of Jacob but capitulating to the hand of Esau." The Mackenzie administration expressed great disappointment. Galt contemplated retaliatory duties. Macdonald, who returned to power in 1878, soon prepared to inaugurate his "National Policy" based on the principles of "go it alone," although he still desired reciprocity.[8]

Meantime, in January, 1876, influenced in part by recommendations of several American chambers of commerce, the House Committee on Commerce reported a basis for a mutually beneficial reciprocity treaty. Suggesting a limited customs union, it recommended the adoption of a joint resolution for the appointment of a joint Anglo-American commission to consider the subject.[9]

In December, 1878, Evarts was asked by a special committee of the National Board of Trade whether he had any objection to its coöperation and conference with a delegation from the Dominion Board of Trade with a view to arriving at an understanding concerning a draft of a reciprocity treaty. He replied that, although there was "no objection to business men putting their heads together," the action of the Board of Trade could carry no official weight whatever on the question of the negotiations of a reciprocity treaty.[10]

By 1879, unable to obtain from the American government an agreement for reciprocity of trade, Macdonald adopted a high protective tariff policy which he designated as the completion of Canadian concurrence in a policy of "reciprocity of tariffs." His so-called national policy tariff which became effective in March, 1879, was regarded by Americans as a retaliatory measure and a threat against the United States, although it contained a provision authorizing the Governor-General in Council to revoke the duties on imports from the United States whenever the Washington government extended the same favor to American imports from Canada. The increased influence of the Canadian protectionists Hincks attributed to the failure of the negotiations in 1874. In reply Professor Goldwin Smith said that the attempt of Canadian statesmen to sever Canada from the American continent was an expensive effort to reverse the order of nature. Instead of partial reciprocity he advocated the necessity of a permanent commercial union.[11]

Apparently, the American government felt no disposition to favor closer trade relations, although it observed with interest the beginning of the Canadian protective policy in 1878 and the increasing Canadian migration movements to the United States and to Manitoba. In a period of increasing prosperity, and with little friction except that concerning fisheries, it offered little encouragement to Canadian lingering hopes for trade reciprocity. Instead of encouragement, it precipitated a new source of controversy by placing a tariff on Canadian coal, lobsters and eggs, and on Canadian tin cans or other containers of free fish. The latter, to which Canada objected on the ground that it was practically a prohibition on American importation of Canadian fish, resulted in additional Canadian retaliation by tariffs on American tin cans and peach baskets.[12]

In some instances retaliation was moderated by reciprocal mercy or courtesy. In January, 1880, in response to an American complaint of unreciprocal Canadian imposition of a tonnage tax on American fishing vessels and a duty on empty barrels carried as containers in which to ship to the United States the fish obtained in Canadian waters, Evarts received a Canadian disclaimer of any right to collect duties on empty barrels. In the following July, in response to a British complaint of an American duty of forty per cent on pure cod-liver oil, unchanged by no process after the original process of manufacture, was exempt from duty when imported into the United States.[13]

Later, in February, 1883, arose a new question concerning tariffs. Frelinghuysen requested Canadian remission of a duty imposed on tea imported by an American firm from Japan to Canada via New York, where it had been detained for a short time without seeking a market there.[14]

Coincidently with the beginnings of the Canadian national tariff policy, the American government felt some apprehension concerning the purpose of the Canadian government in prohibiting importation of American cattle (by an order in council). Early in 1879, Evarts objected to British regulations concerning American cattle shipments to Great Britain through Ontario, and authorized a notice to Salisbury that any restriction of American cattle trade would be regarded as "unjustifiable by any condition here." Later, on March 7, following American adoption of preshipment inspection of all cattle for export, he forwarded a notice that, because of pleuropneumonia at Hull, England, the American government had temporarily prohibited all importation of cattle from Great Britain. The British restriction still continued unadjusted in July, 1885.[15] Possibly this may have influenced Blaine's complaint, of May, 1881, that Canadian immigrants had introduced smallpox into the manufacturing districts of Massachusetts, and his suggestion that the American government might be compelled by necessity to consider the propriety of adopting measures of self-defense.[16]

Meantime, in April, 1880, a House committee resolution recommended the appointment of a commission of experts to obtain information as a basis for the consideration of the question of a reciprocity treaty. It was strongly opposed, however, by the minority of the committee, which doubted the constitutionality of the proposed plan to refer to secret and compromising diplomacy the work which should be done in the light of publicity by the Ways and Means Committee. In view of the events of the preceding two years, Rice of the minority suggested that the time was not favorable to approach Canada with fresh negotiations. "It would be best," said he, "to settle our rights under the present treaty before we seek to make a new one." He regarded just reciprocity impossible so long as Canada continued its "present relation" with Great Britain.[17]

By 1880 a new Canadian movement for adjustment of commercial relations was begun. It was especially agitated by Professor Goldwin Smith who in 1877, in a magazine article on the "Destiny of Canada," had referred to Canadian nationality as a lost cause and had urged preparation for ultimate peaceful political union with the United States by adoption of a plan of commercial union. It was also later promoted by Erastus Wiman, who had the coöperation of Sir Wilfrid Laurier, Sir Richard Cartwright, and Edward Farrer (a writer for the *Toronto Globe*).

In September, 1880, while Macdonald was at London seeking money for railway construction, George Anderson (a member of Parliament) voiced the fear that a customs-union or zollverein would soon result in the separation of Canada from the empire and suggested that Canadian annexation would probably become a leading American political question in the Garfield administration.[18]

In reply to Anderson's apprehension, William Clark expressed the opinion that the American government at that time showed no strong desire to acquire Canada. He thought, however, that North America should unite to avoid the problems of frontiers and boundary lines and that Canada would seek annexation with a view to its future interests. Similar in tone was an article of F. G. Mather, who wondered why Canada should construct railways and canals to avoid contact with the United States in which almost every Canadian family had a representative and which did not seek to hasten Canadian decisions concerning its own destiny. Similar views were expressed by P. Bender who stated that the large body of Canadians preferred annexation to reciprocity.[19]

A marked feature of the two decades of Canadian development after 1879, especially after 1884, was the increase of secret price-fixing combinations which, if they were unable to secure undisturbed control through Canadian tariffs, formed agreements with similar secret combinations in the United States to regulate prices in both countries or to prevent further sales to independent dealers (to non-members of the combination).[20]

By 1878, the American government had found new sources of disagreement concerning the fisheries provisions of 1871. The first source arose from colonial regulations. In June, 1873, Fish complained that provisions of the Newfoundland legislative act to carry into effect the fishery articles of the treaty were contrary to the treaty. Nearly five years later Evarts submitted a complaint that on a Sunday in January, 1878, in Fortune Bay, on the southern coast of Newfoundland, Americans who were fishing there (in violation of a local Sunday law) were interrupted and driven off by a mob of excited citizens (with religious scruples) while the pious islanders continued to fish. In the sharp discussion which arose he was confronted by the British contention of the applicability of local colonial laws to American fishermen within the British territorial water. In reply he presented counter-arguments which induced the British government to agree to the payment of compensation (seventy-five thousand dollars) for the incident on the ground that Newfoundland citizens had acted without authority to exercise control.[21]

A second source of disagreement concerning the fisheries arose from the Halifax award. In April, 1875, after considerable delay in the choice of commissioners to execute the fishery provisions of the treaty of 1871, and following the Senate's failure to assent to the draft treaty of 1874, Fish received from Thornton a statement of the British wish to proceed with the fisheries compensation arbitration at Halifax under the terms of 1871. In accord with the earlier expressed wish of Canada, which he had at first opposed, he finally agreed reluctantly to accept the Austrian appointment of Maurice Delfosse (the Belgian minister at Washington) as a third commissioner to act with A. T. Galt of Canada and Ensign H. Kellogg of the United States. The commission held its first meeting at Halifax on June 15, 1877. After the examination of evidence and the presentation of extensive arguments, Delfosse (on November 23) announced the unexplained award of $5,500,000 (payable in twelve annual installments) in favor of the British government, as the excess value of the inshore fishing privileges which Americans received from Canada by the treaty of 1871. This award was signed by Delfosse and Galt, but not by Kellogg who expressed his formal dissent.

The American government was disappointed by the decision, and was especially surprised by the large sum awarded —a sum which far exceeded earlier Canadian expectations, and to which should be added twelve annual payments of about $350,000 each for remission of duties on Canadian fish and fish-oil. On May 17 the President submitted to Congress the documents and proceedings of the commission with a recommendation that the amount of the award should be appropriated, but that concerning the payment the President should be invested with such discretion as the public interests might seem to require. This recommendation Congress adopted.[22]

On September 27, 1878, Evarts submitted to Welch at London an argumentative statement of American views as to the invalidity of the award, but he gave a warning instruction that the legation should not intimate that the award would not be paid. Early in November, following a tactful reply from Salisbury, he forwarded instructions that the payment of the award, if made, must be made under protest. On November 21, in delivering to the British government a draft in payment, he stated that his government protested against any consideration of the payment as an acquiescence in the award as a just measure of the value of American participation in the inshore fisheries.[23]

The American government later continued to speak firmly its views in opposition to the colonial policy of fishery regulations. In May, 1882, Secretary Frelinghuysen asserted the American claim that fishery rights conceded by the treaty of Washington should be exercised "wholly free from the restraints and regulations of the statutes of Newfoundland," and requested action in recognition of this claim. In reply, Sir Lionel Sackville-West, the British minister at Washington, submitted a proposed revision of the regulations.[24]

Influenced especially by the excessive money award and by declarations of the Gloucester fishermen that access to the Canadian inshore fisheries had become of little value, the President and Congress finally decided to favor the abrogation of the fishery articles of 1871. Congress, by joint resolution of March 3, 1883, provided for termination of these articles (Articles XVIII to XXV) and a water transshipment article (Article XXX) of 1871—an act which also resulted in the termination of the article on transit in bond (Article XXIX). Four months later, on July 2, at the earliest time possible, Frelinghuysen submitted the required two years' notice for abrogation of the fishery-barter clauses. On October 16 he gave notice of the desire to terminate Article XXII (concerning Newfoundland) coincident with the other fishery articles.[25]

Later executive action was influenced by the determined action of the New England fishermen in December, 1884, in urging the American government to repudiate the fishery clauses of 1871 and to restore the rights claimed before 1818, and by the later insistent demands of New England members of Congress. On January 31, 1885, President Arthur gave public notice that, by joint resolution of March 3, 1883, the legislation of March 1, 1873, for execution of the fishery articles, would expire on July 1, 1885.[26]

By a temporary Anglo-American agreement concluded on

June 22, 1885, to avoid misunderstanding and difficulties and in accord with an amicable spirit of good neighborhood, Canada (and Newfoundland) courteously extended the privileges of the treaty from July 1 to the end of the fishing season, in return for an understanding that the American government would negotiate for the development of trade between the two countries.[27]

The Cleveland administration, confronted with the determined purpose of Canada to use the fisheries as a weapon to gain commercial concessions, had decided to adopt a policy for satisfactory adjustment of all Anglo-American neighborhood questions. This policy included plans to recommend the appointment of a joint commission to consider and settle the entire question of fishing rights upon a just, equitable and honorable basis.[28]

For the timely and temporary good-will arrangement of June 22, practically extending treaty provisions which had been abrogated, Bayard was criticized by certain American fishing interests which had expected the abandonment of reciprocal fishing rights to result in an increase in the price of sea food by the tariff method.[29]

In July, 1885, the question of the effect of the abrogation of the fishery articles upon the treaty article for conveyance in bond caused some alarm on the Lakes. On July 2 the Secretary of the Treasury (Manning) issued a circular prohibiting transit of Canadian goods through the United States—a prohibition which, however, was reversed on July 24. On July 11, T. R. Merritt of the Welland Railway doubted whether the result of the prohibition would be injurious to Canadian railways. He expected that the threatened injury to American eastern ports and lake ports (except Buffalo and Erie) would stimulate sufficient American pressure of opposition to remedy the evils of the situation. Considering the effect in relation to the Welland Canal, he stated that only American vessels bound for American ports and the route via Oswego and Ogdensburg would be injuriously affected. He suggested that Canada, in any efforts to prevent interference in a just international trade, would have an advantage from the completion of the Canadian Pacific and the leverage of the Canadian trade of the Canadian North- [illegible]hich was largely carried through the United States by all- [illegible]nd by combined water and rail via Duluth. He said that the object of the bonding clause of 1871 was mainly in the interests of Canadian shipping with a view to its return to the position held before July, 1866. He stated that until 1882 it certainly benefited all the Canadian railways. He mentioned especially the Northern, which had a daily line of Canadian steamers between Collingwood and Chicago and between Toronto and Ogdensburg, and which carried millions of bushels of American grain before the opening of the Welland Canal enlargement made the privilege of little advantage except for goods brought to Sarnia and Collingwood, and other ports, for all-rail transportation to eastern points in the United States.[30]

Sackville-West sensed the danger that the abrogation of the fishery articles and the conveyance-in-bond article would seriously affect trade unless a reciprocal trade arrangement could be reëstablished. He apprehended that abrogation of the conveyance article, which allowed American merchandise free transit across Canadian territory between two American points, would result in a heavy loss to the Canadian Southern and Grand Trunk railways between Sarnia and Ogden on the west and the Niagara suspension bridge on the east. He also apprehended that the Canadian government would retaliate by rescinding its order of December, 1883, by which Canadian goods had free transit through American territory between two Canadian ports. He desired to avoid this retaliation which would force shipments from Ontario to the maritime provinces by the Intercolonial route instead of the cheaper route to Portland and thence by water to St. John and Halifax, and which would also force freights between eastern Canada and the Canadian Northwest to take the route around the northern shore of Lake Superior instead of the shorter route via St. Paul. With a view to prevention of retaliatory measures, he prepared a memorandum which (on July 13) he proposed to submit to Bayard if he could obtain the approval of the British and Canadian governments. In it he suggested that the object to be sought was "to assimilate as far as possible the commerce at the two countries to the interstate commerce of the Union and to remove all impediments to free interchange of commodities and to the carrying trade."[31]

In December, 1885, in accord with his previous suggestion, President Cleveland recommended in the interests of "good neighborhood" that Congress should provide for the appointment of a joint international commission to settle upon an equitable and honorable basis the entire question of fishing rights on the northeast coast, and he suggested the propriety of considering in connection therewith "other general questions dependent upon contiguity and intercourse." This proposition, which met loud protests from the New England fishermen, Congress considered adversely.[32]

In 1886, coincident with act of American revenue cutters in the Bering Sea against Canadian seal-hunters, the American government was confronted by various zealous acts of Canadian revenue cutters and guard boats on the Atlantic coast fishing grounds, acts which rigidly restricted American fishermen to the strict letter of treaty privileges as interpreted by Canadian authorities. These acts, originating in response to American tariffs and directed in responsive competition to the activity of American fishing boats, prevented American vessels from fishing within the three-mile limit and from entering Canadian ports to purchase bait or to ship cargoes or for any other purpose not authorized by treaty. Denouncing these restrictions as unneighborly and as an unfair use of a club to force the opening of American markets to Canadian products, the Cleveland administration determined to maintain American rights under the treaty of 1818. It was finally driven to the consideration of retaliatory measures.[33]

In March, 1886, in reply to Earl Rosebery's inquiry whether the American government intended to notify American fishermen that they were now precluded from fishing in British North American territorial waters, Bayard stated that his government had found no necessity for such notification, that since the President's recent formal proclamation notice of the termination of the fishery articles of 1871 Americans claimed fishing rights under provisions of the treaty of 1818 (to take fish within the three-mile limit and to dry and cure fish under certain conditions). On May 10 he complained of the seizure of American vessels in Nova Scotia. On May 22 he cabled a request for British orders to prevent Canadian execution of the treaty of 1818 except under imperial authority, and he suggested that negotiations might be facilitated by release (without prejudice) of vessels already seized. On May 29, after seeing a copy of the pending Canadian bill proposing forcible search and seizure and confiscation of any foreign vessel which entered Canadian waters for any purpose not permitted by law or treaty, he again complained. Referring to certain Ottawa orders which assumed to execute the provisions of the treaty of 1818 he cabled Phelps at London to protest to the British government and to give notice that the American government would hold it liable for all losses and injuries to American citizens and property resulting from the unauthorized and unfriendly action of the Canadian officials (in search, seizures and detention).

In June Bayard was provoked by information that the masters of American fishing vessels were not allowed to land fish at Halifax for transportation in bond across Nova Scotia and that they had been warned not to enter the waters north of an imaginary line drawn from Canso Head to St. Esprit on the Cape Breton coast, nor the bay of Prince Edward Island inside a line drawn from North Cape to East Point, nor the Bay of Chaleur. On June 14, he expressed his feeling against the attempt to revive unwarranted pretensions of extra-territorial authority which had been settled long ago, and he requested prompt remedial orders by the British government.[34]

In the following month Bayard learned from the Consul-General at Halifax that the local authorities at Pictou, acting on orders from Ottawa, had denied an American registered merchant steamer the right to purchase coal and ice or to transship fish in bond through Canada free of duty, and had compelled it to leave Pictou without fuel necessary for a lawful voyage on a dangerous coast. Against this inhospitable treatment he submitted instant and formal protest and stated that the British government would be held liable for any loss or injury.[35]

The serious situation resulted in some irresponsible annexation agitation which evidently was not regarded as representative of public opinion on either side of the boundary.[36]

In the following November (1886) an effort at adjustment of difficulties was made in conferences at Washington, at which the larger part of the time was used in the discussion of tariffs. On November 15 Sir Charles Tupper proposed unrestricted reciprocity, which Congress refused to discuss under pressure of threats concerning fisheries, and concerning which it was unwilling to conclude an agreement before the settlement of the fishery question.[37]

Near the close of the year S. J. Ritchie, an American capitalist with large business interests in Canada, sought to revive reciprocity negotiations, both by unofficial conferences with Bayard and members of Congress and by encouraging reports to Macdonald. To Macdonald he reported that Bayard regretted the refusal of Congress to appoint a commission as the President had requested, and that he was ready to negotiate a reciprocity treaty whenever he had any reason to hope that the Senate would ratify it. He expressed his opinion that a large portion of the Senate favored reciprocity but did "not want the Democratic President to have the credit of accomplishing it." He reported that Sherman of the Committee of Foreign Relations agreed to support a treaty combining reciprocity with the fisheries, and that even Frye declared a wish to invite Canada to participate in the proposed pan-American congress if it could be done without inviting the British government to which America could not offer reciprocal trade relations. In the House also he found an increasing reciprocity sentiment. From Benjamin Butterworth and other Republican members he received promises to favor a bill requesting the administration to negotiate with Great Britain a treaty for liberal trade relations with Canada. On December 12 he urged Macdonald to forward to Washington an official report to aid the plans in Congress.[38]

Early in 1887 the Canadian policy of using the fisheries as a club to force a renewal of a reciprocity agreement, under which it desired free admission of Canadian fish, threatened to result in an American retaliatory policy. The action of Canadian authorities in seizing four hundred American vessels, for violation of Canadian regulations, produced much American hostile feeling and resulted in renewed complaints by the American government.[39]

On February 4, while awaiting a reply to a proposition of settlement, and while the House committee was considering a Senate bill to authorize and direct the President to proclaim suspension of commercial intercourse with Canada if the latter continued its unfriendly treatment of American fishermen, Bayard cabled London that prompt action was essential to avert a policy of retaliation. Twenty days later Senator Hoar submitted in the Senate a resolution advising against any negotiations relating to a reciprocity treaty with Canada with a purpose of reduction or change or abolition of duties. In the consideration of the resolution Senator Morgan opposed the object to forestall the negotiation of a treaty which he urged was a constitutional right of the President.[40]

Finally, on March 3, influenced by the Canadian teasing and wearying fisheries policy which was applied with the aim to force American trade concessions, Congress enacted a retaliatory law authorizing the President, whenever satisfied that American fishing vessels were unjustly vexed or harassed in British North American dominions, to deny by proclamation the entrance of vessels of British dominions into American ports except as a necessary safety measure, and to forbid the importation of fish or merchandise from the British North American dominions. This act, however, the President declined to enforce because he was never willing to use the authority which it conferred upon him. It was never used by American executives, although it was still regarded as in force two decades later.[41]

President Cleveland favored conciliation which might prevent the need of retaliation, and, therefore, still sought an attempt at settlement by the appointment of a commission. To the American Fisheries Union, which urged him to adopt a policy of non-importation of Canadian fish, he explained that any arrangement with Canada must not favor a particular class of American economic interests. By his subsequent December message on the tariff he drew from Blaine and others an extravagant responsive defense of infant industries.[42]

The United States, prosperous and content and with a divided authority which made the success of negotiation difficult, still seemed indifferent to the advances of Canada. It regretted that Canada was embarrassed by its colonial connection, which was also embarrassing to Great Britain. Although many expected the situation to result in ultimate peaceful annexation of Canada, the American government made no effort to realize these expectations. It would not take the initiative in any movement for annexation and was not seeking to induce Canada to take the initiative in such action. Many Americans, however, were interested in a new Canadian agitation (of 1887) for political union which was chiefly supported by the widely known Professor Goldwin Smith of Toronto, and which provoked a movement in favor of Canadian independence.[43]

Many Canadians were encouraged to hope for a commercial union or zollverein, involving free trade with the United States. The leader in stimulating this movement was Erastus Wiman, a Canadian who had prospered in New York. He was largely influenced by the views of two Americans: Samuel J. Ritchie who was interested in Canadian ores, and Benjamin Butterworth who was an Ohio member of Congress. In pushing the policy in Ontario, he had the support of Goldwin Smith and of Edward Farrer, both of whom believed that Canadian political union with the United States was inevitable. From his office in New York he forwarded to Macdonald many newspaper extracts in favor of closer commercial relations. By some he was regarded as an annexationist. In the fall of 1887 a young English journalist attributed to him a plan to settle the northeast fishery dispute by American purchase of the Canadian maritime provinces, by a payment of $5,500,000 (!).[44]

In Congress Butterworth, coöperating with Wiman and Ritchie, became the active leader of the movement for a zollverein or commercial union, which according to his plan substantially included the ten propositions of the draft treaty of

1874. He introduced a bill for free entrance of all Canadian products whenever Canada should provide for free entrance of all American products. In this bill for reciprocal trade by concurrent legislation, he had the support of Nelson Dingley and other influential protectionist leaders in Congress. In Canada his policy was approved by Sir Richard Cartwright and by many other Liberals who in the following session of the Canadian Parliament favored a proposal to re-open at Washington negotiations for unrestricted trade reciprocity.[45]

Meantime, Governor-General Lord Lansdowne became somewhat apprehensive of the growth of the movement in favor of the new policy. On October 31 he wrote the Colonial Secretary an "extremely confidential" letter, especially directing attention to the bearing of the question upon British interests. Macdonald, whose policy had been to allow the cry of commercial union "to blaze, crackle and go out with a stink," later received this letter as an enclosure from Tupper after its force was lost by the logic of events. Accurately estimating the evidences of increasing sentiment against commercial union, he wrote Tupper (in January, 1888): "Commercial Union is a dead duck." Concerning Lansdowne's dispatch, he significantly said: "We can afford to be perfectly indifferent as to what the private opinions of Governors General may be as to our policy or our personnel. He must obey our behests if supported by the Canadian people."[46]

Meantime, the retaliatory act of March 3, 1887, which largely repressed causes of complaint in regard to the fisheries, had prepared the way for more active negotiations for adjustment. This act, although unexecuted, was probably the origin of a new Canadian effort to arrange a settlement of fishing difficulties on a basis which included improved commercial relations.

For this new Canadian effort, the American adminstration furnished some encouragement. President Cleveland, tired of Bayard's inconvenient and unsatisfactory attempts at indirect transaction of Canadian business through the London Foreign Office, and with a view to a remedy of dilatory methods and obstruction of adjustments, initiated a proposal for a conference at Washington at which the interests of Canada and Newfoundland should be directly represented.

Apparently the way for this proposal was prepared by Dr. Charles Tupper in the Canadian Parliament by a speech in which he stated that Canada, by the construction of the Canadian Pacific and Intercolonial railways, was independent of the United States in means for free intercourse between the Canadian provinces. Following this speech, which attracted much attention in the American press, Dr. Tupper learned from Wiman that Secretary Bayard had recently intimated a wish or willingness to have an opportunity to discuss, either with the Canadian premier or with Tupper, the mutual relations of the United States and Canada. Therefore, at the suggestion of Wiman and with the authority of the Canadian government, he arranged a trip to Washington at the Easter holidays. He was presented to Bayard with whom he had an interview on May 21, 1887, and from whom he later received a letter (of May 31) concerning direct negotiations on the subject of commercial relations in connection with fisheries.[47]

Apparently Bayard welcomed this opportunity for a direct conference. He recognized that it offered a way of relief from the embarrassment experienced by him in conducting with Great Britain negotiations concerning Canada which, although gradually becoming emancipated from British control, still had an imperfectly developed sovereignty. In a letter of May 31 to Tupper, he wrote: "It is evident that the commercial intercourse between the inhabitants of Canada and those of the United States has grown into too vast proportions to be exposed much longer to the wordy triangular duel, and more direct and responsible methods should be resorted to."[48]

As a result of the direct conference with Tupper, Bayard later decided to coöperate in the appointment of a commission for negotiation at Washington. In the following October, on his own responsibility after the Senate had deliberately expressed its conviction that such action was inadvisable, he selected William L. Putnam of Maine and President James B. Angell of Michigan to serve with himself on a commission to confer with British representatives. This commission, upon which the

British and Canadian governments were represented by Lionel Sackville-West and Joseph Chamberlain and Tupper, held its first formal meeting at Washington on November 22, 1887, and continued its conferences until the following February.

The commission considered carefully Tupper's proposal of trade reciprocity as a concession for reciprocity in fishing rights enjoyed under the treaty of Washington. This proposal the American members declined on the ground that they could not agree to grant trade concessions as compensation for immunity from what they regarded as hostile and unneighborly aggression. They proposed to submit to an arbitration tribunal the question of damages for illegal conduct of Canadian officials concerning the fisheries. The Canadian members proposed to determine the question by decision of the Canadian courts.

In the conferences the Canadians especially complained of the recent American decision that American grain and other produce carried in Canadian vessels from Duluth to Canadian ports (Sarnia and Georgian Bay), and thence shipped by rail to American seaboard ports, would be liable to duty on entering the United States. They complained that the decision had resulted in the exclusion of the Canadian steamers from participation in the grain traffic, and, consequently, in a serious loss to the Canadian owners of the vessels.[49]

On December 10, at the suggestion of Tupper, Chamberlain confidentially sounded Bayard upon a proposition to exchange certain American reserved rights to fish (in territorial waters) for a new concession, of facilities expressly denied by the convention of 1818, combined with a license system permitting American fishermen to obtain supplies and transship their catch. In reply Bayard declined to consider any proposal which involved renunciation of American rights in British territorial waters. Although he admitted that these rights tended to impair the sovereignty of Canada and Newfoundland and were probably of little value, he was convinced that Congress would not at that time agree to renounce them.

Subject to the approval of his colleagues and the President, Bayard suggested as a solution: (1) the appointment of an expert commission to settle the limits of territorial waters and to adopt regulations to make treaty rights effective; (2) concession of commercial facilities to fishing vessels in British waters and absolute renunciation of the American right to take fish in exclusive territorial waters of Canada and Newfoundland; and (3) a concession of free import of Canadian fish and fish oil into the United States. He was willing to treat Bay des Chaleurs as British waters and to consider the question of exceptional treatment for other bays or estuaries. He added that personally he had always been in favor of a reciprocity treaty, which had become impossible by the action of the Senate but which might later become possible by American voluntary action.[50]

The indisposition of the American plenipotentiaries to consider reciprocity on the basis of 1854 was disappointing to the Canadian members who had expected to obtain for concession of American demands concerning the fisheries an equivalent to satisfy Canadian opinion. President Cleveland, whom Chamberlain interviewed confidentially on December 14 in accord with a request of Bayard, stated that a renewal of the Reciprocity Treaty of 1854 was at that time impossible as a matter of bargain. He suggested, however, that even more than that might later be secured by voluntary changes in the American tariff. He was willing to concede free fish and fish oil which Chamberlain was willing to accept with the hope that it might be sufficient to secure Canadian assent to the proposed treaty. He suggested, however, that the concession should be in the form of an hypothesis—that the fishery concessions and modifications of the proposed convention should become operative only in case Congress should remove the duty on fish. On the latter point he later decided that positive provisions were better than a hypothetical statement.

Immediately after this interview Chamberlain handed to Secretary Bayard a draft of proposals for settlement. In it he specifically mentioned whale and seal oil which the Americans had refused to admit under the treaty of 1871 (on the ground that whales and seals were not fish). Satisfied that Bayard would offer no objection, he offered to do his best to secure the assent of the colonial governments. A few days later he visited Canada where he made arrangements with the Canadian government "for giving effect to Mr. Bayard's propositions." [51]

Meantime, Bayard had tried to impress upon senators from the Pacific coast, and also upon members of the other house, the importance of accepting a policy which would not allow "such a paltry matter as the duty on a few fish" to imperil good neighborhood and intercourse. He also acquainted his colleagues with the proposals supported by Chamberlain. Later, on January 6, 1888, at his home, he again conferred with Chamberlain—particularly on the result of the latter's visit to Canada. He agreed to minor details concerning the fishery settlement, especially approving the abolition of the irritating pilotage dues and the suggestion of licenses as an alternative. Through the latter he saw the possibility of inducing Congress to enact legislation to remove the duty on fish in case the Senate should decide to reject the treaty.[52]

Near the close of the conferences Bayard asked the British commissioners what modification of the American proposal would make it acceptable. Chamberlain proposed to strike out fishing privileges and to make the right of purchasing bait and supplies contingent upon the removal of the American duty on Canadian fish. To his colleagues he seemed disposed to concede to the Americans transshipment without license if necessary to obtain agreement on an arrangement. Tupper feared that if the British refused on this point the Americans would denounce bonded transit.[53]

During the negotiations, there was considerable speculative talk concerning a lack of accord between Tupper and Chamberlain. Apparently Chamberlain was more conciliatory than Tupper.[54]

At one time the conference was disturbed by a new source of dispute. On January 31, after learning that the Halifax authorities had forbidden the sale of the cargoes of fresh fish from two American vessels which had stopped for repairs, and that the refusal would result in the necessity of throwing the fish overboard, Bayard courteously appealed (by cable) to the British government to prevent such violation of international law and comity, pending amicable adjustment. He received a prompt and satisfactory British response that the collector at Halifax had been instructed to allow the fish to be landed and sold on payment of the duty. Later, on February 22, Tupper, after his return to Ottawa, invited the attention of Macdonald and his colleagues to Chamberlain's suggestion of the expediency of discontinuing admiralty court proceedings at Halifax against the American fishing smacks—as an effective evidence of a Canadian conciliatory spirit and of willingness to accept the arrangements as a termination of every cause of unfriendly feeling.[55]

The draft fisheries treaty, known as the Chamberlain-Bayard treaty, which was completed on February 7, contained (in Article XV) a provision that the United States, on condition of its admission of Canadian fish and fish oil to the American market free of duty, would obtain for its fishermen a grant of certain bait and trading privileges in Canadian ports. It agreed to refer to a special joint board or commission the determination of the waters in which Americans might fish. It provided for British abandonment of the headland theory of imaginary lines of jurisdiction, and affirmed the American right of uninterrupted navigation of the Strait of Canso. It also provided safeguards to prevent oppressive or arbitrary Canadian action against American fishermen, who were required to obtain licenses (without charge) in order to prevent abuse of the reasonable local privileges incident to fishing rights. It recognized the right of Canada and Newfoundland to regulate sales of bait and other fishing supplies within their jurisdiction. It contained no provision affecting tariff duties, but it left to Congress the question of additions to the free list of fish, fish oil, whale oil and seal oil.[56]

In submitting the treaty to the Senate, on February 20, the President expressed his approval of it as a satisfactory, practical and final adjustment of a difficult question. He stated that it had been "framed in a spirit of liberal equity and reciprocal benefits, in the conviction that mutual advantage and convenience are the only permanent foundation of peace and friendship," and that its adoption would establish a beneficial and satisfactory intercourse which would secure perpetual peace and harmony. For information of the popular mind concerning the history and adjustment of the long-continued disputes, and to satisfy the public interests, he suggested the advisability of immediate publication of the proposed treaty, and also of the important related documents which he submitted with the message and with a later message of March 5.[57]

With the treaty the President submitted for the information of the Senate an amicable *modus vivendi* arrangement, offered by the British plenipotentiaries after the conclusion of the treaty, and completed by exchange of notes signed on February 15. This temporary arrangement extended treaty advantages to American fishermen pending the period (not exceeding two years) required for consideration and ratification of the treaty and for enactment of necessary legislation for enforcement, if approved. It admitted American vessels to port privilege on payment of a license fee of a dollar and a half per ton. Under it arose one early small question (concerning its application to Newfoundland) which was promptly and satisfactorily settled.

Later (in August, 1893) Sir Charles Tupper expressed to Bayard the opinion that this arrangement, by serving to allay all friction and difficulties, practically resulted in a substantial success of the fishery negotiations of 1888—an opinion in which Bayard agreed. Under its continuance, by yearly renewal, the fishery issue slumbered and "lapsed into blessed oblivion" until 1905—when Newfoundland precipitated a threatened conflict by attempts to prevent foreign fishing vessels from securing bait or supplies on the island. Meantime, the American fishermen's need for the privileges of Canadian harbors was reduced by the introduction of steam-power fishing vessels.[58]

During the treaty negotiations Canada had continued to urge the importance of closer commercial relations. Confronted with the possible danger of the secession of Nova Scotia, and with a mutinous spirit in Manitoba and provincial demands for subsidies and larger freedom of trade, the Canadian government emphasized the necessity of a reciprocity treaty designed to cultivate closer relations, to terminate disputes and to prevent a serious crisis which was apprehended as inevitable. Early in 1888, at a Quebec conference, the provincial prime minister favored unrestricted trade relations by a commercial union—a policy which was urged by the boards of trade of leading Canadian cities and by over fifty farmers' institutes.

At Washington, after considering the situation, and possibly influenced by the favorable declaration of Joseph Chamberlain, the House Committee on Foreign Affairs recommended a joint resolution to promote commercial union with Canada whenever Canada should declare a desire for this policy, and to confer power on the President to appoint three commissioners to meet with commissioners which Canada might decide to appoint; but this resolution the House failed to approve.[59]

About the same time, early in March, Secretary Bayard unofficially reminded the Canadian government that Congress by act of March 3, 1883, had accepted the Canadian offer of May, 1879, providing for free admission of certain products, and that for five years the Canadians had failed to make the act effective. A few days later, on April 4, in response to a telegram from Sackville-West, Sir Charles Tupper finally announced to the Canadian House of Commons that these articles were placed on the free list.[60]

In the Senate the fisheries treaty encountered strong and determined opposition. Among the five members who signed the committee report in opposition to it was John Sherman who later (after his failure to obtain the Republican nomination for the presidency) proposed complete reciprocity as a preparation for more friendly relations and for eventual union by annexation, and who also proposed a joint resolution to submit to arbitration disputed questions which diplomatic negotiations failed to adjust. On May 29 Sherman moved that the Senate proceed to consider the treaty in open session. He had already moved to print the President's message of February 20, submitting the treaty and the accompanying documents from which the injunction of secrecy had been removed. Frye was somewhat disturbed by the necessity of speaking in open session without more preparation. He did not hesitate to say, however, that he regarded the treaty as a dishonorable, humiliating and cowardly surrender in which the President had practically taken the side of the Canadians.[61]

In the prolonged debates which followed in the Senate, possibly influenced by preëlection partisan purposes, the opposition majority denied the authority of the President to appoint commissioners without previous consent of the Senate. It also contended that difficulties with Canada should properly be settled by concurrent domestic legislation instead of by treaty, and that the British government should have no part in the settlement of the Canadian fisheries. In connection with the debates several members injected other subjects of controversy or difference relating to commerce and transportation, especially questions concerning railways competition, transit trade in bond, and Canadian discriminating canal policy. On August 6 Blair introduced a proposition to open negotiations with Great Britain for political union of Canada with the United States.[62]

In a consideration of the treaty in open executive session, on August 7, Senator Sherman, after denying that senators were influenced by a caucus decree, declared his belief that the treaty, instead of contributing to the peace of the two neighboring countries, would raise new questions and new issues and embarrassments which would create fresh ill feeling.[63]

August 21 the Senate (in open executive session), by a vote of thirty-one to twenty-nine, rejected a motion to commit the treaty to the Committee on Foreign Relations with instructions to frame and report amendments to remove ambiguities and to remedy defects, or to report a plan for arbitration of all differences as to fishery rights. After rejecting proposed amendments, it rejected Morgan's ratification resolution by a vote of twenty-seven to thirty.

Probably the chief factors in the defeat of the treaty were the opponents of reciprocity and the influence of American fishing interests which opposed free admission of Canadian fish and advocated the American payment of a definite lump sum for a renewal of the privilege. The bonding issue, which was injected into the debates, was probably only a minor influence. The heat of the presidential campaign was a contributory influence.[64]

Promptly after the rejection of the treaty by the Republican majority in the Senate the President, by the seizure of another controversy by the horns, outwitted his partisan opponents and regained the initiative which he had lost in the prolonged debates in Congress. In a special message of August 23, he reviewed the conditions of the pending controversy and contemplated the question of retaliation under the inadequate act of Congress of March 3, 1887. Suggesting that the treaty provision for bonded transit (Article XXIX) had terminated on July 1, 1885, he recommended that Congress without partisanship empower him to suspend by proclamation the operation of all pre-treaty laws or regulations which permitted the transit of goods or wares or merchandise in bond across American territory to or from Canada, unless Canada would agree to permit a similar American right to ship fish in bond across Canadian territory; and he also recommended that Congress should adopt some rule of discrimination on American canals, as a response to the Canadian unequal toll policy in favor of Canadian routes and ports. "If we enter on the policy of retaliation," said he, "let us pursue it firmly only with a determination to subserve the interests of our people and maintain the high standard and becoming pride of American citizenship." [65]

On August 24 Senator Morgan introduced a bill in accord with the President's recommendation of August 23. Sherman proposed to consider the President's message first, and, on August 30, submitted a motion to that effect. Incidental to the discussion Senator Cullom submitted a resolution requesting information on the subjects proposed in the message. On September 12, in response to a request of August 28, the President submitted to the Senate correspondence relating to the unfair Canadian canal policy (through discriminatory refunds of tolls) and the refusal of the Canadian government (since 1886) to allow entry of American fish for transportation in bond to the United States. His recommendations, however, remained without action by Congress.[66]

Unfortunately, the President's changed tone after the rejection of the treaty was interpreted by some as a political expediency, incident to the campaign preceding the presidential election. Late in October he created much surprise by demanding the recall of the British minister, Sackville-West, who with entirely friendly intention, in replying to a political "trap-trick" letter seeking advice concerning what candidate was most favorable to British interests, had stated his belief that the President was still desirous of settling all Canadian questions which had been "unfortunately re-opened since the retraction of the treaty by the Republican majority in the Senate and by the President's message." In presenting the demand for recall Bayard said: "This government cannot regard with indifference interference by foreign ministers in our domestic issues."[67]

In his annual message of December 3, a month after the election in which he was the defeated candidate, the President again invited the immediate attention of Congress to the important question of the fisheries. He repeated his statement (of September 12) that since March 3, 1887, the Department of State had received no complaint of any unlawful Canadian treatment of American fishing vessels, except cases for which prompt and satisfactory reparation had been obtained at Halifax. He repeated his opinion that the recently proposed treaty had presented "a satisfactory, practical and final adjustment, upon a basis honorable and just to both parties, of the difficult and vexed question to which it related"; and he significantly added that he had hoped that the legislation which he had subsequently and unavailingly recommended to Congress would have been sufficient to meet the exigency created by the rejection of the treaty.[68]

Meantime, influenced by the American attitude, Canadians were provoked to offer obstruction to a solution or adjustment of other problems, including that of pelagic sealing in Bering Sea. In the period of discussion which followed the Senate's rejection of the treaty and the President's later "thunderbolt out of the blue," Goldwin Smith expressed the Canadian disgust excited by the American campaign arguments against an arrangement for reciprocal trade. Referring to Blaine's policy to continue opposition to commercial union with Canada so long as Canadians continued to wave the British flag, he suggested that on the same principle he would not buy of a woman or sell to her without marrying her.[69]

In the last three months of the Cleveland administration appeared considerable public discussion of closer relations with Canada either by commercial union or by political union. This discussion was stimulated by Benjamin Butterworth in Congress and by Goldwin Smith in Canada. On December 13 Butterworth, deciding that America should take the initiative in a policy of closer relations, introduced in the House a joint resolution to prepare the way for the annexation by negotiations with the Dominion and with Great Britain for "unity and assimilation." Later, on February 19, he proposed to authorize the President to invite the members of the Canadian Parliament and the premiers and cabinets of the several provinces to visit the United States as personal guests of the nation. On March 1, speaking approvingly of Hitt's report in favor of removal of the barriers to commerce with Canada, he announced that political union, which promised a solution of irritating problems, was inevitable, and he declared that America, which had already welcomed to its soil one-fifth of the Canadian people, was waiting for the accession of the other four-fifths.[70]

At the same time, on recommendation of Mr. Hitt, the House adopted a joint resolution authorizing the President, whenever the Canadian government should declare a desire to establish commercial union with a uniform revenue system, to appoint three commissioners to meet Canadian commissioners for preparation of a plan for assimilation of the revenues and equitable division of the receipts. In the Senate this resolution was reported favorably (by Senator Sherman) but its immediate consideration was prevented by objection of Senator Blair.[71]

In Canada, at the close of the Cleveland administration, appeared evidences of considerable resentment at the failure of the recent negotiations at Washington—resentment which increased the opposition to a tariff regulated at Washington, or to a commercial union which might make Canada tributary to New England, New York and other parts of the American Union. J. G. Schurman, a native Canadian who occupied the chair of professor of philosophy at Cornell University, declared that, notwithstanding the Monroe Doctrine, "Canada is the arbiter of her own destiny."[72]

REFERENCES

1. *H. Misc. Docs.*, 43–2, Vol. 2, No. 50, Jan. 25, 1875; *H. Rps.*, 46–2, Vol. 4, No. 1127, Apr. 23 and June 7, 1880; *N. Am. Rev.*, July, 1880 (G. SMITH), and Dec., 1881, pp. 523–33 (Kasson on the Monroe Doctrine); *State Dept. Pamphlets, U. S. Dipl. Questions,* II; *Contemp. Rev.*, Sept., 1880 (GEORGE ANDERSON, M.P.).
2. J. W. FOSTER, *Dipl. Memoirs,* II, 178; *N. Am. Rev.*, Apr., 1880, pp. 338–55 (F. HINCKS); *3 Drafts of Treaties, U.S. and G.B.;* SHORTT and DOUGHTY, IX, 13.
3. *3 Drafts of Treaties, U.S. and G.B.; 3 Reciprocity Treaties, 1898–1907, Canada* (KASSON).
4. *16 G.B., Notes to,* p. 386, July 15, 1874; *3 Drafts of Treaties, U.S. and G.B.*
5. *16 G.B., Notes to,* pp. 402–05, July 18, 1874; *Macdonald Papers, Washington Treaty, 1888,* Vol. 6, pp. 313–17; *3 Reciprocity Treaties,* 1898–1907, *Canada* (KASSON); *N. Am. Rev.*, Apr., 1880, pp. 338–55 (HINCKS); *Canadian Leaves,* N.Y., 1887; RICHARDSON, VII, 266–67.
6. *16 G.B., Notes to,* pp. 402–05, July 18, 1874; *Ib.*, p. 512, Feb. 11, 1875; *Cong. Record,* 43–2, Vol. 3, Part 2, p. 929.
7. *State Dept. Pamphlets, U. S. Dipl. Questions,* II, 1827–83, No. 14875 (Morrill's speech, Feb. 3, 1875); *H. Rps.*, 46–2, Part 2, No. 1127, June 7, 1880.
8. *Ib.*, p. 4; *9 Can. Mo.*, May, 1876, pp. 350–59; *N. Am. Rev.*, 1880, p. 14.
9. *H. Rps.*, 44–1, Vol. 1, No. 9, Jan. 18, 1876; *Ib.*, Vol. 2, Part 2, No. 389, Apr. 11, 1876.
10. *3 Drafts of Treaties, U.S. and G.B.*, Dec. 14, 1878.
11. *H. Rps.*, 46–2, Vol. 4, June 7, 1880, p. 5; *N. Am. Rev.*, Apr., 1880 (HINCKS); *Ib.*, July, 1880 (G. SMITH), pp. 14–25.
12. SHORTT and DOUGHTY, IX, pp. 132 and 157; *U. S. Stats.*, Vol. 18, p. 308; *Imperial Asiatic Rev.*, Jan., 1898 (T. HODGINS).
13. *17 G.B., Notes to,* pp. 531 and 580, Mar. 11 and July 18, 1878.
14. *19 G.B., Notes to,* p. 198, Feb. 14, 1883.
15. *17 G.B., Notes to,* p. 699, Feb. 20, 1879; *25 G.B., Instrs.*, p. 327, Tel., Feb. 1, 1879; *Ib.*, p. 329, Feb. 7; *Ib.*, pp. 1–3, No. 640, July 25, 1883.
16. *18 G.B., Notes to,* pp. 513–16, May 26, 1881.
17. *H. Rps.*, 46–2, Vol. 4, No. 1127, June 7, 1880.
18. *131 N. Am. Rev.; 6 Forum; 11 Can. Mo.*, June, 1877, pp. 596–614 (G. SMITH); *27 Nation,* Oct. 3, 1878, p. 211; *40 Contemp. Rev.*, Sept., 1881 (G. SMITH), pp. 386–89; *152 N. Am. Rev.*,

May, 1891, p. 549; *38 Contemp. Rev.*, Sept., 1880, p. 396 (GEO. ANDERSON).

19. *Ib.*, Nov., 1880; *3 American*, Jan. 14, 1882, pp. 213–14; *N. Am. Rev.*, Aug., 1881, pp. 153–66; *Ib.*, Apr., 1883, and July, 1884 (pp. 42–50).
20. SHORTT and DOUGHTY, IX, 189–91; *Rp. of House of Commons Select Com. on Combinations*, 1888.
21. *16 G.B., Notes to*, p. 128, June 25, 1873; *N. Am. Rev.*, Jan., 1879, pp. 1–14 (G. F. EDMUNDS).
22. *Sen. Exec. Docs.*, 45–2, No. 44, Aug. 21, 1873; *Ib.*, No. 100; *For. Rels., 1878*, p. 291.
23. *Ib.*, pp. 290, 316 and 334; *25 G.B., Instrs.*, pp. 195–245, No. 145, Sept. 27, 1878; *Ib.*, p. 285, No. 173, Nov. 8, 1878.
24. *19 G.B., Notes to*, pp. 55–62, Mem. to West, May 9, 1882.
25. HENDERSON, *Dipl. Questions*, pp. 520–22; *Sen. Exec. Docs.*, 52–2, Vol. 2, No. 40, Feb. 2, 1893; *110 G.B., Notes from*, Oct. 9, 1883; *27 G.B., Instrs.*, p. 37, No. 688, Oct. 16; *For. Rels., 1883*.
26. *Bul. U. S. Fish Commis.*, Vol. 5 (1885), pp. 447–48; MALLOY, *Treaties*, I, 734–37.
27. *Macdonald Papers, Washington Treaty, 1888*, Vol. 2, pp. 81–82 and 96–104; *20 G.B., Notes to*, p. 68, June 19, 1885; *Ib.*, pp. 70–71, June 20 and 22; *For. Rels., 1888*.
28. *19 G.B., Notes to*, pp. 684–87, Personal, Bayard to West, Apr. 22, 1885; *112 G.B., Notes from*, June 5, 1885.
29. *20 G.B., Notes to*, p. 63, June 19, 1885; *Ib.*, pp. 68 and 70–71, June 19, 20 and 22; *For. Rels., 1885; Macdonald Papers, Washington Treaty, 1888*, Vol. 2, pp. 81–104; MALLOY, *Treaties*, I, 729; *42 Nation*, p. 26; *43 Nation*, p. 468.
30. *19 Cong. Record*, 50–1, Part 8, p. 7205, Aug. 3, 1888; *Macdonald Papers, Washington Treaty, 1888*, Vol. 1, *Negotiations of 1874–88*, pp. 69–72.
31. *Ib.*, p. 61, Sackville-West to Lansdowne, July 13, 1885.
32. RICHARDSON, VIII, 332.
33. O. D. SKELTON, *The Day of Sir Wilfrid Laurier*, p. 105.
34. *20 G.B., Notes to*, pp. 214–15, Mar. 23, 1886; *Ib.*, pp. 293–95, May 29; *Ib.*, pp. 303–05, June 14; *28 G.B., Instrs.*, p. 48, Tel., May 10 (also May 11, 12, 22 and 29), 1886.
35. *20 G.B., Notes to*, pp. 385–86, July 10, 1896; *28 G.B., Instrs.*, p. 96, No. 372, July 30; *Exec. Docs.*, 49–2, Dec. 8, 1886.
36. *N. Am. Rev.*, Apr., 1883, and July, 1884 (pp. 42–50); *Mag. of Am. Hist.*, Aug., 1886; *Canadian Leaves*, N.Y., 1887.
37. *Macdonald Papers, Washington Treaty, 1888*, I, *Negotiations of 1874–88*, pp. 259–60.
38. *Macdonald Papers, Commercial Union, 1886–87*, pp. 7–10, and 20–24, Ritchie to Macdonald, Dec. 9 and 12, 1886.

39. *Sen. Exec. Docs.*, 49–2, No. 55, Jan. 26, 1887; *Ib.*, 50–1, No. 265, Sept. 12, 1888; *Sen. Misc. Docs.*, 49–2, No. 54, Feb. 5, 1887.
40. *28 G.B., Instrs.*, p. 259, Tel., Bayard to Phelps, Feb. 4, 1887; *18 Cong. Record*, 49–2, Part 3, pp. 2191 and 2235.
41. *27 G.B., Notes to*, pp. 564–81 and 589–91, May 3 and 9, 1906; *18 Cong. Record*, 49–2, pp. 928–30, 2127–50, 2582–84, and 2611.
42. *Nation*, Apr. 14, 1887, p. 306; RICHARDSON, VIII, 580–91, Dec. 6, 1887.
43. O. D. SKELTON, *Life and Times of Sir Wilfrid Laurier*, II, 365, 369; *13 American*, Feb. 26, 1887, p. 295.
44. *Macdonald Papers, Commercial Union, 1886–87*, pp. 8, 53, 162 (July 25, 1887); *Century Mag.*, June, 1902, pp. 318–19 (LEUPP).
45. *Macdonald Papers, Commercial Union*, 1886–87; *18 Cong. Record*, 49–2, p. 1735, Feb. 14, 1887.
46. *Macdonald Papers, Commercial Union, 1886–87*, pp. 187–205.
47. RICHARDSON, VIII, p. 630, Sept. 12, 1888; *Macdonald Papers, Washington Treaty, 1888*, Vol. 5, *Proceedings of the Conferences*, pp. 1–28 (p. 22, Nov. 22, 1887); *Ib.*, Vol. 8 (*Documents and Debates*), pp. 1–22; *Ib.*, I, *Negotiations*, 1874–88, pp. 259–60; *29 G.B., Instrs.*, pp. 363–77, No. 659, July 12, 1887.
48. *11 Can. Mag.*, Sept., 1898, pp. 409–12 (TUPPER); *U. S. and G. B. Political Pamphlets*, I, No. 21,043; *Sen. Rps.*, 51–1, Part 2, No. 1530, pp. 1225–36 (NIMMO), July 21, 1890; *Laurier Papers, Cor.*, pp. 963–65, L. H. Davies to J. G. Blaine, May 4, 1889.
49. *Cong. Record*, 49–1, Part 4, p. 3440; *Sen. Exec. Docs.*, 50–1, Vol. 10, No. 127, pp. 2–3; *Ib.*, Vol. 9, No. 113; *N. Y. Times*, Nov. 18, 1887; *Macdonald Papers, Washington Treaty*, Vol. 3, pp. 9–11, John D. Thompson to Macdonald, Nov. 21, 1887; *Ib.*, Vol. 6 (especially pp. 336–37), and Vol. 7.
50. *Ib.*, Vol. 3, *Thompson-Tupper Corres.*, pp. 392–416 (Chamberlain's secret mem. of interviews), Tupper to Macdonald, Jan. 25, 1888.
51. *Ib.*, pp. 400–09.
52. *Ib.*, pp. 411, 412 and 415.
53. *Ib.*, pp. 378–79, Jan. 22, 1888.
54. *Ib.*, Vol. 4, *Tupper Corres.*, pp. 229–34, Feb. 22, 1888.
55. *Ib.; 28 G.B., Instrs.*, p. 435, Tel., Jan. 31, 1888; *Ib.*, p. 439, Tel., Feb. 1.
56. *3 Reciprocity Treaties, 1898–1907, Canada* (KASSON), Inclosure in State Dept. to Albert Clark, Mar. 25, 1904; *Sen. Exec. Docs.*, 50–1, No. 176 (1892); *23 Cong. Record*, 52–1, Part 1, p. 8274; RICHARDSON, VIII, 604–06.

57. *Ib.*, 603–08; *Sen. Exec. Docs.*, 50–1, No. 113, Mar. 5, 1888 (142 pp.).
58. RICHARDSON, VIII, 607; MALLOY, I, 738–39; *20 G.B., Notes to*, p. 633, Apr. 21, 1888; *F.R., 1888; 175 G.B., Desps.*, Sept. 19, 1893, Bayard to Gresham.
59. *19 Mag. of Am. Hist.*, Jan., 1888, pp. 21–27; *H. Rps.*, 50–1, Vol. 4, No. 113 (HITT), Mar. 16, 1888.
60. *Sen. Rps.*, 51–1, No. 1530, p. 924, July 21, 1890 (NIMMO).
61. *Nation*, Aug. 16, 1888, p. 122; *Ib.*, Aug. 30, p. 159; *19 Cong. Record*, 50–1, May 29, 1888, pp. 4694–4708.
62. *Nation*, May 17 (p. 399), May 24 (pp. 420–21), June 24 (pp. 482–83), and July 19 (pp. 41–42); *U. S. and G. B. Political Rels. Pamphlets*, I; *19 Cong. Record*, 50–1, pp. 7261 and 7392.
63. *Ib.*, pp. 7285–88, Aug. 7, 1888.
64. *Ib.*, pp. 7766 and 7768, Aug. 21, 1888.
65. *H. Exec. Docs.*, 50–1, Vol. 11, No. 257; *Ib.*, No. 434; RICHARDSON, VIII, 620–27; *Nation*, Aug. 30, 1888, p. 162.
66. *19 Cong. Record*, 50–1, p. 7914 (also see p. 1039); *Sen. Exec. Docs.*, 50–1, No. 1039 (on transport of bonded goods); *Ib.*, No. 265 and No. 406; also see *Sen. Exec. Docs.*, 49–2, Nos. 19 and 55; RICHARDSON, VIII, 628–30.
67. *Ib.*, 780–81; STOWELL and MUNRO, *International Cases*, I, 10–16; *Parl. Papers*, 1888, CIX, 619–20; *28 G.B., Instrs.*, p. 607, Tel., Oct. 25, 1888; *Ib.*, pp. 609–10, Oct. 30; F.R., 1888.
68. RICHARDSON, VIII, 780.
69. *6 Forum*, Nov., 1888, pp. 243–56; G. SMITH, *Canada and the U.S.*
70. *Laurier Papers, Cor.* 1870–91, p. 925, John A. Barron to Laurier, Dec. 29, 1888; *20 Cong. Record*, 50–2, pp. 234 and 2055; *Ib.*, Appendix, p. 211, March 1, 1889; *6 Public Opinion*, Dec. 22, 1888, pp. 214–16; *Toronto Globe*, Dec. 14; *Buffalo Courier*, Dec. 15, 1888; *H. Rps.*, 50–2, Vol. 3, No. 4155, Mar. 2, 1889.
71. *20 Cong. Record*, p. 2539, Mar. 1, 1889; *H. Rps.*, 51–1, Vol. 6, No. 1870, May 2, 1890.
72. *Macdonald Papers, Commercial Rels. with U.S.*, 1890–91, p. 52 (from John Hallam of Toronto), Feb. 27, 1889; *21 Mag. of Am. Hist.*, Feb., 1889, pp. 123–28; *7 Forum*, March, 1889, pp. 1–17.

CHAPTER XVI

INDIANS, RAILWAYS, WATERWAYS AND EXTRADITION, 1872–89

CONTEMPORARY with the discussions and negotiations concerning the questions of reciprocal trade and fisheries were movements toward the disappearance of the last Indian barrier and the last border frontier along the international boundary west of Minnesota, and also other movements toward the removal of obstacles to satisfactory American neighborhood relations with Canada.

Along the American northwest frontier, before the extension of transcontinental railroads across this unsettled or sparsely settled region, were international Indian problems which had originated in the flight of part of the Sioux tribe across the border from Minnesota in 1862. Along the Red River and Saskatchewan regions these problems of border relations were affected by American migrations of settlers across the Indian country. They were also affected by the results of Canadian extension of jurisdiction over the great hunting preserve of the Hudson's Bay Company in 1870—by the prospective advance of the Canadian Pacific railway, by the immigration of new Canadian settlers, by the consequent reduction of the buffalo herds which had furnished the chief support of the half-breeds (Métis), and by the armed revolt of the half-breeds under Riel against the new regime (in 1870 and in 1885).

Near the close of President Grant's administration the border Indian problem became prominent. In seeking a solution of it the American government showed a disposition to favor coöperation of authorities on the frontier. In June, 1875, following a Canadian complaint that horses stolen by the Assiniboine Indians had been taken across the line to the United

States, it promptly ordered American Indian agents to adopt measures for the return of the stolen property and for prevention of similar depredations. In July it instructed American army officers to afford every courtesy to the commander of the Canadian militia whom Canada had sent on an official tour to British Columbia with tentative plans for adoption of a uniform system of police and military measures on both sides of the northwest, with a view to coöperation with American authorities in repression of crime.

In one instance Canada declined an offer of coöperation from American border authority. In October, 1875, when American citizens were held at Winnipeg for trial under a charge of the murder of Assiniboine Indians in Canada in 1873 the Canadian Privy Council regarded as inexpedient and impracticable the suggestion of the governor of Montana that Montana witnesses for the accused would attend the trial if furnished a guarantee of their freedom from arrest.[1]

In 1876, following the destruction of General Custer's forces on the Little Big Horn by Sitting Bull's small band of Sioux Indians, a new source of border complications arose from the escape of these belligerent Indians into Canada. When Canada planned an increase of border posts to enable it to meet its increased responsibility, Secretary Fish coöperated in response to the Canadian request for permission to send supplies through the American Indian reservation.[2]

In the first year of the Hayes administration Secretary Evarts found the Canadian authorities ready to agree upon coöperative action concerning the Indian problem. In response to his request of June, 1877, for permission for representatives of the Department of the Interior to attend a Grand Council of the Indians, west of Manitoba, he received from the Canadian authorities an offer of a proper escort from the frontier to Sitting Bull's camp. In August, in response to a request of the Canadian Privy Council for steps to provide for the return of the fugitive Sioux who had crossed the border into Canada, he considered with the British minister a proposal for a joint American-Canadian commission to treat with the Sioux for removal to their American reservation. In February, 1878, he was assured that Canada had adopted measures to prevent any hostile Indian incursions from Canadian territory. On March 18 he forwarded a request of General Miles that Canada by April 10 should intern all Sioux found north of the boundary.[3]

In 1879 the Indian problem became more serious. Early in the year the American government became apprehensive of the erratic, wandering movements of the "lately hostile Indians under the lead of Sitting Bull" who were now regarded as British Indians. Evarts invited the attention of the British-Canadian government to complaints of their encroachment upon the hunting grounds of the peaceful Indians of Montana whom they damaged by scattering the buffalo herds and by theft of horses. Recognizing the menacing danger of the marauding trans-border operations which might necessitate American military operations to repel the attacks within American jurisdiction he suggested the importance of a friendly understanding by which an adequate Canadian force along the border would coöperate in punitive measures, either by compelling the pursued alien offenders to surrender to the American forces as prisoners of war or by disarming them and constraining them from further trans-border hostilities. Later, in August, he suggested that the Canadian government should surrender fugitive Indians who had committed outrages in the Yellowstone Valley and that it should return the property stolen by them. He received from the Ottawa government a reply that it had no evidence, and that it felt justified in complaining of injuries resulting from the flight of these American Indians into Canadian jurisdiction. Apparently, he did not approve the later Canadian suggestion that all the Sioux refugees should be induced (or allowed) to return to American territory. He also disapproved the subsequent Canadian requests for hunting privileges for Canadian Indians or for reciprocal hunting rights for Indians.[4]

Nearly two years later, following reports of some improvement in the situation through the cheerful coöperation of Canadian frontier officers within the limited range of their duties, the American government was still confronted with the problem of predatory Indian incursions alternating with Indian flights to asylum north of the border, from which Sitting Bull continued to renew evasive and futile parleys for submission while Indians south of the border threatened counter attacks. On February 5, 1881, Evarts again renewed a suggestion of the urgent necessity for a distinct understanding on measures to terminate the incursions. He urged that "the British government, in the fulfillment of its obligations of neighborly comity and good will, should repel any new attempt . . . of Sitting Bull and his unsubmissive adherents to cross the border into British territory in evasion of pursuit, or should take such active and effective steps as will prevent his recrossing into the territory of the United States, and [should] domicile him as a British Indian under due restraint of surveillance and subjection." Meantime, he had complained that a Canadian trading establishment at Woody Mountain, about thirty miles north of the American Blackfoot reservation in Montana, was a rendezvous for hostile Indians who obtained both arms and ammunition there.[5]

Later, in May, 1881, Secretary Blaine notified Thornton that the gravity of the Indian situation was increased by recent depredations (the killing of cattle and the stealing of horses) by bands of British Cree Indians and half-breeds who after the Riel rebellion had encamped upon the American reservation near Beaver Creek and who, defying orders to move, threatened to fight in case of an attempt at their forcible removal. Apprehending the imminence of a popular uprising of the American border settlers for self-preservation against the marauding savages, and the possible precipitation of a general Indian war whose calamities both governments should seek to avert, he urged the duty of Canadian coöperation in efforts to persuade the dangerous Canadian Indians to return to their home in British territory and a determined Canadian effort to disarm and control and restrain them after they recrossed the frontier. In the following August, reporting that a large body of Canadian Indians had passed Fort Belknap on their way to drive the buffaloes away from the American agency Indians, he urged prompt steps to prevent such an invasion which at that time was liable to provoke grave Indian disturbance.[6]

In 1882 conditions seemed worse. On February 25 Frelinghuysen announced that the American government (after full consideration) had determined to prevent Indian raids from the United States into Canada, even by force if necessary, and that it expected Canada to reciprocate and to aid in efforts to secure cordial coöperation of Canadian and American military authorities. On March 29, after Canadian authorities had failed to prevent Canadian dependent Indians from crossing the boundary, he announced that American troops might find stricter measures necessary. He was inclined to regard Canada as responsible for lack of coöperation. On April 7, after receiving from Sackville-West some British suggestions as to reciprocal treatment of migratory frontier Indians, he requested a statement of the views of Canada as to the proposed forcible ejection of Canadian Indians from Montana. On April 10, and again in June, he announced that American troops had driven the Canadian Indians across the line into Canada and would use force to prevent their return.

In the following December, he urged a better system of cooperation, resulting in a Canadian proposal of measures which he regarded as inadequate.

On April 17, 1883, following a statement that thereafter the property of trespassing Indians would be seized and destroyed and that the Indians would be driven back to Canada, Frelinghuysen submitted a proposed arrangement for reciprocal right of pursuit across the boundary line—an arrangement which was similar to one recently accepted by Mexico, and which Canada declined in the following August.

Meantime, on April 13, he had asked permission for General Sherman to pass through Canada in the summer with an armed cavalry escort to visit points of military interest in the United States near the Canadian frontier—a request which was promptly granted (by May 12). In June he reported that a good understanding existed between the border military authorities of the two countries.[7]

On August 5, following a Canadian complaint that the American South Pigeon Indians had stolen some horses in Canada, Frelinghuysen received officially a Canadian request to consider a proposed arrangement by which offending Indians on either side of the line might be surrendered for trial in the country where their offenses were committed, although such offenses might not be included in provisions of existing extradition treaties.[8]

Early in 1884 he received a Canadian proposal to return to the United States the remnants of Sitting Bull's band on a promise of amity. In reply, although he indicated a willingness to give a guaranty of indemnity for the past if the Indians would give a guaranty of good behavior for the future, he stated that an appropriation of Congress would be a necessary preliminary. The question, therefore, was submitted to the appropriate committee of Congress. Apparently it was still unsettled five years later (in June, 1889) when Secretary Blaine inquired concerning the attitude of Canada towards the proposed voluntary return of the fugitive Sioux who upon their return would be subject to a control adequate to prevent further disorder.[9]

Meantime, in October, 1885, Secretary Bayard was asked by the Department of the Interior to arrange with Canada for return of the British Cree Indian refugees who, after implication in the recent Riel rebellion, had settled on American territory and were regarded as well behaved. He declined to return them except upon a specific demand of the Canadian authorities acting under provision of the extradition treaty. He especially stated that American authorities could not connive at their kidnapping as a plan for renewal of the extradition treaty. Later, in December, 1886, he complained that the destitute Crees were eating the cattle of the American white settlers who threatened them with violence. Therefore, he requested their removal to Canada. Their removal, however, was delayed nearly ten years, until the summer of 1896 when, in accord with a Canadian suggestion of April, 1892, and under an act of Congress approved in May, 1896, the American authorities delivered them at the boundary.

Other Indian questions arose in 1885–86. In December, 1885, in reply to complaints of reported Montana sales of whiskey and ammunition to Canadian Indians, Bayard stated that the American Attorney General would investigate and stop such traffic if found.[10]

In the summer of 1887 the American authorities rendered useful aid in relation to Indian disorders (between the Blood Indians and the Gros Ventres) on the Montana-Canadian frontier.[11]

Meantime, coincident with the period of the crisis in the discontent of the Canadian half-breeds of the Saskatchewan Valley who invited the banished Louis Riel to return from Montana to Canada to stimulate and direct a second rebellion of the Canadian Northwest, arose a new problem of neutrality on the Manitoba border. In March, 1884, Frelinghuysen directed an investigation of an unfounded but persistent and widespread newspaper rumors of an alleged Fenian movement in the American Middle Northwest, with plans for an early armed invasion of Manitoba. Through the reports of the War Department and the United States district attorney at St. Paul he discovered that the rumors had originated in an invented communication which an unscrupulous and irresponsible "reporter" (of Fargo, Dakota) had sent to the Chicago *Tribune;* and he promptly reported that they had no basis in fact or in verified evidence.

In March, 1885, Bayard was asked to investigate rumors of violation of American neutrality by transit of men and arms across the border to aid the insurgents at Winnipeg. He acted promptly, and reported no basis for the rumor. At the same time he directed precautionary measures to prevent any invasion of Canada by Indians. In April, in reply to rumors of apprehended Fenian movements to aid the insurgents in Manitoba, he again reported no evidence and stated that steps had been taken to prevent any unlawful acts.[12]

A year later the American government coöperated in efforts to prevent an apprehended Indian uprising from the United States to avenge the recent Canadian execution of Louis Riel.[13]

By the middle of the eighties American railways, contributing to expansion of settlement and the disappearance of the American frontier and resulting in new problems of policy, were decreasing the necessity of military protection against the frontier Indians. Two transcontinental lines between Lake Superior and Pacific waters, one opened in 1883 and the other not completed until nearly a decade later, were the chief factors in stimulating west of Minnesota the development (by 1889) of a range or belt of four new border commonwealths (North Dakota, Montana, Idaho and Washington) with which were also associated two other new neighboring commonwealths (Wyoming and South Dakota).

In 1887, by the Canadian construction of the Canadian Pacific line which had been delayed for a decade by difficulties, the American government was confronted with new international border problems concerning railway competition and transboundary transit.

Even before its completion, the new Canadian line, by its advancing construction, stimulated at its western terminal the promotion of improved means of communication which required coöperation of the American government. In January, 1884, Frelinghuysen declined to grant the application of Canada to establish on the coast of Washington Territory a terminal of a telegraph cable which was expected to compete with the line of the Puget Sound Telegraph Company. On January 16, however, he explained that permission would be granted if Canada would agree to grant to the Puget company the same privileges in British Columbia, to land a cable at Victoria and to establish local offices there.

In the following June Frelinghuysen complained of the action of Canadian authorities at Winnipeg in declining to permit trains (of passengers or mails or freight) to pass the international boundary on the St. Paul, Minneapolis and Manitoba Railway during non-business hours unless the railway authorities would agree to pay the extra expense required for local officials. In April, 1885, Secretary Bayard repeated the complaint and suggested some modification of the regulation in order to prevent the obstruction of international railway traffic.[14]

With the completion of construction on the trans-Rocky or Pacific division of the Canadian Pacific line arose a new source of American complaint concerning Chinese, whose immigration for labor had been encouraged until 1885 but thereafter was restricted by a gradually increasing head-tax. In April, 1885, Secretary Bayard, acting on a complaint from an American commissioner in Washington Territory, submitted a brief statement of difficulties arising from the refusal of British Columbia authorities to receive from the United States returned Chinese laborers who had crossed the border from Canada against American laws which prohibited their immigration.[15]

The Canadian Pacific, after the completion of its line from coast to coast in 1885, and while awaiting the development of local traffic, was vigorous in its efforts both to monopolize the Canadian traffic along the route of its line and to obtain American east and west traffic, including the foreign transit trade between Asia and the American East and the domestic transit trade between San Francisco or Puget Sound and the American East. In the Red River region it aroused strong opposition by its efforts to prevent diversion of Canadian traffic to American transportation routes. These efforts it sought to justify under an earlier contract with the Dominion government by which the latter agreed to refuse to authorize the construction of any competing railway between the pioneer Canadian transcontinental railway and the American border. Early in 1886, acting in favor of the new railway, the Canadian authorities surreptitiously attempted to prevent the shipment of Manitoba grain, in bond, over American railroads between two Canadian points. Manitoba, whose population was growing far more slowly than that of the Dakotas and whose struggling pioneers paid for shipment of wheat from Winnipeg to Montreal at a rate of ten cents per bushel more than the rate from St. Paul to New York, protested against this Dominion policy to compel it to trade with the Canadian East via the Canadian Pacific Railway. With this protest certain interested American railways were in full accord.[16]

Influenced especially by unfair methods of competition between the transcontinental railways, the American Congress had sought a remedy. In 1885, when the Senate and the House were unable to agree upon a national policy of railway regulation, appeared the report of the Cullom Committee on railway conditions. Action on it was hastened by the Supreme Court decision of 1886 in the Wabash case which limited state power to regulate local railway traffic. In 1887, therefore, Congress created the Interstate Commerce Commission. Immediately thereafter the American transcontinental lines, which were placed under the control of the commission, complained of the unfair and disturbing Canadian competition from which certain American shippers profited. They stated that this competition was especially unfair by its unpunishable underbidding against American rival lines restricted by provisions of the Interstate Commerce Commission. This situation was somewhat (although inadequately) moderated by the entrance of the Canadian Pacific into the Transcontinental Rates Association in 1889, and was finally better regulated by a Canadian railway commission (created in 1904).

For their complaints in 1887 the American railways apparently had a basis of justification. The Canadian Pacific, favored by bonding privileges, had recently and successfully demanded from the American transcontinental lines (the American Transcontinental Traffic Association) a cash payment of five hundred thousand dollars for withdrawal from the traffic of San Francisco for one year, enforcing its demand by a threat of a cut-rate which would have prevented to American roads any profit for the transcontinental traffic.

Confronted by this situation the Americans stimulated a controversy concerning railway domestic transit of merchandise in bond, which had been legalized by act of 1866 and provided with an additional guarantee by the treaty of 1871, but which since the abrogation of the treaty article (in 1885) had no legalized basis except the revived statute of 1866.[17]

Before the abrogation of the treaty articles, the control of shipment in bond (under American regulations submitted on June 17, 1874) had been a subject of some complaint by Canada. In May, 1875, the American government received a Canadian complaint that the American customs officials at Island Pond, Vermont, acting under recent Treasury regulations concerning commercial intercourse between Canada and the United States, had unloaded from sealed cars, for inspection, the Canadian merchandise destined for Portland or other ports for exportation. On August 10 the Department of State replied that the manner of enforcing the regulations was not regarded as repugnant to the treaty or to the statutes enacted in accord therewith. In November, 1876, it received a request for revocation of the detention order, and for restoration of the earlier regulation. In July, 1878, after some further correspondence on the subject, it received official notice that in order to carry out the stipulations of Article XXX of the treaty of 1871, concerning transportation of dutiable merchandise between the two countries, the British and Canadian governments would abide by the American regulations submitted in January, 1874.[18]

In the later controversy, which especially attracted wide attention in connection with the vigorous retaliatory policy suggested in President Cleveland's special message of August 23, 1888, the Americans were the complainants. In the face of the unfair demands of the Canadian Pacific, and influenced also by its unfair competitive traffic bidding, the American rival lines suggested that a remedy might be found in the discontinuance of the domestic transit trade in bond. The unfair competition to which they objected was also opposed by the opponents of the Canadian attitude on the fisheries, but it was regarded with favor by certain American shippers—especially by shippers of Minnesota where the Canadian Pacific had recently formed an alliance with the American Sault Ste. Marie line. By the middle of 1887, Secretary Bayard was requested to state the views of the American government concerning Article XXIX of the treaty of 1871.[19]

In the spring of 1888 the railway question was a subject of some public discussion. In an article of May 14, 1888, in the *New York Tribune*, Joseph Nimmo, Jr. presented a summary of the question in a review of the causes of American grievances against Canada. Soon thereafter he published at Washington a pamphlet on the political railways of Canada and strategic military preparations.[20]

Later, in connection with the debates on the fisheries treaty of 1888, Congress seemed to threaten to terminate the arrangement for the eastern foreign transit trade in bond, as it had already abrogated (in 1885) the treaty provision which had legalized the domestic transit trade. On July 25 Senator Cullom submitted a resolution directing the Committee on Interstate Commerce to inquire into reports that the Canadian Pacific Railway had recently obtained control of the Minneapolis, Sault Ste. Marie and Atlantic and the Duluth, South Shore and Atlantic railways—lines which controlled all approaches to the St. Marys River boundary bridge which was owned by the Canadian Pacific. This resolution also directed an inquiry as to whether American legislation was necessary to protect American interests and to prevent the diversion of commerce from its natural and legitimate channels. By another resolution (of July 31) the Senate proposed the appointment of a select committee of that body to report fully on Canadian relations—including the subjects of commerce and business, Canadian railways and canals, and American claims against Great Britain for any Canadian violations of the obligations of treaties and international law. The subject of railways, however, was referred to the Interstate Commerce Committee which by consent of the Senate expected to undertake a thorough investigation of American-Canadian relations connected with the subject of transportation both by rail and by water.[21]

On August 3 Senator Cullom offered for immediate consideration a more extensive resolution directing the Committee on Interstate Commerce to report to the Senate (1) whether any railroad lines in the United States were owned or operated or controlled by the Grand Trunk Railway Company, by the Canadian Pacific Railway Company, or by any other Canadian railroad corporation, (2) whether commerce originating in the United States was diverted from American to Canadian lines of transportation (with the means of any such diversion), and (3) whether Canada in charges for tolls on the Welland and St. Lawrence canals discriminated against American vessels using those canals. This resolution also requested the Committee to report whether any regulatory legislation concerning commerce between the United States and Canada was necessary for the protection of American commercial interests or for promotion of the enforcement of the "act to regulate commerce" approved February 4, 1887. Referring to the newspaper information that the Canadian Pacific controlled the American roads between Sault Ste. Marie and Duluth and to Minneapolis, and was reaching for other feeders, Cullom asserted that proper legislation should be enacted to prevent British methods of diverting to the Canadian Pacific the China and Japan trade which would naturally seek American transcontinental lines.

In the resulting debates Senator Gorman spoke especially on the transit trade which permitted the competition and participation of a foreign railroad in the business of the American side of the boundary. Stating that it had its origin in an emergency and was inaugurated as an expedient for subserving American interests, he said that at the time of the eventful completion of the railway suspension bridge below Niagara Falls (in April, 1855), which permitted a connection between the New York Central and the Michigan Central via the Great Western Railway of Canada, no one had anticipated that the Canadian railroads would become rivals of American lines or would seriously jeopardize the business of the United States.[22]

At the same time the administration had new complaints in regard to Canadian policy concerning importations. On August 4, with a purpose to ameliorate the trade relations of neighboring countries, Bayard presented for the attention of the Canadian authorities a memorial of New York citizens who were prominently engaged in trade with Canada and who especially complained of a feature of Canadian laws alleged to discriminate against importations of merchandise produced in countries east of the Cape of Good Hope and arriving in Canada via the United States.

On August 23 the President recommended to Congress that it should conditionally authorize him to suspend the operation of all pre-treaty laws or regulations which permitted Canadian transit in bond across American territory.[23]

On August 30, following the President's statement that Article XXIX of the treaty of 1871 was no longer in force, and following Senator Morgan's introduction of a bill in accord with the President's recommendations, Senator Cullom submitted a resolution directing the Secretary of the Treasury to report whether the transit in bond of merchandise from Canada over or across American territory, free of duty, had been permitted since July 1, 1885—which had been named as the date for the cessation of Article XXIX. On the following day, in the discussion of the resolution, Senator George of Mississippi suggested that the resolution was unnecessary. He stated that all the operations of commerce which were permitted by Article XXIX of 1871 were already in force and practice under existing American statutes of July 14, 1862, and June 7, 1864, preceding an act of 1866 which provided for the reverse operation (the transfer of imported goods from Europe or other countries through the United States to Canada). Whether for this reason or otherwise, Congress did not act further upon the President's conditional suggestion of a suspension of the laws concerning bonded transit.

Hitt of Illinois opposed the retaliatory withdrawal of Canadian transit in bond, on the ground that the withdrawal would result in the diversion of Canadian traffic via the Intercolonial Railway to St. John and Halifax and in the consequent reduction of the natural carrying trade of the New England railways. He suggested that there was something mysterious about the alleged demise of Article XXIX (of 1871).[24]

The controversy concerning canals, which culminated (in August, 1888) in the President's recommendation of retaliatory American canal discriminations in response to Canadian discriminatory canal tolls, was one which often had engaged the attention of the American government since the early seventies.[25]

In the half decade after the treaty of 1871 the question of Canadian use of the New York State canals was a subject of considerable correspondence. Promptly after the completion of the treaty President Grant wrote the governors of states affected by it, notifying them of the provisions of Article XXVII. In December he received from the governor of New York a reply that under New York laws there were no restrictions on the equal use of the state canals by British subjects and American citizens. Three years later, following official information (of November 23, 1874) that under Canadian regulations American vessels with or without cargo clearing from ports on the Hudson were "allowed to pass through the Chambly canal to the St. Lawrence and thence from Montreal through the Lachine canal and through the canals on the Ottawa to Ottawa or any other destination," Secretary Fish received through the British legation a Canadian complaint that discriminating duties were levied on Canadian vessels entering American canals and especially that Canadian vessels were excluded from the use of the Whitehall (Champlain) and Erie canals. In reply he promptly submitted a report of the governor of New York stating that New York canals were used by British and American citizens on equal terms. Later, after considerable correspondence and a thorough investigation, he learned that this complaint was terminated in February, 1875, by a Canadian minute in council admitting that no case of exclusion could be found.[26]

A few months later the American government was confronted with the Canadian demand for the right to transport cargoes in bond from Canada to the port of New York via the Champlain Canal. Early in September, 1875, Fish was requested to decide a question arising from a Canadian claim to a right of unrestricted navigation of American canals—a claim arising from restrictions recently placed upon the navigation of Champlain Canal by Canadian vessels. He received from the British minister a complaint of the Canadian minister of customs that the American collector of customs at Rouse's Point had refused to permit a Canadian cargo of lumber to pass through the Champlain Canal to the port of New York, and also that the American collector at Plattsburg would not permit Canadian barges to pass from Rouse's Point to New York City with foreign merchandise in bond. In a prompt reply (of September 23) he submitted the decision of the Treasury Department that Canadian vessels had free use of American canals only on condition that they made entry at no port except that for which they were bound at the time they started to the United States. Early in October he submitted the opinion that Canadian vessels were authorized to use the Champlain Canal to carry cargoes to its southern terminus but not to transport cargoes in bond from Canada to New York. He frankly reminded the

British minister that Canada had no treaty right to the free navigation of the Hudson River (without which Canada regarded the navigation of the canal as practically useless). Late in November he submitted the Treasury decision that Canadian vessels had no right to carry goods in bond from Canada via the Champlain Canal to the port of New York—that they had no right to navigate American interior rivers.[27]

Later, in 1876, in order to authorize the unobstructed passage of Canadian vessels and cargoes to the terminus of the canal at Albany (the first Hudson port below the canal), the American government modified an old Treasury regulation which (under a law of 1799) had required Canadian vessels at the frontier to unload goods destined to an American interior port. In June, after some correspondence, Fish notified Thornton of the British legation that the Treasury Department had issued an order to the customs office at Plattsburg to allow Canadian barges and other vessels with cargoes of imported goods to pass that port on a clearance to Albany or to intermediate ports under conditions and regulations governing American vessels coming from Canada, and also to allow free transit to return cargoes destined for Canada. He stated that similar orders would be issued to collectors at Buffalo and Oswego, New York, and at Burlington, Vermont.

In the following month, therefore, he was evidently surprised to learn that under recent Canadian regulations American tugboats had been refused clearance to proceed beyond Chambly on the way from Lake Champlain via St. John and the Chambly Canal to the Richelieu River and the St. Lawrence, and that they were prevented from navigating the St. Lawrence between Sorel and Montreal.[28]

In 1884, two years after the abolition of tolls on the Erie Canal, the American government encountered a new Canadian canal issue. The Canadian government reduced canal tolls by offering a rebate of ninety per cent to all grain cargoes (of both American and Canadian vessels) which, after passing through the Welland Canal, continued down the St. Lawrence to Montreal, but not to cargoes for Oswego or Ogdensburg. This discrimination it sought to justify on the ground that it was aimed only against American routes and ports and not against American vessels.

In 1888 this subject attracted increased attention in Congress. On January 4 Mr. Dingley submitted in the House a resolution relating to the Canadian order in council which authorized the rebate. In the following July, after further information from the Treasury Department concerning the alleged Canadian discrimination against American vessels, and after a resulting inquiry as to whether the power of Congress to impose tolls on vessels passing through the St. Marys Canal or the St. Clair Flats Canal had any legal limit besides that of the treaty of 1871, Secretary Bayard registered a complaint. He asked Sackville-West to remind the Canadian government of the treaty provisions of 1871 concerning the use of canals.[29]

Meantime, an old question concerning the regulation of aid to wrecked or disabled vessels on the inland border waters remained unsettled. By act of June 19 (approved July 19), 1878, Congress had provided a reasonable method of regulation which was designed to avoid the harshness of previous practice in Canada, and required only Canadian concurrent legislation to make it operative. In August, 1879, therefore, Evarts was surprised by the Canadian expression of unwillingness to enter into such a reciprocal arrangement unless combined with the coasting trade and towing privileges.[30] In November, 1888, Bayard declined to agree with the British chargé (Herbert) upon the expediency of a treaty on the coasting trade including wrecking and towing privileges. He also expressed surprise that Canada was unwilling to enter into an arrangement for aid to wreck vessels as proposed by Congress in June, 1878.

Early in December, 1888, the President informed Congress that Canada had never taken the concurrent action necessary to make effective the American act of 1878 and he urged the need of an agreement with the British government for removal (or humane regulation) of obstacles to reciprocal assistance to wrecked or stranded vessels with a purpose to alleviate the damages to life and property on the Great Lakes.[31]

Incidently, in 1886, arose a question concerning tugs. In September, Bayard complained that American tugs in Canadian waters did not receive treatment as favorable as that received by Canadian tugs in American waters. In the following May, however, he was officially informed that Canadian regulations had been changed to conform to the American.[32]

Other problems of navigation, chiefly concerning rivers, arose in the period after 1878. Among these was one on Red River in July, 1879. Evarts requested the removal of recent Canadian restrictions which required American vessels to pay duties at North Pembina before they were allowed to proceed northward with cargo. He represented that such restrictions were contrary to the treaty of 1871 and to later practice under the Governor-General's order of June 13, 1871. Another arose on the St. John in July, 1883. Frelinghuysen remonstrated against obstruction of American lumber trade on the St. John by booms and dams constructed by a British firm.

Another navigation problem arose on the River St. Clair in May, 1884. Frelinghuysen presented the protest of the manager of the Port Hudson and Northwestern Railway against Sarnia's grant of an exclusive ferry privilege between Port Huron and Sarnia, a grant which in its application to American citizens was regarded as an obstruction of the free commerce granted by treaty. In approving the protest he said the navigation of the boundary waters by vessels of both nations had been "contemplated and provided for on an entirely free and equal footing" in all Anglo-American treaties from 1783 to 1842, subject to local regulations. In concluding that the Sarnia grant could not be justified he asserted that the adoption of similar action by Port Huron "could only result in giving rise to a state of unfriendly and unneighborly feeling between the two municipalities." In the following November he received through the British legation a suggestion of the Canadian government that, preceding any attempt to settle the complications at Port Huron, the two governments should confer with a view to an international agreement concerning ferries between the United States and Canada. To this Frelinghuysen agreed.[33]

A related question arose in March, 1888. Bayard complained of Canadian discriminating duties (entrance and clearance fees) charged on American vessels in Ontario, not involving the claim that American vessels should be admitted to the privileges of the Canadian coasting trade.[34]

In addition to questions of the regulation of navigation on the Lakes were questions concerning the need of fishery regulations in border waters. In December, 1875, the Grant administration, following a suggestion from the British minister, invited the attention of state executives to the need of such regulations to protect and promote the increase of fish in the border waters.

In August, 1879, influenced by recent action of Canadian local authorities to prevent Americans from fishing on the Canadian side of Lake Ontario at points near the mouth of the Niagara, Evarts asked the British minister to request the Canadian government to prevent Canadians from fishing on the American side.[35]

For almost two decades after 1869, extradition was a subject of extended controversy, which increased in importance coincidently with the increase of business and development of facilities of communication, and which increasingly affected American-Canadian relations. In 1870–74 Fish declined British invitations to negotiate a new treaty with provisions which were regarded as practically subservient to acts of the British Parliament.[36] In 1876, he denied the British claim of a right (under a British act) to refuse extradition under the treaty of 1842 unless the application was accompanied by the assurance that the fugitive would be tried only for the extraditable offense specifically named in the request for surrender. He declined to admit that the British had a right to alter or restrict a treaty provision by domestic legislation,[37] or to withhold advantages of the old treaty after failure to agree upon provisions for a new one.[38] Finally, in June, 1876, after British refusal to deliver certain fugitives, he announced the suspension of the treaty clause of 1842 by British failure to execute its terms. In the following September he declined to renew operation of the suspended clause unless the British government should arrange to reverse its action.[39]

In October, 1876, Fish received a British proposal temporarily to revive the provision of 1842 without the British restriction (in order to avoid serious inconvenience and the encouragement of crime).[40] This proposal he accepted in December and promptly proceeded to submit requests for extradition of new fugitives from justice. On December 28 he formally submitted a draft for a proposed new treaty. In February, 1877, apprehensive that a pending case of a fugitive to Canada might result in the termination of the temporarily revived provision of 1842, he sought to hasten the completion of a proposed permanent treaty which seemed necessary to prevent possible hindrances to the administration of justice. A few days later, on March 2, he expressed entire satisfaction with the British change of position and the resulting concession of all that the American government had demanded.[41]

In April, Evarts submitted a draft of a new provision which would permit trial of an extradited person for any crime enumerated in the treaty but negotiations reached a standstill by September 12.[42]

New negotiations for a new treaty were begun early in 1883, but were soon ended because Frelinghuysen refused to accept the principle of non-trial for other than the surrender offense,[43] and could not agree to certain amendments suggested by the British.[44]

In 1886, following renewed negotiations at London, Phelps agreed with Rosebery upon the terms of a modernized enlarged convention to which the Senate was unable to agree because of political considerations in relation to certain new kinds of crimes, and which remained unapproved until the close of the Cleveland administration.[45]

In contrast with controversies and irritations arising from railway competition and canal tolls, and from lake fishing and extradition, appeared many evidences of improved neighborhood relations in the period of the seventies and eighties. These may be seen especially in agreements concerning postal arrangments. In 1874–75, in accord with precedents beginning in 1851, the American government concluded with the Dominion a postal agreement which practically extinguished the international boundary so far as the postal service was concerned. Twelve years later, in January, 1886, Bayard received a British proposal for a parcel post convention. He replied that the Postmaster General, although he agreed to the desirability of such extension of mail service, decided that it was then inadmissible by lack of legislative authority.[46]

An interesting question concerning reciprocal postal arrangements arose in 1888, near the close of President Cleveland's administration. Bayard negotiated with Canada another postal convention which caused Sackville-West to express by confidential *note verbale* the British wish that "all communications on postal matters affecting the British colonies or possessions should pass through the regular diplomatic channels, either at Washington or in London." He explained that the postal administration had reasonably assumed that the colonial administrations in inviting such arrangements had acted under the sanction and permission of the imperial government, or under its statutes authorizing colonial self-management of postal affairs. Later, on June 17, in reply to an inquiry he was confidentially informed that the British government, although it suggested that all postal conventions with the crown colonies should be negotiated directly with the imperial government, had no desire to ignore the history of past postal arrangements between the United States and the British colonies, or to urge any general or extensive changes of practice in regard to agreements with the colonial government for conventions with self-governing colonies like Canada.[47]

REFERENCES

1. *99 G.B., Notes* [*from*], July 10, 1875; *16 G.B., Notes to,* p. 577, June 5 and 12, 1875; *Ib.*, p. 596, July 20; *Ib.*, p. 599, July 24; *17 G.B., Notes to,* pp. 29–30, Sept. 13, 1875; *Ib.*, pp. 79–81, Jan. 5, 1876; *C.A.*, G Series, Oct. 12 and 15, 1875.
2. *17 G.B., Notes to,* p. 216, Aug. 30, 1876; *Sen. Exec. Docs.*, 44–1, No. 52; *H. Exec. Docs.*, 44–2, I; *Ib.*, 45–3, I; *Sen. Docs.*, 73–1, No. 68.
3. *17 G.B., Notes to,* pp. 425–26, June 26, 1877; *Ib.*, p. 450, Sept. 4; *Ib.*, pp. 423 and 442, June 23 and Aug. 14; *Ib.*, pp. 520 and 535, Feb. 23 and Mar. 18, 1878.
4. *For. Rels.*, *1879*, pp. 488, 500, 508, and 510; *Ib.*, *1880*, p. 498; *18 G.B., Notes to,* pp. 59–65, May 27, 1879 (also pp. 11 and

37, Mar. 15 and Apr. 19); *Ib.*, pp. 107–10, Aug. 11; *Ib.*, p. 210, Feb. 5, 1880.

5. *Ib.*, pp. 442–45, Feb. 5, 1881; *Ib.*, p. 204, Dec. 2, 1880.
6. *Ib.*, pp. 517–18, May 26, 1881; *Ib.*, p. 593, Aug. 25, 1881.
7. *Ib.*, p. 685, Feb. 25, 1882; *For. Rels., 1882*, pp. 315–16, 319, 323–24, 496, 503; *19 G.B., Notes to,* pp. 17–18, Apr. 7, 1882; *Ib.*, p. 246, Apr. 13.
8. *Ib.*, p. 328, July 30, 1883; *For. Rels., 1883.*
9. *Ib., 1884*, pp. 234 and 239, Dec. 12, 1883, and Feb. 18, 1884; *19 G.B., Notes to,* p. 417, Jan. 18, 1884; *21 G.B., Notes to,* p. 84, June 10, 1889.
10. *157 Dom. Letters,* p. 352, Oct. 13, 1885; *20 G.B., Notes to,* p. 436, Dec. 22, 1886; *Ib.*, pp. 156–57, Dec. 2, 1886.
11. *Ib.*, p. 528, Aug. 10, 1887.
12. *19 G.B., Notes to,* pp. 438–40, Mar. 27, 1884; *Ib.*, p. 467, Apr. 24, 1884; *Ib.*, p. 653, Mar. 28, 1885.
13. *20 G.B., Notes to,* p. 246, Apr. 28, 1886.
14. *19 G.B., Notes to,* pp. 442–43, Jan. 10, 13 and 16, and Feb. 16, 1884; *Ib.*, pp. 679–80, Apr. 18, 1885; *110 G.B., Notes from,* June 25, 1884.
15. *19 G.B., Notes to,* p. 681, Apr. 20, 1885; *20 G.B., Notes to,* p. 110, Sept. 1.
16. *Sen. Rps.*, 51–1, No. 1530, Part 2, p. 923.
17. *Sen. Rps.*, 49–1, No. 46; *118 U.S., 557;* Dewey, *National Problems,* Chap. VI; Shortt and Doughty, IX, 161–62; *3 A Reciprocity Treaties,* 1898–99, Kasson, *Rp. of the Republican Club of N. Y. City,* Jan. 18, 1897.
18. *17 G.B., Notes to,* pp. 8–9, Aug. 10, 1875; *Ib.*, p. 281, Nov. 24, 1876; *Ib.*, July 18, 1878.
19. *Sen. Exec. Docs.*, 52–2, No. 40, July 6, 1887, pp. 11–12.
20. *State Dept. Pamphs., G. B. Political Rels.*, I.
21. *19 Cong. Record,* 50–1, pp. 6769, 7062, 7203–21, 8103 and 8130; *Sen. Rps.*, 51–1, No. 1530.
22. *Ib.*, 51–1, Vol. 4, No. 847; *19 Cong. Record,* 50–1, pp. 7203–10, 7213–21, 7262 and 7885.
23. *20 G.B., Notes to,* pp. 680–81, Aug. 4, 1888; Richardson, VIII, 620–27.
24. *19 Cong. Record,* 50–1, pp. 7914, 8103, 8130–31 and 8268–76.
25. Richardson, VIII, 620–27.
26. *3 Can. Parl.*, 3rd Sess., No. 111, pp. 1, 2, 4, 11, 14; *22 G.B., Notes to,* pp. 221–24, Dec. 31, 1892; *17 G.B., Notes to,* pp. 211–13, Aug. 19, 1876; *16 G.B., Notes to,* p. 491, Dec. 8, 1874.
27. *C.A.*, G Series, Haly to Thornton, No. 20, Aug. 30, 1875 (with enclosures); *17 G.B., Notes to,* p. 27, Sept. 7, 1875; *Ib.*, pp. 29–30, Sept. 23; *Ib.*, p. 59, Nov. 24; *22 G.B., Notes to,* pp. 221–24, Dec. 31, 1892.

28. *Ib., 17 G.B., Notes to,* pp. 179–80, June 7, 1876; *Ib.,* pp. 211–13, Aug. 19.
29. SHORTT and DOUGHTY, IX, 160; *Sen. Rps.,* 51–1, No. 1530, Part 2, pp. 921–22, July 21, 1890; *20 G.B., Notes to,* pp. 674–75, July 21 and 22, 1888; *Misc. Letters,* July 9; *Nation,* Oct. 31, 1912, pp. 406–07 (C. D. ALLIN).
30. *17 G.B., Notes to,* p. 646, Dec. 17, 1878; *18 G.B., Notes to,* p. 110, Aug. 11, 1879; *21 G.B., Notes to,* pp. 18–21, Nov. 16, 1888; *Misc. Letters,* Nov. 20, 1878; *125 Domestic Letters,* p. 334.
31. *21 G.B., Notes to,* Nov. 16, 1888; *For. Rels., 1888;* RICHARDSON, VIII, 781.
32. *20 G.B., Notes to,* pp. 353–56, Sept. 24, 1886.
33. *C.A.,* G Series, O'Grady Haly to Thornton, No. 18, Aug. 28, 1875; *Gov.-Genl.'s Letter Book,* 1870–75, p. 332; *For. Rels., 1879, 1883 and 1884; 18 G.B., Notes to,* p. 98, July 30, 1879; *27 G.B., Instrs.,* pp. 1–3, No. 640, July 25, 1883; *19 G.B., Notes to,* pp. 480–82, May 21, 1884; *Ib.,* p. 592, Nov. 21; *110 G.B., Notes from,* May 24.
34. *20 G.B., Notes to,* pp. 615–18, Mar. 24, 1888; *F.R., 1888.*
35. *17 G.B., Notes to,* p. 72, Dec. 18, 1875; *18 G.B.,* p. 112, Aug. 16, 1879; *F.R., 1880.*
36. *24 G.B., Instrs.,* p. 257, No. 887, May 22, 1876; also see *C.A.,* G Series, Jan. 9 and Aug. 2, and *passim;* also *Ib., Gov.-Genl.'s Letter Book,* Dufferin to Thornton, Confid., No. 39, Dec. 15, 1875 (also Dec. 3 and 13).
37. *24 G.B., Instrs.;* No. 864, Mar. 31, 1876; *F.R., 1876;* J. B. MOORE, *Int. Law Digest,* IV, 306–09.
38. *24 G.B., Instrs.,* p. 257, No. 887, May 22, 1876.
39. *Exec. Docs.,* 44–1, No. 173; *24 G.B., Instrs.,* pp. 347–51, No. 6, June 22, 1876; *Ib.,* pp. 372–74, Tels., July 20 and 26; *Ib.,* p. 400, No. 34, Sept. 18; *17 G.B., Notes to,* p. 193, June 22, 1876.
40. *Ib.,* pp. 342–48, Feb. 23, 1877; *Ib.,* pp. 265–68, Oct. 30, 1876.
41. *Ib.,* p. 295, Dec. 23, 1876; RICHARDSON, VIII, 414–17; *F.R., 1877,* pp. 271–89; *24 G.B., Instrs.,* p. 467, Tel., Dec. 27; *Ib.,* p. 485, No. 95, Feb. 2, 1877; *Ib.,* pp. 503–09, No. 107, Feb. 23; *Ib.,* pp. 512–21, No. 108, Feb. 24; *Ib.,* pp. 526–27, No. 115, Mar. 2; *17 G.B., Notes to,* pp. 342–48, Feb. 23.
42. *Ib.,* p. 389, Apr. 23, 1877; *27 G.B., Instrs.,* pp. 251–63, No. 915, July 15, 1884 (Review).
43. *Ib.* (pp. 259 and 261); *19 G.B., Notes to,* p. 204, Feb. 16, 1883.
44. *27 G.B., Instrs.,* p. 306, No. 979, Sept. 11, 1884; *Ib.,* p. 308, Tel., Sept. 15; *Ib.,* pp. 524–35, No. 73 (Confid.), Aug. 4, 1885; *G.B., Desps.,* No. 884, Aug. 26, 1884.
45. RICHARDSON, VIII, 332; *27 G.B., Instrs.,* pp. 678–85, No. 229,

Mar. 3, 1886; *Nation,* Aug. 12, 1886, p. 130; *109 G.B., Notes from,* Mar. 17, 1883.

46. *19 Cong. Record,* 50–1, p. 3687; *H. Exec. Docs.,* 50–1, No. 293, Apr. 30, 1888; *20 G.B., Notes to,* p. 182, Jan. 25, 1886.

47. *Ib.,* pp. 624–27, Personal, Apr. 9, 1888; *19 Cong. Record,* 50–1, p. 3687 (also pp. 2113 and 2486–2500); *115 G.B., Notes from,* June 17, 1888.

CHAPTER XVII

POLICY OF THE HARRISON ADMINISTRATION 1889–93

FOLLOWING the rejection of the draft reciprocity-fisheries treaty of 1888 and the renewed discussions of commercial union, Harrison was elected president with expectations that his administration would direct a more vigorous American foreign policy, and especially that it would try to find a satisfactory settlement of the chief problems in Canadian relations. These expectations received new promise of realization by the selection of James C. Blaine as head of the Department of State, and they also stimulated in the leaders of the Canadian Liberal party a desire to re-open discussion of plans for unrestricted reciprocity.[1]

By 1889 American foreign policy concerning Canada was influenced by American increasing strength of the eighties, by the British movement for imperial federation, and also by an initial American excursion into the field of extra-American dependencies. After 1889–90 it was influenced by the Pan-American Congress, which stimulated the principle of reciprocity and possibly also contributed to a brief Canadian flirtation with Jamaica.[2]

American-Canadian policy was determined in part by the American feeling that the British and other foreign governments were insidiously seeking advantages over American competitors in commerce. This feeling was expressed in the discussions preceding the McKinley tariff act of October, 1890, which was followed by rejection of renewed Canadian overtures for reciprocity and which foreshadowed the beginning of a series of strategic struggles relating to tariffs and counter-tariffs.

Early in 1892, recognizing the importance of problems concerning the northern neighbor, the Senate unanimously consented to the approval of Senator Hoar's resolution to make the committee on relations with Canada a standing committee of the Senate.[3]

Incident to the main principles and purposes of American Canadian policy re-appeared considerable annexation sentiment, which was considerably increased by the effect of the McKinley tariff in decreasing Canadian trade across the border, and which was associated with expressions of sentiment in favor of a future American policy to assert American rightful influence and power on the American continent.[4] This sentiment, however, was partially neutralized by publication of opposing views.[5]

Secretary Blaine's views of policy in relations with Canada were probably summarized in an unsigned and undated confidential typewritten memorandum on the union and peace of the continent which is filed in the archives of the Department of State. This memorandum, which evidently was instigated or provoked by anti-American sentiments of Canadian protected manufacturers and the Canadian Pacific Railway, declared that the most vital foreign policy for consideration of American statesmanship was "to unite the continent, secure its independence and prevent the northern part of it from being turned into an outpost of European reaction antagonistic in spirit and institutions to the rest." It stated that union "would exclude war from the continent" and solve all the American Canadian questions which seemed to open "an endless vista of dispute." Referring to the unwisdom of a policy of annexation by coercion, it suggested the probable acquiescence of the sensible British government in the transfer of the allegiance of Canada whose nominal subjection had contributed to the empire only "onerous liabilities and dangerous disputes." It concluded with the statement that "Union is likely to be promoted by everything which asserts the commercial autonomy of the continent and helps to make Canada feel that to enjoy her full measure of prosperity she must be economically a community of this hemisphere, not an outlying dependency of a European power."[6]

Near the close of Harrison's administration American newspapers expressed considerable sentiment in favor of "continental union" (without consultation of Great Britain). They seemed to recognize, however, that American annexation of Canada could originate only in Canadian initiative or as a contingency resulting from an attempt of Great Britain to meddle in American relations with Hawaii. Evidently American annexation sentiment, largely subsided before the change of administration,[7] had practically vanished by 1896. Goldwin Smith, consistent with his earlier views, was still an annexationist, but on that platform he stood practically alone.[8]

Although the development of Canadian nationality and autonomy was evident, the American government was consistently careful in avoiding any act which might be interpreted as a recognition of Canadian independent status in the conduct of foreign affairs. Both Blaine and Foster deferred to the British minister in arranging conferences with Canadian official representatives. In November, 1892, in reply to an inquiry from London whether Canada had been invited to participate in the proposed silver conference, Foster stated that the American government, although it did not plan to send a direct invitation to Canada, would heartily approve the appointment of Canadian delegates by the British government.[9]

In the period of Harrison's presidency the chief subjects of American Canadian policy, after the dominating Bering Sea seals controversy (which is treated in a separate chapter), were the problems of extradition, Chinese immigration across the Canadian frontier, jurisdiction along the Lakes water boundary, cattle and pork regulations, railway competition and bonded transit, canal tolls and aid to wrecked vessels, trade reciprocity, Lake defenses, and copyrights.

The proposed new extradition convention which had been delayed until the beginning of the administration was finally concluded by Blaine and Sir Julian Pauncefote on July 12, 1889. In the following December the President, in announcing the new treaty, stated that it greatly lessened the chances that neighboring territory would be used as a secure harbor for evil doers. On March 25, 1890, following approval of the amended treaty by the Senate on February 18, he issued the proclamation which was required to make it effective.[10]

This treaty greatly extended the list of extraditable crimes beyond those mentioned in the treaty of 1842. To the list it added voluntary manslaughter, counterfeiting or the altering of money or the circulation of such money, embezzlement and larceny, fraud, perjury, rape, abduction or kidnaping, burglary, piracy, revolt or conspiracy to revolt on a ship on the high seas, and crimes or offenses against the laws of both countries for suppression of slavery and slave-trading. Among the crimes omitted were bribery and offenses against bankruptcy law which were added to the list of 1905.[11] Another omission was conspiracy to defraud which was a subject of some correspondence in 1892.[12]

By October, 1890, the American government was confronted with increasing difficulties of enforcing along an unguarded inland frontier a policy of restricting immigration of Chinese laborers whose illegal entrance into American territory had been facilitated by the completion of the Canadian Pacific Railway. The State Department instructed Lincoln, the American minister in London, to submit to Lord Salisbury a concurrent resolution of Congress inviting negotiation for treaty stipulations to prevent this illegal entry from Canada. Lincoln, who acted promptly, found that Salisbury must consult with the Canadian government which seemed indifferent and delayed its reply.[13]

Early in the new administration the Department of State was apprehensive of Canadian regulation of importations of American livestock. Even after Congress placed upon the newly created Department of Agriculture the duty to inspect cattle and fresh meat offered for export, it found reason to express some anxiety concerning Canadian restrictions on the admission of American cattle.[14]

Questions relating to boundaries arose early in the new administration. In December, 1889, with a view to accuracy in the settlement of jurisdictional questions, the President recommended to Congress provision for an international agreement for visibly marking the water boundary in the narrow channels connecting the Great Lakes. In the following year (in September) Congress enacted a law extending the criminal jurisdiction of the United States circuit and district courts to the Great Lakes and their connecting waters.[15]

In 1893 the United States Supreme Court decided that the United States courts, irrespective of the statute, had jurisdiction to try one Rodgers for criminal assault committed on an American vessel on the Canadian side of the Detroit River (in February, 1888). The decision was based on the ground that the connecting Lakes are interior high seas and that the Detroit River from shore to shore is within the admiralty jurisdiction of the United States. In the following year, and again in 1895, the Department of State decided that this doctrine of the "high seas" did not confer fishing rights, but that concerning the latter each country had exclusive jurisdiction on its side of the international boundary line.[16]

Late in June, 1892, Blaine prepared a draft of a proposed convention providing for a commission to direct the demarkation of portions of the boundary not permanently marked. On July 27 he announced that the Senate had consented to its ratification.[17]

Another subject of some controversy in the period was the Canadian amended copyright law of 1889 which the imperial Parliament had suspended pending the discussion of the protection of British authors from sales of cheap reprints imported into Canada from the United States. On June 16, 1891, Salisbury explicitly declared that the law of copyright in all British possessions permitted American citizens the benefit of copyright on "substantially the same basis as to British subjects." On the basis of this official assurance, President Harrison extended the benefit of the American copyright to citizens or subjects of Great Britain and the British possessions. In the following December, learning that the Canadian government had denied that the American enactment and proclamation constituted an international copyright treaty and had refused to admit American citizens to the privilege of registration of copyright in Canada under provisions of the Canadian statute, Blaine insisted that the declaration of Salisbury and its acceptance by the American government constituted an international arrangement which should be fulfilled in good faith. He submitted a request for an explanation of the discrepancy between British assurances and the course of the Canadian government, and inquired whether Salisbury's declaration of 1891 applied to Canada. In January, 1892, he received from London a statement that the Colonial

Secretary had requested the Canadian government to report on the question. In June and August, 1894, the Department of State complained that it had received no reply on the inquiry. In the following year it was relieved of further doubt by the Canadian enactment of a more satisfactory copyright law.[18]

In the early nineties the problem of opening deeper waterways between the Lakes and the Atlantic attracted some attention. It especially appeared in renewed efforts to obtain national aid for construction of a ship canal from the Lakes to the Hudson River, which was advocated for both commercial and military reasons. In modified form it appeared in a proposed diversion of water from the St. Lawrence to Lake Champlain. In March, 1892, in connection with the discussion, Blaine received an interesting request of Verplank Colvin of Albany to consider a proposal to purchase a triangular strip of Canadian territory, west of a line extending directly from Rouse's Point to Valleyfield, Canada, which he regarded as "necessary for the section of the St. Lawrence Valley Canal, northward of Clinton and Franklin counties, New York."[19]

The discussion of railway competition and bonding regulations was continued from the first Cleveland administration. Some leading Americans who were interested in the problems of American transcontinental transportation, and of steamship connections on the Pacific, regarded Canada as an aggressive and gradually encroaching competitor on the American Northwest. They especially mentioned the encroachments of the Canadian Pacific Railway which was encouraged by British aid and was practically protected by being exempt from the provisions of the recently created American Interstate Commerce Commission. Contemplating retaliatory legislation they stimulated the collection of a large amount of information on Canadian political organization and all other subjects which had a bearing upon American policy in Canadian relations. Much information, collected by authority of Senate resolutions, was submitted to the Senate in committee reports of May 3 and July 21, 1890.

In the hearings before the Senate select committee, Joseph Nimmo, Jr., chief of the Bureau of Statistics, stated that the earlier American retaliatory acts were too vague and general, and that President Cleveland's proposal to suspend transit trade was too radical. He proposed an American policy of retaliation by a tonnage tax on Canadian vessels passing through the American Sault Ste. Marie Canal which had been free of all tolls since its transfer from Michigan to the United States in 1881, and whose traffic had been greatly increased by recent development connected with the west end of Lake Superior. The Senate Committee upon Interstate Commerce recommended to Congress "such action as will give American railroads an even chance in competition with the railroads of Canada doing business in the United States." Referring to the sharp competition in navigation on the ocean and on the Lakes and to Canadian discriminatory entrance and clearance fees on American vessels on border water, it especially recommended as a "reciprocal proposition" American collection of similar fees on Canadian vessels in American ports; and, in retaliation for the Canadian discriminatory tolls on American products passing through the Welland Canal, it proposed an American discriminatory toll on the tonnage of all Canadian vessels passing through the Sault Ste. Marie Canal. Later, William Windom, Secretary of the Treasury, immediately preceding his death in January, 1891, had in preparation plans for abolition of bonding regulations.[20]

In connection with the discussions of tariff policy, preceding the adoption of the McKinley bill in October, 1890, appeared considerable sentiment in favor of reciprocal trade with Canada. On May 2, 1890, Mr. Hitt submitted from the House Committee on Foreign Affairs an interesting proposed substitute for the resolution which had been adopted by the House on March 1, 1889. This report recommended that, when Canada desired to enter into a commercial arrangement for removal of all duties between the United States and Canada, the President should appoint three commissioners to meet with Canadian commissioners to consider the best methods of extending trade relations.[21]

By the encouraging tone of American views, such as those of Hitt and of Butterworth, the Liberals of Canada felt a revival of its remaining hopes for freer trade. During the entire period of the consideration of the tariff problem in 1890,

Macdonald was exposed to influences which later induced the Canadian Conservative government to send a mission to Washington to renew the Liberal efforts for a reciprocity arrangement.[22]

Early in 1890 S. J. Ritchie, an American who had large business interests in Canada, and who in the preceding year had planned to arrange a Canadian trip for several members of Congress with a view to their casual call upon Macdonald at Ottawa, became very active in voluntary personal efforts to initiate a renewal of Anglo-American reciprocity negotiations. He was possibly influenced by the opinions of Mr. Butterworth whose bill for reciprocity was before the House. He was especially anxious to arrange a meeting between Macdonald and Butterworth. Writing Macdonald of plans to appear before the Ways and Means Committee to "talk annexation or anything else which will seem most likely to secure the necessary concessions," he repeated a suggestion that Tupper should be sent to Washington to confer, without the aid of the British minister. Later, in April, he interviewed Macdonald and the Canadian council at Ottawa. A few days later he wrote Macdonald to explain that there was no understanding between Butterworth, Hitt and McKinley.[23]

Later, he conferred with Butterworth, who, although too busy to go to Ottawa for a talk with Macdonald, agreed to offer a reciprocity amendment to the tariff bill. He also conferred with McKinley, who authorized the statement that after the passage of the tariff bill he "would then agree upon a bill for free exchange of all or a certain number of articles between the two countries." At Ottawa, on May 4, he reported to Macdonald this encouraging promise and "substantially the same promises from the Senate." Suggesting the importance of grasping this unusual opportunity, and expressing no faith in arrangements through the Department of State which required the approval of the Senate Committee on Foreign Relations, he tactfully advised an immediate cable call to Sir Charles Tupper to return from London and to proceed at once to Washington where meantime he proposed to prepare the ground for negotiations.[24]

On August 1, immediately following a lengthy and satisfactory interview with Macdonald at Ottawa, Ritchie submitted to Senator Aldrich, Macdonald's offer to agree to a mutual removal of the tariff on coal—an offer which was intended for use in framing the American tariff bill, and which he regarded as especially advantageous to the United States whose citizens largely owned the mines of Nova Scotia and Vancouver. He added a warning that if Congress failed to accept the offer of Macdonald, "the responsibility of not having profitable and friendly relations with Canada must rest with us." Less than three weeks later he went to Bar Harbor, Maine, to visit Secretary Blaine, with whom he fully discussed the whole Canadian question and whose attitude he regarded as both fair and friendly. After his return to Washington, he reported to Macdonald his belief that Blaine and Macdonald could arrive at a satisfactory conclusion, by an arrangement for concurrent legislation and without intervention of Downing Street. He hoped to fasten to the tariff bill in the Senate the articles to which Macdonald had agreed, but he apprehended a real struggle in the House.[25] On September 1 he saw his hopes partially realized in the Senate by Senator Sherman's notice of a reciprocal "free coal" amendment to the tariff bill, and also by a proposal to empower the President to appoint a commission to confer with the Canadian authorities on the general subject of reciprocal trade whenever those authorities should indicate a wish to consider the subject. Although still uncertain whether he and the advocates of reciprocity could force the proposed reciprocity amendment through the Senate, and still expecting a great struggle in the House, he was confident that in case of failure a fair arrangement might be obtained from Blaine.

Four weeks later Ritchie explained to Macdonald that the friends of Canadian reciprocity, deciding not to risk failure of their measure by attaching it to a party tariff bill to which the south American reciprocity measure was already fastened, had agreed to postpone the Canadian measure until December. Later, on November 11, at Montreal, he wrote Macdonald that he had no doubt that Congress at its next session would authorize the commission and that he expected to have a part in determining the provisions to suit Macdonald's wishes. He especially expressed his personal satisfaction that the latter intended to sit with Blaine upon a commission which he expected to settle all Canadian questions.[26]

In the following December, at Washington, Ritchie reported to Macdonald two interviews with Blaine who he said was "quite in favor of the proposed joint commission to discuss and recommend terms of settlement of questions in dispute (or in an unsatisfactory condition) and had expressed much satisfaction with the information of Macdonald's intention to sit on the commission if Blaine also would agree to sit.[27]

Meantime, Canadian hopes for reciprocity were again revived both by Blaine's progressive policy to restrict the principle of tariff protection and by the American elections of 1890 which gave the Democrats control of the House. While the Canadian Liberals hoped to hasten negotiations by an attempt to defeat the Conservative Macdonald government at the next Canadian election, Macdonald was preparing to modify his recent views. While intervening in the American trade negotiations with Newfoundland, he proposed, through the British minister at Washington, a joint commission to consider all American-Canadian issues, including a modified renewal of the Reciprocity Treaty of 1854.

Possibly the overtures for the later Canadian conferences with Blaine originated in the protests of the Macdonald government against an American reciprocity treaty with Newfoundland, which Blaine finally negotiated with Robert Bond in November, 1890, and which the British government failed to approve (because of the Canadian opposition to it).[28] According to John W. Foster, who on October 2 had been invited to conduct contemplated reciprocity negotiations with various countries, the Canadian government initiated the later arrangement for a conference by submitting through the British minister at Washington, in December, 1890, a request to Blaine to open negotiations for commercial reciprocity—a proposal which Goldwin Smith later characterized as a strategic move for effect upon plans for an approaching election. After considerable delay, Blaine finally agreed to hold a private (unofficial) conference with the British minister and one or more agents of Canada for consideration of every subject of relations with a view to possible formal negotiations if the proposed conference should indicate a probability of agreement upon any of the subjects discussed informally. This basis was accepted by the British minister and by the Canadian government, but the conference was delayed by various reasons of convenience or policy.[29]

Early in 1891, the Macdonald government, in connection with its decision strategically to favor a moderate plan of reciprocal trade (enough to pull the chair from under the opposition Liberal party), sought to create a public impression that the initiative for reciprocity negotiations had been taken by the American government. Confronted by Secretary Blaine's caustic note to Pauncefote denying that he had opened negotiations, it arranged to send Sir Charles Tupper to Washington on a visit of explanation. It continued to emphasize the importance of trusting the negotiations to a safe and moderate statesman of the Conservative party who advocated a national policy.[30]

In March, 1891, preceding the Canadian elections, Tupper in a speech at Toronto said he had every reason to believe that Blaine saw his way to propose a plan of commercial reciprocity with Canada which would interfere neither with the autonomy of Canada nor the operation of the American tariff. Later, however, he was unable to arrange with Blaine a definite date for a post-election conference. Further negotiations for a commercial truce, which were announced in April, were interrupted by the crossing of telegrams and the countermand of a special train between Washington and Ottawa. The three members of the Canadian cabinet who started to Washington were turned back at the frontier by a telegram from the British minister stating that the date of the meeting had not yet been fixed.

In the Canadian election campaign Macdonald's party won by the effective efforts of anti-reciprocity forces. It won chiefly through the active influence of the Canadian Pacific Railway in spreading propaganda to secure a vote against too intimate trade connection with the United States, and to avoid the risk of a diversion of Canadian traffic to American railways whose competition it sought to restrict through projects for entry into Chicago by control of lines southward across Minnesota and Wisconsin.[31]

After Macdonald's death (on June 6) further unsuccessful requests for a conference were made by the Canadian government under the new Prime Minister, Sir John Abbott, who, although he had signed the annexation manifesto of 1849, had risen to the leadership of the Conservatives in the Canadian Senate.[32]

Early in 1892 the chances of success for reciprocity seemed more hopeful. One sign appeared in a resolution of Senator Hale proposing to inquire into the practicability of an agreement relating to a reduction of revenue and the equalization of duties on imports. This resolution some regarded as a last despairing American gesture in favor of friendly overtures to Canada.[33]

After a delay of several months, resulting largely from the Canadian announcement that the conference was to be held "by the initiative of the American government," Blaine finally agreed to receive the Canadian representatives at Washington, and by authority of President Harrison he designated John W. Foster to participate in the informal conference. On February 1, 1892, he notified Pauncefote that he would receive the "gentlemen of Canada" informally on February 10 to discuss reciprocity.[34]

In the meantime Blaine had received information and suggestions which somewhat affected the scope and nature of the conferences. In September, 1891, he had received from the American Lake Carriers' Association of Buffalo complaints concerning the inequality and discriminatory nature of Canadian canal tolls at the Welland Canal. These complaints he had promptly submitted to Pauncefote with a statement that the tolls were regarded as a violation of a provision of the treaty of 1871. Later, on February 2, 1892, he received from Blanchard, of the Committee on Rivers and Harbors, a suggestion of the adoption of a policy of retaliatory tolls on commerce passing through the St. Clair and Sault Ste. Marie canals for Canadian ports.[35]

At the sessions of the conference which continued from February 10 to February 15, Blaine (aided by J. W. Foster) received the Canadian views presented by Sir John Thompson, George E. Foster, Mackenzie Bowell and Sir Julian Pauncefote. He courteously declined to accept a proposal for reciprocity on the basis of the treaty of 1854 (natural products), with necessary or desirable modifications and extensions but without including manufactured products which he especially desired. He unsuccessfully proposed the addition of a list of manufactured goods and the exclusive application to American-Canadian trade. He especially urged that the favors granted must not be enjoyed gratuitously by other countries. He declared that the American government could not be satisfied with any arrangement except one providing for Canadian preferential treatment to American manufactures, discrimination against Great Britain and other foreign countries and adoption of a uniform tariff (practically the American tariff). He insisted that, in any trade arrangement, assimilation of the Canadian and American tariffs and discrimination against Great Britain were necessary. He elaborated a plan for a complete commercial union which the Canadians said they could not accept and which Edward Farrer later described as the result of a policy to induce Canada to elect to enter the Union in order to avoid starvation.[36]

Blaine also declined to accept an offer for reciprocal removal of all duties on fish and fish products and on all containers or coverings, and he refused to consider a proposal for reciprocal opening of the privileges of the coasting trade on the Atlantic and the Lakes.[37]

On February 15 the conference reached an agreement to cooperate in efforts to adjust several subjects of controversy. It agreed to a proposal to appoint a joint commission of two experts to report upon complaints of American poaching in the fisheries of Canadian waters of the Great Lakes, for which Canada sought protection through some arrangement under joint legislation. It agreed that this commission should consider and report upon suitable restrictions and regulations to prevent destructive fishing in contiguous waters, to prevent pollution and obstruction detrimental to fisheries and navigation therein, and to provide for preservation and increase of fish life by restocking and replenishing the waters with fish ova. It also cooperated in agreements for a joint survey of the boundary between Alaska and the British possessions of British Columbia and Northwest Canada, from 54°40′ north latitude to the meridian of 141° west longitude, and for the appointment of two commissioners to decide upon a method of marking more accurately the boundary in the waters of Passamaquoddy Bay in front of and adjacent to Eastport, Maine.[38]

Toward the close of the conference, after the discussion of other questions (including the Alaska boundary and concurrent jurisdiction concerning wrecking regulations on the Lakes), Blaine made a strong torrential protest against the Canadian discrimination in tolls on the Welland Canal, a subject suggested to him by Foster. In vehement language he characterized these tolls as a plain and unjustifiable violation of Article XXVII of the treaty of 1871. In the Canadian reply he felt that he had the friendly assurance or promise that the objectionable discriminations would be removed by withdrawal of the toll rebate which gave preference to the port of Montreal. On February 18 he announced that the Canadian commissioners had given assurances that the question of withdrawal of the discriminations would receive prompt consideration. He soon found, however, that in their sanguine assurances they had left the impression of a promise which they could not fulfill, because of difficulties which they reported in the following June on a second visit to Washington.[39]

At Washington, in the month following the earlier conferences J. W. Foster was also in touch with Goldwin Smith of Toronto, who courteously suggested that the chief object of the Conservative Canadian visitors was to strengthen their political party, and who sought from the Washington government some expression favorable to the Canadian Liberal party which he regarded as the indispensable organ of progress in Canada.[40]

In the debates in the Canadian Commons, following the publication of the Canadian report of the Washington conferences, the Conservatives greeted with "deafening cheers" the statement that reciprocity was dead.[41]

Later, at London, Earl Grey urged that the Canadian government should plan to guard against injury from the McKinley tariff by seeking a remedy in free trade and new openings for trade elsewhere, and not by resort to retaliatory duties which he thought would increase the damage to Canada.[42]

In April, 1892, Blaine was embarrassed by a Canadian report that he had told Tupper that Bond, in the interview at Washington, had expressed the intention of the Newfoundland government to exclude Canadians from bait. He promptly telegraphed to Bond a denial, in which he had the supporting evidence of Pauncefote who was present at the Blaine-Bond conference.[43]

Following the Anglo-American conferences of February, the President delayed to send to Congress a report of the conference discussions which was prepared by John W. Foster. In this delay he was influenced by the desire to avoid any action which might be construed as an effort to aggravate the situation resulting from the Bering Sea seals question which was still pending. In fact he did not receive a written report from Foster until April 15.[44]

Meantime the American government received further complaints that Canada had not modified its canal-tolls practice and a suggestion of the question whether introduction of a retaliatory bill in Congress was advisable. Later, after learning that a new Canadian order in council (on April 4) had reenacted the rebate provisions, he complained in an informal conference with the British minister who consequently proposed a Washington visit of members of the Canadian ministry to discuss anew the question of removal of the discriminating tolls.[45]

On June 3, in response to the desire of the British minister, Blaine (again aided by Foster) held another conference with two of the Canadian commissioners, Mackenzie Bowell and George E. Foster. He again declined to agree to reciprocity limited to exchange of natural products and insisted that the arrangement should include an important list of manufactured articles. Concerning the question of the adjustment of the canal-tolls controversy, he received from the Canadians an explanation that they had intended no assurance beyond the promise that the American complaint would be considered by the Canadian ministry, and an acknowledgment that they had been remiss in their failure to advise the American government of the decision of the Dominion government. Requesting a proposition by which an understanding might be reached, he was surprised by the reply that the canal tolls and rebates, although arranged to favor the export route through Montreal, were not regarded as discriminations against Americans nor as in violation of either the letter or the spirit of Article XXVII of the treaty of 1871. In response to this statement he urged that the discrimination against American ports and lines of transportation to the seaboard was in plain violation of Article XXVII, and that the conduct of Canada was in marked and unfavorable contrast to that of the United States which allowed free transit through its Great Lakes canals to all commerce without regard to route to the sea. On the following day, the day on which he resigned from the office of Secretary of State, he declined to entertain the Canadian proposal to modify the order in council "by allowing the transshipment in American ports of cargoes destined for Montreal without loss of rebate" on condition that the American government would agree to allow to Canadian vessels free navigation of the Hudson from the end of the New York State canals to New York City.

He also received from the Canadians a tentative suggestion (not a formal offer) that an adjustment of the canal tolls might be reached by abolition of all rebates, on both the Welland and St. Lawrence canals, on condition that the United States would assure Canada of the continued free use of the Sault Ste. Marie Canal and the revival of the transshipment arrangement (Article XXX) of the treaty of 1871. To this he replied that Canada was still bound by Article XXVII after the termination of Article XXX and could not reasonably expect the United States to yield to suggestions of further concessions. Before the close of the conference he had the assurance that the question of the removal of the tolls rebate would be resubmitted promptly to the Dominion ministry with a view to the presentation of a new proposition to the American government within two weeks—a proposition which was never formulated.[46]

Finding that the Canadian ministry had declined to withdraw the unequal rebate of canal tolls, the President in a message of June 20 submitted to Congress a recommendation of deliberate but prompt steps to secure the just rights of American citizens. This he supplemented on June 28 by an explanation that the American termination of Article XXX could not properly be regarded as a penalty for the Canadian canal policy. In a message of July 1 to the Senate he asserted that discrimination was the purpose, and not the incident, of Canadian regulation; and he declared that the American government could not yield to the suggestion of further American concessions to secure treaty rights for which it had already given a consideration.

Secretary Foster, who (on June 29) had succeeded Blaine, promptly notified Pauncefote of the President's action. Thereby he evidently hastened British and Canadian efforts for partial adjustment.[47] On July 19, before action by Congress, he received from Herbert a personal note announcing the revocation of the Canadian discriminatory order which had excluded from the benefit of the rebate tolls in the St. Lawrence canals the grain cargoes originating in American ports on Lake Ontario and "destined for export from Montreal or a port further eastward." He replied that the removal had no practical benefit.[48]

On July 20 a committee of the House recommended a bill to vest in the President the power to regulate the tolls on the Sault Ste. Marie as a means to secure American rights. In justification it stated that all efforts to secure a just interpretation of treaty rights had been met by Canada in a spirit of evasion, avoidance and delay. The House acted promptly upon the recommendation, which was also accepted by the Senate. At the same time, by the Hitt resolution which especially contemplated investigation of the Canadian Pacific Railway, it requested the President to submit information concerning regulations as to bonded transit of American goods or merchandise across Canadian territory from one American port to another (under Article XXIX of the treaty of 1871), whether further legislation was necessary, whether careful inspection of such merchandise should be made at frontiers on departure and arrival, and whether a custodian of customs should accompany each car as an inspector at the expense of the foreign carrier. Meantime, Senator Frye had introduced a bill proposing to prohibit the transportation of goods through the United States in Canadian cars and, in certain contingencies, to suspend the transportation of Canadian goods in bond to or from any American port.[49]

On July 26 the President approved a mandatory, retaliatory act of Congress to enforce reciprocal commercial relations. By it, if the Canadian government continued to discriminate against Americans in the use of the Welland Canal, he was authorized to suspend the right of Canadian free passage through St. Marys Falls Canal so far as it related to Canadian vessels or to cargoes or passengers in transit to Canadian ports, and to collect tolls not to exceed two dollars per ton for freight and five dollars for each passenger. Under this authority he acted promptly, but not precipitately. On August 20, after a brief period of friendly delay and after learning that Canada contemplated no relief for the current season of canal navigation, he issued a proclamation suspending Canadian free passage through the St. Marys Canal for a period no longer than that of the Canadian discriminations, and establishing temporarily a toll of twenty cents per ton on all freight passing through it in transit to any Canadian port.

On August 24, in reply to a British belated notice that Canada would agree not to re-adopt its canal policy for the next season on condition that the President refrain from enforcing the proposed tolls on the St. Marys Canal, Foster submitted to Herbert a reminder that the American government was not responsible for the "grave difficulties" concerning unneighborly canal tolls which since 1888 it had sought to avoid by repeated remonstrances and protests. Referring to the popular support of the American policy, he declared: "Until the Canadian government is prepared to resume its obligations under the treaty there can be found no safe basis of friendly commercial intercourse." [50]

Thereafter, the American discussion of the question of Canadian canal tolls was part of a broader discussion of bonded transit and other problems of trade and neighborhood relations.

Among the problems of neighborhood relations which remained unsettled was the question of preventing illegal Chinese immigration via the Canadian border. In August–September, 1892, recognizing that the situtaion had become serious by the encouragement given to this immigration by the transportation facilities of the Canadian Pacific Railway to Chicago and Detroit and other points, Foster submitted a complaint to the British legation. He requested an immediate investigation and invited a "prompt response befitting the friendly intercourse of the two countries." Early in October he instructed Lincoln at London to ask whether the Canadian Privy Council had declined the American overtures (of October 22, 1890) for a special convention on the subject. Late in November he received a reply which largely relieved the Canadian Pacific from the imputation of unfriendliness, denying that it sold to Chinese through tickets from China to the States, and also denying the reported congregating of Chinese at Vancouver to await opportunities to enter the United States. The Canadian denial of any foundation for assertions of Canadian indifference to the enforcement of the American law, however, Foster could not accept. He stated that his assertions had "abundant foundation in the silence with which the Canadian authorities treated the proposal . . . nearly two years ago, inviting negotiations." [51]

In the following December, in the regular annual message to Congress, the President expressed regret that in many of the controversies with Canada the negotiations with the British government had been thwarted or retarded continuously by "unreasonable and unfriendly objections and protests from Canada." He suggested that, if the political relations of Canada and the disposition of the Canadian government should remain unchanged, the American government (without any disposition to interfere with Canadian political relations) should undertake a somewhat radical revision of its trade relations. Referring to the competition of Canadian railway lines for American traffic and the sustenance of these lines by commerce originating or terminating (or both) in the United States, and to American opportunity for greater trade advantages, he suggested a consideration of the question whether American interchanges upon lines of land transportation should be put upon a different basis. He also suggested that entire American independence of Canadian canals and the St. Lawrence, as an outlet to the sea, should be secured by construction of an American canal around Niagara Falls and by the opening of ship communication between the Great Lakes and one of the American seaports. Advocating American withdrawal of the support which Canadian railways and steamship lines had unfairly obtained from American traffic, he suggested that a consideration of the propriety of a modification or abrogation of the treaty article concerning transit in bond was probably involved in any compete solution of the question.[52]

Following this message, which was regarded as "vigorously anti-Canadian in tone," reporters for the newspapers announced a possible "complete disintegration of relations between the United States and Canada." In this premature opinion, based partly upon views expressed by several members of Congress, they were probably influenced by certain recent proposals to abrogate or modify the Anglo-American agreement of 1817—proposals which resulted chiefly from the recent decision of the Navy Department that the agreement prevented the acceptance of lower bids offered by Lakes firms for construction of naval practice vessels, and which produced a temporary general discussion terminating in the conclusion that an attempt at modification at that time might invite serious and disadvantageous complications.[53]

Near the end of December, somewhat provoked by a report or memorandum of the Canadian Minister of Railways, Foster in the interest of a clear understanding was again tempted into a renewal of unpleasant controversy. In his reply (to Pauncefote) to sustain his assertion that the Canadian government had pursued an "unneighborly course," he intimated that the discriminating canal tolls were conceived as a retaliation for American refusal to concede to Canadians the free navigation of the Hudson River. He contradicted the allegations that for five years after the treaty of 1871 Canadian vessels were denied their treaty privilege to use the New York State canals. He also denied any treaty basis for Canadian efforts to obtain the free navigation of the Hudson, the use of which by Canada (he said) probably had not been considered in the conferences and negotiations of 1871. As a preliminary to an appeal for exertions to secure a better understanding upon a basis of a faithful observance of treaty obligations, he declared that the American government, fully convinced of the justice of its claims, could not consent to purchase a compliance with a solemn treaty stipulation by grant of a further concession not required or contemplated by the treaty.[54]

In the adoption of a tolls policy at the Sault Ste. Marie Canal the American government planned only to hasten the adjustment of the question of Canadian canal tolls. In this it was successful. On February 13, 1893, Foster informed Pauncefote that, following satisfactory Canadian action concerning tolls on Canadian canals, the President would withdraw the Sault tolls. Immediately Canada adjusted the dispute by substitution of a more equitable schedule of charges at the Welland Canal, ten cents per ton upon cargoes of cereals bound to and from American ports by that route. It also changed its regulation by charging a single toll on either the Welland Canal or the St. Lawrence canals, and by making the latter free to cargoes which had paid the Welland toll. Five days later (on February 28) President Harrison suspended the retaliatory discriminating tolls upon British transit through the American Sault Ste. Marie.[55]

Meantime, on February 2, in reply to a House resolution of the previous July, President Harrison submitted to Congress a full review of the question of American treaty obligations concerning bonded transit. After a review of the legislation upon the whole subject of the transit of goods "from, to, or through Canada," he presented a brief summary of his conclusions.

He agreed with his predecessor that the transshipment provision of the treaty of 1871 (Article XXIX) was abrogated, or at least (by lack of legislation) was not operative. Stating that neither government had placed itself under restraint as to merchandise intended for its own people and coming from its own territory, he declared that the American government could unload and inspect every vehicle arriving at the American border with imported merchandise which had first arrived at a Canadian port for transportation to the United States, or every vehicle carrying merchandise from the United States through Canada to the United States. The question of sealing and examining cars, when they crossed the American border, he said was one to be settled by American laws according to American convenience and American interests. Referring to a practice by which American shipments from China and Japan (or any other non-contiguous country) through Canada (in cars sealed by the transportation company) were allowed to cross the border into the United States without any inspection except examination of the seals, he declared the system was unauthorized by the law which provided for sealing in Canada of cars containing merchandise imported from a contiguous country, and that it improperly favored Canadian ports of entry. With a view to prevention of possible frauds, by the introduction of Canadian products not subject to free entry, he recommended revision of the statutes. He especially recommended a declaration of policy to remedy certain conditions resulting in part from the construction of the Canadian Pacific Railway which was free to offer competitive rates unfair to American railways. For a time, however, the American railways, possibly influenced by the populist spirit of antagonism in the West, feared to press the matter upon Congress.[56]

Parallel with the questions of canal tolls and bonded transit was the question of aid to wrecked vessels on the Lakes. By act of May 24, 1890, amendatory of an earlier act of June 19, 1878, Congress provided for common wrecking and salvage privileges to aid vessels wrecked or disabled in the waters conterminous to the United States and the Dominion of Canada, the Welland Canal, the water improvements between Lake Erie and Lake Huron, the St. Marys River and the Sault Ste. Marie Canal. This act was subject to concurrent Canadian legislation. In July, 1892, following the reception of a copy of the Canadian reciprocal act of May 10, Foster asked assurance that the latter would be applied to all Canadian waters as provided in the American act. He also explained that, after the President's proclamation, the Treasury Department would issue instructions that the "aid and assistance" provided in the act would include "all necessary towing" incident thereto, unrestricted by coasting and customs laws. Later, learning that the Canadian government denied that any salvage operations by American vessels in the Welland Canal were authorized by the Canadian wrecking act, he urged that the canals and other improved connecting waters were logically incidental to contiguous waters, and declared that the President was powerless to omit them from the reciprocal arrangement. A few days later, in a note to the Lake Carriers' Association, he expressed his hope of reaching an understanding with the British legation.[57]

In September, not satisfied with the British construction of the Canadian wrecking act, Foster explained that, in view of experience with Canadian authorities, the President could not issue a proclamation for enforcement of the American wrecking act until he was advised that the reciprocal privileges applied to the Welland Canal as fully as to other connecting waterways. Late in the following December, although the Canadian Minister of Railways and Canals had admitted that distress of a temporary nature should be within the purview of the intended reciprocity if not otherwise provided, he was requested by the Lakes Carriers' Association to secure from Congress an amendment to the statute of 1890 by an omission of the reference to the Welland Canal. After another effort to open the way to an agreement with Pauncefote, he apparently referred the Lake Carriers' request to Congress, which later provided for the requested omission by an amendatory clause in the appropriation act of March 3, 1893.[58]

On March 24, Foster's successor (Gresham), in a note inviting an immediate and modified disposition of the subject, suggested the expediency of a consistent extension of the concurrent legislation to the lesser casualties to which tugs and their tows and self-propelled vessels were liable in the confined and shallow waters of canals. In the following July, while still awaiting a reply and with a friendly desire to avoid any appearance of trying to force an unwilling reply, he advised the President to put the American wrecking act in force without further delay. In this advice he was influenced by the expectation that American navigation in the Welland Canal would be treated in the just and liberal spirit foreshadowed in letters of the Canadian Minister of Railways and Canals.[59] On July 17, acting under the legislative provisions of Congress and in accord with a Canadian concurrent order (in council) of May 17, 1893, the President proclaimed that Canadian vessels and wrecking appliances had the privilege of aiding Canadian and other vessels and property wrecked or disabled or in distress in American waters contiguous to Canada, including the canals and water improvements connecting Lake Huron with Lake Erie and Lake Superior.[60]

Probably the most important act of the Harrison administration concerning problems in Canadian relations was the negotiation of a convention of February, 1892, under which the Bering Sea fur-seals controversy (treated in the next chapter) was arbitrated at Paris early in the succeeding Cleveland administration.[61]

REFERENCES

1. *28 G.B., Instrs.*, pp. 458–61, No. 791, Feb. 17, 1888; *Laurier Papers, Cor. 1870–91*, pp. 963–65, L. H. Davies to James G. Blaine, May 4, 1889, Strictly Confidential.
2. *29 G.B., Instrs.*, p. 183, Tel., Dec. 30, 1889; I. N. Ford, *Tropical Am.*, p. 395; *Ib.*, p. 251.
3. *23 Cong. Record*, 52–1, p. 285, Jan. 13, 1892.
4. *State Dept. Pamphlets, U.S. and G.B., Political Rels.*, I; *Ib.*, I, No. 21,043; *Sen. Rps.*, 51–1, pp. 4 and 885–934, July 21, 1890; *Parlia. Debates*, Mar. 7, 1892, pp. 175–80.
5. *152 N. Am. Rev.*, May, 1891, pp. 557–66; *153 N. Am. Rev.*, Oct., 1891, pp. 468–80.
6. *3 Reciprocity Treaties, 1898–1907, Canada* (Kasson), 23–27.

7. *Cong. Record,* 52–2, p. 1104; *State Dept. Pamphs., Reciprocity,* I, No. 14,445; *14 Public Opinion,* Jan. 14, 1893, p. 349; *Ib.,* Feb. 11, p. 442; *4 Am. Jour. of Politics,* Dec., 1893, and Feb., 1894 (pp. 201–13 and 132–37).
8. *3 Bookman,* June, 1896, pp. 333–36; Mayor N. S. Boynton of Port Huron, Mich., to J. M. Callahan, Oct. 12, 1896; Interviews of the writer with G. Smith and others at Toronto, Aug., 1896.
9. *153 N. Am. Rev.* (1891), p. 468 *et seq.; 30 G.P., Instrs.,* p. 112, Tel., Nov. 11, 1892.
10. *29 G.B., Instrs.,* pp. 215–17, No. 193, Feb. 25, 1892; *Ib.,* p. 234, No. 220, Mar. 25; RICHARDSON, IX, 35.
11. MALLOY, I, 740–43; *21 G.B., Notes to,* p. 182, Feb. 19, 1890; *29 G.B., Instrs.,* pp. 215–17 and 234, Nos. 193 and 220, Feb. 25 and Mar. 25, 1890.
12. *21 G.B., Notes to,* p. 643; *120 G.B., Notes from,* June 11, 1892.
13. *22 G.B., Notes to,* pp. 162–63, Aug. 10, 1892.
14. *30 G.B., Instrs.,* p. 78, No. 910, Oct. 7, 1892; *Ib.,* p. 118, No. 969, Nov. 21; *Ib.,* p. 166, No. 1042, Jan. 21, 1893.
15. *21 Cong. Record,* 51–1, p. 9455, Sept. 1, 1890.
16. *150 U.S.,* p. 249 (1893); *197 Domestic Letters,* p. 118; *200 Dom. Letters,* p. 121; MOORE, *Int. Law Dig.,* I, 672–75.
17. *21 G.B., Notes to,* pp. 285–88, June 22, 1892; *22 G.B., Notes to,* p. 24, Tel., July 27.
18. MALLOY, I, 105; *21 G.B., Notes to,* pp. 573–75, Dec. 19, 1891; *29 G.B., Instrs.,* pp. 586–88, No. 656, Dec. 19, 1891; *30 G.B., Instrs.,* pp. 594–96, No. 424, June 15, 1894; *Ib.,* pp. 667–68, No. 493, Aug., 1894; *F.R., 1892,* pp. 221–27, 240, 257.
19. *H. Rp.,* 52–1, Feb. 1, 1892; *Misc. Letters,* Mar. 11; *185 Domestic Letters,* Mar. 18.
20. *Overland Mo.,* Oct., 1889, pp. 414–28 (JAMES O'MEARA, *The Union or the Dominion*); *Sen. Rps.,* 51–1, No. 1530, July 21, 1890, pp. 84– , 874– , 921–22, 933– , 980– and 1149; *Ib.,* No. 1531 (Vol. 10), pp. 937–1224; *Ib.,* No. 847 (Vol. IV), May 3, 1890; RICHARDSON, IX, 315; *Ib.,* 43–1, No. 307 (Windom report on transportation routes to the seaboard); *3A Reciprocity Treaties, 1898–99* (KASSON), *Rp. of Repub. Club of N. Y. City,* Jan. 18, 1897.
21. *H. Misc. Docs.,* 51–1, Vol. 16, No. 195, May 2, 1890; *H. Rps.,* 51–1, Vol. 6, No. 1870, May 2, 1890; *21 Cong. Record,* 51–1, p. 9454, Sept. 1, 1890.
22. SKELTON, *Life and Times of Sir Wilfrid Laurier,* I, 411–14; *Laurier Papers, Cor. 1870–91,* pp. 963–65, L. H. Davies to James G. Blaine, May 4, 1889.
23. *Macdonald Papers, Commercial Relations with the U.S. and Nickel, 1890–91,* p. 147, Jan. 19, 1890; *Ib.,* p. 19, Apr. 21.
24. *Ib.,* pp. 23–26, Confidential, May 4, 1890.

25. *Ib.*, pp. 162–65, Aug. 1, 1890, pp. 150–55, Aug. 23.
26. *Ib.*, pp. 153–54, Sept. 2, 1890 (and inclosure); *21 Cong. Record, 51–1*, p. 9454, Sept. 1; *Macdonald Papers, Com'l. Rels. with the U.S. and Nickel*, pp. 173–74, Sept. 29; *Ib.*, pp. 178–80, Private, Nov. 11, 1890.
27. *Ib.*, pp. 29–30, Dec. 16, 1890.
28. *33 G.B., Instrs.*, pp. 283–90, No. 241, Nov. 10, 1899; FOSTER, *Dipl. Memoirs*, II, 178; SHORTT and DOUGHTY, IX, 173 and 175; *Sen. Exec. Docs.*, 52–1, Vol. 6, No. 114, Jan. 20, 1892, pp. 3 and 43.
29. *Ib.*, pp. 3–5.
30. *Toronto Globe*, Nov. 20, 1891; SHORTT and DOUGHTY, IX, 167; FOSTER, *Dipl. Memoirs*, II, 179.
31. SKELTON, *Life and Times of Sir Wilfrid Laurier*, I, 418.
32. *132 N. Am. Rev.*, Oct., 1892, pp. 468–69.
33. *23 Cong. Record*, 52–1, pp. 612–15.
34. *21 G.B., Notes to*, p. 593, Feb. 1, 1892.
35. *Ib.*, p. 537, Oct. 10, 1891; *Misc. Letters*, Sept. 18, 1891; *H. Exec. Docs.*, 52–1, Vol. 6, No. 114; *H. Rps.*, 52–1, Vol. 10, No. 1957, July 20, 1892.
36. *Exec. Docs.*, 52–1, No. 44; *3 Reciprocity Treaties, 1898–1907, Canada* (KASSON), No. 28, pp. 29–30; *House of Commons Debates, 7th Parl., 2nd Sess.*, Mar. 28, 1892, pp. 363–66; *U. S. Tariff Com., Reciproc. and Commercial Treaties* (1919), p. 24; *25 Forum*, Aug., 1898, pp. 652–53.
37. *Sen. Exec. Docs.*, 52–1, No. 114; *3 Reciprocity Treaties, 1898–1907, Canada* (KASSON), No. 28, pp. 29–30.
38. *Ib.*, June 6, 1892; SHORTT and DOUGHTY, IX, 183.
39. *Sen. Exec. Docs.*, 52–1, Vol. 6, No. 114; FOSTER, *Dipl. Memoirs*, II, 180–82; *22 G.B., Notes to*, pp. 221–24, Dec. 31, 1892; *Misc. Letters.*
40. *J. W. Foster Papers*, Mar. 3, 1892; *3 Reciprocity Treaties, 1898–1907, Canada*, March 21, 1892.
41. *Ib.*, J. D. Edgar to J. W. Foster, Mar. 23, 1892.
42. EARL GREY, *Commercial Relations of the Br. Colonies and the McKinley Tariff* (1892).
43. *21 G.B., Notes to*, p. 698, Tel., Apr. 7, 1892.
44. *3 Reciprocity Treaties, 1898–1907, Canada* (KASSON), Foster to J. D. Edgar, Mar. 26, 1892; *Ib.*, Foster to the President, June 6; *Sen. Exec. Docs.*, 52–1, No. 114, pp. 3 and 43.
45. *Ib.*; *Misc. Letters*, Feb. 12, Mar. 11 and Apr. 12, 1892; *3 Reciprocity Treaties, 1898–1907, Canada* (KASSON), Foster to the President, June 6, 1892.
46. *Ib.*; *Sen. Exec. Docs.*, 52–1, Vol. 6, No. 114.
47. *Ib.*; RICHARDSON, IX, 240–42; MALLOY, I, 712–13 and 243; *21 G.B., Notes to*, p. 697, July 2, 1892; *F.R., 1892.*

48. *22 G.B., Notes to,* p. 14, July 19, 1892.
49. *H. Rps.,* 52–1, Vol. 10, No. 1957; *Sen. Exec. Docs.,* 52–2, Vol. 2, No. 40, Feb. 3, 1893; *23 Cong. Record,* 52–1, pp. 5483, 6428, 6680, 6950 (June 25, July 19 and 30, 1892).
50. Richardson, IX, 290–92; *22 G.B., Notes to,* pp. 164–65, Aug. 24, 1892.
51. *30 G.B., Instrs.,* p. 76, No. 906, Sept. 7 and Oct. 6, 1892; *22 G.B., Notes to,* p. 167, Oct. 3.
52. Richardson, IX, 313–15.
53. *Exec. Docs.,* 52–1, No. 95, May 6, 1892; *Ib.,* 52–2, No. 9, Dec. 7, 1892, p. 34; *Journal of the Senate,* Apr. 8; *N. Y. Recorder,* Mar. 8, 1892; *Chicago Tribune,* Apr. 9; *Washington Post,* Dec. 8, 9, 22, 24, 25, 27.
54. *22 G.B., Notes to,* pp. 221–24, Dec. 31, 1892.
55. *Ib.,* p. 259, Feb. 13, 1893; *Ib.,* pp. 267–68, Feb. 21; *Ib.,* p. 272, Feb. 27.
56. *Sen. Exec. Docs.,* 52–2, Vol. 2, No. 40, Feb. 2; Richardson, IX, 335–46; *3A Reciprocity Treaties, 1898–99, Canada,* Jan. 18, 1897.
57. *21 G.B., Notes to,* p. 698, July 9, 1892; *22 G.B., Notes to,* p. 162, Aug. 2; *Misc. Register,* Aug. 2 and 10.
58. *22 G.B., Notes to,* p. 166, Sept. 6, 1892; *Ib.,* pp. 285–90, Mar. 24, 1893.
59. *Ib.,* pp. 358–59, July 24, 1893.
60. Richardson, IX, 396–98 (July 17, 1893).
61. Malloy, I, 746–50.

CHAPTER XVIII

THE BERING SEA FUR-SEALS CONTROVERSY AND AFTER

AT the close of President Harrison's administration the famous Bering Sea fur-seals controversy, which first arose in the previous administration, reached a situation which demanded early adjustment to prevent further increase of hostile feeling.

This controversy arose from the American claim to the right to exercise exclusive authority in the extraterritorial waters of the eastern part of Bering Sea in the protection of the herds of seals which during the summers resided on the Pribilof Islands and reared their young there. This claim to jurisdiction beyond the three-mile limit of the islands was based upon three main lines of argument: (1) the interpretation of the Alaska treaty of 1867 defining the western water limit; (2) the precedent Russian system of protection in which Great Britain had acquiesced; and (3) the continuation of this system in American practice.[1]

Congress, by act of July 27, 1868, required the Secretary of the Treasury to prevent the killing of fur seals within the limits of the new acquisition. Two years later, by act of July 1, 1870, it directed him to lease for twenty years, at an annual rental of not less than $50,000, the right to take on two Pribilof islands a limited number of fur seals annually within a limited season (June–October). Under this law the Alaskan Commercial Company (a private corporation) obtained a lease under which it conducted the sealing industry, under protective conditions adopted from the Russian period of control. For over a decade it encountered no difficulty from attempts to violate the regulations by which its monopoly was protected.

In 1885, following the completion of the Canadian Pacific

Railway, the American government was requested by the Alaska Commercial Company to protect the decreasing herd against sealing vessels which about 1880 had begun to pursue them along the coast northward toward the Pribilof Islands, and which later had pushed the pursuit to the vicinity of the islands where they could conveniently watch for the opportunity to continue the slaughter of the female seals whenever the latter temporarily left the islands on sea trips to search for fish-food. Influenced by the solicitation of the Alaska company, which was represented by a lobbyist at Washington, the Secretary of the Treasury sent to its revenue-cutter service a copy of its usual annual instructions, which were interpreted as an authorization of seizures.

In this way, in 1886–87, the American government became responsible for seizing on the "high seas" a few Canadian vessels (from Victoria), which (with their cargoes) were promptly condemned by the American court at Sitka on the ground that pelagic sealing in Bering Sea east of 193° was a violation of the act of Congress making illegal the killing of seals within the limits of Alaska or the waters thereof.[2]

Following British protests and presentation of claims for damages, Secretary Bayard, without discussing the grounds or legal aspects of the seizures, proposed an international arrangement for coöperation of the United States, Great Britain and Russia for better protection of the seals from extermination. Through E. J. Phelps, the American minister at London, he conducted with Salisbury negotiations which practically reached an agreement in 1888. The proposed agreement, however, failed to obtain the approval of the Canadian government, which probably was influenced by the failure of the American Senate to approve the draft treaty for settlement of the Atlantic fisheries controversy, and which suddenly requested the British government to suspend further negotiations.[3]

In connection with the negotiations Phelps in an official interview (of November 11, 1887) obtained from Salisbury a cordial agreement that "a code of regulations should be adopted for the preservation of the seals from destruction at improper times by improper means." Later, in February, 1888, after other interviews in which the Russian ambassador participated and in answer to Salisbury's request, he submitted regulations (for a closed season from April 15 to November 1 between 160° and 170° west longitude) which the American government desired to establish by a mutual concurrent arrangement between the governments interested, and to which Salisbury assented. In the following April the American government was further assured by Salisbury's suggestion to extend the regulations to the whole of Bering Sea and to the portions of the Okhotsk Sea and the Pacific Ocean north of 27° north latitude, and by his promise to submit a form of draft convention which he proposed to make effective by a British Order in Council. It had no reason to doubt that the whole dispute was practically settled. Five days later (on April 28), however, White was notified that the necessary Order in Council and Act of Parliament could not be drafted "until Canada is heard from." On June 20, after repeated inquiries, he learned from Salisbury that Canada in reply to an urgent telegram had agreed to consider the matter at once. On July 28 Phelps cabled Bayard his fear that Canadian opposition would prevent the expected convention. On September 12, after other interviews at which he pressed for a completion of the convention, he forwarded Salisbury's statement that the Canadian government objected to the proposed restrictions.[4]

In December of the following year, after other efforts to establish by international coöperation measures for prevention of the extermination of the seals, President Cleveland announced his hope soon to submit for approval of the Senate an effective conventional arrangement with the maritime powers.[5]

Later, in 1889, Secretary Blaine resumed negotiations at Washington by conferences with Pauncefote and the Russian representative with a view to an arrangement for protection of both American and Russian herds of seals. Finally, in January, 1890, after additional seizures of Canadian vessels and consequent increase of Canadian excitement, and in response to repeated British protests against the seizures for which damages were claimed, he undertook to defend the seizures and the condemnation of the Canadian vessels on the ground that they were engaged in a pursuit which was *contra bonos mores*. In a brilliant discussion with Lord Salisbury he also submitted allegations that Russia, with the acquiescence of Great Britain, had treated Bering Sea as a *mare clausum* and had issued and enforced rules against pelagic sealing. These allegations were not sustained by authentic documents, and they later caused the American government considerable embarrassment in connection with the presentation of its case before the arbitration tribunal.[6]

Claiming that Canadian methods of taking the fur seal destroyed the power of reproduction and would eventually result in the extermination of the species, Blaine urged that such violations of the common rights of mankind were preventable under the principles of the law of nations. He declared that American forcible resistance to Canadian lawlessness in Bering Sea seal fishing was demanded "not only by the necessity of defending the traditional and long established rights of the United States, but also [in defense of] the rights of good morals and of good government the world over." He hoped that all friendly nations would "concede to the United States the same rights and privileges on the lands and waters of Alaska" which they had always conceded to the empire of Russia.[7]

In March and April Blaine held several conferences with M. De Struve of the Russian legation, and with Pauncefote and Charles H. Tupper (the Canadian minister of marine and fisheries); but he could reach no agreement.

Later, after deciding that an immediate agreement with the British was not possible, he continued to expect the coöperation of Russia. This hope was based upon conferences with M. Rosen, the Russian representative at Washington, who apparently favored his proposal of a plan for an American and Russian concurrent proclamation forbidding the killing of seals in Bering Sea and for use of a joint police force if necessary, but it was never encouraged by the Russian government, which (according to Rosen's memoirs) decided that the plan might result in complications with leading maritime powers.[8]

At first Blaine recognized a disposition of Pauncefote to reach a reasonable and friendly adjustment on practically the same basis as that previously suggested by Salisbury, and without American presentation of any obstacle such as the *mare clausum* doctrine. Suddenly, however, he found that negotiations were again halted by the interposition of Canada. On April 30, 1890, he received from Pauncefote a proposal for a mixed commission of experts to decide the questions at issue, and also a proposition that pelagic sealing should be prohibited in Bering Sea only during the months of May, June, October, November and December, and that British vessels should be allowed to kill seals within ten miles of the Pribilof Islands. To the latter proposition he (and the Russian minister) objected. He maintained that the proposed open season of June and July and August was one in which the area around the islands was most crowded with female seals hunting food for their young, and that the Canadian respect of the ten mile limit would be the same as that of a wolf for a flock of sheep located so that no shepherd could guard them.[9]

On May 29, expressing surprise at Salisbury's protest against the American policy in Bering Sea, Blaine stated that the British position and policy had changed by the demands of Canada with whose laws the British executive could interfere. He protested "against the course of the British government in authorizing, encouraging and protecting vessels which are not only interfering with American rights in Bering Sea, but which are doing violence as well to the rights of the civilized world." Determined to find a suitable time to continue undisturbed the delayed negotiations, he submitted as a preparation for friendlier relations the President's proposal that the British government should agree not to permit Canadian vessels to enter Bering Sea for the season.[10]

On June 2, he submitted to Pauncefote the President's statement that arbitration, which was of little value unless conducted with careful deliberation, could not be concluded in time for the season. Therefore he submitted an anxious and friendly inquiry whether Salisbury, in order to promote a friendly solution, would agree to establish for a single season the regulation which in 1888 he had agreed to make permanent. In reply he received a prompt and unexpected rejection. On

June 4 he expressed the President's disappointment at Salisbury's change of views. A few days later (June 9) he received from Pauncefote the statement of Salisbury that the British government had no power to exclude British or Canadian ships from any portion of the high seas without legislative sanction, and that it must hold the American government responsible for the consequences which might ensue from acts contrary to the established principles of international law.[11]

In a lengthy note of June 30 Blaine argued that the Pacific Ocean did not include Bering Sea. He stated that both the United States and Great Britain (by the treaties of 1824 and 1825 with Russia) had acquiesced in the Russian jurisdictional claims north of the parallel of 60°. In reply he received a statement of denial (of August 2) in which Salisbury proposed arbitration. Later, on December 17, he declared that the American government had never demanded that Bering Sea be pronounced a *mare clausum,* and that it expressly disavowed such a claim. Possibly (as later suggested by John W. Foster) the fallacies in his earlier argument on American jurisdiction over Bering Sea were due to "false assertion of historical facts and erroneous judicial decisions put forth during the preceding administration."[12]

In the later discussion Blaine declared that the American claim to the right to protect the seals did not require arguments of American sovereignty over Bering Sea. He contended that the United States, by its property right in the Pribilof seal herd and its interest in the sealing industry, was entitled to preserve the herd from destruction in the water of Bering Sea, even by force if necessary. He asserted that the law of the sea should not be perverted to justify immoral acts such as the destruction of American seals while swimming in search of food. This doctrine of right of property in the seals had already been suggested by General B. F. Tracy, Secretary of the Navy, who later prepared upon the subject an exhaustive study which served as the basis of the American contention before the arbitration tribunal. It was founded upon the idea that seals were domestic animals; and it was strongly opposed by the British who, influenced by the protests of the Canadian government, urged that the American government could not properly exercise jurisdiction over wild animals in waters beyond the three-mile limit of territorial waters.[13]

Confronted with a hopeless disagreement in the Blaine-Salisbury correspondence, the Harrison administration was unwilling either to abandon the American jurisdictional claim and pay the damages claimed for seizure of the Canadian vessels or to reject the British protests and continue a policy of seizures which would not justify the hazard of war between friendly English-speaking neighbors. By cabinet agreement it wisely adopted a policy of arbitration. This policy, which was proposed by the British government, met with general approval.

On December 17, 1890, after renewing and amplifying the arguments concerning Russian jurisdiction over Bering Sea before 1867, Blaine proposed for arbitration five questions. Four of these were related to the jurisdictional rights of Russia and their transfer to the United States. The fifth was related to American fur-seal fishery rights in Bering Sea beyond ordinary territorial limits, whether obtained by Russian cession or as an incident to ownership of the breeding islands of the seals and the relation of the seal fisheries to American territorial possessions.[14]

In connection with later correspondence Blaine also suggested a *modus vivendi* for suspension or restriction of sealing pending the result of the proposed arbitration of the questions at issue. On May 4, 1891, he proposed to Pauncefote to limit both American and British seal-taking on the islands and in the waters of Bering Sea pending the arbitration of questions in controversy. On May 26, influenced by reports of departure of many Canadian sealers for the fishing grounds while American revenue cutters were still waiting for definite orders concerning their protective duties, he urged that the situation demanded prompt action. On June 9, after further correspondence on seals regulations, he expressed regret that Salisbury had suggested new conditions after the two governments had practically reached an agreement, and he insisted that negotiations should be brought to a speedy termination.[15]

On June 15, the American government (through Assistant

Secretary Wharton) signed with Pauncefote a sensible agreement for a temporary *modus vivendi* concerning the regulation of the seal fisheries until May, 1892, with a view to avoidance of irritating differences and the promotion of a friendly settlement of pending questions relating thereto.

On November 27 (1891) Blaine objected to Salisbury's proposed reservation that regulations should not be obligatory on Great Britain until accepted by other maritime powers—a proposal which was regarded as a material change in the arbitration terms already agreed upon.[16] On December 10, he intimated that the injection of new questions, which could have no effect except to exhaust the time allotted for arbitration, was only a pretext for further delay. Four days later he expressed to Pauncefote the President's matured conclusion that the arbitration should proceed on the seven points as agreed, without any change in their meaning in any particular.[17]

Finally, on December 18, 1891, Blaine and Pauncefote signed a preliminary agreement on the text of articles for insertion in the Bering Sea arbitration, and also another providing for the appointment of a joint commission of four (two by each government) to investigate and report all the facts concerning seal life and the measures necessary for proper protection and preservation. On February 29, 1892, they concluded a convention (framed by Foster) by which they agreed to submit to a judicial arbitration tribunal of seven jurists of distinguished reputation the settlement of the questions of American jurisdictional rights in Bering Sea, the preservation of the seals therein and the sealing rights of American and British citizens. This convention provided for the appointment of the arbitrators—two by the executive head of each of the contending governments, one by the President of France, one by the King of Italy and one by the King of Sweden and Norway. It designated that the selecting powers should be "requested to choose, if possible, jurists acquainted with the English language." It named Paris as the place of meeting.[18]

On February 24, 1892, near the end of the negotiations for arbitration, Blaine had submitted to Pauncefote a suggestion of the importance of an immediate arrangement for revival of the temporary *modus vivendi,* with more efficient measures for its execution during the pendency of arbitration. On March 22 Acting Secretary Wharton notified Pauncefote of the President's views of the extreme urgency and gravity of the situation, illustrated by the fact that already forty-seven Canadian vessels had hastened their departure for the sealing grounds in order "to escape notice of a possible *modus.*" Surprised and disappointed at the British assumption that another year of suspension of pelagic sealing was not necessary, and also at the suggestion that such restriction would furnish Canadian sealers a basis of claim for compensation, he presented considerations to support the American "just demand that property which is the subject of an agreed arbitration shall not be subjected to spoliation pending the arbitration." He declared that the American government could accept nothing less than a renewal of the *modus* of the previous year. On this point an agreement was promptly reached on April 18.[19]

On April 20, 1892, Blaine notified Pauncefote that the Senate had given its advice and consent to both the convention of February 29 for arbitration and the convention of April 18 for renewal of the *modus vivendi.*[20]

The members of the arbitration tribunal, chosen in accord with the arbitration convention, were as follows: Justice John M. Harlan of the United States Supreme Court; Senator John T. Morgan of the Committee on Foreign Relations of the American Senate; Lord Hannen of the British High Court of Justice; Sir John Thompson, Minister of Justice and Attorney-General of Canada; Baron Alphonse de Courcel of France; Marquis Emilio Visconti Venosta (a nephew of Cavour) of Italy; and Prime Minister Gregors Gram of Sweden and Norway. The American agent was John W. Foster, who in the preparation of the case was assisted by Robert Lansing (junior counsel). The British agent was Charles H. Tupper, son of Sir Charles Tupper. The senior American counsel was Edward J. Phelps. The associate counsel was James C. Carter. Another associate, Judge Henry M. Blodgett, was restricted in his service by impaired health. Assistants were Frederick R. Coudert and Robert Lansing. The senior British counsel was Sir Charles

Russell, Attorney-General of England (and later Chief Justice). His chief associate-counsel at Paris was Sir Richard E. Webster (later Baron Alverstone, Lord Chief Justice). These were assisted by Christopher Robinson of Canada.[21]

Foster, who had assisted Secretary Blaine in framing the treaty for arbitration and in the collection of the evidence for the American case, and who had continued the direction of the preparation of the case while discharging the duties of Secretary of State as successor of Blaine, continued his duties as agent under the Cleveland administration, at the special request of the American counsel and of W. Q. Gresham who had been selected as his successor as Secretary of State. He was fitted for his work both by his long diplomatic experience and by his careful study of the case.

After the presentation of the case Foster was much embarrassed by the discovery that a special clerk (Ivan Petroff) had submitted a fraudulent translation of some Russian documents—an imposition which was discovered by William C. Mayo, a regular clerk at the Department of State. He promptly explained the imposition, both to the British chargé at Washington and to the British agent, and hastened to correct the error by submitting to the British agent a revised translation.

The tribunal met informally at Paris on February 23, 1893, but adjourned for one month. It reassembled on March 23. It chose Baron de Courcel as president. Although M. Ribot, the French Minister of Foreign Affairs, had ventured to suggest that French was "still considered to be the diplomatic language of the world," it decided that the proceedings should be conducted in English. On July 10, following the admission of evidence and the presentation of oral arguments, it began its secret and confidential consideration of the case. On August 15, in open court, it announced its decision, against the American government on all points except on regulations for protection of the seals on the high seas.[22]

In the expectation of Russian assistance by proper moral support in the arbitration at Paris, based on previous Russian assurances of coöperation and identity of interest, the American government was disappointed. On June 21, through the

British presentation of a recent Anglo-Russian sealing agreement to the tribunal, it learned the reason for the Russian change of attitude. On July 14 Secretary Gresham wrote Foster of his conviction that Russia desired the American government to fail before the tribunal.[23]

The decision of the arbitrators on each of the five points submitted to them was as follows: (1) Russia after 1824 had never asserted or exercised any exclusive jurisdiction as to the seal fisheries in Bering Sea beyond the ordinary limit of territorial waters (decided by a vote of 6 to 1); (2) Great Britain had never recognized or conceded any such claim of Russian (decided by a vote of 6 to 1); (3) Bering Sea as used in the Anglo-Russian treaty of 1825 was included in the phrase "Pacific Ocean" (unanimous decision); (4) By the Russo-American Alaskan Treaty of 1867 all rights of Russia as to jurisdiction, and as to seal fisheries in Bering Sea east of the designated water boundary, were transferred unimpaired to the United States (unanimous decision); (5) The United States has not any right of protection or property in the seals in Bering Sea outside of the ordinary three-mile limit of the American islands which they frequent (decided by a vote of 5 to 2).

From the determination of these five questions the tribunal reached the conclusion that the concurrence of Great Britain with the United States was necessary to establish regulations for the proper protection and preservation of the fur seal in the Bering Sea. In accord with this conclusion it submitted concurrent regulations regarded as necessary to protect the seals from destruction. These restrictive regulations prescribed a closed season east of 180° and north of 35° from May 1 to July 31, established a permanent prohibited zone of sixty miles around the Pribilof Islands, forbade the use of firearms and explosives, and fixed other restrictions concerning vessels, licenses and fitness of the men employed. They were subject to concurrent modification every five years, or to abolition by agreement. They were more strict than the terms previously proposed by Bayard and Blaine; and, both in Canada and in the United States, they were regarded as practical evidence of an American victory from the standpoint of the main purpose of the American contention.

The tribunal, which also recommended further restrictive legislation, urged that each government should decide upon means necessary to make effective the regulations determined by the arbitral decision.[24]

Early in October, after receiving Bayard's confident opinion that an effective execution of the award would be agreed upon at an early date, Gresham wrote Foster that if the award had recognized the American right of property in the fur seals and the right to protect them, "there would have been little necessity for regulations."[25]

In the transition decade between the fur-seals arbitration and the Alaskan boundary arbitration arose a series of other American-Canadian questions which were subjects of considerable diplomatic discussion.

For several years the most pressing question was the establishment of a suitable arrangement for effective execution of the provisions of the award of 1893 in regard to regulations for the protection of the fur seals. The American government, which promptly forbade American citizens to engage in pelagic sealing, soon complained that the Canadian government failed to enact similar legislation. On November 21, 1893, Gresham instructed Bayard to press negotiations without waiting for acquiescence of other powers concerned. On December 5 he consented to the British request to transfer negotiations to Washington, although he regretted the necessity therefor. In a cablegram of January 5, 1894, after the British minister had urgently requested him to agree to admit a Canadian negotiator for concurrent action to make the regulations effective, he instructed Bayard to inform Lord Rosebery that "this government will treat with the Imperial government only." On January 24, seeking to avoid further delay, he submitted to the British ambassador a draft of a proposed convention. At a conference of March 7–8 with the British ambassador, he renewed an expression of his preference for a convention to enforce protection as contemplated by the award. Finding that the ambassador did not think this necessary, and apprehensive that the British government was determined to have another open season for the Canadian sealers, he proposed (on March 21) an extension of the existing *modus vivendi* for one year with an amendment to include waters to 42° N. for the months of May, June and July; and he instructed Bayard that, if this were not accepted, Congress would probably provide legislation for American enforcement for the season.[26]

On March 23, influenced by the dilatory policies (obstacles and counter-proposals) which threatened to defeat efforts to renew in modified form the previous *modus vivendi,* he suggested a concentration of efforts on plans to obtain needed concurrent legislation. Objecting to a stipulation of Lord Kimberley which implied a possible violation of the agreement by the United States, he cabled Bayard on March 28 that before August 1 Congress would enact enforcement legislation with the expectation that Great Britain would do the same, but that neither party should have the right to denounce the treaty if enforcement should be delayed. Three days later he wired that British delay had created some feeling of irritation in Congress. Again on April 10, he urged the necessity of reaching an understanding for a permanent arrangement, or at least for a *modus vivendi.* Meantime, the proposed legislation was introduced in the Senate on April 2 and completed four days later.[27]

On May 1 Gresham cabled to Bayard a copy of the regulations which the British ambassador and the agent of Canada had accepted to meet the situation for the season—regulations in accord with the American act of April 6 which Canada had strenuously opposed as "unfair and not in accordance with the Paris award." A few days later he received from Bayard a confidential dispatch enclosing British orders to the Pacific fleet to coöperate in the execution of the Paris award as to protection of seal life.[28] Meantime, he completed with the Russian government an agreement for a *modus vivendi;* and he had the assurance that Russia would negotiate and sign with the United States, England and Japan a treaty for application of the principles and regulations of the Paris award to all the waters of the Pacific north of 35° N.[29]

Early in 1895, considering the unsatisfactory situation and recognizing the immediate necessity of further regulations to preserve the seals from increasing slaughter, Gresham suggested to the British ambassador an immediate *modus vivendi* and speedy arrangement for a commission of representatives of the United States, Great Britain, Japan and Russia. He especially insisted that the only way effectually to prevent the use of firearms in seal fishing in Bering Sea was to prohibit the possession there of firearms adapted to such purpose. He suggested as a remedy provisional absolute closing of Bering Sea and a *modus vivendi* to which Japan and Russia should become parties.[30]

In June, 1895, Secretary Olney expressed disappointment that the British government had refused to agree to concurrent regulations for 1895. Through Roosevelt at London, he complained of the action of the British naval authorities in releasing two Canadian sealing schooners, which (in accord with a British order) had been seized by American patrol vessels for violation of the Paris award regulations and had been delivered to the British authorities. He urged that in future such cases should be submitted to the proper admiralty court.

On December 2, the President reported to Congress that the ineffectiveness of efforts to enforce the regulations to prevent the slaughter of the seals was partly a result of the insufficiency of the British patrol of Bering Sea.[31]

Meantime, the American government had considered the question of British claims for American seizure of Canadian sealing vessels. On August 21, 1894, in reply to the British proposal of a mixed commission to agree upon an adjustment, Gresham submitted the President's suggestion that direct settlement might be more practicable and advantageous. Subject to the action of Congress he proposed a payment of $425,000 which the British government agreed to accept in full payment of the claims estimated at over $542,000; but the uncompromising Congress refused to appropriate the money for payment. On December 2, 1895, the President recommended to Congress further consideration with a view to confirmation of the arrangement. He also suggested a possible alternate treaty arrangement for speedy adjustment. Later, the two governments, acting under a convention signed by Olney and Pauncefote on February 8, 1896, appointed a joint commission (of two), which met at Victoria, British Columbia, and after discussions lasting until December, 1897, finally awarded the British government $473,151 which Congress promptly appropriated.[32]

In accord with the earlier policy of seal protection the McKinley administration continued to propose a joint agreement to prevent extermination of the seals. In April, 1897, Secretary Sherman cabled to London an urgent request for an agreement on a *modus vivendi* for suspension of all killing for the season, and also for an arrangement for an early joint conference of the powers concerned to agree upon necessary permanent protective measures. At the same time he notified Pauncefote that John W. Foster, by commission from the President, had been given full charge of all correspondence relating to Bering Sea matters and full power in negotiations.[33]

The President was greatly surprised and disappointed by the British rejection of the protective proposals. He promptly authorized a continuation of negotiations. On May 10, Sherman sent to Hay instructions in which, after reviewing American efforts and British evasions concerning the proposed international conferences on seal protection, he placed upon the British government the blame for eventual difficulties. A copy of these instruction was procured in some unknown way by the *New York Tribune* which published it in full on July 14, without authority of the Department of State and after the President had declined to send the Bering Sea correspondence to Congress.[34]

Meantime, early in July, 1897, Ambassador Hay received from Salisbury a reply that the question was a colonial one in which Great Britain was acting only as trustee. This led to a proposition for reference of the question to Canada, and to a consequent delay of negotiations and a complication of the adjustment of other pending questions.[35]

On July 16, at London, following a conference with Chamberlain in which Sir Louis Davies had participated, Laurier wrote Foster his opinion that an understanding might be reached on a conference if limited to purposes of expert inquiry; but he suggested that certain recent American statements, accusing the British government of deceit and bad faith, were not calculated to facilitate negotiations.[36]

Late in September Hay expressed his surprise that the British government, after agreeing to a conference of sealing experts at Washington, suddenly refused to attend a proposed conference to which Russia and Japan were invited. In October, in a letter to Foster concerning the recent negotiations in London, and the British suppression of his note of July 29, he said that never before had he imagined that English diplomacy was tricky.[37]

Later, on November 6, 1897, the American negotiations with the Japanese and Russian governments, concerning measures to remedy the grave situation in Alaskan and Pribilof waters, finally culminated in the signing of a tripartite convention for absolute prohibition of seal-hunting by their citizens for one year, subject to the adherence of the British government. Hay was much disappointed that the British declined to adhere, apparently on the ground of pending American negotiations with Canada.[38]

In connection with the seals conferences, Sir Wilfred Laurier and Sir Louis Davies, as Canadian representatives with British authority, visited Washington as observers, without invitation by the American government and apparently not without producing "some feeling on the part of the British embassy." There, in the presence of a British representative, on November 13 and 16, they discussed the sealing question with Foster and received a hearty welcome from the President and other members of the government. To Foster they stated that the Canadian government, confronted by political exigencies, was unwilling to agree to the American proposal to abolish or suspend pelagic sealing without adequate compensation or some adequate offset concession in adjustment of other questions.

In reply Foster urged the importance of immediate action for protection of the seals, which otherwise would "cease to be a matter worth negotiating about"; but he was willing to negotiate for treaty settlements on the other questions whenever Laurier was ready, and (if necessary) even to consider the

Lakes fisheries at once in connection with the Bering Sea seals question. Apparently he failed in his efforts to impress upon the Canadian government the American view "that pelagic sealing was unneighborly and ought to be voluntarily given up without compensation or off-set." Finally, after objecting to Davies's alternate proposal to proceed with negotiations with a view to concluding them before August and without any *modus vivendi* for the year, he received from Laurier a promise to obtain promptly a decision of the Privy Council which by telegraphic notice he requested to meet him at Ottawa.[39]

On November 29 Sherman wrote to Hay concerning information that the Canadian government would not consent to the suspension of pelagic sealing pending the negotiations. At the same time he submitted a copy of the conditional tripartite convention (of November 6) and he forwarded with it instructions to urge prompt British adhesion by the British Foreign Office so that the President could submit to Congress the whole subject of seals protection. In a cablegram of December 27, directing Hay to inform Salisbury that all Canadian proposals had been declined and that no negotiations with Canada were pending, he again urged British adhesion to the convention.[40]

On the same day (December 27), Hay wrote Foster an interesting confidential letter in which he referred to Salisbury's comparison of Canada to a coquettish girl who had two suitors and played one against the other. Concerning British policy he said: "They frankly avow their slavery to Canada and chafe under it; and yet they rather resent our talking to Canada directly and make this a pretext for declining adhesion to the convention." Stating that America could end pelagic sealing by excluding the pelagic catch from the American market, he said: "I hope that no further attempt at negotiation with Canada will be made for the present." Three weeks later, after reporting to Foster that Salisbury had based his non-adherence upon American negotiations with Canada and American non-suspension of seal-catching on the Pribilof Islands, he wrote: "It is as you have known from the beginning. They cannot act here independently of Canada, and Canada will do nothing unless she is bought off. We are on the right track in acting on our own responsibility inside of our own rights. There will be some squealing on the part of the ladies, but there is some friction in all legal processes and the new law if executed discreetly will stop pelagic sealing." [41]

In 1898, the question of fur-seals protection, added to a list of other subjects, was submitted to a special joint high commission which in its negotiations failed to reach an agreement. Later, in referring to the negotiations of 1898–99 in which Canada seemed more agreeable on the Bering seal problem and which were wrecked by the rock of the Alaskan boundary controversy, Foster wrote: "We were so near an agreement on the fur-seal question, it seems too bad that such a useful herd of animals should be gradually destroyed because of the failure to agree about the ownership of some glaciers." [42]

Meantime, in the decade after 1893, the American government in its Canadian relations was confronted by many other problems, arising both from the hardening of earlier differences and from the emergence of new issues, and resulting in occasional exaggerated expressions that Canada as a part of the British empire was a standing menace to peace.[43]

In 1893, following an exploratory discussion of trade reciprocity initiated by Tupper and Bayard at London, Bayard repeated President Cleveland's earlier views that a policy of liberal reciprocal exchanges of natural products was wise and expedient but that the end should be reached by concurrent and independent legislation in preference to international agreement through treaty negotiations.[44] Later, at the close of 1896, when Laurier sent Canadian representatives to Washington to discuss informally the question of negotiations, American officials suggested that American farmers and the British government might object to their proposed reciprocity treaty.[45]

In 1895, the American government was again interested in the discussion of bonded transit which was revived by the initiation of American railway interests in proposing abrogation of such traffic regulation on the ground that it diverted traffic to the Canadian railways.[46] Meantime, too, it complained of Canadian action in several minor routine cases relating to trade or transit.[47] It also complained of the difficulty encountered by American authors in their efforts to secure copyrights in Canada—a subject of correspondence since 1891.[48] In 1894–96, in considering difficulties involving conflicting claims of jurisdiction, it suggested the need of more definite demarcation of certain parts of the boundary between Lake Superior and the Lake of the Woods and in the western part of Lake Erie.[49]

In 1895–96 it revived the consideration of the question of regulations for navigation of the Great Lakes and their connecting and tributary waters, concerning which Pauncefote offered the friendly but surprising suggestion that the difficulties involved might be settled by direct negotiations between the American and Canadian governments.[50] Between 1893 and 1896 it considered other types of problems relating to the undisturbed use of connecting boundary waters of the Lakes.[51] At the same time it showed an increased interest in the conditions of navigation on the upper St. Lawrence.[52] In 1895 it was asked to consider the larger problem of control of the waters of the Lakes, especially the maintenance of uniform levels,[53] and also various proposals of plans for completion of a deep waterway from the Lakes to the sea either via the St. Lawrence or via the Hudson.[54] It coöperated with the Canadian government in the appointment of canal commissioners to confer on the feasibility of internal waterway improvements (canals) adequate for passage of ocean vessels to the Lakes.[55] At the same time it was engaged in a correspondence concerning fishing problems on the Lakes, resulting in proposed measures of coöperation for protection and preservation of the fisheries in contiguous waters between the United States and Canada—a subject which by agreement of December, 1892, had been referred to a joint commission for investigation.[56]

In 1895–96, American relations with Canada were somewhat disturbed by American policy in the dangerous British-Venezuelan boundary dispute, and especially by Olney's famous instructions on American continental responsibility and policy in which he asserted that because of distance a permanent political union formed by a European "permanent encampment on American soil" was unnatural and inexpedient.[57] Coincident with this disturbance appeared a new American agitation for abrogation or modification of the Agreement of 1817, which at first was based upon refusal of the Navy to award contracts to shipbuilding firms on the Lakes for construction of unarmed gunboats for ocean use,[58] and which later was stimulated with a view to the creation of a Lakes naval force to "protect" the commerce of the Lakes.[59] The latter was probably influenced by a brief Canadian agitation for defenses.[60] After the subsidence of the Venezuelan crisis, followed more harmonious Anglo-American relations which were especially expressed in the negotiation of a treaty in 1896 for settlement of disputes by a general system of arbitration—a treaty which, however, the Senate failed to approve.[61]

Although by 1898 many evidences of the improved Anglo-American relations appeared,[62] the American government encountered in new situations and incidents the sources of new difficulties and new controversies which complicated efforts to adjust old ones.[63] It also found that its new tariff under the Dingley act was a source of increased irritation to the Laurier government,[64] which thereby was diverted to a policy of retaliatory trade legislation and search for foreign markets.[65]

In seeking a satisfactory adjustment of all American-Canadian controversial questions, the McKinley administration supported the wishes of Laurier who on a visit to Washington (in November, 1897) conferred with Secretary Sherman. The latter referred him to a special agent, John W. Foster, for conferences[66] in which he sought to obtain, as compensating concessions for agreement to abolition of pelagic sealing, several arrangements relating to changes in the American alien labor law, protection and regulation of fisheries in contiguous waters, free admission of Canadian fish, reciprocity in the coal trade, and removal of the discriminating tariff on lumber and logs.[67] From the discussions emerged an American friendly proposal to refer all outstanding questions to a joint high commission of ten members, five for each government.[68] By specific agreement of joint conferees, twelve main subjects were selected with a view to adjustment by agreement of the commission:[69] (1) the Bering Sea fur-seals fisheries, (2) coastal and inland water frontier fisheries, (3) Alaskan boundary, (4) trans-territory transit, (5) trans-boundary transit, (6) alien labor laws, (7) mining rights, (8) tariff concessions, (9) revision of the Agreement of 1817, (10) demarcation of the frontier boundary, (11) conveyance of prisoners, and (12) reciprocity in wrecking and salvage rights. Other recent controversial subjects were omitted: certain problems relating to new development in the Klondike; [70] diversion of Lakes waters; [71] questions concerning plans for a deep waterway from the Lakes to the sea via the St. Lawrence [72] or via the Hudson; [73] American timber industries in Canada.[74] Following the organization of the commission, Secretary Day especially urged an adjustment of the question of bonded transit privilege.[75]

The commission, to which the various selected subjects were submitted by protocol of May 30, 1898, organized at Quebec in the following August by selection of Lord Herschell as its president. Its later meetings, from November 10 to February 20, were held at Washington and were terminated chiefly because of the development of irreconcilable difference of views on the Alaskan boundary question.[76] On February 3 Fairbanks reported to the President that substantial agreement had been reached on seven subjects and on most points of two others, and that he expected early agreement on the Bering Sea question by American concession.[77] After the Alaskan question, the subjects which encountered the greatest difficulties were trade reciprocity and Atlantic fisheries.[78] In efforts to harmonize vexatious differences on tariffs, the Americans were restricted by the Canadian contention that any accepted arrangement must be extended to all "favored nation" treaty countries and by the practical realization that approval of Congress was necessary to validate any change of tariff schedules.[79] Among the several subjects upon which the commissioners reached agreement were travel across the border, revision of the convention of 1817, differences concerning the water boundary and fisheries in contiguous waters.[80] Failing to induce the Canadians to agree to refer the difficult Alaskan question to a separate settlement by diplomatic negotiation and to proceed with efforts to formulate a treaty for adjustment of the other questions, the American commissioners were finally forced to agree to an adjournment of the commission without any definite settlement.[81]

The President, hoping to find some way to avoid a fruitless result of months of labor and careful study as a result of failure to agree upon a single question, authorized Hay to ascertain from the British government whether some way might be found to remove the obstacle which seemed to make further deliberations of the commission useless. In May, by a cablegram from London, he learned definitely that Canada would not be ready to proceed with other questions at issue until the two governments reached an agreement on the arbitration of the Alaskan boundary question which had become the chief bone of contention.[82]

In the period of suspense between 1899 and 1903, America awaited more favorable auspices for a new series of negotiations. In connection with routine problems resulting from development on the Yukon arose new irritating questions relating to Alaska which emphasized the importance of an early agreement on the Alaska boundary.[83] Farther east along the older boundary frontier, fortunately no serious difficulty appeared. Minor routine questions relating to trade and transportation were promptly adjusted.[84] The American government, however, regarded proposed negotiations for a reciprocity treaty as impracticable and inexpedient—especially because of the prolonged non-action of the Senate upon several pending trade treaties.[85] While awaiting the final decision on the Alaskan boundary it apparently had less interest in reciprocal trade than it had in the various questions relating to the conditions, use, diversion and protection of conterminous boundary waters.[86]

REFERENCES

1. John W. Foster, *Diplomatic Memoirs,* II, 20–50.
2. *Ib.,* II, 22–23; *28 G.B., Instrs.,* p. 243, No. 508, Jan. 17, 1887.
3. *Ib.,* pp. 362–63, No. 685, Aug. 19, 1887; *Ib.,* p. 410, No. 733, Nov. 25, 1887; J. B. Moore, *Int. Arbitrations,* I, 776–84; *Sen. Exec. Docs.,* 50–2, No. 106, p. 84; *For. Rels., 1888.*
4. *21 G.B., Notes to,* pp. 215–26, May 29, 1890; *Ib.,* pp. 227–31, June 4; *28 G.B., Instrs.,* p. 442, No. 782, Feb. 7, 1888.

5. Richardson, *Messages*, VIII, 781.
6. *N. Am. Rev.*, Dec., 1895 (Foster); *21 G.B., Notes to*, pp. 164–74, Jan. 22, 1890; Moore, *Dip. Arb's.*, I, 785–87; *For. Rels., 1890*, pp. 366–70, 419, 437; Foster, *Dipl. Memoirs*, II, 25–26.
7. *21 G.B., Notes to*, pp. 164–74, Jan. 22, 1890; Moore, *Int. Arb's.*, I, 786–87.
8. Foster, *Dipl. Memoirs*, II, 24–25; Rosen, *Forty Years of Diplomacy*, I, 80.
9. *For. Rels., 1890*, pp. 410–17; *21 G.B., Notes to*, pp. 215–26, May 29, 1890.
10. *Ib.*; Moore, *Int. Arb's.*, I, 790.
11. *21 G.B., Notes to*, p. 226, June 2, 1890; *Ib.*, pp. 227–32, June 4; Moore, *Int. Arb's.*, I, 790–92.
12. *Ib.*, I, 794–95; *For. Rels.*, 1890, pp. 437–48.
13. *Ib.*, 1890, p. 366; Foster, *Dipl. Memoirs*, II, 27–28.
14. *Ib.*, pp. 29–30; Moore, *Int. Arb's.*, p. 797; *21 G.B., Notes to*, p. 309, Dec. 17, 1890.
15. *For. Rels., 1891*, pp. 552–70; *21 G.B., Notes to*, pp. 424–26, May 26, 1891; *Ib.*, pp. 455–58, June 9.
16. Malloy, *Treaties*, I, 743–44; Moore, *Int. Arb's.*, I, 798; *For. Rels., 1891*, pp. 552–73; *21 G.B., Notes to*, p. 561, Nov. 27, 1891.
17. *Ib.*, p. 567, Dec. 10, 1891; *21 G.B., Notes to*, p. 568, Dec. 14.
18. Malloy, *Treaties*, I, 744–50; *11 Can. Mag.*, Sept., 1898, pp. 409–12 (C. H. Tupper).
19. *21 G.B., Notes to*, p. 607, Feb. 24, 1892; *Ib.*, p. 609, Feb. 26; *Ib.*, pp. 620–21, March 22.
20. *Ib.*, p. 645, Apr. 20, 1892.
21. Foster, *Dipl. Memoirs*, II, pp. 32, 35–44.
22. *Ib.*, 44, 48; *N. Am. Rev.*, Dec., 1895 (Foster); *Ib.*, Vol. 185, p. 432; Moore, *Int. Arb's.*, I, 809–960.
23. Foster, *Dipl. Memoirs*. II, 46–48; *Foster Papers*.
24. Malloy, *Treaties*, I, 753; *Forum*, May, 1899; D. S. Jordon, *Imperial Democracy*, pp. 220–35.
25. *175 G.B., Desps.*, No. 63, Sept. 19, 1893; *Foster Papers*, Oct. 9, 1893.
26. *30 G.B., Instrs.*, p. 400, No. 212, Nov. 21, 1893; *Ib.*, pp. 423–24, No. 232, Dec. 5; *Ib.*, pp. 441–42, Tel., Jan. 5, 1894; *Ib.*, pp. 498–502, No. 320, Mar. 17, 1894; *Ib.*, p. 507, Tel., Mar. 22; *22 G.B., Notes to*, p. 315, Jan. 24, 1894.
27. *Ib.*, pp. 509–12, Apr. 20, 1894 (also pp. 499–503, Apr. 10); *30 G.B., Instrs.*, pp. 509–10, Tel., Mar. 28, 1894.
28. *Ib.*, pp. 546–50, Tel., May 1, 1894; *Ib.*, p. 560, No. 392, May 12.
29. *Ib.*, No. 394, May 14, 1894.
30. *22 G.B., Notes to*, Jan. 2, 1895; *23 G.B., Notes to*, pp. 68–79, No. 99, May 10; *Ib.*, p. 149, No. 151, July 11.

31. *31 G.B., Instrs.*, p. 176, No. 740, June 12, 1895; *Ib.*, pp. 183–88, No. 749, June 18; RICHARDSON, *Messages*, IX, 630.
32. *22 G.B., Notes to*, p. 600, July 26, 1894; *State Papers*, Vol. 87, p. 1134; RICHARDSON, *Messages*, IX, 630–31; MALLOY, *Treaties*, I, 766–70; *H. Exec. Docs.*, 53–3, No. 132; MOORE, *Int. Arb's.*, I, 960–61.
33. *23 G.B., Notes to*, pp. 591–95, No. 636, Apr. 9, 1897; *Ib.*, p. 546, Apr. 10.
34. *32 G.B., Instrs.*, pp. 65–86, No. 28, May 10, 1897; *Ib.*, p. 177, Tel., July 14, 1897.
35. *For. Rels., 1897*, p. 299.
36. *Foster Papers*, July 16, 1897.
37. *Ib.*, Hay to Foster, Oct. 18, and (Confid.) Nov. 20, 1897; *For. Rels., 1897*, pp. 300, 304–10; *G.B., Desps.*, No. 126, Sept. 25, 1897; *Baltimore Sun*, Oct. 7 and 8, 1897.
38. *34 G.B., Instrs.*, pp. 453–55, Personal, Hay to Choate, July 28, 1903.
39. *For. Rels., 1897*, p. 113 (Nov. 8), and p. 320; *32 G.B., Instrs.*, pp. 314–17, No. 326, Sherman to Hay, Nov. 29, 1897; *48 Sp'l Agents, 1893–97*, Nov. 13 and 16, and (Confid.) Dec. 3, 1897 (Foster to Sherman).
40. *32 G.B., Instrs.*, pp. 314–17, No. 326 (also No. 325), Nov. 29, 1897; *Ib.*, p. 348, Tel., Dec. 27.
41. *J. W. Foster Papers*, Hay to Foster (Confid.), Dec. 27, 1897, and Jan. 17, 1898.
42. FOSTER, *Dipl. Memoirs*, II, 189.
43. WALTER MILLIS, *The Martial Spirit . . .*, pp. 5, 7 and 27; SKELTON, *Life and Letters of Sir Wilfrid Laurier*, II, 120–21; *Sen. Misc. Docs.*, 53–3, Vol. 1, No. 30; *148 Cong. Record*, Vol. 27, Part 1.
44. *175 G.B., Desps.*, No. 63, Sept. 19, 1893; *30 G.B., Instrs.*, pp. 359–60, No. 161, Oct. 10; *Ib.*, p. 386, No. 192, Nov. 2; *Sen. Exec. Docs.*, 53–2, Vol. 4, No. 106, May 26, 1894.
45. *16 Rev. of Revs.*, Dec., 1897, pp. 712–14 (E. V. SMALLEY); *Arena*, Dec., 1899, pp. 667–82 (L. E. MUNSON); *23 G.B., Notes to*, p. 596, Apr. 10, 1897.
46. *Sen. Misc. Docs.*, 53–3, Vol. 1, No. 89, Feb. 2, 1895; *3A Reciprocity Treaties, 1898–1907, Canada* (KASSON), *Rp. of Republican Club of N.Y.*, Jan. 18, 1897.
47. *22 G.B., Notes to*, Sept. 25, 1893; *123 G.B., Notes from*, Nov. 17; *23 G.B., Notes to*, pp. 147–48, No. 149, July 11, 1895; *Ib.*, p. 149, No. 151, July 11; *Ib.*, p. 198, No. 202, Sept. 21; *Ib.*, p. 236, No. 239, Nov. 2; *Ib.*, p. 309, No. 331, Feb. 18, 1896; *Ib.*, p. 497, No. 540, Nov. 23.
48. *Ib.*, p. 548, No. 593, Feb. 4, 1897; *32 G.B., Instrs.*, p. 57, No. 19, May 4.

49. *23 G.B., Notes to,* pp. 140–43, No. 143, July 3, 1895; *Ib.,* pp. 227–29, No. 225, Oct. 17; *Dept. of State, U. S. Dipl. Pamphs., U.S. and G.B.,* 1810–96, No. 20, 346.
50. *23 G.B., Notes to,* p. 19, Feb. 21, 1895; *Ib.,* pp. 203–04, No. 204, Sept. 27; *Ib.,* pp. 320–21, No. 343, Mar. 11, 1896; *31 G.B., Instrs.,* No. 1025, Mar. 12, 1896 (Inclosure); *135 G.B., Notes from,* Sept. 23, 1895.
51. *22 G.B., Notes to,* pp. 352–53, July 6, 1893; Moore, *Int. Law Digest,* I, 678; *31 G.B., Instrs.,* pp. 421–26, No. 1076, Apr. 14, 1896; *23 G.B., Notes to,* p. 165, No. 167, Aug. 6, 1895; *Ib.,* p. 54, No. 80, Apr. 17, 1895.
52. *22 G.B., Notes to,* pp. 375–77, Aug. 16, 1893; *Ib.,* p. 296, No. 314, Feb. 5, 1896.
53. Hon. Calvin S. Brice to J. M. Callahan, Dec. 24, 1895; *Papers rel. to the Work of the Int. Joint Commis.,* p. 103.
54. *Spl. Consular Rps., Highways of Commerce,* XII (1899), 26–27; *Baltimore Herald,* Oct. 14, 1895; Verplank Colvin to J. M. Callahan, Oct. 1.
55. *For. Rels.,* 1895, I, 705–07; *Ib.,* 1896, lxxiv; *23 G.B., Notes to,* p. 252, No. 251, Nov. 12, 1895; *Ib.,* p. 294, No. 312, Feb., 1896; Richardson, IX, 747–48; *H. Rps.,* 54–1, No. 423, Feb. 18, 1896 (Historical review); *Special Consular Reports, Highways of Commerce,* XII (1889), Supplement, p. 26.
56. *Chicago Times Herald,* Sept. 18, 1895; *H. Rps.,* 60–1, No. 1760; *Domestic Letters,* State Dept. to Treas. Dept., Nov. 20, 1894; *Misc. Letters,* Nov. 30, 1894; *23 G.B., Notes to,* pp. 285–88, No. 298, Jan. 21, 1896; Richardson, IX, 751; *H. Docs.,* 54–2, Vol. 58, No. 315, Feb. 24, 1897.
57. J. B. Henderson, *Dipl. Questions,* pp. 425, 428 and 438–39.
58. *Philadelphia Ledger,* Oct. 25, 1895; *Chicago Times Herald,* Oct. 27 and 29; *Toledo Blade,* Oct. 29; *Baltimore Sun,* Nov. 4; Hon. Geo. E. Adams to J. M. Callahan, Nov. 4, 1895; *Marine Record,* Oct. 31; *Chicago Post,* Nov. 2, 1895; *Philadelphia Times,* Nov. 3; *Baltimore Sun,* Nov. 4; *Nation* (N.Y.), Nov. 7; *Detroit Tribune,* Nov. 9 and 18.
59. *Detroit Evening News,* Nov., 1895; *Detroit Free Press,* Nov. 27; *Washington Times,* Dec. 24; Richardson, IX, 632; *Ib.,* 655; Henderson, *Dipl. Questions,* p. 417; *Chicago Times Herald,* Dec. 20, 1895; *Baltimore Herald,* Dec. 21; *Superior Leader* (Wis.), Dec. 24.
60. *For. Rels., 1895.*
61. *23 G.B., Notes to,* pp. 354–57, No. 365, Apr. 11, 1896; *Ib.,* p. 618, No. 662, May 12, 1897; Richardson, IX, 722 and 746–47; Dunning, *The British Empire and the U.S.,* pp. 318–19.
62. *Ib.,* X, 184.

63. SKELTON, *Life and Letters of Sir Wilfrid Laurier,* II, 46, 49, 123–25; SHORTT and DOUGHTY, IX, 185; RICHARDSON, IX, 631.
64. *Sen.* [*Misc.*] *Docs.*, 55–1, Vol. 6, No. 158, June 25, 1897; *N. Am. Rev.*, Jan., 1897, pp. 710–18 (JNO. W. RUSSELL); *23 Public Opinion,* Oct. 21, 1897, pp. 517–18; *16 Rev. of Revs.*, Dec., 1897, pp. 712–14.
65. SHORTT and DOUGHTY, IX, 206–15; *Baltimore Sun,* Apr. 5 and Oct. 1–7, 1897; *23 Public Opinion,* Oct. 21, pp. 517–18; *11 Can. Mag.*, Sept., 1898, pp. 371–80.
66. *25 Forum,* Aug., 1898, pp. 652–53 (EDW. FARRER); *3 Reciprocity Treaties, 1898–1907, Canada* (KASSON), Dept. to Albert Clarke, Mar. 25, 1904; *24 G.B., Notes to,* p. 61, Sherman to Laurier, Nov. 12, 1897.
67. *48 Spl. Agents, 1893–97; 24 G.B., Notes to,* p. 62, Nov. 15, 1897.
68. SKELTON, *Life and Letters of Sir Wilfrid Laurier,* pp. 123–26; MALLOY, I, 770–73; *3 Reciprocity Treaties, 1898–1907, Canada* (KASSON); *27 G.B., Notes to,* pp. 564–81, May 3, 1906.
69. MALLOY, I, 770–73; *3 Reciprocity Treaties, 1898–1907, Canada* (KASSON).
70. *24 G.B., Notes to,* pp. 123–24, No. 915, Feb. 16, 1898; *129 G.B., Notes from,* Feb. 21 and Mar. 17, 1898; *24 G.B., Notes to,* p. 146, No. 945, March 16, 1898.
71. *Ib.*, p. 108, No. 893, Feb. 2, 1898.
72. *Marine Rev.*, May 26, 1898; *3A Reciprocity Treaties, 1898–99, Canada* (KASSON), McDougall to Eugene T. Chamberlain, Mar. 10, 1898; *Ib.*, Kasson to McDougall, Mar. 31; *Ib.*, McDougall to Kasson, Apr. 22 and May 30.
73. *Ib.*, John A. C. Wright to Pres. McKinley, June 10, 1898; *Ib.*, Weed to Kasson, June 14 and Oct. 12, 1898.
74. *24 G.B., Notes to,* pp. 220–22, No. 1057, June 15, 1898.
75. *3A Reciprocity Treaties, 1898–99.*
76. *Baltimore Sun,* Aug. 24, 1898; MALLOY, I, 773; W. R. THAYER, *Life and Letters of John Hay,* II, 205; *3 Reciprocity Treaties, 1898–1907, Canada* (KASSON), Nos. 72–73.
77. Annex, *3 Reciprocity Treaties, 1898–1907; 27 G.B., Notes to,* pp. 564–81, May 3, 1906.
78. *Independent,* Mar. 2, 1899 (also Feb. 23, p. 571), and Sept. 29 (pp. 920–22), 1899; *12 Can. Mag.*, Jan., 1899, pp. 198–201.
79. *27 G.B., Notes to,* pp. 564–81, May 3, 1906; Annex, *3 Reciprocity Treaties, 1898–1907* (Fairbanks to the President, Feb. 3, 1899, Confidential Mem., and Draft of Treaty); *Expansionist,* 1900.
80. *Ib.* (Draft of Treaty); *27 G.B., Notes to,* pp. 602–04, No. 457, Root to Durand, June 6, 1906; *22 Opinions of Atty. Gen.*, p. 214; *195 G.B., Desps.*, Tel., Dec. 30, 1898.
81. *33 G.B., Instrs.*, No. 87, Hay to Choate, Apr. 19, 1899; J. W. FOSTER, *Dipl. Memoirs,* II, 188; *Arena,* Dec., 1899, pp. 667–82.

82. *33 G.B., Instrs.*, No. 87, Apr. 19, 1899; *197 G.B., Desps.*, May 15, 1899; *Rev. of Revs.*, June, 1899; MALLOY, I, 773 and 777–78; J. W. FOSTER, *Dipl. Memoirs*, II, 188–89; [*Br.*] *Treaty Series*, No. 19, 1899; SKELTON, *Life and Letters of Sir Wilfrid Laurier*, II, 133–34.

83. *4 Spl. Missions*, pp. 384–85; *24 G.B., Notes to*, pp. 622–23, No. 1561, Sept. 15, 1899; *25 G.B., Notes to*, pp. 378–87, No. 1990, Nov. 27, 1900; *26 G.B., Notes to*, pp. 17–18, Dec. 16, 1901; *Ib.*, pp. 20–21, Dec. 18; *Ib.*, p. 36, Jan. 7, 1902.

84. *25 G.B., Notes to*, p. 504, No. 2128, Apr. 3, 1901; *Ib.*, pp. 554–55, No. 173, June 3, 1901; *26 G.B., Notes to*, pp. 215–18, No. 2509, Adee to Raikes, Aug. 6, 1902; *Ib.*, pp. 428–29, No. 132, May 25, 1903.

85. *7 Reciprocity Treaties, 1898–1907, Misc. Letters*, Kasson to Erastus Wiman, Nov. 26, 1902; *3 Reciprocity Treaties, 1898–1907, Canada* (KASSON), Aug. 26, 1903.

86. *26 G.B., Notes to*, pp. 382–83, No. 95, Mar. 28, 1903; *Ib.*, p. 557, No. 204, Oct. 7; *34 G.B., Instrs.*, p. 200, No. 947, July 1, 1902; *Ib.*, No. 1275, Oct. 2, 1903 (also No. 1280); *Papers rel. to the Work of the International Joint Commis.*, p. 103.

CHAPTER XIX

THE ALASKAN BOUNDARY CONTROVERSY

THE question of the location of the eastern boundary of the panhandle of Alaska was a subject of serious controversy from 1898 until its adjustment by a joint commission in 1903. It had its origin in the language and purpose of the Anglo-Russian treaty of 1825 which determined the American claim under the Russo-American treaty of 1867. Probably it could have been satisfactorily settled without serious difficulty concerning interpretation of treaty provisions if a joint survey had been arranged promptly after the American purchase. Unfortunately it was left unsettled, like two previous controversies, until it became involved in new problems resulting from new conditions and new development unforeseen by British statesmen who agreed to a western boundary for British America in 1825.

In the diplomatic negotiations preceding the treaty of 1825 the British government, in proposing a treaty of limits, especially sought by tactful means to secure the withdrawal of Russia from its extravagant claim to exclusive jurisdiction in the northern Pacific southward to 51°. The Russian government, rejecting the British proposal of a "seaward base," especially insisted upon a strip of continental coast which would establish a Russian barrier to the encroachments of the English agents of the Hudson's Bay Company. Reluctantly yielding to the British insistence upon a specific limit on the mainland north of 54°40′, and without knowledge of Canning's willingness to accept a line one hundred miles east of the ocean, it agreed to accept a continuous strip including all the inlets of the sea and with a width of ten marine leagues (thirty miles) unless within that limit was a chain of mountains which constituted a natural international watershed boundary. The part of the treaty line of 1825 which was later a source of controversy between the United States and Great Britain was described as follows:

> "Commencing from the southernmost point of the island called Prince of Wales Island, which lies in the parallel of 54°40′ north latitude . . . the said line shall ascend to the north along the channel called Portland Channel as far as the point of the continent where it strikes the 56th degree of north latitude; from this last mentioned point the line of demarcation shall follow the summit of the mountains situated parallel to the coast as far as the point of intersection of the 141st degree of west longitude. . . . Whenever the summit of the mountains which extend in a direction parallel to the coast . . . shall prove to be at a distance of more than 10 marine leagues from the ocean, the limit between the British possessions and the line of coast which is to belong to Russia, as above mentioned, shall be formed by a line parallel to the winding (sinuosities) of the coast, and which shall never exceed the distance of ten marine leagues therefrom."

In 1827 the Russian government authorized the publication of a map on which the boundary of Russian American possessions was drawn from the head of Portland Channel ten marine leagues from tidewater and around the heads of all inlets to the meridian of 141°W., and on 141° to the Arctic Ocean. This map was adopted by the British and Canadian governments and was later used as evidence for the American claim under the Russian treaty of cession of 1867.[1]

In 1867, the American government authorized a map delineating the panhandle strip on the mainland exactly as it had been claimed by Russia for over forty years. For the next thirty years American ownership and jurisdiction of the unbroken panhandle strip, reaching eastward beyond the inlets of the sea, was admitted and respected by the British government.

In 1872, following the discovery of gold in the Stikine region of British Columbia, appeared the first proposal for a joint survey. At that time both Canadian and British officials understood that the boundary crossed the rivers above the inlets. In reply to the Canadian suggestion of the necessity of some early action to define the boundary line, Secretary Fish expressed agreement as to the expediency of a survey but doubted whether Congress would grant the necessary funds. In the correspondence there was no intimation that the line was in dispute. In

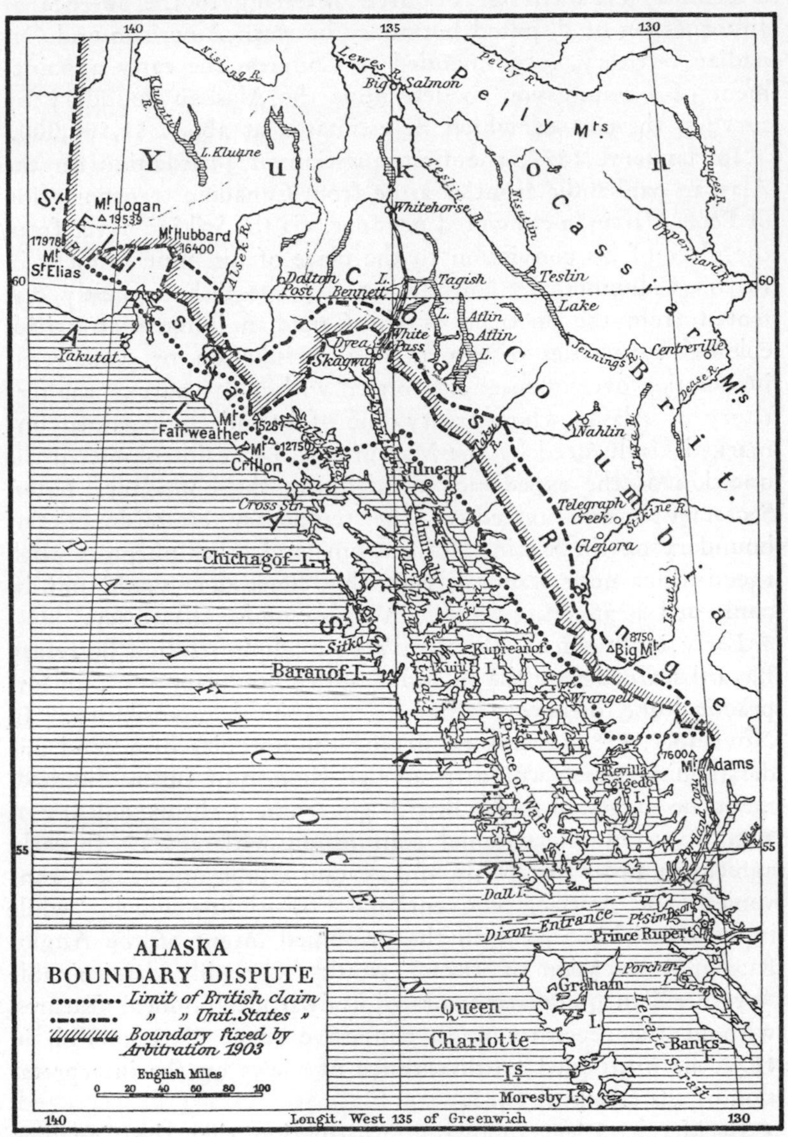

From Carl Wittke's "A History of Canada," F. S. Crofts & Co., Publishers.

December, President Grant, after referring to the absence of any question of disputed boundary between American and Canadian territory, recommended to Congress the early appointment of a commission to determine the Alaskan boundary by surveys, the cost of which he estimated at about $1,500,000.[2]

In January, 1877, the first question of jurisdiction on the Alaskan panhandle frontier arose from Canadian transportation of Peter Martin, a convicted prisoner, via the Stikine River from the place of his conviction to the place of his imprisonment in British Columbia. In considering the case Fish explicitly dissented from the doctrine of the Canadian judge that British colonial authorities or courts had jurisdiction or concurrent jurisdiction over offenses committed within any part of the territory of Alaska whose treaty line of boundary remained unmarked. Influenced by the Martin case, he again submitted the question of the expediency of defining the boundary. Later, Secretary Evarts agreed to the temporary establishment of boundary on the Stikine, for customs and other purposes, with the distinct understanding that this concession would not be construed as affecting American rights under the treaty.[3]

Early in President Cleveland's first administration Secretary Bayard learned that the inland frontier boundary was "an impractical one to survey, if not a geographical impossibility." In November, 1885, therefore, urging the necessity of a good understanding which would remove all chances of future disagreement, he suggested to the British government the expediency of appointing an international commission with a view to early agreement upon the speedy and certain establishment of a convenient and practical conventional line—a line which, "while in substantial accord with the presumed intent of the Anglo-Russian convention of 1825," would be readily determinable "by meridian observations or by known geographical features, without the necessity of an expensive survey." Like Fish in 1872, he mentioned no divergence of views on the interpretation of the treaty of 1825.[4]

In March, 1886, following information that the Canadian government had agreed to the principle of a preliminary survey by a joint commission, Bayard instructed Phelps that he might soon be able to conclude at London negotiations for a convention for that purpose. Over two years later (in October, 1888) he directed Phelps to ask the British government to induce the Canadian government to prepare its surveying party to cooperate with the American party. Action was delayed, however, partly by postponement of consideration of the subject in Congress.[5]

In December, 1888, President Cleveland recommended to Congress a prompt and adequate appropriation for a reconnaissance and survey of the geographical features with a view to prevention of complications of international jurisdiction, but Congress was not ready to act.[6]

In 1892 diplomatic consideration of the subject was renewed. In February, the Canadian commissioners at Washington proposed the selection of an impartial authority to determine the boundary and a commission of four experts to determine the mode of delimitation under the consequent award. On July 22 Secretary Foster and Michael H. Herbert (the British chargé), concluded a convention authorizing the appointment of commissions to make a coincident or joint survey to obtain data necessary to the permanent delimitation of the entire eastern boundary of the Alaskan panhandle, as contemplated in the treaties of 1825 and 1867. Nearly a year later Secretary Gresham and Pauncefote signed a convention extending the term for completion of the work of these commissions.[7]

In 1895, following the Klondike gold discoveries which soon made the valley of the Yukon a highway through the previously unexplored wilds of Alaska, the Department of State received from the British legation a suggestion of the practical importance of early determination of the precise jurisdictional limits of the two governments in the region north of Mount St. Elias along the meridian of 141°, and a proposal for a preliminary survey to determine provisionally a line of convenient points on the meridian of 141°. In reply Adee suggested that the proposed survey should be deferred until the meeting of Congress, from which an appropriation was necessary.[8] In December President Cleveland directed the attention of Congress to the expediency and vital importance of further effective measures necessary to complete the exact location of the entire eastern boundary line of Alaska. In the following February, he submitted as evidence a report on the establishment of Canadian post routes across American territory in Alaska and also on the use of American territory by Canadian mounted police—a report which influenced Congress to approve a responsive joint resolution contemplating permanent marking of convenient points on the meridian of 141° by conventional provisions.

On March 11, 1896, Olney proposed to Pauncefote a new convention to agree upon certain points of the boundary at the intersection of the principal streams—points which could be connected later by convenient joint surveys as occasion might require. Finally, on January 30, 1897, he signed with Pauncefote a draft convention for appointment of commissioners to make the survey.[9]

Apparently the first British proposition for an arbitration of the Alaskan panhandle boundary appeared in a note of Pauncefote to Secretary Sherman on February 23, 1898, before the creation of the Joint High Commission. It was evidently stimulated by the increasing traffic to the upper (Canadian) Yukon by trails northward (by the shortest route) through certain passes at the head of Lynn Canal at Dyea and Skagway whose consequent increase in population and importance precipitated a threatened danger of difficulties from conflict of authority concerning collection of customs and caused Canada to claim them by an entirely new interpretation of the treaty of 1825.[10]

In August, 1898, the American government first learned that a difference of views existed in regard to the interpretation of the Anglo-Russian boundary treaty of 1825. From the statement of the Canadian commissioners at Quebec it learned that the British government would claim that the boundary line should be run from the extremity of Prince of Wales Island, along the Pearse Canal, to the head of Portland Canal at 56°, thence directly west to the coast, and then northward to Mount St. Elias following the mountains nearest to the outer coast and crossing all the inlets of the sea.[11]

In the conference discussions of the joint commission of 1898–99, the Americans claimed that the boundary of the panhandle strip, north of the Portland Channel, was ten marine leagues from the inner (mainland) coastline at all points except at White Pass and Chilkoot Pass, following the sinuosities of the coast around the inlets of the sea and marking the eastern limit of an unbroken belt on the mainland. This contention was sustained by the provisions of the Anglo-Russian treaty of 1825, by the anterior concurrent negotiations which explained the motives and objects of the treaty, and by the many interpretative acts of Russian and American occupation and sovereignty in which the British and Canadian governments had acquiesced without protest or complaint. It was opposed by the Canadians who insisted upon their new claim to the mountains nearest the outer shore line, crossing ten or twelve inlets whose eastern waters would thereby be transferred to British possession. On February 3, Fairbanks reported to the President that the chief points in dispute were two small islands at the mouth of Portland Canal, Pyramid Harbor on Lynn Canal, and a strip of territory (from five to ten miles in width) extending from that harbor up Chilkat Valley to the frontier (about ten or fifteen miles distant).[12]

Unable to agree, after sessions of several months, the Canadian commissioners proposed adjustment by a conventional boundary, giving to Canada (by cession or perpetual grant) Pyramid Harbor and a strip of land to connect it with Canadian territory toward the northwest, and locating the remainder of the boundary to conform with the American contention.

The Americans, although they did not finally accept this proposition, were at first disposed to agree to a reasonable compromise—before their liberal views were adversely affected by protests from the American Pacific coast states. They practically concluded an arrangement which, through a proposed lease, would have placed Pyramid Harbor under Canadian jurisdiction for fifty years with a provision for reversion to the United States in case the Canadian government should choose no longer to occupy it. This arrangement, however, was opposed by strong American influence on the Pacific coast and it finally failed to secure consent of the Canadian commissioners.[13]

The Americans were then asked to consider the Canadian

plan to adjust the Alaskan boundary by arbitration with an umpire. To this they declined to agree. They preferred settlement without an umpire. They especially declined to accept a European umpire, while the Canadians refused to accept a South American umpire. They stipulated that in any case the territory of American settlements on the shore of Skagway (the seaboard terminus of the overland route to the Klondike), and also the settlements elsewhere, should continue as American territory.

In declining the British-Canadian insistent alternate proposition for arbitration of the entire boundary on the terms of the recent arbitration of the Venezuelan boundary dispute the American commissioners explained that they did not regard it as a similar or analogous case. They especially objected to the proposed arbitration concerning territory which they insisted had been in practically unchallenged and unquestioned American possession for thirty years, and which since 1825 had constituted part of a solid coast barrier (*lisiére*) around the head of the inlets by which Russia had intended to shut Canada from the coast harbors. Although they had proposed to submit to a mutually satisfactory arbitral tribunal all questions which had arisen before the creation of the commission, they were unwilling to subject to the peril of arbitration the territory upon which (under American authority) cities and towns had been built, and valuable interests and industries established, without a word of protest or objection from either the British or Canadian governments.

Finally, influenced to make some concession, the Americans confidentially and unsuccessfully proposed, as a substitute means or adjustment, the plan which had been included in the Olney-Pauncefote draft treaty of arbitration of 1897: to submit the territorial claims to a joint tribunal of six judges of the highest standing, three appointed by each government, but with a condition that any tidewater settlements already under American jurisdiction should remain so. After the Canadian rejection of this plan, they joined in a British proposition for adjournment with the understanding that the boundary question should be returned to the two governments for further diplomatic negotiations and that until the completion of an arrangement for its adjustment the adjournment would continue.[14]

Before the final adjournment the Americans proposed to proceed with the other questions of difference which were so far advanced toward settlement; but the British commissioner declined to consider these questions further until after the adjustment of the boundary question.[15]

Sir Wilfrid Laurier, in explaining the final failure of the negotiations, said: "This arrangement [for lease of Pyramid Harbor] provoked such a storm in the Pacific states that our fellow Commissioners withdrew their consent. There was nothing left but to arbitrate. We wanted to arbitrate upon the terms of the Venezuela treaty. This they would not consent to. There was nothing else to do but to stop then and there. They offered to go on with the other subjects referred to us, but this we declined to do, and insisted, before we proceeded with the other articles, that they should either settle the boundary question by agreement or by reference to arbitration." [16]

For the difficulties in the negotiations and the disappointing failure of the commission Secretary Hay was inclined to blame the attitude of Lord Herschell who insisted on his way concerning the boundary, even at the risk of the abandonment of all the other subjects of proposed adjustment. He found the British government more inclined to compromise or to offer compensations elsewhere. By cable of February 15 he learned from Henry White that Salisbury had assured him that if the commission should reach an agreement the British government would promptly assent to the recent American proposal to modify the old Clayton-Bulwer treaty of 1850.[17]

In a letter of February 21 to White, after expressing deep regret at the failure of the negotiations, Hay declared that the American commissioners had gone "to the very verge of concessions to induce the Canadians to make a treaty." Concerning the policy of the Canadians, he said: "They refused to consider any form of arbitration, except that which they themselves proposed . . . and finally they refused to consider the proposition to isolate the Alaska question and to agree upon all the rest, leaving that open for future negotiation, although such progress had been made in the discussion of the other matters that an agreement was, in almost every one of them, clearly in sight." [18]

From London Hay soon received more hopeful news. On February 25, after submitting confidentially the American offer of arbitration by a mixed tribunal of six jurists, White reported Salisbury's hopefulness that the two governments could reach an agreement in August when the commission was expected to reconvene.[19]

After the final adjournment of the Commission with provision that it might reassemble upon the call of the two chairmen, Secretary Hay requested Foster to prepare a memorandum on the situation. In a prompt response, after stating that further meetings were then useless, Foster suggested the possibility and expediency of a temporary *modus vivendi* concerning the line in the vicinity of the head of Lynn Canal where early trouble was threatened. On March 20, in accord with this suggestion and after interviews concerning it, Hay proposed to Pauncefote to fix without prejudice a provisional line thirty miles from Pyramid Harbor and to establish immediately, by international cooperation, a provisional boundary monument at each of three points determined.[20]

Later, on April 19, 1899, after considering the failure of the Commission to reach an agreement and the irreconcilable difference of views in regard to an arrangement for final establishment of the boundary, Hay sent to Choate at London a suggestive draft of a convention for determination of the boundary and instructed him to impress upon Salisbury the President's earnest wish to obtain some friendly boundary agreement which would remove the obstacle to the completion of the Canadian negotiations for peaceful and mutually satisfactory adjustment of other questions of difference. On May 5 Choate found Salisbury embarrassed by the fact that the British government, in acting under an agreement with the United States, must consult with Canada although it did not seem to agree with the Canadian objection to the proposed method of settlement. He promptly reported that Salisbury could neither propose nor agree to anything without consulting the Secretary for the

Colonies who would probably say that he must consult with Sir Wilfrid Laurier. In a cablegram of May 15, however, he reported Canadian willingness to an arbitration of the Alaskan boundary on the lines of the British-Venezuelan adjustment.[21]

In his interviews with Pauncefote, at London, Choate considered a tentative plan for American retention of the American ports of Dyea and Skagway and for submission of the whole boundary question to an arbitral tribunal of seven members, the seventh to be chosen by the six jurists selected by the two governments. He soon learned that this plan was rejected by the Canadian authorities, who suggested that Pyramid Harbor on the Lynn Canal should be given to Canada. On May 18 he cabled that Salisbury, after consultation with Canada, could not concur in the previously approved arrangement, but that he now proposed as a substitute that Dyea and Skagway, if found (by arbitration) to be in British territory, would remain in American occupation and jurisdiction, and that Pyramid Harbor, if found to be within American territory, would remain in British occupation and jurisdiction. The latter novel demand, a Canadian strategic bargaining attempt to secure a much-coveted port "without basis of legal right," he regarded as unreasonable and astounding, and as "utterly inadmissible." In this opinion Hay concurred. He promptly informed the British legation at Washington that the new propostion was unacceptable and that he had so instructed Choate.[22]

Meantime, as a temporary expedient in deference to Canadian customs authorities, and without any purpose to prejudice American rights under the treaty of 1825, the American government had recently withdrawn its customs outposts on the trails or passes leading from the head of Lynn Canal.[23]

On May 22, at London, Pauncefote wrote Choate of the distress and disappointment caused by the failure of their efforts, which (he said) illustrated "how difficult it is to satisfy politicians whose tenure of office is at stake." In explanation of the situation he said: "The Canadians must know quite well that under the terms of the rules laid down in the Anglo-Venezuelan treaty, it is quite certain that Dyea and Skagway must be and remain American territory; but they dare not put it in the treaty in so many words as it looks as a concession granted without an equivalent, for which they would be attacked by their opponents in Parliament and in the press." He suggested an agreement that the tribunal in determining the boundary should not interefere with previous occupation or exclusive political control by either party.

On the same day Hay sent Choate a copy of the recent correspondence with the British legation which had resulted in an American agreement to suspend for the time the dispatch of troops to Pyramid Harbor, but without prejudice of American rights pending a determination of the issue. He had explained to Tower that the sole purpose in the contemplated establishment of a small military post in this tidewater territory, which had long been peacefully occupied by American citizens, was to prevent collision and to preserve public peace.[24]

Meantime, the question of a frontier line had been a subject of continued negotiations which had been delayed by constant British reference to Canada. By May, 1899, such a line was regarded as imperatively necessary. In June it became more necessary because of the attempts of Canada to exercise jurisdiction south of the Klehini River of which the United States had undisputed possession. On May 27 Hay suggested to Choate a provisional boundary at the summit of the White and Chilkoot passes and on a line north of Klukwan on the Dalton Trail. A week later he wrote Foster that the status of the *modus,* which had almost reached an agreement, had suddenly become involved in mystery, and that the news dispatches from London and Ottawa were contradictory. By Choate's dispatch of June 16, he learned that Salisbury, although impressed with the reasonableness of the American modifications of the British terms, awaited the opinion of Canada—resulting in the usual inevitable delay at a time when a speedy agreement was regarded as necessary. On June 27 he sent a cablegram earnestly urging prompt acceptance of the American proposal. On July 5 he wrote Foster, "We will not give them another inch of concession on the Dalton trail." On July 6 he cabled Choate that the American government could not recede from the line of Klehini as proposed.[25]

At London, Choate became increasingly anxious. On June

28, after receiving from Salisbury the Canadian proposition to establish a *modus vivendi* boundary at the junction of the Klehini and Chilkat rivers, he earnestly urged the prompt adoption of the earlier American proposition. On July 15, after receiving from Salisbury a suggestion that the Canadians must yield on the *modus vivendi,* and also the assurance that they would not break the peace, he reported the situation as hopeful.[26]

A few days later, in view of the uncertainty of pending negotiations, the contemplated meeting of the Anglo-American Joint Commission (set for August 2) was postponed without date, although Sir Wilfrid Laurier inferentially suggested that a meeting should be held in October.[27]

After the concessions already made Hay felt unable to recede any farther to the south. The British objection to the line of the Klehini as vague and ill-defined he endeavored practically to meet by proposing a "more feasible and definite line a little north of the Klehini"—an offer which the British regarded as "a considerable increase in demands." Finally, on August 3, he proposed two alternatives, slight variations of his previous offer.[28]

Early in August, anxious to clear the way for the negotiation of a modification or abrogation of the old Clayton-Bulwer treaty independent of Canadian matters, Hay was inclined to accept a proposition to lease to Canada some of the territory in dispute (at the head of Lynn Canal) and with a right of way for a railway thence to British territory on the Yukon, especially because such a lease would imply unquestioned American possession and sovereignty; but he doubted whether approval of the necessary two-thirds of the Senate could be obtained, and he was opposed both to the British proposition of a perpetual lease and to the Canadian plans to secure exclusive control of the leased port on the Lynn Canal and a proposed transit zone from that point across Alaska toward the British territory on the upper Yukon. Later, feeling that the lease of a terminal and a right of way was the only chance of an advantageous settlement of many questions, and that it should have the assent of the Senate, he asked Foster to use his influence in convincing Senator C. K. Davis that a lease was not a surrender but rather a success. On September 6 he notified Tower that he would accept the modification of the line proposed by Canada through Salisbury, along the high bank of the Klehini River, and he suggested a text for an agreement. On the following day he was somewhat disturbed by a recent *London Times* statement indicating that the British, contrary to the American assertion, had claimed a portion of Lynn Canal before 1898.[29]

During these negotiations arose new practical situations which indicated the necessity of an early understanding concerning the boundary. On September 19 Adee, in a note to Tower, raised a question concerning the appearance of Canadian mounted police in uniform at Skagway. Recognizing the propriety of an earlier Canadian suggestion that members of the American armed service should not wear uniform north of the summits of the Chilkoot and White passes, he suggested that within Alaskan jurisdiction the Canadians should observe the converse of their requirement.[30]

The necessity for an immediate permanent adjustment was finally lessened by the conclusion of the previously proposed temporary *modus vivendi* (of October 20, 1899). By this temporary concession, without prejudice to the claims of either party in the later negotiations for permanent adjustment, the American government agreed to fix, in the region of the Lynn Canal and the Dalton transmontane trail, a provisional boundary line which gave to Canada a temporary possession of several points which had always been regarded as American territory. Thereby, it probably encouraged Canada to hope for permanent possession.[31]

Meantime, on July 2, 1899, at London, in response to an invitation for a written formal proposal for permanent settlement of the boundary, Choate received from Salisbury a repetition of the earlier British-Canadian arbitration proposal, on the Venezuelan boundary basis, which the Americans had rejected. Against this proposal to place in peril American territory which had long been held in undisputed possession, Hay promptly directed Foster to draft a suitable answer. On July 20 he sent Choate a lengthy reply. In it, after reviewing the history of the boundary and the nature of the recent controversy, and after suggesting that Great Britain might properly be estopped from setting up its new claims, he expressed a possible disposition to consider an arbitration under fair and reasonable provisions, especially excepting towns and settlements and industries established before this recent British claim.[32]

In the subsequent discussion with Salisbury, Choate especially explained the American objection to arbitration on the basis of the British-Venezuelan arbitration and urged that the Alaskan boundary dispute was not an old one. He was unable to persuade him to recede from the position of the Canadian government or to accept the American proposition of settlement by a joint tribunal of six jurists and only animated him to a renewed attempt to maintain that the Alaskan boundary line had been in dispute since 1872.[33]

In November Hay sent to Choate the evidence that the Alaskan boundary was not in dispute in 1872. In concluding the instructions he declared that at no time previous to August 3, 1898, had the British government intimated a claim to waters of any of the inlets extending into the strip of territory to which Russia obtained title by the treaty of 1825. Therefore, he was unwilling to submit to arbitration any point which might question the American right to a continuous strip of territory on the mainland and to the waters of the sea enclosed by it as settled by the Russo-British treaty of 1825. He suggested that any arbitration arrangement should be limited in its scope to the boundary questions raised by the British government before 1898.[34]

In November, 1899, the American position in the controversy was very fully explained by John W. Foster in a lecture delivered before the American Geographic Society and widely circulated in the Society's magazine and in pamphlet form.[35]

In 1900–01 the American government unsuccessfully continued discussions with the British government in efforts to induce the Canadian government to recede from its position. In May, 1901, Hay submitted the drafts of two separate treaties which Canada later declined to approve—one for settlement of the Alaskan boundary and the other for adjustment of the remaining Canadian questions except trade reciprocity and the Atlantic fisheries. Six months later, in obtaining British consent to the Hay-Pauncefote canal treaty, he escaped any compensating concessions which the Canadian government had hoped to obtain in Alaska. Soon thereafter President Roosevelt, pressed by Pacific coast interests to avoid concessions on the Alaskan frontier, expressed determined opposition to any proposal to arbitrate any unquestionable American rights such as the American claim to the seacoast under the Anglo-Russian treaty of 1825.[86]

Late in June, 1902, Choate was urged by Lansdowne to confer with Laurier who was then in London, and who desired to explain the urgency of the situation. This conference the Department promptly authorized by confidential cable cipher of June 30, which mentioned the President's opinion that the Canadian claim had not a leg on which to stand and that compromise was impossible.

Early in July the President received through Hay information (from Henry White) that Laurier was anxious to have the boundary question settled—and that he no longer hoped to get Lynn Canal but wanted to save his face by having the matter decided against him, or possibly by compensation elsewhere. On July 10 he replied that in his judgment compromise was not possible. Referring to the recent Canadian claim as "outrageous and indefensible," he said: "I could not submit to any arbitration in the matter. I am entirely willing to appoint three commissioners on our side to meet three commissioners on theirs and try to fix the line, but I should definitely instruct our three . . . not to yield any territory whatsoever, but . . . to insist upon our entire claim." He was not willing to make concessions to relieve the Canadians from the possible effects of their own "false claim."[87]

Hay, although he agreed that Canada had "no leg to stand on," favored some sort of reference of the controversy to a judicial commission for settlement. On July 14 he explained to the President that his suggestion was to submit the question of the interpretation of the treaty of 1825 to a mixed tribunal of six (three on each side), with provision for a majority decision. Concerning the latter suggestion, he said: "In this case it is impossible that we should lose, and not at all impossible that a majority should give a verdict in our favor." He also explained that "Sir Wilfrid's suggestion concerning compensation does not mean . . . that compensation should be given in case the commission should decide in our favor—but that in case of decision in their favor they would not insist on possession of Dyea and Skagway but would consider the subject of compensation for American retention of the strip." [38]

In a confidential cablegram of July 17, following Choate's interview with Laurier, and immediately after receiving Roosevelt's letter of July 16, Hay expressed to Choate the opinion that negotiation of an arrangement for a boundary tribunal acceptable to the Senate would be found very difficult. Apparently he especially desired to find some basis of adjustment which would avoid any excited debate in the Senate. He suggested to the President that "a debate in Congress on the subject, with Champ Clark and Tillman with open throttle on the floor, would be a portent to the civilized world." [39]

In the autumn the Roosevelt administration was favored in its plans by Sir Michael H. Herbert (the brilliant young successor of Pauncefote) who was able to influence his government and the Canadian government to accept the American proposition for adjustment.

Finally, in December, 1902, following an interview with Laurier at Washington, and deciding to make a last effort for a peaceful settlement "with due regard to England's honor," President Roosevelt accepted Hay's view in favor of arbitration. On January 24, 1903, after Lansdowne's frank reversal of his policy in the contemplated joint Anglo-German debt collecting expedition against Venezuela, Hay signed with Herbert a convention establishing a joint judicial tribunal of six "impartial jurists of repute" (three appointed by each government) to meet at London to consider judicially the questions involved in the interpretation of the Anglo-Russian treaty of 1825, and to settle the boundary line. For this achievement, in the face of strong opposition, Foster stated that the chief credit belonged to President Roosevelt and Secretary Hay and Sir Wilfrid Laurier.[40]

The President promptly applied his efforts to secure the assent of the Senate. In this task he encountered certain newspaper editorial opposition which urged rejection of the treaty on the ground that it made a concession concerning territory long in undisputed American possession. He also found his efforts opposed by the lobbying influences of a legal representative of the Northern Pacific Railway. He was doubtless aided by a published newspaper communication of Mr. Foster which by order of Secretary Hay was re-published in pamphlet form and distributed to all members of the Senate. He was also aided by political expedience in consulting with leaders in the Senate concerning the choice of American members of the tribunal. He secured the Senate's approval of the treaty on February 11, 1903, with unusual promptness and little debate.[41]

After learning that members of the Supreme Court had expressed doubt whether they could consistently accept an invitation to sit on a diplomatic and political tribunal, and in accord with an understanding with the leaders of the Senate, the President judiciously appointed as the American members of the tribunal Elihu Root (Secretary of War), Senator Henry Cabot Lodge (of Massachusetts) and Senator George Turner (of Washington). These he properly regarded as eminent lawyers, although they were not considered as "impartial" by Canadian authorities. In a personal and confidential letter of March 25, notifying them of their appointment, he stated that he regarded as untenable the Canadian claim to Skagway and Dyea (and Pyramid Harbor) which Laurier recently had asserted in open Parliament at Ottawa. In justification of his opposition he said the claim was in violation of the evident intention of the Anglo-Russian treaty of 1825 and of the British interpretation of it until 1898.[42]

To act as counsel in presentation of the American side of the case the American government selected John W. Foster whose ability as an agent was already widely recognized. The proposal of the President and Hay that Ambassador Choate should present before the commission the American case, which was prepared by Foster, was declined by Choate on the ground of international impropriety resulting from his many conferences upon the subject with British ministers from whom he had acquired much information which he did not feel free to use before the judicial tribunal.

For British members of the tribunal King Edward appointed Baron Alverstone (Lord Chief Justice) of England, Lieutenant-Governor Louis Jetté of Quebec, and Allen Bristol Aylesworth of the Ontario bar. W. R. Thayer in his biography of Hay suggested that the appointment of Alverstone was a concession to President Roosevelt who had declared his determination that, in case the mixed commission failed, he would obtain authority of Congress "to run the line as we claim it, by our own people, without further regard to the attitude of England and Canada."

Hay received some criticism for proposing the place of meeting at London, as designated in the treaty. One protest, which referred to the strong London "magnetic influences that the English use to debilitate the American," he forwarded to Foster with the jocular note of comment, "I do not know whether the appropriation will provide lightning rods for each of you, but, if possible, I will strain the point that far." [43]

Late in June Lodge protested against a British proposal to delay the meeting of the tribunal until October, especially objecting to the personal inconvenience to himself, and even suggesting that the proposed delay to a time so near the meeting of Congress was a British attempt to keep himself and Senator Root from serving on the tribunal. To the President he suggested a preference for a longer delay until the next summer.

The President promptly acted to prevent any delay. To Hay he wrote (on June 29):

"I don't want the thing pending during a presidential campaign, and moreover if the English decline to come to an agreement this fall, under any pretense, I shall feel that it is simply due to bad faith,—that they have no sincere desire to settle the matter equitably. I think that they ought to be made to understand that . . . the agreement must be kept . . . I hope Choate will gently convey to them the substance of our conversation that afternoon on the White House portico, . . . that I shall probably, if they fail to come to some agreement, bring the matter to the attention of Congress and ask for an appropriation so that we can run the line ourselves. I do not want to make this as a threat, and of course it may be that it would be inadvisable to do it." [44]

Lodge, who apparently was willing to locate the Portland Channel line on either side of the channel, desired to undertake preliminary *pourparlers* at London to facilitate or advance the work of the tribunal. On July 1, in a letter to the President, he offered to attempt to hasten the settlement by going to London three or four weeks ahead of Root and Turner; and he requested the President to direct Hay to issue the proper instructions to enable him to speak with authority to the British members of the tribunal and Lord Lansdowne, and to secure for him the coöperative backing of the American embassy. On July 8, he renewed the suggestion. On July 10, in referring to it again he said: "I think when we get to London and put a gentle pressure on them we can get the matter disposed of in a reasonable time." [45]

Late in July Lodge arrived at London, but without any formal or official instructions. On July 30, after he had met Alverstone at a dinner at Choate's, he wrote the President that the whole difficulty concerning the settlement of the boundary was due to the Canadians. Later, from Paris, he wrote: "The only question is whether Lord Alverstone will go with us on the main points. . . . Very likely he will, but England is in such mortal terror of Canada that I feel more than doubtful in regard to it. . . . The fact is that Canada is in that worst of all possible positions of possessing power unaccompanied by any responsibility." [46]

The American government sought to avoid further proposals for delay. On August 5, in a personal note to Foster, Hay expressed amazement at the written request of the Canadian agent, Clifford Sifton, for postponement of the tribunal. In conclusion he wrote: "The fact is they are beaten and they know it—and they think we are 'hard on them' because we do not allow them all the pettifogging delays they ask for. We must of course be excessively courteous and indulgent with them so as not to make it too difficult for them to agree."

On August 21, in a personal note to Hay, Roosevelt wrote: "I most certainly hope the English will ultimately act with sanity and propriety in that Alaska business. It will be a great misfortune if they do not—a misfortune for us and a much greater one for England and Canada." [47]

On September 3 the tribunal was satisfactorily organized at London with Lord Alverstone as president. After an adjournment of nine days for convenience of counsel, it reconvened on September 12 for the beginning of oral arguments which closed on October 8.

On September 5, from Paris, Lodge wrote President Roosevelt: "I think there is no doubt we shall finish so I can get away on October 21 . . . Choate and Foster and Harry White (especially Choate and White) have strong hopes that we shall get a decision. . . . Root and Turner and myself from the general tone of things, do not feel hopeful."[48]

Throughout the oral presentation of the arguments the two Canadian members of the tribunal seemed to fear that Alverstone would favor the Amercians in his decisions. On October 8 they probably contemplated withdrawal, against which Laurier forwarded his disapproval. The harmony of intercourse, however, was not marred by any harsh word nor by any unpleasant incident. Throughout the period of the sessions the members and official staff were recipients of many courtesies of the British government and also of many social attentions in their honor. The only really disagreeable feature of the stay in London was the miserable weather.[49]

Foster in his Memoirs refers to the marked contrast between the British and American lawyers in their manner of argument before the tribunal. The British spoke with marked deliberation and dignity, usually in a quiet tone and without gestures, and the Americans with vigor and with frequent emphasis, rather active in gesture and happy in their occasional use of witticisms and amusing anecdotes to illustrate their points of argument.

The two leading points of controversy before the joint tribunal were (1) whether the land boundary of the Alaskan panhandle included the heads of all salt-water inlets and (2) whether the water boundary through the Portland Canal in the vicinity of 54°40′ was located south or north of a few uninhabited islands. Of most importance was the American contention for a line about thirty miles inland, claimed on the basis of the purpose and terms of the Anglo-Russian treaty of 1825, and opposed by the Canadians who wished access to the ocean through the inlets. Foster, before he left Washington, had suggested to Secretary Hay that the question of the islands in the Portland Canal might afford an opportunity for a satisfactory compromise decision by the tribunal, and he was authorized by Hay and by Roosevelt to agree to such a proposal. In a personal note from Oyster Bay, on September 15, Roosevelt wrote to Hay: "I agree with all you say about those little islands. I shall be glad to use them as a makeshift in the Alaska boundary matter. If we can come to an agreement over them, all right; if not, arbitrate—before the Hague court by preference."[50]

Meantime Foster and Lodge reported evidence of Canadian efforts to influence opinion concerning the issue. On September 13 Lodge wrote Roosevelt: "We begin to hear the arguments today. The Canadians have been filling the newspapers with articles of the most violent kind, threatening England with all sorts of things if the decision should go against Canada. They are all aimed, I suppose, at Lord Alverstone." On September 24, after a week and a half of argument, he wrote: "Meantime Lord Alverstone has been saying a great many things to Root and me, who sit on either hand. . . . He takes very decisively the British view on the Portland Canal."

On September 20, after hearing of pessimistic forecasts of the verdict, Hay wrote Foster that Lord Alverstone, with the knowledge that this was the last chance for an honorable and graceful British retreat from an absolutely untenable position, would hardly shut his eyes to the law and evidence in favor of the American contention.

On the following day, after reading Foster's letter and clippings indicative of Canadian press propaganda at London, Roosevelt sent to Hay a personal letter in which he said: "I wonder if they realize that while it may be unpleasant to us, it will be far more unpleasant to them, if they force the alternative upon us, if we simply announce that the country is ours and will remain so."[51] Later, in a personal note of October 5, he wrote Lodge: "Of course we can yield on the islands, if Alverstone goes with us on the main contention (on the line around the heads of the inlets). . . . The plain fact is that the British have no case whatever, and . . . Alverstone ought to be satisfied with the very minimum—simply enough to save his face and bring an adjustment. Rather than give up an essential we should accept a disagreement. . . . We must not weaken on the points that are of serious importance."[52]

On October 15, before a formal vote had been taken on any question, and when an American stand on the ten marine leagues throughout seemed to involve a disagreement, Choate cabled Hay a secret and urgent inquiry. He asked whether an adjournment for a year to await completion of a survey to the ten marine leagues line, by experts to be employed by the tribunal, would be preferable to an immediate vote which would result in a disagreement except on one question (Question 5). Hay promptly cabled a reply that if the tribunal had decided the fifth question in favor of the American contention, the President would not object to an adjournment, and confidentially suggested that, if necessary, the American commissioners might decide (on the third question) in favor of the English contention as to the North Channel of Portland Canal.[53]

On October 20, Lord Alverstone delivered to the agents of the two governments the majority decision of the tribunal (the two Canadian members dissenting). This decision fixed the land boundary in accord with the American contention and agreed upon a compromise water boundary by which Canada obtained two of the four uninhabited islands, which it had regarded as of great strategic value in commanding the probable terminus of the Grand Trunk Pacific. President Roosevelt announced that the result of the settlement was the greatest diplomatic victory of a generation. Secretary Hay regarded it as one of the greatest transactions of his life.[54]

On October 29, 1903, Hay sent to the President a few extracts from an interesting letter of Henry White indicating certain diplomatic influences in reaching the settlement. In this letter, after referring to Hay's terse statement of September 30 that the British "must see what the result of a failure to agree would be," he told of a visit with the Prime Minister (on October 2–4) and of a long talk with him (on October 4) which left upon his mind no doubt as to the importance of a settlement nor as to the result of a failure to agree. "I explained to him very fully the position of Alverstone," said White, "and intimated that I thought it would be very desirable that he should be told that the Government, without in any way wishing to influence him, was very anxious for a decision." Two days after this talk he learned from the Prime Minister's confidential secretary (Saunders) that the latter had had two interviews with Alverstone. Later, when a deadlock was threatened, he "never for one moment doubted that the undercurrents of diplomacy would bring about a decision in the end."

Possibly the settlement was also influenced and hastened by a talk of Choate with Lansdowne on the Wednesday before the decision, by the intimacy between Lodge and Alverstone in discussing the delicate problems involved, and by the conciliatory attitude of Foster. Choate reported that in his unofficial and confidential interview with Lansdowne he had urgently pressed the views of the President as expressed to him in June, and had asserted that this was the last chance to settle the question by agreement on a line which might partly satisfy Canadian wishes. In his report he said: "I left satisfied that he and Mr. Balfour would, if they had not already done so, tell Lord Alverstone what they thought as to the necessity of agreeing upon that line, and that the present chance of settling the controversy ought not to be lost."[55]

Coincident with the announcement of the award, the rejoicing over the peaceful settlement of a source of discordant excitement, and over the removal of a serious obstacle to the improvement of neighborhood relations, was somewhat clouded by a published interview of the Canadian members of the tribunal who asserted that the decision was not judicial in its character and improperly arraigned their colleague for wrong motives and inconsistent conduct. The Canadian agent (Clifford Sifton), however, announced that Canada would accept the decision and carry it into effect in good faith.

In the Canadian Parliament, on October 23, Laurier was vigorously attacked for failing to link the Alaskan question with the isthmian canal treaty, for failure to demand the appointment of three Canadians on the tribunal, and for failing to make the award subject to the ratification of the Canadian Parliament. In reply, after stating his disappointment, he expressed regret that Canada did not have in its control the treaty-making power necessary to direct its own affairs and definitely to locate responsibility. Later he steadily advanced the Canadian impulse to independent control of foreign policy—although in 1909, in reply to a proposal for the appointment of a Canadian minister or chargé at Washington, he asserted that so long as James Bryce was British ambassador at Washington Canada needed no special minister there.[56]

In reply to Sir Wilfrid's frank opinion that the decisions could not be supported on judicial grounds, Lord Alverstone wrote him: "I desire to state most emphatically that the decisions, whether they were right or wrong, were judicial and founded on no other considerations. I alone am responsible for them." If he was influenced by the diplomatic consideration that the Alaskan strip of territory was not worth enough to justify a war, he was probably correct, for its importance to Canada decreased with the decline of gold production on the Yukon. Whether influenced by non-judicial considerations or not, he apparently suffered a loss of Canadian esteem. Later, in 1908, when the American Bar Association planned to invite him to give an address at its annual meeting which would have involved also a question of a visit to Canada, Bryce in a note to Governor-General Grey at Ottawa suggested that he would not accept, because he was not *persona gratissima* in Canada.[57]

On March 25, 1905, by exchange of notes, Acting Secretary Adee and the British minister (Durand) accepted the report of the commissioners to complete the award concerning the boundary.

Meantime, Hay had renewed American efforts to secure a satisfactory settlement of other questions, chiefly those which had been postponed since 1899 by the refusal of the Canadians to separate them from the Alaskan question.

REFERENCES

1. *National Geographic Mag.*, Nov., 1899, pp. 429–30, 434–36, 439–40 (J. W. Foster); *Fur Seal Arbitration, Papers*, 1893, IV, 370, 405, 424, 428, 430, 434, 441, 446–47.
2. *Nat. Geog. Mag.*, Nov., 1899, pp. 443, 452–53; *33 G.B., Instrs.*,

pp. 283–90, No. 241, Nov. 10, 1899; *Can. Law Rev.*, Sept., 1902, pp. 525–37 (THOMAS HODGKIN); *Can. Session Papers*, 1878, No. 125, pp. 6–8; *27 G.B., Instrs.*, pp. 592–610, No. 144, Nov. 20, 1885.

3. *17 G.B., Notes*, pp. 307–12, Jan. 10, 1877, and p. 340, Feb. 20, 1877; *Can. Law Rev.*, Sept., 1902, p. 532; *For. Rels., 1878*, p. 346; *107 G.B., Desps.*, May 22, 1899.
4. *27 G.B., Instrs.*, pp. 592–610, No. 144, Nov. 20, 1885; *33 G.B., Instrs.*, pp. 283–90, No. 241, Nov. 10, 1899; *Sen. Exec. Docs.*, 49–1, No. 143, p. 3; RICHARDSON, *Messages*, VIII, 333.
5. *27 G.B., Instrs.*, pp. 692–93, No. 240, Mar. 16, 1886; *28 G.B., Instrs.*, p. 26, No. 280, Apr. 26, 1886; *Ib.*, pp. 596–97, No. 970, Oct. 1, 1888.
6. RICHARDSON, *Messages*, VIII, 781.
7. *3 Reciprocity Treaties, 1898–1907, Canada,* JNO. A. KASSON, Nos. 29–30; RICHARDSON, IX, 631; MALLOY, *Treaties*, I, 763–66.
8. *125 G.B., Notes from,* Pauncefote to Olney, Aug. 20, 1895; *23 G.B., Notes to,* pp. 181–82, No. 184, Sept. 6, 1895.
9. RICHARDSON, IX, 631, 665; *Sen. Docs.*, 54–1, Vol. 4, No. 112, Feb. 10, 1896; *23 G.B., Notes* [*to*], pp. 324–26, No. 345, March 11, 1896; *Can. Law Rev.*, Sept., 1902, p. 533.
10. *33 G.B., Instrs.*, pp. 283–90, No. 241, Nov. 10, 1899; O. D. SKELTON, *Life and Letters of Sir Wilfrid Laurier*, II, 46–49.
11. J. W. FOSTER, *Diplomatic Memoirs*, II, 454; *Nat. Geog. Mag.*, Nov., 1899, p. 455 (J. W. FOSTER).
12. *Ib.*, p. 436; Annex to *3 Reciprocity Treaties, 1898–1907* (Kasson's draft of a treaty on Canadian questions).
13. *Nat. Geog. Mag.*, Nov., 1899, p. 455; *33 G.B., Instrs.*, pp. 143–51, No. 87, Apr. 19, 1899; *Ib.*, Tel., May 19, 1899; *Misc. Archives*, 1893–98; SKELTON, *Life and Letters of Sir Wilfrid Laurier*, II, 132.
14. *Nat. Geog. Mag.*, Nov., 1899, p. 455–56; *33 G.B., Instrs.*, No. 87, Hay to Choate, Apr. 19, 1899; SKELTON, *Life and Letters of Sir Wilfrid Laurier*, II, 135–38.
15. MALLOY, *Treaties*, I, 773.
16. SKELTON, *Life and Letters of Laurier*, II, 132; *Baltimore American*, June 5, 1899.
17. *Hay Papers,* Hay to Henry White, Feb. 14, 1899; *196 G.B.*, Tel., White to Hay, Feb. 15, 1899.
18. *Hay Papers*, Feb. 21, 1899.
19. *196 G.B., Desps.*, No. 699, Feb. 25, 1899.
20. FOSTER, *Diplomatic Memoirs*, II, 192; *24 G.B., Notes to,* pp. 684–85, No. 1381, Mar. 20, 1899.
21. *33 G.B., Instrs.*, No. 87, Apr. 19, 1899; *197 G.B., Desps.*, No. 81, May 5; *Ib.*, Tel., May 15.

22. *Ib.*, Tels., May 12, 15 and 18; *Ib.*, Private and Confidential, May 24, 1899; *24 G.B., Notes to,* p. 527, May 18; *Ib.*, pp. 531–33, No. 1454, May 19; *33 G.B., Instrs.*, No. 138, May 22, 1899; *197 G.B., Desps.*, Private and Confidential, May 19, and No. 85, May 19, 1899.
23. *Ib.*, May 22, 1899.
24. *Ib.*, Choate to Hay, May 24, 1899 (Enclosure of Pauncefote's private and confidential note); *33 G.B., Instrs.*, No. 138, May 22; *24 G.B., Notes* [*to*], p. 527, May 17.
25. *33 G.B., Instrs.*, p. 183, Tel., May 27; *Ib.*, pp. 188–89, Tel., June 8; *Ib.*, No. 164, June 23, and Tel., June 25; *Ib.*, p. 210, Tel., July 6; *197 G.B., Desps.*, Nos. 94, 95, 99, 109, 110, 112, of June 2, 6, 14, 23, and July 1, 5, and "Private" of June 16; *24 G.B., Notes* [*to*], p. 527, May 17; *Foster Papers,* Hay to Foster, June 14, and July 5.
26. *197 G.B., Desps.*, No. 110, July 1, 1899 (with inclosure); *Ib.*, No. 118, July 12; *Misc. Archives,* 1893–98, Private, Choate to Hay, July 15, 1899.
27. *Foster Papers,* C. W. Fairbanks to Foster, July 26, 1899.
28. *24 G.B., Notes to,* pp. 590–92, Aug. 3, 1899.
29. *33 G.B., Instrs.*, pp. 236–37, No. 198, Aug. 21, 1899; *Misc. Archives,* 1893–98; *Foster Papers,* Sept. 26 (and Sept. 10), 1899; *24 G.B., Notes to,* pp. 614–17, No. 1552, Sept. 6, 1899.
30. *Ib.*, pp. 629–31, No. 1564, Sept. 19, 1899.
31. J. W. Foster, *Diplomatic Memoirs,* I, 777; Malloy, *Treaties,* I, 777–78; *For. Rels., 1899,* pp. 330– ; *British Treaty Series,* 1899, No. 19; *Rev. of Revs.*, XXVIII, 527.
32. Foster, *Diplomatic Memoirs,* II, 193; *197 G.B., Desps.*, No. 112, July 5, 1899; *33 G.B., Instrs.*, pp. 219–25, No. 183, July 20, 1899.
33. *Ib.*, pp. 237–38, Nos. 199 and 200, Aug. 21, 1899.
34. *Ib.*, pp. 283–90, No. 241, Nov. 10, 1899.
35. Foster, *Dip. Memoirs,* II, 192.
36. Malloy, *Treaties,* I, 782; Skelton, *Life and Letters of Sir Wilfrid Laurier,* II, 141.
37. *205 G.B., Desps.*, Tel., June 29, 1902; *34 G.B., Instrs.*, p. 198, June 30, 1902; *Hay-Roosevelt Papers,* Hay to T. R., I, 1901–02; *Ib.*, T. R. to Hay, Vol. 5, 1897–1903.
38. *Ib.*, Hay to T. R., I, 1901–02.
39. *34 G.B., Instrs.*, p. 212, Tel., July 17, 1902; *Hay-Roosevelt Papers,* Hay to T. R., I, 1901–02.
40. Foster, *Dip. Memoirs,* II, 194, 209; Malloy, *Treaties,* I, 787–92.
41. *Hay-Roosevelt Papers,* Hay to T. R., Vol. 2, 1903–05 (Feb. 7, 1903); Foster, *Dip. Memoirs,* I, 194–95; *For. Rels., 1903; 26 G.B., Notes* [*to*], pp. 339–40, Feb. 2, and No. 73, Feb. 13, 1903.

42. Skelton, *Life and Letters of Sir Wilfrid Laurier*, II, 144–46; Foster, *Dip. Memoirs*, II, 199; Thayer, *Life of John Hay*, II, 209; T. R., *Personal Letter Book*, Vol. 9, p. 230; *Ib.*, Vol. 10, June 29, July 8, and Aug. 16; *Ib.*, Vol. 11, p. 367; *Selections from the Corres. of Theodore Roosevelt and H. C. Lodge*, Vol. 2, pp. 4–5.
43. Thayer, *Life of John Hay*, II, 210 and 212; *Foster Papers*, June 4, 1903.
44. *T. R. Papers*, Lodge to T. R., 1901–03 (July 2, 1903); *Ib.*, T. R. to Hay, Vol. 5, 1897–1903; *Foster Papers*, Hay to Foster, July 2, 1903.
45. *T. R. Papers*, Lodge to T. R., July 1, 8 and 10, 1903.
46. *Selections from the Corres. of Roosevelt and Lodge*, Vol. 2, pp. 41–43, 48.
47. *Foster Papers*, Aug. 5, 1903; T. R. to Hay, Vol. 5, 1897–1903.
48. Hay to T. R., II, 1903–05; *T. R. Papers*, Lodge to T. R., 1901–03.
49. Foster, *Dip. Memoirs*, II, 207–09.
50. *Ib.*, 202–03; T. R. to Hay, Vol. 5, 1897–1903.
51. *Selections from the Corres. of Roosevelt and Lodge, 1884–1918*, Vol. 2, pp. 55–59; Foster, *Dip. Memoirs*, II, 205–06; T. R. to Hay, Vol. 5, 1897–1903.
52. *President Roosevelt's Letter Book*, Vol. 12, pp. 406–07.
53. *208 G.B., Desps.*, Tel., Oct. 15, 1903; *34 G.B., Instrs.*, pp. 498–99, Tel., Oct. 16.
54. *208 G.B., Desps.*, Tel., Oct. 20, and No. 1222, Oct. 21, 1903.
55. Hay to T. R., II, 1903–05.
56. Skelton, *Life and Letters of Sir Wilfrid Laurier*, II, 155–56, 347.
57. *Ib.*, 157, 159; *Laurier Papers, Gov. Gen'l's Cor.*, Grey, 1908, Bryce to Grey, Confid., Feb. 1, 1908.

CHAPTER XX

THE WAY OF TRANSITION TO EASIER ADJUSTMENTS

IN the first decade of the new era of reciprocal neighborhood friendliness after 1903, characterized by an increased American interest in Canada, practically all remaining questions of importance in Canadian relations were amicably discussed and adjusted, leaving little source of border irritation except the inconvenience of high tariffs.

In the earlier years, until May, 1906, only two questions reached the stage of a treaty settlement: the question of a supplementary extradition convention which was finally signed at London in April, 1905, and the question of demarcation of the Alaskan boundary on the meridian of 141° W. which was concluded at Washington in April, 1906.

The general preliminary discussion of the more important questions, however, set the stage for the later negotiations which finally resulted in several other adjustments by treaties.

For these adjustments the way was prepared by Secretary Hay who led the advance toward broader American views of world policy, by Secretary Root who visited Ottawa in 1907 to discuss international questions, and by James Bryce (the British ambassador at Washington) who visited Ottawa each year and otherwise showed a live interest in Canadian affairs. In Canada the way was also made easier by the watchful direction of Governor-General Grey and later by the cautious coöperation of Prime Minister Laurier.

On both sides of the boundary appeared obstacles which restricted and delayed executive action. In the United States President Roosevelt found that Congress was "evidently prepared to be a little sensitive" concerning its prerogatives. In

1903, seeking to forestall possible criticism of the House, which he had seen foreshadowed in the slightly nervous attitude of the Speaker "Uncle Joe" Cannon, he suggested to Hay the advisability of keeping in close touch with Hitt, of the Committee on Foreign Affairs. Later he encountered greater difficulty from the necessity of considering the attitude of the Senate upon the subjects of negotiation.[1]

The prominent remaining problems of the first decade after the settlement of the Alaskan boundary controversy Root summarized in May, 1906, after a period of general tandem negotiation upon certain subjects without any general plan of parallel negotiations. He especially reflected an increasing American interest in coöperation in the use and disposition of international waters. In compliance with a request of H. Mortimer Durand, he submitted a list of sixteen outstanding questions pending between Canada and the United States. He proposed to resume consideration of the chief ones at the point reached by the Joint High Commission of 1898–99 and to dispose of them by direct negotiation. To the earlier list of twelve questions formulated by the Washington conference of May, 1898, and left unsettled by the Joint High Commission, he added four or five questions which had subsequently arisen: (1) the uses and disposition of international waterways (under consideration by the International Waterways Commission) including the diversion of water which threatened destruction of Niagara Falls; (2) the use of logging booms on the St. John River; (3) various pecuniary claims (on both sides); (4) minor questions relating to an American immigration head tax on Canadians temporarily entering the United States; and (5) an American requirement of bills of health from Canadian vessels arriving from Atlantic ports of the Dominion. Concerning the pecuniary claims, he saw no reason why they could not be settled by direct negotiation but was willing to resort to arbitration if necessary or expedient. For settlement of other questions he proposed concurrent legislation for some and conventions for others.[2]

Root's memorandum to Durand was the result of renewed efforts earlier in 1906 to secure a friendly settlement of all pending questions at a favorable time, before the next election.

On January 19, in a letter to Governor-General Earl Grey, President Roosevelt said he was anxious to do everything possible to increase the good feeling between Canada and the United States. This feeling Grey reciprocated. In a private letter of April 3 to Lord Elgin of the Colonial Office, written at New York where he and Root had attended a "Pilgrims Dinner" on March 31, he urged that the time furnished a really good opportunity for "cleaning the slate" of all outstanding questions if a meeting of Prime Minister Laurier with Secretary Root could be arranged. Seeking to prepare the way before possible unfavorable changes which might result from the next election, he strongly recommended that Laurier should be allowed to send to Washington, officially, a Canadian expert to help Durand in the negotiations with Root. "The closer you bring Ottawa and Washington together," he said, "the greater the chances of cleaning the slate." Three weeks later he received additional evidence that Root was anxious to "clean the slate." Meantime he reported that Laurier was opposed to the opening of formal negotiations without preliminaries insuring beforehand agreement between the two governments.

Although indifferent to the possible hostility of the Senate, Laurier desired to avoid the possibility of a breakdown in negotiations which might arouse angry feelings in both countries. However, he was ready to consider private communications conveying Root's proposals and privately to submit his own proposals to Root through the British ambassador; and, if convinced of a chance of settlement, he was willing to send to Washington an expert to help the British ambassador as a plenipotentiary. His proposal, approved by Grey and Elgin, resulted in British instructions to Durand to submit the plan to Root and also in a trip of Durand to London to talk with the Foreign Office on the various questions.

Incident to the plan Grey courteously invited Root and family to visit him at Ottawa in the following winter—an invitation which Root promptly accepted. Coincidently, the British government obtained from Laurier his consent to a proposal to exclude pecuniary claims from the scope of general settlement, leaving these claims for reference to arbitration.[8]

The résumé of the situation in regard to pending questions, which Root submitted on May 3, Laurier did not receive from Grey until May 23. Then, busy with Parliament, he delayed to reply. After several official reminders transmitted from Washington and London through Grey, he announced that he could not possibly prepare a statement before July 1. In August, still delayed, he received a more urgent reminder through a private letter which Grey received from Elgin and which was stimulated by the expressed anxiety of Sir Edward Grey of the Foreign Office. Finally, on September 25, he submitted his views. With these Grey agreed, although he tactfully suggested a few changes of words in order to avoid charges which "some people might resent." Over two months later, on November 29, Grey received from Elgin a cable stating that the Foreign Office had instructed the British ambassador to communicate informally Laurier's memorandum to Root with an intimation of the hope that the American government would consider it as basis for discussion.

On December 2, before Laurier's views reached Washington, Root, admitting that he felt "a little discouraged," wrote Grey to propose the beginning of the week of January 21, 1907, as a convenient time for his prospective visit with the Greys at Government House, a proposal which resulted in a definite arrangement for January 19–23.

In planning the incidents of the visit and the courtesies due to Root, Grey especially sought to arrange contacts with Laurier which might result in a better understanding of the situation. In the results of the visit he saw new reasons for hope. At the end of February he received the acceptance of Bryce to an invitation for a similar visit, and by March 2 he received from President Roosevelt a breezy letter which stimulated him almost to believe that the light on the mountain top was descending.[4]

Apparently Roosevelt doubted the practicability of a contemplated attempt to negotiate a general treaty for the settlement of all remaining American-Canadian questions. On April 8, 1907, in a personal letter to Arthur Lee of the British House of Commons, he wrote: "Bryce has started out well.

Whether we can get a general treaty settling the questions between Canada and the United States, I do not know. I should tremble about laying such a treaty before the Senate." [5]

By the beginning of 1908 Root and Bryce had made considerable progress on pending draft treaties for adjustment of several questions. Early in January Root urged the importance of quick progress on all pending questions in order to get the approval of the Senate before the close of the session of Congress. He furnished new evidence of his friendly liberality which especially convinced Bryce and Grey of his sincere desire to reach an agreement on all questions. Bryce regarded both Root and the President as personally friendly and suggested to Grey that if they were not restricted by the Senate he could probably dispose of all outstanding negotiations, but he felt that they apparently would be powerless in efforts to obtain the consent of the Senate. Three weeks later, after Secretary Root by concessions to Canada had considerably facilitated the chances of the completion of the most important negotiations, Howard of the British legation reported that Bacon of the Department of State apparently had little hope that the Senate would agree and especially suggested the importance of an early reply from the Canadian government. On February 1 Grey informed Laurier that Bryce had reported that Root had given way on practically all the important controversial points of recent negotiations and that he had again urged the importance of taking advantage of Root's friendship to Canada by a prompt reply (by February 7) to facilitate efforts to secure the approval of the Senate.[6]

Meantime, near the close of January, Laurier, in response to an indirect invitation from President Roosevelt, took an unexpected step which led the way to easier negotiations. Deciding to consult with the American government concerning coöperation in a policy in regard to restriction of Japanese immigration, he sent Mackenzie King from Ottawa to Washington on a somewhat irregular and delicate but friendly and significant mission, with instructions to confer with Roosevelt and Root. This mission, through the concurrent action of Bryce, resulted in a very friendly exchange of information and views concerning recent negotiations with Japan. On February 1, following a White House luncheon conference with Bryce and King, Roosevelt wrote Laurier a note of appreciation in which he said: "I think it altogether admirable that this step should have been taken, and that there should now be a fair likelihood of both nations working cordially together for their own interests." After a brief acknowledgement of memoranda about wood pulp and lumber he continued: "Believe me, My dear Sir Wilfrid, that it was a particular pleasure to hear from you and to meet Mr. King and that I feel the directness, simplicity and good faith of such a communication is a happy omen for the future. . . . I am exceedingly pleased at the steps that have been taken to bring our several peoples into a closer and more friendly connection."

Apparently as a result of the conference with President Roosevelt and Secretary Root, King visited England with confidential messages from the President to Sir Edward Grey, especially with the purpose to secure British coöperation in communicating to Japan the American assurances calculated to relieve a critical situation concerning restriction of Japanese immigration and to result in a gentlemen's agreement with Japan similar to the British Canadian agreement. Soon thereafter Bryce reported information that Japan, with assurances that it had no intention to quarrel with the United States, had promised to restrict Japanese immigration in a way satisfactory to the American government.

By creating a more liberal attitude of officials, and by suggesting the later practical missions of George C. Gibbons and A. B. Aylesworth (in 1908–09), King's mission to Washington probably tended to facilitate the diplomatic efforts of 1908–11 which resulted in the signing of several important treaties. It also tended to stimulate further steps toward fuller recognition of Dominion autonomy which Laurier had suggested to Grey in 1907, and in the discussion of which Grey later suggested (in January, 1910) that Canada should take the lead.[7]

Among other evidences of a new spirit of friendly coöperation which appeared by 1909 was the American invitation to

Canada to send representatives to a conservation conference at Washington.

The somewhat tedious details of the negotiations on the chief American-Canadian problems of the decade may best be studied tandem from data presented under each separate subject.

The chief problems of diplomatic consideration were those relating to conterminous waters. The most important, and the most difficult, of these finally found a solution in the Boundary Waters Treaty of January 11, 1909.

By 1900, after some recent experience in the consideration of the old problem of navigation rights and new difficulties concerning the diversion and obstruction of boundary waters for sanitary and irrigation purposes or for power development, the American government recognized the necessity of some method of international coöperation for the proper regulation of enterprises which threatened to reduce water levels of the boundary Lakes or to interfere improperly with border streams in which two nations had an interest. Logically, therefore, it proposed to invite Great Britain to join in the formation of an international commission to examine and report upon the diversion of boundary waters. Later, in July, 1902, under authority of a river and harbor appropriation act of Congress, Secretary Hay instructed Choate to invite the British government to coöperate in a plan for the establishment of a temporary joint international waterways commission (of six persons) to investigate questions concerning waters adjacent to the boundary, including the location and erection of a dam at the outlet of Lake Erie. In the following December, and again in June, 1903, he submitted information on the condition of the negotiations. Early in October, 1903, in a note to the British legation, he announced the appointment of the three American members of the proposed commission. In November he cabled Choate to request the British government to notify the Canadian government of the American action.[8]

After considerable delay, the Waterways Commission held its first meeting at Washington on May 11, 1905. Promptly thereafter it was organized and at once began to function. Its establishment may be regarded as the earliest practical recognition of the international status of Canada—as an initial step toward the more advanced step of 1909.[9]

Perhaps the chief water problems which influenced the appointment of the temporary commission were those connected with the St. Mary River and Milk River, which rise in northwestern Montana and flow across the boundary into Canada. By 1902, the apportionment of the waters for irrigation purposes, which had long been a source of irritation to settlers on each side of the international boundary, had developed into a question of difference between the American and Canadian governments. The Americans complained that the Milk, after flowing about one hundred miles through Canadian territory, returned to its native American territory with a reduced volume of water inadequate for the irrigation needs of its lower valley which was tributary to the Missouri. To increase the volume the American Reclamation Service first proposed to divert water from the St. Mary in Canadian territory to the upper Milk Valley, and later it proposed to make the diversion by a canal through American territory to irrigate Montana lands farther west than the lower Milk. Each plan threatened vested Canadian interests, which depended upon a regular supply of water from the St. Mary, and each resulted in a Canadian official protest against any interference with the flow into Canada.

Subsequent conferences and negotiations in efforts to find a basis of agreement, although they failed to harmonize the conflicting claims which threatened to develop a serious situation, prepared the way for Root's draft treaty of June, 1907, providing for equitable apportionment of the waters and for later negotiations.[10]

In May, 1904, coincidently with British complaints concerning obstruction of the St. John River, Hay submitted American complaints against proposed Canadian plans for diversion of a large part of the waters of the Milk River into the Saskatchewan basin. He stated that these plans during dry periods threatened to result in great injury to the people of Montana who at great expense had built irrigating canals to secure the normal flow of the lower course of the river for use in necessary irrigation. As bases of the American opposition to Canadian diversion of the river he mentioned the river's American origin, its return into Montana after a brief detour through Canadian territory, and its natural exit into the Missouri. In October, after he had received a Canadian report on the amount of diversion authorized for Canadian irrigation purposes, he again submitted an opinion that serious injury would result to prior appropriations of water in Montana. At the end of December, after characterizing the Canadian authorization of diversion as an act seemingly lacking in friendliness, he urged the importance of an early understanding and suggested a joint conference with a view to reaching an agreement as to the disposition of the waters of both the Milk and the St. Mary. As a suggestion of a possible method of equitable solution he submitted a report of American engineers upon the practicability of storing in the United States the waters of the St. Mary and of conducting them by an American canal into the Milk—with the double purpose of increasing the flow of the Milk and of restraining the destructive floods of the lower St. Mary. By January, 1905, the prominence of the question of the diversion of the waters of the Milk indicated the necessity of further negotiations.[11]

Meantime the new problems of the Niagara, which contributed to later negotiations concerning conterminous waters, had also increased in importance. In May, 1904, Secretary Hay renewed Sherman's suggestion of 1898 for negotiations for joint action in plans for conservation and protection of the Falls—plans to prevent destruction by diversions of water for manufacturing plants. In November, 1905, Secretary Root, in suggesting an investigation of the subject, stated that action for preservation was within the scope of the authority of the proposed Deep Waterways Commission. On May 3, 1906, in referring to the investigations of questions of contiguous international waters by the Waterways Commission, he suggested the necessity of coöperative concurrent legislation for limitation of the amounts of water diverted for industrial purposes, a subject which was already pending in Congress and which also attracted the attention of the President.

In introducing this subject Root distinguished differences between it and the diversion of water from Lake Michigan by the Chicago Drainage Canal which Canada had desired to consider with it, but which he proposed to refer to diplomatic negotiations with a view to agreement upon a convention.[12]

Meantime, following the appointment of the members of the temporary waterways commission in 1903, a new water problem had arisen on the St. John. In May, 1904, Hay received from New Brunswick a complaint that an American corporation was erecting in the St. John certain piers and booms which were regarded as detrimental to the interests of Canadians engaged in the lumber industry and also as in contravention to Article III of the treaty of 1842. In February, 1905, he received a suggestion of the Canadian government that further plans for construction of additional piers in the St. John should be postponed until the recently appointed Waterways Commission could submit its report. In reply he stated the view of his colleagues that the functions of this commission extended only to the investigation of the problems of water level, water supply, and navigation in the Great Lakes and tributary streams drained by the St. Lawrence into the Atlantic. In the following May the Department explained that American jurisdiction in the consideration of complaints concerning obstructions in the St. John could be exercised only by authority of Congress. He suggested that Congress would coöperate in authorizing a proper arrangement for a special joint commission on which Maine and New Brunswick should be represented. On May 3, 1906, Root submitted information that the Department had requested Congress to authorize the appointment of the proposed special international commission. After considerable delay, resulting from Canadian neglect to enact the necessary concurrent legislation, the commission was finally appointed in 1909.[13]

Meantime, in May, 1905, the American government, engaged in a project of improving Warroad Harbor and River in Minnesota under acts of Congress since June, 1902, sought an agreement with the Canadian government for the maintenance of a normal level of the Lake of the Woods.[14]

Related to the purpose of the temporary international water

boundary commission were several other water questions arising before 1906. In March, 1903, Hay received from Herbert a statement that certain plans for improvements in Maine threatened to result in a diversion of the Allegash River and injury to Canadian lumber operations. In January, 1905, he received from Durand a request temporarily to suspend action on the application of the Minnesota Canal and Power Company for permission to conduct certain operations at Duluth. In February, 1906, Root received from Durand a suggestion of the Canadian government that the American government should not grant the application of the Massena Water Power Company for permission to dam the south channel of the St. Lawrence River at Long Sault Island, which seemed to involve a contravention of the treaty of 1842. In November, 1906, he invited the views of the Canadian government on rules concerning the navigation of the St. Marys River which had been in force for ten years. By January, 1907, in connection with problems relating to water power companies, he was asked to consider questions concerning American limitation of Canadian export of electric energy into the United States.[15]

Early in 1907, following a visit to Governor-General Grey at Ottawa, Root sought to find a way to facilitate negotiations on problems and disputes relating to the distribution or diversion and the obstruction of boundary waters. In June he submitted a draft treaty which provided for equitable apportionment of the waters, and for later negotiations. In the subsequent negotiations he was guided and influenced by the reports and recommendations of the temporary international joint investigating commission, the International Waters Commission. In the plans to enlarge the powers of the commission he recognized the feasibility of avoiding any extensive enlargement which practically might destroy the chance of approval by the Senate.[16]

For a time, both before and after Mackenzie King's friendly visit to Washington, negotiations toward a treaty were especially delayed by Laurier's procrastination, which possibly was partly justified by his conviction of the necessity of prolonged consideration and partly by illness. This procrastination both Bryce and Grey sought to terminate or reduce. On February 5, 1908, repeating to Laurier the reminder of Bryce's request for a prompt answer on a question relating to the delimitation of boundaries, Grey added a reminder of Bryce's request that the Ottawa government should send George C. Gibbons to Washington to help in the negotiations in connection with the international waterways. On February 23 he submitted to Laurier for his signature a memorandum handed to him by Bryce on a visit to Ottawa while Laurier was unwell. On February 26 he returned to Laurier for revision the belated Dominion statement concerning Root's draft treaty for equitable apportionment of the waters of the St. Mary River and the Milk River. He objected to an introductory reflection upon the action of the United States. Intimating the impropriety of such a reflection in beginning a statement for which Root had continuously pressed Bryce since the preceding June, he suggested as a more appropriate beginning an explanation of the real Canadian delay (the necessity of awaiting a report from engineers). As an addition to the Canadian conclusion that the proposed treaty did not give to Canada waters necessary for protection of vested interests, he also proposed an expression of readiness to appoint a representative to act jointly with an American representative in an examination of the rivers and the region with a view to the determination of a basis of agreement for a fair arrangement.

Later, in April, expecting Congress to adjourn in May and regarding every day as precious, Bryce inquired when he might expect Mackenzie King at Washington to consider the Milk River question, by which he hoped to gain a step forward on the general waters question.[17]

In the following July, finding that Root could not fully agree with the British arguments on the possibility of laying down specific principles for the regulation of international waters, Bryce suggested and urged (through Grey) that the Canadian government should make a definite seasoned reply to the serious argument which Root had presented. He also urged that Laurier should consider the desirability of sending two or three strong men to Washington in the following November to confer with American representatives with a view to a satisfactory compromise. He believed that a permanent boundary-waters commission, even with the limited powers to which Root agreed, would soon become practically a board of conciliation and arbitration; and he urged the appointment of this commission (of inquiry and report) to take the place of the Hague tribunal in the consideration of water questions along the Anglo-American boundary.

For a time the Chicago Canal question was a bone of contention and a cause of delay in the negotiations. At first Laurier insisted upon the insertion of a proposed Chicago clause which Bryce regarded as a sure obstacle to ratification of the treaty by the American Senate. Finally, early in January, 1909, he decided to refer his judgment on this subject to George C. Gibbons of Montreal who agreed with the opinion of Bryce. Grey, approving this decision of Laurier, used the occasion to impress upon him the importance of prompt action. In confirmation of Bryce's repeated warnings as to the risk of delaying the settlement of outstanding questions until after the resignation of Root, he stated that Pinchot had told him privately that Root's successor would be "a much more difficult man to deal with."

On January 9, two days before the treaty was signed, a copy of the draft form (which at Ottawa was called the Gibbons treaty) was submitted by Laurier to the Canadian council for its acceptance. On January 12, following the signature at Washington, Grey wrote Laurier, "This is a great personal triumph for you and your Ramrod Gibbons." [18]

Thus from the organization and experiences of the earlier International Waterways Commission, whose duties were limited to the investigation of border lake and river waters, and to reports on lake levels and water conditions and the cause and effect of diversions, finally developed the plans for the creation of a permanent joint international commission of larger powers adequate to the satisfactory adjustment of the annoyingly frequent problems arising from American-Canadian geographic and political relationships—especially from the increasing controversies concerning water supply, water power and waterways.

This permanent international commission-tribunal, designed

especially to settle peacefully and quietly all pending American-Canadian water-boundary controversies involving the rights and obligations or interests of either country or the inhabitants of either along the common frontier, was authorized to provide "for the adjustment and settlement of all such questions as may hereafter arise" and to consider all future questions of difference which might be referred to it by the American and British governments. Before it individual citizens of either country might present cases directly, instead of indirectly through their government.[19]

The Boundary Waters Treaty of 1909, which after five years was terminable by twelve months' notice, marked a notable advance in international arbitration. For the contentions and delays of diplomacy it substituted an international judicial tribunal which might be used both as a means to promote joint economic interests and as an agency to promote peace by conciliation, and which represented the hopes of Root and Bryce to dispense with the Hague tribunal in the decision of questions between the United States and Canada. It also reflected an advance in the diplomatic status of Canada. One of its practical and significant meanings was the British transfer to Canada of the responsibility of conducting its own foreign relations within the scope of jurisdiction defined in the agreement. It promptly stimulated the creation of a Canadian Department of External Affairs, but without any provision for distinct Canadian foreign diplomatic representation. The latter the premier declared unnecessary at Washington so long as James Bryce served as British ambassador there.[20]

The treaty provided for the free navigation of all navigable boundary waters, and also Lake Michigan and all canals connecting boundary waters, and for protection from injuries resulting from diversion of these waters. It gave to the permanent commission mandatory power to control diversions or obstructions—to regulate levels, diversions, obstructions or pollutions of boundary waters and of waters flowing across the boundary. In considering the common right of use of boundary waters, in accord with the Canadian contention, it adopted the principle of equal division for power purposes instead of a division based upon the proportion of the flow on each side of the boundary. At Niagara Falls, as a result of the importance of preserving the scenic beauty and the conditions of previous Canadian legislation (of 1907), it made an apparent exception by allowing Canada a greater diversion. Above the Falls it fixed the diversion at an amount which could be increased only by revision of the treaty and which was later enlarged by a treaty signed in January, 1929. Below the Falls, between the Falls and the whirlpool and below to Queenstown, it established no limit, leaving the question for determination of the commission with no requirement for treaty revision. By Article VI it authorized a combination of the St. Mary and Milk rivers (and their tributaries) into one stream for purposes of irrigation and power, and also an equal apportionment of their waters under direction of the commission. It provided for a practical but difficult project, which included the construction of a canal from a point near the outlet of the St. Mary River (from the St. Mary Lake) to a point on the Milk River to provide for conveyance of the American share of the water to the irrigable lands in Montana. Although it recognized the right to each party to reserve its national jurisdiction and control over the use and diversion of waters flowing across the boundary or into boundary waters, it provided that persons injured by any diversion from the natural channels on one side of the boundary were entitled to legal remedies in the courts of that side. It also stipulated that either of the contracting parties had the right to object to any interference or diversion on one side of the boundary which threatened to produce material injury to navigation interests on the other side. It agreed to the reservation by each country of the right to build on its side of boundary waters governmental works for the benefit of commerce and navigation. In Article VIII it defined the order of precedence for uses of boundary waters: for sanitation, for navigation, and for power and irrigation.[21]

By the treaty the permanent joint commission was assigned four different functions or powers:

(1) Quasi-judicial or administrative justice concerning boundary waters (Article VIII).

(2) Executive, concerning the rules for distributing certain waters for irrigation (Article VI).

(3) Investigation (and report) of questions of frontier difference (Article IX).

(4) International judicial arbitration (Article X).

In acting as an international court, it could make decisions or findings by a majority vote; and in case it should report inability to reach a decision, the two governments were authorized to refer the questions of disagreement to an umpire chosen in accord with Article XLV of the Hague Convention of October, 1907.[22]

The treaty provided an effective means of settling differences by decisions whose enforcement rests with the national governments of the two countries supported by the intelligent public opinion of each. Its provisions were not affected in any way by the later Anglo-American treaty for the advancement of the cause of general peace signed by Secretary Bryan and Cecil Spring Rice in September, 1914.[23]

In approving the treaty, the American Senate added an ambiguous restrictive rider which created in the Canadian Parliament a temporary suspicion of American intentions against the spirit of the convention.[24] This rider, which possibly originated in certain press discussions of the treaty (especially in Canada), resulted from the varying interpretations as to the effect of the treaty upon territorial or riparian rights in the water on either side of the boundary at the rapids of the St. Marys at Sault Ste. Marie. On February 24, with a view to the prevention of outside rumors and gossip during the discussion in the Senate, Bryce suggested to Grey the advisability of sending Gibbons to Washington to help clear up the misunderstanding. A few days later, following a conference with Gibbons and a telegram from Bryce, Grey assured Laurier that the agreement with Root gave Canada all it wanted. Seeking to overcome the apparent hesitation of Laurier, he suggested that the agreement asked for nothing which the Canadian government could not grant. To this he added: "We have not a moment to spare. We must not lose the treaty by one moment's unnecessary delay." On the following day, again urging prompt acceptance, he said: "I hold most strongly that it would be better to lose the battle of the Sault than to lose the treaty. Even at the Sault, Canada appears to be better off with the treaty as amended than without it." [25]

Later, in March, after acceptance of the Senate amendment by the Department of State and approval of the amended treaty by the Senate (on March 3), and in response to further pressure from Bryce and Grey, Laurier sent Gibbons and Aylesworth (Minister of Justice) to Washington to confer concerning the meaning of the amendment. Later, on March 24, he was advised by the British legation at Washington, in a secret telegram to Grey, that the best way to get a satisfactory reply from the American government was to empower Aylesworth and Gibbons to give assurance that, in case the result of the conference should be satisfactory, the Dominion government would consent to ratification at once without waiting for debate in Parliament.[26]

For a year, while the Canadian government continued to delay ratification of the treaty, both Bryce and Grey were diligent in their efforts to secure prompt Canadian action by submitting assurances concerning the purpose and effect of the amendment. In April, 1909, they submitted to Laurier the opinion of Attorney-General Wickersham that the object of the amendment was not to release the American government from any treaty obligation. In May they submitted the confirmatory opinions of both Root and Secretary Knox that the Senate resolution did not affect Canada. On May 24, in showing Laurier and his colleagues, confidentially, a copy of a letter from Bryce, Grey suggested that the evidence indicated that Canada could accept the treaty, without running any risk of impairing its equity or self-respect. In October, following his return from a trip to Vancouver, he again turned to questions relating to the treaty. Early in the following January he submitted to Laurier a private letter and a confidential dispatch from Bryce with the hope that the contents might be regarded by him "as sufficient to justify your acceptance of the treaty before January 11." In the result he was disappointed.

The continued inaction of Canada delayed British ratification until March 3, 1910, and the exchange of ratifications until

May 5. The British ratification of the appended protocol was not deposited with the American government until July 23.[27]

In January, 1911, the British legation at Washington became apprehensive that the principles of the treaty might be infringed by the operations of American private power works on the St. Lawrence by the Long Sault Development Company, under rights obtained from New York State. Apparently its representative was satisfied with the reply of the chairman of the Rivers and Harbors Committee of the House, that the bill recommended to Congress would in no way encroach on the prerogatives of the Canadian government or the International Joint Commission.[28]

Following the negotiation of the boundary waters treaty, Congress showed an increased interest in waterway problems. By an act of March 3, 1909, it created the National Waterways Commission, composed of twelve members chosen from both branches of Congress, to investigate questions in regard to water transportation and the improvements of waterways and to make recommendations on these subjects. On January 24, 1910, this commission, acting through Senator Burton, presented a preliminary report on various transportation subjects such as the decline in inland waterway traffic, increase of Great Lakes traffic, relation between waterway and railway transportation, construction of artificial canals adapted to the passage of seagoing ships, relation of waterway navigation improvements to associated objects (such as irrigation, flood prevention and water power). The consideration of these subjects prepared the way for intelligent consideration of the later problem of the Great Lakes and St. Lawrence deep waterways.[29]

Another prominent subject of diplomatic discussion in the half decade after 1903, which was segregated from other water boundary questions, and which reached a treaty agreement in 1908 while the others were still pending, was regulative protection of fresh-water fisheries in conterminous waters. It was a subject which had been inherited from a draft article of the Joint High Commission of 1898, and which later included border waters tributary to the Pacific. In January, 1904, the

American government suggested the necessity for closer coöperation between American and Canadian interests in efforts to provide uniform regulations for the protection of salmon in the Fraser River and Puget Sound regions. In August, Hay revived the subject by a suggestion of coöperation concerning the fish hatcheries.[30] Later, by 1905, arose the question of the prohibition of seine and net fishing in Lake Champlain, a question which was stimulated by the increasing use of the region as a summer resort, resulting in the coöperation of Vermont with New York in efforts to induce the Canadian government to repeal its laws which permitted such fishing in Missisquoi Bay, the favorite spawning grounds of pike and pickerel. In March, in reply to a petition submitted by Hay, the Department of State received from the Canadian government a suggestion that the subject might be considered in common with other questions which had arisen at various places in waters contiguous to the international boundary.[31]

Later, on May 20, 1905, the Department announced its intention to ask Congress for authority and the necessary appropriation to coöperate in protective regulations for the fisheries in conterminous waters contiguous to the boundary line.[32] In March, 1906, Root submitted to Durand a draft of a proposed treaty which provided for regulation by an international commission. In reply to a Canadian suggestion to include Lake Michigan, Rainy Lake and Rainy River among the enumerated waters, he agreed to add Rainy Lake and Rainy River on condition that Lake Memphremagog should also be added, but he declined to include Lake Michigan which was wholly in American jurisdiction. To the Canadian suggestions that the American government should first obtain adhesion of the various states which might claim any measure of authority over the contiguous waters, he reiterated the American position of 1898 that treaty regulation of fisheries in these waters was unquestionably within the jurisdiction of the American treaty-making power.

Finally, on April 11, 1908, Root joined with Bryce in an agreement for uniform and effective means for protection and propagation of good fish in the boundary waters. This treaty, although opposed by private American interests, was approved by the Senate on April 17 and proclaimed by the President on July 1. It provided for the appointment of an International Fishery Commission (one member appointed by each government) to prepare necessary regulations. It also contained a provision placing upon the Canadian government the duty of protecting, by suitable regulations, the food fishes in the Fraser River.[33]

Another subject of some consideration in 1906 was the protection of shipping in conterminous waters. In February, with a view to a joint arrangement for the prevention of disasters or dangers to navigation in the Strait of Juan de Fuca, Root suggested an invitation for a conference between American and British Columbian lighthouse and life-saving authorities to consider aids to safe navigation. Later he expressed American readiness to coöperate in the establishment and maintenance of a lightship at the entrance of the strait.[34]

In the half decade before 1909, appeared two other questions relating to problems of the Great Lakes. These were the disarmament agreement of 1817 and wreckage and salvage rights.

Possibly the Canadian discussion of the question of the convention of 1817 was stimulated in part by the European political situation since 1900, which forced Laurier to consider the problem of Canadian naval defense in connection with the consideration of the German menace and the tensity of Anglo-German relations. A more immediate source of the discussion was the American occasional need of larger and better equipped naval vessels in connection with the training of state naval militia, as illustrated in April, 1904, by Hay's request for permission to take such an American naval vessel through the St. Lawrence and Canadian canals to Lake Erie for temporary use by Ohio without any contemplated departure from the stipulations of the agreement of 1817. On May 3, 1906, in connection with some discussion concerning the question of a modification of the agreement of 1817, Root suggested that "construction on the Lakes of naval vessels for use elsewhere would not be a violation of the spirit of the treaty or of its terms justly construed," and invited agreement upon a stipulation assenting to this construction. At the same time he stated that, notwithstanding the changed defensive conditions resulting from the construction of the Canadian system of canals, the American government did not wish to speculate upon possible future contingencies which might justify the termination of an arrangement under which adjacent peoples had lived in peace and security for nearly ninety years. In September, in considering the subject with Grey, Laurier suggested a strong response "in favour of an undisturbed continuation of the happy state of things now existing."

Later, in June, 1909, the action of Canada in determining to maintain an improvised armored cruiser on the Georgian Bay was a subject of some criticism in the American press.[35]

Near the close of 1909 apropos an American request to take some torpedo boats via the St. Lawrence to the Lakes, Bryce suggested to Grey that possibly the American government might soon raise the question of revising the agreement of 1817. On December 16, he wrote that this question was the only pending American-Canadian question of 1898–99 "which had not been settled or in a fair way of settlement." Regarding it as a question of vital interest to Canada and also to the Empire, he suggested that the unclouded condition of the diplomatic sky seemed to furnish a favorable time to sound the American government upon its views concerning the conclusion of a treaty to alter the provisions of 1817. Over a year later, early in February, 1911, he informed both Grey and Laurier that the American government had consented to drop its request for passage of torpedo boats from the sea to the Lakes. This action Grey promptly cited to Laurier as another illustration of "American good feeling toward Canada which Bryce's influence has done so much to establish." He promptly suggested to Laurier the advisability of withholding from Parliament certain papers relating to American warships on the Lakes—papers which had been requested by a motion of G. Foster.[36]

In May, 1906, Secretary Root renewed an earlier suggestion of reciprocity in wrecking and salvage rights in contiguous waters, a subject upon which the Joint High Commission (in September, 1898) had favored a conventional agreement. This question had been a subject of diplomatic correspondence and legislation since an initial act of Congress of June 19, 1878, which as amended in 1890 and 1893 had been accepted by a Canadian concurrent act of May, 1893, and had been made effective in July, 1893, by the President's proclamation. Later, however, a controversy had arisen as to whether the privileges thus granted were applicable to waters of the Atlantic and Pacific coasts (which were not regarded as "contiguous waters" within the meaning of the statute). In 1906, Root personally could see no good reason why the privileges should not be extended to Passamaquoddy Bay or the Strait of Juan de Fuca. Two years later, on May 18, 1908, Robert Bacon concluded with Ambassador Bryce a treaty providing for reciprocal rights of the United States and Canada in regard to privileges relating to wreckage and salvage in the Great Lakes and other waters contiguous to the boundary, including the privileges of all necessary towing incident to the salvage operations.[37]

Of incidental interest, reflecting the spirit of Chicago in seeking improved facilities for quicker and cheaper water transportation eastward for the rapidly increasing commerce of lower Lake Michigan, was the favorable report of the House Committee on Railways and Canals, in 1908, on a resolution to authorize a survey of a route for a ship-canal from Lake Erie to Lake Michigan at or near Benton Harbor, and especially mentioning the proposed route via Fort Wayne.[38]

Between 1905 and 1909, in addition to questions relating to conterminous waters, several other questions had been subjects of diplomatic consideration. Among these were extradition, deportation of aliens, demarcation of boundaries, conventions of arbitration and pacific settlement, coöperation on the Japanese problem of 1908, conservation policy and the Atlantic coast fisheries.

On April 12, 1905, at London, Choate and Lansdowne agreed upon a supplementary extradition convention extending the lists of extraditable crimes contained in the extradition convention of July, 1889, and in the supplementary convention of December, 1900, to include bribery offenses against bankruptcy law. To this were later added (by a supplementary convention of May 15, 1922) "willful desertion or willful non support of minor or dependent children." [39]

In the spring of 1905 arose a question concerning the mode of deportation of aliens from the United States into Canada, under an act of Congress approved March 3, 1905. Following a complaint of a Canadian mayor against an American official who had exercised extraterritorial authority in the deportation of a native Canadian who had become a public charge at Duluth, the American Department of State suggested an arrangement for delivery at the border to properly authorized officers.[40]

In May, 1906, Secretary Root suggested to Durand the expedience of some reciprocal arrangement for conveyance of prisoners in custody of one government through the territory of the other, a subject upon which the Joint High Commission had reported the text of an agreement on September 27, 1898. Two years later this question was adjusted by new negotiations, resulting in a treaty, signed on May 18, 1908, by Robert Bacon and Ambassador Bryce.[41]

A later source of some irritation (in 1911) was the American application for leniency for certain Americans who were imprisoned or convicted under Canadian law for crimes committed in Canadian territory.[42]

In May, 1906, in connection with a general statement of chief pending American-Canadian questions, and following a convention (of April 21) which provided for a joint survey to trace and mark the location of the meridian of 141° from Mt. St. Elias north to the Arctic Ocean, Root had expressed a willingness to join in informal arrangements or formal conventions for completion of the surveys and definite marking or re-marking of the entire international boundary line by land and water—a project which had been initiated by the Canadian government through a communication of Lord Pauncefote to Hay on July 23, 1900. He submitted a summary of the condition of the various parts of the boundary from Passamaquoddy Bay and the St. Croix to Puget Sound, with chief difficulties and recommendations. Among the incidental difficulties in connection with the boundary in well-settled regions he mentioned the "line houses," many of which were "undoubtedly used for . . . facilitating evasions of the law." He suggested that each government should forbid the erection of buildings within a specified number of feet from the line.[43]

On April 11, 1908, he concluded with Bryce a treaty providing for a more complete definition and demarcation of the entire international boundary from the Bay of Fundy to the Pacific Ocean, including the determination of the small undetermined boundary in Passamaquoddy Bay and also the determination of the center of the main channel of the St. Croix River from its mouth to its source. This treaty in its provisions indicated eight geographic divisions. As a concession to Canada the work for one of these, the division of the St. Lawrence and the Great Lakes, was assigned to the international Waterways Commission, which had been authorized in 1902. The work for each of the other seven divisions was assigned to a special commission of two members (expert geographers or surveyors), one appointed by each of the contracting parties.

The undetermined boundary in Passamaquoddy Bay was through Lubec Narrows Channel, between Campobello Island and the mainland, where controversies had arisen concerning Pope's Folly Island and certain fishing grounds. Upon it the commissioners reached an agreement after the time designated by the treaty. Finally, on May 21, 1910, Secretary Knox signed with Bryce a treaty which definitely provided for completion of the location of the boundary.[44]

Meantime, early in 1908, the question of agreement upon the terms of a general arbitration had become prominent. The two governments found some difficulty in the negotiations. In February Bryce and Grey unsuccessfully sought an official decision from Laurier who, instead of accepting Root's proposal for a commission of limited powers, apparently insisted upon a general commission for the settlement of all future questions (which the British legation at Washington regarded as impossible of attainment). In March Grey obtained from him the unofficial statement that he would "agree to any kind of arbitration provided the award is binding on the contracting parties," and discovered that he planned to propose a binding clause which Bryce and Grey regarded as unnecessary and which they opposed upon the ground that it might be interpreted as an imputation against the good faith of the United States.

On April 4, after further discussion, Root and Bryce finally concluded the treaty, which was similar to an earlier general draft treaty (of 1897) which the Senate had refused to approve and also similar to a draft treaty which had been negotiated by Hay and defeated by the Senate in 1904. By it they agreed to submit to the Hague Permanent Court of Arbitration any Anglo-American "differences of a legal nature or relating to the interpretation of treaties" provided that they did not affect the vital interests or the independence or the honor of the two contracting parties and did not concern the interests of third parties. In it they also agreed to the British reservation of the right to obtain the concurrence of the Dominion government before concluding any special agreement in any matter affecting the interests of the self-governing Dominion. At the same time by exchange of notes they recorded their understanding that the treaty would not apply to existing pecuniary claims nor to the negotiation and conclusion of the proposed special treaty (on boundary waters) recently recommended by the International Waterways Commission.

On August, 1911, the representatives of the two governments signed a more comprehensive arbitration treaty which was emasculated by the Senate in March, 1912, and finally abandoned. Meantime, however, the sources of future dispute had been lessened by the provisions of the Boundary Waters Treaty of January, 1909.[45]

On August 18, 1910, under the provisions of the Hague convention (of October, 1907) for the pacific settlement of international disputes, Secretary Knox and Ambassador Bryce signed a special agreement for submission of outstanding pecuniary claims to arbitration by a tribunal composed of one arbitrator appointed by each party and a presiding umpire chosen by the two arbitrators. The tribunal did not open its first meeting until May 13, 1913.[46]

Within the decade before 1912 American relations with Canada were affected by two subjects of negotiation concerning Newfoundland: (1) reciprocity, from 1902 to 1904; and (2) fisheries, in the half decade after 1905.

In September, 1902, by request of the British legation, Hay received Sir Robert Bond's propositions for separate reciprocity negotiations with Newfoundland. After a conference with Bond, he reached an agreement upon a draft convention which provided reciprocal freedom from customs duties on certain articles and conceded the right of American fishermen to purchase bait and supplies in Newfoundland.[47]

The negotiation was followed by a three-sided conflict which prevented ratification of the draft treaty. Newfoundland, using as a lever its control of the supply of bait, demanded access to the American markets. Canada opposed ratification and insisted upon a veto by the imperial Parliament. In this policy it was influenced by its desire for free entry of its fish into American ports, by its feeling that the agreement would deprive it of a lever which it had used in its various efforts to induce the American government to agree to a general reciprocity agreement and by its hope for a situation which might result in the union of Newfoundland with the Dominion. America was influenced by New England fishing and canning interests (led by Senator Lodge) and by preëlection conditions which prevented a favorable vote in the Senate. In 1904 all hope of ratification was abandoned. Root later stated that refusal of the Senate to confirm the convention was due to unwillingness to repeat the unsatisfactory experiments of 1854 and 1871 on free entry of British fish to the American markets. In the determination of this policy Senator Lodge was an active leader.[48]

Meantime, in April, 1903, Hay had received from Herbert a complaint of Newfoundland against an American head tax (of March 3) on alien immigrants except those from Canada, Mexico and Cuba. He replied that Newfoundland, forming no integral part of the Dominion of Canada and not contiguous to the United States, had no reason for complaint.[49]

In 1905 the American fishery industry in Newfoundland again became a subject of confusion and controversy. Under a new retaliatory law the Newfoundland officials made a distinction between American registered vessels and ordinary licensed fishing vessels and sought to prohibit fishing under an American register. The operation of the new policy resulted in a strong feeling among the American fishermen who were not allowed to buy bait, and also among Newfoundland fishermen from whom many Americans had been in the habit of buying bait and for whom the trade had been a principal means of support. In August, following the dispatch of an American fishing schooner to the Newfoundland coast to make a scientific study of the movements of schools of mackerel, Senator Lodge urged the importance of sending a naval vessel to the coast to prevent a possible repetition of the Fortune Bay outrage.[50] In October, Root expressed to Durand his apprehension concerning threats of violence by Newfoundland fishermen. Recognizing the danger of conflict which might result from an attempt to execute the threats, he urged that the British government should take speedy steps to induce Newfoundland authorities to control the Newfoundland fishermen.[51]

In 1906, following a repeal of the ineffective law of 1905, Newfoundland proposed a new law which forbade American captains to hire Newfoundland crews; but this law was opposed by diplomatic representations and never became effective.

In April, 1906, Grey suggested that in any attempt at general settlement of all pending questions the Atlantic fisheries would be the crux. Three weeks later he received from Washington information that Root wanted to be reasonable and fair but that he must contend with Lodge and his son-in-law (Gardiner).[52]

On May 3, 1906, in proposing to Durand to resume consideration of chief pending questions of 1898–99 and to dispose of them by direct negotiation, Root reviewed the various efforts to adjust the questions concerning the Atlantic coast fisheries and the irritating effects of the unfriendly British colonial legislation and administration concerning the fisheries, and he suggested the advisability of seeking to terminate the fisheries difficulties by efforts to ascertain existing American rights with a purpose to maintain them by fair and liberal treatment of colonial authorities. He significantly referred to the fact that the unexecuted American act of March 3, 1887, authorizing the President to retaliate, was still in force. Further discussion soon followed. On June 30 Root used vigorous language which Governor-General Grey later characterized as a "claim to convert a liberty in common into an unrestricted right to destroy our fishing industry."[53]

Four months later, in October, 1906, by exchange of notes between Ambassador Reid and Sir Edward Grey of the British Foreign Office, and with the coöperation of Lord Elgin, the American and British governments agreed to a *modus vivendi* concerning the question of the Newfoundland fisheries. By this arrangement American fishermen were required temporarily to renounce Sunday fishing and to pay light dues, and they were allowed, temporarily (for the next season), to use purse seines which they had been driven to use by the local regulations of 1906 against the employment of Newfoundlanders (who had used the form of net previously prescribed). The arrangement in modified form, the Americans waiving the use of purse seines for a British waiver of interference with the use of Newfoundlander labor on American fishing vessels outside the three mile limit, was continued by renewals in 1907, 1908 and 1909, although it was resisted by Sir Robert Bond.[54]

Early in January, 1907, in connection with the consideration of Root's proposals for a settlement of all pending questions, and before Root's visit to Grey at Ottawa, Grey expressed to Laurier regret that no prompt reply had been submitted in refutation of Root's statement of 1906 on American fishery rights. A few days later, on January 11, he found occasion to soften Laurier's draft cable concerning Root's proposals, by reminding him that Root in requesting a definition of American rights had not suggested any renunciation of Canadian rights in the Atlantic fisheries.[55]

Apparently the chief obstacle to agreement on the fisheries was Sir Robert Bond, who still resisted the *modus vivendi* and whom Bryce regarded as difficult to divert from an independent course which seriously affected Canada. On September 24, 1907, following receipt of a letter from Bryce, Grey suggested to Laurier the expediency of representing to Bond the desirability of withholding from any action which might lead to complications in plans for arbitration. Two months later, in response to the suggestions of Grey and Laurier that the American government should be asked to submit its terms of reference to the Hague, Bryce emphasized the importance of settling first with Bond in order to avoid giving him a possible pretext for another grievance.[56]

Finally, acting under the general treaty of arbitration of April 4, 1908, and after accepting many changes which Laurier considered important, Root signed with Bryce a special agreement of January 27, 1909, by which the old fisheries questions arising under the convention of 1818 were submitted to arbitration by the Hague tribunal of impartial jurists. Under the agreement the two governments submitted to the tribunal seven questions for decision: (1) Whether the right of regulating reasonably the liberties conferred by the treaty of 1818 resides in Great Britain; (2) whether the American fishermen had a right to employ non-Americans as members of their fishing crews; (3) whether the Americans, in the exercise of their fishing liberties, were properly subject to local requirements; (4) whether American fishing vessels, in entering ports for shelter or repairs or wood or water, were subject to local dues and reports; (5) from where must be measured the "three marine miles"; (6) whether Americans had the liberty to take fish in the bays, harbors and creeks of the coast; (7) whether American fishing vessels could properly claim commercial privileges accorded to American trading vessels on the treaty coasts.[57]

On February 18, 1909, the American Senate gave its consent and advice to the ratification of the special agreement subject to the understanding of the two governments that the question "from where must be measured the three marine miles of any of the coasts, bays, creeks or harbors" did not include any questions as to the Bay of Fundy or as to innocent passage through the Gut of Canso.[58]

Early in March, Bryce (through Grey) pressed for prompt action by Canada in the selection of the arbitrators. In reply, complaining of the pressure, Laurier asked Grey why the selection of the arbitrators should be a condition precedent to the ratification. He objected to the selection of a South American arbiter and also suggested that Newfoundland had not been consulted. On March 7, however, Bryce wired Grey that the final steps in the fisheries arbitration agreement had been taken.[59]

In the decision on the seven questions, in September, 1910, the tribunal sustained the Canadian contention on most points. In opposition to the American contention against unreasonable interference with fishing within the three-mile limit on the treaty coast (by requirements such as observance of the Newfoundland Sabbath and specific restrictions on methods of fishing), it stated that the United States had been admitted to a regulated fishery, concerning which Great Britain had a right to make and enforce regulations within the bounds of reason; but it created a commission of fishery experts to decide upon the reasonableness of the regulations and to consider American objections. It decided in favor of the American contention for the right to employ non-Americans as members of the fishing crews of American vessels; but it added the statement that such non-American employees (either foreign or British) could derive no benefit or immunity from the treaty. Concerning the American contention for complete exemption of American fishing vessels from certain local dues, it decided that such vessels must pay the same light and harbor dues imposed on Newfoundland fishermen; but it added that these vessels should not be subjected to the commercial formalities relating to report and entry and clearance at a customhouse, nor to dues not imposed on Newfoundland fishermen. On the basis of duties of hospitality and humanity it decided in favor of the right of unrestricted entry to obtain shelter, repairs, wood and water; but it recognized that American fishermen remaining beyond forty-eight hours should report to a customs official if opportunity was reasonably convenient. Against the American contention that all bays or creeks or harbors of a width of six miles or more should be considered part of the open sea it adopted the British headland-to-headland doctrine with the provision that bays of a width of ten miles or less should be considered closed. On the question of the liberty of Americans to fish in the Newfoundland harbors, and bays and creeks, it decided in favor of the Americans by the interpretation that these were included under the term "coast." It decided that American fishing vessels when duly authorized by the United States were entitled to commercial privileges accorded to American trading vessels on the treaty coasts, but with the condition that they could not exercise their treaty rights and enjoy their commercial privileges during the same voyage.[60]

In making its award the tribunal recommended for consideration certain rules and methods of procedure for determination of all future questions concerning liberties of fishing (under the treaty of 1818). These rules and methods the American and British governments finally accepted with some modification by an agreement signed at Washington on July 20, 1912, by Chandler P. Anderson of the Department of State and Alfred Mitchell Innes, chargé of the British legation.

For a time before this agreement on acceptance, these rules, requiring the British or colonial authorities to submit to the American government for its information and approval all future regulatory acts, were a source of renewed controversy. By the American government they were regarded as essential to the execution of the treaty. By Laurier they were regarded as unacceptable—as beyond the powers of the commission and an unnecessary imposition upon Canada whose regulations (he said) had never been offensive or unneighborly. Grey promptly explained to the British Foreign Office that on January 12, 1911, the United States, in signing with Sir Allan Aylesworth (the Canadian agent) a memorandum accepting the recommendations, had the understanding that Canada accepted (an understanding shared by Bryce). According to Bryce, the American government argued that Sir Charles Fitzpatrick (of Canada) had committed Great Britain to the acceptance of the recommendations, but, wishing to protect the Chief Justice of Canada from embarrassment, it refrained from insisting.[61]

For a time Laurier refused to be bound by Fitzpatrick's unauthorized and unreported promise at The Hague. In his explanation to Grey he stated that the provision that Canadian regulations would be rendered inoperative by a mere American objection was a very serious infringement upon Canadian sovereignty, and that acceptance of it would subject the Canadian government to very serious inconvenience and trouble with the Canadian fishermen, and would precipitate a formidable parliamentary attack which possibly might result in his defeat. Early in August, in a confidential letter and a telegram, Bryce expressed to Grey his feeling that the matter was not as serious as Laurier had contemplated. He confidentially stated that the only cause for disquiet was the possibility that the question of the Canadian private assurance might be raised in the Senate—which he said he would try to prevent. Satisfied with Bryce's letter, Laurier wrote Grey that he proposed to ask Fitzpatrick to explain his Hague assurances, the only remaining point against Canada.[62]

Following the adjudication and the later supplemental agreement of 1912, the waves of controversy concerning the northeast fisheries became quiet under the *modus vivendi* of 1888 which was continued in force (by statutory authority) until January 1, 1924.[63]

In 1911, the American government was successful in its effort to remove from the field of negotiation and discussion another important long-pending question, the protection of fur seals in Bering Sea.

In 1903, Hay had renewed American efforts to secure a satisfactory international agreement on this question. He had asked Herbert to use his friendly efforts with British authorities in connection with a proposed visit to England. At the same time he had authorized Choate to act in concert with Herbert at London to secure agreement on the plan of a convention which could be completed at Washington after Herbert's return, and which might be followed by negotiations between Russia and Japan in the same direction. He had suggested the substance of the draft convention prepared with the co-operation of Lord Herschell in the conferences of 1898–99. By August, 1904, the American and British governments had reached a full agreement as to concurrent patrol of the prohibited pelagic zone of thirty miles around Commander and Copper Islands, in addition to the three miles of territorial waters of the islands. In April, 1906, Root submitted to Durand a project of a treaty which reflected American policy of co-operation to stop pelagic sealing.[64]

In November, 1908, after further delay, the American government made a compromise proposal that Canada might share in the skins taken by land, but it declined to entertain any claim of British Columbia sealers against the United States. At the end of December Bryce wrote Grey that he thought this offer was the last word, and Grey promptly informed Laurier who had not yet made a formal reply.

In July, 1909, Grey tactfully pressed Laurier to hasten action. Submitting a confidential memorandum on the seals negotiations since April, 1906, he suggested that, unless wide considerations of international policy would justify further delay in the settlement of a question concerning which American offers and arguments had been waiting for three years for a formal Canadian reply, the time had arrived for a reasoned official statement of the Canadian position. In September, after returning from a summer trip to British Columbia, he again suggested the desirability of considering the proposed co-operation. In November he again sought to stimulate Laurier to send the reply for which the American government had been waiting so long.[65]

Finally, after further delays, the governments reached a satisfactory agreement. On February 7, 1911, at Washington, Secretary Knox and James Bryce signed a treaty providing for preservation and protection of fur seals by prohibition of pelagic sealing in the Bering Sea and in the Pacific north of latitude 35° and east of 180°, effective upon the conclusion and ratification of an international agreement between the United States, Great Britain, Japan and Russia, and not terminable before expiration of fifteen years. On July 7, 1911, at Washington, representatives of the four powers signed a similar treaty which became effective on December 15 and superseded the Anglo-American treaty of the preceding February.[66]

The only important remaining unsettled question in 1911 was that of a proposed reciprocal trade arrangement which, when it seemed within reach of attainment, was suddenly defeated by the results of a Canadian political campaign. This question the Department of State had revived in 1904 by the preparation of convenient information concerning the several attempts at negotiation of a reciprocity treaty since 1866. President Roosevelt had become interested in negotiations upon the subject, and apparently had sought to avoid or reduce opposition in Congress. Some obstacles had appeared in Canada, which recently had placed tariff discriminations on tea and coffee imported from the United States[67] and which both Senator Lodge and Henry White had reported as unfavorable to reciprocity negotiations.[68]

By 1906 the reciprocity problem was no longer complicated with the question of canal tolls in Canada or the question of Canadian use of New York canals;[69] but Laurier was unwilling to make concessions in favor of American manufactures and therefore he doubted whether the American government would offer any concession which Canada would accept. In 1908, the Laurier government apparently was still willing to adopt the Chamberlain-Bayard draft treaty of 1888; but the latter was opposed by the American fisheries interests of Gloucester, Massachusetts, and by the American political "standpatters."[70]

The reciprocity negotiations of 1911 originated in the American aggressively protectionist Payne-Aldrich tariff of 1909, which directed the President to apply a special schedule of prohibitive maximum rates as a club of retaliation against any country whose tariff discriminated unduly against its imports from the United States. Before the close of 1909, wishing to avoid any friction with Canada which recently had discriminated against the United States by the negotiation of more favorable trade concessions with France, President Taft sought to secure similar concessions for the United States,[71] or a liberal trade arrangement which would furnish him an excuse to extend to Canada the benefit of the minimum tariff rates. In this liberal policy, he was partly influenced by the western insurgent movement in the Republican party and partly by the logical conclusion that the conditions of neighborhood contact and common interests required friendlier relations. For it he was partly prepared by the recent creation of a new tariff board which early in 1910 proposed an unofficial American mission to Canada for "backstairs negotiations" (without the regular authority of the State Department). With a purpose to avoid an unpremeditated tariff war, and aided by the coöperation of Bryce and Grey, he arranged to open with Laurier and Grey at Ottawa informal secret negotiations. Later, on March 19, 1910, at Albany, he personally met Fielding, who later went to Washington for more formal negotiations which finally reached a satisfactory compromise by a Canadian nominal concession [72] and resulted in a friendly reciprocal agreement of January 26, 1911, providing for mutual simultaneous concurrent legislative action.[73]

In the American border states, the agreement met with strong approval, which in some instances unfortunately was supported with irresponsible and impolitic annexation sentiment not conducive to the promotion of confidence among sensitive Canadian neighbors.[74]

In Canada it was promptly accepted by the surprised Laurier who recognized that it was in accord with the lower tariff demands of western Canada and with the recent Canadian policy concerning direct negotiation of new trade agreements, and who was also influenced by the expediency of a pacification policy calculated to quell the insurgent movement of farmers in the Canadian West which had recently menaced his political life.[75] At the same time, apparently without consultation with Grey, Laurier informed Bryce that he contemplated the appointment of a trade commissioner at Washington—a proposal which Grey regarded as a "black eye" to the British embassy, and as a poor return to Bryce for his services in clearing the slate of Canadian differences with the United States.[76]

President Taft encountered some difficulty in obtaining

legislative approval of the Senate to the House reciprocity bill. In June, two months after he was sustained by the House, he started a back-fire of public opinion to force the Senate's hand. He especially criticized the opposition of the American lumber and wood-pulp interests.[77] On July 22, in the face of strong opposition, he finally obtained for his policy a favorable majority vote in the Senate, aided by the Democrats and the melting temperature of midsummer weather.[78]

In Canada, whose action Taft confidently awaited, and whose premier and cabinet hoped to celebrate a belated triumph for a long period of earlier consistent Canadian diplomacy, the agreement for restricted reciprocity was defeated by a surprising conservative partisan reaction which disappointed the expectations of Sir Wilfrid and the Liberal government and resulted in a patriotic sacrifice of Canadian interests in an effort to prove Canadian independence in the consideration of trade policy.[79]

The American act of 1911 was not promptly repealed. Until 1922 most of it would have become operative if approved by the Canadian Parliament. Section 2, relating to the importations of wood pulp and paper, was repealed by the tariff act of 1913, and the remaining sections by the tariff act of 1922.

Although the inconvenience of tariffs remained, the important adjustments of the decade had removed the chief sources of irritation and thereby had prepared the way for a new era of friendly relations along the unfortified frontier.

REFERENCES

1. Skelton, *The Day of Sir Wilfrid Laurier*, pp. 256–57; *Laurier Papers, Governor General's Cor.*, Grey 1904–11; *T. R. Papers*, T. R. to Hay, Vol. 5, 1897–1903.
2. *27 G.B., Notes to*, pp. 564–81, May 3, 1906; *Ib.*, pp. 589–91, No. 445, May 19.
3. *Laurier Papers, Gov. Gen'l's Cor.*, Grey 1906, pp. 6–7, T. R. to Lord Grey, Jan. 19, 1906; *Ib.*, pp. 114–18, Private, Grey to Elgin, Apr. 3; *Ib.*, p. 115A, Low to Grey, Apr. 21; *Ib.*, p. 156, Secret, Grey to Elgin, Apr. 14; *Ib.*, p. 157, Secret, Elgin to Grey, Apr. 23; *Ib.*, pp. 163–64, Root to Grey, Apr. 29; *Ib.*, p. 171, Secret cable, Elgin to Grey, May 2.

4. *Ib.*, pp. 220 (May 21), 266–97 (June 14), 321 (June 14), 332 (June 21), 475 (Aug. 19), 513 (Oct. 9), 589–91 (Nov. 29), and 603, *B.C.* (Dec. 2); *Ib.*, 1907, pp. 33–44 (Jan. 11), 47–51 (Jan. 12), 63–65 (Jan. 14), 70–78 (Jan. 22), 138 (Bryce to Grey, Feb. 28), and 152 (Mar. 2).
5. *T. R. Papers,* I–L, Vol. 7.
6. *Laurier Papers, Gov. Gen'l's Cor.*, Grey 1908, pp. 16–18 and 20–22, Grey to Laurier, Private, Jan. 8, 1908; *Ib.*, pp. 112–13, Howard to Grey, Private, Jan. 28; *Ib.*, pp. 101–08, Grey to Laurier, Feb. 1.
7. *Laurier Papers, Gov. Gen'l's Cor.*, Grey 1907, pp. 401–07, Grey to Laurier, Oct. 6; *Ib.*, pp. 613–14, Nov. 27 (with inclosures, pp. 618–20); *Ib.*, pp. 645–46, Grey to Elgin, Dec. 9; *Ib.*, pp. 676 and 692–93, Sir Claude McDonald to Grey, Dec. 20; *Ib.*, 1908, pp. 35–36, Jan. 6; *Ib.*, pp. 151–54, Jan. 22; *Ib.*, pp. 116–24, Grey to Laurier, Feb. 5; *Ib.*, pp. 125–27, Bryce to Grey, Confid., Feb. 1; *Ib.*, pp. 109–11, Bryce to Grey, Jan. 28; *Ib.*, pp. 141–42, Bryce to Grey, Confid., Feb. 4, 1908; *Ib.*, pp. 316–19, Sir Edward Grey to Lord Grey, Feb. 29; *Ib.*, pp. 372–76, McDonald to Lord Grey, Mar. 17; *Ib.*, p. 290, Hearn to Young, Mar. 2; *San Francisco Chronicle*, Feb. 27, 1908; *Ib.*, 1910, pp. 12 and 15A–E, Grey to Laurier, Jan. 10; *T. R. Papers*, I–L, Vol. 7, Feb. 1, 1908.
8. *4 Compilation of Sen. Rps. on For. Rels.*, pp. 503–04; SHORTT and DOUGHTY, IX, 219–20; *27 G.B., Notes to,* pp. 564–81, May 3, 1906; *Ib.*, pp. 589–91, No. 445, May 19; *34 G.B., Instrs.*, p. 200, No. 947, July 1, 1902; *T. R. Papers,* Hay to T. R., I, 1901–02, Dec. 19, 1902; *Ib.*, II, 1903–05, June 10, 1903; *26 G.B., Notes to,* p. 557, No. 204, Oct. 7, 1903; *Ib.*, No. 202, Oct. 2; *34 G.B., Instrs.*, No. 1280; *Ib.*, p. 524, Tel., Nov. 12, 1903; *G.B., Desps.*, No. 1275, Oct. 2, 1903.
9. *27 G.B., Notes to,* pp. 261–62, No. 230, May 11, 1905; SKELTON, *The Day of Laurier*, p. 287.
10. *Papers Rel. to the Work of the Int. Joint Com.*, pp. 125–26; *U. S. Geol. Survey, Water Supply and Irrigation Papers,* 1905–06, No. 172, pp. 54–55; *U. S. Reclam. Service An. Rps., 1903–04,* pp. 79–82; *Ib., 1907,* pp. 114–19; *Laurier Papers, Gov. Gen'l's Cor.*, Grey 1908, pp. 194–96 and 198–202.
11. *26 G.B., Notes to,* pp. 679–80, May 9, 1904; *27 G.B., Notes to,* pp. 5–6, May 12; *Ib.*, pp. 105–06, Personal, Oct. 13; *Ib.*, pp. 148–50, No. 154, Dec. 30; *Ib.*, pp. 159–60, Personal, Jan. 25, 1905.
12. *24 G.B., Notes to,* p. 108, No. 893, Feb. 2, 1898; *26 G.B., Notes to,* pp. 677–78, No. 72, May 6, 1904; *Ib.*, May 7; *Laurier's Papers, Gov. Gen'l's Cor.,* Grey 1906, pp. 186–200, May 9 and 10; *27 G.B., Notes to,* pp. 425–26, Nov. 3, 1905; *For. Rels., 1905;*

Ib., pp. 564–81, May 3, 1906; *Ib.*, p. 674, Aug. 14; *President's Mess. to Cong., Mar. 27, 1906.*

13. *27 G.B., Notes to,* pp. 5–6, May 12, 1904; *Ib.*, pp. 182–83, No. 173, Feb. 24, 1905; *Ib.*, May 29; *Ib.*, pp. 276–77, May 31; *Ib.*, pp. 281–82, June 7; *Ib.*, pp. 564–81, May 3, 1906; *Laurier Papers, Gov. Gen'l's Cor.*, Grey 1908, pp. 362 and 369, Mar. 29 and Apr. 8.
14. *27 G.B., Notes to,* pp. 253–54, No. 223, May 6, 1905.
15. *26 G.B., Notes to,* pp. 382–83, No. 95, Mar. 28, 1903; *Ib.*, p. 385, No. 98, Apr. 3; *27 G.B., Notes to,* pp. 589–91, No. 445, May 19, 1906; *Ib.*, pp. 159–60, Personal, Jan. 25, 1905; *State Dept., Numerical Files* (to Br. Legation), No. 574, Nov. 30, 1906; *Laurier Papers, Gov. Gen'l's Cor.*, Grey 1907, pp. 53–56, Grey to Laurier, Jan. 12, 1907, inclosing Howard's unofficial aide-memoir of Jan. 9.
16. *Sessional Papers, to Canada,* Vol. 47, 1913, 19a, No. 12, p. 340; *Am. J. Int. Law,* Apr., 1928, pp. 293–318 (Robt. A. Mackay); *Laurier Papers, Gov. Gen'l's Cor.*, Grey 1909, pp. 409–32, Grey to Laurier, Confid., June 5; *Ib.*, 1908, pp. 1–14, Jan. 8, 1908.
17. *Ib.*, pp. 386–87, Bryce to Chief Justice Charles Fitzpatrick, Apr. 7; *Ib.*, pp. 388–89 and 391–94 (Apr. 6); *Ib.*, pp. 128–32, Feb. 5; *Ib.*, pp. 184–88, Feb. 23; *Ib.*, 192–93, Feb. 26.
18. *Ib.*, pp. 608–20 and 621–24, Grey to Laurier, July 23; *Ib.*, 1909, pp. 8–21, Jan. 4; *Ib.*, pp. 38–40, Jan. 11; *Ib.*, pp. 41–42, Jan. 12.
19. Charles, *Treaties bet. the U.S. and Other Powers,* III, 39–47; Falconer, *The U.S. as a Neighbor* (1925), p. 78; Skelton, *Life and Times of Laurier,* II, 363.
20. *Ib.*, p. 347; Shortt and Doughty, IX, 219; *Laurier Papers, Gov. Gen'l's Cor.*, Grey 1909, pp. 343 and 346, May 6 and 7.
21. Shortt and Doughty, IX, 219–20; *Papers Rel. to the Work of the Int. Joint Com.* (Ottawa, 1919), pp. 11–15.
22. *Ib.*, p. 16; *Am. J. Int. Law,* Apr., 1928, pp. 292–318.
23. *Papers Rel. to the Work of the Int. Joint Com.*
24. *Laurier Papers, Gov. Gen'l's Cor.*, Grey 1909, pp. 127–29 *et seq.* (Feb., March, April, May).
25. *Ib.*, pp. 101–02, Lord Crewe to Lord Grey, Jan. 29; *Ib.*, pp. 127–29, Grey to Laurier, Feb. 26; *Ib.*, pp. 130–32, Bryce to Grey, Feb. 24; *Ib.*, pp. 139–41, Grey to Laurier, Mar. 1; *Ib.*, pp. 146–49, Mar. 2.
26. *Ib.*, pp. 158–69, Grey to Laurier, Mar. 7; *Ib.*, pp. 170–71, Mar. 9; *Ib.*, p. 217, Innes to Grey, Secret Tel., Mar. 24; *Ib.*, pp. 328–31, Grey to Laurier, Apr. 30; *Ex. O and U,* 60–2 (injunction of secrecy removed from treaties with Gr. Br., providing for settlement of international differences).
27. *Laurier Papers, Gov. Gen'l's Cor.*, Grey 1909, pp. 294–95, Grey to Laurier, Apr. 17; *Ib.*, pp. 328–31, Apr. 30; *Ib.*, pp. 384–87,

May 19; *Ib.*, pp. 388–91, May 20; *Ib.*, p. 401, Bryce to Grey, May 19; *Ib.*, pp. 381–83, Grey to Laurier, May 24; *Ib.*, pp. 592–93, Oct. 22; *Ib.*, pp. 595–611, Oct. 25; *Ib.*, 1910, p. 8, Jan. 8.

28. *Ib.*, 1911, p. 17, Innes to Lord Grey, Jan. 20.
29. *Sen. Docs.*, 61–2, No. 301, Jan. 24, 1910.
30. *26 G.B., Notes to,* pp. 609–10, No. 22, Jan. 29, 1904; *27 G.B., Notes to,* pp. 52–56, No. 118, Aug. 11.
31. *Ib.*, pp. 172–74, No. 168, Feb. 16, 1905; *Ib.*, pp. 209–10, No. 185, Mar. 23.
32. *Ib.*, p. 272, No. 242, May 20, 1905; *Ib.*, pp. 602–04, No. 457, June 6, 1906.
33. *Ib.*, pp. 564–81, May 3, 1906; *Ib.*, pp. 602–04, No. 457, June 6; Shortt and Doughty, IX, p. 219; Malloy, I, 827–29.
34. *Ib.*, p. 476, Feb. 1, 1906; Ib., pp. 529–30, Apr. 2.
35. *26 G.B., Notes to,* Apr. 27 and May 4 (p. 676), 1904; *27 G.B., Notes to,* pp. 564–81, May 3, 1906; *Laurier Papers, Gov. Gen'l's Cor.*, Grey 1906, pp. 482–501, Laurier to Grey, Sept. 25; *Ib.*, p. 513, Grey to Laurier, Oct. 9; *State Dept., Numerical Files,* Nov. 20, 1906; *Pittsburgh Dispatch,* June 9, 1909.
36. *Laurier Papers, Gov. Gen'l's Cor.*, Grey 1909, pp. 680–82, Bryce to Grey, Nov. 29; *Ib.*, pp. 713–15, Dec. 16; *Ib.*, 1911, pp. 33–37, Feb. 3; *Ib.*, p. 30, Grey to Laurier, Feb. 2; *Ib.*, pp. 33–37, Feb. 3.
37. *27 G.B. Notes to,* pp. 564–81, May 3, 1906; Malloy, I, 830–32.
38. *H. Rps.*, 60–1, No. 1760.
39. Malloy, I, 798–99.
40. *27 G.B., Notes to,* pp. 226–27, No. 198, Apr. 10, 1905.
41. *Ib.*, pp. 564–81, May 3, 1906; Malloy, I, 830–32.
42. *Laurier Papers, Gov. Gen'l's Cor.*, Grey 1911, Laurier to Grey, May 29.
43. Malloy, I, 803–05; *27 G.B., Notes to,* pp. 564–81, May 3, 1906.
44. Malloy, I, 815–27; *Laurier Papers, Gov. Gen'l's Cor.*, Grey 1908, Jan. 8; *Ib.*, 1909, Bryce to Grey, Apr. 22; Charles, *Treaties of U.S.*, III, 47–50; *Treaties Affecting Canada,* pp. 352–53.
45. *Laurier Papers, Gov. Gen'l's Cor.*, Grey 1908, pp. 203–08, Feb. 26; *Ib.*, pp. 235–40, Howard to Grey, Feb. 28; *Ib.*, pp. 292–93, Grey to Laurier, Mar. 13; *Ib.*, pp. 300–01, Mar. 14; *Ib.*, pp. 308–10, Mar. 15; Malloy, *Treaties,* I, 814–15; *Treaties Affecting Canada,* pp. 297–99.
46. *Ib.*, pp. 354–60; Charles, *Treaties,* III, 50–59; F. K. Neilson, *Am. and Br. Claims Arbitration.*
47. *26 G.B., Notes to,* p. 254, Personal, Sept. 26, 1902; *Ib.*, pp. 256–57, No. 2536, Oct. 1; *Ib.*, p. 261, No. 2541, Oct. 9; *Ib.*, p. 264, Oct. 14.
48. *Ib.*, p. 406, Apr. 24, 1903; *Nineteenth Century,* Vol. 53 (1903); Shortt and Doughty, VIII, 705; *27 G.B., Notes to,* pp. 564–

81, May 3, 1906; *T. R. Papers,* Lodge to T. R., 1904–06, Vol. 2.

49. *26 G.B., Notes to,* p. 299, Apr. 14, 1903.
50. *27 G.B., Notes to,* pp. 398–406, No. 336, Oct. 19, 1905; *Ib.,* pp. 329–30, July 25; *T. R. Papers,* Lodge to T. R., 1904–05, Vol. 2, Apr. 10 and Aug. 16.
51. *For. Rels., 1905; 27 G.B.,* pp. 398–406, No. 336, Oct. 19, 1905; *Ib.,* p. 444, Dec. 16.
52. *Laurier Papers, Gov. Gen'l's Cor.,* Grey 1906, pp. 114–18, Grey to Elgin, Private, Apr. 3; *Ib.,* p. 155A, Maurice Low to Grey, Apr. 14.
53. *27 G.B., Notes to,* pp. 564–81, May 3, 1906; *35 G.B., Instrs.,* No. 239, June 30; *Laurier Papers, Gov. Gen'l's Cor.,* Grey 1907, pp.1–8, Grey to Laurier, Jan. 3.
54. Malloy, I, 805–08, 811, 832–34, 844–47; *For. Rels., 1906; 35 G.B., Instrs.,* Telegrams, Sept. 10, 14, 18, 24, 29, and Oct. 6 and Nov. 13, 1906; *Ib.,* No. 325, Oct. 25; *Ib.,* Dec. 4.
55. *Laurier Papers, Gov. Gen'l's Cor.,* Grey 1907, pp. 1–8, Grey to Laurier, Jan. 3; *Ib.,* pp. 36–44, July 11.
56. *Ib.,* pp. 375–83, Sept. 24, 1907; *Ib.,* p. 384, Grey to Bryce, Sept. 21; *Ib.,* pp. 605A–B, Bryce to Grey, Private, Nov. 25.
57. Malloy, I, 835–44; *Laurier Papers, Gov. Gen'l's Cor.,* Grey 1909, Bryce to Grey, Jan. 25.
58. Malloy, I, 841–45.
59. *Laurier Papers, Gov. Gen'l's Cor.,* Grey 1909, p. 150, Laurier to Grey, Mar. 2; *Ib.,* pp. 158–69, Laurier to Grey, Mar. 7.
60. *For. Rels.,* 1910, pp. 549, 556–57, 559, 561, 569; Keenleyside, *Canada and the U.S.,* pp. 275–89; *Treaties Affecting Canada,* pp. 325–48.
61. *Ib.,* pp. 456–69; Charles, *Treaties bet. the U.S. and Other Powers,* III, 66–70; *Laurier Papers, Gov. Gen'l's Cor.,* Grey 1911, pp. 119–20, Laurier to Grey, May 29; *Ib.,* p. 164, May 29 (Private); *Ib.,* pp. 158–60, Grey to L. V. Harcourt, June 15.
62. *Ib.,* pp. 211–12, Laurier to Grey, Aug. 7, 1911; *Ib.,* p. 170, July 27; *Ib.,* pp. 173–76, July 28; *Ib.,* p. 189, Bryce to Grey, Aug. 2.
63. Dunning, *The Br. Empire and the U.S.,* p. 280.
64. *34 G.B., Instrs.,* pp. 453–55, Personal, Hay to Choate, July 28, 1903; *Ib.,* p. 669, Tel., Adee to Choate, Aug. 4, 1904; *27 G.B., Notes to,* Apr. 18, 1906 (also see pp. 564–81 for Root's later reference); *Laurier Papers, Gov. Gen'l's Cor.,* Grey 1909, pp. 677–79, Bryce to Grey, No. 29.
65. *Ib.,* pp. 5–7, Bryce to Grey, Dec. 31, 1908, and Grey to Laurier, Jan. 3, 1909; *Ib.,* pp. 444–48, July 27 (with Mem. on pp. 449–52); *Ib.,* pp. 465–66, Grey to Laurier (Skagway), Aug. 11; *Ib.,* pp. 473–86 and 487–90, Sept. 9 (with documents on pp. 491–509); *Ib.,* pp. 654–56, Nov. 13.

66. Charles, *Treaties between the U.S. and Other Powers,* III, 56–66; *U. S. Stats.,* Vol. 37, p. 499.
67. Shortt and Doughty, IX, 202, 205; *3 Reciprocity Treaties, 1898–1907, Canada* (Kasson), Mar. 25 and Aug. 3, 1904; *T. R. Papers,* Lodge to T. R., 1904–06, June 6, 1904.
68. *Ib.,* Lodge to T. R., Nov. 15, 1904 (Vol. 2); *Ib.,* Hay to T. R., II, 1903–05, Dec. 28, 1904; *Selections from the Correspondence of T. R. and Lodge, 1884–1918,* Vol. 2, pp. 110–12, Jan. 6, 1905; *Ib.,* pp. 209–11, Oct. 31.
69. *Sen. Docs.,* 67–2, No. 114, p. 166.
70. *27 G.B., Notes to,* pp. 564–81, May 3, 1906; Skelton, *Life and Letters of Laurier,* II, 356; *Laurier Papers, Gov. Gen'l's Cor.,* Grey 1906, pp. 482–91, Laurier to Grey, Sept. 25; *Ib.,* 1908, pp. 355–64, Grey to Laurier, Sept. 9.
71. *U. S. Tariff Commission Rp.* (1920), on the proposed reciprocity agreement of 1911; Skelton, *Life and Letters of Laurier,* II, 364–65; *Laurier Papers, Gov. Gen'l's Cor.,* Grey 1909, pp. 657–58, Grey to Fielding, Nov. 13; *Ib.,* Bryce to Grey, Private, Nov. 24.
72. *Ib.,* 1910, pp. 87–90, Geo. Young to Grey, Confid., Feb. 18; *Ib.,* pp. 91–93, Emery to Young, Feb. 16; *Ib.,* p. 98, Innes to Grey, Feb. 19; *Ib.,* pp. 99–111, Grey to Laurier, Feb. 23, 26, 27; *Ib.,* p. 112, Bryce to Grey, Feb. 28; *Ib.,* pp. 131–32, Mar. 5; *N. Y. Herald,* Feb. 19, 1910; Skelton, *Life and Letters of Laurier,* II, 367; *Cong. Digest,* May 19, 1933, pp. 130–32; *U. S. Tariff Com. Rp.* (1920), pp. 33–37.
73. *Ib.,* II, 368; *Pres. Mess.,* Dec. 6, 1910; *Cong. Rec.,* Jan. 26, 1911, pp. 1516–19.
74. *Ib.; Can. An. Rev.,* 1910, p. 622; *H. Docs.,* 61–3, No. 1418.
75. *107 Annals Am. Acad. of Pol. Sc.,* p. 194 (J. A. Stevenson, *Canadian Tariff*).
76. *Laurier Papers, Gov. Gen'l's Cor.,* Grey 1911, pp. 39–42, Grey to Laurier, Feb. 6; *Ib.,* pp. 43–47, Mem. of Geo. Young, Jan. 24; *Ib.,* pp. 33–37, Grey to Laurier, Feb. 3.
77. *Journal of Polit. Econ.,* XIX, 513–26.
78. Shortt and Doughty, IX, 225; Skelton, *Life and Letters of Laurier,* II, 369.
79. *Ib.,* II, 370–80; *Cong. Digest,* May, 1933, pp. 130–32; *H.R.* 4412, 62–1, July 26, 1911; *H.R. 7753* and *7779,* 66–1; *Cong. Record,* Oct. 9 and 10 and 11, 1919, pp. 7021, 7029, 7053 and 7098.

CHAPTER XXI

THE LATEST ERA OF EASIER ADJUSTMENT

IN the quarter century after 1911, the permanent International Joint Commission of six members (three Americans and three Canadians) was an important factor in the reduction of the labors and difficulties of diplomatic adjustment of American-Canadian problems. This interesting tribunal, which the treaty of 1909 was authorized to provide for adjustment of many troublesome international border problems previously referred to diplomatic negotiations, met at Washington on January 10, 1912, for organization. After providing for chairmen (one for each section) and for permanent offices at Washington and Ottawa, it adopted rules of procedure concerning joint sessions, hearings, and consideration of cases submitted for its decision. Immediately thereafter it became a constant medium for direct communication to settle questions at issue between two neighbors and to prevent disputes by amicable and impartial judicial methods. It blazed a new trail for the judicial settlement of international disputes.[1]

By February, 1915, the Commission had adjusted several controversies and had under consideration serious long-pending cases. Among the important adjusted cases were the St. Marys power works which had entirely obstructed the natural outlet of Lake Superior. Among the cases under consideration were the Lake of the Woods controversy which had been pending since the construction of the Norman Dam at the outlet of that lake in 1888, a similar controversy which had arisen from the construction of the international dam at the outlet of Rainy Lake (a tributary of the Lake of the Woods) and the

Livingstone Channel controversy in the Detroit River where the American government had expended eleven million dollars in the interest of navigation. Others had arisen from applications for approval of a proposed dam at Kettle Falls in Rainy Lake, for approval of a proposed Rainy River log boom which threatened injury to navigation and private interests, and for approval of a proposed daily diversion of a hundred million gallons of water from the Lake of the Woods to Winnipeg.

Besides the consideration of cases, the Commission had made an investigation and report upon the pollution of boundary waters and waters flowing across the boundary.[2]

Within two decades after 1915, the Commission received for final determination or investigation many other cases of difference involving a variety of important interests, both public and private, extending from the St. Croix and St. John boundary waters in the East to tributaries of the Columbia River in the West. Among the more important problems were the Sault Ste. Marie power cases which involved the levels of Lake Superior, the Lake of the Woods investigation, the St. Lawrence navigation and power investigation, and the diversion of waters of the St. Mary and Milk rivers for irrigation in Montana and Alberta and Saskatchewan.[3]

By April, 1928, the Commission had disposed of fifteen cases under Article VIII of the treaty of 1909. Of these fifteen applications, nine sought approval for specific obstructions (such as timber booms, submerged weirs, dams, fishways and bridge abutments) in boundary waters or in water flowing therefrom, and six contemplated diversions (five for electric power and one for domestic and sanitary purposes).

The nine applications which sought approval for obstructions in boundary waters were based upon problems relating to six rivers: the Rainy, the St. Clair, the St. Lawrence, the St. Croix, the St. John and the Niagara. The five applications for diversions for power were based upon problems relating to the St. Marys and the St. Croix. The application for diversion for domestic and sanitary purposes was submitted in 1913 by the Greater Winnipeg Water District which sought approval for the use of the waters of Shoal Lake and the Lake of the Woods. Other applications for diversions were based upon development problems on the St. Marys, the St. Lawrence and the St. John.[4]

A minor question of lake levels, originating (in 1920) in certain Vermont complaints of flood damages resulting from a dam at the outlet of Lake Memphremagog was later submitted to engineers for investigation.[5]

In the consideration of the applications relating to obstructions and diversions of border waters the Commission was uniformly successful, deciding by unanimous opinion all but one case (which was later dismissed by a four to two vote, for lack of jurisdiction). In its orders it encountered no dissatisfaction, no opposing appeals, and no disobedience.[6]

In 1920, in connection with its administrative duty to direct American reclamation officials and Canadian irrigation officials in the execution of the treaty provision concerning the St. Mary River and the Milk River, the Commission encountered a controversy which necessitated its determination or interpretation of the meaning and scope of its mandate. After listening to the conflicting arguments of the Canadian and American lawyers, on the question whether the provision applied to all tributaries of the streams or only to tributaries which crossed the boundary, it visited the region of the streams to confer informally with the farmers and other interested parties. Finally, in 1921, it issued an order which disposed of the controversy on an equitable basis, by including only the eastern or Saskatchewan tributaries which flow into Montana and by recommending a joint irrigation plan involving construction partly in the United States and partly in Canada—a plan which apparently was regarded as satisfactory.[7]

By 1928 the Commission completed four investigations under Article IX of the treaty of 1909.

One of these, on the Livingstone Channel in the Detroit River, it conducted in 1913 primarily on the application of the American government in order to ascertain the effect of certain excavations and dredging upon the level and flow of waters on the Canadian side of the river. In a report, later adopted and followed by the American government, it recommended compensatory works and a dyke which was extended in 1919 and 1921.

Another investigation (a more extensive one), on the pollution of boundary waters, it began in 1913. In 1915 it reported that the conditions of pollution were found serious only in certain areas along the Lakes, notably in the Detroit River where the water was contaminated with sewage from Detroit and in the Niagara where it was contaminated by the sewage from Buffalo. Later it made a careful study of suitable remedies. In August, 1918, it made a final report and offered recommendations which resulted in great improvement of sanitary conditions. In October, 1920, in response to a request of the two governments, it drafted rules and regulations (relating to pollution) which were embodied in a draft treaty.[8]

Meantime, in June, 1917, it had reported upon the question of the most advantageous fixed levels for the Lake of the Woods, a question which had been a subject of some correspondence with the British legation in 1913–15. Incident to this question it also had undertaken to investigate complaints of the Minnesota authorities concerning the inundation of American lands resulting from the high gauge of a dam at Kenora, Ontario. In August, 1915, with a view to inquiry into these complaints in connection with a general investigation of water problems, it called meetings at Warroad, International Falls, and Kenora. In connection with its report of 1917 it submitted various recommendations concerning (1) the maintenance of a fixed level advantageous to both countries (by a joint board of control under the surveillance of the commission), (2) a compensation to property owners for any resulting injuries to their interests, and (3) the prohibition of diversions from this watershed to another without authority of the Commission—recommendations subsequently embodied in the Lake of the Woods treaty of 1925.[9]

In 1920–22 it investigated the problems of the proposed St. Lawrence waterway. In these problems of engineering and economic development it included a determination of what further improvements in the river channel or canals alongside were necessary to enable vessels of ocean draft to navigate between Montreal and Lake Ontario, the feasibility of linking hydro-electric power development with the navigation enterprise, a program for execution of administrative features of the proposal, an estimate of the capital and operating costs, and the basis of apportioning these costs between the two countries. In January, 1922, it submitted to Secretary Hughes an elaborate report which included detailed plans and recommended further investigation of engineering features and negotiations for a treaty arrangement for plans of waterway improvement between Lake Ontario and Montreal.[10]

In the reports on various investigations under Article IX the Commission was in substantial accord on conclusions and recommendations. Its recommendations, like its decisions under Article III, were usually unanimous.

As a result of its investigation of the levels of boundary waters and methods of controlling them, the Commission's jurisdiction was extended by the Lake of the Woods treaty of February 24, 1925, which required its approval for any subsequent diversion of water from the Lake of the Woods watershed to any other watershed. In 1925 it began an investigation of certain questions relating to the levels of Rainy Lake which were referred to it by the two governments. In December, 1928, it was requested to investigate and report the effects of certain intensive drainage into the Roseau River (a tributary of the Red River) in Minnesota, and certain proposed improvements in the lower channel (in Manitoba) which had caused complaints on both sides of the boundary.[11]

Under its quasi-judicial power the Commission had other cases still pending early in 1928, and it received other cases thereafter. Among the pending cases was an application for permission to construct certain permanent works in the Kootenay (Kootenai) River at Creston, British Columbia. Later, in 1929, it received an application of a power and light company for permission to construct and operate in the channel of the Kootenay, at Granite, British Columbia, certain permanent works, which were later a subject of complaint by Idaho citizens whose agricultural lands were damaged by the rise of the water above the dam, and who requested the removal of all obstructions in the river or in the connecting lake.

In 1928 the Commission was requested to investigate a border problem on the upper Columbia—a problem involving complaints from landowners of Stevens County, Washington, concerning damages to their property by fumes from a copper smelter which had been erected at Trail in British Columbia in 1895. In 1932, after careful investigation, involving various hearings and arguments, it decided the case against the copper smelter by a judgment for damages. These damages Canada paid in November 1835 in accord with the provision of a convention of April 15, 1835, which also provided for arbitration of any claims for damages after January 1, 1932.

Early in 1934 (May 1) it settled a Rainy Lake case (of Isaac Walton) involving a conflict between recreation-tourist interests and power interests. Desiring to leave the way open for later approval of reasonable development of storage facilities on waters above Namaken Lake, it expressed the opinion that a reasonable use of the waters for economic (power) development, properly controlled and regulated, might be permitted without serious injury to the beauty and recreational interests.[12]

Besides the questions referred to the International Joint Commission for adjustment, the chief problems or subjects of American-Canadian relations since 1912 may be grouped under four or five general heads: World War questions, protection of fisheries, water and waterways, trade and trade policies and economic penetration.

For a half decade diplomatic relations were affected by questions related to the World War, which was precipitated in the midst of Anglo-American preparations for coöperation in an international celebration of a century of Anglo-American peace and immediately preceding the completion of Anglo-American negotiations of 1914 for a new arbitration treaty especially designed to facilitate the settlement of disputes. Early in the war Americans admiringly expressed increasing interest in Canadian achievement; and, in the face of a neutrality proclamation, they expressed opinions of sympathy with the

Allied cause in which many American citizens enlisted with Canadian military forces. In the latter part of the war they felt an increased friendliness and respect resulting from the experiences of official coöperation and common sacrifice both at home and on the battlefield.

In a recent volume on Canada and the United States a Canadian writer states that, through influences of the tense atmosphere of the World War and of the aftermath of discussion, Canada became less friendly toward the United States than it had been in 1914. This change of attitude he attributed to the American failure to protest against German violation of Belgian neutrality in 1914, to American expressions of gratification at its position of peaceful isolation from the European military contest including the President's declaration that Americans should be neutral in thought as well as in deed, to American disagreement with Great Britain on questions of blockade and definition of contraband, to American development to a powerful creditor nation by loans to the belligerents during the heat of the struggle, to provocative American assertions concerning the importance of America's military participation in the war, and to the later American attitude toward the questions of the inter-Allied debts and the League of Nations.[18]

In 1915, in connection with the problems of the war, arose several cases relating to American neutral duties. In February Secretary Bryan received through Cecil Spring-Rice an application for extradition of Vernil Horne on a charge of attempting to destroy the Vanceboro bridge in New Brunswick. With it he also received a suggestion that the American government, with a view to the prevention of similar outrages, should place guards on the American side of all international bridges between Canada and the United States. This suggestion he refused to consider, claiming that the United States was neutral and that in such cases the American government would act only upon application of the local authorities. Later, through Rice, he complained of the appearance of uniformed Canadian soldiers on the streets of Detroit and requested a discontinuance of the practice. Later, both Bryan and Lansing denied the Canadian request for permission for passage of Canadian uniformed soldiers from New Brunswick through Maine to other points in Canada. In 1916 Lansing refused a request to allow Jamaican soldiers to travel via New York *en route* from Halifax to Jamaica. Two years later, however, after America entered the war, he signed with the Earl of Reading, British ambassador on a special mission, a treaty relating to the military service of citizens of one country in the territory of the other.[14]

In 1916 the large exodus of Americans to Canada attracted some attention in Congress. Apparently many were enlisted in the Canadian army. In the Senate, on January 13, Townsend discussed the question of the status of Americans who thus enlisted with expectation to return to the United States as full citizens, although they had taken an oath of allegiance to King George.[15]

In the war period arose several routine questions which had no direct relation to war problems. Among the most prominent was the case of the accidental shooting of two Buffalo citizens in Canada, by Canadian militiamen who claimed that their purpose had been only to frighten the fore-warned violators of the Canadian duck-hunting law. Early in 1915, the American State Department submitted the case for British consideration. Later the American authorities insisted upon a trial of the militiamen. The trial was finally avoided on the ground that a representative of the Canadian government had succeeded in effecting a settlement by which a compensation of ten thousand dollars had been paid to the mother of the deceased and five thousand dollars to the wounded man.[16]

An interesting convention for restriction of bird hunters was negotiated at Washington in August, 1916. Its purpose was to protect certain migratory birds in their spring transit from the Caribbean to Hudson Bay and other northern regions used by them as summer resorts for mating and reproduction and incidental pleasure.[17]

Within the decade before 1920 also arose an interesting question of jurisdiction over Hudson Bay. It first arose in 1912 from a Canadian legislative fisheries act of 1906 under which the Canadian government required American vessels to obtain a Canadian license to catch fish or to hunt whales in Hudson Bay waters. In 1920, following an opinion of the American State Department that a claim to territorial jurisdiction had never been made, the Canadian claim was renewed. Later the question received new significance from the plans of the Canadian government to complete a railway from Winnipeg to Fort Churchill on Hudson Bay to facilitate the movement of Canadian wheat to European markets by diversion from American to Canadian ports on a shorter and cheaper navigation route.[18]

Meantime, since 1912, the two governments had directed their attention to certain new fishery problems, less serious than the former northeastern fisheries problem which had now become quiescent. On certain pending questions relating to the northeastern fisheries they began negotiations in June, 1917. In December, following a conference, they appointed commissioners who proceeded to consider by "open diplomacy" the question of the privileges of the fishing vessels of each country in the ports of the other—a question especially connected with shipment in bond by fishermen of either country through the territory of the other. They promptly found a satisfactory settlement for the period of the war by concurrent instructions of each government to collectors of customs. Early in 1918, through agreement of the joint commission and by war legislation under pressure of war conditions, they reached a reciprocal agreement by which each country conceded to the fishing vessels of the other all the port privileges enjoyed by domestic vessels. This arrangement terminated with the American cancellation of war legislation in July, 1921, and with the consequent seizure of American "poaching" vessels by Canadian patrol boats. The situation in 1921 was complicated by the American Fordney tariff bill which erected an almost prohibitive wall against the American importation of Canadian fish.

At the end of 1923, following the failure of a Washington conference which had been arranged with a view to negotiation of a new agreement for regulation of international fisheries, the Canadian government gave official notice of the discontinuance of the privileges so long extended to American fishing vessels in Canadian ports. This official notice, which became effective in 1924 and to which the American government seemed rather indifferent, was based upon the Canadian expectation that it would prove a makeweight in bargaining negotiations for trade reciprocity (at least on fish) or for better tariff relations. Thus efforts to reach a mutually satisfactory solution of the problem of international fisheries of the northeast coast were terminated or postponed.[19]

The conference of 1917 also considered the questions of the rehabilitation and protection of the sockeye salmon of the Fraser River system, the protection of the Pacific halibut fishery off the coast of Alaska and northern British Columbia, fishing by American well-smacks off the Canadian coast, the unwarranted requirements imposed by Canadian fishing vessels passing through territorial waters of Alaska, the protection of pike and pickerel in Lake Champlain and of sturgeon fisheries in the Great Lakes and off Nova Scotia, and the protection of whales in the ocean.[20]

The importance of the sockeye salmon question arose especially from the fact that blasting operations in the construction of the Canadian Northern railway road-bed had caused a rock slide which prevented the down-stream return of the salmon from their resting place in the bay-like indentation of the river just above Hell's Gate. This barrier necessitated the restocking of the river below, involving an agreement on a period of suspension of fishing operations there. To secure proper regulation the commissioners recommended a treaty or convention for a period of fifteen years and with a provision for the appointment of a special commission to study the situation by aid of experts.

For the Pacific halibut grounds the commission recommended a closed season, from November 16 to February 16 annually for ten years, with supervision by the special salmon commission. For the protection of sturgeon fisheries it suggested the necessity of a suspension of such fishing in all contiguous interior waters for a period of at least five years, and it recommended similar prohibitory legislation for non-contiguous waters. For the protection of whales it advised the calling of a post-war international conference to consider world-wide action.[21]

On September 2, 1919, at Washington, the representatives of the British and American governments reached an agreement on regulations for the protection of the sockeye salmon of the Fraser River from injury resulting from American methods of taking these fish before they entered the river.[22]

In December, 1922, after various investigations and negotiations, Secretary Hughes submitted through the British ambassador for consideration of the Canadian government the draft of a treaty providing for a closed fishing season in Alaska for protection of the halibut on the Pacific coast during the spawning period. This treaty was signed for the Dominion on March 2, 1923, by the Canadian Minister of Marine and Fisheries, Ernest Lapointe, who was designated as the British plenipotentiary in the negotiations, and who strenuously opposed the addition of the signature of the British ambassador. In the American Senate, which at first proposed amendment, it was finally approved (in 1924) in its original form.[23]

By this treaty Canada obtained its treaty-making power and a basis for its renewed argument in favor of a resident Canadian minister at Washington. It stubbornly declined to accept a proposed amendment by which the American Senate sought to extend the provisions of the treaty to nationals and vessels of "any other part of Great Britain."

In this independent action Canada was in accord with recent development of policy. A year before the World War, it had aspired to establish at Washington a permanent Canadian office, of semi-ambassadorial character, to coöperate freely with the British embassy in close and constant communication with the American government concerning questions of common interest. Incident to the events of the war it had continued to advance toward a position of national status, as an equal among the self-governing "autonomous nations of an Imperial Commonwealth." At the end of the war, it had participated as an equal in the negotiation and ratification of the treaty of Versailles and had received separate representation in the League of Nations. In May, 1919, its government had expressed the opinion that a Canadian representative at Washington was necessary to the adequate protection of Canadian interests resulting from increasing business with the United States. A year later it had obtained from the British government a decision to appoint a Canadian minister, which, however, was delayed without explanation. In 1921, opposing a renewal of the Anglo-Japanese alliance of 1902, it had influenced the British government to support the American proposal for the Washington disarmament conference. At this conference it was represented on the British delegation by Sir Robert Borden who individually signed treaties resulting from the discussion.[24] After the conference, which contributed to the growth of Canada's international status, its direct negotiations with Washington had increased. Following a postal conference, Prime Minister King (by arrangement with the British minister) had visited Washington to confer with Secretary Hughes on several questions: a waterways treaty, the development of navigation and electric power on the St. Lawrence, the problem of prohibition enforcement and the question whether the agreement of 1817 should be replaced by a formal treaty of explicit and definite terms. Possibly, as Hughes suspected, he may have had an ulterior motive to prepare the way for direct negotiation through a Canadian minister at Washington. Apparently the British government had withdrawn its earlier objections to Dominion direct diplomatic representation in the conduct of international relations.[25]

Within the two years after the fisheries treaty of 1923 Secretary Hughes negotiated several other conventions which he signed with Lapointe (the Canadian Minister of Justice who represented the British government). On June 6, 1924, he and Lapointe signed an anti-smuggling convention, which was supplemental to the Hughes-Geddes treaty (of January 23, 1924) for British coöperation in American enforcement of legislation to prevent the importation of intoxicating liquors. On January 8, 1925, they signed another Anglo-American convention in respect to Canada, to provide extradition for crimes or offenses against narcotic laws. In the following month (on February 24) they signed a treaty to provide for the maintenance of an effective boundary between the United States and Canada, and between Alaska and Canada, in accord with the treaties of April 11, 1908, and May 21, 1910. On the same day they signed a treaty and protocol to regulate the levels of the Lake of the Woods, by extending the jurisdiction of the International Joint Commission in the determination of subsequent cases relating to water diversion therefrom to another watershed.[26]

Meantime, at the imperial conference of 1923, Canada had obtained a further confirmation of its new international status by a formal agreement that any part of the empire acting alone might negotiate and sign treaties which affected no other part of the empire, and that the parts of the empire affected by imperial agreements must be consulted in advance. In 1925 it received new recognition of its new importance in the empire by the British creation of a new cabinet position for Dominion affairs. In the fall of 1926, at the London imperial conference it was successful in securing recognition of the constitutional right of the dominion governments to send their own diplomatic representatives to foreign capitals. Early in 1927 it established a legation at Washington.

The American government was ready to agree to the Canadian common-sense wish for direct diplomatic communication with a view to the facilitation of further efforts to reach a satisfactory solution of pending questions. Following the Canadian appointment of Vincent Massey of Toronto as the first Canadian resident minister at Washington, it promptly coöperated by the appointment of William Phillips as the first American resident minister to the Dominion government.[27] Probably it would have approved the earlier suggestion that Canada should join the Pan-American Union if Canada had shown any disposition to seek membership in that organization.

Since Canada attained full autonomy in foreign policy, the American government has considered by direct negotiations with the Canadian government several important diplomatic questions resulting in several new conventions or agreements. On January 2, 1929, at Ottawa, William Phillips signed with Mackenzie King a draft convention for the preservation and improvement of the scenic beauty of Niagara Falls, and the rapids below, a question which had been a subject of correspondence for several years (since 1923) and a subject of study and report by the special International Niagara Board since 1925. The American Senate, however, returned it to the President without approval. On March 27, at Washington, the two governments signed a convention for preservation of the sockeye salmon fisheries in the Fraser system. This, too, the Senate returned without approval, but with a suggestion of revision. On May 26, 1930, Secretary Stimson signed with Vincent Massey a (substitute) convention on the same subject, providing for greater flexibility in regulation and extending the area of regulation from the Fraser River and contiguous boundary waters to territorial waters of the Pacific Coast between parallels 48° and 49° and to the adjacent high seas. This, too, the Senate failed to approve.

Meantime, several other agreements had been reached by exchange of notes. One of these (at Washington in March and April, 1929) provided for arbitration of the case of the schooner *I'm Alone*. Another (at Ottawa, in October, 1929) provided for health quarantine inspection of vessels entering Puget Sound and adjacent waters or the Great Lakes via the St. Lawrence (by quarantine officers of the government having jurisdiction over the primary port of arrival). Another (at Washington, in October) provided for regulation of civil aircraft. The latter arrangement was an elaboration of the existing understanding governing the flight of American aircraft into Canada by extension since 1920. Later (in October, 1933), it was the subject of an informal Washington conference of American and Canadian radio experts with a view to the conclusion of a new arrangement for division of shortwave lengths.

The prominent case of the *I'm Alone,* which was submitted to arbitration, arose in connection with American enforcement of the American national prohibition law which, while it stimulated the emigration of American delinquents to Canada, increased the illicit importation of intoxicating liquors from Canada into the United States both by land and by sea. With a desire to aid the observance of neighborly obligations and to avoid any difficulties which might arise from enforcement of the amendment along the American coasts, an Anglo-American convention for regulation of the traffic in alcoholic beverages or liquors was signed at Washington on January 13, 1924, by Secretary Hughes and the British ambassador. Under this convention which the Canadian government approved, American authorities were permitted to board and to search suspicious British private vessels outside of the three-mile limit (but not beyond the distance which could be traversed by the suspected vessel in one hour). Acting under this authority, in March, 1929, the American coast guard pursued and sank the Canadian rum-running schooner *I'm Alone* in the Gulf of Mexico near the coast of Louisiana. After considerable courteous correspondence at Washington between Secretary Stimson and the Canadian minister concerning the question of the location of the vessel and the question of hot pursuit, Stimson suggested a willingness to submit the subject to arbitration. This proposal the Canadian government promptly accepted. The commissioners, to whom the Canadian and American briefs were submitted in 1931–32, presented a joint interim report and recommendations on June 30, 1933, and a joint final report on January 5, 1935. They decided that the "admittedly intentional sinking of the suspected vessel was not justified by anything in the Convention." Therefore they recommended that the American government should apologize to the Canadian government for the illegal sinking and pay to it as an amend the sum of $25,000, and that it should pay for the benefit of the unoffending captain and crew as compensation the sum of $25,666.50. In view of the facts concerning the character of the vessel, a rum-runner owned and directed chiefly by American citizens, they stated that no compensation should be paid for its loss or for the loss of its cargo. In accord with the recommendation Secretary Hull promptly tendered an apology and took steps to obtain an appropriation for payment of the compensation.

On May 9, 1930, the American chargé at Ottawa signed with Prime Minister King a new convention for preservation of the halibut fishery of the North Pacific Ocean (to supplant the convention of March 2, 1923). This convention, terminable after five years by a notice of two years, received the consent of the Senate on February 24, 1931. It became effective by exchange of ratifications at Ottawa on May 9 and proclamation of the President on May 14.

On December 9, 1933, Acting Secretary William Phillips signed with the Canadian minister at Washington a convention for exemption, within Puget Sound and neighboring specified sheltered waters, of American and Canadian vessels from the international load requirements (under provision of the London convention of July 5, 1930) when these vessels were engaged in international voyages originating or terminating on these waters. On February 2, 1934, this convention received the consent of the Senate for ratification.[28]

The latest important new subject of negotiations with Canada was the St. Lawrence deep-waterway project which had been considered as a possible coöperative enterprise over a decade before it reached the stage of a draft treaty agreement. This project was especially influenced by the unequal effects of the opening of the Panama Canal upon transportation costs for different geographical sections, causing the Middle West to favor the St. Lawrence seaway route.[29]

As early as 1912–14, plans for coöperation in construction of the proposed deeper waterway from the Lakes to the ocean via the St. Lawrence route were discussed by Prime Minister Borden with the governor of New York, especially with a view to the development of larger hydro-electric facilities. In 1919 increased interest in the proposed enterprise was stimulated by the completion of an improved all-water transportation from the Lakes to the Atlantic by the opening of the terminal pier of the New York state barge canal, which had been designed to divert the large eastward export shipments of western grain from the St. Lawrence route. Following memorials from the legislatures of Minnesota and North Dakota urging American coöperation in the St. Lawrence improvements, the Senate committee on rivers and harbors appropriations proposed an investigation of the project by the International Joint Commission. The bitter opposition from Lodge and others, who doubted whether America should join with its neighbor in construction of a waterway which it could not control, resulted in an additional amendment for an all-American route, authorizing a survey for a ship canal between the Lakes and the Hudson.[80]

On January 21, 1920, the American and Canadian governments referred to the International Joint Commission the question of the feasibility and practicability of the projected improvement of the St. Lawrence for ocean navigation with the incidental development of water power. In December, 1921, the Commission made a favorable report in which it recommended negotiation of a treaty arrangement for a plan of improvements and suggested a provision for apportionment of the cost of the "navigation works" on the basis of the benefits which each country would receive from the new waterway, and also a provision for maintenance of "power works" at the expense of the country in which they were located.[81]

In Congress the introduction of a bill for immediate steps toward construction of the St. Lawrence canal resulted in three counter-measures: (1) one for construction, entirely within New York, of a ship canal by a private corporation under a plan which was advanced by Millard of Buffalo; (2) another (offered by Ten Eyck of Albany) for a route southward from the Canadian St. Lawrence (via Lake Champlain to the Hudson) through Canadian territory which the promoters proposed that the American government should acquire by cession as a part payment of the British war indebtedness to the United States; and (3) a similar but more moderate proposition involving a cession of Canadian territory south of the middle of the St. Lawrence River and west of the Richelieu as a condition precedent to American participation in the St. Lawrence improvement by canalization. These counter-moves temporarily blocked the St. Lawrence canal measure.

Further legislative progress on the project at that time was also postponed by the pro-canal policy of President Harding who insisted that such action should be preceded by the preliminary negotiation of treaties with Canada and Great Britain. The proposed negotiations, which the President directed Secretary Hughes to begin, the Canadian government practically declined.[82]

Soon thereafter, in 1922, Prime Minister Mackenzie King

visited Washington to discuss with Secretary Hughes the problems of a deep waterways treaty and other questions. Following his return to Ottawa, the press reported that the Canadian government was ready to consider a treaty for deepening the St. Lawrence; but, apparently, he desired to consider the subject further before reaching a decision upon an enterprise involving such large expenditures. At the same time the public mind was attracted by private plans for completion and dedication of a boundary peace portal—a proposed new bond of Canadian-American friendship.[33]

Early in 1925 appeared the significant decision of the United States Supreme Court declaring illegal Chicago's large diversion of water from Lake Michigan through the local Chicago sanitary drainage canal. It asserted the right of the American government to regulate the amount or manner of the flow through the local canal. This right, it declared, was implied in the federal power to regulate commerce and the control of navigable waters within its jurisdiction, including the incidental power to remove obstructions to interstate and foreign commerce and to execute treaty obligations to a foreign power bordering upon the connected system of the Lakes.[34]

Meantime, in the spring of 1924, the two governments had appointed a joint board of engineers, whose authority to conduct later surveys and investigations on the St. Lawrence were supplemented by the advice of two national advisory committees (one for each country). In December, 1926, this joint board submitted an elaborate report with detailed plans for construction of the proposed waterway and for development of the water power incidental thereto. A few days later the American advisory commission submitted an opinion that the construction of a shipway from the Lakes to the sea was imperative, and recommended construction on the St. Lawrence route if a suitable agreement for the joint undertaking could be reached.

Adopting the recommendations of the American advisory commission, the American government in 1927 announced its readiness to negotiate an appropriate convention on the subject. Finally, in October, 1928, after many conferences, both governments announced simultaneously that the contemplated treaty negotiations for the joint enterprise would be initiated at once by direct and verbal exchange of views.[85]

In the subsequent negotiations, which were promptly opened with the Dominion government, the two governments agreed on many points and made considerable progress by the early part of 1929. Although an early treaty seemed possible, concluding negotiations were postponed. In September, 1930, the American minister at Ottawa reiterated the information that the American government was ready to proceed with plans, but he encountered some delay. In the following January he accompanied Bennett to Washington for informal conferences with the President and other American officials.[86]

Negotiations were finally re-opened at Washington in November, 1931, by a conference which resulted in an arrangement for reconvening the joint board of engineers to complete its final report upon which the later deep-waterway treaty was based. The renewed conferences at Washington, after the completion of the engineers' report in April, 1932, resulted in the conclusion of an outline of a treaty by the middle of June, and in the formulation of the definite terms at Ottawa by July 12. In the final agreement the American government adopted the Canadian project of a two-stage development in the international section of the St. Lawrence (instead of the original American project of a single-stage development). The chief features of this plan included a dam (and power houses) at Chrysler Island and a dam (and power houses) at Barnhart Island, with a short side canal around each.[87]

On July 18, 1932, at Washington, Secretary Stimson signed with Herridge the completed treaty of ten articles providing for coöperation in construction of the proposed deep-waterway (twenty-seven feet in depth) and the incidental development of a large by-product of water-power—an enterprise which was expected to require ten years for completion and a total cost of $543,000,000 (an estimated total expenditure of $272,000,000 by the United States).

Besides articles of agreement concerning construction of the different sections of the waterway, the treaty contained articles on (1) equal division of water utilized for power purposes and regulation of river-flow to protect down-river shipping facilities, (2) the question of jurisdiction, (3) maintenance of rights of navigation under existing treaties, (4) preservation of water levels and prohibition of water diversion to another watershed except by authority of the International Joint Commission, (5) release of each party for damages or injury of persons or property in the territory of the other, and (6) responsibility of each for acquisition of lands or interests in its territory when necessary to make effective the treaty provisions. Under its terms the disposal of about 1,100,000 horse power on the American side of the international section was reserved as a purely domestic question in the United States. Into Article VIII was incorporated the American Supreme Court decree of 1930 providing for reduction of water diversion from Lake Michigan.

President Hoover promptly announced that completion of the treaty marked "another step forward in this the greatest internal improvement yet undertaken on this continent."[38]

On January 19, 1933, the President submitted the treaty to the Senate with a request for approval. With it he submitted copies of notes, exchanged on January 13 between Stimson and the Canadian minister, clarifying the question of the effect of the treaty on the diversion of water through the Massena Canal and the Grass River for power purposes.

On February 21, after considering three chief sources of opposition to the project, the Committee on Foreign Relations recommended approval subject to an amendment based on certain agreements and interpretations (by the recent exchange of notes) concerning private diversions of water on the St. Lawrence. Further consideration by the Senate was postponed.[39]

President Roosevelt continued the American friendly policy in Canadian relations, as illustrated by his invitation of April, 1933, to Prime Minister Bennett to a conference with him at the White House. On January 12, 1934, he renewed the request of his predecessor for approval of the St. Lawrence deep-waterway treaty by the Senate, to which he submitted proofs that the proposed seaway enterprise would greatly benefit American commerce and transportation without economic harm to special localities or to special interests. He emphasized the economy of the direct seaway route from the Northwest to Europe, via the St. Lawrence instead of via Texas ports or the Mississippi to the Gulf; and he urged that, both in navigation and in the development of water power, the American government should seek to maintain the historic policy of coöperation.[40]

Pending action by the Senate, the battle of the St. Lawrence project was fought in the American newspapers, by expression of views indicating that public opinion was largely influenced by sectional interests (as in Canada).

In the Senate, following strong speeches of La Follette and others in favor of the project, Dietrich of Illinois led the opposition of the Mississippi Valley. He asserted that the power distribution contemplated by the treaty was unfair to the United States and he urged that the American constitutional authority to divert water from one watershed to another for the public interest belonged to Congress as much as to the treaty-making power. Senator Clark, of Missouri, said that the Mississippi Valley opposition to the treaty was especially due to the absolute limitation on diversion of water from Lake Michigan. Senator Overton of Louisiana opposed it on the ground that it released American sovereignty over Lake Michigan.[41]

On March 14, after considerable discussion, the Senate rejected the treaty by a vote of forty-six yeas and forty-two nays (and eight not voting)—a majority of yeas which, however, was less than the two-thirds vote required for approval. Among the chief obstacles which contributed to the rejection were the combined opposition of various interests of the American Atlantic seaboard states (including the opposition of western New York and western Pennsylvania), and the strong opposition of Illinois. On March 26 Mr. Pevey of Wisconsin stated in the House his opinion that the defeat was primarily due to the inactivity of the St. Lawrence Tidewater Association.[42]

A study of the geographic distribution of the vote presents some interesting features. It shows that the treaty was opposed by all the Atlantic seaboard states except South Carolina and by all the Gulf states except Alabama; and that west of New

York and Pennsylvania it was approved by all the border states except Illinois and also by all the states of the Pacific coast, by two states on the Mexican border and by three interior states drained by the Mississippi River.[43]

Along the Lakes, mingled with lamentations, appeared hopeful expectations of final realization of the deep-waterway project by coöperative efforts. Duluth, the prophet of the seaway since 1871, and the dogged spokesman of the large wheat-producing region of the northwest border which had determined its destiny largely by its own efforts, expressed its continued belief that a deep-waterway to the ocean via the St. Lawrence is a major problem in American national and international policy which eventually would find a satisfactory solution.[44] On both sides of the boundary were strong doubts whether Canada would undertake the important enterprise alone; but ultimate completion of the work by piecemeal process seemed likely unless Senate approval of the treaty could be obtained by renewed efforts.

The President, undismayed by the indications of failure and suggesting that the United States could not afford to refuse coöperation in the project, announced that the subject would be submitted again for consideration. In the following October and November he revealed his determination to renew efforts to obtain consent for ratification. With this purpose he authorized a special trip of William Phillips to Ottawa to confer informally on proposals to modify the treaty by slight revisions; and coincidently he obtained an expert report on costs of power distribution.[45] Apparently, however, he decided to postpone the renewal of the struggle to convince the Senate.

Parallel with the problems of waterways were the persistent problems of trade and tariffs whose chances of adjustment had remained in doubt since the failure of the reciprocity plans of 1911.

In the decade after the close of the World War a question of trade diversion was a subject of some discussion and investigation. In 1921 the Canadian Senate appointed a special investigating committee which in 1922 reported a serious condition in regard to the diversion of the western grain trade to New York and other American seaports for export. Seven years later, on May 7, 1928, the American Senate, following apprehensions of diversion from American to Canadian ports, requested the investigation of the subject by a coöperative interdepartmental committee which, in January, 1929, submitted a report indicating a distinct improvement in the position of American ports since 1919 notwithstanding a clear tendency toward increasing diversion of Canadian importations from American to Canadian ports after 1921 (a diversion which had increased steadily since the beginning of the century).

The American joint report, with which a separate report of the United States Shipping Board practically agreed, explained that movement of American grain to Canadian ports, and also the movement of Canadian grain through American ports, was determined chiefly by seasonal conditions or by considerations of service or port facilities or business expediency and not by inland rate situations. The American use of the St. Lawrence route it explained chiefly by geographic advantages, but partly by the fundamental difference between American and Canadian grain inspection laws and dockage assessment. The gradual decline in Canadian imports via American ports it attributed in part to increased facilities of Canadian transportation agencies, to the opening of Canadian public lands to immigrant settlers and to the development of improvements in Canadian port facilities. The large importation of raw silks into the United States via Vancouver, from which they were usually routed by Canadian railways to Buffalo or Ogdensburg, it explained by the shippers' selection of the first fast Pacific steamer. The diversion from American ports it did not attribute to the freight rate situation, either ocean or rail. It admitted, however, that Canadian laws of 1923 and 1926 for reduction of duties on direct shipments from British countries might prove more effective than earlier Canadian measures for diverting traffic to Canadian ports and announced that diplomatic negotiations had already been instituted to consider with Canadian officials the principle involved in the question.[46]

Meantime, originating from experiences under the American reduced tariff of 1913, and especially influenced by the effects of the World War of 1914 upon trade, a new movement for trade reciprocity had appeared. In the United States the author of the original House bill of 1911 had asserted that in any new efforts to make reciprocity a practical issue the initiative must proceed from Canada. In 1919, following the introduction of a bill in Congress for repeal of the American reciprocity law of 1911, the Liberal party in Canada, led by Mackenzie King, had asserted its adherence to the principle of reciprocity with the United States. In 1921, Sir Robert Borden had advocated closer relations with the United States and had urged his successor as prime minister to appoint at once a "minister plenipotentiary" to Washington to propose a reciprocity arrangement similar to that which Canada had refused to accept in 1911. In accord with this policy, the question of reciprocity was again revived, in July, 1922, by discussions of Prime Minister King and W. S. Fielding on visits to Washington. In September, 1922, however, by the Fordney-McCumber act, the American government adopted a policy of a higher tariff and the repeal of the provisions of the reciprocity law of 1911, which had remained ineffective by failure of Canada to enact the required concurrent legislation. For a decade thereafter the question of reciprocity was neglected while interest in tariffs seemed to increase.

Finally, in February, 1934, the Department of State in a press release expressed the hope that in accord with its "good neighbor" policy it would soon be able to take steps toward the conclusion of a trade agreement with Canada. On March 2 the President requested Congress to confer upon him authority to negotiate such agreements, resulting in the prompt passage of the desired legislation (on June 12) and increased executive action. In April, while this legislation was pending he invited Prime Minister Bennett to visit the White House for an informal conference on promotion of trade development. Following this conference, which reached an informal agreement on means of action, informal discussions were continued with a view to negotiations for removal of prohibitions and restrictions, and for reduction of tariffs. The final conclusions probably were influenced by the problems of a drouth in the American Northwest in August and by the recommendations of a joint committee of the American and Canadian chambers of commerce in September.

In the following November Secretary Hull received from the Canadian minister at Washington information that Canada was ready to join in a declaration in favor of gradual preparation for the freest possible exchange of natural products, and a suggestion that there was no barrier to the immediate initiation of exploratory negotiations to improve existing trade relations. Near the end of December he replied that the American government was ready to begin immediate preparations on the proposed basis for discussion. On January 21, 1935, in accord with Section 4 of an act (of June 12, 1934) amending the tariff act of 1930 and a consequent executive order (of June 27) he gave notice of his intention to negotiate a trade agreement with Canada and arranged for oral presentation of views before a special committee on reciprocity. The later negotiations, although they encountered considerable opposition, both in Canada and in the United States, seemed promising by June, 1935. Early in the following September, preceding the defeat of the Conservative party in the Canadian election, the text of the pre-negotiation correspondence was released to the press.[47]

Early in November, discussions were renewed at the suggestion of Mackenzie King, the new Canadian prime minister, who visited Washington to propose a broadening of the base of the negotiations with a view to removal of barriers to natural trade-flow, and to urge speed in reaching a conclusion. As a result, on November 15, after mutual concessions, the two governments signed a liberal trade agreement, accepting the principle of most favored nation treatment and minimum tariff rates accorded to any country except components of the British empire and American possessions and Cuba, providing for free admission of a small list of products, and a considerable reduction of tariffs on a large comprehensive list, including reductions on certain farm and forest products and Canadian reductions on machinery and other American manufactures. Articles I, III and IV became operative on January 1, 1936, and the remainder after ratification by the Canadian Parliament in the following April.

Of particular interest in this connection are the statistical evidences of the overflow of American capital and business enterprise into Canada, through investments which in form and volume tend toward a continuous tightening of the ties of common interest. American peaceful economic penetration which had begun even before the large American migration into Manitoba in the last decade of the nineteenth century, became prominent within the next two decades. After 1914, partly influenced by tariffs, it found a favorite field in Canada. By 1925 American investors controlled many important branches of Canadian industry. In 1926 they had in Canada investments estimated at three billion dollars, which by the end of 1930 increased to over four billion dollars. The large amount of American direct investment, which was also associated with a considerable American immigration and cultural penetration, was largely due to the establishment of branch or assembling factories in Canada by American corporations with a desire to overcome tariff barriers and to secure the advantage of preferential tariff rates accorded to Canadian products by other members of the British empire.[48]

REFERENCES

1. *Rev. of Revs.*, LIII, Feb., 1916, p. 181 (L. J. Burpee); *Am. J. Int. Law*, VI, 194–96, Jan., 1912.
2. 52 *Cong. Record*, 63–3, pp. 4722–25, Feb. 26, 1915; also see *Papers Rel. to For. Rels. of U.S.*, 1916, pp. 294–95.
3. *Papers Rel. to . . . Int. Joint Com.; Canada Year Book*, 1926, p. 972.
4. *Am. J. Int. Law*, Apr., 1928, pp. 292–318 (Robert A. MacKay).
5. *Papers Rel. to . . . Int. Joint Com.*, p. 171.
6. *Address of W. A. Riddell before the Security Com. of the League of Nations*, Feb. 22, 1928; *Montreal Star*, Feb. 22, 1928.
7. *Kiwanis Mag.*, Sept., 1925, p. 353.
8. *Ib.*, p. 352; *Am. J. Int. Law*, Apr., 1928, pp. 292–318.
9. *Papers Rel. to For. Rels. of U.S.*, 1916, pp. 294–95, 297–99; 19 *Am. J. Int. Law*, pp. 122–33.
10. *Sen. Docs.*, 67–2, No. 114, pp. 176–81.
11. 19 *Am. J. Int. Law* (No. 4), pp. 122–23, 128–33; *Papers Rel. to . . . Int. Joint Com.*, pp. 168–69.

12. *Ib.*, p. 167; *State Dept. Pubs. since 1929*, Nos. 43, 71 and 114 (1930); SHORTT and DOUGHTY, IX, 185.
13. *Rp., Mohonk Lake Conference*, May, 1913, pp. 29–52; KEENLEYSIDE, pp. 365–73, 377–82; *Can. An. Rev.*, 1914, pp. 132ff.; *Ib.*, 1917 and 1918; *N. Y. Times*, Jan. 7, 1916; BEER, *The English-Speaking Peoples* (1918), p. 134.
14. *For. Rels., 1915*, Supplement, p. 890; *Ib.*, pp. 774–75; *Ib.*, 1915–16; *Ib.*, 1916, pp. 704–06 and 776; *56 Cong. Record*, 65–2, pp. 8193–96, June 24, 1918.
15. *53 Cong. Record*, 64–1, pp. 998 and 10548, Jan. 13 and July 7, 1916; *Ib.*, p. 13183.
16. *For. Rels., 1915*, pp. 415–23.
17. *Ib.*, 1916, pp. 279–83; *55 Cong. Record*, 65–1, p. 5412.
18. *6 Am. J. Int. Law* (1912), pp. 409–59 (BALCH); *N. Y. Times*, Nov. 4, 1934.
19. *For. Rels., 1918*, pp. 432–39, 441–68, 471–75, 532–39; *Rp. of U. S. Com'rs of Fisheries*, 1918, p. 94; *N. Y. Times*, Mar. 14, 1918; *Can. An. Rev.*, 1919 and 1923; *Debates, House of Commons*, CLV (1933, I, 112).
20. *For. Rels., 1918*, pp. 459–60, 463–76.
21. *Ib.*, pp. 459–76.
22. *Can. An. Rev.*, 1919.
23. *58 Cong. Record*, 66–1, p. 377, May 28, 1919; *60 Cong. Record*, 66–3, pp. 2823, 4248; *61 Cong. Record*, 67–1, p. 1934, June 1, 1921; *U. S. Treaty Series*, No. 701; *Can. An. Rev.*, 1924–25, p. 79; *Treaties . . . Affecting Can.*, pp. 505–07.
24. *Rp. Mohonk Lake Conference on Int. Arb.*, pp. 59–67; *2 For. Affairs*, p. 15.
25. *2 For. Affairs*, pp. 15–19 (A. L. LOWELL); *86 Lit. Dig.*, Mar. 24, 1923; *The Baltimore Sun*, Jan. 1923; W. L. Mackenzie King to J. M. Callahan, May 25, 1935.
26. *Dept. of State Pubs., Treaty Series*, Nos. 718, 719, 720 and 721; 19 *Am. J. Int. Law* (No. 4), pp. 128–33; *Treaties . . . Affecting Canada*, pp. 511–25.
27. *Current History*, Jan., 1927, pp. 564–69.
28. *Neilson's Rps.*, 1927; *Treaty Information, Bul. 39*, Supplement, p. 150; *70 Cong. Record*, Jan. 21, 1929, pp. 1–3 (No. 34); *Papers Rel. to . . . Int. Joint Com.*, p. 170; *Dept. of State, Treaty Information, Bul. 8*, pp. 11–12; *Ib., Bul. 39*, Supplement; *Ib., Bul. 1*, Oct. 31, 1929, pp. 13–14; *Ib., Bul. 2*, Dec. 31, 1929, pp. 17–19; *Ib., Bul. 32*, May 31, 1932, pp. 27–30; *U. S. Treaty Series*, No. 837, May 14, 1931; *Sen. Exec. Doc. M*, 71–2; *72 Cong. Record*, 71–2, No. 134, May 29, 1930, pp. 1–3; *74 Cong. Rec.*, No. 60, Feb. 24, 1931; *78 Cong. Rec.*, No. 25, Feb. 2, 1934.

29. Tom Ireland, *The Great Lakes and the St. Lawrence Seaway* (1934), pp. 34–35, 105–34, 164–74, and 186–95.
30. *Assoc. Press Reports,* Oct. 19, 1919; Whitford, *History of the Barge Canal of N. Y. State* (1921), p. 548; *57 Cong. Record,* 65–3, pp. 2788, 3347, 3663–77 and 3740.
31. *Dept. of State, Press Release,* July 18, 1932; *Sen. Docs.*, 67–2, No. 114, Jan. 16, 1922, pp. 180–81.
32. Whitford, *Hist. of the Barge Canal of N. Y. State,* pp. 549–50, and 552; *62 Cong. Record,* 67–2, p. 2372, Feb. 10, 1922; *Ib.*, p. 2581, Feb. 14.
33. *Ib.*, p. 4731, Mar. 29, 1922; *The Baltimore Sun,* Jan. 28, 1923.
34. Assoc. Press Reports, Jan. 14, 1925.
35. *H. Docs.*, 68–2, No. 428, Dec. 19, 1924; *Sen. Docs.*, 69–2, No. 183; *Sen. Rps.*, 72–2, No. 1, p. 3, Feb. 21, 1933; *Dept. of State, Press Release,* July 18, 1932; *Ib., Confid. Press Release,* Oct. 7, 1928; *Sen. Journal,* 72–1, p. 718; *Institute of Economics,* N.Y., 1928; Henry C. Harriman, *New Eng. and the St. Lawrence Seaway* (Boston, 1929).
36. *Ib.*, pp. 13–14; *Dept. of State, Treaty Information, Bul. 12,* p. 14; *Assoc. Press Rps.*, Jan. 30, 1931.
37. *Dept. of State, Confid. Press Release,* Nov. 15, 1931; *Ib., Press Releases,* July 18 and 19, 1932; *N. Y. Times,* July 3, 1932.
38. *Dept. of State, Treaty Information, Bul. 34,* pp. 28–36, July 31, 1932; *Dept. of State, Press Release,* July 18, 1932; *The Round Table,* June, 1934, p. 554.
39. *76 Cong. Rec.*, No. 35, p. 2157, Jan. 19, 1933; *Sen. Exec. Rp.*, 72–2, No. 1, pp. 1, 10, Feb. 21, 1933.
40. *Sen. Docs.*, 73–2, No. 110, Jan. 10, 1934; *78 Cong. Record,* 73–2, No. 57, p. 4568, Mar. 14, 1934.
41. *Ib.*, Appendix, p. 1556, Jan. 29, 1934; *Ib.*, Feb. 15, pp. 2643–48; *Ib.*, p. 1584, Jan. 30; *Ib.*, pp. 1763–97, Feb. 1; *Ib.*, Appendix, pp. 2333–34, Feb. 9; *Ib.*, p. 4671; *N. Y. Herald Tribune,* Feb. 7 (Walter Lippmann's article).
42. *N. Y. Times,* Mar. 14, 1934; *78 Cong. Record,* No. 57, p. 4573, Mar. 14; *Ib.*, Appendix, p. 5609, March 26; *H. Docs.*, 68–2, No. 498.
43. *Cong. Record,* Feb. 12, 1934, pp. 2440–44; *Ib.*, Feb. 5, pp. 1949–50.
44. *N. Y. Times,* Mar. 14, 1934; *Collier's,* Apr. 28, 1934, pp. 14–15.
45. *Round Table,* June, 1934, pp. 559–60; Associated Press news, Oct. 12, 1934; *N. Y. Times,* Nov. 11, 1934.
46. *Sen. Docs.*, 70–2, No. 212 (154 pp.), Jan. 29, 1929; *Ib.*, No. 183.
47. *53 Cong. Record,* Aug. 25, 1916, p. 13183; *Cong. Record,* 66–1, July 23 and 24 and Oct. 9 and 10, 1919; *The Monetary Times* (Toronto), Aug. 8, 1919; *N. Y. Evening Post,* Oct. 18, 1919;

Annals Am. Acad. Pol. and Social Science, 1921, p. 8 (J. A. Cooper); *Cong. Record*, June 29, 1922; *N. Am. Rev.*, CCXIV, 751–60, Dec., 1921 (D. M. Le Bourdais); *Lit. Dig.*, Sept. 23, 1922, p. 9; *N. Y. Times*, Jan. 22, 1922; *16 Current History* (1922), p. 844; *Boston Transcript*, July 6, 1922; *Can. An. Rev.*, 1922, pp. 90–2; *Canadian Hansard*, Feb. 27, 1933; Associated Press news, Sept. 29, 1934; *Dept. of State, Press Releases*, Jan. 21 and Sept. 8–9, 1935; *Washington Post*, Oct. 17, 1935.

48. *8 Can. Hist. Rev.*, pp. 31–40 and 137–41; *2 For. Affairs*, pp. 716–19 (July, 1933); *H. Docs.*, 57–62, I, No. 305 (1902); *Sen. Docs.*, 71–3, No. 258 (1931); *Fortnightly Rev.*, Aug., 1934; *World's Work*, Apr., 1929, p. 128; *State Dept., Confid. Press Release*, Sept. 7, 1935.

INDEX

Abbott, Sir John, 422.

Abercrombie, Fort, road from, to Fort Barton, 293.

Aberdeen, Earl of, 218, 220, 222, 228, 231–32, 233, 234, 243.

Adams, Charles Francis, 275.

Adams, John, 9, 10, 11, 15, 25.

Adams, John Quincy, 51, 90, 91, 93, 94, 98, 106, 107, 110–11, 114, 124, 127–28, 131–32, 138, 141, 219.

Adee, Alvey A., 469, 478.

Agreement of 1817, motives and purpose, 91–92; negotiations, 92–100; proclaimed, 101; effects, 101–02; proposals to abrogate, 278, 281, 284, 286, 430; proposals to modify or revise, 457, 512–13 (*see also* Armaments); later expressions of desire to continue the principle, 181, 272, 286, 287, 430, 513. *See also* Disarmament.

Alabama claims, negotiations on the, 331, 332, 338, 342, 348; relation to the annexation movement, 304–05, 318, 319–20; Russian policy concerning, 318, 321–22; plan for settlement, 319–20 (Sumner's proposal, 320).

Alaska, motives in purchase of, 307–09.

Alaskan boundary, agreement for survey of, 424; convention for demarkation of, 515.

Alaskan boundary dispute, origin, 465–66; early proposals for a joint survey, 466, 468–69; first question of jurisdiction, 468; proposals of surveys after 1895, 469–70; effect of Klondike gold discoveries, 470; first proposal of arbitration, 470; opposing contentions and proposals of 1898–99, 470–74; disagreements on proposed arbitration, 472; proposal to submit to joint commission of jurists, 472, 474, 480–81, 481; *modus vivendi,* 474, 477, 478; tedious adjustment discussions with the London government, 474–81; Hay-Herbert convention of 1903, 481; members of the mixed commission, 482–83; Roosevelt's policy for prompt settlement, 483, 484; Lodge's *pourparlers* at London, 484; sidelights and diplomatic influences, 484, 485, 486, 487–88; the arguments before the tribunal, 485–87; the decision, 487; Canadian criticism of the award, 488–89.

Alaskan rivers, navigation of, 339.

Alien immigrants (from Newfoundland), head tax on, 518.

Aliens, mode of deportation of, 515.

Allegosh River, 503.

Allen, Ethan, 2.

Alliance, with France, 6; Anglo-American (suggested), 26, 27, 41, 47.

Alverstone, Baron, 483–89 *passim. See also* Webster (Charles E.).

Amenities and courtesies, 243, 247, 258, 273, 363–64, 377, 495, 496.

American Revolution. *See* Revolution.

Amherstburg, 65, 138.

Anderson, David, 61, 74.

Andrews, Israel DeWolf, 243, 245–46, 248, 250, 251, 253, 254, 255–57.

Annexation, early policy and proposals, 2, 5, 6, 7, 8, 12, 46, 57, 61–65, 67, 70–71, 84–85, (1848) 243; Canadian mid-century sentiment, 243, 245, 248, 299, 300; expectations of the fifties, 300–301.

Annexation expectations after 1871,

views of 1875, 356–57; new agitation of 1887, 370; later disappearance of annexation sentiment, 413.
Annexation movement of 1865–70, 299, 304; motives, 304, 308; plans (peaceful), 304–05, 318; resolutions in Congress, 311, 317–18; British policy concerning, 312, 316, 317, 318; diplomatic negotiations, 312–13, 315–20; Russian policy concerning, 318.
Arbitration, 141, 143–44, 148, 338, 348, 445–49, 481–88, 517, 521–23, 539, 548; suggested or proposed, 91, 228–29, 341, 343, 443, 444, 457, 470, 472, 473, 475, 478, 479, 480, 494, 495.
Arbitration treaties (general), negotiation of, 457, 516–17, 517 (arbitration provisions of the treaty of 1909, 506).
Armaments, increase of, 174, 175, 178, 179, 180, 277–78; contemplated or suggested increase of, 166, 168–69, 173, 178, 272, 273, 274, 277, 281–82, 283, 291–92.
Arnold, Benedict, 2, 3, 4.
Aroostook war, 188–89.
Ashburton, Lord, 198, 200–205 *passim*, 207, 209.
Astor, John Jacob, 56, 89.
Astoria, 56–57, 72, 90–91, 128, 130.
Atcheson, Nathaniel, 73.
Aylesworth, A. B., 498, 509.

Bacon, Robert, 514.
Bagot, Charles, 94–99 *passim*, 106, 142, 181.
Banks, N. P., resolution of, 305.
Barnhart's Island, 122–23, 137, 138, 206, 552.
Bayard, Thomas F., 364, 366–67, 372, 373–74, 375, 381, 392, 393, 394, 395, 403, 404, 406–07, 440, 455, 468.
Beckwith, George, 25, 26, 27.
Bender, P., 361.
Bennett, Richard B., 553, 557.
Bering Sea fur-seals controversy, origin, 438–40; seizure of Canadian vessels, 439, 440; proposals for international protection of the seals, 439, 440; Blaine's arguments in defense of the seizures, 440–41; Salisbury's counter arguments, 443; submission to arbitration, 444, 445; *modus vivendi*, 444–45, 446, 454; the arbitration, 446–49 (decision, 448–49); later negotiations for regulations for protection of the seals, 449–51, 452–55 (tripartite convention, 453), 524–26; adjustment of the British claims for seizures, 451–52; conventions of 1911, 524–26.
Birds (migratory), protection of, 541.
Blaine, James G., 359, 381, 390, 411, 412–13, 415, 419–26 *passim*, 440–44, 445, 446.
Blaine-Bond conference, 420, 425.
Bond, Sir Robert, 420, 425, 518, 520, 521.
Bonded transit. *See* Transit in bond.
Borden, Sir Robert, 545, 549, 557.
Boundaries, proposed original: instructions on (1779–81), 8, 9, 10; discussion of (1782), 11–12, 13–14, (in 1813–14), 70–83; as designated by treaty of 1783, 14–15; questions of demarkation of, 71–72; later proposals for revision of, 73, 76–77.
original, 13–14; proposed rectification from Lake Superior to the Mississippi, 35, 47, 48, 50, 51, 81–82, 128; question of the St. Croix, 35, 37, 42; northeastern, 42, 47, 50, 51, 73, 75–77, 83–84, 149, 183 (*see also* Northeastern boundary dispute); Lakes line problems (islands), 42, 205–06, 207–08; northern limit of Louisiana, 51, 82, 128–29, 294, 347–48; proposed definite designation between Lake Superior and Lake of the Woods, 192, 456; demarkation of, 414, 415, 456, 470, 493, 515–16, 545–46. *See also* Alaskan boundary, Alaskan boundary dispute, Northwestern boundary dispute, Oregon boundary dispute.
Boundary barriers, proposed, 39, 75, 76, 88.
Boundary waters, pollution of, 537.

Boundary waters treaty, origin, 499–503, 505; negotiations, 503–05; provisions, 505–08; significance, 506, 508; effect upon the diplomatic status of Canada, 506; ratification, 508–10.
Bowell, Mackenzie, 423, 425.
British apprehensions of American post-war aggression (1865), 285.
British Canadian policies, 1783–1812, 18, 22, 27, 28, 29, 31, 33, 34, 46, 52, 58. *See also* Trade.
British Columbia, American influence in, 300–301; annexation movement in, 306, 316; enticement into the Dominion, 322, 331.
Brown, George, 245, 354.
Bryan, W. J., 540.
Bryce, James, 489, 493, 497, 504–05, 508, 513, 514, 516, 517, 521, 523–24, 525.
Buchanan, Israel, 328.
Buchanan, James, 223, 225, 226–27, 228–30, 232–33, 237.
Bullock, James D., 274.
Bulwer, Sir Henry Lytton, 246, 248.
Butterworth, Benjamin, 369, 370–71, 382, 418.

Calhoun, John C., 221, 226, 232.
Canada, proposed annexation of, *see* Annexation; defensive military invasion of, 2–6, 62–65; proposed Franco-American attack on, 7; increase of American trade with, 52 (later decline, 58); independence of, predicted, 52, 244, 245; British suggestions of withdrawal of control over, 181–82; American threats of non-intercourse with, (1830) 120, (1864) 282; struggle for reciprocity, 242–49, 250–51; British apprehensions of American post-war aggression in (1865), 285; national policy of (1878), 357, 358. *See also* Annexation, Canadian trade policy, Fisheries, Reciprocity.
  direct negotiations with, in 1888, 407; in 1892, 413; Pauncefote's suggestion, 456; through the International Joint Commission, 534; treaty-making power obtained in signing of the halibut treaty of 1923, 544; establishment of direct communication, 546.
  independent status of, antecedents, 181–82, 407, 412–13, 415, 442, 453, 454, 456, 474, 498, 500, 506, 527, 544; developed incident to events of the World War and peace negotiations, 544–45; reflected in Washington conferences, 545; confirmed by imperial conferences of 1923 and 1926, 546. *See also* Treaties (Canadian-American).
Canadian confederation, origin of first steps in, 303; American opposition to, 307, 313, 315; opposed in maritime provinces, 309; completed, 322, 331.
Canadian Pacific Railway, influence in border relations, 394, 395. *See also* Railway competition.
Canadian "pilgrimages" to Washington, 258, 288–90, 313, 319, 326, 327, 329, 354–57, 372, 373, 421, 422, 425, 453, 455, 457, 498, 527, 551, 557, 558.
Canadian rebellion of 1837, causes, 161–63; incidents, 163–66; American neutrality problems in, 164–69, 171–74; effect on Anglo-American relations, 169–71, 175; effect on British policies, 171, 181–82; effect on American public opinion, 182.
Canadian trade policy, prominent influences affecting (1842–46), 242, 243, 244, 245; question of transit across American territory, 242–43; legislative gesture of 1848, 244; struggle for reciprocal trade (1846–54), 242–49, 250–51. *See also* British Canadian policies, Reciprocity, Trade.
Canadian westward expansion policy, 301–02, 308, 309–10, 313–14; American opposition to, 310.
Canal competition, 117, 123, 242; use of, 259.
Canal tolls, Canadian discriminatory, 400, 402, 403, 422–23, 424, 425–27, 431.
Canals, American, 338, 339; question of use by Canadians, 400–402, 426,

431; proposed retaliatory discriminations on, 403, 430–31; proposed canal across Michigan, 514.
Canadian, 203, 263, 284, 336, 337, 339, 355, 402, 403.
Canning, George, 116, 118, 131, 133, 134.
Canso Strait, 242, 376.
Caroline affair, 165, 166, 175, 182, 208–09.
Carroll, Charles, 4.
Carroll, John, 4.
Cartwright, Sir Richard, 360, 371.
Cass, Lewis, 89, 95, 99, 226, 261.
Castine, British seizure of, 66.
Castlereagh, Lord, 58, 76, 91, 93, 94, 99, 100, 110–11, 127, 129.
Catacazy, Constantine, 318, 321–22.
Cattle shipments, British prohibitions on, 359; Canadian restrictions on import of, 414.
Chamberlain, Joseph, 373, 374, 375, 376.
Chamberlain-Bayard draft treaty of 1888, origin of the commission, 371–72; conference negotiations, 373–75; provisions, 376; opposition in the Senate, 378–79.
Champlain, Lake. *See* Lake Champlain.
Chauncey, Isaac, 65.
Chesapeake case, 275–76; effect on American commercial regulations, 276, 279.
Chicago Drainage Canal, 502, 505, 551.
Chinese illegal immigration via Canada, 414, 429.
Choate, Joseph H., 474, 475, 476, 478, 480, 481, 482, 483, 487, 488, 514.
Civil War (U.S.), effect on Canadian relations, 270; Canadian enlistments in the, 270, 280; trade restrictions in the, 276, 279, 282, 287, 288; influence on Canadian confederation, 303–04, 307, 309.
Clarendon, Lord, 313, 317.
Clark, George Rogers, expedition of, 8.
Clay, C. C., 276, 278, 286.
Clay, Henry, 80, 81, 108, 113, 116–17, 119, 122–23, 134–35, 136, 137, 142–43, 145–47, 153–54, 208.
Clayton, J. M., 244.
Clayton-Bulwer treaty, proposed modification of, in connection with Canadian negotiations, 473, 477, 480.
Cleveland, Grover, 364, 366, 369, 372, 374, 376, 380, 381, 397, 399, 403, 440, 451, 468, 469.
Coasting trade, 327, 330, 333, 334, 337, 403.
Columbia River, 56, 128, 129, 130, 134, 135, 223, 230, 233, 234, 246.
Colvin, Verplank, proposal to purchase territory for a ship canal, 416, 456.
Commercial negotiations, 1815–18, 107–09. *See also* British Canadian policies, Trade.
Commercial (customs) union, movement for (1887–89), 238, 357, 360, 370, 371, 378, 382; later sentiment for, 411, 423.
Commissions, mixed, 35, 37, 82, 90, 128, 136–39, 139–40, 236, 238, 259, 261, 293, 319, 321, 331–32, 341, 345, 348, 372, 415, 452, 455, 456, 457–58, 469, 470, 499, 506–08, 512, 516, 522, 542, 548, 551; unilateral, 188, 194, 510.
Commissions proposed, 194, 197, 330, 348, 357, 360, 364, 368, 388, 417, 419, 420, 423, 442, 468, 499, 502, 543–44.
Confederate operations from Canada (1861–65), 270, 271, 275–81 *passim,* 283.
Continental Congress, acts of, 1, 4–11 *passim,* 23, 25.
Continental policy, 1, 6, 61, 62, 169, 303, 304, 307, 308, 319, 412–13, 456.
Coöperation, proposals and practice of, 46–47, 133, 275, 293, 294, 387, 388, 389, 390, 391, 439, 440, 456, 494, 497–98, 499, 501, 502, 511, 514, 539–40, 544, 546, 549. *See also* Alliance.
Copyright laws, 330, 415–16, 456.
Corn laws, British, 242.
Crampton, J. F. T., 244, 248, 251, 252, 253, 254, 258, 261.
Crimean War, British recruiting in the United States during, 261.
Criminal jurisdiction on the Lakes, 414–15.

Crises, 33, 165, 169–70, 175, 188–89, 195, 196, 225–26, 227, 254, 272–73.
Cullom, S. M., 395, 396, 398.
Cushing, Caleb, 348.

Davies, Louis, 452, 453.
Debts, pre-war, 16, 24, 35.
De Grey, Earl, 331, 334, 335, 340, 341, 342, 343, 344, 346, 347.
Derby, E. H., 306, 326, 327–28.
Detroit, British surrender of, 39; in the War of 1812, 62–63.
Detroit River, islands in, 137–38, 206, 535, 536, 537.
Dingley, Nelson, 403.
Dingley act, 457.
Diplomatic delays on colonial questions, remedy proposed by Madison, 48.
Disarmament on the Lakes, antecedents of, 36, 59, 71, 73, 75, 76, 77, 78, 79, 84, 87, 88. *See also* Agreement of 1817.
Dix, John, military order of, 282.
Dorchester, Lord, 26, 27, 28, 31, 32, 34.
Douglas, Stephen A., 246, 247.
Drummond's Island, 88, 137.
Durand, H. Mortimer, 494, 495.
Durham, Lord, 170, 171.

Economic penetration, 559.
Electric energy, export of, 503.
Electric (hydro) power development, 538, 539, 549, 550, 552, 553.
Elgin, Lord, 243, 244, 245, 248.
Embargo act, 57–58, 60, 66.
Evarts, William M., 358, 359, 362, 388, 389, 390, 404, 405, 406.
Everett, Edward, 222, 250, 251.
Executive policies, restricted and delayed by legislative branch, 493–94, 495, 497, 503.
Extradition, 208, 405–06, 413–14, 493, 514–15, 545.

Farrer, Edward, 360, 370.
Fenian movement against Canada, 271, 283, 291, 292; sympathizers in Congress, 291, 305; effects of, 292; rumors of a new movement in 1884, 393.
Fenian raids, Canadian claims for, 348.
Fielding, W. S., 527, 557.
Fillmore, Millard, 250, 251.
Fish, Hamilton, 312–13, 315–16, 317, 318, 320, 321, 328, 329, 331, 332, 333, 336, 338, 341, 344, 354, 355, 356, 361, 388, 397, 401, 402, 405–06, 466.
Fisheries, northeastern, 12, 16, 52–53, 72, 74, 75, 81, 87, 88, 105–06, (negotiations of 1818) 107, (1836–46) 241, (1850) 246, (1851–53) 249–50, 251, 252, 290; Morrill's views concerning (1866), 327; Canadian policy after 1866, (1868–70) 328; American views, (1870–71) 330; negotiations of 1870–71, 331, 332, 334, 335, 341, 343, 344, 345; negotiations of 1874, 354–55; Halifax award, 361–63; termination (in 1885) of articles of 1871, 363, 366–67, 426; used as a Canadian club to force renewal of reciprocity, 368; Chamberlain-Bayard negotiations, 373–75; *modus vivendi* of 1888, 377, 524, 542–43; negotiations concerning Newfoundland acts, 518–21; *modus vivendi* of 1906, 520–21; arbitration by the Hague tribunal, 521–23; later controversy concerning regulatory acts, 523–24.
Fisheries in common inland waters, proposed protection and regulation of, 355, 405, 423–24.
Fisheries protection, question of, in 1917, 543.
Floyd, John, 130–31.
Forsyth, John, 156, 157–58, 164–65, 166, 175, 185, 186, 189–90, 191, 192–93.
Fort Harmar treaty (1789), 25, 30.
Foster, George E., 423, 425.
Foster, John W., 413, 420, 422, 423, 424, 427, 428, 429, 430–31, 433, 443, 446, 447, 452, 453, 457, 469, 474, 479, 482, 486, 488.
Fox, Henry S., 166, 167, 169–70, 171, 172, 175, 176, 178, 180, 181, 190, 191–92.
France, 6.
Franklin, Benjamin, 6, 11, 12.

Fraser River, American influence on, 237, 300–301; protection of salmon in, 543, 544, 547.
Frelinghuysen, Frederick T., 359, 363, 391, 393, 394, 404.
Frye, William P., 428.
Fuca Strait, 512, 514.
Fur seals. *See* Bering Sea.
Fur trade, Canadian, influence of, 22–23.

Gallatin, Albert, 78, 79, 81, 82, 83, 108, 117–18, 119, 123, 129, 135, 136, 144, 148.
Galt, A. T., 262, 326, 327, 357, 362.
Ghent, negotiations of, 70–82; American aims, 70–72; British demands, 73–75; discussions, 75–82; results, 82; problems for post-Ghent adjustment, 87–102.
Gibbons, George C., 498, 504, 505, 508, 509.
Gladstone, W. E., 227.
Grand (Long) Isle, 137, 167.
Grant, U. S., 313, 318, 319, 321, 330, 331, 356, 400, 405, 468.
Granville, Lord, 350.
Great Lakes, armaments, 32, 36, 71, 97 (*see also* Agreement of 1817); boundary questions, 42; British plans to control, 22, 29, 31–32, 36, 38, 46, 59, 70, 73, 79, 84, 93, 117; questions concerning navigation of the, 59–60, 71–72, 73; settlements retarded on, 60. *See also* Fisheries, Waterway.
Greeley, Horace, 279.
Greenland, purchase of, proposed by R. J. Walker, 309.
Greenville, Indian treaty of (1795), 38.
Gresham, W. Q., 433–34, 447, 448, 449–50, 451, 469.
Grey, Earl (George), 425, 493, 495, 496, 497, 504, 505, 508, 509, 514, 516, 519, 524.
Grey, Sir Edward, 498, 520.

Hague tribunal arbitration of the Northeast fisheries, 521–23; the decision, 522–23; rules recommended become a source of temporary controversy, 523–24.
Haliburton, R. G., 326.
Halibut protection, Pacific coast, 543, 544.
Halifax award on shore fisheries, origin, 330, 335, 340, 341, 345, 346; organization of the commission, 362; the award, 362–63 (American opposition to, 363).
Hall's stream, 140, 205.
Hamilton, Alexander, 15, 26, 27, 28, 29, 33, 38, 41.
Hammond, George, 27–28, 29, 30.
Hampton Roads Conference, Confederate misrepresentations concerning, 285.
Harding, Warren G., 550.
Harrison, Benjamin, 415, 425, 427, 428, 429–30, 431–32.
Harrison (B.) administration, chief subjects of policy, 413; discussion of railway competition and bonding regulations, 416–17; discussion of trade reciprocity and canal tolls, etc., 417–28; Bering Sea fur-seals discussion and treaty for arbitration, 438–47.
Harrison, William H., 60, 64, 178.
Hatch, Isaac T., 263, 264, 311.
Hay, John, 452, 453, 454, 473, 474, 476–81 *passim*, 484, 486, 499–503 *passim*, 511, 517, 518, 519, 524.
Head, Sir Francis, 162, 163, 168.
Headland interpretation (to restrict fishing limits), 241, 328–29, 522.
Henry, John, 57–58.
Herbert, Michael H., 427, 469, 481.
Herschell, Lord, 473.
Hincks, Francis, 248, 256, 258.
Hitt, Robert R., resolutions of, 382, 417, 427, 494.
Hoar, George F., 369, 411.
Holcombe, J. P., 276, 279, 281.
Hoover, Herbert, 553.
Hudson Bay, question of jurisdiction over, 541–42.
Hudson River, Canadian desire for free navigation of, 426, 431.
Hudson's Bay Company, 36, 89; claims of, in Oregon, 238, 294; claims of, in Alaska, 294; jurisdictional rights in Canada (acquired by Canada),

294, 309, 313–14, (sought by United States) 310, 314.
Hughes, Charles E., 544, 545, 547, 548.
Hull, Cordell, 558.
Hull, William, 62–64.
"Hunters' Lodges," 169, 171–72, 173.
Hunting restrictions, 541.
Huskisson Canada Trade Act of 1822, 112; injurious effects, 113; U.S. retaliatory act of 1823, 114; later British proposals, 115, 118.

I'm Alone, case of the, 447–48.
Immigration, Canadian, into the U.S., 359, 387; American, into Canada, 387.
Indian neutral barrier, Canadian proposals of, 39, 65, 75.
Indian policy in the Northwest, 23, 25, 29, 30, 33, 36, 38–39, 47.
Indians, early frontier trans-boundary trade with, 36, 59–60.
Indians of the Lakes Northwest, American policies as to, 23, 25, 29, 30, 33, 36, 38–39, 47; Canadian influence over, 22, 25, 27, 61; treaties with, 25; St. Clair expedition against, 25, 27; suggestions of British mediation with, 27, 28, 29, 30.
Indians west of Lake Superior, problems concerning, 293, 387–93; question of trans-border pursuit, 391; question of extradition, 392.
International Joint Commission, origin, 505; purpose, 505, 506; powers and functions, 506–08; organization, 534; its work and achievements, 513, 515, 516, 517, 534–39, 546, 549, 550, 553.
International Waterways Commission (1903), 494, 499, 501, 502, 516.
Isle Royale, 138, 139, 206.

Jackson, Andrew, 150–54 *passim.*
Japan, Canadian coöperation in relations with, 495–96, 497–98, 524, 525–26.
Jay, John, 2, 12, 13, 24, 33–34.
Jay-Grenville agreement, 33.
Jay mission to London, purpose, 33; instructions, 34; discussions, 35–36.
Jay treaty, provisions, 35–37; criticism and defense of, 37–38; opposition in the House, 38; efforts to renew, 52.
Jefferson, Thomas, 3, 8, 27, 29, 30, 46–47, 48, 49, 54, 56, 57, 62, 70, 79.
Johnson-Clarendon convention, 311.
Joint High Commission of 1871, 321; Canadian influence in securing, 328, 331; purpose, 331; members, 331–32; subjects discussed by, 332; the negotiations, 332–45 (Macdonald's position and views in, 333–34, 335, 337, 342, 343, 344, 347); results, the provisions of the treaty of 1871, 345; subjects not admitted, 347–48.
Joint High Commission of 1898–99, 455, 457–59, 477.

Kimberley, Earl of, 349, 350.
King, Rufus, 40, 41, 42, 47, 49, 50; draft treaty of, 51.
King, W. L. Mackenzie, 497, 498, 503, 504, 545, 546, 548, 550–51, 557, 558.
Klondike gold discoveries, effects of, 469–70.
Knox, Philander C., 509, 517, 525.
Kootenay River, 538.

Labrador, 351.
Lake Champlain, jurisdiction over, 292, 336, 337; fisheries, 511, 543, 550.
Lake Memphremagog, 511, 536.
Lake Michigan, navigation of, 123, 258, 259, 327, 335, 336, 338, 506; diversion of water from, 502, 551, 553, 554; fisheries, 511.
Lake of the Woods, 502, 534, 536, 538; treaty, 537, 546.
Lakes, Great. *See* Great Lakes.
Lansdowne, Lord, 371.
Lansing, Robert, 446, 541.
Lapointe, Ernest, 544.
Larned, J. N., 328.
Laurier, Sir Wilfrid, 360, 452–57 *passim,* 473, 477, 480, 481, 488, 489, 493, 495, 503–04, 505, 509, 513, 516, 523–24, 526, 527.
Lincoln, Abraham, 279, 285.
Lincoln, Robert, 429.
Linn, Senator Lewis F., 217, 218, 219.
Lisgar, Lord, 349.

Liston, Robert, 39, 40, 41.
Livingston, Edward, 136, 150, 151, 153, 154, 155.
Livingston, Robert R., 48.
Lodge, H. C., 482, 483, 484, 485, 518, 519, 526.
Louisiana, northern limits, 51, 55; not open to British trade with the Indians, 51, 55.
Loyalists, 11, 12, 16–17; emigration of, 17–18; influence in Canada, 18, 66, 161, 162.
Lyons, Lord, 275, 278.

Macdonald, Sir John, 173, 249, 336–47 *passim*, 357, 358, 360, 371, 418, 419, 420, 422, 532, 533–35.
McDougall, William, 309, 314, 315.
McGee, Thomas D'Arcy, 303.
Mackenzie, William Lyon, 163–64, 168, 174, 245.
McKinley administration, problems of, inherited, 455–57; new situations, 457, 459; efforts to solve or adjust, 457–59.
McLane, Louis, 120, 123, 153, 155, 156, 223, 228, 230–32, 233.
McLeod, Alexander, arrest and trial, 175–80, 209.
McLoughlin, Dr. John, 219.
Madison, James, 48–52 *passim*, 55, 56, 84, 95–96.
Maine, border irritations and contentions, 141–43, 145–48, 151, 157; commissioners of 1842, 199, 201; disputed territory fund, 207. *See also* Northeastern boundary dispute.
Malden, in 1811, 61; in the War of 1812, 62, 63; Indian visits to, 89; search of American vessels at, 95, 99.
Manitoba, 314.
Map, the old "red line," 198, 203.
Marcy, William L., 251–55 *passim*.
Maritime provinces, anti-Dominion attitude in, 316.
Mars Hill, 147, 148, 149.
Massey, Vincent, 546, 547.
Mediation, British suggestions of, between the United States and Indians, 27, 28, 29, 30, 39; proffered Russian, 70.
Memphremagog, Lake, 511, 536.
Merritt, T. R., 364.
Merritt, W. H., 243, 244.
Metcalf, Lord, 225.
Michigan, Lake. *See* Lake Michigan.
Michigan, the, 179, 275, 280, 291, 292.
Michilimackinac, 60, 63, 87, 88.
Middleton, Henry, 133.
Milk River (and St. Mary River) problem, 500–501, 506, 536.
Mississippi, navigation of the, 16, 29, 36–37; U.S. refuses Canadian access through American territory, 55; British loss of, 81, 128, 129.
Mississippi-Louisiana problem, influence on Anglo-American relations, 46, 47–49.
Monck, Lord, 275, 277.
Monroe, James, 48, 51, 52, 53, 55, 61, 70–72, 87, 92–102 *passim*, 109, 114, 132, 141.
Monroe doctrine, 225, 307, 311, 456. *See also* Non-colonization doctrine.
Monroe-Pinckney draft treaty (1806), 54; objections to, 55.
Montgomery, Richard, 2, 3, 4.
Montreal merchants, 15, 29, 59–60, 61.
Moose Island, 90.
Morrill, Justin S., 289, 326, 327, 350, 356–57.
Morris, Gouverneur, 8, 9, 10, 26, 79.
Motley, J. L., 312, 316, 317, 320.

National (American) Waterways Commission, 510.
Naturalization question, 292–93 (convention of 1870).
Naval armaments. *See* Disarmament on the Lakes, Agreement of 1817.
Navigation of the Lakes, questions concerning, 59–60, 71–72, 73. *See also* Water, Waterway (deep).
Navigation of the St. Lawrence (to the sea), American claim to, 108, 113, 114, 117, 119, 120, 122–24, 233–34, 243–44, 246, 247, 248, 251, 258, 290, 319; discussions, (1866) 327, (1868) 328, (1870) 329, (1871) 332, 333, 335, 336, 338; provision of the treaty of 1871, 348. *See also* St. Lawrence River, Great Lakes.

Navy Island, 165, 167.
Neutrality, British policy of (1861–65), 272, 274, 275; Canadian, 270 (*see also* Confederate operations); U.S. policy, 293, 593.
New Brunswick, 17, 18, 145–51 *passim,* 156, 257, 345, 357.
New England, defection in (1814), 80.
Newfoundland, 16, 256, 334, 345, 346, 351, 363, 420, 518–23. *See also* Fisheries.
Newspapers, speculation, criticism of, 231.
Niagara Falls, protection of, 494; treaty, 546–47.
Niagara Falls canal, suggested, 430.
Niagara River, 501, 506, 535.
Nimmo, Joseph, Jr., 317, 397.
Non-colonization doctrine, 91, 131–32, 136.
Non-intercourse, in trade with West Indies, 112, 119; threatened against Canada, (1830) 120, (1864) 282.
Nootka Sound convention, 26, 223.
North American act, 303–04.
Northeastern boundary dispute, origin of, 42, 73, 75, 82–83, 84; commission to settle, 136–37, 139–40; diplomatic negotiations, 141, 143–44; influenced by border irritations, 141–43, 145–48, 151, 156–57; submission to arbitration, 144, 148–49; award not accepted, 150–51, 152–54, 156; attempts at renewal of negotiations, 154–58; later negotiations (1837–41), 185–95 (influenced by new border situations, 185–86, 188–94); Webster-Ashburton negotiations (for a conventional line), 195–207 (connection of Maine and Massachusetts therewith, 195, 198–200, 201, 203, 204, 205, 206); the treaty settlement, 207–08 (Senate debates on, 210, 211).
Northwest coast, 56.
Northwest water boundary (1871–72), 332, 338.
Northwestern boundary dispute, 55, 73, 91, 105, 127–36; negotiations of 1842–45, 215, 218, 220, 221; Polk's views on, 222; negotiations of 1845–46, 222–35; treaty of settlement, 235; later San Juan Island controversy, 236–37, 301. *See also* Oregon.
Northwestern frontier, between the Pacific and Minnesota, 300–302; problems (1872–89) of the, 387–96, 397–99, 404.
Nova Scotia, early trade with, 18, 74; "Hovering Act" of 1836, 241; northwest angle of, 139, 148, 204; question of direct communication with Quebec, 73, 75, 109, 110, 112, 115; missions of Andrews to, 245–46, 253–54, 255–57; opposition to treaty of 1854, 246, 260; ports used by Confederates in the Civil War, 276, 288. *See also* Fisheries.

Oliphant, Laurence, 258, 260.
Olney, Richard, 451, 452, 456, 470.
Ordinance of 1787, 25.
Oregon, joint occupation of, 130, 136; proposed settlements in (postponed), 130; beginnings of immigration to, 215, 217; proposals to extend American jurisdiction to, 216, 217; apprehensions of British activities in, 216–17; trail to, surveyed, 217; increase of settlements resulting in a settlers' government, 219; increase of American interests northward and eastward from Oregon (1857–64), 300–301.
Oregon boundary dispute, forecast, (in 1806) 55, (in 1814) 73, 91; bases of American claims to, 90–91, 128, 130, 132, 223, 224; early discussions on, 127–36; early adjustment by joint occupation, 130, 136; negotiations of 1825–27, 133–36; later negotiations of 1842–46, 215, 218, 220, 221, 222–35; question of termination of joint occupation, 225, 227, 232; termination of, 234; treaty of settlement, 235; question of Hudson's Bay Company claims, 238, (settled) 294. *See* Northwestern boundary dispute.

Pacific coast fisheries, 543–44, 547, 548.
Pacific Fur Company, 56.

Pakenham, Richard, 221, 224, 226, 243.
Palmerston, Lord, 170, 176, 196, 197.
Pan-American Congress, question of Canadian participation, 368; influence of, in Canadian relations, 411.
Pan-American Union, suggestion of Canadian membership in, 546.
Passamaquoddy Bay, 42, 50, 83, 90, 137, 200, 424, 514, 516.
Passport system, 279, 283, 287.
Pauncefote, Sir Julian, 413, 423, 425, 440, 441, 442, 443, 452, 470, 475.
Peace, the basis of American policy, 412. *See also* Continental policy.
Peace negotiations, of 1782–83, 11–14; with northwest Indians (1793), 30; of Ghent, 70–82.
Peace portal, 551.
Peaceful economic penetration, 559.
Pecuniary claims, 494, 495; arbitration, 517.
Peel, Sir Robert, 224–25, 232, 241, 242.
Pembina, 292, 294, 348.
Perry, Oliver H., 64.
Phelps, E. J., 439–40, 446.
Phillips, William, 546, 549, 555.
Philo Parsons affair, 280; effect, 281, 285.
Pickering, Timothy, 7, 40, 41.
Pierce, Franklin, 251, 253.
Pigeon River (Long Lake), 139, 206.
Pinckney, William, 53, 54, 55.
Plattsburg, 66, 168.
Polk, James K., 222–26 *passim*, 235.
Pollution of boundary waters, 537.
Portage duties, resisted by Canadians, 59.
Postal agreement with Canada, 406–07, 545.
Posts on the Lakes, British retention of the, 22; purpose, 22, 25, 28, 29; excuse for, 24; final British evacuation of, 35; relation to the Mississippi question, 40.
Preble, William Pitt, 148, 150, 152, 153.
Pribylof Islands, 439, 448.
Prince Edward Island, 249, 256, 260, 334, 345.
Prisoners, conveyance in custody through foreign territory (treaty of 1908), 515; request for leniency in trial of, 515.
Prohibition enforcement, 545, 547–48.
Puget Sound load requirements exemption, 549.
Puget Sound Telegraph Company, 394.

Quebec act, 1, 12.

Railway competition, 261, 264, 299–300, 330, 394–99, 416–17, 427–28, 430.
Railways, in 1842, 242; of the Northwest, influence of, 394; Cullom's report on, 395; resolutions on, 398, 399.
Rainy Lake (and River), 511, 534, 535, 538, 539.
Randolph, Edmund, 33.
Reciprocity in trade, sought by the U.S., 53, 109; sought by Canada (1846–54), 242–49, 258, 261–64, 288–89, 326–28, 518; bill of 1848–49, failure of (in Senate), 243; causes of American objections to, 243–50 *passim;* negotiations of 1850–54, combined with fisheries negotiations, 249, 251; treaty of 1854 (*see* Reciprocity treaty of 1854); proposals of 1866, 310, 311; negotiations of 1871, 329, 333, 340, 341, 342; negotiations of 1874, 354–57; suggestions of 1878, 358; proposed reference to a commission, 360; new discussions at Washington (1886), 368; Chamberlain-Bayard draft treaty, 372–79 (in the Senate, 378–79); later sentiment in favor of, 417–18; efforts to renew negotiations for, 418–22; conferences at Washington, 1892, 420–27; discussions of 1893 and 1896, 455; discussions of 1898, 458–59; American proposals of 1911, defeated in Canada, 526–28; reciprocity trade agreement of 1935, 557–58.
Reciprocity treaty of 1854, origin, 241; preparatory background, 241–52; chief difficulties in the negotiations for, 243–49 *passim*, 251, 252–54, 255–57; opposition to, in the maritime provinces (how conciliated), 255–57; completed by negotiations of Lord Elgin at Washington, 257–58; American motives in the,

250, 251, 259, 300; provisions of, 258–59 (defect in, 259, 262); ratification of, 259–60; effects and operation of, 261–63, 284; proposals to abrogate, 278, 283, 284; causes of abrogation, 262–65, 284; Canadian efforts to renew, 326–27, 329–30; American refusal to renew, 287, 288, 289, 326–27; Canadian continuation of the American privileges under the treaty, 290.

Reciprocity treaty agreement of 1935, 557–58.

Recruiting, British, in the U.S. (1855), 261.

Red River valley (Selkirk), American influences in, 301–02, 304–05; annexation sentiment in (1861), 302–03, 316; Canadian expansion to, 314 (effects, 314, 331); American investigation in, 315–16; discontent in, 316; American annexation policy, motives of, 316–17.

Retaliation, experiments in, 330–31, 357, 358, 359, 428; threatened or recommended, 330, 380, 417, 427; in Canadian trade legislation of 1898, 457.

Retaliatory act of Congress, 1887, 369, 371, 380, 520.

Revolution, the American, purpose and policies of, 1.

Riel, Louis, insurrection under, 294, 314, 393.

Ritchie, S. J., 368, 418–20.

Roosevelt, F. D., 553–54, 555.

Roosevelt, Theodore, 480–87 *passim*, 494–98 *passim*, 526.

Roosevelt (Theodore) administration, chief problems of (after Alaska), 493, 494–95; negotiations, 495–509, 510–17, 518–21, 524–25, 526; apprehensions of interference of legislative branch, 493–94, 495, 497, 503, 505, 524, 526; obstacles and delays in negotiations, 496, 503–04, 522, 526; influence of Earl Grey in hastening decisions, 495, 496, 503–04, 505, 508–09, 513, 516, 520, 521; Canadian participation in negotiations at Washington (after 1906), 495, 503–04, 505; treaties and conventions completed by, 493, 505, 512–17 *passim*, 521.

Root, Elihu, 482, 493, 494, 495, 497, 500–504 *passim*, 509–20 *passim*.

Rose, Sir John, 238, 288, 294, 313, 319, 320, 321, 327, 329, 331, 349–49.

Roseau River, 538.

Rosebery, Earl, 366.

Rouse's Point, 140, 149, 150, 207.

Royale, Isle, 138, 139, 206.

Rush, Richard, 91, 100, 108, 114, 115, 116, 129, 133.

Rush-Bagot agreement. *See* Agreement of 1817.

Russell, Lord, note to Richmond authorities, 285; opposition to arbitration of the *Alabama* claims, 305.

Russia, pretensions on the Northwest coast, 131; American negotiations with, in 1823–24, 131–34; treaties with, 133, 307–08; opposition of, to the Anglo-American treaty negotiations of 1871, 318, 321–22; policy in the Bering Sea fur-seals problem, 441, 447–48, 450, 453, 524–26.

Sackett's Harbor, 65, 66, 74, 101, 102, 168.

Sackville-West, Sir Lionel, 363, 365, 373; recall, 380–81, 407.

St. Albans raid, 280; effect, 282, 283, 285; claims for, 350.

St. Clair, Arthur, 25, 27, 28.

St. Clair Flats, 336, 337, 339.

St. Clair River, 535.

St. Croix River, 13, 42, 535.

St. George's Island, 138, 205.

St. John River, 152, 155, 156, 157, 158, 192, 196, 198–207 *passim*, 253, 254, 258, 337, 339, 340, (booms) 494, 502, 535, 536.

St. Lawrence islands, 56.

St. Lawrence-Lakes water boundary, commissions to establish, 137–39.

St. Lawrence River, navigation to the sea; America denied right to, 108, 113, 118, 120; Monroe's views on, 114, 117; diplomatic discussions on, 122–24; Clay's views (against offer of concessions for), 122–23;

negotiations of 1848–54, 242–43, 244, 246–47, 248, 258; negotiations of 1871, 330, 332, 333, 335–39 *passim*, 348. *See also* Navigation of the St. Lawrence.

St. Lawrence waterway project, 549–55; investigation of the problems of, 537–38; counter measures, 550; joint board of engineers, 551; negotiations, 551–52; treaty of 1932 (provisions, 552–53; opposition in the Senate, 553–55; renewed efforts in favor of, 555).

St. Mary River, 500–501, 506, 536.

St. Marys River, 138, 205, 503, 508, 534, 535, 536.

Salisbury, Lord, 362, 415, 439–45 *passim*, 452, 454, 473, 474, 476, 478.

Salmon, sockeye, protection of, 543; draft treaty, 547.

Sanders, G. N., 279, 286.

Sandwich Islands influences, 219–20.

San Juan Island, water boundary dispute, 292, 301, 308.

Sault (Long) islands of the St. Lawrence, 137, 138, 206, (dam) 503, 510, 553.

Sault Ste. Marie, Canadian free port at, 263, 327; American canal at (1870), 293, 336, 337, 426, 427, 428, 431; power, 535.

Schurman, J. G., 382.

Schuyler, Philip John, 2, 3, 4.

Scott, Winfield, 166, 167, 174, 190–91, 236.

Security, as basis of American policy, 70.

Settlement (American) on Lakes, 32, 72, 102.

Seward, William H., 177, 179, 247, 271, 273–80 *passim*, 281–83, 284–89 *passim*, 302, 306, 326.

Sherman, John, 368, 378, 379, 380, 420, 452, 470.

Sherman, W. T., 391.

Sifton, Clifford, 484.

Simcoe, John Graves, 29–33 *passim*.

Smith, Goldwin, 311, 358, 360, 370, 381, 382, 413, 420, 424.

Smuggling, convention to prevent, 545.

Sodus Point, 32.

Sparks, Jared, 170, 198, 199.

Sprague, Peleg, 152, 153, 200.

Spring-Rice, Cecil, 540.

Stimson, Henry L., 547, 553.

Sumner, Charles, 311, 320, 321.

Taft, W. H., 527, 528.

Taft administration, treaty negotiations of the, 517, 523, 524, 525–26; reciprocity policy of, 526.

Tariffs, Canadian policy concerning, 262, 263, 327, 358–59; American, 359, 411, 416–20, 457, 526, 556–57.

Taylor, James W., 264, 304–05, 315.

Territory, proposal to purchase, for a ship canal from the St. Lawrence to Lake Champlain, 416, 456; restitution of, 71, 80, 87, 88, 90–91 (*see also* Posts on the Lakes); violations of, 272.

Thompson, Jacob, 278, 281, 285, 286.

Thornton, Edward, 47, 51.

Thornton, Sir Edward, 312, 317, 318, 329, 333, 346, 350, 354, 355, 362.

Tippecanoe, battle of, 61.

Tracy, B. F., 443.

Trade, colonial, 1815–30: early British policy concerning, 18–19, 35–36, 108, 109, 115, 120–21, 161; American opposition to British policy, 52–53, 109, 111; temporary change in British policy (1808), 58; negotiations of 1815, 108; negotiations of 1818, 110–11; Canadian policy, 109, 121; retaliatory and discriminatory acts, 110, 111, 112, 119; injurious effects of Huskisson's Canada trade act of 1822, 112–13; U.S. retaliatory act of 1823, 114; later British proposals, 115, 118. *See also* Canadian trade policy, Reciprocity, West Indian trade.

early trans-border, with the Indians: (*see* Fur trade), reciprocal provision of Jay treaty, 36, 40; not extended to Louisiana, 51; American objections to renewal (in 1806), 53, 54, 55, 61, 71, 72; Canadian complaints against restriction, 54, 59–60; interdicted by United States law (1816), 88, 89; American refusal

to renew, 108, 110, 129. *See also* Fur trade.
illicit, via Vermont, 66; via the maritime provinces, 110.
Trade diversion, 119, 123, 242–43, 245, 247, 262, 263, 264, 395–96, 398–99, 417, 426, 430, 555–56.
Trade of the Northwest, the Pacific coast, 56; the Red River (with St. Paul), 302.
Trade reciprocity. *See* Reciprocity in trade.
Trade treaty of 1935, 558.
Trail copper smelter, 539.
Transit in bond, origin, 36, (proposal of 1836) 121–22, 242, 260–61, 337, 348; proposed change of, 284, 289, 290, 350; Grant's proposal to suspend, 330; questions of effects of termination of article of 1871, 363, 364, 365–66; discussed in Senate, 379; Cleveland's special message on, 380; origin of opposition to, 396–400; Senate resolutions and debates on (1888), 397–400; later questions and discussions on, 401, 402, 416–17, 428, 429, 430, 431–32, 455.
Transshipment, 339, 348, 350, 363, 426, 432.
Treaties and conventions (ratified), Anglo-American: relating to Canada, 1783, 14–75, 16–17; 1794 (Jay), 35–37; 1814 (Ghent), 82; 1815, 105, 108–09; 1817, 92–100; 1818, 105, 107, 109, 130; 1827, 105, 136, 144; 1842, 207–08; 1846, 234–35; 1854, 258–59; 1863 (Hudson's Bay Co. claims), 238; 1870 (naturalization), 293; 1871 (naturalization), 293; 1871, 321, 332–48; 1889 (extradition), 415–16; 1891, 445; 1892, 434, 445–46; 1892 boundary demarkation), 415; 1899 (*modus vivendi,* Alaska boundary), 478; 1903, 481, 482; 1905 (extradition), 314–15; 1906 (boundary demarkation), 493; 1908 (fisheries), 511–12; 1908 (prisoners), 515; 1908 (wreckage), 514; 1908 (boundary demarkation), 516; 1909, 505–09; 1909 (fisheries arbitration), 521; 1910 ((Passamaquoddy), 516; 1911 (fur-seals protection), 525–26; 1916 (birds), 541; 1919 (salmon protection), 544; 1923 (halibut protection), 457; 1923 (anti-smuggling), 545; 1924 (prohibition, 545; 1925 (extradition), 545.
(draft or unratified), 50, 54, 90, 311, 312, 355, 376, 406, 457, 472, 517, 518, 546, 552–53, 558–59.
Canadian-American: since 1922, 539, 544–49 *passim,* 552–53, 558.
with Russia (1824), 133, (1867) 307–08.
Treaty of 1871, origin, 312–21, 326–31; negotiations, 321; Russian efforts to prevent, 321–22; conditions of Canadian agreement to, 322; provisions, 339–41, 348; ratification, (by the U.S.) 348, (by Canada), 349; abrogation of the fishery articles of, 363.
Trent affair, 272, 273.
Tugs and tows, 433, 434.
Tupper, Charles H., 441, 446.
Tupper, Sir Charles, 333, 334, 337, 341, 346, 368, 372, 375, 376, 377, 378, 418, 421, 425.
Tyler, John, 179–80, 197, 199, 204, 218, 220, 221.

Upshur, A. P., 220–21.

Van Buren, Martin, 120, 148, 166, 167, 173, 189, 192.
Vancouver Island, 221, 230, 235, 236, 301, 306.
Van Rensselaer, Rensselaer, 164, 165, 168.
Vaughan, Charles R., 142, 146, 147, 155, 156.
Vermont, apprehension concerning, 15, 24, 32, 57–58; illicit trade through, 66.
Vessels wrecked on inland waters, old question of regulations of aid to, 403–04, 432–33; wrecking and salvage rights, 513–14.

Walker, R. J., 308–09.
War of 1812, causes and motives, 46,

61–62, 70–72, 75; military and naval operations in, 62–66; peace negotiations of, 70–82.
War on border, threatened, 31, 57, 94, 165, 178, 181, 188–89, 193–94, 222, 227, 236–37, 283, 291.
Warroad Harbor, 502.
Washington, George, 4, 5, 7, 25, 26, 29, 30, 32, 37.
Water levels, 538.
Waters, conterminous: regulations for navigation in, 456; diversion, obstruction, and sanitation problems of, 456, 499–503; negotiations concerning, 499, 503–05; treaty concerning, 505–08 (amendment and ratification of, 508–10); problems of regulative protection of fresh-water fisheries in, 510–12 (resulting in a treaty of 1908); protection of shipping in, 512; wrecking and salvage rights in, 513–14.
Waterway (deep), Great Lakes and St. Lawrence to the sea, proposed, 416, 456, 510; plans for, 549–54; treaty rejected, 554–55; proposed canal route from the St. Lawrence via Lake Champlain to the Hudson, 416, 456, 550.
Waterways, coöperation in the use of, 424, 456, 458, 494, 500, 501, 502, 549–54.
Waterways Commission, National (American), 510.
Wayne, Anthony, expedition of, 30, 32.
Webster, Charles E. (later Baron Alverstone), 447. *See also* Alverstone.
Webster, Daniel, 176–77, 179, 180–81, 182, 188, 190, 195–99 *passim,* 202–06 *passim,* 209, 210, 211, 218, 219–20, 226, 232, 247, 249, 250.
Webster-Ashburton Treaty, historic background, 139–57, 185–200 (*see also* Northeastern boundary dispute); negotiations, 200–207; provisions, 207–08; coincident adjustments, 209–10; Webster's defense of, 211.
Welland canal, Canadian toll rebate policy on (1860), 263, 402, 403; traffic interrupted on, 291; free use requested (1870), 329, 333, 336, 337, 339, 364, 365; American complaints concerning discriminating tolls on, 422–23, 424; question of salvage operations in, 433, 434.
West Indian trade, Jay treaty provision, 35, 37, 38; Monroe's negotiations concerning, 52–53; discussion, (in War of 1812) 74, (in 1815) 108; commercial struggle to 1830, 108–32; Huskisson's proposal (1825), 115; American contention and policy (Clay), 116–17 (results, 118–20); renewed negotiations and result, (1830) 120; later American complaints, 121.
White, Henry, 473, 480, 487–88, 526.
Wilkinson, James, (at Detroit) 39–40, 51, 65.
Wiman, Erastus, 360, 370, 372.
Windom, William, 417.
World War questions, 540–41.
Wrecking and salvage rights in contiguous waters, 513–14.

York (Toronto), 65.

Zollverein. *See* Commercial union.